Physical Education Methods for Elementary Teachers

THIRD EDITION

Katherine T. Thomas, PhD
Iowa State University

Amelia M. Lee, PhD
Louisiana State University

Jerry R. Thomas, EdD
Iowa State University

Human Kinetics

Library of Congress Cataloging-in-Publication Data

Thomas, Katherine T., 1948-
    Physical education methods for elementary teachers / Katherine T. Thomas, Amelia M. Lee, Jerry R. Thomas. -- 3rd ed.
        p. cm.
    Includes bibliographical references and index.
    ISBN-13: 978-0-7360-6704-1 (soft cover)
    ISBN-10: 0-7360-6704-3 (soft cover)
    1. Physical education for children--Study and teaching (Elementary) 2. Physical education for children--Curricula. I. Lee,
Amelia M., 1938- II. Thomas, Jerry R. III. Title.
    GV443.T495 2008
    372.86'044--dc22
                                    2007034002

ISBN-10: 0-7360-6704-3
ISBN-13: 978-0-7360-6704-1

The Web addresses cited in this text were current as of September 2007, unless otherwise noted.

The four guiding principles on pages 35, 39-41, 63-65, 93-95, 128-129, and 161-162 are adapted, by permission, from K.T. Thomas and J.R. Thomas, 2008, "Principles of motor development for elementary school physical education," *Elementary School Journal* 108(3): 181-195.

Acquisitions Editor: Bonnie Pettifor Vreeman; **Developmental Editor:** Ray Vallese; **Assistant Editor:** Derek Campbell; **Copyeditor:** Susan Campanini; **Proofreader:** Red Inc.; **Indexer:** Marie Rizzo; **Permission Manager:** Carly Breeding; **Graphic Designer:** Nancy Rasmus; **Graphic Artists:** Denise Lowry, Angela K. Snyder, and Yvonne Griffith; **Cover Designer:** Keith Blomberg; **Photographer (cover):** Paul S. Howell/Getty Images; **Photographer (interior):** © Human Kinetics, unless otherwise noted; **Photo Office Assistant:** Jason Allen; **Art Manager:** Kelly Hendren; **Associate Art Manager:** Alan L. Wilborn; **Illustrator:** Argosy, unless otherwise noted. Illustrations on pages 43, 60, 86, 100, 127, 146, 175 (third from top), 176 (middle), 177 (bottom), 182 (top), 190, 243, 261-262, 266 (top and middle), 278, 324, 327 (top), 336, 345 (top), 348, 370, and 387 by Tim Offenstein; on page 10 by Jenny L. Parum; on page 42 by Nina Laidlaw; and on page 357 by Kelly Hendren; **Chapter- and Part-Opening Drawings:** Students at Barkstall Elementary School, Champaign, Illinois; **Printer:** Total Printing Systems

Printed in the United States of America   10   9   8   7   6   5

The paper in this book is certified under a sustainable forestry program.

Human Kinetics
Web site: www.HumanKinetics.com

United States: Human Kinetics
P.O. Box 5076, Champaign, IL 61825-5076
800-747-4457
e-mail: humank@hkusa.com

Canada: Human Kinetics
475 Devonshire Road Unit 100, Windsor, ON N8Y 2L5
800-465-7301 (in Canada only)
e-mail: info@hkcanada.com

Europe: Human Kinetics
107 Bradford Road, Stanningley, Leeds LS28 6AT
United Kingdom
+44 (0) 113 255 5665
e-mail: hk@hkeurope.com

Australia: Human Kinetics
57A Price Avenue, Lower Mitcham, South Australia 5062
08 8372 0999
e-mail: info@hkaustralia.com

New Zealand: Human Kinetics
P.O. Box 80
Torrens Park, South Australia 5062
0800 222 062
e-mail: info@hknewzealand.com

E3886

To our children and grandchildren, who have taught us so much. Every day they demonstrate the joy of movement, reinforce that teaching is a noble profession, and show us why physical education is important.

—Jerry R. Thomas and Katherine T. Thomas

To my doctoral students through the years, for all I have learned from them.

—Amelia M. Lee

CONTENTS

Contents

PREFACE

The second edition of *Physical Education Methods for Elementary Teachers* was published in 2003; changes in physical activity and physical education policy since then shape the third edition. First, the national content standards have changed; there are now six rather than seven standards. Second, more detailed recommendations for physical activity have been developed for toddlers, preschoolers, and young children. Finally, physical activity continues to dominate public health, as evidenced by the new Dietary Guidelines for Americans and Local School Wellness Policies. Physically active lifestyles continue to be an important part of programs of disease prevention and health promotion. Physical education is an important part of becoming physically active. Thus, elementary physical education remains the first step in creating a healthy population.

This emphasis on healthy students and healthy schools leads to suggestions for integrating information on nutrition and wellness. Integration can and should occur in both physical education lessons and in other academic content. This edition is designed to motivate beginning teachers to create healthier schools and to help them feel confident in presenting information and creating exciting learning activities for their students.

In addition to policy change, physical education is evolving. Emphasis continues to shift to standards and benchmarks, variety in teaching styles, and the inclusion of new and exciting developmentally appropriate activities. This third edition extends existing information on how to integrate academics and physical activity. New in this edition are a section on character development, the positive youth development model, and more on teaching skills using forms, progression, and contextual practice. More emphasis is directed at goal orientation and motivational climate, two factors associated with maintenance of physical activity. This edition outlines strategies for creating an environment where students choose to participate in physical activity with confidence, enthusiasm, and a desire to learn.

We continue to establish a foundation for teaching and learning based on motor development. Thus, the third edition focuses on developmentally appropriate physical education. New in this edition are four principles of motor development, which serve as the foundation for chapters 3 through 7. In those chapters, the content is introduced with an example of each principle from elementary physical education, followed by more detailed information about physical growth and maturation; motor performance during childhood; cognition, learning, and practice; physical activity for children; and psychosocial factors in physical education. In addition, information about gender, students with special needs, and expertise is now integrated into other chapters.

Our goal is to assist classroom teachers of physical education and to provide physical education specialists with the skills and knowledge necessary to offer an excellent physical education program while supporting the academic mission of the school. We hope that the information presented in the third edition will encourage and assist all school personnel in working toward healthier schools.

A Well-Rounded Approach

In this edition of *Physical Education Methods for Elementary Teachers*, you will find

- the content knowledge from over 100 years of studying children (motor development), which provides a sound foundation for teaching physical education effectively;
- insights into how you can become the most effective physical education instructor;
- practical information on how to enhance the elementary school mission through physical education while assisting students to reach intended outcomes;
- down-to-earth suggestions for effective class management; and
- ready-to-use, proven lesson plans to help guide you as you develop and hone your teaching skills in this content area.

Whether you are a preservice or inservice teacher, *Physical Education Methods for Elementary Teachers, Third Edition*, will provide you with a wealth of practical, researched, and field-tested information and application ideas for your situation.

Why Teach Physical Education?

As you will learn in this book, physical activity is a necessary and important part of childhood. Physical education is one aspect of physical activity. Current recommendations suggest beginning structured physical activity experiences in preschool; physical education is considered part of a healthy childhood. The American Academy of Pediatrics recommends *the reinstatement of mandatory daily physical education in all grades* as a primary strategy to fight the epidemic of childhood obesity. Similarly the Centers for Disease Control and Prevention (CDC) and the American Heart Association recognize the contributions of physical education to healthy children.

Some states and school districts have responded by increasing physical education requirements. Quality physical education includes student–teacher ratios similar to other academic subjects, well-supported and -trained specialist teachers, and a minimum of 150 minutes of physical education each week (preferably at least 30 minutes a day). A challenge for all schools is to find trained specialist teachers and the facilities necessary for daily physical education in all grades. Therefore, the reality is that sometimes classroom teachers will be providing all or some of the physical education instruction in the elementary school. In schools where the specialist provides all physical education instruction, the classroom teacher who understands the role of physical education in the development of healthy children will be a better prepared partner for the specialist.

One goal of this book is to develop a team approach to educating children. The vision is physical education specialists who work with classroom teachers to support student learning and classroom teachers who support student learning in physical education. The integrated approach is discussed in more detail in chapter 2.

We continue to observe many wonderful elementary physical education programs. The renewed interest in physical education because of public health concerns has energized the profession. Developmentally appropriate programs are being recognized for quality and for contributing to healthy, active children. While there is a long way to go before every child has daily physical education, and the existence of some programs is still threatened by budget and other issues such as high-stakes testing, physical education is making progress. There is considerable hope, optimism, and as a result, pressure surrounding physical education.

Physical education for children in elementary school prepares them to make decisions about physical activity for life. Certainly we want children to be active during childhood—and many of them are—but we also want them to have physically active lifestyles for life. This means caring and competent teachers have a significant responsibility to the children and to their future health. As more resources are invested in physical education, the responsibility and pressure increases. Thus, preparing to be a highly qualified teacher begins by understanding how children learn and develop, what motivates them to be active, and how to use physical education time effectively.

Guiding Principles

The purpose of this book is twofold:

1. To prepare teachers to do their best teaching
2. To support quality physical activity programs—emphasizing physical education—for elementary school children

In order to accomplish these goals, you will need to be an informed advocate for children and physical activity. The information in this book will help you do this as well as help parents and other concerned people who want to advocate for your students.

Several specific principles guide our selection of the activities and information in this book:

- Children are naturally active; therefore, we are fostering a normal behavior by teaching physical education.
- Children are naturally motivated in that they participate in sport and physical activity to have fun, be with friends, and learn new skills.
- Each child is unique. Differences in motor skill within and between children are

normal. This means that a child may find some skills easier than other skills. This will vary from child to child.

- Boys and girls are more alike than different when doing physical activities.
- Motor skills develop as a result of practice.
- Improving, having appropriate levels of challenge, being with friends, and having fun are important in physical education. Competition is not an essential ingredient. Remember this is physical *education*, through which *all* children should be able to grow in competence in a supportive environment.

This leads us to the question: What is important in elementary physical education? Two major themes provide the answer:

- Elementary physical education is firmly placed on a foundation of motor development. Thus, it is more than a collection of activities or teaching skills.
- Physical activity and skill development are the goals of elementary physical education. Thus, the important learning outcomes describe what children know and can do related to physical activity.

A program that implements these two themes through effective teaching within an enjoyable, non-threatening context will encourage children to be

- more active outside of school,
- physically active across the lifespan, and
- more healthy overall.

Special Features of This Edition

Lesson plans with many activities for all grade levels are included at the end of most chapters to demonstrate the concepts in the chapter. The same lesson plans are included on the DVD-ROM (detailed below). The breadth and depth of these lessons provide guidance for the student teacher and a starter set of lessons for the practicing teacher.

A **lesson plan finder** makes it easy to refer to the lesson plans now and throughout your career. See pages xiii to xvii.

Mastery activities at the end of each chapter provide activities that will help you better grasp main points and put that knowledge to use when you teach.

Sidebars throughout the book provide teachable moments, tips on putting concepts discussed in the book into practice, and at-a-glance facts that provide you with opportunities to see how key points play out in the real teaching environment.

Electronic ancillaries offer support materials for instructors, including a slide presentation package of key points from each chapter, a comprehensive test bank with questions from each chapter, and an instructor guide with learning activities and a sample syllabus.

A DVD-ROM bound into the book includes lesson plans and video clips.

- All the lesson plans from the book are available as PDF files, making them easy to access and print.
- Video clips demonstrate how three expert elementary physical education teachers and two young teachers conduct lessons. The clips include a mastery lesson, a contextual practice lesson, a station teaching lesson, a locomotor skill lesson using a whole group approach, and a manipulative skill lesson using a small group approach. In the book, we identify discussions that are supported by a video clip and mark them with a DVD icon so you'll know when to check the disc.
- In interviews, the five teachers address the role of physical education in a school's mission, their personal physical education goals, challenges facing educators, and other important topics.

For more details on using the DVD-ROM, please see page 453.

Organization of the Text

This book is organized into four main parts to guide you toward implementing effective, developmentally appropriate physical education. It also includes more than 70 lesson plans and a glossary.

Part I: Introduction to Physical Education

Chapters 1 and 2 set the stage as you begin to understand why physical education is an important part of child development and health. Accountability has led to standards-based education, which means that teacher expectations are stated as outcomes. In addition, national standards for physical education describe what students should know and do when they finish secondary school. Elementary physical education has a responsibility to address those standards so that students will be ready for the new challenges of middle and high school.

You will also see how health and child development are part of the mission of the elementary school. Integration is a key concept for teachers working to support the mission of the school.

Part II: Addressing the Child's Needs

Chapters 3 through 7 provide a foundation that is the basis for developmentally appropriate physical education. You will understand typical growth and development, individual differences, and how these apply to physical education classes. You will learn about physical growth and maturation (chapter 3); motor performance during childhood (chapter 4); cognition, learning, and practice (chapter 5); physical activity (chapter 6); and psychosocial factors (chapter 7).

Part III: Preparing to Teach Physical Education

Chapters 8 through 12 help prepare you to teach. You will learn about planning a curriculum (chapter 8); organizing for teaching (chapter 9); managing students (chapter 10); teacher's rights, responsibilities, and best practices (chapter 11); and equipment and facilities (chapter 12).

Part IV: Teaching Physical Education

Chapters 13 through 15 offer you specific information on how to provide effective instruction (chapter 13), conduct assessments (chapter 14),

and grow as a teacher (chapter 15). We hope that this book will provide the knowledge you need to succeed in a physical education setting but also arm you with additional strategies to teach across the curriculum.

Lesson Plans

Chapters 2 through 14 include lesson plans related to the concepts in those chapters. Most of the lesson plans are from *Physical Education for Children: Daily Lesson Plans for Elementary School, Second Edition* (Thomas, Lee, and Thomas 2000 [Champaign, IL: Human Kinetics]). The information in the chapters will guide you through the four components of effective, developmentally appropriate physical education programs: objectives, planning, instruction, and evaluation. The activities are divided by grade and the type of activity so that you can select appropriate activities for your objective or standard. The lesson plan finder (pages xiii through xvii) allows you to find appropriate activities at a glance.

Glossary

The glossary (pages 435 through 439) provides a useful reference. Lists at the beginning of each chapter present the relevant glossary terms in order of appearance. Within each chapter, each term is presented in boldfaced type when it is defined, not necessarily when it first appears.

Our Challenge to You

Throughout *Physical Education Methods for Elementary Teachers, Third Edition*, we challenge you to provide the best possible physical education experience for your students. At the same time, we offer concrete information and reality-based advice to make that possible, no matter your background or teaching experience. Through your efforts, you can make a difference in the health and school experiences of your students—now and throughout your career.

LESSON PLAN FINDER

Use this resource to find at a glance the type of activity you want to plan for the grade level you are teaching.

(continued)

PART I

Introduction to Physical Education

Most of you have firsthand experience of how schools work, and a part of that experience concerns physical education. However, since you were in elementary school, many changes have taken place that influence what you will do as a teacher. Perhaps more important, your role changes dramatically as you move from being a student to being a teacher. Therefore, because you have accumulated a great deal of knowledge and experience with education, your perspective changes. Instead of seeing only from the student's point of view, you now also see things as the teacher sees them. The first two chapters in this book are designed to help you make the transition from student to teacher. These chapters set the stage in two ways: First, you learn why physical education is important. As a result, you understand why being a competent physical education teacher is important. Teaching competency is defined in part by standards for teachers, which are introduced in chapter 1, Health and Developmental Benefits of Physical Education. This book covers material inherent in the 10 standards. Second, you see that physical education is integral to the mission of the school. Therefore, in physical education, what you teach and how you teach it are important to the success of the students and of the school.

CHAPTER 1

Health and Developmental Benefits of Physical Education

ANNIKA. AGE 9

Most children attend school, so schools are the best place to reach children. Schools nurture all aspects of development. Schools today are charged with delivering a message about the importance of physical activity as well as helping children learn motor skills that allow them to remain active throughout their lives. Physical activity is the single most important controllable health risk factor, and teachers play a major role in helping children achieve physically active lifestyles.

By July 1, 2006, most school districts in the United States were required by Congress to have a local school wellness policy. The policy addresses four goals: nutrition education, physical activity, all foods available on campus, and other wellness promotions. School and community programs that promote regular physical activity among young people could be the most effective strategy for reducing the public health burden of chronic diseases associated with sedentary lifestyles. Programs that provide students with the knowledge, attitudes, motor skills, behavioral skills, and confidence to participate in physical activity may establish active lifestyles among young people that continue into and throughout their adult lives. These programs must also be fun and part of a plan to address childhood obesity in schools (Wechsler, McKenna, Lee, and Dietz 2004).

Learner Outcomes

After studying this chapter, you should be able to do the following:

- Demonstrate the value of physical activity by describing its importance.

- Provide examples of effective developmentally appropriate physical education programs.

- Document personal achievement of the standards of the Interstate New Teacher Assessment and Support Consortium (INTASC).

Glossary Terms

physical activity

developmentally appropriate

coordinated school health program

physical education

INTASC standards

skill

Stand outside any elementary school and watch as the doors burst open for recess. You'll see children running, excited, and engaged. The same images are replayed every day with younger children at playgrounds and parks. The joy of movement is evident in these children at play. If you followed those children to effective physical education classes, you would see that same energy and joy as they are challenged to master new skills. Continuing to watch those children after school, you could see them engaged in play that might include riding their bikes or more formal sport experiences such as soccer or tee ball. **Physical activity**—in the forms of sport, exercise, physical education, and play—makes an important contribution to child development. And, what is more, it is a joyful time for children.

Everywhere you look, you see examples of exercise, sport, and physical activity in American culture. For example, an entire section of the daily newspaper is devoted to sports. The same is true of the evening television news: Entire television networks are devoted to sports and some to specific sports! In nearly every community, you can see people walking, jogging, or riding their bicycles for exercise. Entire industries, from those selling athletic shoes to those offering aerobics classes, serve people seeking health through exercise. Clearly, you don't have to look very far to see that exercise is popular. Being physically active includes lifestyle activity (gardening, walking, and cycling) and vigorous activity (jumping rope, running, and cross-country skiing). Because physical activity includes sport, exercise, and more general movements that expend energy, you can see that physical activity is also important in our culture.

Why Value Physical Activity?

One reason to value physical activity is the health benefit associated with a physically active lifestyle. Other reasons are developmental needs:

- To explore and master your environment
- To express yourselves through movement
- To feel satisfaction resulting from successful movement

Physical activity also provides an opportunity for affiliation. Being part of a group—as a fan, a team member, or a walking partner—meets an important human need. Physical activity and sport allow people to test their skill, fitness, and determination. People derive pleasure from the effort and accomplishments found in physical activity. Physical activity is often fun—another reason to value it. So, whether we are an elderly person or an infant reaffirming its independence by mastering its environment, a fan identifying with his or her team, a child expressing joy through movement, a middle-aged adult exercising for health, or an adolescent working hard to learn a new skill and succeeding, physical activity is important to us as individuals and as a culture.

Standards

Three sets of standards (Content Standards in Physical Education, INTASC, and Developmentally Appropriate Physical Education) set the framework for this book and guide elementary physical education instruction. The National Association for Sport and Physical Education (NASPE) defines a physically educated person (NASPE 2004) with six statements of behavior (figure 1.1). These content standards provide a model for all educators: for physical education

Children are naturally active and enjoy games that provide vigorous physical activity.

A physically educated person follows these standards:

Standard 1: Demonstrates competency in motor skills and movement patterns needed to perform a variety of physical activities.

Standard 2: Demonstrates understanding of movement concepts, principles, strategies, and tactics as they apply to the learning and performance of physical activities.

Standard 3: Participates regularly in physical activity.

Standard 4: Achieves and maintains a health-enhancing level of physical fitness.

Standard 5: Exhibits responsible personal and social behavior that respects self and others in physical activity settings.

Standard 6: Values physical activity for health, enjoyment, challenge, self-expression, or social interaction.

Figure 1.1 Content standards in physical education.

Moving Into the Future: National Standards for Physical Education, 2nd Edition (2004) adapted with permission from the National Association for Sport and Physical Education (NASPE), 1900 Association Drive, Reston, VA 20191-1599.

programs and for your behaviors as physical educators. Of course, this model also applies to classroom teachers who provide physical education for children in the classroom and in the gymnasium. (See the DVD-ROM for teacher interviews on the importance of the NASPE standards.)

Ten learning outcomes for teachers were developed by the INTASC to guide teacher education programs. These suggest the content of teacher education programs and provide guidance for teachers to demonstrate their level of preparation (table 1.1). The INTASC standards apply to all teachers: elementary classroom, secondary classroom, and special subject (e.g., art, physical education, and music). To help students become physically educated, you need to have and apply knowledge about how children grow, move, and learn. Furthermore, you need to know about teaching to be able to communicate effectively and to evaluate yourselves and your students. Finally, you need to have knowledge of subject matter. Knowledge of subject matter in physical education includes how the body responds to exercise, how the body moves efficiently, how students learn motor skills, and how they perform the actual activities (e.g., in dance, gymnastics, games, and team sports). Compare this with the subject matter knowledge for secondary education, where the content is relatively narrow and specific, such as in teaching chemistry. The elementary classroom teacher must have content knowledge of each subject area (e.g., mathematics, reading, and social studies), and the physical education teacher must understand and

be able to apply the science of movement (e.g., physiology, biomechanics, and motor learning) and the forms of movement (e.g., activities) to meet this standard. Clearly, teaching elementary children is a challenge for physical education teachers and a double challenge for elementary classroom teachers! NASPE developed the initial physical education teacher preparation guidelines for the National Council for the Accreditation of Teacher Education (NCATE). NASPE (1999) used the INTASC standards as a model; therefore, the standards are similar (see table 1.1).

Perhaps the most important standards are those describing **developmentally appropriate** physical education. Developmentally appropriate programs meet the needs of children according to their age, maturation, and interests. Quality physical education programs are developmentally appropriate. More information on developmentally appropriate physical education is provided in chapter 8, Planning Your Curriculum. The information in this book is guided by a perspective that recognizes that development is qualitative, sequential, directional, cumulative, multifaceted, and individual (NASPE 1994). Qualitative change focuses on process—the way a skill or behavior looks rather than the product or outcome. Development is orderly or sequential; therefore, predictions can be made about performance and used to plan programs. This means that children of different ages do different activities. Development is a building process; it is cumulative. Early experience and competence are a foundation for later skill learning. Motor development is based

Table 1.1 Standards for Teacher Preparation

INTASC	NASPE/NCATE
1. Subject matter: The teacher understands the central concepts, tools of inquiry, and structures of the disciplines he or she teaches and can create learning experiences that make these aspects of subject matter meaningful for students.	1. Content knowledge: A physical education teacher understands physical education content, disciplinary concepts, and tools of inquiry related to the development of a physically educated person.
2. Student learning: The teacher understands how children and youth learn and develop and can provide learning opportunities that support their intellectual, social, and personal development.	2. Growth and development: A physical education teacher understands how individuals learn and develop and can provide opportunities that support their physical, cognitive, social, and emotional development.
3. Diverse learners: The teacher understands how learners differ in their approaches to learning and creates instructional opportunities that are adapted to learners from diverse cultural backgrounds and with exceptionalities.	3. Diverse learners: A physical education teacher understands how individuals differ in their approaches to learning and creates appropriate instruction adapted to these differences.
4. Instructional strategies: The teacher understands and uses a variety of instructional strategies to encourage the students' development of critical thinking, problem solving, and performance skills.	4. Management and motivation: A physical education teacher uses an understanding of individual and group motivation and behavior to create a safe learning environment that encourages social interaction, active engagement in learning, and self-motivation.
5. Learning environment: The teacher uses an understanding of individual and group motivation and behavior to create a learning environment that encourages positive social interaction, active engagement in learning, and self-motivation.	5. Communication: A physical education teacher uses knowledge of effective verbal, nonverbal, and media communication techniques to foster inquiry, collaboration, and engagement in physical activity settings.
6. Communication: The teacher uses knowledge of effective verbal, nonverbal, and media communication techniques to foster active inquiry, collaboration, and supportive interaction in the classroom.	6. Planning and instruction: A physical education teacher plans and implements a variety of developmentally appropriate instructional strategies to develop physically educated individuals.
7. Planning instruction: The teacher plans and manages instruction based on knowledge of subject matter, students, the community, and curriculum goals.	7. Learner assessment: A physical education teacher understands and uses formal and informal assessment strategies to foster physical, cognitive, social, and emotional development of learners in physical activity.
8. Assessment: The teacher understands and uses formal and informal assessment strategies to evaluate and ensure the continuous intellectual, social, and physical development of learners.	8. Reflection: A physical education teacher is a reflective practitioner who evaluates the effects of his or her actions on others (e.g., learners, parents and guardians, and professionals in the learning community) and seeks opportunities to grow professionally.
9. Reflection and professional development: The teacher is a reflective practitioner who continually evaluates the effects of his or her choices and actions on others (students, parents, and other professionals in the learning community) and who actively seeks out opportunities to grow professionally.	9. Collaboration: The teacher fosters relationships with colleagues, parents and guardians, and community agencies to support learners' growth and well-being.
10. Collaboration, ethics, and relationships: A teacher communicates and interacts with parents and guardians, families, school colleagues, and the community to support the students' learning and well-being.	

Data from NASPE 1995; INTASC 1992.

on the concept of improvement—that is, as people get older, they get better. In part II, this and other principles of motor development provide evidence for a developmentally appropriate physical education program. The developmentally appropriate curriculum recognizes this by using increasingly difficult benchmarks with lessons to help students achieve the standard. Development is a composite of the cognitive, social, affective, and psychomotor domains, which means that development is multifaceted. Each child is a unique individual; therefore, instruction and programs must be sensitive to the individual learner. Children of the same age learn at different rates and in different ways, but children of the same age are more alike than different.

Current Practices in Physical Education

Many states mandate physical education in elementary school but neither specify the amount of time required nor indicate who should teach the classes. The method for implementing state guidelines varies within the states as well. Only one state, Illinois, has been recognized as requiring physical education K-12.

Since the *U.S. Surgeon General's Report on Health Promotion and Disease Prevention* (U.S. Department of Health and Human Services 1979), physical activity has been on the national health agenda. In 1990 (HHS), *Healthy People 2000: Surgeon General's Report* included specific goals for the nation for elementary and secondary physical education. In 1997, *Guidelines for School and Community Programs to Promote Lifelong Physical Activity Among Young People* from the Centers for Disease Control (CDC) emphasized the need for daily physical education in grades K-12.

Few states or schools have responded to the U.S. Surgeon General, the CDC Guidelines for Physical Activity, U.S. Congress Resolution 97 (which encourages daily physical education for grades K-12) (NASPE 1997), or *Healthy People 2000*. Currently, 36 states require elementary physical education (NASPE 2006). For example, certified physical education teachers are required in 28 states; classroom teachers are allowed to teach physical education in other states. Thirty-three states have their own state physical education standards.

Although states have not responded to the increasing concern by the CDC, Surgeon General, and U.S. Congress, these agencies and many others continue to support physical activity and physical education programs for children and adolescents:

- The United States Department of Agriculture (with Team Nutrition), U.S. Congress (Physical Education for Progress grants), and the President's Council on Physical Fitness and Sport have programs or funding to provide physical education and activity for children and adolescents.

- Parents support physical education and recognize the contribution that physical activity makes to the reduction and control of obesity.

The focus of initiatives has changed slightly since 1990 as scientists have come to recognize the importance of skill development, fun, and confidence building to lifelong activity. Previously, early programs for young children focused more on physical fitness and less on skill. Current programs balance physical activity, fun, and the learning of lifelong motor skills (e.g., lifetime sports). An example of this shift is the President's Challenge, which offers two levels of group participation—Active Lifestyle (beginners) and Presidential Champions (already active)—and Fitnessgram, which has added Activitygram to track physical activity. Both programs focus on the amount of physical activity and increasing physical activity rather than on fitness. Because physical activity drops dramatically during adolescence, especially among girls, the focus of programs has shifted to middle school and high school students. The physical activity goal for the U.S. Department of Health and Human Services' *Healthy People 2010* is the following: "Improve health, fitness, and quality of life through daily physical activity." The impact of physical activity on health is outlined in *Healthy People 2010*. The objectives for 2010 include the following:

- Increase the proportion of adolescents who engage in at least 30 minutes of moderate physical activity on five or more of the previous seven days from 20 to 30 percent.

- Increase the proportion of adolescents who engage in vigorous physical activity that promotes the development and maintenance of cardiorespiratory fitness on three or more days per week for 20 or more minutes per session from 64 to 85 percent.

- Increase the proportion of the nation's private and public schools that require daily physical education for all students from 17 to 25 percent in middle school and from 2 to 25 percent in high school.

- Increase the proportion of adolescents who participate in daily school physical education from 27 to 50 percent.
- Increase the proportion of adolescents who spend at least 50 percent of school physical education class time being physically active from 32 to 50 percent.
- Increase the proportion of children and adolescents who view television two or fewer hours per day from 60 to 75 percent.

Clearly, the first objectives do not apply directly to elementary school children. However, a healthy base of physical education for children in elementary school may increase the chances of meeting those objectives as the children become adolescents and adults. Furthermore, those first objectives do apply to teachers and college students! The objectives target adolescents, who are in the upper elementary grades, middle school, and high school. The final objective targets all elementary school students. Elementary physical education is viewed as an important factor in developing a physically active lifestyle. In addition, elementary physical education provides some of the daily activity children need to grow and develop.

Physical activity is associated with reduced health risk. People who are physically active are less at risk for obesity, diabetes, cardiovascular disease, cancer, and other diseases (Dietz 2004). Quality daily physical education is recommended as a primary strategy to fight obesity and reduce the risk of other diseases by the American Heart Association (Pate, Davis, Robinson, Stone, McKenzie, and Young 2006), the American Academy of Pediatrics (AAP 2006), and the National Association of State Boards of Education (NASBE 2006).

In addition to the direct influence of physical education, schools influence physical activity indirectly. Sometimes, this influence is evidenced by modeling the value of physical activity. For example, using physical activity as a punishment (by withholding recess or physical education) related to an academic issue suggests to the student that academic issues are more important than physical activity (and health). Other times, the messages are sent directly: "We are cutting recess so we have more time to read" or "We are reducing physical education so we can employ a math specialist."

Consider the student who sits in school from 8:30 a.m. to 3:30 p.m., rides the school bus home, does homework or plays video games from 4:00 to 5:00, eats dinner from 5:00 to 5:30, watches television for two hours from 5:30 to 7:30, bathes, and goes to bed at 8:00. Where are the time and opportunity for physical activity? The three most frequently cited barriers to being physically active are

- time,
- access to convenient facilities, and

Helping children learn motor skills is an important part of teaching physical education.

- access to a safe environment in which to be active.

Clearly, these barriers affect children. (See the DVD-ROM for teacher interviews on challenges facing educators.) Schools have not only the opportunity but also the responsibility to provide for students to be physically active every day. Physical activity experiences for children should include structured and unstructured movement—physical education, sport, exercise, play, and recess.

Young children are naturally active as they explore their environments and master skills such as walking and running. As children enter school, activity levels drop, partially because the children are required to sit throughout the school day. Children who are the least active—those who sit still and are quiet—are often rewarded the most by classroom teachers. During preschool and elementary school, children should have two movement opportunities: structured and unstructured. Structured experiences include physical education, sport, and adult-organized exercise. Children learn motor skills, knowledge, behavioral skills, and confidence during these structured experiences.

Unstructured experiences, in which children engage in physical activity, learn behavioral and motor skills, and gain confidence, include play and recess. Both unstructured and structured experiences are important because each provides unique learning experiences for children. Elementary school provides both types of experiences, in which teachers are involved as supervisors, facilitators, and instructors. This text focuses on structured experiences. Classroom teachers and physical educators are responsible for providing time for physical activity in a safe and nurturing environment and for helping children learn important motor skills.

Many organizations support the idea that physical activity beyond the physical education program is an important part of the school day. The NASBE extends the role of schools in encouraging physical activity to providing after-school programs. NASBE policy includes recommendations for

- daily physical education for grades pre-K through 12,
- recess, and
- voluntary before- and after-school activity programs such as intramural clubs, joint school and community recreation programs, and programs involving the students' families.

The CDC has developed the **coordinated school health program** with the following eight components (figure 1.2):

1. Health education
2. Physical education
3. Health services
4. Nutrition services
5. Staff health promotion
6. Counseling and psychological services
7. Healthy school environment
8. Parent and community involvement

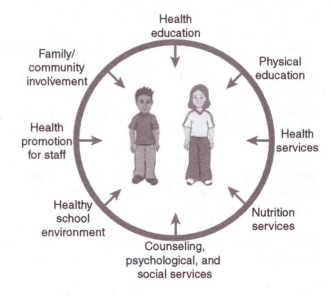

Figure 1.2 The eight components of a coordinated school health program.

www.cdc.gov/healthyyouth/cshp/index.htm.

Physical education is defined as "a planned sequential K-12 curriculum that provides cognitive content and learning experiences in a variety of activity areas such as basic movement skills; physical fitness; rhythms and dance; games; team, dual, and individual sports; tumbling and gymnastics; and aquatics. Quality physical education should promote, through a variety of planned physical activities, each student's optimum physical, mental, emotional, and social development, and should promote activities and sports that all students enjoy and can pursue throughout their lives. Qualified, trained teachers teach physical activity" (CDC 2007).

The message is clear and consistent: Physical education for children is important!

The NASBE Policy to Encourage Physical Activity

Every student shall be physically active—that is, shall develop the knowledge and skills necessary to perform a variety of physical activities, maintain physical fitness, regularly participate in physical activity, understand the short- and long-term benefits of physical activity, and value and enjoy physical activity as an ongoing part of a healthful lifestyle. In addition, staff are encouraged to participate in and model physical activity as a valuable part of daily life.

Perspective

We have designed the material in this book to prepare teachers to meet the **INTASC** (and NASPE and NCATE) **standards** and to provide children with developmentally appropriate physical education programs. Performing sport skills and other physical activities successfully requires practice to acquire skill and success to develop confidence. **Skill** (competence) and confidence are associated with physically active lifestyles in adults. The information in this book is grounded in motor development; we take a developmental perspective and apply it to developmentally appropriate physical education for children. Although reaching this teaching goal may seem overwhelming—especially to those who do not see themselves as athletic—it is not. First, your desire to be a teacher is likely driven by concern and caring for children. All teaching tasks are easier when the students know you like them, care about their welfare, and believe they can learn. Second, you have time to learn and practice teaching physical education. Finally, you can work through the material in this book with your peers under the guidance of a knowledgeable and caring instructor.

Model for This Book

A single conceptual model guides this book—that is, the relationship among developmentally appropriate objectives, planning, instruction, and evaluation (figure 1.3). The NASPE physical education standards ("a physically educated person") are the overall goal of physical education. These standards are first translated into curricular objectives, then unit objectives, and finally lesson objectives. As a teacher, you should select units, lessons, and activities that help children and adolescents meet the standards. A variety of units and activities help children explore sport and physical activity. Note that children ages 6 through 12 years are in the "sampling" stage of sport: They try a variety of different activities and do not and should not specialize in one sport (Soberlak and Côté 2003). Specializing too early may lead a child to drop out of a sport (Côté, Baker, and Abernethy 2001) or to become less active as an adult (Robertson-Wilson, Baker, Derbinshyre, and Côté 2003). Each recommendation for physical activity for children stresses variety, skill development, and fun as important factors in developing physically active lifestyles. You should test their progress using age-appropriate benchmarks. Instruction that includes demonstration, directions, cues, practice, and feedback is designed to help students achieve the objectives of the lesson so that evaluation of the teaching and learning is focused on achievement of the objectives. Effective physical education programs translate the standards into developmentally appropriate activities and evaluations: Children at each age, grade, or skill level participate in different activities to master the same standard in a developmentally appropriate program.

One way to assess the effectiveness of the translation of the standards is to assess how obvious the relationship is among the four components in figure 1.3. For example, if you watch instruction, can you determine the objective? Or, by looking at the evaluation, can you identify the lesson plan? The CDC uses this model in the Physical Education Curriculum Analysis Tool (PECAT) to help schools assess their physical education programs. Another way to assess the effectiveness of the translation is to observe for differences among age, grade, and skill levels in the objectives, lesson plan, instruction, and evaluation. Developmentally appropriate programs are planned based on three principles:

1. The goal is to help all students become physically educated by achieving the content standards.
2. Plans are based on typical performance for the age, grade, and skill level of the students.
3. Planning and instruction accommodate individual differences.

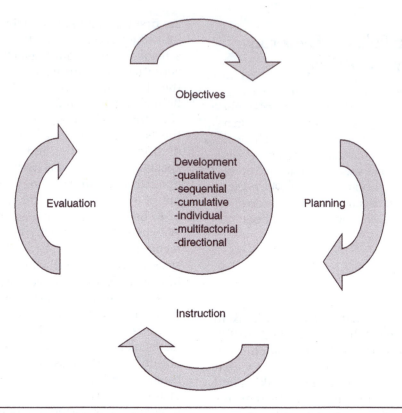

Figure 1.3 The relationship among objectives, planning, instruction, evaluation, and developmentally appropriate practice.

Summary

Teaching is demanding. Helping elementary school children learn to be physically active is a challenge for both specialists and classroom teachers. The benefits to individual health and well-being, as well as the benefits to the public health, make this an important part of the elementary school curriculum. The long-term goal of elementary physical education is twofold: nurturing an important part of child development (the psychomotor domain) and ensuring physically active lifestyles. Developmentally appropriate physical education programs, which recognize the similarities and differences among children while considering progression and age issues, address these two important goals. (See the DVD-ROM for teacher interviews on personal physical education goals.) Those who meet the standards for new teachers (either NCATE or INTASC) are ready to assume the challenge. Well-prepared teachers know what, how, and why to teach in order to maximize student learning. Children are naturally active and generally enjoy physical activity; this facilitates teaching physical education. Motor skills and the physical development associated with being active are important parts of child development and therefore essential ingredients in the elementary school curriculum. We explore this concept further in the next chapter.

Mastery Learning Activities

1. Find the licensing requirements for physical education in your state. Could you find this on the Department of Education Web site?

2. Find the state mandates for physical education in your state. Could you find this on the Department of Education Web site?

3. Select a school district. How many sessions per week and minutes per session of elementary physical education are taught? Who provides elementary instruction in this district?

4. Go to one of the Web sites listed under "Resources" at the end of this chapter. Find a "new fact," that is, something you did not know before going to the site.

5. Find one physical education or physical activity Web site not listed under "Resources." What information does this site provide and how could you use the information?

References

American Academy of Pediatrics. 2006. Active healthy living: Prevention of childhood obesity through increased physical activity. *Pediatrics* 117: 1834-1841.

Centers for Disease Control and Prevention (CDC). 1997. *Guidelines for school and community programs to promote lifelong physical activity among young people.* [Online.] Available: www.cdc.gov/mmwr/preview/mmwrhtml/00046823.htm [September 25, 2002].

CDC. 2007. *Healthy Youth! Coordinated school health program.* [Online.] Available: www.cdc.gov/Healthy Youth/CSHP/ [June 13, 2007].

Côté, J., J. Baker, and B. Abernethy. 2001. Stages of sport participation of expert decision-makers in team ball sports. In *Proceedings of the 10th World Congress of Sport Psychology.* Vol 3. Edited by A. Papaioannou, M. Goudas, and Y. Theodorakis, 150-152. Skiathos Island, Greece: International Society for Sport Psychology.

Dietz, W.H. 2004. The effects of physical activity on obesity. *Quest* 56: 1-11.

Interstate New Teacher Assessment and Support Consortium (INTASC). 1992. *Model standards for beginning teacher licensing and development: A resource for state dialogue.* Washington, DC: Council of Chief State School Officers.

National Association of Sport and Physical Education (NASPE). 1994. *Looking at physical education from a developmental perspective: A guide to teaching.* Reston, VA: NASPE Publications.

NASPE. 1995. *Moving into the future: National standards for physical education.* Boston: WCB/McGraw-Hill.

NASPE. 1997. *Shape of the nation report.* Reston, VA: NASPE Publications.

NASPE. 1999. *Guidelines for teacher preparation in physical education NASPE/NCATE guideline.* 4th ed. Reston, VA: NASPE Publications.

NASPE. 2004. *Moving into the future: National standards for physical education.* 2nd ed. Boston: McGraw-Hill.

NASPE. 2006. *Shape of the nation report.* Reston, VA: NASPE Publications.

National Association of State Boards of Education (NASBE). 2006. *Fit, healthy, and ready to learn: A school health policy guide.* [Online.] Available: www.nasbe.org/healthy_schools/FHRTL.htm [December 1, 2006].

Pate, R.R., M.G. Davis, T.N. Robinson, E.J. Stone, T.L. McKenzie, and J.C. Young. 2006. Promoting physical activity in children and youth: A leadership role for schools. *Circulation* 114: 1214-1225.

Robertson-Wilson, J., J. Baker, E. Derbinshyre, and J. Côté. 2003. Childhood sport involvement in active and inactive female adults. *AVANTE* 9: 1-8.

Soberlak, P., and J. Côté. 2003. The developmental activities of elite hockey players. *Journal of Applied Sport Psychology* 15: 41-49.

U.S. Department of Health and Human Services. 1979. *Surgeon general's report on health promotion and disease prevention.* Washington, DC: Government Printing Office.

U.S. Department of Health and Human Services. 1990. *Healthy people 2000: Surgeon general's report.* Washington, DC: Government Printing Office.

U.S. Department of Health and Human Services. 2000. *Healthy people 2010: Conference edition.* Washington, DC: Government Printing Office.

Wechsler, H., M.L. McKenna, S.M. Lee, and W.H. Dietz. December 2004. The role of schools in preventing childhood obesity. *The State Education Standard* 4-12.

Resources

Byers, T., M. Nestle, A. McTiernan, C. Doyle, A. Currie-Williams, T. Gansler, and M. Thun. 2002. American Cancer Society guidelines on nutrition and physical activity for cancer prevention. *CA: A Cancer Journal for Clinicians* 52: 92-119.

Centers for Disease Control and Prevention (CDC). Winter 2000. Chronic disease notes and reports. *National Centers for Disease Prevention and Health Promotion* 14(1): 7.

Lee, A.M., K.T. Thomas, and J.R. Thomas. 2000. *Physical education for children: Daily lesson plans for middle school.* 2nd ed. Champaign, IL: Human Kinetics.

Thomas, K.T., A.M. Lee, and J.R. Thomas. 2000. *Physical education for children: Daily lesson plans for elementary school.* 2nd ed. Champaign, IL: Human Kinetics.

www.healthypeople.gov

www.pbs.org/teachersource/health.htm

www.aahperd.org

www.cdc.gov

www.fns.usda.gov/tn/

www.presidentschallenge.org/the_challenge/joining_a_group.aspx

CHAPTER 2

Meeting the Mission
of the Elementary School

NICK, AGE 9

Elementary schools help children learn skills that are an essential part of child development. Mastering skills allows children to become productive members of society. Thus, the mission of the elementary school is to facilitate the transition from childhood to being a productive member of society. Physical education is generally acknowledged to be a contributor to child development: The psychomotor domain is one of the recognized domains of development. Furthermore, physical education can make an important contribution to individual well-being and therefore to public health.

Learner Outcomes

After studying this chapter, you should be able to do the following:

- State the goal of education.
- Describe why physical education is an essential part of the elementary school curriculum.
- List several ways physical activity and physical education contribute to the elementary school mission.
- Define an integrated physical education curriculum from three perspectives.
- Provide examples of integration.

Glossary Terms

mission	learning	allocated time
best practice	educational outcomes	academic learning time

The **mission** of elementary schools is to help children become contributing members of society. The schools serve children, their parents, and the broader community. In their mission statements, schools generally recognize individual differences and the need for a variety of approaches to meet the needs of all students. The long-term outcome of education is independence for the student. Specifically, at the end of their school careers, students should

- be financially self-supporting,
- understand how to continue to learn,
- have reached their potential in all three domains (affective, cognitive, and psychomotor), and
- understand their rights and responsibilities as citizens.

The Foundation

Elementary school establishes a foundation for students as they move toward independence. Each subject in the elementary school curriculum is meant to help all children, although some subjects may become the focus for certain children. For example, some children will dedicate their lives to music. Others develop mathematical skills into a vocation, and still others use language skills to enjoy reading and employment as a writer.

Citizens can be negative or positive members of a society. For example, a person who lives a healthy lifestyle, works to meet a need of society, and finds personal satisfaction with life contributes to the community. That person has value and is valued—by self and others. It is important that each person feel valued for his or her contributions and be valued by himself or herself and by others.

Each person contributes in his or her own unique way. During childhood, children learn about the importance of contributing and begin to identify and develop the skills necessary to make contributions. Poor health, unlawful behavior, and lack of skills are factors that drain the resources of society. These same factors may contribute to feelings of low self-worth in children. Therefore, as they influence children, elementary schools and, more specifically, the teachers that staff them make critical contributions to the well-being of society.

Mission Statements

Most elementary schools have mission statements that differ in wording and emphasis but emphasize the following common characteristics:

- Respect
- Individual differences
- Learning
- Citizenship

Respect includes the child's behavior toward the school and the teachers, and your behavior toward the child. Related to this is the notion that everyone is different. Children represent a variety of cultures, ethnicities, religions, and value sets. They enter school with a variety of abilities and potentials. Society expects schools and teachers to embrace those differences. In fact, the **best practice** is to use the differences among children to enhance learning by all children.

Learning is a broad term that focuses on acquisition of new skills or information retained over long periods or used under new circumstances. Often, learning is viewed as specific to content—for example, subjects such as mathematics, reading, or physical education. Learning in those content areas is often defined in terms of learning or **educational outcomes**. However, elementary schools facilitate other learning as well. As part of learning citizenship, children have opportunities to learn how to be members of a group, how and why to follow rules, and how to be leaders.

Elementary schools are increasingly adopting programs that are cross-curricular and that address specific needs. Often, these programs are not related to academic content. Character education programs are popular examples. Whether or not your school has a schoolwide program to address important but nonacademic learning, as a teacher, you have an impact on your students' beliefs and values. Your goal is to be a positive influence, helping the children become independent and contributing members of society. Children admire and model their teachers, who are important figures in a child's life. And the children—your students—are always watching. (See the DVD-ROM for teacher interviews on the role of physical education in a school's mission.)

Schools demonstrate what is valued in many ways; one way is in their mission statement. Many states now require schools to produce a school report card demonstrating the effectiveness of the school in educating students. Other schools use annual goals with benchmarks of performance. All of the teachers in the school are expected to make positive contributions to these schoolwide efforts.

Characteristics of Successful Schools

Successful schools often have three characteristics:

1. A shared mission—all teachers, staff, and often students and their parents, all working toward the same goals

2. Recognition of individual differences—a clear understanding of and plan to accommodate the strengths and weaknesses of everyone in the school

3. Developmentally appropriate curricula, with breadth, depth, and progression—a plan that respects the essential contributions of each subject area to the development of the whole child

In chapter 15, Growing as a Teacher, we examine collaboration and professional development as we revisit the school mission. Although chapter 8, Planning Your Curriculum, covers curriculum development in physical education, we cover the schoolwide curriculum issues in the rest of this chapter. A critical point is the balance between meeting general school goals and covering specific content. Everyone—teachers, administrators, and students—feels the pressure of time. Allocating time to one initiative means taking time from another. Childhood is a time for considerable learning—all of which is important. Therefore, it is difficult to prioritize, especially when adding something to the curriculum may mean deleting something else. Schools and teachers face challenging decisions about the overall curriculum and what happens in each classroom. One method used to address this problem is integration, or the idea of teaching two things at once. For example, reading a book about science reinforces the reading curriculum while simultaneously teaching about science. There are other ways of integrating as well.

Physical Activity and the Elementary School Mission

Physical activity can be integrated in the curriculum from four perspectives. The first is an integrated approach as presented in chapter 8, Planning Your Curriculum, where the three domains (cognitive, psychomotor, and affective) are targeted as objectives in each unit and lesson. The second is integration with class units of instruction. For example, third graders might include playing a traditional Native American game as part of a social studies unit on Native American culture. Third, physical activity can be integrated into a schoolwide event, such as National Reading Week. A fourth interpretation of integration is to make physical activity and the health benefits of a physically active lifestyle central to the mission of the school, as discussed in chapter 1, Health and Developmental Benefits of Physical Education.

Physical activity and physical education make important and independent contributions to child development and to the school curriculum. Children need physical activity to enhance the cardiovascular and muscular systems, to grow strong bones, to develop skills that allow them to be physically active and thereby healthier as adults, and to participate in important social activities during childhood. Motor skills and fitness are taught in physical education, but not in other academic areas. Therefore, physical education programs should not need to be justified by suggesting that physical education contributes to the learning of academic content. However, physical education programs must be consistent with the mission of the school and should contribute through integration as appropriate to academic learning. (See the DVD-ROM for teacher interviews on the importance of physical education for students.)

As a teacher, you need to understand integration for several reasons:

- To maximize student learning
- To ensure that all subject areas work together
- To address the needs of the whole child

Integrating the Domains

In chapter 8, Planning Your Curriculum, we target the three domains as objectives in each lesson. The cognitive domain objectives focus on knowledge of motor skills, fitness, and physical activities—concepts taught in the lesson. The cognitive objectives do not focus on concepts taught in other subject areas. Integration by addressing the three domains is important because knowing must precede doing or develop in concert with doing. The general cognitive skills, such as recall and decision making, can be practiced on any content—from algebra and aquatics to zoology and the zone defense. Learning in physical education depends as much on cognition as learning in mathematics or reading. This means that

Cognitive objectives teach important physical education content and support other subject areas.

18

cognitive objectives are appropriate and important in physical education. In many physical activities, teamwork, arousal, and moral behavior become important factors for success; therefore, cooperative or affective objectives are appropriate for physical education. Integration of the three domains is critical for success in many physical activities. Regardless of who teaches physical education—a specialist or a classroom teacher—physical education helps children practice important skills from the cognitive, affective, and psychomotor domains. In addition, physical education is likely to be the only place where students learn and demonstrate skills from the psychomotor domain.

Sample Cognitive Objectives

The student will

- name three locomotor skills;
- correctly identify skip, hop, and gallop;
- list two benefits of physical fitness; and
- state when a runner is "out" in baseball.

Classroom teachers may recognize success—and value—in some students when observing motor skills. A physical education specialist may find that a child with less motor skill contributes as a leader during class. In either case, two underlying beliefs are essential:

1. Each domain and objective of the elementary school is important and makes a contribution.
2. Children must be allowed to maximize their individual potential within each domain and must be recognized and valued for success in any domain.

What does this mean for you in the real world of teaching?

- If you are a physical education specialist, seek value in those children who are not as fit or as skilled.
- If you are a classroom teacher, recognize the value of physical education and children who find success in the psychomotor domain.

Accepting and acting on these beliefs helps all teachers meet the mission of the school. Consequently, physical education becomes a core value of the school as it contributes to health, wellness, and child development.

Integration With Schoolwide Initiatives

Two factors make the integration of physical education with schoolwide initiatives essential:

1. Physical education is uniquely qualified to demonstrate and foster what it means to be a team player. Schoolwide initiatives, such as National Reading Week or a character education program, succeed only when everyone has bought into the program. Teachers in every subject area need to engage themselves in the program activities, support the program, and work toward the success of the program for it to be successful. (See the DVD-ROM for teacher interviews on the Word Wall.)

2. The physical education specialist is often isolated, sometimes because the school does not convey information on schoolwide initiatives to the physical education teacher and, at other times, because the teacher chooses not to participate actively in schoolwide events. In contrast, schoolwide initiatives provide an excellent opportunity for physical education specialists to be a more integral part of the school and to further promote their curriculum to their students. Often, this means being proactive, however, and finding ways, on their own, to contribute.

So, how could a physical education teacher contribute to National Reading Week? How could a classroom teacher use physical activity to contribute to a National Reading Week initiative? Here are some ideas:

- Identify books about physical activity in the school library and suggest that your students read them.
- Select a theme from a book and develop physical education class activities related to that book.
- Assign a reading activity related to physical education.
- As a physical education teacher, volunteer to read to one or more classes.
- As a classroom teacher, lead the class in the physical activity from the selected book.

Table 2.1 Mrs. Braden's Reading Project

Overview of project	The book *Flat Stanley* is about a boy who becomes flat like a piece of paper. He has many adventures, as you learn from reading the book. This project creates an adventure for each second grader: A paper image of each child is mailed to another school with a cover letter and return envelope. The school's second grade teacher is asked to take a photo of the little visitor participating in the class' favorite physical activity. The class writes a description of that activity and returns everything (the photo, the visitor, and the description). Our class posts the photos with the "flat second graders" and then plays the games during physical education class.
Timeline	Who, what, when, where
Month 1	Contact second-grade classroom teachers about the project.
Month 2	Contact the librarian and make arrangements to check out the book *Flat Stanley*. Make a list of schools and address labels. Write a letter explaining the project.
Month 3	The art teacher assists in making "flat second graders." Mail "flat second graders" to schools with letters explaining the project.
Months 4-5	Wait.
Month 6	Open mail, post "flat second graders," and play games.

Ideas for integrating physical education into schoolwide programs are presented in table 2.1 and figure 2.1; these use a reading campaign and Team Nutrition (a USDA nutrition and physical activity program) as the targets of the integration. Sources for award-winning books are available on the American Library Association Web site (www.ala.org). For example, *The Story of Jumping Mouse: A Native American Legend*, retold and illustrated by John Steptoe (Lothrop; Caldecott Honor Book in 1985), and *Casey at the Bat: A Ballad of the Republic Sung in the Year 1888*, illustrated by Christopher Bing, written by Ernest Lawrence Thayer (Handprint Books; Caldecott Honor book in 2000), can both be integrated into a physical education lesson or unit. Many more similar books are available. Your school media specialist should be able to help you find them.

Integration With Subject Matter

There are two approaches to integrating physical education with subject matter (e.g., social studies or mathematics). One approach is to work with the teacher and plan a systematic integration. The other approach is less formal.

Systematic Integration

When the classroom teacher teaches physical education, the communication is simple, but the process still requires planning and thought. Finding time to plan can be a barrier to integration.

Classroom teachers have many subjects to plan and may feel less comfortable or knowledgeable about integrating physical activity. One solution, especially in the upper grades, is to have your students help with integration! In social studies, the students can research games or dances from another culture; in other subject areas, teams of students can create games or activities that meet criteria that you establish. For example, to integrate with math, the game must be scored using numbers divisible by 7, or, for a reading unit, the game must use characters or sayings from a book or story the class read recently. Although it is helpful to collaborate with colleagues or physical education specialists on ideas, this is not always possible or practical. Do not be discouraged: Take the risk and try integration.

Concepts Into Practice

As part of its summer enrichment program, a local elementary school selected the Philippines as their project. The school adopted a recently immigrated family and the students read books about the country, tasted ethnic foods, and made traditional costumes. The physical education teacher taught tinikling—a Filipino dance using bamboo poles. The summer unit culminated with a program for parents in which the students wore the clothes, served the snacks, and performed the dance of the Filipino culture.

Team Nutrition Iowa
Hop, Jump, and Dance Like Betsy

Arrange the children in a long line facing you.

Betsy is a frog in the book "Hop, Jump" (by Ellen S. Walsh, 1993, Harcourt, Brace & Co). This activity copies Betsy's movements and allows the children to create movements of their own. Betsy watches the other frogs hop and jump, but she wants to try other movements. At first the other frogs say "no room for dancing," but after watching her, they try dancing and like it. Then they say "no room for hopping and jumping," but Betsy tells us there is room for everyone.

Begin by jumping forward (jumping is with both feet at the same time). Try short quick jumps, long jumps, and jumps up into the air.

Next try hopping (jumping on one foot at a time, several hops at a time). Repeat on the other foot.

Betsy leaped (long running step) and did twisting and turning. Show the children leaping, and have them try it. Repeat with several turns.

Betsy and the frogs began to dance, combining jumps, hops, turns, leaps, and other movements. Expand by having everyone hop-jump while one person dances, then reverse.

Figure 2.1 Team Nutrition curricular materials focus on integrating nutrition and physical activity across the curriculum.

From *Physical Activities and Healthy Snacks for Young Children*, Iowa Department of Education, Bureau of Food and Nutrition (2001) by L. Sands (snacks) and K.T. Thomas (physical activity). Reprinted by permission.

Informal Integration

The physical education specialist may be able to infer from what the children say or what he or she can learn from the curriculum about how to use classroom skills in the gym. Classroom teachers can help physical education specialists by sharing information; we elaborate on such collaborations in chapter 15, Growing as a Teacher. Regardless of who teaches physical education, one example of integration is to use numbers in scoring that challenge the math skills of the students. For example, rather than using 1 point for each score, use 7 or 9 points; then for penalties you can divide the score by 0.25 and really challenge the students! If the students are studying Native Americans in social studies class, playing games or performing dances from that culture would be an excellent integration. This requires some research but is worth the effort.

Two important things should guide your decisions about this type of integration, whether you are a classroom teacher or a physical education specialist:

1. Make sure your content information is accurate—do the research!

2. Do not sacrifice physical education content to reinforce subject area knowledge. Physical education is important, and the content stands alone.

However, when integration is possible and practical and information is reliable, all areas of education can benefit.

Concepts Into Practice

In physical education in the primary grades, challenge your students to think of a new word learned in each physical education class. Write these words on poster paper and tape them high on the gym wall. After a few weeks, ask the children to read and think creatively to meet the challenge of identifying the new words!

Final Notes About Integration

Although integration is a sound and generally accepted educational approach, the idea of integration has been confused with and confounded by two other educational issues. One is the feeling that more time is needed for academics and therefore time should not be allocated to physical education. This has led physical educators to the second issue: They tend to justify their programs based on the programs' contributions to academic performance rather than to performance in physical education. There is little evidence that either of these approaches works in successfully promoting physical education (Kavale and Matson 1983). Trying to improve reading or math skills by performing certain skills in physical education (e.g., balancing or bouncing a ball) and teaching academic skills while doing movements (e.g., tossing a ball into a target exhibiting the answers to math problems) have not improved academic skills and have often interfered with the learning of motor skills, an undesirable outcome.

Several studies have looked at time spent in physical education. The results show that more time in physical education does not lower standardized test scores (Sallis, McKenzie, Kolody, Lewis, Marshall, and Rosengard 1999). Furthermore, more time spent in school or academic classes does not necessarily enhance test scores or grades (Berliner 1990). In fact, there is evidence that **allocated time** (the time spent in school for instruction and practice) does not predict student learning for most students (Berliner 1990). Increased **academic learning time** is associated with improved outcomes for some sectors of the population (e.g., students from socioeconomically low, at-risk homes). Learning is probably enhanced to a greater degree by the quality rather than the quantity of time. There is some evidence that both physical education and recess may enhance academic performance and classroom behavior in some children (e.g., in girls and special-needs children; Keays 1995; Sallis et al. 1999; Shepard 1983). There is no evidence that 25 to 50 minutes of physical activity during each school day negatively affect academic performance. There is a great deal of evidence, however, that physical activity is an important part of child development and has a long-term positive impact on health.

Integration does not mean replacing physical education and the learning of motor skills with practice time for academic skills. But integration does mean supporting all areas of the curriculum and teaching the whole child. The goal for all physical education programs is to develop positive lifestyles and skills in students, to make physical activity central to the mission of the school, to work toward the school mission (including schoolwide programs), and to integrate physical activity into academic subjects as appropriate.

Teaching the Whole Child

Many theories of child development and learning have influenced elementary education. This wealth of influences has come from educators and psychologists who have developed curriculum and instruction based on a theory or a blend of theories. Two currently popular theories are Gardner's theory of multiple intelligences (MI; Gardner 1983) and constructivism (Perkins 1992).

Unfortunately, educators often view theories as methodologies. Yet theory does not automatically translate into effective teaching methodology. In addition, educators often think that no two theories have anything in common but are mutually exclusive. To clarify, theories provide a testable framework to explain observations and to make predictions. Testing and predicting are usually done in research studies, often with several teams of scholars conducting experiments. Sometimes theories are either adopted as truth with very little empirical evidence (e.g., research studies testing the theory) or dispensed with when one study or case fails to support the theory. This means that, as practitioners (teachers), you must think through theories carefully before depending on them.

Although theories are often perceived as mutually exclusive, most theories have a great deal in common. The studies testing the theories have similar findings. Think about what might cause the theories to be similar. Two factors indicating that educational theories have many similarities focus

1. on how children learn, and, often,
2. on how teachers facilitate that learning.

For example, information processing theory and Piaget's theory both identify the same ages for critical changes in how children solve problems (Thomas, Gallagher, and Thomas 2000). The two theories explain the changes differently and use different methods, but both have been tested extensively by scholars around the world.

A practical approach is to examine the theories and follow those that reflect commonalities and themes that run through several dominant theories. Those themes are likely to be the most important for you to use as you plan curriculum and instruction.

Gardner's Theory of MI

Gardner challenged the traditional view of intelligence (Brualdi 1996; Gardner 1983, 1991). Intel-

Games and other physical activities provide opportunities to practice cooperation and motor skills.

ligence had previously been viewed as a singular dimension, representing a person's ability to solve problems. The traditional view of intelligence is that you are born with it, that it cannot be changed, and that it can be measured. Traditional views hold intelligence to be an innate ability that represents potential for learning and cognitive performance. Tests of intelligence were designed to help schools identify areas in which students might need assistance. Those tests typically focus on numeric skills and literacy (e.g., the Scholastic Aptitude Test [SAT] and the Stanford–Binet IQ Test).

In contrast, Gardner has suggested that these tests do not accurately represent a person's ability because they are limited in focus. In response, he posits the existence of seven different intelligences: musical, logical-mathematical, linguistic, spatial, interpersonal, intrapersonal, and bodily kinesthetic intelligence (Gardner 1983). Subsequently, he added naturalistic as an eighth intelligence and suggests that there may be additional intelligences (Checkley 1997).

Impact on Education

The impact of traditional intelligence testing on education has been its focus on literacy and numeracy as primary values and therefore cur-

ricular areas. Students who did not excel in one or both of those areas were often left out of the educational plan. Gardner suggests that tests, teachers, and schools use a broader array of markers and widen the focus of the curriculum to include all seven intelligences and others as well. The critical feature of this theory is to find value in each child and to find a path to success for each student. Furthermore, educators need to use multiple and creative sources of information to assess children's abilities. Clearly, Gardner advocates that educators move away from multiple-choice tests and toward more authentic assessments of a broad range of content.

Controversy

MI theory is controversial, especially in the area of bodily kinesthetic intelligence (Checkley 1997). One reason for dispute is that intelligence has traditionally been viewed as stable and innate. This definition is more consistent with the traditional definition of performance, which is unstable and influenced by both innate and learned factors. Gardner has used examples of athletes to demonstrate bodily kinesthetic intelligence. Movement is controlled in the brain and is important across cultures, and it varies among individuals, meeting Gardner's criteria for an intelligence. Three criticisms of MI are that (1) Gardner does not deal with the issue of practice, (2) considerable research indicates that only a small portion of athletic performance is biological (or inherited), and (3) sport experts are often experts because of their cognitive decision making.

Gardner states that MI is best implemented in schools because "a teacher takes individual differences among children very seriously" (Checkley 1997). Teachers often confuse MI with learning styles, according to Gardner. For example, a visual learner is not the same as a person with high bodily kinesthetic intelligence. The descriptions Gardner uses for the seven or eight intelligences are similar to descriptions of talent—a fair description according to Gardner. Gardner does not suggest that an appropriate use of MI theory is to teach math or reading by having children who are high in bodily kinesthetic intelligence use movement to learn that content. Clearly, however, he does encourage teachers and schools to respect and nurture a variety of ways for students to contribute.

Constructivism

Constructivism is another theory that has been used to guide educational practice. Constructivist theory advocates for students to create their own understanding through active involvement in the learning process. The theory has evolved from information processing theory (Anderson, Reder, and Simon 1998) and Piaget's theory. Bruner (1973) noted the benefits of active versus passive learning during his information processing research, making him a pioneer in constructivist theory. Social and cognitive constructivism have further defined the theory.

Social Constructivism

Social constructivism suggests that information is interpreted by the learner based on personal experience and context, so what is learned in the same situation varies from person to person.

Cognitive Constructivism

Cognitive constructivism is the basis for some language, math, and science practices, so educators often refer to this as "constructivist theory." Cognitive constructivism has two dimensions:

1. How information is presented forms one dimension.

- "BIG" means taking the activity Beyond the Information Given by the teacher. In this case, a constructivist teacher would have students create learning to extend what the teacher had presented.
- "WIG" means the students create learning Without Information Given by the teacher (Perkins 1992). Instead, students create all of the information.

2. The other dimension concerns how far the theory has moved away from information processing.

- Radical constructivists do not believe in practice, assessment, or instruction and would be more likely to follow WIG.
- Conservative constructivists tend to rely on the empirical evidence from information processing and extend that to classroom practice with a focus on active learning and contextual accuracy.

Strengths and Weaknesses

A weakness of constructivism, unfortunately, is the lack of empirical evidence supporting the theory—especially radical constructivism (Anderson, Reder, and Simon 1998). However, as chapter 5, Cognition, Learning, and Practice, indicates, considerable empirical evidence supports information processing theory. Conservative constructivism is grounded in theory that has empirical support and the major premise of the theory—active learning—is well respected.

The idea is that understanding, learning, and memory are enhanced when the student is actively involved in the process. For example, rather than explain in a lecture several ways to solve a math problem, the teacher might challenge students to create as many ways as possible to arrive at the correct answer. Many physical education lessons use this approach as well. For example, you might ask, "How many ways can you move your body without moving your feet?" The students would then be challenged to demonstrate many nonlocomotor tasks, such as swaying, bending, twisting, stretching, or wiggling. Motor learning theory has demonstrated the benefit to active rather than passive practice for many years (Schmidt and Lee 1999).

Mission: Possible

At this point, your choice to be a teacher may seem overwhelming! You are going to teach content to children, help them become citizens, and identify the value in each child. In addition, you will be expected to bring theories into realistic practice. Yes, it is a challenge—but one with great rewards. The mission of the school is met because each teacher contributes to it. One lesson, one classroom, one child at a time, you help children become productive members of society. Your decision to become a teacher shows your compassion, caring, and dedication to that goal. You harvest rewards in terms of student learning, attainment of goals, and the value your students have in their communities. You enjoy two more rewards as a teacher: being a member of a community of professional educators and having the opportunity to share in the joy of your students' achievements. You share values and goals with other teachers; therefore, you find special collegiality in your school. Furthermore, you experience the personal joy of teaching, of your other accomplishments, and of the accomplishments of your students. Teaching is not a job: it is a career and a profession. What a wonderful calling!

Regardless of the educational philosophy or theory to which you and your school subscribe, the information in this book is likely to help you support the mission of your school, and physical activity and physical education do not operate in a vacuum. The psychomotor domain is an important component of child development; it makes unique contributions and is mastered in ways similar to other domains. Consequently, physical education activities directly and indirectly support the mission of the school.

Summary

As a teacher in an elementary school, you help your school accomplish its mission. Likewise, each subject area makes a contribution to the development of the child and to the mission of the school—including physical education. Teachers and students have different strengths and therefore make different contributions. The fact that each person is unique creates a richer learning environment and supports accomplishing the mission of the school. Integration of content is an efficient and effective way to address the multifaceted mission of the school and to help children develop across all domains. Make decisions about curriculum and instruction based on theory, practical issues, knowledge about child development, and the school mission.

Consider using the following principles to guide your decisions as a teacher:

1. Active participation enhances learning.
2. Each child is different and valuable.
3. Using a variety of approaches is desirable.
4. Each domain is important.
5. All teachers—including you—contribute to the school mission and influence a student's development in each domain.

The next section of the book provides information about child development, specifically motor development. This information helps you understand the science of children's physical activity—the "why" of the teaching and learning process.

Mastery Learning Activities

1. Find an elementary school Web site that gives the school's mission statement. Identify three ways that physical education helps support the school's mission statement.

2. Read Kavale and Matson and, in 75 words or less, discuss what is wrong with perceptual motor programs.

3. Read about two theories of education and identify two differences and two similarities between the theories.

4. Make two lists, one for classroom teachers and one for physical education specialists. One list should identify five ways classroom teachers can support physical education goals (e.g., facilitating physically active lifestyles and skill development) in the classroom. The other should identify at least five ways the physical education teacher can support classroom learning.

References

Anderson, J.R., L.M. Reder, and H.A. Simon. 1998. Radical constructivism and cognitive psychology. In *Brookings papers on education policy: 1998*, edited by D. Ravitch, 227-255. Washington, DC: Brookings Institution.

Berliner, D. 1990. What is all the fuss about instructional time? In *The nature of time in schools: Theoretical concepts, practitioner perceptions*, edited by M. Ben-Peretz and R. Bromme, 3-35. New York: Teachers College Press.

Brualdi, A.C. 1996. *Multiple intelligences: Gardner's theory.* [Online.] ERIC Digest (ED410226). Available: http://ericir.syr.edu/ [September 8, 2002]. Washington, DC.

Bruner, J. 1973. *Going beyond the information given.* New York: Norton.

Checkley, K. 1997. The first seven . . . and the eighth: A conversation with Howard Gardner. *Educational Leadership* 55 (September):1-7.

Gardner, H. 1983. *Frames of mind.* New York: Basic Books.

Gardner, H. 1991. *The unschooled mind: How children think and how schools should teach.* New York: Basic Books.

Kavale, K., and P.D. Matson. 1983. One jumped off the balance beam: A meta analysis of perceptual motor training programs. *Journal of Learning Disabilities* 16: 165-173.

Keays, J.J. 1995. The effects of regular moderate-to-vigorous physical activity on student outcomes: A review. *Canadian Journal of Public Health* 86: 62-65.

Perkins, D.N. 1992. Technology meets constructivism: Do they make a marriage? In *Constructivism and the technology of instruction: A conversation,* edited by T.M. Duffy and D.H. Jonassen, 45-55. Hillsdale, NJ: Erlbaum.

Sallis, J.F., T.L. McKenzie, B. Kolody, M. Lewis, S. Marshall, and P. Rosengard. 1999. Effects of health-related physical education on academic achievement: Project SPARK. *Research Quarterly for Exercise and Sport* 70: 127-136.

Schmidt, R.A., and T.D. Lee. 1999. *Motor control and learning: A behavioral approach.* 3rd ed. Champaign, IL: Human Kinetics.

Shepard, R.J. 1983. Physical activity and the healthy mind. *Canadian Medical Association Journal* 128: 525-530.

Thomas, K.T., J.D. Gallagher, and J.R. Thomas. 2000. Motor development and skill acquisition during childhood and adolescence. In *Handbook of sport psychology,* 2nd ed., edited by R.N. Singer, H.A. Hausenblas, and C. Janelle, 20-52. New York: Wiley.

Resources

Sources for children's books:

U.S. Department of Education: www.ed.gov

American Library Association: www.ala.org

Lesson Plans

The organization lesson plan for grades 4 and 5 uses journal writing to stimulate thinking about physical education. Practice at writing supports language arts and is one way of integrating subjects to meet the school mission. Journal writing does not detract from physical education content; instead, the journals help teachers understand student learning and beliefs. The rhythmic lesson for grade 6 presents tinikling, which was used as an example of integration with social studies earlier in this chapter. Cognitive concepts important in physical education and in the classroom are presented in lessons. The concepts for grades K and 1 are body parts and relationships (over and under), and the concepts for grades 2 and 3 are directions.

Lesson 2.1

Body Parts

Student Objectives 2 5

- Demonstrate various relationships between beanbags and their bodies (high, behind, on knees).
- Balance the beanbag on various body parts when moving.
- Demonstrate following the rules in a simple game using beanbags.
- Cooperate when playing Over and Under.

Equipment and Materials

- 1 beanbag per child, minimum
- Signal

Safety Tips

- For the warm-up game, stress touching body parts gently, not bumping, banging, or hitting.
- Remind the children to respect other children's personal space (space they can be in without touching anyone else).

Warm-Up Activities (5 minutes)

Run and Touch

Arrange the children in a widespread scatter formation.

1. Explain the activity:
   - I call a body part, and you each run to another child and touch those body parts together. For example, when I call, "Knees," run and touch your knees to a partner's knees.
   - On each call, find a new partner, never repeating partners.
2. Have the children play Run and Touch.

Skill-Development Activities (15 minutes)

Movement Challenges

Arrange the children in scatter formation; each child has a beanbag.

1. Tell the children: "Put your beanbag up high. (Child's name)'s beanbag is really high (low)!"
2. Ask the children: "How low can you hold your beanbag? Can you hold it in front of you (behind you, under you, beside you, between high and low)?" Tell the children: "Touch your foot (head, neck, knee, ankle, shoulder, elbow, calf, chest, shin, forearm, wrist, hip, tummy, back, chin) with your beanbag."
3. Discuss any body parts that the children have trouble recognizing, such as shin, chin, or forearm.

4. Tell the children: "Balance your beanbag on your forearm (head, elbow, knee, shoulder, wrist, ankle, chest, foot). Balance your beanbag on your hand (arm, thigh, head, shoulder, chest) and walk slowly."

Concluding Activities (10 minutes)

Over and Under

Arrange the children in a circle facing counterclockwise. Give a beanbag to each of 3 to 6 children spaced around the circle so that approximately the same number of children are between each beanbag.

1. Describe and demonstrate the game:
   ○ On the start signal, pass the beanbags alternately over one child's head and between (or under) the next child's legs.
   ○ Do not drop beanbags, never go over or under two children in a row, and try to move as many beanbags as quickly as possible around the circle.
   ○ I will gradually increase the number of beanbags and the speed. When you make mistakes (drops or two overs or unders), I will stop the game and slow down the speed or take away one or more of the beanbags.
   ○ I am looking for you to really cooperate with each other.
2. Have the children play Over and Under.

From K.T. Thomas, A.M. Lee, and J.R. Thomas, 2008, *Physical education methods for elementary teachers*, 3rd ed. (Champaign, IL: Human Kinetics). Adapted, by permission, from K.T. Thomas, A.M. Lee, and J.R. Thomas, 2000, *Physical education for children: Daily lesson plans for elementary school*, 2nd ed. (Champaign, IL: Human Kinetics), 97-98.

Lesson 2.2

Hopping

Student Objectives 1 2 5

- Move through space using various combinations of hopping steps.
- Work cooperatively when playing Follow the Leader.
- Identify hopping (as opposed to jumping).

Equipment and Materials

- Polyspots, polydomes, paint, chalk, or tape to mark 1 hopscotch area per group
- Signal

Warm-Up Activities (5 minutes)

Sneaky Tag

Arrange the children into two groups, one group on a start line and the other group on Xs (see figure on this page). (You can make the lines and Xs on a hard surface with polyspots or polydomes and on grass or dirt with paint.) The children on the start line are the "Sneakers," and the children on the Xs are the "Taggers."

1. Describe and demonstrate the game:
   - On the signal, the Sneakers move through the Taggers, trying to get to the end line without being tagged. Sneakers must stay within the boundaries, and Taggers must keep at least one toe touching their X.
   - If you are tagged, run around the outside trackway and back to the start line during the next round (from finish line to start line).

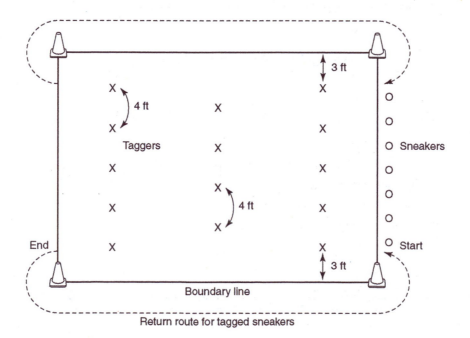

Lesson 2.2 *(continued)*

- After several rounds, switch Taggers and Sneakers.
- Sneakers use this strategy: When a Tagger is trying to reach you on one side, run by on the other side.

2. Have the children play Sneaky Tag.

Skill-Development Activities (15 minutes)

Hopping Skills

Arrange the children in scatter formation.

1. Challenge the children with the following tasks:
   - Hop forward and backward (then side to side).
   - Hop and change direction (speed, pathway) on the signal.
   - Hop a figure eight.
   - Hop as far as you can.
   - Hop and land facing another direction.
2. Have them repeat the challenges on the other foot.

Follow the Leader

Divide the children into groups of 4 to 6.

1. Describe the game:
   - Choose one child to lead, and the rest follow, imitating the leader's actions.
   - The leader must use a hopping pattern (changing combinations of right- and left-footed hopping).
   - Change the leader when you hear the signal.
2. Children play Follow the Leader, signaling groups to change leaders every 60 seconds.

Name That Skill

1. Ask a child to demonstrate hopping and then jumping.
2. Demonstrate jumping and ask another child to name the skill.
3. Repeat with hopping.

Concluding Activities (10 minutes)

Hopscotch

Arrange the children in groups of 4 to 6, and place each group at a hopscotch area.

1. Describe the activity:
   - Hop through the diagrams, first on your right foot and then on your left.
   - Repeat, going backward.
   - If you step on a line or lose your balance, start again.
2. Have the children play Hopscotch.

From K.T. Thomas, A.M. Lee, and J.R. Thomas, 2008, *Physical education methods for elementary teachers*, 3rd ed. (Champaign, IL: Human Kinetics). Adapted, by permission, from K.T. Thomas, A.M. Lee, and J.R. Thomas, 2000, *Physical education for children: Daily lesson plans for elementary school*, 2nd ed. (Champaign, IL: Human Kinetics), 521-523.

Lesson 2.3

Forming Groups, Journal Writing

Student Objectives   2   5   6

- Form groups of various sizes quickly and quietly.
- State your feelings about physical education in writing.

Equipment and Materials

- 1 notebook and pencil per child
- 1 color-shape-number card per child

Warm-Up Activities (10 minutes)

Forming Groups

Continue to work on forming groups with the following adaptation.

1. Make cards before class and distribute them to the children as they enter the gym.
2. Cards should be four colors (red, blue, yellow, green). Stamp them with various shapes (circle, triangle, rectangle, square).
3. Number the cards from 1 to the number of children in the class.
4. Present the following tasks:
   - Find a partner who has the same color.
   - Find a partner who has the same shape.
5. Form two groups: Red and blue make the first group, and yellow and green make the second group.
6. Continue with other combinations:
   - Form two groups: Group 1 = first half of numbers; Group 2 = second half of numbers.
   - Form four groups: Group 1 = circles; Group 2 = squares; Group 3 = rectangles; Group 4 = triangles.
7. Continue using color and shape combinations to form groups.

Skill-Development Activities (15 minutes)

Feelings About Physical Education

Arrange children in scatter formation, each child with a notebook and pencil.

1. Ask the children: "What were your feelings when you were in physical education last year?"
2. Stimulate children's thinking by asking them to complete the following open-ended statements:
   - I feel good in physical education when I . . .

- The activity I enjoyed most was . . .
- It was my favorite activity because . . .
- The times I feel uncomfortable in physical education are when . . .
- I believe physical education is (or is not) important for children because . . .

3. Insist that this be a serious activity and that you will keep the children's responses private and not discuss them in class.
4. Read the journals to get ideas about what children think and feel about their experiences in physical education.

Concluding Activities (5 minutes)

Discussion

Arrange children in an advanced information formation. Continue the discussion of the importance of rules:

- Why is it important to stop and listen quickly on the teacher's signal?
- What might happen if some children do not use the equipment in the way it is intended?

Describe what a good physical education class would look like to a stranger.

From K.T. Thomas, A.M. Lee, and J.R. Thomas, 2008, *Physical education methods for elementary teachers*, 3rd ed. (Champaign, IL: Human Kinetics). Adapted, by permission, from K.T. Thomas, A.M. Lee, and J.R. Thomas, 2000, *Physical education for children: Daily lesson plans for elementary school*, 2nd ed. (Champaign, IL: Human Kinetics), 762-763.

Lesson 2.4

Tinikling

Student Objectives   1

- Perform the Basic Tinikling Step.

Equipment and Materials

- 1 short jump rope for each child
- Record: "Tinikling," Kimbo (KEA 8095, 9015)
- 6 to 8 sets of bamboo poles (8 to 12 feet [2.4 to 3.7 m])

Warm-Up Activities (5 minutes)

Rhythmic Patterns With Ropes

Arrange the children in scatter formation with their jump ropes in circles on the ground.

1. The children jump in and out of the circles in a 3/4 rhythm: for example, 2 jumps in and 1 jump out.
2. The children continue jumping rhythmically to a drumbeat. Have them try 1 jump in and 2 jumps out.

Skill-Development Activities (20 minutes)

Basic Tinikling Step

Arrange the children in groups of 4 in scatter formation. Each group has a set of tinikling poles.

1. Have the children listen to tinikling music, clapping and counting the 3/4 time.
2. The children in each group begin by standing with right sides to the poles.
3. Describe and demonstrate counts 1 to 3.
   - Count 1: Step in place with the left foot (the foot away from the pole).
   - Count 2: Step with the right foot between the poles.
   - Count 3: Step with the left foot between the poles (lift up the right foot).

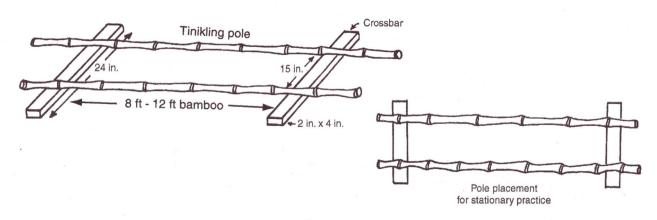

Tinikling pole

Crossbar

24 in.

15 in.

8 ft - 12 ft bamboo

2 in. x 4 in.

Pole placement
for stationary practice

4. Arrange the sticks on the floor and practice with the sticks stationary. In each group, all children practice at the same time.

5. Have the children practice counts 1 to 3. Say to the children: "Step left, right between, left between."

6. Describe and demonstrate counts 4 to 6.

   ○ Count 4: Step with the right foot out to the right of the poles.

   ○ Count 5: Step with the left foot between the poles.

   ○ Count 6: Step with the right foot between the poles (lift up the left foot).

   ○ Count 7: Step with the left foot to the left side of the poles. (Count 7 becomes count 1 for the second step.)

7. Have the children practice all of the counts. Say to the children: "Step left, right between, left between, right out, left between, right between, left out."

8. Have the children repeat the Basic Tinikling Step, counts 1 to 6.

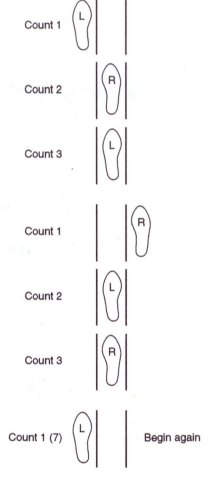

Concluding Activities (5 minutes)

Basic Tinikling Step

The children perform the Basic Tinikling Step, one child in each group at a time, to music; on count 7, the second child enters and the first child exits. Repeat until each child in each group has had several turns.

From K.T. Thomas, A.M. Lee, and J.R. Thomas, 2008, *Physical education methods for elementary teachers*, 3rd ed. (Champaign, IL: Human Kinetics). Adapted, by permission, from A.M. Lee, K.T. Thomas, and J.R. Thomas, 2000, *Physical education for children: Daily lesson plans for middle school*, 2nd ed. (Champaign, IL: Human Kinetics), 196-198.

PART II

Addressing the Child's Needs

Children are not miniature adults—if they were, teaching would be easier and parenting would be less of a mystery! Each of the five chapters in this section covers a different aspect of motor development:

- Physical growth and maturation
- Motor performance during childhood
- Cognition, learning, and practice
- Physical activity for children
- Psychosocial factors in physical education

The first section of each chapter is organized around the four principles outlined in the following paragraph, with the goal of demonstrating the principle within each aspect of motor development. The principles are followed by a section with greater detail on that aspect of motor development. Every chapter ends with lesson plans that apply the motor development information to teaching.

We selected the following principles because each one of them is important in understanding how children develop and what that means for physical education.

- *Children are not miniature adults.* AKA: As people get older, they get better. Childhood lasts for about 12 years and is followed by adolescence, which continues for several more years. There is a reason for this extended period of development. Development is a process that takes time and nurturing in order to reach a successful conclusion.

- *Boys and girls are more alike than different.* Although in each chapter we use the example of gender as a difference, the fact is that all children are more alike than different. The focus of this principle is, of course, inclusion—whether the difference between two children is race, ethnicity, culture, gender, disability, or socioeconomic status.

- *Good things are earned.* If environment did not matter, schools would be unnecessary—as would teachers. The educational system is based on the notion that environment (and nurturing) does matter. The foundation of physical education is effort, practice, and improvement for mastery. Motor development research suggests that good things come to those who work hard.

- *No body is perfect.* Good teachers embrace the uniqueness of each child. There is variability among children and within each child. The educator's job is to leverage the potential of each child by understanding how children are different, how they develop, and how they learn.

CHAPTER 3

Physical Growth and Maturation

TINA. AGE 6

During childhood and adolescence, children grow larger and become mature. Proportions change because body parts and systems grow and mature at different rates. Age-related differences in body size, proportion, and composition influence motor performance. Boys and girls are comparable in these areas prior to puberty. Even after puberty, however, the differences should be small and have a relatively small impact on performance of motor skills.

Learner Outcomes

After studying this chapter, you should be able to do the following:

- Define growth and maturation.

- Describe the impact of puberty on growth for boys and girls.

- Relate growth to performance.

- Distinguish among growth factors that are genetic and environmental.

- Use knowledge of growth and maturation to select, plan, teach, and modify appropriate activities for children.

Glossary Terms

maturation	development	puberty	body composition
growth	experience	stature	physique

Every teacher should understand how children mature, grow, and develop. **Maturation** is the rate of progress toward an adult state, which is controlled genetically by the child's chronometer (biological time clock). This means that the environment has little influence on maturation and that each child has a unique maturational calendar. Characteristics appear in the same order for all children, but at different chronological ages among children. **Growth** is a change in body size that results from more and bigger body cells and more intercellular material. Growth and maturation are related; that is, growth patterns are influenced by and indicative of maturation. **Development** is the change in a child's level of functioning. Development is a combination of growth, maturation, and experience. **Experience** is external or environmental and includes factors such as nutrition, education, and home life. This chapter focuses on growth and maturation as components of development.

You should understand growth, maturation, and development for three reasons:

1. You should monitor growth, maturation, and development in your students. If unusual deviations occur, advise the principal, nurse, or parents so that the child can be evaluated by appropriate professionals.

2. You should select and teach activities based on your knowledge about growth, maturation, and development.

3. You need to be able to answer questions that children ask about their bodies and the process of development.

Physical growth and some aspects of maturation are observable biological characteristics. In fact, physical growth is measurable in inches (centimeters) and pounds (kilograms). Some measures of maturation are also observable, but others are not. The best-known process of maturation during childhood is "going through puberty." Puberty is controlled by a biological time clock, which varies among children (Malina 1984). As facial and body hair appear on young males and breasts develop on young females, the process of sexual maturation has begun. This beginning of puberty is called pubescence. However, no observable indicators determine when sexual maturation is fully attained. For females, the onset of menstruation is used as a marker of sexual maturation, but this point does not necessarily mean that reproductive capacity has been reached. For males, there is no clear marker. Growth and maturation are related; for example, from 9 to 11 years of age, boys and girls typically experience a prepubescent growth spurt.

The Four Guiding Principles

Now we explore in more detail the four guiding principles outlined on page 35 in regard to growth and maturation. Keep in mind as you study this chapter that each of the principles is important to understanding how children develop and what this means for physical education.

Principle 1. Children Are Not Miniature Adults

Children are smaller than adults. But, if you drew a child and adult to the same scale, they would look very different because children have different capacity, proportions, and composition. Their capacity changes during puberty as reproductive function is achieved.

Children have relatively larger heads, shorter extremities, and smaller torsos than adults (Malina 1984). Compared to an adult, the younger the child is, the greater is the difference in proportion. Progress toward the adult form is gradual across childhood and adolescence. At birth, the head is about 25 percent of the total body length; for an adult the head is about 12 percent of the total height. Similarly, adult leg length accounts for at least half of the total height; at birth, the legs are about 30 percent of total body length. If all body parts grew at the same rate during childhood, adults would have the same proportions as infants. The extremities grow faster than the torso,

which grows faster than the head. Consider how difficult tasks such as balancing and jumping are for young children based on their short legs and large heads.

Select activities and equipment to meet the needs of each developmental level. For example, when teaching gymnastics, using special wedge-shaped mats helps young children overcome the mechanical disadvantage of their relatively large heads and short arms and legs. Professional physical educators understand how to select activities that are appropriate for the age, developmental, and experience level of the children. They also select modified equipment, such as larger, softer balls (e.g., foam balls) instead of baseballs, to help younger children master skills.

Principle 2. Boys and Girls Are More Alike Than Different

The bodies of girls and boys are more alike than different during childhood; however, differences emerge during puberty that give males a performance advantage in certain activities (Malina 1984). At puberty, or about 12 to 13 years of age, the growth of girls slows dramatically and then stops completely at about 15 to 16 years of age. Males reach puberty about two years later than girls and therefore reach their adult size at about 17 to 19 years of age, thus growing two years longer than girls. As a result, boys are typically taller, have longer legs (and arms), and broader shoulders. These longer levers (arms, shoulder girth, and legs) provide mechanical advantages for males in many tasks. Girls who mature later also typically have longer legs and a performance advantage. Prior to puberty, boys and girls are very similar in height and leg length; in fact, in elementary school the advantage may go to the earliest maturing girls, who are likely to be taller than everyone else.

Take care when grouping children for participation in physical education. Optimally, children of similar skill should work together. Grouping by skill provides at least three benefits:

- First, it is often safer. For example, a ball thrown with great force is more difficult to catch, so children of more equal throwing and catching skills are less likely to be injured.

- Second, motivation for success peaks when the challenge is appropriate; therefore equal skill levels provide a greater balance in challenge for the partners.

- Third, physical size may be important in partner tasks, especially when one child helps the other.

Do not group elementary school children based on an arbitrary characteristic, especially gender, in physical education. In a physical education class, children of similar size or skill should be working together, depending on the activity. Grouping is not as complex as it might sound, however. Most of the time, physical education teachers group children randomly because differences among children are too small to matter.

Principle 3. Good Things Are Earned

Bones increase in length, circumference, breadth, and density during childhood. This growth is partially a result of weight-bearing physical activity and the presence of an adequate supply of calcium. Calcium is used during muscle contraction and to make bones dense, so a calcium-rich diet (1,300 mg of calcium [three or four glasses of milk] is recommended) is critical during child-

hood and adolescence. Bailey (2000) estimates that 1.5 hours daily of weight-bearing physical activity during growth is necessary to ensure bone density. Increased physical activity during childhood is associated with a more robust skeleton (for example, wider shoulders), increased bone mineralization, slightly increased height, less fat, and more muscle (Broekoff 1985). Increased body fat is associated with Type 2 diabetes during childhood.

More muscle is important: Muscle uses energy, which means that less energy is stored as fat. Muscle is associated with better performance of many motor skills, greater physical fitness, and better health outcomes. During puberty, girls gain fat associated with menstruation and experience an increase in estrogen associated with sexual maturation. Unfortunately for many girls, puberty is also a time of decreased physical activity, so fat increases more than is necessary and healthy. Males typically maintain just under 15 percent body fat during childhood and adolescence, whereas girls increase from 15 to 25 percent during the same ages (Morrow, Jackson, Disch, and Mood 2005). Optimally, girls would maintain 15 to 24 percent body fat and males would remain below 19 percent body fat (American College of Sports

Notice the differences in height among these children that are the same age and in the same grade.

Medicine 1995). The current obesity epidemic in the United States suggests that many children and adolescents have too much fat (U.S. Department of Health and Human Services 2001).

Bones and muscles are heavy tissues. Fat is less dense, and too much fat is unhealthy. However, all children need some fat. Physical education class provides an opportunity for children to learn about muscle and bone growth and to practice activities that keep their bones healthy and muscles strong for their entire lives. To strengthen any muscle group, there are multiple exercises from which to choose. For example, if a child cannot do a pull-up, substitute a modified or assisted pull-up. With practice, bones and muscles become stronger, so the critical issue is to find an activity that works on increasing strength rather than focusing on a child's failure to accomplish one task. Vary warm-up and fitness activities to maintain interest and modify activities so that all children can succeed and improve.

Principle 4. No Body Is Perfect

Physique is described by three body shapes: the apple- or pear-shaped body (endomorph), the muscular body (mesomorph), and the linear body (ectomorph) (Carter 1980). Many individuals have balanced physiques, involving a bit of each type. Early maturing females tend to be endomorphs, early maturing males tend to be mesomorphs, and later maturing children tend to be ectomorphs. Since maturation is inherited, individuals may have little control over their physique (Malina 1984).

Physical activity and healthy eating allow people to make the most of their physiques. A variety of positive experiences during physical education helps children find enjoyable activities, maintain a healthy body, and select activities that are suited to their physical attributes. As their physical education teacher, you can help children understand that

- there is no ideal body shape,
- we are more alike than different, and
- all of us can have healthy bodies.

Daily quality physical education develops the knowledge, skills, and behaviors to ensure healthy skeletons, strong muscles, and appropriate amounts of fat. You can help children understand changes that occur in their bodies during puberty, distinguish between what can be changed (e.g.,

fat) and what cannot, and accept responsibility for maintaining a healthy body. So, although physical education classes are typified by movement, they also integrate knowledge about health and growth as appropriate.

Providing Great Detail

In the following sections, we provide greater detail on many aspects of growth and maturation. Depending on your level of interest and need, these sections can add considerably to your knowledge base.

Maturation

Maturation can be measured in many ways. Maturational age (MA) describes the age of a person based on his or her progress toward a mature state. The MA and the biological age (BA) are essentially the same. The chronological age (CA) is the amount of time since birth. Without knowing the terms themselves, you may have noticed, for example, an early maturing person who has an MA greater than his or her CA. So the person might be 12 years old but look 15 years old, whereas a later maturing person could look 4 years old and actually be 7 years old.

Estimating MA

MA can be estimated using skeletal age, sexual maturation, dental age, and physical growth. Some measures of MA are used for specific periods (e.g., sexual maturation is used during puberty). Others require expensive testing (skeletal maturation requires an X-ray). Yet all of the measures reveal important and consistent information about an individual's MA. Although they are estimates of maturation, the important point is that these measures provide valuable information about a child's development that may be the same as or more helpful than CA.

For example, many children replace baby teeth with permanent teeth during kindergarten and first grade (ages 5 to 7 years). When you see a boy who has lost a front tooth, you can guess that he is in kindergarten or first grade. He may be a late maturing child, however, and actually be 9 years of age. So his CA is 9, but his MA is 6. Since maturation is determined genetically, the boy has no control over his slower rate of maturation.

Accepting MA

A teacher who understands that the boy is less physically mature than his classmates is likely to be more compassionate toward him. You may, for example, help him to understand this difference as both a natural variation among children and one that he will outgrow. Remember, once people are mature—that is, once they are adults—early and late maturation no longer matter because everyone is finally an adult. As a wise teacher, you can challenge a worried child (or parent) to try to pick out which classmate now running on the playground learned to walk first. He or she will not be able to guess correctly except by pure luck.

Children who mature early or late compared to their classmates may feel odd and may not understand that the process of maturation is both normal and out of their control. However, early maturing children often experience a temporary advantage in performance during puberty. Several factors explain this advantage: First, early maturing children experience their circumpubertal growth spurt earlier than other children, so they are taller than their classmates. *Circumpubertal* means "around puberty" and describes the accelerated growth between childhood (where growth is steady) and adulthood (where growth has ended). Second, other advantages of maturity are also likely to be present, such as greater muscle mass, and thus greater strength, or earlier maturation of the ner-

vous system, which translates into greater movement control. This advantage is brief; for example, other girls grow steadily for a longer time and then rapidly during the circumpubertal growth spurt. Generally, the early maturing child is shorter as an adult than an individual who matures later.

Boys and girls are very similar in maturation until at least 9 or 10 years of age and even longer for many characteristics, suggesting that expectations of maturity should also be similar. You need to consider variation among children as well. Some girls are more mature than other girls, and some boys are more mature than other boys. Variation is normal (figure 3.1). Having discussed height in relation to maturation, we examine, in the next section, the growth factors that explain the increase in height during childhood and adolescence.

Differences in maturation matter most during childhood and adolescence. Explaining this to your students—whether they are early or late maturing—may help them accept and understand differences in maturation.

Puberty

Maturation determines when a child will go through puberty. **Puberty** is when the genital organs mature, the secondary sex characteristics (facial and body hair and a deeper voice) develop, and sexual maturity (ability to reproduce) is complete. Pubescence (the beginning of puberty)

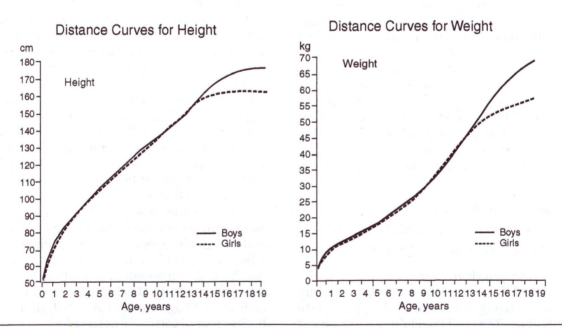

Figure 3.1 Average height and weight curves for American boys and girls.

Reprinted, by permission, from R.M. Malina, C. Bouchard, and O. Bar-Or, 2004, *Growth, maturation, and physical activity*, 2nd ed. (Champaign, IL: Human Kinetics), 49; data from R.J. Kuczmarski et al., 2000, "CDC growth charts: United States," *Advance Data from Vital and Health Statistics*, no. 314 (Hyattsville, MD: National Center for Health Statistics). www.cdc.gov/growthcharts.htm.

begins for boys with growth of the testicles, followed by a growth spurt in height at about 9 or 10 years of age. For girls, a growth spurt signifies pubescence around 9 to 10 years of age, followed by development of the breasts. Menarche (the beginning of menstruation in girls) occurs, on average, at 13 years of age. Puberty ends when individuals are able to reproduce. Figure 3.1 demonstrates one of the changes associated with maturation and puberty—notice how the growth curve levels off for girls at about 13 years of age.

When girls begin to menstruate, their growth slows dramatically. The figure also shows that boys mature about two years later than girls. Growth and maturation are clearly related, so one predicts the other.

Skeletal Maturation

Skeletal maturation is another way to assess MA. X-rays of the hand and wrist are examined for replacement of cartilage with bone, appearance of adult shape and size, and closure of the growth plates (epiphyses). The skeleton continues to change throughout the life span. Consider the fingers of a grandmother or elderly aunt—how the joints tend to be enlarged and the fingers bent—compared with the hands of a younger adult. Toddlers have short fingers with relatively large palms. An X-ray would reveal more cartilage and less bone in a toddler's hand than in yours.

Physical Growth

Physical growth can also be used to assess maturation. One example is age at peak height velocity: Growth is steady from 3 to about 9 years of age (averaging about 2.3 inches [6 cm] per year), and then the rate of growth for height increases rapidly. Peak height velocity is the point at which the rate is the highest. Usually, this rate is more than 4 inches (10 cm) per year and occurs at 11 to 12 years of age for girls and 14 to 15 years of age for boys.

As children grow, their height and weight increase steadily. The average heights and weights for boys and girls are nearly the same during childhood. However, the average adult male is taller than the average adult female. Boys mature later; therefore, they grow two or more years after girls have stopped growing. The difference in average height between adult males and females is the growth that occurs in males during those years.

Children gain about 2.3 inches (6 cm) in **stature**, or height, each year during childhood. Figure 3.2 shows, however, that the changes are more complex than the body getting larger. At birth, the head accounts for about 25 percent of the infant's length and is 2.3 times larger in circumference than an adult's head compared to body size. By school age, the head is approximately 20 percent of total stature and nearly 2 times larger than an adult's compared to body

| 2 mo (fetal) | 5 mo | Newborn | 2 yr | 6 yr | 12 yr | 25 yr |

Figure 3.2 Changes in form and proportion of the human body during fetal and postnatal life.

From K.M. Newell, 1984, Physical constraints to the development of motor skills. In *Motor development during childhood and adolescence*, edited by J.R. Thomas (Minneapolis, MN: Burgess), 108. Adapted by permission of Jerry Thomas.

size. During childhood, the proportional size of the head decreases until it is at about 12 percent—the proportional size of an adult's head! Think about trying to do motor tasks if your head were twice its current size. Performing a forward roll or balancing on one foot, for example, would be more difficult with a larger head. Head size is just one of the challenges of movement during childhood.

The extremities (arms and legs) grow rapidly from birth to maturity, more rapidly than the head or torso. The torso grows more rapidly than the head, but not as rapidly as the extremities. This is why the legs increase from 30 to 50 percent of total stature from birth to maturity. Legs are the levers for many movements, so during childhood the levers that send the body up or out while running and jumping are relatively short. Clearly, part of the reason children do not run as fast or jump as far as adults is that their levers are shorter.

To summarize, we have made several observations:

- Children increase steadily in stature during childhood.

- Children increase rapidly in stature at the beginning of puberty.

- Children increase in stature because the legs grow faster than other body parts.

- Children increase in stature because the torso grows, but it does not grow as fast as the legs.

- Children improve in motor skills partly because the relative size of the head decreases.

- Boys and girls are similar in stature and pattern of stature during childhood.

- Stature, because of leg length, influences performance.

- Boys continue to grow after girls stop growing (because of differences in maturation); therefore, as adults, males are, on average, taller than females.

As the legs and arms grow longer, the bones also increase in diameter and circumference. A typical pattern of growth is length, then breadth, and circumference; finally, the bones "fill in," becoming denser. Strong bones are wider, bigger around, and denser. Broader and denser bones are associated with more physical activity. Bones should be the heaviest tissue in the body. Dense bones are important because as we age, we experience a gradual loss of calcium. Bones that have more density at the beginning of this loss will be stronger and therefore less likely to fracture as bone density decreases during old age.

As children grow taller, body breadth also increases. The distance between the outsides of

Children of all shapes, sizes, and backgrounds enjoy physical activity; it is the teacher's job to nurture that natural interest.

the hip bones and the shoulder bones is the same until puberty, when the males' shoulders grow more than the females' shoulders. There are three important concepts:

- First, boys and girls are alike prior to puberty.
- Second, the differences after puberty are attributable to the boys' shoulders (and not the girls' hips) being relatively larger. So, after puberty, boys have an advantage in some activities because of broader shoulders.
- Third, the larger hip circumference observed in females is not a reflection of wider hip bones but is related to greater soft tissue (e.g., fat and muscle).

Using **body composition**, the body can be divided in two parts: lean tissues and fat. Lean body mass (LBM) is the weight of all lean tissues, including bone, muscle, and organs. Fat is all fat tissues, including subcutaneous (fat just under the skin), visceral (deep body fat found around organs), and other fats such as cholesterol. Boys and girls gain lean tissue as they grow; the increase is dramatic for boys at pubescence. Boys and girls also gain fat during growth. By dividing absolute fat by total body weight, we estimate relative fatness, or percentage of body fat. The average percentage of body fat for boys is relatively stable at less than 15 percent during childhood and adolescence. The

percentage for girls climbs steadily during this same period, from 15 to 25 percent. Two factors influence the increase in body fat in girls: First, at puberty, a minimum of 15 percent body fat is necessary for menstruation to begin. If the increase is caused only by the preparation for menstruation, the increase in fat would resemble lean body mass in males, with a more abrupt change. The second factor is physical activity: Girls tend to be less active than boys. (This idea is discussed in greater detail in chapter 5, Cognition, Learning, and Practice.) In short, girls gain body fat rapidly because of a combination of biological factors (e.g., menstruation) and cultural factors (e.g., less physical activity).

Physique

Somatotype rating is a specific way of assessing **physique** so that changes attributable to age, diet, exercise, or disease can be traced. Physique is the way the body looks. It includes three prototypes (figure 3.3):

1. Endomorphy is assessed using the sum of three skinfolds, corrected for height, and is typically seen as a soft, round, or pear-shaped body.

2. Mesomorphy is determined with humerus and femur breadth and calf and biceps circumference, corrected for skinfolds and height. This is a muscular body that may be relatively short and large boned.

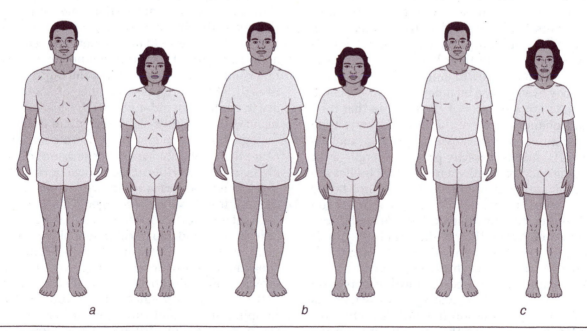

a   b   c

Figure 3.3 The three types of body types are *(a)* mesomorphs, *(b)* endomorphs, and *(c)* ectomorphs.

Reprinted, by permission, from A. Faigenbaum, 2000, Age- and sex-related differences and their implications for resistance exercise. In *Essentials of strength training and conditioning*, 2nd ed., edited by T.R. Baechle and R.W. Earle (Champaign, IL: Human Kinetics), 173.

3. Ectomorphy is based on ponderal index (mass corrected for height) and is a linear or tall, lean body.

Most people are balanced in body type, so they do not look exactly like any of the prototypes but are a combination of two. A relationship exists between physique (or somatotype) and maturation. Late maturing children tend to be ectomorphic. Early maturing males tend to be mesomorphic, whereas early maturing females tend to be endomorphic. These physiques can be observed as early as preschool, in which as many as 50 percent of the girls (but only 25 percent of the boys) show a tendency toward endomorphy, whereas more than 50 percent of the boys (and only 16 percent of the girls) tend toward mesomorphy. World-class athletes have a high occurrence of ectomorphy, indicating a tall, lean, and probably late maturing body. The soft tissues (fat and muscle) change over time because of exercise, diet, and disease, whereas height and bone breadth remain stable after maturity. Somatotype can change, however, and the changes are more subtle after growth stops.

Children, especially older children who are nearing puberty, are often concerned about their body type or physique. Physique is difficult to change at any age. Often, what society considers the ideal body type—for example, the Barbie Doll body—is impossible to achieve. Most people look like one of their parents or a blend of their parents. What is important for children and adolescents to understand is that larger bones and a healthy amount of muscle are good. Physical activity can help their bodies by increasing muscle and bone growth and reducing extra fat. They may even grow a bit taller as a result of being active. There are parts of their shape that they cannot change, however. A specific body type neither guarantees success in any area, including sports, nor necessarily prevents people from attaining success. Understanding that bodies are different and that one body type is not better than another is essential. Having too much or too little fat increases health risk. Therefore, children need to understand their bodies, including their physique. You can help children by accepting as equally valuable each physique and encouraging healthy, active bodies. Furthermore, you should never decide which sport or activity is best for a child based on the child's body type. As a teacher, you have the opportunity and the power to influence the way children think and feel about their bodies.

Inherited Versus Environmental Factors

Height and maturational rate are inherited. Therefore, physical activity has little impact on sexual maturation or stature. One predictor of height is the average of the height of the parents. If both parents are tall and matured later, the child is likely to be tall. Conversely, a child who inherits early maturation from parents of average height is likely to be of average or below-average height. The location of fat on the body is inherited, as demonstrated earlier in the discussion of physique. Some aspects of bone density are inherited, as indicated by the mineral content of bones for different ethnic groups. This means people are less likely to have osteoporosis if they are African American and more likely to have it if they are Caucasian. Variables such as body weight and percentage of body fat are influenced by the environment. Physical activity has a positive impact on the skeleton (mineralization and density, robustness), body weight and fat (less fat), and body composition (more muscle, less fat).

Growth and Motor Performance

Children age and grow simultaneously; motor skills change as well during that time. Pinpointing the factors that influence changes in motor skill is difficult because so many elements are changing at the same time. Is it additional practice, growth, or a combination that explains the improvement in skill? Why is the performance of some skills at a lower level in older children? Clearly, performance does improve—older boys run faster than younger boys and a girl jumps farther at 10 years of age than when she was 6. Performance of motor skills improves with increased age during childhood. Often, performance improves only because the children have grown larger. This point is of particular importance when considering changes that children undergo during a school year: Are the changes attributable to a good physical education program or simply a result of growth? For boys, growth and maturation nearly always result in better motor performance—that is, running faster, jumping higher, and throwing farther. For girls, the picture is a bit different. Girls show steady improvement in motor performance of most skills during childhood, until adolescence. During ado-

Physical activity is good for health and development—and it's fun!

physical activity is a general misconception. The contributions of biology—growth, maturation, and other biological factors—are rather small. In world-class athletes, the differences in physical factors may be as small as 10 to 20 percent, and biology explains very little of the differences among average people. Thus, careful interpretation is necessary with respect to changes in skill (either positive or negative) during growth.

Furthermore, you must be careful not to judge skill based on a physical characteristic. For example, allowing children to specialize in a sport or a position within a sport at an early age—especially when the decision is based on body type or size—may have a negative impact on lifelong participation (Robertson-Wilson, Baker, Derbinshyre, and Côté 2003). A child who seems big for his or her age is likely to be maturing early, which means that child may be smaller relative to others after maturity. There are three reasons why you should help children and their parents avoid early specialization: First, children who sample a variety of activities before adolescence are more likely to remain active and also to achieve greater expertise within a specific sport (Robertson-Wilson et al. 2003). Second, there seems to be very little correlation between biological factors and performance in the typical adult (Ransdell and Wells 1999; Thomas and Thomas 1988, 1999). Third, the success of predicting which children will excel and which activity a child is suited for is very low, and the advantage from early maturation and increase in size is very short in duration.

Summary

As a teacher, you need to understand growth and maturation so you can monitor your students' health and development. Furthermore, understanding growth and maturation allows you to plan more effectively by selecting and modifying activities as necessary to accommodate individual needs. You also need to understand the problems that children face when trying to learn new skills. The challenges that movement presents to children are different than those facing adults because children are not miniature adults. Information empowers you to avoid stereotypes and to help children and adolescents understand the normal and natural processes of growth and maturation. Both you and your students need to know the difference between variables that can be changed (e.g., environment) and those that must be accommodated (e.g., genetics). Finally, understanding the processes of growth and maturation

lescence, growth and maturation have a negative impact on some aspects of motor performance. For example, running speed, jumping distance, and aerobic capacity decrease after puberty. The decrease is caused largely by an increase in body fat. (Girls who remain lean tend to maintain their performance.) In addition, girls tend to become less active during adolescence. This inactivity can result in larger increases in body fat and a decrease in skill caused by a lack of training and practice; the situation becomes self-perpetuating. The gender differences should be smaller than what is observed because the biological contribution is small (about 10 percent).

Bigger children tend to be stronger than smaller children of the same age. This observation is similar to the improvements in skill noted in children as they grow taller, and heavier children have an advantage when throwing or kicking. However, those same larger children are at a disadvantage for running and jumping. Clearly, growth influences performance, but the impact can be either positive or negative, depending on the skill considered. That physical or biological factors are very important in predicting success in allows you to make wise decisions when faced with gender issues. Keep in mind that, generally, boys and girls are more alike than different during childhood in terms of growth and maturation.

Mastery Learning Activities

1. Develop a profile for grades K, 3, and 5 based on what you have learned about growth and maturation. What would the children in each grade look like? Would they have their front teeth? How tall would they be? What about leg length? Would there be secondary sex characteristics?

2. Observe a group of children. See if you can determine how old they are based on what you learned in this chapter.

3. Measure the weight, stature (standing height), and sitting height of several boys and girls at ages 5, 9, and 13. Average the data and graph the averages. Do your data look the way you expected?

4. Compare the gymnastics lessons in this chapter (starting on page 50). What accommodations are made for the different ages (and sizes) of the children?

5. Review the following concepts. Provide supporting information for each concept by using definitions, examples, and applications.

There are specific techniques for measuring maturation (MA) and growth (anthropometric techniques):

a. MA and CA are not the same.

b. MA is biological age and is controlled by genetics. CA is time since birth.

c. Some techniques for estimating MA are valid for a brief period or are retroactive. Other techniques are valid for the life span.

d. Usually, MA is of concern at the younger end of CA, but it is also useful at other times of change (e.g., menopause and old age).

Body proportions change during growth:

a. Extremities grow relatively fast.

b. Length, breadth, and then circumference increase.

c. Changes influence performance.

Body composition changes with age and, after puberty, differs for the genders:

a. All children gain LBM during childhood.

b. At puberty, males gain more LBM than females, and the gain in LBM in males is rapid.

c. At puberty, females gain more fat than males.

Somatotype rating is a specific way of assessing physique so that changes caused by age, diet, exercise, or disease can be traced:

a. Endomorphy is assessed using the sum of three skinfolds (corrected for height).

b. Mesomorphy is determined with humerus and femur breadth, calf and biceps circumference (corrected for skinfolds), and height.

c. Ectomorphy is based on ponderal index (mass corrected for height).

d. Soft tissue (fat and muscle) changes over time because of the effects of exercise, diet, disease, and growth.

e. Early maturing males are mesomorphs; early maturing females are endomorphs.

f. Late maturing children are ectomorphs, and athletes are ectomorphs.

References

American College of Sports Medicine. 1995. *ACSM's guidelines for exercise testing and prescription.* Philadelphia: Lea & Febiger.

Bailey, D.A. 2000. Is anyone out there listening? *Quest 52*: 344-350.

Broekoff, J. 1985. The effects of physical activity on physical growth and development. In *The Academy papers. Effects of physical activity on children,* edited by G.A. Stull and H.M. Eckert, no. 19, 75-87. Champaign, IL: Human Kinetics.

Carter, J.E.L. 1980. *The Heath-Carter somatotype method.* San Diego: San Diego State University Syllabus Service.

Malina, R.M. 1984. Physical growth and maturation. In *Motor development during childhood and adolescence,* edited by J.R. Thomas, 2-26. Minneapolis: Burgess.

Morrow, J.R., A.W. Jackson, J.G. Disch, and D.P. Mood. 2005. *Measurement and evaluation in human performance.* 3rd ed. Champaign, IL: Human Kinetics.

Ransdell, L.B., and C.L. Wells. 1999. Sex differences in athletic performance. *Women in Sport and Physical Activity* 8: 55-81.

Robertson-Wilson, J., E. Baker, E. Derbinshyre, and J. Côté. 2003. Childhood sports involvement in active and inactive female adults. *AVANTE* 9: 1-8.

Thomas, J.R., and K.T. Thomas. 1988. Development of gender differences in physical activity. *Quest* 40: 219-229.

Thomas, K.T., and J.R. Thomas. 1999. What squirrels in the trees predict about expert athletes. *International Journal of Sport Psychology* 30: 221-234.

U.S. Department of Health and Human Services. 2001. *The surgeon general's call to action to prevent and decrease overweight and obesity.* Washington, DC: Government Printing Office.

Resources

Baxter-Jones, A., P. Helms, N. Maffull, J. Baines-Preece, and M. Preece. 1995. Growth and development of male gymnasts, swimmers, soccer and tennis players: A longitudinal study. *Annals of Human Biology* 22: 381-394.

Espenschade, A.S. 1963. Restudy of relationships between physical performances of school children and age, height, and weight. *Research Quarterly* 34: 144-153.

Gallahue, D.L., and J.C. Ozmun. 1995. *Understanding motor development.* 3rd ed. Madison, WI: Brown & Benchmark.

Nelson, K.R., J.R. Thomas, and J.K. Nelson. 1991. Longitudinal changes in throwing performance. Gender differences. *Research Quarterly for Exercise and Sport* 62: 105-108.

Payne, G.V., and L.D. Isaacs. 1998. *Human motor development: A lifespan approach.* Mountain View, CA: Mayfield.

Rarick, G.L., and Smoll, F. 1967. Stability of growth in strength and motor performance from childhood to adolescence. *Human Biology* 39: 295-306.

Scammon, R.E. 1930. The measurement of the body in childhood. In *The measurement of man,* edited by J.A. Harris, C.M. Jackson, D.G. Jackson, and R.E. Scammon, 171-215. Minneapolis: University of Minnesota Press.

Tanner, J.M. 1978. *Foetus into man: Physical growth from conception to maturity.* Cambridge, MA: Harvard University Press.

Thomas, K.T., J.D. Gallagher, and J.R. Thomas. 2001. Motor development and skill acquisition during childhood and adolescence. In *Handbook of sport psychology,* 2nd ed., edited by R.N. Singer, H.A. Hausenblas, and C. Janelle, 20-52. New York: Wiley.

Lesson Plans

The four gymnastics (tumbling) lesson plans at the end of this chapter are designed to accommodate the differences in growth, especially proportion, by age. Gymnastics skills are challenging for younger children, who have relatively larger heads and shorter legs and torsos than older children. Notice that the slanted triangle (wedge) mat is used to help younger children master Forward Rolls. Younger children benefit from practice with activities that are adapted to their smaller bodies.

For example, the rope-climbing task allows younger children to practice the movement without having to support body weight while learning the movement at the same time. The wedge mat is used for the Backward Roll for children in grades 2 and 3; this allows gravity to do part of the work. Children at this age still have relatively short legs and little strength, so gravity makes the task easier. Once they master the mechanics of the Backward Roll, have them practice it on a flat mat. As children practice on the balance beam, looking at a stationary spot (not at their feet or the beam) makes balance easier in two ways: First, looking at the stationary spot allows ambient (peripheral) vision to make rapid corrections in balance. Second, keeping the head over the body, rather than in front of the body, maintains equilibrium (balance).

The lessons cover similar skills with adaptations that consider developmental differences in children. The skills allow for progression from level to level (e.g., from grades K and 1 to grades 2 and 3, and then to grades 4 and 5). In addition, learning motor skills, children learn about independent practice in lessons using stations. You can and must practice time management during station lessons. Gymnastics is a popular activity with children in elementary school. Gymnastics lessons allow children to learn skills; practice independently; and work on muscle strength, endurance, and flexibility.

Lesson 3.1

Tumbling Using Triangle Mat

Student Objectives 1 5

- Work effectively in a small group.
- Look at a target while walking a balance beam.
- Demonstrate two ways to roll on a mat.
- Complete a sequence of three or more activities.
- Demonstrate jumping up onto a stationary platform.

Equipment and Materials

- 6 to 8 mats
- 1 long thick rope (10+ feet [3+ m] long and 1 inch [2.5 cm] or more in diameter)
- 1 vaulting box (or stack of mats) 24 inches (60 cm) high
- 1 balance beam
- 1 poster or target
- Tape for the poster or target
- 1 wedge mat (or 1 regular mat placed at an angle on another stacked mat)

Warm-Up Activity (5 minutes)

Arrange the children in four groups facing you.

Stretching

Ask the children to do each of the following stretching challenges as you demonstrate and do the activity with the children:

1. Reach for the sky with both hands, slowly bend at the waist and hips (keep legs straight, but do not lock knees), and reach for the floor. Sweep the dust bunnies with your hands. Repeat several times.

2. Place your right hand behind your right shoulder, reaching as far down and back as possible. Put your left hand on your right elbow and push gently. Repeat several times and reverse to stretch the left shoulder.

3. Standing with feet shoulder-width apart, rise to toes, slowly return to stand, then bend knees and lower yourself to a partial squat position so that your thighs are parallel to the ground. Return to stand and repeat several times.

4. With the arms straight and extended in front of your body, push palms together for the count of 5. Slowly move the arms sideward and then back, trying to touch palms behind you. Hold the back-most position for a count of 5. Repeat several times.

5. Complete 5 vertical jumps in place. (Challenge the children to jump as high as possible. After you demonstrate and complete 5 jumps, walk around to groups of children asking them to jump and touch your hand. Hold your hand at a challenging but reachable point above the child's head.)

Skill-Development Activities (20 minutes)

Arrange children in four groups, one group at each station.

Stations

Each group practices at each station for approximately 4 minutes. Use 2 minutes to explain what happens at each station and approximately 30 seconds to rotate groups at the end of each 4-minute practice time. Arrange the jumping and tumbling stations near each other so that you can supervise both of them.

ROPE

The rope is tied to a sturdy object (a door handle works well). The children lie on their backs with their feet in the air pointed toward the ceiling. The object is to pull yourself, head first, from the loose end of the rope toward the secure end of the rope, in a manner similar to climbing a rope. Hint: This works best on the smooth gym floor (i.e., no mat necessary). Cue words: "Reach and pull."

JUMPING

Place the jumping cube or a stack of mats at the joint of two mats placed together lengthwise. One at a time, children run to the jumping cube and jump or climb to a standing position on top of the cube. Children jump forward off the cube onto the mat.

TUMBLING

Place two mats next to each other. Place the wedge mat on top of one. Children do the Log Roll on the flat mat and the Forward Roll on the wedge mat.

- **Log Roll.** Lying on one side, with your arms and legs together and stretched out (extended), roll onto your tummy and quickly over onto your other side. Continue rolling over until you reach the other end of the mat. (Remind children to go straight and stay on the mat at all times! Cue words: "Stay straight.")

- **Forward Roll.** Begin in a squat with your feet on the tall side of the wedge mat. Your hands are on the wedge mat, shoulder-width apart. Chin is on the chest; look at your tummy. Bend your arms to bring your shoulders closer to the mat, overbalance, roll onto your shoulders, and continue to roll with your legs tucked. Keep your heels close to your bottom and your knees close to your chest until your feet touch the ground and you are squatting again. The object is to roll down the slant of the wedge mat. (Cue words: "Pushing hands.")

BALANCE BEAM

The beam is placed on a mat (or more than one mat). Tape the target or poster to the wall at eye level for the children. Place the beam on a mat so that the target or poster is about 10 feet (3 m) from one end of the beam. Children should walk, one at a time, the length of the beam while looking at the target or poster. Cue words: "Heads up."

Concluding Activity (5 minutes)

Keep the children in their four groups at stations.

Obstacle Course

Individual children rotate through all activities. State the order as Beam to Rope, Rope to Tumbling, Tumbling to Jumping, and so forth. Each child in the group completes the activity for that station and then moves to the next station and waits for a turn. This continues until all of the children have been to all of the stations or the time is up.

From K.T. Thomas, A.M. Lee, and J.R. Thomas, 2008, *Physical education methods for elementary teachers*, 3rd ed. (Champaign, IL: Human Kinetics).

Lesson 3.2

Stations

Student Objectives 1 5

- Cooperate by working in small groups at stations.
- Change levels (bend and stand) while standing on a balance beam.
- Demonstrate a Backward Roll.
- Demonstrate a sequence of skills from memory.

Equipment and Materials

- 6 to 8 mats
- 1 wedge mat (or 1 regular mat placed at an angle on another stacked mat)
- 1 long thick rope (10+ feet [3+ m] long and 1 inch [2.5 cm] or more in diameter)
- 1 vaulting box (or stack of mats) 36 inches (91 cm) high
- 1 balance beam

Warm-Up Activity (5 minutes)

Arrange the children in four groups.

Stretching

All children count aloud as they do the repetitions for each exercise. Demonstrate each stretch and then have the children do the stretch:

1. Reach for the sky with both hands, slowly bend at the waist and hips (keep legs straight, but do not lock knees), and reach for the floor. Sweep the dust bunnies with your hands. Repeat 10 times.
2. Place your right hand behind your right shoulder, reaching as far down and back as possible. Put your left hand on your right elbow and push gently. Repeat 5 times and reverse to stretch 5 times for the left shoulder.
3. Standing with feet shoulder-width apart, rise to toes, slowly return to stand, then bend knees and lower yourself to a partial squat position so that your thighs are parallel to the ground. Return to stand and repeat 10 times.
4. With the arms straight and extended in front of your body, push palms together for the count of 5, slowly move the arms sideward and then back trying to touch palms behind you. Hold the back-most position for 5 counts. Repeat 5 times front and back.
5. Complete 3 sets of 5 vertical jumps in place (jump 5 times, rest a few seconds, and repeat). (Challenge the children to jump as high as possible.)

Skill-Development Activities (20 minutes)

Keep the children in four groups, one group at each station.

Stations

Each group practices at each station for approximately 4 minutes. Use 2 minutes to explain what happens at each station and approximately 30 seconds to rotate groups at the end of each 4-minute practice time. Arrange the jumping and tumbling stations near each other so that you can supervise both of them.

ROPE

The rope is tied to a sturdy object (a door handle works well). The children lie on their backs with their feet in the air pointed toward the ceiling. The object is to pull yourself, head first, from the loose end of the rope toward the secure end of the rope, in a manner similar to climbing a rope. Repeat going feet first. To make this more challenging, do this on a mat, which creates more resistance. Cue words: "Reach, pull."

JUMPING

Place the jumping cube or a stack of mats at the joint of two mats placed together lengthwise. One at a time, children run to the jumping cube and jump to a squat and then rise to a standing position on top of the cube. Children jump forward off the cube onto the mat. Cue words: "Heads up."

TUMBLING

Place two mats next to each other. Children do the Forward Roll on one mat and the Backward Roll on the wedge mat.

- **Forward Roll.** Begin squatting with your hands on the mat, shoulder-width apart. Chin is on chest; look at your tummy. Bend your arms to bring your shoulders closer to the mat, overbalance, roll onto your shoulder blades, and continue to roll with your legs tucked. Keep your heels close to your bottom and your knees close to your chest until your feet touch the ground and you are squatting again. (Cue words: "Shoulder blades.")

- **Backward Roll.** Squat (feet on the top end of the wedge mat) with your back to the down slant of the mat. Put your hands on your shoulders, with your palms turned upward. Tuck your chin tightly to your chest, looking at your tummy. Lean backward slightly, overbalancing so that your bottom touches the mat. Keep rolling backward until your back touches the mat. Stay tightly tucked in a ball, with chin on chest and knees against chest. Continue rolling so that your hands touch the mat (your hands are still on your shoulders). Push with your hands and begin to straighten your arms. As your body passes over your head so that your hands are pushing on the mat, let your chin leave your chest. Recover by landing on your feet. (Young children often land on their knees but, with practice, should learn to land on their feet. Cue words: "Push up.")

BALANCE BEAM

The beam is placed on a mat (or more than one mat). Children walk, one at a time, the length of the beam. Encourage children to look forward and not at the beam. Children walk forward, backward, and forward, bending to touch the beam on various turns. Cue words: "Look up."

Concluding Activities (5 minutes)

Children remain in four groups at the stations.

Obstacle Course

Individual children rotate through all activities. State the order as Beam to Rope, Rope to Tumbling, Tumbling to Jumping, and so forth. Each child in the group completes the activity for that station and then moves to the next station and waits for a turn. This continues until all of the children have been to all of the stations or the time is up.

From K.T. Thomas, A.M. Lee, and J.R. Thomas, 2008, *Physical education methods for elementary teachers*, 3rd ed. (Champaign, IL: Human Kinetics).

Lesson 3.3

Planet "School Name"

Student Objectives | 1 | 5 |

- Work with a group so that all group members accomplish each challenge.
- Demonstrate the following skills: vaulting, holding weight on a rope or chin-up bar, walking on a balance beam while stepping over objects, balancing and rolling.

Equipment and Materials

- 6 to 8 mats
- 1 climbing rope (or chin-up bar)
- 1 vaulting box (or stack of mats) 36 inches (91 cm) high
- 1 balance beam
- Music

Warm-Up Activities (5 minutes)

Arrange the children in four groups facing you.

Stretching

Demonstrate the first stretch. Have one child in each group lead that stretch for the group. Repeat with the remaining stretches.

1. Reach for the sky with both hands, slowly bend at the waist and hips (keep legs straight, but do not lock knees), and reach for the floor. Sweep the dust bunnies with your hands. Repeat 10 times.

2. Place your right hand behind your right shoulder, reaching as far down and back as possible. Put your left hand on your right elbow and push gently. Repeat 5 times and reverse to stretch 5 times for the left shoulder.

3. Standing with feet shoulder-width apart, rise to toes, slowly return to stand, then bend knees and lower yourself to a partial squat position so that your thighs are parallel to the ground. Return to stand and repeat 10 times.

4. With the arms straight and extended in front of your body, push palms together for the count of 5. Slowly move the arms sideward and then back, trying to touch palms behind you. Hold the back-most position for a count of 5. Repeat 5 times front and back.

5. Complete 3 sets of 5 vertical jumps in place (jump 5 times, rest a few seconds, and repeat). (Challenge the children to jump as high as possible.)

Skill-Development Activities (20 minutes)

Arrange children in four groups, one at each station on the planet.

Planet "School Name"

Each group practices at each station for approximately 4 minutes. Use 2 minutes to explain what happens at each station and approximately 30 seconds to rotate groups at the end of each 4-minute practice time. Arrange the jumping and rope-climbing stations near each other so that you can supervise both of them. Play appropriate but popular music; children rotate when you stop the music.

ROPE

Children climb the vertical rope. Children hold the bottom of the rope for group members. If you do not have a climbing rope, do pull-ups on the pull-up bar, also with group members spotting each other.

JUMPING

(Place the jumping cube or a stack of mats at the joint of two mats placed together lengthwise. One at a time, children run to the jumping cube and vault over the cube.) The two vaults are the tuck vault and the side vault. For the tuck, place hands shoulder-width apart on the cube and bend legs, bringing knees to the chest and between the arms. For the side vault, place both hands near one end of the cube; jump while swinging straight legs over the end of cube opposite from the hands. For both vaults, land on the far side of the cube on your feet. Keep the head up by looking forward during the vault. Cue words: "Head up."

TUMBLING

Place two mats next to each other. Children do the Forward and Backward Rolls on one mat and Elbow–Knee Balances on the other mat.

- **Forward Roll.** Begin squatting, with your hands shoulder-width apart and chin on chest while looking at your tummy. Bend your arms to bring your shoulders closer to the mat, overbalance, roll onto your shoulders, and continue to roll with your legs tucked. Keep your heels close to your bottom and your knees close to your chest until your feet touch the ground and you are squatting again. Cue word: "Tuck."

- **Backward Roll.** Squat with your back to the length of the mat, and put your hands on your shoulders, with your palms turned upward. Tuck your chin tightly to your chest, looking at your tummy. Lean backward slightly, overbalancing so that your bottom touches the mat. Keep rolling backward until your back touches the mat. Stay tightly tucked in a ball, with chin on chest and knees against chest. Continue rolling so your hands touch the mat (your hands are still on your shoulders). Push with your hands and begin to straighten your arms. As your body passes over your head so that your hands are pushing on the mat, let your chin leave your chest. Recover by landing on your feet. Cue words: "Roll, push, stand."

- **Elbow–Knee Balance.** Squat; place your hands on the mat. Arms are inside your legs, and knees touch your elbows. Hold your head up; looking straight ahead helps. Shift your weight from your feet to your hands, and rest your knees on your elbows. The critical point is to maintain balance with only your hands supporting your body weight. Cue words: "Look up."

- **Tripod.** Begin in a squat, with your hands and arms placed on the mat outside your knees and legs. Bend forward until your forehead (at the hairline) touches the mat. Your head serves as a balance point but supports very little weight. Bend your arms and make your knees touch your elbows. Support most of your body weight with your arms. Stop moving when your knees are resting on your elbows, your head is resting on the mat, and your feet are off the mat. Support most of your weight with your arms. Your head touches the mat but does not support much body weight. Cue words: "Head touching."

BALANCE BEAM

The beam is placed on a mat (or more than one mat). Beanbags are scattered around on the mat near the beam. Children walk, one or more at a time, the length of the beam. Children are to pick up as many of the scattered beanbags as possible without falling. If one child falls, all of the beanbags are returned to the mat and the group starts again to pick up the beanbags.

Concluding Activities (5 minutes)

Join two groups together to form two large groups.

Planet "School Name" Challenge

One of the groups goes to the jumping cube, the other to the balance beam. The object is to get as many group members as possible successfully through the challenge. For the vaulting, all group members go over the cube using either of the two vaults. For the balance beam, members walk the beam, picking up one beanbag each. Repeat until all of the beanbags are picked up. If someone steps off, the group starts again. When either group finishes the challenge successfully, the groups reverse stations (so that the group on the beam moves to the cube and vice versa) and complete the other challenge.

From K.T. Thomas, A.M. Lee, and J.R. Thomas, 2008, *Physical education methods for elementary teachers*, 3rd ed. (Champaign, IL: Human Kinetics).

Lesson 3.4

Tumbling

Student Objectives 1 2

- Demonstrate the Forward Roll and the Run and Take-Off.
- Attempt a Straddle Roll and a Heel Slap.
- State two important things to remember about the Forward Roll.
- Practice a variation of the Forward Roll.

Equipment and Materials

- 1 or more mats (4 by 8 feet [1.2 by 2.4 m]) per group

Warm-Up Activities

Warm-Up Routine for Grades 4 and 5

Keep the children in small groups on the mats. Cue the children to perform the entire routine straight through as follows:

FLOOR STRETCHING

- 4 Straddle Stretches right, 4 left
- 4 Overhead Straddle Stretches right, 4 left
- 4 Pike Stretches with toes pointed and then repeat with ankles flexed

BACK FLEXIBILITY

- 4 Back Arches
- 4 Leg Rollovers
- 4 Back Push-Ups

STANDING STRETCHES

- 4 Torso Stretches
- 4 Bent-Leg Hamstring Stretches

ENDURANCE EXERCISES

- 1 minute each of running and skipping
- 20 Sit-Ups
- 10 Push-Ups
- 10 Dorsal Back Curls

Skill-Development Activities (18 to 20 minutes)

Forward Roll

Organize small groups of children, and assign each to a mat.

1. Describe and demonstrate the stunt:
   - Bend over and place your hands on the mat shoulder-width apart and, looking at your belly and bending your arms, shift more and more body weight onto your hands as your legs provide less and less support.
   - As your center of gravity moves forward, your body overbalances and rolls forward, hitting the mat on your shoulder blades. Continue to roll in a curved position.
   - Bend your legs at the knees and accept weight on your legs as your shoulders leave the mat.
   - Return to standing with your arms extended overhead.
2. Have the children practice the Forward Roll.

Straddle Forward Roll

Arrange partners on the mats.

1. Describe and demonstrate the stunt:
   - This is actually two consecutive rolls. Start by doing a Forward Roll and then add the straddle part. Begin in closed standing position with feet together and arms extended overhead, and then bend, placing your hands on the mat shoulder-width apart.
   - Look at your belly, bend your arms, and accept more and more of your body weight onto your hands as your legs decrease support.
   - As your center of gravity moves forward, your body overbalances and rolls forward as you hit the mat on the shoulder blades. Continue to roll in a curved position.
   - This stunt differs from a regular Forward Roll. Keep your legs straight and spread apart in the straddle position so that you land on your legs for the first roll with your feet spread, body bent slightly forward, and arms extended forward.

- Begin the second roll immediately from the straddle position, with your head tucking under and your body moving forward to a landing on your shoulder blades.
- Recover to standing with your feet closed, as in the regular Forward Roll.
- Work with your partner—one partner stands in front of the Roller after the roll phase to help him or her recover. Roller, reach out to your partner and try to shake hands as you come up. This gets your arms and weight forward by moving your center of gravity forward.

2. Have the children practice the Straddle Forward Roll.

Backward Roll

Continue with the same setup except that partners are not necessary.

1. Describe and demonstrate the stunt:
   - Begin standing, arms extended overhead (palms up) and your back toward the length of the mat and your chin moving to your chest. Lower your body to a tuck position by bending the knees. Overbalance your body backward to begin the roll, and remain in tuck position as your shoulders and hands contact the mat.
   - Push with your hands to lift your body (hips, legs, and torso) over your head. Your head and neck should not support your weight, and you should touch the mat as little as possible.
   - As your feet touch the mat, straighten your arms until your feet are supporting your weight. Rise to standing with your arms extended overhead.

2. Have the children practice the Backward Roll.

Straddle Backward Roll

Continue with the same setup.

1. Describe and demonstrate the stunt:
   - Begin standing in a straddle balance position, with your back toward the length of the mat.
   - Move your hands between your legs as your torso moves forward to lower your body, with your hips moving back and down, until your seat touches the mat.
   - Move your hands to your shoulders as in the regular Backward Roll. Immediately roll your body backward, while your legs remain in the straddle position.
   - Recover to the straddle balance position (as shown in figure).

2. Have the children practice the Straddle Backward Roll.
3. Have the children extend the skill by beginning in closed standing position, rolling to a straddle balance, and then rolling again from the straddle balance to a closed standing position (2 rolls).

Heel Slap

Continue with the same setup.

1. Describe and demonstrate the stunt:
   - The object is to touch your heels with your hands just under your seat and then land on both feet.
   - Jump up from both feet, lifting both feet toward your seat while reaching back with your arms.
2. Have the children practice the Heel Slap.

Run and Take-Off

Continue with the same setup.

1. Describe and demonstrate the stunt:
   - Many sports use this movement (e.g., springboard diving).
   - Begin with several quick (running) steps leading to a hurdle.
   - To hurdle, raise one leg so that your thigh is parallel to (flat as) the ground and your lower leg is at a 90-degree angle to the thigh (like the corner of a square).
   - Reach your arms high overhead as your body lifts off the ground. Both your raised arms and lifted thigh help your body gain momentum. Momentum helps you gain height in the hurdle.
   - Land from the hurdle on both feet (spread about shoulder-width apart).
   - Follow the landing immediately with a jump to full extension.
   - This movement can come right before a tumbling stunt or end with a jump.
   - Practice finishing with a jump and landing on two feet.
2. Have the children practice the Run and Take-Off.

Needle Scale

Continue with the same setup, except match partners; one partner practices the Needle Scale while the other helps balance by gently holding the knee of the nonsupporting leg.

1. Describe and demonstrate the stunt:
   - The object is to stand on one foot and grasp the ankle of your supporting leg, making your legs move as close to a split position as possible.
   - Begin in a scale, balancing on one leg, with your arms to the sides and your other leg extended to the rear.
   - Bend your torso and grasp the ankle as you lift your nonsupporting leg as high as possible into the air, balance, then recover by reversing the movements.
2. Have the children practice the Needle Scale.

Concluding Activities (5 minutes)

Splits

Continue with the same setup.

1. Tell the children: "A split is a position in which the legs are fully extended away from each other."
2. Describe and demonstrate the Straddle Split and the Regular Split.

Lesson 3.4 *(continued)*

STRADDLE SPLIT

Begin in the straddle balance position and end with your legs extended as far apart as possible. If you are very flexible, recover into a Regular Split. Otherwise, lean forward, taking your weight on your arms and chest, and then swing both legs together to the rear to lie on your front.

REGULAR SPLIT

Begin with your feet together in a "T" position, where one foot faces front and the other foot is perpendicular to and behind the front foot, with the feet meeting the heel of the front foot to the arch of the rear foot. Slowly slide one foot forward and the other backward until your legs are fully extended.

Note: A child may also do the Regular Split with only one leg moving while the other leg remains stationary. To recover, the child leans forward with the torso over the front leg and swings the back leg around to the side until it is touching the front leg.

Discussion

Arrange the children in a semicircle. Discuss what the children have learned today:

- What should you remember about the Forward Roll? (Head tucked, weight on hands.)
- How is the Straddle Forward Roll different from the Forward Roll? (Legs apart.)

From K.T. Thomas, A.M. Lee, and J.R. Thomas, 2008, *Physical education methods for elementary teachers*, 3rd ed. (Champaign, IL: Human Kinetics). Adapted, by permission, from K.T. Thomas, A.M. Lee, and J.R. Thomas, 2000, *Physical education for children: Daily lesson plans for elementary school*, 2nd ed. (Champaign, IL: Human Kinetics), 1013-1018.

CHAPTER 4

Motor Performance During Childhood

TREVOR, AGE 9

Motor skills develop in an orderly and predictable way, and, with practice, children improve the efficiency and effectiveness of their performance. You can facilitate skill development by adapting the environment so that tasks are challenging. At the same time, children must be allowed to be successful at the tasks.

Learner Outcomes

After studying this chapter, you should be able to do the following:

- Define and describe locomotor, nonlocomotor, and manipulative skills.
- Track changes in fundamental skills during childhood.
- List the environmental factors that affect skill performance.
- Identify the skill level of a child on a task and adapt the environment so that the task is challenging and the child achieves success.

Glossary Terms

fundamental movement patterns	fundamental skills	opposition
ontogenetic skills	locomotor skills	effect sizes
phylogenetic skills	manipulative skills	speed–accuracy trade-off
motor milestones	proficiency barrier	nonlocomotor skills

Developing the motor skills that are important within the American culture is a complex process that involves both inherent abilities and practice during childhood and adolescence (Thomas 2000). During infancy, children master a variety of skills that are motor milestones: sitting, standing, and walking. Infants master the skills of locomotion and manipulation so that they can function in their environments. Then they learn general movement patterns, called **fundamental movement patterns**, such as throwing, catching, running, and jumping. Finally, they acquire specific sport skills, such as throwing a baseball or striking a tennis ball. You need to be aware of how movements develop in order to influence those skills. Furthermore, you need to understand the characteristics of movements to know what aspects of a movement can be changed to increase its efficiency and effectiveness. You can use motor skill assessment similarly to MA to estimate developmental age, which, like MA, is not always the same as CA.

Children and adults both are more likely to participate in sports, exercise, and physical activity when they are skilled (Thomas 2000). Enjoyment and success are closely linked and related to higher skill levels. Therefore, motor skills and skilled movement should be viewed as prerequisites to a physically active lifestyle. Fitness and skill are related as well. Adequate levels of physical fitness are necessary for successful participation in sport activities; otherwise, participants become fatigued before the activity is completed. At the same time, participation in vigorous sports promotes physical fitness as the person breathes hard and sweats. Finally, when a person has very low skill, the level of participation may be inadequate to result in health benefits.

Regardless of the grade or discipline that you teach, you should understand how motor skills develop and what is normal at each age. There are four reasons why you should acquire this knowledge:

1. You should monitor motor skills; unusual deviations should be referred to the parents, principal, or nurse for further evaluation.

2. You should base movement experiences for children on the normal sequential development of motor skills.

3. You need to be able to differentiate between factors that are a result of practice and those that emerge without practice.

4. Because motor skills, especially sport skills, are important in American culture, an understanding of motor skills is part of your being an educated person.

Motor skills are used from birth through childhood for assessment. The earliest movements, reflexes, reactions, and motor milestones are used by pediatricians to determine the soundness of the central nervous system and the progress of development. Later, children use fundamental skills to judge each other. Motor skills allow children to explore their environment, exert independence, and socialize. Specialized skills allow children to participate with their families and friends and to compete and perform.

The Four Guiding Principles

Now we explore in more detail the four guiding principles outlined on page 35 in regard to motor performance. Keep in mind as you study this chapter that each of the principles is important to understanding how children develop and what this means for physical education.

Principle 1. Children Are Not Miniature Adults

Skills generally fall into three categories: locomotor (moving from one place to another), nonlocomotor (staying in one place while moving), and manipulative (working with an object). Manipulative (throwing, catching, kicking, and striking) and locomotor skills (walking, running, jumping, sliding, galloping, hopping, and skipping) change systematically for children from 2 years of age through early elementary school age (Roberton

1984). For example, you would expect to see a 2-year-old run with arms high, extended, and straight (i.e., picture Frankenstein walking), feet shoulder-width apart, and a short, flat-footed step. You would not expect to see this kind of movement in an adolescent or an adult. Fundamental skills follow a pattern of change from rudimentary form to adult form. Children typically progress through the same stages of change, but at different rates.

Why do these skills change? Several factors influence the early observed differences and the process of change. Some change is caused by growth; for example, as legs get relatively longer, the step length in walking (and running) increases. Similarly, as relative head size decreases and balance is less of a problem, the torso and head move more and thus facilitate performance. As muscle mass and strength increase, stride length in walking and running also increases. So, growth explains part of the improvement in fundamental motor skills.

The central nervous system is maturing in two dimensions: increases in synapses and myelination and better integration of information. These developments allow better motor control as age increases during childhood. The biological changes work with practice to improve the execution of skills.

The vertical alignment of a developmentally appropriate physical education program is designed to recognize the individual differences in rate of change in the fundamental skills and to capitalize on the consistency of the order of these changes. You should plan for the average and then accommodate variation by individualizing up or down within the lesson. This process is evident when you observe the differences in lessons about the same concept (e.g., throwing or jumping) at two grade levels (e.g., grades 1 and 4). For younger children, there may not be a target or the target is very large when they are practicing throwing. On the other hand, for children in grade 4, you may use a target or have children throw to a partner. In younger children, jumping is often practiced from a standing or an elevated position, but older children combine jumping with other locomotor skills such as running.

Principle 2. Boys and Girls Are More Alike Than Different

The difference between boys and girls performing motor skills such as running, jumping, and swimming is very small before puberty (Thomas and French 1985). The range of performance on most skills during elementary school is greater within a gender than the difference between genders. In adults, in whom the biological difference between males and females is fully developed, the amount of difference explained by biology is about 10 percent (Ransdell and Wells 1999). The difference between male and female world-class athletes, based on Olympic and world records, is 10 percent or less, yet the difference between the average performance of average males and females is often very great: for example, for throwing, it has been observed that girls only throw 57 percent of the distance boys throw (Nelson, Thomas, Nelson, and Abraham 1986). Why is this the case?

Opportunity, practice, and encouragement are the prime environmental variables that explain differences in the average population. You can understand these environmental factors by considering the one skill in which large gender differences appear during childhood: Gender differences in throwing are large between boys and girls as young as 4 years of age in most cultures

Practice is an important variable in skill development, particularly for girls, who don't always get the same amount of attention or practice during childhood.

worldwide (Thomas and Marzke 1992). This is the only skill for which differences are large at an early age. Unfortunately, most Americans recognize when a child "throws like a girl"—there is no step, the arm motion resembles a dart throw, the torso is motionless, and the outcome is an arching ball that travels little distance forward. Furthermore, you can predict that, when a father sees his little girl throwing this way, he probably thinks, "Well, she is a girl." However, if his son threw using the same motion, the result would be different: The boy would practice with his Dad until his throwing skill improved.

In 1972, Title IX, legislation stating that no person could be excluded from participation in educational programs supported by federal funds, was passed into law. Physical education was specifically addressed three years later in guidelines stating that physical education must be the same for males and females and coeducational. There was an option to separate contact sports. (Title IX will be discussed more in chapter 11.) Since Title IX, opportunities have evolved for the elite female athletes. However, opportunity, practice, and encouragement are still typically different for girls than boys, which results in many observed gender differences. For many females after puberty, different expectations and opportunities probably have negative consequences that result in decreased physical activity. Physical education is organized so that all children have an opportunity and are encouraged to practice important motor skills. The children have the guidance of an expert teacher who understands that gender differences should be very small, even after puberty. Motor development research suggests that boys and girls should have the same physical education experience in terms of curriculum, expectations, and assessment.

Principle 3. Good Things Are Earned

Earlier in this section, we discussed skills that children in every culture perform (e.g., reflexes, reactions, and fundamental skills). Conversely, skills that are specific to either a culture or a peer group are called **ontogenetic skills**. Many of these are extensions and variations of fundamental skills; for example, although the skills are very different in execution, bowling a cricket ball and pitching a baseball are extensions of throwing. These activity-specific skills, which include dance and gymnastics, team and individual sport, extreme and adventure sport, and exercise, do not develop naturally. These skills are learned as a result of effortful practice and, often, in a systematic program. Consider the challenge of an infant beginning to walk; yet infants master this skill without lessons or coaching. Contrast that with the effort, time, and money spent trying to learn to strike a golf ball; this contrast demonstrates the value of practice in the acquisition of ontogenetic skills.

A developmentally appropriate physical education curriculum in the elementary school begins with fundamental skills, builds to transitional skills, and provides all of the children with an opportunity to learn ontogenetic skills. For many children, especially low-income students, physical education may be the only opportunity to learn these skills. Skill practice, rules and strategy, and game play are important components of the elementary school physical education curriculum. Although children may play at recess and some children may participate in after-school programs, physical education is the only place where all of the children are systematically exposed to these important skills.

In a physical education class, small groups of children may work together in "mini-games" to practice specific aspects of a game or sport. You can group these children so that the skills are similar and all of the children are challenged and can be successful. Practice on these skills is maximized in small groups, as is enjoyment. Physical educators recognize when the fundamental skill is weak and often return to the "basics" for review and mastery before returning to more advanced skills and application of skills.

Principle 4. No Body Is Perfect

As children get older, performance on motor skills improves in both process and outcome. Process is the way the skill looks and how closely this performance resembles the "ideal." Outcome is usually measured in terms of speed, distance, or accuracy. With practice and instruction, most children master the fundamental skills (e.g., manipulative and locomotor skills). Without practice and instruction, skills improve up to a point, called the proficiency barrier, but then improvement slows or stops (Haubenstricker and Seefeldt 1986). More practice, with feedback, is necessary at this point for improvement to continue.

Because practice and feedback are critical at this time, children vary greatly in their performance. This is normal, but it is also confusing to children. Skill varies within a child, so the child may be very good at kicking because of soccer practice but not so good at throwing because that skill is not used in soccer. Skills also vary between children, so one child is good at soccer but another is better at baseball. Often, children think that these differences are because of inherent characteristics—talent—when, in fact, most of the differences in children are attributable to learning (e.g., practice and feedback). Elementary physical education is an opportunity for children to try a variety of activities, to master fundamental skills, and to develop some more advanced skills. Therefore, elementary physical education curricula and equipment rooms are filled with developmentally appropriate activities and all of the "right stuff" for children of all sizes, experience levels, and interests. You can often begin instruction with statements such as this: "When I first did this activity, I had trouble—but with practice I got better and really liked it." You can also adapt equipment to accommodate the varying skills of children; for example, use a fatter bat for less skilled children and a regulation bat for those who are more skilled.

In the following sections, we provide greater detail on many aspects of motor performance. Depending on your level of interest and need, these sections can add considerably to your knowledge base.

Reflexes and Reactions

Reflexes and reactions are the earliest movements observed in humans; these movements do not disappear with age, however. Instead, more complex voluntary movements often replace the reflexes and reactions observed as the primary movements of infancy. The primitive reflexes of infancy are simple motor responses to stimuli, followed by reactions that are responses to changes in the movement environment. For example, when people lose their balance, their arms move to "catch" them before they fall. You can observe reflexes and reactions in children most often during the first two years of life. As voluntary movements become more frequent, you observe reflexes and reactions less frequently. Sometimes you can observe reflexes and reactions to varying degrees in both children and adults. Most of the time, you see reflexes under a specific environmental circumstance; one example is the Moro (or startle) reflex, evident in most people when something unexpected happens. When startled, the person inhales and exhales (often making a loud sound, even yelling), opens and closes the hands (which may cause dropping of objects), and flails the arms in the Moro reflex. However, even when startled, adults often manage to override part of the reflex. If they could not do this, they would drop whatever they were holding in their hands every time they were startled, because part of the reflex is the opening and closing of the hands. Thus, when adults are startled but do not drop the cup of coffee they are holding, they have successfully suppressed the reflex. When they drop the cup of coffee, however, they have failed to suppress the reflex. When reflexes dominate movement and persist past the age at which the reflex should be suppressed, there is cause for concern. Often, this is a result of a neurological problem.

Reactions are movements that are neurologically linked to environmental stimuli. Generally, reactions help people control their bodies without being aware of the reaction. For example, when they begin to lose their balance, reactions automatically make small, rapid corrections in order to maintain a stable body position. Reactions do not have to be learned or practiced. Reflexes and reactions are considered bases or building blocks for other skills for two reasons. First, reflexes and reactions appear earlier than other skills; second, these movements may prepare the muscles and nervous system for the voluntary movements that emerge later (figure 4.1).

Rudimentary Movements

Phylogenetic skills are movements that are observed in all of the people in a group. The

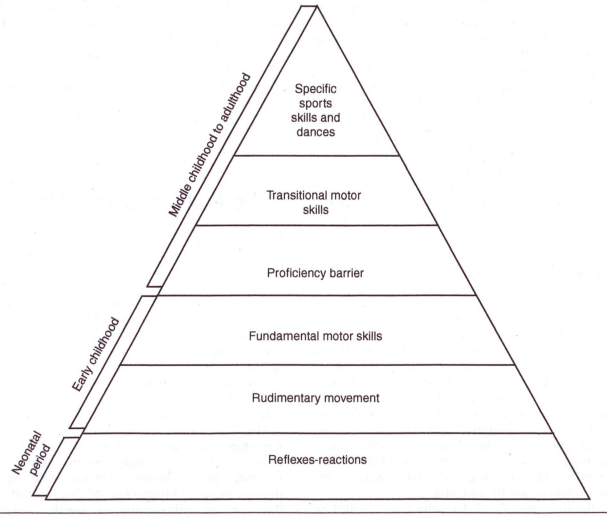

Figure 4.1 Developmental motor skill acquisition.

From J.D. Gallagher, 1984, Making sense of motor development: Interfacing research with lesson planning. In *Motor development during childhood and adolescence,* edited by Jerry Thomas (Minneapolis, MN: Burgess), 125. Reprinted by permission of Jerry Thomas.

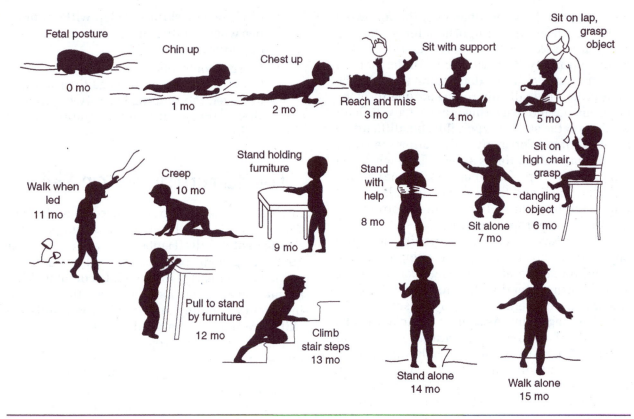

Figure 4.2 Motor milestones.

Reprinted, by permission, from M.M. Shirley, 1931, *The first two years: A study of twenty-five babies*, Vol. I, Institute of Child Welfare Monograph No. 7 (Minneapolis, MN: University of Minnesota Press), 100. Copyright © 1931 by the University of Minnesota, renewed 1959.

rudimentary movements observed during the first year of life (infancy) are sometimes called **motor milestones** because these movements are important markers of child development, including sitting, standing, and walking. Children who do not demonstrate motor milestones during infancy are developmentally delayed. Long delays may be symptoms of serious developmental disorders. Typical ages for attaining the motor milestones are presented in figure 4.2.

Nature Versus Nurture

You have probably read about at least one of the three classic studies that examined nature and nurture in the development of motor skills: McGraw's study of Johnny and Jimmy (1935), Dennis' study of Del and Rey (1935), and Dennis and Dennis' study of Hopi Indian babies (1940). Johnny and Jimmy, twins, were compared on skills such as roller skating, tricycle riding, and climbing slanted boards. The purpose was to investigate the influence of early training on motor skill acquisition. One twin lived a "normal" life; the other was trained at an early age to perform

the motor tasks that would normally be learned weeks or months later. The results showed the following:

1. There was a short-term benefit to the intervention—the trained twin did perform the skills earlier than the untrained twin or other children.

2. There were no long-term benefits to early training—the untrained twin and other children performed the skill as well as the trained twin did, and the untrained twin caught up at the time the other children naturally completed the skill.

3. Skill acquisition was easier and took fewer trials when it was learned at the typical age.

4. Infants and young children can learn and benefit from early training (McGraw 1935; Roberton 1984).

Was the cost of the early intervention worth the benefits? The trained twin often cried and was frustrated when practicing; however, he was able to perform the task at an earlier age. Because there were no long-term benefits, the following question arises: Is it important for a child to perform the skill a few weeks before the skill would normally be performed? Under normal circumstances, children demonstrate skills in the same order, gradually improving the quality of the performance and mastering increasingly difficult versions of the skill. It is possible, but difficult, to force children to do many skills earlier than their developmental readiness allows. Even when you can push earlier performance of skills, the benefits are often small and the costs are great. It is more important for children to have an opportunity to practice age-appropriate skills.

Del and Rey, female twins, participated in a deprivation study focusing on reaching and grasping and on sitting and standing (Dennis 1935). The opportunity and motivation to do the skills were removed by eliminating toys, visual models, and encouragement. As soon as the majority of a group of girls who were the same age performed the skill, Del and Rey were given the opportunity to try it. The twins were able to complete each task successfully and very quickly. For example, one of the twins reached for and grasped a brass ring within the first few tries! The results of this study indicate that practice did not influence the onset of these skills; as soon as there was opportunity and incentive, the girls performed the skills.

The Hopi Indians have a tradition of keeping infants on a cradle board (Dennis and Dennis 1940). The babies stay on the board for most of their first year. The babies are bound to the board with cloth and removed for brief periods to change swaddling and for cleaning. At the time of this study (in the 1930s), some Hopi Indians lived in the traditional villages, whereas others lived in modern villages. The Hopi living in the modern villages did not use the cradle boards. The results indicated that both modern and traditional Hopi babies walked about three months later than white babies did, but there was no influence from the cradle board. In other words, environment had little impact on walking, but there are genetic influences on phylogenetic skills such as walking.

Considered together, these studies suggest the following:

1. Some skills—phylogenetic skills—are influenced by genetics, and environment has little impact. This supports what you already learned about maturation in chapter 3, Physical Growth and Maturation.

2. Phylogenetic skills develop without practice when children are given even a modest opportunity.

3. Learned (ontogenetic) skills are susceptible to training at an earlier age than normal; however, the training is likely to produce short-term benefits and frustration for the child.

Fundamental Motor Skills

Phylogenetic skills also include some of the fundamental skills, both locomotor and manipulative. **Fundamental skills** (Haubenstricker and Seefeldt 1986) are general patterns that emerge and are refined during early childhood. **Locomotor skills** are movements from one place to another, including running, jumping, and hopping. **Manipulative skills** are movements used to interact with an object, such as object projection (kicking, striking, throwing) and object interception (catching). The normal evolution of these skills is orderly and predictable, which helps you as a teacher; once you can identify a child's performance level, you know what should happen next. The rubrics presented in tables 4.1 and 4.2 provide a summary of the changes in these skills. The optimal performance for children is shown in the column labeled "most effective." Children move from "rudimentary" to "most effective" with age and practice, and you can facilitate this journey by planning appropriate practice, goal setting, and corrective feedback.

The rubrics are based on intratask sequences that describe each movement by component (e.g., body part) and level (e.g., increase in effectiveness). The manipulative and locomotor skills observed in children change with growth, practice, and development. The normal progression from an inefficient and ineffective skill to an efficient and effective skill charts a course for elementary physical education. You can observe a child, determine his or her present level of performance, and predict what should occur next in the skill. Instruction can increase consistency at the current level and guide the child to the next level of performance; the rubrics serve as maps for instruction, feedback, and evaluation. Another way to consider skill development is the intertask sequence. Rather than follow the same skill from ineffective to effective, the intertask sequence operates across skills. This familiar approach is reflected in the saying "You have to walk before you can run."

Table 4.1 Locomotor Skills Rubric

	Most effective	Improving	Needs improvement	Rudimentary
Walking	• Arms swing in opposition, proportional to step size • Steps on the midline, heel strike • Trunk rotates with step • Head within 2 inches (5 cm) of same plane	• Hands and arms are stationary, or at side • Arms extend with step on same side • Longer strides, narrower steps	• Hands and arms held waist high and stationary • Steps may be ataxic (too much knee flexion)	• Hands and arms held high and stationary • Short, wide steps, flat-footed • No trunk rotation
Running	• Foot contact on ball of foot or heel–toe, support leg at full extension, leg swings 180 degrees • Humerus drives independent of spine, elbow at 90 degrees, opposition	• Foot and knee cross midline on forward swing, leg swings 90 degrees or less • Spine rotates arms	• Arms flailing, locked or bent	• Flat-footed, foot swings outside legs • Arms in at shoulder or waist and stationary
Jumping	**Take-off** • Symmetrical and full extension of legs and arms • Neck aligned **Flight and landing** • Hips and knees flex separately • Arms lower and reach forward for landing	**Take-off** • Neck flexed • Arms not extended **Flight and landing** • Hips and knees flex during flight, extending for landing • Trunk flexes 30 degrees for flight, flexes more for landing • Arms shoulder high for flight, or windmill	**Take-off** • Symmetrical, but not extended • Trunk leans less than 30 degrees, neck aligned • Shoulders retract, winging **Flight and landing** • Asymmetrical legs and one-foot landing • Trunk hyperextends and flexes for landing • Arms wing for flight and parachute for landing	**Take-off** • One-foot asymmetrical take-off • Trunk forward 30 degrees and neck hyperextended • Arms in opposition or stationary **Flight and landing** • Asymmetrical, one-foot landing • Trunk 30 degrees • Arm opposition
Hopping	• Swing leg leads projection • Weight transferred smoothly from foot to ball for take-off • Arm opposition	• Swing leg pumps but is in front of body • Projected take-off for several steps • Arms assist from front of body position or • Arms are in semi-opposition	• Swing leg inactive in front • Body leans forward • Arms reactive and winging	• Swing leg high in front or to side • Momentary flight from pulling motion for 1-2 steps • Arms stationary

Intertask sequences, like intratask sequences, are orderly and predictable progressions. For example, locomotor skills develop in a predetermined order: A child learns to crawl (abdomen on the surface), creep (on all fours), walk, run, leap, jump, gallop, hop, and skip. Within each task, form changes considerably with practice and growth and as variations are added. For example,

a child can gallop forward and then learn to gallop sideward (which is actually sliding). When children are asked to perform a skill that has not been learned, they substitute a different skill that they have mastered. For example, when asked to skip, children substitute a gallop if they cannot skip. By observing, you can learn a great deal about the child's developmental level.

Table 4.2 Manipulative Skills Rubric

	Most effective	Still improving	Improving	Needs improvement	Rudimentary
Throwing	• Delayed forearm lag • Hand going back while hips move forward • Differentiated trunk rotation (hips and shoulders move separately) • Step with opposition—half body length (vigorous)	• Downward and circular back swing • Forearm lags behind ball • Step with opposite foot	• Upward backspin to ear • Elbow may point skyward • Hand leads elbow and arm • Blocked trunk rotation (hips and shoulders move together) • Step with same foot as throw	• Dartboard—anterior–posterior motion • Body stationary or sways • No step	• Shot put—pushing motion • Body stationary
Catching	• Correct hand position depending on line of flight • Moves to ball • Absorbs shock	• Can change position to catch ball not thrown directly to hands	• Arms at side before catch • Control with hands	• Active—arms move before contact • Attempt to catch but will trap	• Passive—ball strikes hand or arm before movement begins • Trapping—ball is captured against chest
Kicking	• May take a step first • Arms may lift body off ground at impact		• Forward lean in preparation • Arm and leg opposition • Follow-through	• Active—leg moves before ball hits (ball often rolls under leg)	• Passive—ball strikes foot before movement begins • Pushing—the leg and foot push ball • No backspin
Striking	• Spiral motion of body • Wrists uncock at impact • Body weight		• Swing does not cross midline • Body position perpendicular to line of flight	• Active—moves hand, arm, or object before ball hits • Anterior–posterior motion • Stands facing line	• Passive—ball strikes hand or arm before movement begins • Pushing—the hand or arm pushes ball • No backspin

Proficiency Barrier and Transitional Skills

Fundamental skills begin to develop in virtually all children (Haubenstricker and Seefeldt 1986); with experience, children master these skills. Mastery means that the child can execute the skill correctly without having to think about the movements. Practice and instruction (especially feedback) facilitate the mastery of these skills. The **proficiency barrier**, an explanation for children not mastering the fundamental skills, is usually a result of too little practice and ineffective instruction. Children who do not break through the barrier find it difficult or impossible to move on to transitional and sport skills. Transitional skills are those activities that help children make the leap from fundamental skills to sport, dance, gymnastics, and exercise applications. Transitional skills focus on combining the fundamental patterns in unique and demanding ways to create new movements, such as jumping rope.

Specific Sport Skills

Specific sport skills are learned and mastered with a great deal of practice (French and McPherson 1999). These are called ontogenetic skills—learned skills that vary by cultural and peer group. In-line skating and snow skiing are two examples of skills that some people do and others do not. Many dances are good examples of the peer influence that is observed in ontogenetic skills: For example, dances that may have been popular with

Once children have mastered the fundamental skills, they can move on to transitional and specific sport skills to successfully enjoy activities like climbing a traverse wall.

your great-grandparents (the Lindy), grandparents (the jitterbug), and parents (the twist) seemed old-fashioned to each new generation, whereas dances popular with you and your friends are probably labeled as passing fads by previous generations.

Reflexes, reactions, motor milestones, and fundamental motor skills are most frequently evaluated by time of onset. These become markers of development based on the age at which a child completes the skill. Developmental age (similar to MA) is sometimes assessed using these motor skills. Fundamental motor skills are also assessed

using process or qualitative instruments such as the rubrics. Skill efficiency is the measurement. Other ways to assess motor skills are by the outcome (or product measurements), such as time, distance, and accuracy, and by observing the child using the skill in a real-world setting such as a game or a dance.

Sport, dance, and gymnastics require use of a combination of skills, often in novel ways and often quickly. During middle childhood, these skills become the focus of physical education (Thomas and Thomas 1999). The taxonomy of psychomotor and cognitive domains (table 4.3),

Table 4.3 Taxonomy of Psychomotor and Cognitive Domains

Psychomotor	Action descriptors	Cognitive	Action descriptors
Perceiving	Name, identify	Knowledge	Define, list, state
Patterning	Demonstrate	Comprehension	Give example, compare
Adapting	Modify	Application	Demonstrate, calculate
Refining	Transfer, use in game	Analysis	Distinguish, test, examine
Varying	Combine, create	Synthesis	Propose, design, construct
Valuing	Judge, correct	Evaluation	Judge, predict, choose

which is similar to Bloom's taxonomy of cognitive performance, provides a way of thinking about how motor skill progresses from the most basic level of recognizing or naming a skill to the highest level of evaluating that skill. You are expected to evaluate motor skill, and therefore you must have mastered many aspects of the psychomotor domain.

Concepts Into Practice

Benjamin Bloom (1956) brought the notion of mastery learning to the United States. (See "Lesson #1 Rhythmic Lesson" on the DVD-ROM for a video clip showing a mastery learning approach to teaching.) He also identified six levels of cognition that recognized different demands and understanding of cognitive tasks. The simplest level is knowledge that represents definitions and memorization; the next level is comprehension that demonstrates understanding, such as actions and providing examples. Application is the next level, which takes place when information can be used, for example, in calculating an answer. The next two levels are analysis and synthesis: breaking apart knowledge and using it in a new way. The highest level is evaluation: making a judgment. Bloom suggests that mastery of all levels of the taxonomy leads to wisdom. Bloom's taxonomy has been examined, refined, and criticized, but it remains an important basis for research and thinking. For example, cognitive assessment is based on the level of the question, using Bloom's taxonomy. A teacher can also use Bloom's taxonomy to individualize instruction. For example, after most of the class was asked to apply the concept, one child might be challenged to give an example of the concept, while another child is asked to evaluate the concept. Each student would be working on the same material but at a different level—a level appropriate for the individual students.

Locomotor Skills

As children grow and age, performance of motor skills improves. Part of the improvement is caused by increases in size; another part is attributable to increased efficiency of the movement. The rubrics summarize the changes in efficiency. This section examines the locomotor skills in greater depth and covers the changes in motor outcome (e.g., speed and distance).

Walking and Running

The major difference between walking and running is the nonsupport (flight) phase that defines running. In walking, the pattern is right foot, both feet, left foot, both feet, and right foot. At least one foot is always on the ground, and part of the time both feet are in contact with the ground. In a mature walk, the head remains in the same plane, deviating no more than 2 inches (5 cm) in any direction (up to down, front to back, side to side). The heel touches the ground first, followed by the ball of the foot; then the push-off from the ground for the next step is from the toes. The arms are relaxed at the sides of the body, moving in opposition to the legs. **Opposition** means that, as the right arm goes forward, the left arm goes back. So, as the step is taken on the left foot, the right arm swings forward. The arm opposition should be proportional to the size of the step. One final characteristic is that the step touches the ground on an imaginary line that runs through the middle of the body from front to back.

In running, the pattern used is right foot, (air), left foot, (air), and right foot. Running speed increases during childhood because stride length increases. The stride increases as the legs grow longer and stronger and as the pattern becomes more efficient. As children progress, they take longer steps or strides and stay in the air longer. When young children are asked to run faster, they generally take quicker steps—often in place. Rather than saying "Run faster," you should say, "Take bigger steps." The fastest runners use their arms to pull themselves forward. The arms move in opposition, with the upper arm (humerus) driving forward forcefully. In young children, the arms may be stationary or may flail in no particular pattern. As skill increases, the arms begin to rotate in opposition, but this movement is generated by a twisting of the spine rather than by conscious movement of the humerus. Girls demonstrate the mature running form described in the rubric at a slightly earlier age than boys; most children demonstrate a mature run by 7 years of age. You should identify the following problems in running for remediation: arms swinging too much or too little, crossing the midline of the body, or flailing; feet toeing in or out or producing flat-footed steps; or trunk leaning too far forward and twisting.

The average running speed for boys and girls is nearly the same during elementary school (figure 4.3; Thomas and French 1985). At puberty, boys continue to increase running

Dash

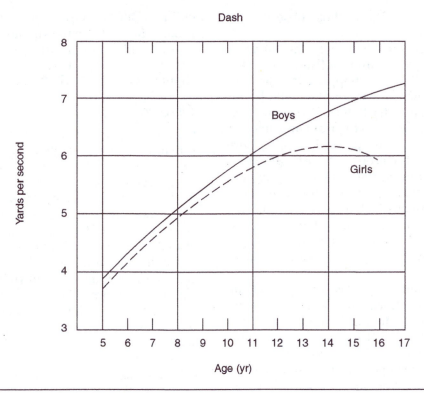

Figure 4.3 Running speed during childhood.

Reprinted, by permission, from A. Espenschade and H. Eckert, 1974, Motor development. In *Science and medicine of exercise and sport*, 2nd ed., edited by W.R. Johnson and E.R. Buskirk (New York, NY: Harper & Row), 329.

speed, whereas girls' running speed tends to level off or decrease slightly. The differences during the elementary years are attributed to different treatment of girls and boys (Thomas and French 1985; Nelson, Thomas, and Nelson 1991). For example, boys have greater opportunity, encouragement, and expectations for achievement in sports and physical education than do girls. Considering the factors that influence running speed (e.g., leg length), there is no reason to expect differences during elementary school. Therefore, you need to provide equal opportunity, have similar expectations, and encourage boys and girls equally.

Jumping, Hopping, Galloping, Sliding, and Skipping

Jumping has several forms, each of which has intratask sequences of development. The intertask sequence for jumping begins with a step down and progresses as follows (Wickstrom 1983):

1. Jump down from one foot, landing on the other.
2. Jump up from two feet, landing on two feet.
3. Jump down from one foot, landing on two feet.
4. Jump down from two feet, landing on two feet.
5. Run and jump forward from on one foot; land on the other foot (leaping).
6. Jump forward from two feet; land on two feet (standing long jump).
7. Run and jump forward from one foot; land on two feet (running long jump).
8. Jump over an object from two feet; land on two feet.
9. Jump rhythmically from one foot to the same foot (hopping).

Hopping and leaping are variations of jumping. By 10 years of age, approximately 60 percent of boys and girls demonstrate a mature pattern for the standing long jump. Typical problems you should identify for the long jump include poor initial crouch, failure to use the arms or to extend the body, and poor balance at landing. Boys and girls from 5 to 10 years of age jump forward on two feet (standing long jump) about as far as they are tall. The differences between boys and girls are similar to those observed for running.

Hopping is mastered between 7 and 8 years of age by 60 percent of children (Haubenstricker and Seefeldt 1986). Early hopping is characterized by children jumping forward on both feet or losing balance as they try to hop. Young children hold the nonsupport leg to the front and actually look at the foot. They are probably making sure that the foot is off the ground. Several problems may persist, including flat-footed hopping; too much arm movement; failure to maintain balance; inability to hop equally well on both feet; and lack of a smooth, rhythmic movement. Girls often hop greater distances and on either foot at earlier ages than boys. However, by age 9, there are no longer gender differences.

You can cue galloping most easily in young children by saying "Move like a horse." Immediately, children step forward on one foot, draw the other foot close, and continue this pattern with the same foot leading. Galloping evolves into sliding. Children generally master one foot leading before the other, but they should be able to lead effectively with either foot during early elementary school.

Skipping is a combination of hopping and walking; the pattern is step-hop, step-hop. Most children can skip proficiently by age 7; however, some children learn to skip during the preschool years. Gender and age differences are related to experience and, primarily, to practice. Skipping should be a smooth, rhythmic movement.

Climbing

Climbing up is accomplished before climbing down, likely because going up, children are not aware of the height because they are focused on the goal at the top. Climbing down, they look at the goal, which makes them more aware of the height. This awareness of height also makes them aware of the possibility of falling! So, like kittens who get stranded in trees, children sometimes have more difficulty climbing down than they do climbing up. They first climb up or down in a creeping position (on all fours). This is followed by climbing in a standing position but while "marking time," which means that children lead with the same foot for every step. Finally, children climb using alternate feet. Children often mark time going up and creep back down or step alternately going up and mark time going down. The pattern a child uses gives insight into his or her confidence as well as skill level.

See "Lesson #4 Games and Sport Lesson" on the DVD-ROM for a video clip showing a locomotor skills lesson using whole-group instruction.

Concepts Into Practice

Suppose that you asked your students to skip across the gym floor. Most of the second graders can perform this skill, but one child is galloping. You see the difference in the movement pattern because, in galloping, the same leg is always in the front, while legs alternate moving forward in skipping. What you do not know is why the child is galloping instead of skipping. Consider each of the following possible reasons:

- The child cannot skip.
- The child doesn't know the difference between skipping and galloping.
- The child is trying to gain your attention by doing the wrong skill.
- The child is testing to see if you care whether the skills are done correctly.

Regardless of the reason, you must address this matter with the child. Why is he or she galloping?

Manipulative Skills

Most sports require interaction with objects. The pyramid of skills suggests that the fundamental skills of catching, kicking, striking, and throwing become more refined and specific as they are applied in various sports. During childhood, games require the use of these skills. Therefore, children who have poor skills often have less opportunity to interact with their peers. Manipulative skills are important during childhood and adolescence.

Catching

Catching requires prediction, anticipation, and coordination; however, most children master catching an 8.5-inch (21.5 cm) ball by the time they are in grade 3. This means that most of the time the children demonstrate efficient form and catch the ball. The easiest catch is a ball thrown in an arc that approaches the child's chest at a 45-degree angle. In this scenario, the ball, ideally 8.5 inches (21.5 cm) in diameter, should be tossed from 10 to 15 feet (3 to 4.5 m) away. By grade 5, children are able to catch a tennis ball

Children should practice catching balls of different sizes.

because the gender differences are larger and appear earlier than for other skills. Figure 4.4 compares overhand throwing by girls and boys using effect size. **Effect sizes** are calculated by dividing the difference between two means (e.g., boys' throwing distance minus girls' throwing distance) by the standard deviation of the means. If the answer is zero or close to zero, the effect size suggests that the two groups are not different. An effect size of 0.5 is moderate, and 0.8 is large. Measuring effect size is advantageous because the results of many studies can be combined, providing a more accurate picture of the true differences. The effect sizes for overhand throwing are larger than for any other motor task (Thomas and French 1985). The differences begin very early (about 3 to 4 years of age) and continue to increase throughout childhood and adolescence.

consistently under similar conditions. Boys and girls are similar in skill level when catching. Large differences are observed between children who have practiced and those who have not practiced catching balls thrown with force, line drives, and ground balls. These differences tend to be interpreted as gender differences because boys have traditionally had more practice.

Striking and Kicking

Striking and kicking are similar in their intratask sequences and performance curves (Roberton 1984). Boys demonstrate mature patterns at 7 years of age, about a year and a half before girls. Boys kick farther and with 40 percent more velocity than girls during elementary school. Both patterns begin as passive reactions; that is, the ball touches the child before any attempt at movement occurs. Younger children also involve as few body parts as possible in kicking and striking; with age and practice, more body parts are incorporated into the pattern, generating more force and greater velocity and distance.

Throwing

The overhand throwing motion is used in many sports (e.g., with the javelin, the tennis serve, the football pass, and baseball pitching). Other methods of projecting the ball include rolling and tossing; however, the word "throw" usually means overarm throwing. Throwing is, perhaps, the most interesting skill because it is important and

Most of you know what the phrase "throws like a girl" means: The throw is a slow, weak lower-arm motion, accompanied by a short step on the same foot as the throwing hand (Yan, Payne, and Thomas 2000). The arm motion often looks like a dart throw. Contrast this motion with the typical throw for a boy, which is vigorous: The entire body coils backward; as a large step is taken forward, the hips rotate forward, followed by the shoulder, then upper arm, and finally the lower arm and hand. The throw ends with the body leaning forward over the stepping leg.

Several explanations for the difference include evolution, sociocultural factors, and the emergence of gender-specific forms of throwing (Thomas and Marzke 1992). One theory suggests that, although evolution favored males who could throw effectively, this trait did not influence the evolution of women. Another theory suggests that men develop one throwing pattern and women a different pattern and that they therefore develop different skills. Finally, a third theory suggests that the sociocultural importance of throwing well for males creates an atmosphere in which girls who throw poorly are allowed to continue throwing poorly and boys who throw poorly are trained until they throw well. The answer may well be a combination of the three theories. The fact is that sizable throwing differences exist between males and females, and training reduces those

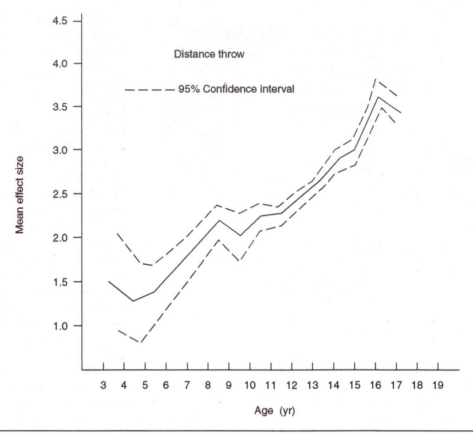

Figure 4.4 Effect size for overarm throwing.

From J.R. Thomas and K.E. French, "Gender differences in motor performance: A meta analysis," *Psychological Bulletin* 98(2): 260-282. Copyright © 1985 by the American Psychological Association. Adapted with permission.

differences but does not eliminate them (Thomas, Michael, and Gallagher 1994; Thomas 2000).

All children should be expected to throw with an efficient pattern. As children practice, encourage them to take a large step, throwing with force. Do not worry about accuracy until a mature pattern is well established—that is, until the child consistently demonstrates a mature throwing pattern. For most boys, this occurs at around 5 years of age; for most girls, it occurs around age 8 (Haubenstricker and Seefeldt 1986).

See "Lesson #5 Games and Sport Lesson" on the DVD-ROM for a video clip showing a manipulative skills lesson using small-group organization.

Speed–Accuracy Trade-Off

One of the most robust phenomena in movement science is the **speed–accuracy trade-off**: As the demand for accuracy increases, the speed of movement decreases. In tasks for which force (or distance) is important, such as throwing, demanding accuracy increases movement time and therefore reduces force. Generally, practice forceful or fast movements first and then add accuracy gradually. Your students

should practice without a target. Children switch from an overhand throw to tossing underhand when accuracy demands are increased. Practicing tossing will not develop overhand throwing skill.

The speed–accuracy trade-off applies to many skills (e.g., kicking and hitting); as the demand for speed increases, accuracy decreases because of errors (Yan, Thomas, and Stelmach 2002). In skills that are dangerous (e.g., in climbing), reducing speed usually makes the skill safer because errors are reduced. Consider the speed–accuracy trade-off as you plan lessons and provide instruction.

Other Groups of Motor Skills

Numerous techniques have been used for classifying motor skills. We have covered phylogenetic and ontogenetic (e.g., classifying by inherent or learned skills) as well as locomotor and manipulative skills. Another group—**nonlocomotor skills**—encompasses virtually all other skills. Balancing, stretching, and bending are nonlocomotor skills. In this chapter, we divide manipulative skills into tasks of object reception and object projection. By adding body projection (locomotor) and body stability (nonlocomotor) categories, we have included virtually all basic movements (table 4.4). Many terms have the same meaning; we use the terms in order to be able to consider groups of skills in a logical way. As we develop curriculum, one technique is used to cover all of the categories in a classification system to ensure that the curriculum is comprehensive.

Table 4.4 Classifying Skills

Locomotor skills	Manipulative skills	Nonlocomotor skills
Walking	Throwing	Standing
Running	Catching	Bending
Jumping	Kicking	Stretching
Hopping	Striking	Curling
Galloping		Wiggling
Sliding		Swaying
Skipping		

These skills represent the broad base of movements children should master in early elementary school that allow them to perform more advanced sport, dance, and gymnastics skills.

Motor Abilities Underlying Performance

Some children find it easier to acquire and perform certain skills than other children. As with any task (e.g., reading, mathematics, and language), inherited abilities that underlie performance vary from child to child. Abilities such as balance and speed influence skill acquisition and sometimes performance. The amount of influence depends on the importance of the ability to the task (Thomas 2000). For example, in the 100-meter dash, speed is critical. However, in dancing the waltz, speed is not critical. In sports where strategy is important (e.g., where there is an offense and defense), underlying abilities do not predict skill level. Reaction time is often cited as a critical component of the abilities of expert athletes, yet reaction time may not matter as much as other factors in most sport settings. For example, in a swimming race that lasts 60 seconds from start to finish, the difference between the fastest and slowest reaction time accounts for less

than one-fifth of a second! The majority of the time is spent on strokes, which are learned through practice. So the advantage gained by fast reaction time in a swimming race is so small that it probably makes no difference in the outcome to the typical swimmer, even the typical athlete. However, it could be the difference between breaking a world record and not breaking it.

Some sports or events are more related to underlying abilities than others. For example, the balance beam logically demands good balance. Other important attributes for success on the beam include strength and flexibility. So good balance alone does not guarantee success. Underlying abilities are complicated to measure, usually requiring more than one test and often yielding surprising results. The average effect sizes for several tests of balance indicate that boys and girls have similar balance during childhood, but, at several ages, small differences favor the boys. At adolescence, the differences increase, favoring the boys, which is contrary to the popular opinion that girls have better balance. Why? Girls may perform better on some balance tasks, and girls were better at balance at ages 3 and 4 years. However, when balance is inverted (e.g., headstand, handstand), boys' strength and endurance are an advantage. (Thomas and French 1985). So, even on a task that seems as simple as balance, the answer is complex. Remember two important things when considering gender differences in underlying abilities: First, underlying abilities in the normal range probably do not hinder performance, and better-than-average abilities provide a very small advantage—and then primarily only during early skill learning or at the world-class level. Second, stereotypes are often incorrect and always limit opportunities. In the development of skilled movements, underlying abilities are not nearly as important as opportunity, encouragement, and practice.

Modifying Task Demands

You can modify the same task in many ways to meet the individual needs of children. For example, adding a target or changing the size of a ball makes a task more or less difficult. Some motor skills are carried out when the person decides to initiate the skill; for example, in golf, the player swings at the ball when he or she is ready. Tennis is different from golf because, once the ball is in play, the player must respond when the ball is hit. Golf is a self-paced task because the golfer establishes the timing; tennis

Using a batting tee is an example of modifying task demands of striking to fit the skill level of the participants.

such as football. In football, the object is to change the conditions (e.g., the predictability of the offense or defense) as often as possible. In addition to the strategy of making the game unpredictable, players have to deal with environmental issues such as wind and field conditions.

Applying the concepts of stability of the environment and pacing (figure 4.5) to more basic skills, you can regulate the difficulty of motor tasks. As children master the tasks, increase the difficulty so that the task remains challenging. Shifting a task from self-paced to externally paced or from stable to unstable accomplishes this goal. The organization of baseball in many communities applies this principle. The youngest players play tee ball (where they hit the ball off a tee); next, they play coaches pitch (where their own coach pitches); then, the opponent's pitcher pitches. This progression gradually makes the task less predictable because batting from the tee is very stable, whereas trying to hit a ball thrown by another 12-year-old is most often unpredictable!

Most motor tasks have many dimensions that influence the difficulty of the task. Locomotor tasks can be modified by changing speed of the movement, direction of the movement, number of skills, level of the movement, and pacing of the movement (table 4.5).

Tables 4.6 through 4.8 present various ways to modify manipulative tasks, including using characteristics of targets, implements, and object projections. This list is not all-inclusive but provides samples of environmental variables that can be used to challenge children or accommodate lower skill levels.

volleying is an externally paced task because the player does not decide when to hit the ball. Certain tasks, such as bowling, change very little from time to time. In bowling, the lanes and other conditions remain constant, especially compared with a sport

	Skill Initiation	
	Self-paced	Externally paced
Open	Golf Softball pitching Jogging	Tennis Softball batting Soccer
Closed	Bowling Balance beam T-ball batting	Speed swimming 100-meter dash Cotton-eyed Joe

Movement Environment

Figure 4.5 Matrix of task difficulty.

Table 4.5 Modifying Locomotor Skills

	Easiest	Moderate	Most difficult
Speed of movement	Slow	Medium	Fast
Direction of movement	In place	Forward	Backward
Number of skills	One	Two	Three or more
Level of movement	Medium	Low	High
Pacing	Self-paced		Externally paced

Table 4.6 Modifying Tasks That Use a Target (e.g., throwing, kicking, striking)

	Easiest	Easy	Challenging	Difficult
Target size	No target	Very large—an area (e.g., a wall)	Moderate size for distance (e.g., 4 by 4 from 10 feet [3 m])	Small (1 square foot [0.1 sq m] from 20 feet [6 m])
Target distance	No distance	5 feet (1.6 m)	10-20 feet (3-6 m)	Long distance
Target movement	None	Moderate speed and predictable	Fast	Fast and unpredictable

Table 4.7 Modifying Striking Implements

	Easiest	Challenging	Difficult
Handle length	None	Short	Long
Striking surface size	Large (oversized tennis racket)	Moderate (paddle)	Small (e.g., bat)

Table 4.8 Modifying Object Interception Tasks (e.g., striking, kicking)

	Easiest	Easy	Challenging	Difficult
Speed of the object	None	Moderate	Slow	Fast
Direction of the object	In front	From front	From side	From rear
Predictability of object	Stable			Unstable
Size of object	Large—13 inches (33 cm) diameter	Moderate—8.5 inches (21.5 cm) diameter	Small (tennis ball)	Very small (golf or Ping-Pong ball)
Object projection	None (object is waiting)	Directly to interceptor	Requires one step adjustment	Requires several steps or change of direction
Object trajectory	None	On ground	45-degree angle interception point at chest	Line drive

Summary

You apply your knowledge of how motor skills develop to plan lessons and provide instruction. The notion of developmentally appropriate physical education is grounded in knowledge of skill development. Furthermore, you have the opportunity to influence the sociocultural environment so that expectations and opportunities are optimal for both boys and girls. Some skills evolve naturally, whereas others require considerable practice and instruction. Children who practice are able to maximize their potential. You need to understand the factors that influence task difficulty so that instruction can demonstrate progression (e.g., in assessing the speed–accuracy trade-off). If you understand how skills develop, you can deliver a developmentally appropriate physical education program that is challenging to children and allows children to be successful.

Mastery Learning Activities

1. Working with a partner, watch as your partner walks toward you on a line. Be sure your partner is looking at you. Look for the characteristics of a mature walk (head on same plane, arm opposed and proportional, step on midline, heel strike). Reverse roles and repeat. Alternatively, go to a public place and record the various deviations from a mature walk that you observe in adults.

2. Using the information from this chapter and the previous chapter, consider the following concept and the statements explaining the concept. What evidence supports the concept and the statements?

   Human behavior and performance are results of both nature and nurture.

   a. Early in the development of children (birth to 2 years), most observable behavior and performance are attributable to genetics (nature).

   b. During childhood (3 to 18 years), environment becomes increasingly important.

   c. At puberty, genetics, maturation, and nature are very important.

   d. Most observable child behavior and performance are caused by environmental influences.

   e. Enrichment tends to have short-term benefits; deprivation has little influence on phylogenetic skills.

3. Motor skills can be classified in various categories, as follows:

   a. Phylogenetic and ontogenetic

   b. Locomotor, nonlocomotor, and manipulative

   c. Object projection, object interception, body projection, and stability

   Define and give examples of each of these classifications. How can you use classifications such as these?

4. Make a checklist of problems that may persist for each locomotor skill and the age at which you should expect the skill to be mastered.

5. Boys and girls perform most motor skills similarly during childhood, but one skill is performed differently by each gender. Name that skill, describe the differences between genders, and present at least two possible causes for the large gender differences in that skill.

6. Select a skill not covered in this chapter and describe the speed–accuracy trade-off for that skill.

7. Compare the activities in the lesson plans. What changes are made based on the age of the children? Are there opportunities in the lessons to accommodate varying skill? How would you achieve this balance?

References

Bloom, B.S. 1956. *Taxonomy of educational objectives: Cognitive domain.* New York: McKay.

Dennis, W. 1935. The effect of restricted practice upon the reaching, sitting, and standing of two infants. *Journal of Genetic Psychology* 47: 17-32.

Dennis, W., and M.G. Dennis. 1940. The effect of cradling practices upon the onset of walking in Hopi children. *Journal of Genetic Psychology* 56: 77-86.

French, K.E., and S.L. McPherson. 1999. Adaptations in response selection processes used during sport competition with increasing age and expertise. *International Journal of Sport Psychology* 30: 173-193.

Haubenstricker, J., and V. Seefeldt. 1986. Acquisition of motor skills during childhood. In *Physical activity and well-being*, edited by V. Seefeldt, 41-102. Reston, VA: American Alliance for Health, Physical Education, Recreation and Dance (AAHPERD).

McGraw, M.B. 1935. *Growth: A study of Johnny and Jimmy.* New York: Appleton-Century-Crofts.

Nelson, J.K., J.R. Thomas, K.R. Nelson, and P.C. Abraham. 1986. Gender differences in children's throwing performance: Biology and environment. *Research Quarterly for Exercise and Sport* 57: 280-287.

Nelson, K.R., J.R. Thomas, and J.K. Nelson. 1991. Longitudinal changes in throwing performance: Gender differences. *Research Quarterly for Exercise and Sport* 62: 105-108.

Ransdell, L.B., and C.L. Wells. 1999. Sex differences in athletic performance. *Women in Sport and Activity* 8: 55-81.

Roberton, M.A. 1984. Changing motor patterns during childhood. In *Motor development during childhood and adolescence,* edited by J.R. Thomas, 48-90. Minneapolis: Burgess.

Thomas, J.R. 2000. C.H. McCloy Lecture: Children's control, learning and performance of motor skills. *Research Quarterly for Exercise and Sport* 71: 1-9.

Thomas, J.R., and K.E. French. 1985. Gender differences across age in motor performance: A meta-analysis. *Psychological Bulletin* 98: 260-282.

Thomas, J.R., and M. Marzke. 1992. The development of gender differences in throwing: Is human evolution a factor? In *The academy papers—Enhancing human performance in sport,* edited by R. Christina and H. Eckert, 60-76. Champaign, IL: Human Kinetics.

Thomas, J.R., D. Michael, and J.D. Gallagher. 1994. Effects of training on gender differences in overhead throwing: A brief quantitative literature analysis. *Research Quarterly for Exercise and Sport* 65: 67-71.

Thomas, K.T., and J.R. Thomas. 1999. What squirrels in the trees predict about expert athletes. *International Journal of Sport Psychology* 30: 221-234.

Wickstrom, R.L. 1983. *Fundamental motor patterns.* 3rd ed. Philadelphia: Lea & Febiger.

Yan, J.H., V.G. Payne, and J.R. Thomas. 2000. Developmental kinematics of young girls' overarm throwing. *Research Quarterly for Exercise and Sport* 71: 92-98.

Yan, J.H., J.R. Thomas, and G.E. Stelmach. 2002. How children and seniors differ from adults in controlling rapid aiming arm movements. In *Motor development research and reviews,* edited by J.E. Clark and J. Humphrey, 191-217. Reston, VA: NASPE.

Resources

Fitts, P.M. 1954. The information capacity of the human motor system in controlling the amplitude of movements. *Journal of Experimental Psychology* 47: 381-391.

Halverson, L., M.A. Roberton, and S. Langendorfer. 1982. Development of the overarm throw: Movement and ball velocity changes by seventh grade. *Research Quarterly for Exercise and Sport* 53: 198-205.

Isaac, B. 1987. Throwing and human evolution. *The African Archaeological Review* 5: 3-17.

Roberton, M.A., L.E. Halverson, S. Langendorfer, and K. Williams. 1979. Longitudinal changes in children's overarm throw ball velocities. *Research Quarterly for Exercise and Sport* 50: 256-264.

Seefeldt, V., and J. Haubenstricker. 1982. Patterns, phases, or stages: An analytical model for the study of developmental movement. In *The development of movement control and co-ordination,* edited by J.A.S. Kelso and J.E. Clark, 309-318. New York: Wiley.

Thomas, K.T., J.D. Gallagher, and J.R. Thomas. 2001. Motor development and skill acquisition during childhood and adolescence. In *Handbook of sport psychology,* 2nd ed., edited by R.N. Singer, H.A. Hausenblas, and C. Janelle, 20-52. New York: Wiley.

Wild, M.R. 1938. The behavior pattern of throwing and some observations concerning its course of development in children. *Research Quarterly* 9: 20-24.

Lesson Plans

The four lesson plans that follow demonstrate the progressive use of locomotor, nonlocomotor, and manipulative skills at three age levels (grades K-1, 2-3, and 4-5). The first three lessons trace the activity of catching from kindergarten through grade 5 and are appropriate at the beginning of the year. Catching a tossed object is easier than catching a thrown object. Therefore, combine catching with tossing in the early grades. In grades K and 1, you can use beanbags because they are easier to grasp than balls and require less chasing when missed, whereas, in grades 2 and 3, children can throw both beanbags and balls. At the beginning of the school year, activities should include reviewing skills taught the previous year. In grades 2 and 3, you can follow a review of beanbag throwing and catching by throwing a ball. In the early grades, children practice with self-tossed beanbags; follow this activity by tossing and catching or using a beanie launcher. Teacher tossing is also a good way for beginners to practice. Partner work comes after children have mastered the basics and move under control.

The last lesson follows nonlocomotor skills in grades 4 and 5. In grades 4 and 5, combine nonlocomotor and locomotor skills. Children master individual skills first and then experiment with combinations; the ultimate goal is to be able to create novel movements as necessary.

Lesson 4.1

Throwing and Catching Beanbags

Student Objectives   1

- Toss a beanbag above their heads and catch it, toss a beanbag from hand to hand successfully, and toss and catch a beanbag with the same hand.
- Demonstrate a high and low toss and throw.
- Practice tossing into a hoop from varying distances (kindergarten children).
- Toss a beanbag into a hoop from 10 feet (3 m) away (first-grade children).
- Demonstrate cooperation when playing Beanbag Rope Toss.
- Correctly identify 5 body parts (wrist, elbow, arm, chest, head) by placing the beanbag on the part during Movement Challenges.

Equipment and Materials

- 1 beanbag per child, plus extra beanbags
- 1 hoop per group (30 to 36 inches [76 to 91 cm])
- 1 rope (at least 20 feet [6 m] long)
- 1 foam ball per group (first-grade children)
- 2 standards and rope

Safety Tip

- Remind the children to respect each other's personal space.

Warm-Up Activities (5 minutes)

Throw and Fetch

Arrange the children in a line facing a long, open area; each child should have a beanbag.

1. Describe the activity:
    - Throw your beanbag as far as possible.
    - On the signal, run to the beanbags, pick one up, and return to the line. It doesn't matter which beanbag you get.
    - Continue this several times as quickly as possible.
2. Have the children play Throw and Fetch.

Skill-Development Activities (20 minutes)

Movement Challenges

Arrange the children in scatter formation; each child should have a beanbag.

1. Ask the children: "Can you walk and balance the beanbag on your head?"
2. Have the children practice balancing the beanbag on their shoulders, wrists, arms, or chests.

Tossing a Beanbag

Keep the children in scatter formation; each child should have a beanbag.

1. Ask the children: "Can you toss the beanbag up and catch it, like this?"
2. Demonstrate. Cup a beanbag in both hands and toss it 4 to 6 inches (10 to 15 cm) into the air.
3. Tell the children: "Keep it low! Now try a little higher." Look for tosses above the children's heads. They should still be tossing, using both hands. "This is harder. Try with one hand; start low! Put the other hand behind your back. Try throwing above your head with one hand."
4. Stop the children. Demonstrate tossing from hand to hand. Tell the children: "You try! Can you make the beanbag arc up high?"

Beanbag Rope Toss

Arrange partners in two lines, facing each other 6 to 10 feet (1.8 to 3 m) apart, with a rope suspended in the air, midway between the lines, at the children's eye level (use two standards to hold the rope). Give each pair of children a beanbag.

1. Describe the game, "Partners toss one beanbag back and forth over the rope for 4 or 5 minutes. Try to toss so that it is possible to catch, and try hard to catch."
2. Have the children play Beanbag Rope Toss. If this is too easy, raise the rope or move the children farther from the rope (or move pairs who are successful farther apart, or move the rope at one end higher to make the activity more challenging).

Beanbag Hoop Toss

Divide the children into groups of 4 or 5, with each group around a hoop laid on the ground.

1. Have the children practice tossing beanbags into the hoops for 4 or 5 minutes.
2. Ask the children, "How far can you toss and hit inside the hoop?"

Concluding Activities (5 minutes)

Play Teacher Ball or Circle Toss Ball, depending on the age group.

Teacher Ball (kindergarten children)

Divide the children into small groups, arranged in circles. For each group, select a child to play the role of Teacher to stand in the middle with a beanbag.

1. Describe and demonstrate the activity:
   - The Teacher tosses the beanbag to one of the other children, who in turn tosses it back to the Teacher.
   - Continue tossing the beanbag until each child in your group has had one turn.
   - Then the Teacher chooses a new Teacher.
2. Have the children play Teacher Ball.

Circle Toss Ball (first-grade children)

Divide the children into groups of 4 to 6, standing in a circle. Place one child in the middle with a foam ball. Scatter the circles. The first time, you will probably want to play as one large group. After the children have learned the game, divide into groups to play. Note: This is a good game for helping the children get to know each other's names at the beginning of the school year.

1. Describe and demonstrate the game:
   - The child in the middle of the circle tosses the foam ball high (and straight up) into the air and calls the name of one of the other children.
   - The child whose name is called tries to catch the ball before it hits the ground.
   - The Tosser joins the circle, and the Catcher becomes the Tosser.

   Note: If the children do not try to catch the ball, replace the Tosser only when the ball is successfully caught.

2. Have the children play Circle Toss Ball.

From K.T. Thomas, A.M. Lee, and J.R. Thomas, 2008, *Physical education methods for elementary teachers*, 3rd ed. (Champaign, IL: Human Kinetics). Adapted, by permission, from K.T. Thomas, A.M. Lee, and J.R. Thomas, 2000, *Physical education for children: Daily lesson plans for elementary school*, 2nd ed. (Champaign, IL: Human Kinetics), 99-101.

Lesson 4.2

Throwing, Catching, and Dribbling

Student Objectives   1

- Dribble while moving.
- Refine skills of throwing and catching with a partner.
- Contrast dribbling and bouncing.
- Work cooperatively in Circle Stride Ball or in small groups in Keep Away.

Equipment and Materials

- 1 playground ball (8+ inches [20 cm]) per child
- Polyspots, polydomes, or tape to mark lines
- 1 playground ball (13 inches [33 cm]) per group
- Signal

Warm-Up Activities (5 minutes)

Delivery Relay

Arrange the children in groups of 4 divided between 2 lines marked about 60 feet (18 m) apart. Give one child in each group a ball.

1. Describe and demonstrate the game:
   - On the signal, the child with the ball delivers (carries) the ball to a teammate at the other line.
   - That child returns the ball to a child at the first line, and so on, until each child in the group has carried the ball over the distance.
2. Have the children play Delivery Relay.

Skill-Development Activities (15 minutes)

Throwing and Catching Tasks

Arrange pairs in scatter formation; each pair is 10 feet (3 m) apart with one playground ball.

1. Challenge the children with the following tasks:
   - Toss (throw underhand) and catch with your partner.
   - Back up one step at a time until you can no longer catch and toss.
   - Each of you should toss from each distance before moving.
   Move the pairs back to 10 feet (3 m) apart.
2. Have them throw (overhand) and catch and then back up after each successful round, as in step 1. After several trials, move them back to 10 feet (3 m) apart.
3. Have them bounce and catch the ball, following the same procedure.

Lesson 4.2 *(continued)*

Dribbling

Arrange the children in scatter formation; each child should have a ball.

1. Ask the children, "What is the difference between dribbling and bouncing a ball?" Demonstrate while explaining to them, "Dribbling is with one hand."
2. Have the children practice dribbling.
3. Tell the children: "Dribble the ball rhythmically, keeping the ball below your waist and close to your body so that your elbow stays bent when the ball is at its peak. Spread your fingers so that your fingers and palm cover as much of the surface of the ball as possible."
4. Have the children perform some dribbling tasks: "Dribble with your left hand. Don't move your feet. Now try with your right hand." Repeat several times.
5. Line up the children across one end of the play area.

    Ask the children: "Can you dribble and walk to there?" Point out an end line or opposite side of the play area. Have the children go back and forth several times.
6. Arrange partners in scatter formation.

    Have one partner dribble around the other; then have partners switch roles. Do this several times.

Concluding Activities (10 minutes)

Circle Stride Ball

Use this activity with second graders. See Keep Away (next activity) for third graders. Divide the children into groups of 6 to 9 each. Have the children stand in a circle with their feet spread apart so that they touch the feet of each of their neighbors. Place one child in the center of each circle with a large ball.

1. Describe and demonstrate the game:
    - The child in the center tries to roll the ball out of the circle between another child's legs.
    - If the child in the center is successful, the two players exchange places; if not, play continues.
    - Players may not move their feet and must stop the ball with their hands.
2. Have the children play Circle Stride Ball.
3. You can also have the children play this game with the circle facing outward and the children looking back through their legs.

Keep Away

Use this game with third graders. See Circle Stride Ball (previous activity) for second graders. Arrange groups of 3 children in scatter formation.

1. Describe and demonstrate the game:
    - Two of you in each group play catch (you may bounce, roll, toss, or throw the ball) while the third child tries to gain control of the ball.
    - Anyone who loses control of the ball switches roles with the child who gains control of the ball.
    - At set intervals (e.g., 30 to 60 seconds), I will signal when the child trying to gain control is allowed to switch places with one of the other children if he or she doesn't get to switch by gaining control of the ball.
2. Have the children play Keep Away.

From K.T. Thomas, A.M. Lee, and J.R. Thomas, 2008, *Physical education methods for elementary teachers*, 3rd ed. (Champaign, IL: Human Kinetics). Adapted, by permission, from K.T. Thomas, A.M. Lee, and J.R. Thomas, 2000, *Physical education for children: Daily lesson plans for elementary school*, 2nd ed. (Champaign, IL: Human Kinetics), 473-475.

Lesson 4.3

Throwing and Catching

Student Objectives 1

- Toss up a ring and catch it with right and left hands.
- Work cooperatively with a group to achieve a goal.

Equipment and Materials

- 1 ring (quoit) per child
- 1 hoop per group
- Polyspots, polydomes, or tape for marking Cooperative Ring Toss areas
- Cones or other markers for marking jogging course

Warm-Up Activities (5 minutes)

Walk or Jog

Mark a jogging course and arrange the children on the starting line.

1. Start with a walk or jog for 5 minutes.
2. Increase to 10 to 12 minutes, encouraging the children to increase gradually the distance they cover.

Skill-Development Activities (15 minutes)

Throwing and Catching Tasks

Arrange the children in scatter formation; each child should have a ring.

1. Challenge the children with the following tasks:
   - Throw your ring up and catch it with the same hand.
   - Practice until you can catch it 5 times without a miss.
   - Throw your ring up with one hand and catch it with the other.
   - From a low level, throw your ring up and catch it.
   - Throw your ring up and jump high to catch it.
   - Jump high and then throw your ring and catch it.
2. Repeat all tasks several times.
3. Challenge the children: "Throw your ring up and turn around (or touch the ground, clap 3 times, click your heels) before you catch it."
4. Ask the children to think of other stunts to perform.

Lesson 4.3 *(continued)*

Concluding Activities (10 minutes)

Cooperative Ring Toss

Divide the children into groups of 4 to 6, give each child a ring, and place each group at a game area. Mark each game area with lines 6, 12, and 24 feet (1.8, 3.7, and 7.4 m) from a hoop. Mark a square around the hoop about 1 inch (2.5 cm) larger than the hoop.

1. Describe and demonstrate the game:
   - The goal of the game is for a group to achieve a combined score of 24 points.
   - During each round, each child has a turn and the group decides if the throw is from 6, 12, or 24 feet (1.8, 3.7, and 7.4 m).
   - Team members can throw from various lines, but the team with a total score closest to 24 points wins.
   - A ring landing in the hoop scores 4 points from 6 feet (1.8 m), 6 points from 12 feet (3.7 m), and 8 points from 24 feet (7.4 m). All rings landing in the square around the hoop score 2 points.
2. Have the children play Cooperative Ring Toss.
3. Repeat the game several times, encouraging the children to decide the best way for their team to score close to 24 points total.

From K.T. Thomas, A.M. Lee, and J.R. Thomas, 2008, *Physical education methods for elementary teachers*, 3rd ed. (Champaign, IL: Human Kinetics). Adapted, by permission, from K.T. Thomas, A.M. Lee, and J.R. Thomas, 2000, *Physical education for children: Daily lesson plans for elementary school*, 2nd ed. (Champaign, IL: Human Kinetics), 857-858.

Lesson 4.4

Locomotor and Nonlocomotor Combinations

Student Objectives   1   5

- Combine locomotor and nonlocomotor movements into a sequence.
- Create a movement sequence for a partner to copy.
- Work cooperatively with a group to achieve a goal.

Equipment and Materials

- 2 rhythm sticks
- 1 drum
- 1 tambourine
- Skill cards (listing locomotor and nonlocomotor skills)

Warm-Up Activities (5 minutes)

Movement to Sounds

Arrange the children in scatter formation.

1. Explain the activity:
   - The sound of the sticks hitting together is the signal to move forward.
   - The sound of the drum is the signal to move backward.
   - The sound of the tambourine is the signal to move in place.
   - Respond to the instrument in time with the beat and in the correct direction while running.
2. Have the children practice responding, repeating each sound several times.

Skill-Development Activities (20 minutes)

Movement Combinations

Make sure that the children are still in scatter formation.

1. Have the children perform the following movement combinations:
   - Leap forward (4 counts), leap backward (4 counts), leap while turning (4 counts), jump in place (4 counts), and collapse.
   - Hop right (4 counts), hop left (4 counts), run forward (4 counts), stretch (2 counts), and curl (2 counts).
   - Swing right leg forward and back (8 counts), and swing left leg forward and back (8 counts).

Lesson 4.4 (continued)

- Hop in place (4 counts), hop forward (4 counts), hop backward (4 counts), hop in place (4 counts).
- Walk forward (8 counts), jump in place (8 counts), walk backward (8 counts), jump in place (8 counts).
- Slide right (8 counts), slide left (8 counts).
- Run (3 counts), leap (1 count). Repeat several times.
- Run (2 counts), leap (2 counts). Repeat several times.

2. Repeat challenges as time allows.

Partner Copy Activity

Arrange partners in scatter formation.

1. Select 2 or more locomotor or nonlocomotor skills you wish to target and a variety of counts (e.g., 4, 8, 12, 16, 24).
2. Explain the activity:
   - The goal of the activity is for the leader to use the skills in a sequence with the specified number of counts. For example, the task might be to use walk, hop, and jump for 16 counts. The sequence could be walk (8 counts), hop (4 counts), and jump (4 counts).
   - One of you creates the movement sequence and the partner watches.
   - The partner then repeats the sequence.
   - Then trade roles and repeat the activity using other skills and counts.
3. Present the following tasks for partners:
   - Walk, run, stretch, and twist for 12 counts.
   - Gallop forward, gallop backward, jump forward, jump backward for 24 counts.
   - Walk forward, walk backward, hop in a circle for 12 counts.
   - Skip and slide for 16 counts.
4. After several practice trials, have the children select their own movements and number of counts.

Concluding Activities (5 minutes)

Skill Cards

Divide the class into groups of 4 to 6. Have prepared a number of cards listing various locomotor and nonlocomotor skills.

1. Describe the activity:
   - Each group selects 4 or more cards from the stack of cards.
   - The group has to prepare a sequence using the skills on the cards.
2. Allow the groups time to create and practice their sequences.

From K.T. Thomas, A.M. Lee, and J.R. Thomas, 2008, *Physical education methods for elementary teachers*, 3rd ed. (Champaign, IL: Human Kinetics). Adapted, by permission, from K.T. Thomas, A.M. Lee, and J.R. Thomas, 2000, *Physical education for children: Daily lesson plans for elementary school*, 2nd ed. (Champaign, IL: Human Kinetics), 955-956.

CHAPTER 5

Cognition, Learning, and Practice

RACHEL, AGE 9

Children have less knowledge and fewer cognitive strategies than adults. A child's performance usually improves when he or she practices appropriately while using adult strategies.

Learner Outcomes

After studying this chapter, you should be able to do the following:

- Distinguish between learning and memory.
- Describe the age-related changes in information processing.
- Define three methods to organize practice and describe the influence of each on learning.
- Organize practice appropriately, based on the learning objective and the learner.
- Design instruction to facilitate learning.

Glossary Terms

cognition	information processing	constant practice
learning	declarative knowledge	variable practice
memory	procedural knowledge	blocked practice
practice	strategic knowledge	random practice
attention	control processes	variability
capacity	extrinsic feedback	readiness
vigilance	intrinsic feedback	expertise
overexclusive attention	reinforcement and general encouragement	relative age effect
overinclusive attention		
selective attention		

Teaching and learning are two sides of the same process; you need to understand how children learn in order to teach effectively. In physical education, you must understand how children learn concepts, facts, and motor skills. This creates a unique challenge, because motor skills include typical errors of learning, such as problems with memory and decision making. However, motor skill learning includes a unique source of error—motor execution error, or skill error. When a child makes an error on a story problem in math, inability to write the number is not likely to be the source of error. However, in physical education, the error could be decision making, memory, or execution. For example, the child is supposed to throw the ball to second base when the first batter hits the ball. The child throws the ball between first and second base. What type of error was this? Did he or she know where to throw it? Was the child trying to throw it to first or second base? This could be a decision error (not knowing where to throw), a skill error (not throwing where he or she intended), or both. Skill is an issue at all levels of sport. The best professional baseball players know that the object of batting is to hit the ball safely into fair territory, but even the best batters do this only about one-third of the time. Skill makes sport unique and challenging. As an expert teacher, you can understand how children learn, especially how they learn motor skills.

Children have to learn motor skills, work with a body that is significantly different than an adult body, and figure out how to interpret outcomes of performance. In addition, children have to learn how to learn motor skills and the knowledge of when to do what. Of course, some of the developmental changes in learning motor skills parallel learning in other areas such as math or reading. The major difference is in the execution phase. Generally, the error in math is computational, not in actually writing the answer. In motor skill performance, however, the error can be in either area; that is, the child may know what to do but cannot execute it or may not do either effectively.

The Four Guiding Principles

Now we explore in more detail the four guiding principles outlined on page 35 in regard to cognition, learning, and practice. Keep in mind as you study this chapter that each of the principles is important to understanding how children develop and what this means for physical education.

Principle 1. Children Are Not Miniature Adults

Prior to age 11 years, children need help with the activities that support learning (Thomas, Gallagher, and Thomas 2000). One part of learning is remembering. There are many strategies to assist memory, for example repeating the information to be remembered. At 7 years of age, children begin to repeat information to assist remember-

ing; however, at 5 years of age, children do not repeat unless told to do so. By 11 years of age, children use adultlike strategies to remember. In physical education class, children have key skill components to remember (e.g., bend the knees, look forward, use fingertips) and execute. So they must know what to do and then practice executing the skill. You can help students remember key aspects of performance by using mnemonic strategies. For example, "BEEF" (Bend knees, Eyes up, Elbows in, Feet still) describes the characteristics of a good free throw in basketball.

Principle 2. Boys and Girls Are More Alike Than Different

Feedback and reinforcement are important to improving motor performance. Feedback about performance allows girls and boys to correct errors; teacher reinforcement is valuable for correct performances. In fact, Smoll and Smith (2002, p. 216) suggest a model for coaches to provide feedback and reinforcement that applies well to teachers of children in physical education:

- Desirable performance yields a positive reaction ("good try," "good effort").
- Mistakes in performance yield one of two reactions:
  - Mistake contingent encouragement ("good try").
  - Mistake contingent technical instruction (i.e., information necessary to correct the error).

The sandwich approach is useful in combining reinforcement, feedback, and technical instruction for both boys and girls. Essentially, the idea is to sandwich the feedback and technical instruction between reinforcing comments. For example, suppose a 6-year-old girl is learning to catch a tossed ball. When the ball is tossed, she drops it; then using the sandwich approach, you might tell her:

- Really good try! You almost caught it.
- Next time, if you keep your fingers relaxed and give with the ball, you'll be sure to catch it!

You can vary this approach by the skill level and age of the children, but it is equally useful in improving the performance of both girls and boys.

Principle 3. Good Things Are Earned

Several studies have examined the differences between expert and novice children in sport and dance. One misconception is that expert athletes are "naturals" or have special talent. The research suggests that more appropriate words to describe experts are "hard workers" or "dedicated."

During childhood, two types of experts are found: short term and long term. Short-term experts have an expiration date and are no longer experts as adults. The explanation is the relative age effect, an advantage for older children (Thomas and Thomas 1999). The older children in a cohort or group have a temporary advantage over the younger (and less mature) children. For example, in baseball, the oldest players on a youth team play the skill positions, pitching and infield. When all of the children reach maturity, the advantage of the relative age effect disappears. Unfortunately, an outcome of the relative age effect is that children who might become true experts do not have the same level of practice, experience, and encouragement as the older or more mature children. This often leads less mature and younger children to drop out.

The long-term experts differ from novices in their game play competence. Interestingly, in youth basketball players, the factor that changes during a season for experts and novices is knowledge (French and Thomas 1987). Skill does not improve during a season, especially for the novices. The experts tend to get more skill practice and playing time. Game playing competence is best explained by decision making. Children often begin the season with limited knowledge about what to do, and knowing what to do often precedes being able to do the skill. For example, young tennis players were able to explain what they wanted to do in a match well before they were able to do the skill (McPherson and Thomas 1989). Expert players could accurately and rapidly make decisions that they described as "if-then-do" statements: "if this happens, then I will do this . . ."

Expert physical education teachers understand the relative age effect and the need for students to know what to do before performing in a game situation (Thomas and Thomas 1999). Elementary physical education teachers see and encourage quality practice in all students regardless of age, maturity, or skill. You may often remind your students during game play or practice about what should be done next depending on the circumstances; you are thereby providing one or more "if-then-do" cues. This type of practice leads to expertise.

Principle 4. No Body Is Perfect

In sport expertise, the question is "How much skill is due to genetics and how much to practice?" (Starkes 2003). That question is not easily answered and varies by sport; for example, to become an expert basketball player is more difficult if you are short rather than tall. However, being a tall gymnast is a disadvantage. Girls and boys clearly have individual differences in heritable characteristics such as size and speed. However, opportunity, encouragement, and prac-

Opportunity, practice, and encouragement are the most critical factors as children develop sport expertise.

tice are clearly important to skill development. In fact, for the so-called typical boy or girl, opportunity, encouragement, and practice are critical in acquiring the level of skill needed to participate in most sports and physical activities. Although a moderate level of skill is important in order to enjoy a sport, you do not have to be an expert to enjoy sports and physical activity. If expertise were required to enjoy and participate in sport, most golfers, tennis players, swimmers, and joggers would not be participating.

Thus, the task for elementary physical education is to provide all children with a variety of skills so that they can choose physical activities in which they can enjoy success. Success does not mean winning; success means participating regularly and performing effectively relative to skill level and expectations.

In the following sections, we provide greater detail on many aspects of cognition, learning, and practice. Depending on your level of interest and need, these sections can add considerably to your knowledge base.

Cognition, Learning, and Memory

Learning, memory, and cognition are related but different. **Cognition** is thinking; it is the basis for learning and memory. **Learning** has four definitive characteristics: It results from practice, it is permanent, it is dependent on feedback, and it is demonstrated by retention and transfer. **Memory** comprises two parts: working (short-term) memory, which is limited in capacity, and long-term memory, which is the unlimited repository for knowledge. Learning depends on memory, and **practice** is both the repetition required to facilitate memory and a critical ingredient in learning. Learning motor skills has been described in three stages.

Learning Motor Skills: Stage 1

Stage 1, "getting the idea," is characterized by many mistakes and large errors (Fitts and Posner 1967). This stage is primarily cognitive: The learner tries to figure out how to do the task the first time, often without getting hurt and with as little embarrassment as possible. You can help students in Stage 1 by giving hints and modeling how to make the first attempt at the skill and by identifying the relationship between practice and improvement.

Learning Motor Skills: Stage 2

Stage 2 starts when the performances become stable; there are still errors, but the learner tends to make the same mistake over and over (Fitts and Posner 1967). Sometimes a learner stays in this stage indefinitely. The learner can detect errors but cannot correct them. Your feedback is essential in Stage 2. This feedback should focus on how to correct errors.

Learning Motor Skills: Stage 3

Finally, in Stage 3, the learner performs the movement consistently, with few errors (Fitts and Posner 1967). The learner is now able to detect and correct errors. The movement is automatic; that is, the learner does not have to think about the movement once it starts. During Stage 3, instruction shifts from skill execution to the more strategic or conceptual aspects of performance. The goal of learning for all skills is to reach Stage 3, the autonomous stage, when the learner is independent.

You need to understand cognition, learning, and practice for four reasons:

1. You are responsible for monitoring cognition and learning; if you discover unusual deviations, you may need to refer the child for evaluation.

2. You cannot assume that children will do anything to help themselves learn compared to the many specific activities adults and older children do to learn. Certainly, children do not do the same things adults do to facilitate memory and learning; you must know the difference in order to help them learn.

3. You need to understand how the organization of practice influences learning so that you can select practice regimens appropriate for children of various skill and maturational levels.

4. You need to be able to explain to children how learning occurs so that they become responsible for their own learning.

Attention

Attention has three usages: It means cognitive **capacity** or space; this is used interchangeably with short-term memory. Short-term memory and attention are limited. Have you heard of Miller's magical number seven, plus or minus two? It means that the typical person has the short-term memory capacity to deal with seven items at once (Thomas 2000). People with greater capacity may remember up to nine items, whereas those with less capacity can only deal with five items. In the simplest case, think of this as juggling seven single-digit numbers in short-term memory. Short-term memory is the component of cognition that makes decisions and deals with current events. Capacity or attention can be focused on external events (sensory information), on solving problems (decision making and control processes), or on searching long-term memory. This concept is demonstrated in figure 5.1. Attention can also be divided so that you are monitoring sensory information, searching long-term memory, and solving a problem at the same time. For example, you are watching for your friend, trying to remember what ingredients are in a recipe, and deciding if you can actually make the recipe. Later in this chapter, you will see how cognitive systems maximize efficiency, allowing more information to be dealt with simultaneously. In this case, a person can juggle seven complex tasks or units in short-term memory.

A second usage of attention is **vigilance**, which refers to the length of time a person can allocate attention to a particular task. A common misconception is that children have short attention spans. If you have read a favorite bedtime story to a 3-year-old, you have evidence that children do not have short attention spans. When you try to skip a page or miss a word in that favorite story, what happens? The child usually notices! Frequently, very young children ask for the story to be read again. In fact, some popular television shows for very young children use this idea and repeat the story segment during each episode. Children do not have short attention spans; however, they may not be interested in what adults want them to "pay attention to." Therefore, adults conclude that children have short attention spans. Most of you can recall a parent or teacher saying, "Pay attention!" Often you were thinking, *Why? This is boring.*

The third use of attention refers to the focus or object of attention—in other words, what you are paying attention to. Once again, children differ from adults. Three stages of attention are generally recognized: The first, from birth to about 5 years of age, is called **overexclusive attention**. The infant and young child focus on one thing and ignore all others. Attention can be focused inward on cognitive activities or outward on the environment. From 5 to about 12 years, the child is in the **overinclusive attention** stage, trying to take in everything. The result is distraction and the inability to select the critical element to solve a task. Overinclusive children try to solve problems by considering every possible issue. They may seem picky or even petty. However, the process is likely to be important as they work toward strategies for quickly and accurately selecting important information. Sometime around the 12th birthday, children begin to use selective attention. In **selective attention**, children use the appropriate information and ignore all other information. Selective attention enhances their performance on tasks because their attention becomes focused

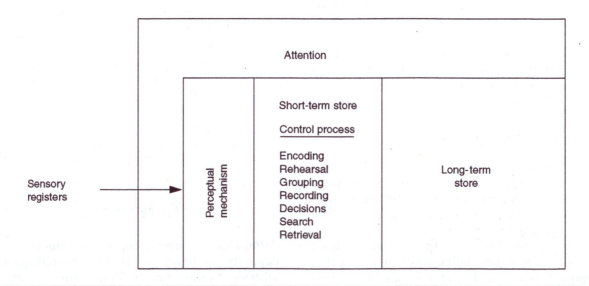

Figure 5.1 The information processing system.

(Ladewig and Gallagher 1994; Thomas, Gallagher, and Thomas 2000).

Expert teachers determine the critical aspects of a task and help their students by informing them—that is, cuing them to consider the critical aspects—and thereby encouraging them to use selective attention to enhance performance. Furthermore, you should not automatically assume that children will not stay on task because of short attention spans. If children are off task (not paying attention), examine the task and the instruction. Is the task too easy or difficult? Are the children improving? Is this fun? Does a child or a group of children demonstrate more on-task behavior on self-selected tasks?

Information Processing

Information processing is a specific part of cognition that includes perception, working memory, and long-term memory. Children use the same information processing system in the classroom as in the gymnasium; the difference is in the output. In the classroom, the output is usually a verbal or written response. In the gym, the response is most often a movement, but it can be verbal or written as well. Children have less experience and therefore less knowledge or information than adults (Thomas, Gallagher, and Thomas 2000). Because knowledge is critical to successful performance, missing knowledge is problematic for children in several ways.

- Children have less information or **declarative knowledge** (e.g., facts and rules) than adults, largely because it takes time to acquire information and children have had less time than adults because they are younger.

- **Procedural knowledge** is information about how to do something and is a result of learning. Because children have learned less than adults during their shorter life spans, they have fewer procedures to help them solve problems.

- Children do not use all (or the same) strategies or control processes that adults use to help them remember and solve problems; this makes learning more difficult for them. These control processes are sometimes called **strategic knowledge. Control processes** are cognitive strategies, such as rehearsal (figure 5.2). During elementary school, children develop mastery of many of the control processes. You can help children learn to use control processes and make learning easier by designing instruction to accommodate the differences between children and adults in cognition, learning, and memory.

Adults understand that, most of the time, they have to do something, such as perform a deliberate act, in order to remember information or learn how to do a task (Helsen, Starkes, and Hodges 1998). However, children do not understand the

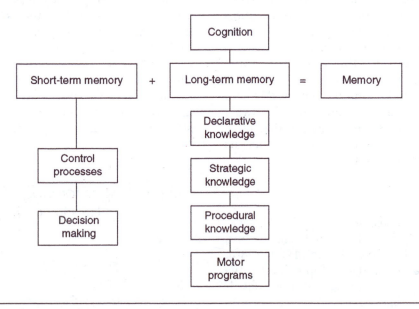

Figure 5.2 *Storage and action components in memory and cognition.*

deliberate part of memory and learning. Even experts have trouble organizing practice, so it is not surprising that children need your guidance (Deakin 2001).

The first thing you can do to help children learn is to describe how to learn. Statements such as "When I want to remember something, I say it over and over quietly to myself" are very helpful. Unfortunately, children are often offered useless or vague information such as "Try harder" or "Put on your thinking cap" (Gallagher and Thomas 1984, 1986; Ornstein and Naus 1985; Thomas, Thomas, Lee, Testerman, and Ashy 1983). An adult does not believe that putting on a thinking cap facilitates learning, so why would this statement be helpful to a child? Children cannot turn "Try harder" into action.

A misconception held by children is that people either can or cannot do something; rarely do children understand the concept of practice as a factor in being able to do a task. When children understand that practice is important, they no longer feel incompetent or abnormal when they fail to do a task correctly on the first try. Furthermore, there is motivation for practice. The more specific the information is about learning and memory, the more helpful the information will be. You can help children understand the role of practice by recounting personal stories of the hard work needed to master tasks. Statements such as "Most of us have to practice a long time to learn how to . . ." are helpful.

The object of learning is to put correct and important information into long-term memory so that the information becomes knowledge. Part of this process is to make information use as automatic as possible. Both declarative and procedural knowledge can be automatic, such as an answer to a multiplication fact (e.g., 3 times 4 is 12) or typing words on a keyboard. As you consider a fact, idea, or problem, it enters short-term memory. If you do not move it to long-term memory, it fades away. Control processes are deliberate actions that move information into long-term memory, sometimes as facts and sometimes as actions.

Labeling

The first control process to emerge in children, at about 2 years of age, is labeling (Ornstein and Naus 1985; Gallagher and Thomas 1984, 1986). Early labels are names, and they typically involve physical characteristics. During childhood, labeling becomes more abstract and children begin to connect the labels to other labels or concepts.

Applying a name or label to an action or object makes it easier to remember and use. For example, if there were no label for the double play in baseball or for parallel parking, these actions would be difficult and time-consuming to describe. Some of the characteristics to remember about movements are end locations, distance or speed, force, amplitude, and acceleration or deceleration. Cues or words that label these characteristics help children remember the important aspects of the movement. Describing the beginning and ending locations of the hands and feet (or other critical body parts), the speed or distance of the movement (e.g., by counting or moving quickly versus slowly), and changes in the speed of the movement (acceleration or deceleration) give children labels they can use during practice to make correct attempts.

Rehearsal

Rehearsal, another control process that children learn, is repetition; it begins at about 7 years of age. Early rehearsal is rote repetition of a single piece of information; the use of mixed rehearsal sets—in which several items are repeated in random order—begins at about 11 years of age (Gallagher and Thomas 1984, 1986). Consider how difficult it would be to remember something if you could not say or write it repeatedly. Children spend two or three years in school before they begin to repeat, but they are asked to memorize information during that time. Teachers often force children to repeat but rarely explain why or how this helps learning. Spelling is a perfect example of how you can use rehearsal strategies for memorization. Each day of the week, you can assign a new task that requires repetition of the spelling words (e.g., Monday, write the word five times; Tuesday, write the word in a sentence; and Wednesday, take a self-test). In physical education, repetition is used as part of instruction; however, to master many skills, children need to practice outside of class.

Typical Ages for Cognitive Processes Used by Children

- Labeling   2 years
- Rote rehearsal   7 years
- Mixed rehearsal   11 years
- Chunking and grouping   11 years

One of the most powerful messages you can send children is the importance of practice (rehearsal) in skill acquisition. Encourage practice, provide time for repetition, and relate improvement to hard work (e.g., practice).

Grouping

Grouping occurs when information is organized logically to combine discrete units. Skipping combines two discrete skills: hopping and stepping. Another example of grouping is arranging information in order from simple to difficult or large to small. You use this technique whenever you use one word to remember a sequence of events such that the first letter in the word stands for the first event and so forth. For example, when you teach kicking, you might use SOFK: Step, Opposite Foot, Kick. Grouping begins in children around 11 years of age. You can use metaphors, acronyms, or other grouping strategies to help children recall information with a short cue. (This concept is discussed in more detail in chapter 6, Physical Activity for Children.)

Search and Retrieval

Search and retrieval occur when you think about something you know (which is in long-term memory) and you move it from long-term to short-term memory. Once something is placed in long-term memory, you must search to retrieve it. The more connections or pathways you have to a piece of information, the more likely it is that you will be able to retrieve it. When you learn new information, you follow a progression from understanding it concretely (e.g., a fact or definition) to thinking of it more abstractly (e.g., application, concept, or theory). As you learn information better, it becomes easier for you to retrieve; often, this means the information is more conceptual.

Have you ever taken an exam during which you remembered the location in the textbook of an answer to a question—the page and place on it—but you could not remember the answer itself? The search led to the appropriate information, but the information stored was superficial, as was the recollection of the information. Bloom's taxonomy, which is discussed in chapter 4, Motor Performance During Childhood, has six levels leading to wisdom: comprehension, knowledge, application, analysis, synthesis, and evaluation (Bloom 1956). Mastery is described in levels from knowledge to evaluation, which reflects the idea of shifting from concrete and superficial understanding to conceptual or abstract representations of information. As children practice, hints about how to remember information facilitate their later recall. The more connections they have to a piece of information, the more likely they are to recall that information.

Decision Making

Decision making is based on simple matching: Either the response matches the stimulus or it does not. You can even break down complicated problems into parts that are eventually answered this simply. Procedural knowledge is a stored set of decisions called "if-then-do" statements. You are probably familiar with many such procedures.

- In math, you learned how to "carry" and what to do with the remainder as you learned division; both carrying and dealing with remainders are examples of procedures.

- Sport and physical activity provide many procedures as well. In youth baseball, when you field the ball after a hit, you then throw the ball to second base. There are several reasons to throw to second base. Running skills are better than throwing and catching skills in young children, so stopping a runner by throwing to second base has a higher probability of success than getting an out at first base. Also, second base is a shorter throw than first base for many hits.

- Another example comes from tee ball: With the 9th or 10th batter, everything (runners and ball) goes to home.

In many activities, rapid and accurate decisions are critical to becoming an expert. Driving a car requires rapid and accurate decisions; so does teaching or playing ice hockey. Experts know many procedures and use them automatically. Physical education requires you to teach motor skills as well as how and when to use the skills (procedures). During game play, expert teachers explain the strengths and weaknesses of various decisions. Reaction time is a simple decision: Young children take longer to make decisions than older children and adults. Generally, strategies are the focus of instruction for children in the third stage of learning motor skills. Children learning and using strategies in a game go through the same stages as they do when learning motor skills.

You can see from figure 5.3 how much error is reduced when children who would not ordinarily use a strategy are given one to solve a specific task. In this case, the task was remembering a distance run, similar to remembering the distance in an offensive football play. The receiver runs a specific distance and turns to catch the ball; if the distance run is inaccurate—no matter how good the throw—the play fails. The children were capable of counting and remembering, but not of figuring out to count! Often, you may find it too difficult to teach the skill and the application at the same time.

Control processes demand attention or capacity. One goal of learning is for responses to become automatic, so the response demands less attention. This allows children to do more than one thing at once, which is usually desirable. Early in skill learning, all of their attention may be devoted to doing the motor skill, so they are unable to consider the context. As they gain skill, more capacity (attention) can be allocated to the context. The context could be the offense and defense of a sport or the music and expression of emotion in a dance. In learning a dance, the initial focus is on the steps; later, in practice, the children can feel the joy of moving to the music and can identify with people from other cultures who perform the dance. You need to focus the content of learning appropriately, based on the stage of learning and the mastery of the three types of knowledge.

Feedback

Feedback is information about performance. **Extrinsic feedback** is information about performance that cannot be obtained by the performer. **Intrinsic feedback** is information the performer receives that could be visual (I missed the target), proprioceptive (it didn't feel right), or auditory (everyone is cheering). The dominant source of sensory or intrinsic feedback is vision; people believe what they see and ignore everything else. This affects learning motor skills because the way something feels is often critical for improving or maintaining performance. Furthermore, in practice situations, visual feedback is often available, but it may no longer be available during an actual performance. For example, a child can practice in front of a mirror so that when you say, "Look at your hand," he or she can receive visual feedback (but during actual performance, looking at the hand does not work). You should cue students to think about and remember how movements feel.

Reinforcement and general encouragement (e.g., "good job" and "keep trying") are often confused with feedback. Although reinforcement and general encouragement are important, they do not serve the same purpose as feedback because they do not provide information that could help the child either correct or repeat the movement.

Feedback is reinforcing, motivating, and corrective. When children make errors that they cannot detect themselves, you should provide corrective feedback. Give reinforcing feedback when a child does something correctly. The critical feature of either reinforcing or corrective feedback is that the learner must be given the information necessary to do the skill correctly on the next try. In overarm throwing, the feedback could include statements such as the following: "Great! You stepped on the correct foot that time; keep it up" or "I can see you are working hard; if you want to take this to the next level, try stepping on the opposite foot the next time. I know you can do it!" In both examples, encouragement is coupled with

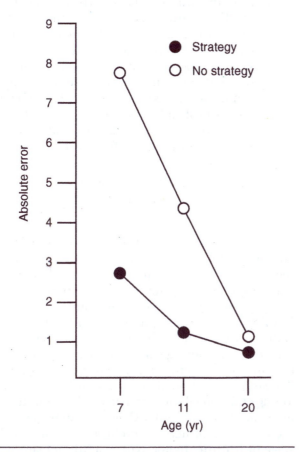

Figure 5.3 A comparison of errors made without a strategy versus with a strategy.

specific extrinsic feedback. This is the sandwich technique—something positive, the corrective feedback, something positive.

Corrective feedback can motivate children because it delivers three important messages from you to them:

- "I am watching and I notice what you do."
- "I believe you can do this."
- "I care about you and this skill; I want you to learn this."

Children have consistently reported preferring coaches who provide corrective feedback to those who provide general encouragement. Unfortunately, physical education teachers seldom give corrective feedback, often only a few statements in a whole class (Thomas 2000). But children want to learn skills and need to see improvement. Feedback can also provide evidence of improvement.

Feedback can document progress during learning; general encouragement cannot document progress. For example, the phrase "great job," repeated over and over, shows no progress, whereas saying "Now I see you stepping on the opposite foot most of the time" does document progress. Because feedback should focus on information not otherwise available to the child, feedback should generally be about the process rather than the outcome. A child can see that the ball missed the target and can usually figure out that hitting 6 out of 10 today is better than hitting 4 out of 10 yesterday. This means that your feedback should indicate knowledge of performance (KP) rather than knowledge of results (KR). The locomotor and manipulative skill rubrics in chapter 4, Motor Performance During Childhood, provide a good source of information for your feedback as well as lesson design and evaluation.

Consider these four factors as you give feedback to children:

1. Postfeedback interval
2. Modality
3. Precision
4. Frequency

Younger children need more time to think about feedback than older children and adults (Thomas, Solmon, and Mitchell 1979). Once children have feedback, they need 10 or more seconds to make a plan to correct the movement before their next

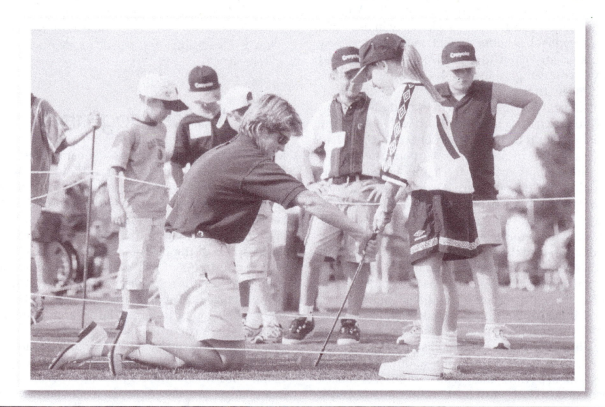

You can be helpful when you offer children specific instructions on how to perform a task.

try. Unfortunately, on their own, children take almost no time to consider the feedback. So you need to allow the time and encourage the children to use the time to make corrections. Providing more time after the feedback (the postfeedback interval) can improve performance. The modality indicates whether the feedback is verbal, visual, or physical. The most familiar is verbal; however, you could demonstrate both incorrect and correct versions of the task. Sometimes you can guide children through the correct movement by moving their body parts through the correct pattern. The first two modalities of feedback are effective, especially when used together. The third modality, guided movement, can be helpful, but guided feedback and practice are not always effective. Clearly, guided movement should not be used exclusively. Precision of feedback refers to the type of information, from general ("Push harder") to specific ("Your elbow was bent two degrees too much"). For younger children, less precise information is better (Newell and Kennedy 1978). In fact, young children ignore information that they consider too precise. Older children select only the part they can understand (e.g., "Your elbow was bent too much"). Feedback should provide information about the direction of the error (e.g., too much, too little, left, right, up, down) and how to correct the error. Frequency of feedback refers to how often you give feedback. Early in learning, more feedback is better; in fact, feedback on every try is great. When the children have practiced more, you can give feedback less often, perhaps half of the time. Late in practice, only give feedback once in a while. If you averaged the amount of feedback across learning, from early to late, the average would be that 50 percent of the tries had feedback. The reason is that learners can become dependent on extrinsic feedback, which means the children do not learn to detect and correct errors themselves. To be independent performers, they must learn to detect and correct their own errors. One of your major responsibilities is to give feedback but, at the same time, help children learn to detect and correct their own errors. Ironically, good teachers may teach themselves out of a job! In a teaching situation, giving feedback to all of the children on half of their trials is almost impossible; a realistic goal is to give feedback as often as possible to as many children as possible.

A common misconception about feedback is that it must be immediate (Adams 1987). Feedback must occur before the next trial of a task, but it does not have to occur immediately. One study

that examined feedback given immediately, one day later, and one week after the performance reported no differences in learning! Immediate feedback is not important to learning motor skills. So, if you cannot give feedback at the end of class on a given day, do it before practice begins during the next class. This effect is so strong that feedback given after several trials about the group of trials (i.e., averaged feedback) is just as good as immediate feedback about one trial at a time.

Give corrective feedback as often as possible. The feedback should be specific so the child can correct the next performance. Children, especially younger ones, need time to make corrections before the next trial. You might want to use the sandwich technique, with praise, feedback, and encouragement given together. Finally, feedback should be directly related to the objectives of the lesson and should target important characteristics of the skill or task.

Concepts Into Practice

Mr. Jones notices Sean making an error. Mr. Jones says, "Sean, I can see you are trying hard; you need to take a larger step if you want to improve. Keep working; I know you can do it!" Mr. Jones used the sandwich technique, providing reinforcement, specific corrective feedback, and encouragement. This is considerably more effective than saying, "Nice job."

Motor Programs

Motor programs are a way to conceptualize how movements are stored in memory. Four characteristics of motor programs are order, overall timing, relative timing, and relative force. Order is the sequence in which movement events occur (e.g., step, then hop in skipping). The overall timing is the speed of the movement. In this case, individual children can run either fast or slow, but running is still the same motor program. However, if you change the relative timing, it will no longer be the same motor program. For example, if children who are running change speed of one leg, but not the other, they are likely to be galloping rather than running. This is a different motor program. The same is true for force; the overall force can change, but the points in a movement with the most force must always have the most force.

So, the children can throw hard or soft (changing the overall force), but the greatest force must still be when they release the ball. Understanding this explains why practice in slow motion may not work. Movements that are rapid or forceful are best practiced in real time or with a normal amount of force. You can provide cues or labels for the order of the movements, design practice so that relative force and timing are constant, and encourage children to recall the "feel" of the movement after each trial.

A motor program is selected at the same time as a decision to move. That program is retrieved from long-term memory (knowledge) and programmed in short-term memory. Once the movement is programmed, it can be executed with minimal attention (Yan, Thomas, Stelmach, and Thomas 2000). Usually, people monitor motor programs during movement but do not have to use much capacity to do so. That means they can use that capacity for other things. One of the outcomes of elementary physical education is developing a variety of motor programs. This leads to the question "How are motor programs learned?" The obvious answer is practice. Practice with intrinsic and extrinsic feedback helps motor programs become efficient and automatic. As children learn a new movement, most of the movement is controlled by sensory feedback. This means that they use vision and proprioception to guide the movement (Meyer, Abrams, Kornblum, Wright, and Smith 1988; Yan et al. 2000). The results are slower movement and many corrections during the movement. For young children and beginners, only the start of the movement is controlled by a motor program. With practice, more of the movement is controlled in this way. With practice, motor programs become larger, controlling more of the movement. Motor programs tend to produce faster and more efficient movements than movements guided by feedback.

Scientists have used the speed–accuracy trade-off to examine motor programs (Plamondon and Alimi 1997; Kerr 1985; Salmoni and Pascoe 1979). The speed–accuracy trade-off was described in chapter 4, Motor Performance During Childhood. As children increase speed, accuracy decreases and vice versa. In order to study motor programs, children and adults were asked to make a series of movements, with targets of varying difficulty, as quickly as possible. The movements were divided into primary and secondary phases. The primary phase is the programmed part; the secondary phase is the portion of the movement controlled by sensory feedback. What happens is this: The child moves quickly toward the target, then slows down and uses vision to guide the movement to the target. Young children (5-year-olds) and the elderly (70-year-olds) have very short primary phases: Most of the movement is controlled by vision (Yan et al. 2000). Their movements include many small corrections. Older children (e.g., 11-year-olds) and adults below age 70 have long primary phases and brief secondary phases: Their movements are smoother and faster. Motor programs reduce reliance on sensory information and reduce corrections and errors.

Changing a motor program once it begins working usually creates large errors. So, once children begin to perform a well-learned movement, they should think about the movement as little as possible and just allow the motor program to select the appropriate sensory information. One example of this technique is how balance can be enhanced by vision. Focal vision is the type of vision you are using to read these words. Information from focal vision goes to short-term memory, is analyzed, and is then incorporated into the motor program and eventually sent to the muscles. This process takes one reaction time (between one fifth and one third of a second). Information about body position from ambient vision, which is peripheral vision that you are not aware of, is sent almost directly to the muscles. Therefore, corrections are made more rapidly—one reaction time faster—in fact, the corrections are made automatically (Thomas 2000; Yan et al. 2000). For a skill such as balance, when you tell a child, "Look at a spot on the wall, and just feel the movement as you walk the beam," you are using this concept. Similarly, when children are batting or catching, you might say, "Watch the ball all the way to the bat or glove." In fact, information from ambient vision makes the last corrections faster and better than focal vision, which is used to watch the ball all the way to the target. So you should be saying, "Watch a spot the ball passes through; watch the thrower's hand, and then feel yourself make contact with the ball." Ambient vision captures the changes in ball position during the end of the ball's flight and allows the arms and hands to react automatically.

In physical education, children learn how to execute and control movements (i.e., motor programs), what movements to select (i.e., decision making or procedures), and why to move (i.e., physical activity is fun and healthy). You can make learning easier and more efficient by understanding how motor programs develop and are used during physical activity.

Designing Practice

Consider two dimensions when designing practice. The first is the amount of the skill to be practiced. Can you divide the skill logically into parts? If the answer is yes, several options for part practice or progressive part practice are possible. If the answer is no, whole practice is the only choice. Part practice means practicing the parts first and then joining the parts together for whole skill practice. Progressive part practice is similar; but, in this system, you teach one part first and then add another part. Once the children have mastered that, add the next part, and so forth until they have mastered the whole skill. You can see examples of the method for progressive part practice in some of the rhythmical lessons at the end of this chapter. The skill of jumping from a height and landing is difficult to divide into parts, so the entire skill is practiced at once. You can divide jumping from a springboard into three parts: the running approach, the hurdle, and the take-off and landing. Children can practice these parts using the progressive part method: They first practice running to the springboard so that the last step is positioned for the hurdle. Then they can practice the hurdle, followed by the run and hurdle. Finally, they can practice the three parts together.

The second dimension for you to consider when designing practice is how to organize trials; use the four practice methods of

1. constant,
2. variable,
3. blocked, and
4. random practice.

Constant practice means doing one skill over and over. In constant practice, children might repeatedly tossing beanbags at the same target. **Variable practice** is similar to constant practice, but one dimension of the task changes (Yan, Thomas, and Thomas 1998). For example, in variable practice, children might toss beanbags into the target from several positions, such as from 4, 8, and 13 feet (1.2, 2.4, and 4 m) away. **Blocked practice** involves several skills; children practice all of one skill and then move on to another skill, practicing all of that skill. For example, in blocked practice, players might strike underhand 10 times, hit 10 backhands, and then hit 10 forehand drives. In **random practice**, players cannot practice the same skill two times in a row; players might complete one forehand drive, one underhand strike, and one backhand until each task had been repeated 10 times.

Constant practice leads to rapid acquisition; that is, improvement is rapid and large. The downside is that retention is low (retention is a measure of learning). So, although performance seems good, learning is not actually occurring; when the learner returns to the task after a period of no practice, the performance is similar to that in the first trials. Blocked practice is similar to constant practice because acquisition is rapid but retention is low. Random practice is the most difficult, with little progress early in practice. Retention is high, however. An interesting point is that children, especially younger children, benefit most from random practice. Practice is also best for tasks

Teachers make sure children are safe and challenged during practice.

that are more difficult—those that are complex or rapid. Variable practice is a format related to random practice. In variable practice, children practice the same skill with varying demands (for example, tossing beanbags at a target from various distances); the skill is tossing, and the variation is distance. Variable practice is usually better than constant or blocked practice, but not as good for learning as random practice.

There are several possible reasons that random practice produces greater learning. Random practice closely simulates how skills are used; that is, random practice provides a more similar context to sport, dance, and exercise. In most sports, players perform a series of tasks, often not knowing the order; they rarely do the same thing over and over. Sports in which the object is to do the same thing over and over are less complex, and random practice is less helpful for those skills. Also, with random practice, the motor program is selected and programmed for each trial; in blocked practice, the same program is run over and over. Practicing retrieving and programming the movement may be one benefit. Finally, random practice is the most difficult, so it may force learners to concentrate or to pay more attention to the practice, which benefits learning.

Often a skill is so difficult that beginners need constant or blocked practice early in learning. In such a case, you should switch practice to a random format as soon as possible, probably as soon as the skill becomes stable and the children recognize error and get the idea; in other words, when they reach Stage 2 of learning. At this stage, you can begin to encourage them to correct their own errors by asking, "What are you doing wrong?" or "What should you do?" Of course, when children cannot identify the error, you must provide feedback. This serves three purposes. You help the children become aware of their responsibility for learning and thinking about what they are doing. You guide the children to detect errors and to associate corrections with errors. Finally, you give them the message "I am confident you can learn this. I care about you and want you to learn."

Regardless of the type, design, and organization of practice, two criteria must be met for practice to be optimal: Every child should be involved and active as much of the time as possible so that the amount of practice is maximized. In chapter 9, Organizing for Teaching, and chapter 10, Managing Students, we cover techniques to assist you in planning these other aspects of a lesson so that practice is optimal.

Variability

Developmentally appropriate practices include two components: those that are age appropriate for a group of children and those that are appropriate for the range of individual children in the group. In chapter 3, Physical Growth and Maturation, chapter 4, Motor Performance During Childhood, and chapter 5, we have presented information about the various aspects of development. After reading these chapters, you should be familiar with one of the most robust and important concepts of child development: **variability**. There is a wide range of variation among individuals in what is considered "normal." Humans are more alike than different; the variations make them unique individuals. As you consider development beyond the normal range—people with disabilities and exceptional abilities—variation increases. Because variability is normal, you need to understand the individual differences associated with variability.

Readiness is the capability of a child to participate in an activity. You can determine readiness by evaluating demands of the tasks involved, converting those to prerequisite skills, and then assessing the child's capability of performing the prerequisite skills. The saying "You have to walk before you can run" summarizes this idea. Readiness is complicated by the multiple dimensionality of most activities. For example, an activity such as a team sport requires motor skills, cognitive skills, and social interaction. To be successful, the child must meet prerequisites from all areas. Often, a child meets some of the prerequisites, but not all of them. Consider soccer: A child may be able to control the ball and understand the goal of scoring but may not be ready to do role taking (understanding the role of another) and therefore not be a good team member. You can observe this in the typical "beehive" soccer game, in which all of the children run after the ball rather than play their respective positions on the field. You should evaluate readiness for any activity in terms of the following task demands:

- Motor skill
- Cognitive readiness
- Physical characteristics (size and maturation)
- Psychological readiness
- Physiological readiness

Considering task demands in view of the normal child's development (prerequisites) helps teachers, parents, and coaches determine whether an activity is appropriate. Baseball provides a good example: The youngest children play tee ball because they cannot strike a tossed ball. Older children play with coaches pitching; it is difficult to find children who can pitch, and, even when the coach throws the pitches, striking is difficult for the children. Baseball is played with a child pitching to a child batter. These alterations are based on motor skill. Because the structure of the game does not take into account cognitive demands or psychological or physiological factors, these alterations are appropriate.

In chapter 4, Motor Performance During Childhood, we discussed competition. Competition is not obvious to young children (Passer and Wilson 2002). After a tee-ball game, parents often ask, "Who won?" The child has to ask the coach because the young players do not view winning as important. As the parent continues to ask, winning becomes important to the child. If you de-emphasize competition, the children will too. Competition may occur at the expense of practice and have a negative impact on motor skill development, delaying readiness and negatively affecting performance. Early and high-intensity competition contributes to children dropping out of sport (Gould, Udry, Tuffey, and Loehr 1996). In extracurricular sport, children have the option of dropping out, and by doing so they send a message to adults. Children in physical education classes are not allowed to drop out directly, so they send the message in other ways: by sitting on the sidelines, asking to go to the bathroom, misbehaving, calling the activity "stupid," or giving low effort. You need to be careful about competition in class. If competition causes highly skilled players to drop out, you can imagine how competition affects those with poor skills! For physical education and sport, it is important to allow children 13 years and younger to sample a number of activities and avoid specializing in one sport (Côté, Baker, and Abernethy 2003).

How do you know when children are ready for competition? Generally, they ask to compete. When a child can do role taking (10 to 12 years), attribute outcomes (10 to 13 years), and understand competition cognitively (12 years), he or she is ready to compete. As children are ready for competition, programs should introduce controlled competition. This means you need to help children keep winning and losing in perspective,

reduce the public aspects of competition, reduce stress and anxiety, and balance winning and losing so that some children are not consistently losers. Finally, you should be sure that children have mastered cooperation before they begin competition. In sport, you can recognize cooperation when children help each other and share (e.g., a child extends a hand to a teammate who has fallen to the ground or a player passes the ball to an open player rather than keeping the ball).

Expertise

Perhaps your greatest challenge is dealing with a wide range of abilities in children. However, those who have exceptional skill—**expertise** (often more skill than you have)—can prove to be a substantial challenge. The goal of teaching is to develop expertise in your students. How does that happen? If you consider an expert, whether it is the best player on a team or the best in the world, certain characteristics come to mind. Sportswriters and broadcasters often use terms such as "quickness," "natural athlete," "talented," and "fast reaction time" to describe superstars. Less often, they use the terms "hard worker" and "dedicated." The characteristics contributing to performance are physiological (e.g., physical size, body composition, speed, and training; Thomas 1994); psychological (e.g., motivation); perceptual (e.g., visual acuity; Starkes and Deakin 1984; Starkes, Deakin, Lindley, and Crisp 1987); cognitive (e.g., declarative and procedural knowledge; Starkes 1987); and experience (e.g., practice and game play; French, Nevett, Spurgeon, Graham, Rink, and McPherson 1996; French and Thomas 1987). A person has little control over many of the biological characteristics, some control over the psychological and perceptual characteristics, and considerable control over the cognitive and experience characteristics (Abernethy, Thomas, and Thomas 1993).

World-class athletes are all motivated, well trained, and well coached. A comparison of males and females in the same sports at the world-record level provides a window on the contribution of biological factors. At this level, males and females differ in performance by about 10 percent; this represents a true biological difference. Tables 5.1 and 5.2 show that the differences between males and females holding world records in 1993 for track (100 and 400 meters) and swimming (100 meters) are between 5 and 11 percent (Ransdell and Wells 1999). However, in comparisons of

Table 5.1   Sex Differences in World-Record Performance in Track (100 m, 400 m)

Record as of	Women's 100 m record (seconds)	m · sec⁻¹ (women)	Men's 100 m record (seconds)	m · sec⁻¹ (men)	Percentage difference 100 m	Women's 400 m record (seconds)	m · sec⁻¹ (women)	Men's 400 m record (seconds)	m · sec⁻¹ (men)	Percentage difference 400 m
1923	12.80	7.81	10.40	9.62	19	60.50*	6.61	47.10*	8.49	28
1933	11.70	8.55	10.30	9.71	12	56.50*	7.08	46.10*	8.49	18
1943	11.60	8.62	10.20	9.80	12	56.50	7.08	46.00	8.70	19
1953	11.40	8.77	10.20	9.80	11	55.70	7.18	45.70	8.75	18
1963	11.20	8.93	10.00	10.00	11	51.90	7.71	44.60	8.97	14
1973	10.80	9.26	9.95	10.05	8	51.00	7.84	43.86	9.12	14
1983	10.79	9.27	9.93	10.07	8	47.99	8.34	43.71	9.15	8
1993	10.49	9.53	9.86	10.14	6	47.60	8.40	43.29	9.24	9

Key: m · sec⁻¹ = speed in meters per second

*Times extrapolated based on conversion from yards to meters

$$\text{Percentage difference} = \frac{\text{Men's speed (m · sec}^{-1}) - \text{women's speed (m · sec}^{-1})}{\text{Men's speed (m · sec}^{-1})} \times 100$$

Adapted, by permission, from L.B. Ransdell and C.L. Wells, 1999, "Sex differences in athletic performance," *Women in Sport and Physical Activity* 8: 55-81.

Table 5.2   Sex Differences in World-Record Performance in Swimming (100 m)

Record as of	Women's 100 m record (seconds)	m · sec⁻¹	Men's 100 m record (seconds)	m · sec⁻¹	Percentage difference
1923	72.80	1.37	58.60	1.71	20
1933	66.00	1.52	57.40	1.74	13
1943	64.60	1.55	56.40	1.77	12
1953	64.60	1.55	55.40	1.81	14
1963	59.50	1.68	53.60	1.87	10
1973	57.54	1.74	51.22	1.95	11
1983	54.79	1.83	49.36	2.03	10
1993	54.48	1.84	48.42	2.07	11

Key: m · sec⁻¹ = speed in meters per second

$$\text{Percentage difference} = \frac{\text{Men's speed (m · sec}^{-1}) - \text{women's speed (m · sec}^{-1})}{\text{Men's speed (m · sec}^{-1})} \times 100$$

Adapted, by permission, from L.B. Ransdell and C.L. Wells, 1999, "Sex differences in athletic performance," *Women in Sport and Physical Activity* 8: 55-81.

males and females in the general population, the differences are much larger, partly because of different opportunities (e.g., training and coaching) for males and females. Another factor is evident in the world records themselves, specifically the improvement from 1923 to 1993. During that 70-year span, both males and females improved; however, the females clearly improved more rapidly than the males and are thus "catching up."

Why? The expectations and opportunities for women are considerably different today than they were in 1923. Many women now train for sport in the same way that men train—sometimes with the same coaches, using the same facilities, and with the same rewards for winning. The improvement for women between 1923 and 1993 was caused largely by factors in the environment. As a teacher, you have an impact on those same factors—opportunity, expectation, and encouragement.

The differences within gender are also large; that is, some males are much better at a particular activity than other males, and some females are better than other females. Thus, depending on the sport, biological and inherited factors make a relatively small contribution. Therefore, you should mention two important considerations with parents and children when discussing "talent," "natural ability," and biological factors (Thomas 1994). First, no one can control or change these factors. Second, the biological factors do not explain much of the difference in performance at any level. Teachers, parents, and coaches need to be aware of the contribution of biological factors. No one should assume that these factors either guarantee or deny expertise in sport, as shown by numerous examples. Mugsy Bogues, at five feet (1.5 m) six inches (15 cm) tall, had a successful career in the National Basketball Association (NBA), where players are considered too short at six feet (1.8 m) tall. Mugsy reported being told to quit the sport at 5 years of age because of his height. Can you imagine how that coach feels about his early assessment of Mugsy and the advice he gave him? You would certainly prefer to be remembered as the person who encouraged children and provided accurate information that allowed them to maximize their potential.

Many professional athletes report being discouraged during elementary school, middle school, or high school; however, they persisted and became successful. This is likely attributable to the **relative age effect**, which means that the oldest athletes in youth sport are identified as the best. Conversely, the youngest and least mature are identified as the poorest. This age effect disappears once everyone is mature. The relative age effect was discovered by examining the age of players on youth all-star teams, where the players with birth dates just after the cut-off date were most frequently on the all-star teams (Thomas and Thomas 1999). These athletes were almost a year older than the other players (French et al. 1996). Similarly, players in the most skilled positions (e.g., the infield in baseball) were the oldest on the team. On a team with 7- and 8-year-old children, the infielders were all 8, and the outfielders and bench-warmers were all 7 years old. The relative age effect suggests two things: First, being more mature than other children and adolescents is an advantage in sport. Second, being older often means having had more experience or practice, which is also an advantage. It is up to you and the coaches to make sure that all of the children—younger, older, mature, and immature—have equal opportunities to learn. The latest maturing children are likely to be ectomorphic, taller, and often the superior athletes; however, they also are the least mature during elementary and middle school. Expert physical education teachers recognize this and provide equal practice and encouragement for all children (Thomas and Thomas 1999). Furthermore, they do not allow more mature children to dominate practice and play.

Sports range from high to low strategy, depending on the amount of offense and defense. In low-strategy sports, such as running 100 meters or swimming 100 meters, biology and motor skill are more important. Characteristics such as speed, strength, and efficient movements are critical to success. Inheritance of biological factors such as speed, cardiovascular endurance, and susceptibility to training are important in some activities, such as running the marathon or performing the 100-meter dash. In sports where offense and defense are important, such as football, soccer, and baseball, cognition is more important. The best players at the beginning of the first year of a sport are those who know what to do. At first, most children have trouble performing the skills. Knowing what to do often precedes being able to do the skill. For example, new badminton players are at an advantage if they know how to play tennis. The object of the game and the format are similar, so, even though the skills are different, there is an early advantage to knowing. Declarative knowledge is a foundation for playing. Experts have both declarative knowledge and procedural knowledge. Procedural knowledge is the "how to" information often referred to as "if-then-do." Experts also have good motor skills. How do experts acquire knowledge and skill? Practice, practice, practice! You and the coaches can help children perform more like experts by teaching procedures and skill together and by providing lots of practice.

Experts recount hours of practice. Research identifies 10,000 hours of practice as the start of expertise (Ericsson, Krampe, and Tesch-Römer 1993; Starkes, Deakin, Allard, Hodges, and Hayes 1996). Help students understand the importance of practice and help them to be patient and allow skill to develop. Spend time on learning skills and developing knowledge. Youth sport and physical education often produce little time for practice (e.g., 10 to 13 trials during a day's practice; Thomas 1994). Experts report 200 to 300 trials per day (Thomas 1994). Good management and planning allow more time for practice. However, if children are to become experts, they must practice outside of class as well as in school.

How does someone become an expert? Learning the declarative and procedural knowledge and being able to execute the skills—both of which are accomplished with lots of practice—are how expertise develops in high-strategy sport. You can help children develop expertise by explaining the role of practice, understanding the influence of maturation and biology, and providing experiences that lead to skill and knowledge.

Summary

Your goal is for students to learn. Children have less experience and knowledge than adults and they learn differently. You must understand how they learn so you can teach them effectively. The content of elementary physical education for children comprises developing skills (or motor programs) and procedures (decision making), learning facts (declarative knowledge), and becoming physically active (understanding why physical activity is important and incorporating it into their lives). You need to

- provide as much appropriate practice as possible,
- help children understand why and how practice works,
- provide learning strategies such as labeling and rehearsal,
- use appropriate cues that help children focus on important sensory information,
- use the sandwich technique as often as possible to give corrective feedback, and
- consider children's variability in readiness and performance when you are planning practice.

Children, especially younger children, benefit from practice in which control processes or spe-

cific strategies are used. Figure 5.3 on page 100 demonstrates how error decreases for children of all ages when they use a specific strategy to remember movement characteristics. A similar pattern, with similar benefits, has been found for labeling, rehearsal, and grouping. As children get older, they get better—with the improvement largely attributable to more efficient cognitive processing.

Mastery Learning Activities

1. Make a list of 20 different words of encouragement, praise, and reinforcement to use after a poor performance.

2. Select a task. Design practice (random versus blocked, constant versus variable) for the task with cues, adaptations for higher and lower degrees of skill, and notes about how to know when to switch from early (constant or blocked) to advanced (random or variable) practice.

3. Select a motor skill. Identify the beginning and ending locations, distance or speed characteristics, and acceleration or deceleration cues. Provide cues for each of those characteristics.

4. Define and provide examples of the following words: motor program, attention, memory, decision making, knowledge, practice, and control processes.

5. Identify specific things that you could do to improve student learning. Find at least one each for attention, information processing, feedback, motor programs, and practice.

6. Count out 12 seconds. Observe another teacher and count the length of the post-feedback interval and the number of feedback statements. Did the teacher use the sandwich technique? Were there at least two feedback statements during class?

7. Fill in table 5.3 with information from the text.

Table 5.3

Type of practice	Definition	Acquisition performance	Retention performance
Constant			
Blocked			
Random			
Variable			

8. Review the following three concepts and provide supporting information for each one using definitions and applications:

   a. Learning is

   - a result of practice,
   - demonstrated with retention and transfer tests (e.g., permanent), and
   - often confused with performance (and memory).

   b. People process information in a predictable way that changes with age and experience.

   - Attention has three meanings: capacity, vigilance, and stage of development.
   - The perceptual mechanism gives meaning to sensory information and is where stimulus identification occurs.
   - Working, or short-term memory, is where decisions are made and all cognitive activities occur; it is limited by attention (capacity). Capacity is 7 ± 2 (Miller's magical number).
   - Children can be forced to use control processes (working memory) to improve their performance; adultlike strategies almost always improve children's performance in cognitive tasks.
   - Response selection occurs in working memory with either decision making or retrieval.
   - Reaction time is a way of examining the simplest of decisions.
   - Children begin to label at 2 years of age, use rote rehearsal at 7 years, and use mixed rehearsal at 11 years.
   - Giving specific strategies to solve tasks helps children perform better, but they are unlikely to use the strategy on their own, even in a similar situation.

   c. Feedback should be information that learners cannot obtain for themselves (it is not intrinsic).

   - Two types of extrinsic feedback are knowledge of performance (KP) and knowledge of results (KR).
   - Feedback reinforces, motivates, and provides information.
   - Sensory modality, skill level, frequency, scheduling, and processing time should be considered when you are planning feedback.

References

Abernethy, B., K.T. Thomas, and J.R. Thomas. 1993. Strategies for improving understanding of motor expertise (or mistakes we have made and things we have learned!). In *Cognitive issues in motor expertise*, edited by J.L. Starkes and F. Allard, 317-356. North-Holland, Amsterdam: Elsevier Science.

Adams, J.A. 1987. Historical review and appraisal of research on the learning, retention, and transfer of human motor skills. *Psychological Bulletin* 101: 41-74.

Bloom, B.S. 1956. *Taxonomy of educational objectives: Cognitive domain.* New York: McKay.

Côté, J., J. Baker, and A.B. Abernethy. 2003. From play to practice: A developmental framework for the acquisition of expertise in team sport. In *Expert performance in sports: Advances in research on sport expertise*, edited by K.A. Ericsson and J.L. Starkes, 89-110. Champaign, IL: Human Kinetics.

Deakin, J. 2001. What they do versus what they say they do: An assessment of practice in figure skating. In *Proceedings of the 10th World Congress of Sport Psychology*, Vol. 3, edited by A. Papaioannou, M. Goudas, and Y. Theodorakis, 153-155. Skiathos Island, Greece: International Society of Sport Psychology.

Ericsson, K.A., R.T. Krampe, and C. Tesch-Römer. 1993. The role of deliberate practice in the acquisition of expert performance. *Psychological Review* 100(3): 363-406.

Fitts, P.M., and M.I. Posner. 1967. *Human performance.* Belmont, CA: Brooks/Cole.

French, K.E., M.E. Nevett, J.H. Spurgeon, K.C. Graham, J.E. Rink, and S.L. McPherson. 1996. Knowledge representation and problem solution in expert and novice youth baseball players. *Research Quarterly for Exercise and Sport* 67: 386-395.

French, K.E., and J.R. Thomas. 1987. The relation of knowledge development to children's basketball performance. *Journal of Sport Psychology* 9: 15-32.

Gallagher, J.D., and J.R. Thomas. 1984. Rehearsal strategy effects on developmental differences for recall of a movement series. *Research Quarterly for Exercise and Sport* 55: 123-128.

Gallagher, J.D., and J.R. Thomas. 1986. Developmental effects of grouping and recoding on learning a movement series. *Research Quarterly for Exercise and Sport* 57: 117-127.

Gould, D., E. Udry, S. Tuffey, and J. Loehr. 1996. Burnout in competitive junior tennis players: A quantitative psychological assessment. *The Sport Psychologist* 10: 322-340.

Helsen, W.F., J.L. Starkes, and N.J. Hodges. 1998. Team sports and the theory of deliberate practice. *Journal of Sport and Exercise Psychology* 20: 12-34.

Kerr, R. 1985. Fitts' law and motor control in children. In *Motor development: Current selected research,* edited by J. Clark and H.H. Humphrey, 45-53. Princeton, NJ: Princeton Book Co.

Ladewig, I., and J. Gallagher. 1994. Cue use to enhance selective attention. *Research Quarterly for Exercise and Sport* 65: s64.

McPherson, S.L., and J.R. Thomas. 1989. Relation of knowledge and performance in boys' tennis: Age and expertise. *Journal of Experimental Child Psychology* 48: 190-211.

Meyer, D.E., R.A. Abrams, S. Kornblum, C.E. Wright, and J.E.K. Smith. 1988. Optimality in human motor performance: Ideal control of rapid aimed movements. *Psychological Review* 95: 340-370.

Newell, K.M., and J.A. Kennedy. 1978. Knowledge of results and children's motor learning. *Developmental Psychology* 14: 531-536.

Ornstein, P.A., and M.J. Naus. 1985. Effects of knowledge base on children's memory strategies. In *Advances in child development and behavior,* edited by H.W. Reese, 113-148. New York: Academic Press.

Passer, M.W., and B.J. Wilson. 2002. At what age are children ready to compete? In *Children and youth in sport: A biopsychosocial perspective,* edited by F.L. Smoll and R.E. Smith, 83-103. Dubuque, IA: Kendall/Hunt.

Plamondon, R., and A.M. Alimi. 1997. Speed/accuracy trade-offs in target-directed movements. *Behavioral and Brain Sciences* 20: 279-303.

Ransdell, L.B., and C.L. Wells. 1999. Sex differences in athletic performance. *Women in Sport and Physical Activity* 8: 55-81.

Salmoni, A.W., and C. Pascoe. 1979. Fitts reciprocal tapping task: A developmental study. In *Psychology of motor behavior and sport—1978,* edited by G.C. Roberts and K.M. Newell, 355-386. Champaign, IL: Human Kinetics.

Smoll, F.L., and R.S. Smith. 2002. Coaching behavior research and intervention in youth sport. In *Children and youth in sport: A biopsychosocial perspective,* edited by F.L. Smoll and R.E. Smith, 211-231. Dubuque, IA: Kendall/Hunt.

Starkes, J.L. 1987. Skill in field hockey: The nature of the cognitive advantage. *Journal of Sport Psychology* 9: 146-160.

Starkes, J.L. 2003. The magic and science of sport expertise: Introduction to sport expertise research and this volume. In *Expert performance in sports: Advances in research on sport expertise,* edited by J.L Starkes and K.A. Ericsson, 3-16. Champaign, IL: Human Kinetics.

Starkes, J.L., and J. Deakin. 1984. Perception in sport: A cognitive approach to skilled performance. In *Cognitive sport psychology,* edited by W.F. Straub and J.M. Williams, 115-128. Lansing, NY: Sport Science Associates.

Starkes, J.L., J.M. Deakin, F. Allard, N.J. Hodges, and A. Hayes. 1996. Deliberate practice in sports: What is it anyway? In *The road to excellence: The acquisition of expert performance in the arts, sciences, sports and games,* edited by K.A. Ericsson, 81-106. Mahwah, NJ: Erlbaum.

Starkes, J.L., J.M. Deakin, S. Lindley, and F. Crisp. 1987. Motor versus verbal recall of ballet sequences by young expert dancers. *Journal of Sport Psychology* 9: 222-230.

Thomas, J.R. 2000. C.H. McCloy Lecture: Children's control, learning, and performance of motor skills. *Research Quarterly for Exercise and Sport* 71: 1-9.

Thomas, J.R., M.A. Solmon, and B. Mitchell. 1979. Precision knowledge of results and motor performance: Relationship to age. *Research Quarterly for Exercise and Sport* 50: 687-698.

Thomas, J.R., K.T. Thomas, A.M. Lee, E. Testerman, and M. Ashy. 1983. Age differences in use of strategy for recall of movement in a large scale environment. *Research Quarterly for Exercise and Sport* 54: 264-272.

Thomas, K.T. 1994. The development of expertise: From Leeds to legend. *Quest* 46: 199-210.

Thomas, K.T., J.D. Gallagher, and J.R. Thomas. 2000. Motor development and skill acquisition during childhood and adolescence. In *Handbook of sport psychology,* 2nd ed., edited by R.N. Singer, H.A. Hausenblas, and C. Janelle, 20-52. New York: Wiley.

Thomas, K.T., and J.R. Thomas. 1999. What squirrels in the trees predict about expert athletes. *International Journal of Sport Psychology* 30: 221-234.

Yan, J.H., J.R. Thomas, G.E. Stelmach, and K.T. Thomas. 2000. Developmental features of rapid aiming movements across the lifespan. *Journal of Motor Behavior* 32: 121-140.

Yan, J.H., J.R. Thomas, and K.T. Thomas. 1998. Children's age moderates the effect of practice variability: A quantitative review. *Research Quarterly for Exercise and Sport* 69: 210-215.

Resources

Gallagher, J.D., and J.R. Thomas. 1980. Effects of varying post-KR intervals upon children's motor performance. *Journal of Motor Behavior* 12: 41-46.

Newell, K.M., and C.R. Barclay. 1982. Developing knowledge about action. In *The development of movement control and co-ordination,* edited by J.A.S. Kelso and J.E. Clark, 175-212. New York: Wiley.

Lesson Plans

The lesson plans provided here demonstrate methods that appropriately help children learn motor skills, make decisions, and learn facts. For grades K and 1 (the Mulberry Bush and Baa, Baa, Black Sheep), grades 2 and 3 (Kinderpolka and rope jumping), and grades 4 and 5 (country dance), lessons use progressive part instruction and repetition to help children remember the skills. The concluding activity is a retention test: doing both dances again after short periods without practice. Another grade K and 1 lesson using jump ropes incorporates cognitive concepts such as over, around, shapes, and letters into movement challenges. The rope-jumping lesson for grades 4 and 5 uses blocked practice to introduce the skills; later lessons practice these skills again and move toward a random practice schedule in routines. In addition to these lessons, the cognitive concepts presented in the fitness lessons at the end of chapter 6, Physical Activity for Children, demonstrate the use of decision making, rehearsal, and other concepts to develop declarative and procedural knowledge.

Lesson 5.1

Baa, Baa, Black Sheep and Mulberry Bush

Student Objectives   1

- Remember the words to the songs.
- Perform the movement sequences to the words of the songs.

Equipment and Materials

- 1 tambourine
- Music (optional): "Baa, Baa, Black Sheep" (Folkraft 1191, Victor E-83) and "Mulberry Bush" (Folkraft 1183, Victor 20806)

Warm-Up Activities (5 minutes)

Move and Freeze

Arrange the children in scatter formation.

1. Tell the children: "Walk freely around the area to a drumbeat and freeze when the drumbeat stops."
2. "When the drum starts again, find another way to travel" (backward; sideways; in a circle; with a jump, hop, leap, [or the like]).

Skill-Development Activities (20 minutes)

Baa, Baa, Black Sheep

Arrange the children in a circle, facing center.

1. Describe and demonstrate the following steps, based on the lyrics:

   Baa, baa, black sheep *(3 claps)*,
   Have you any wool *(3 stamps)*?
   Yes, sir, yes, sir *(nod 2 times)*,
   Three bags full *(hold up 3 fingers)*.
   One for my master *(turn and bow right)*,
   One for my dame *(turn and bow left)*,
   One for the little boy *(turn in place once)*
   Who lives down the lane *(bow forward)*.
   Baa, baa, black sheep *(3 claps)*,
   Have you any wool *(3 stamps)*?
   Yes, sir, yes, sir *(nod 2 times)*,
   Three bags full *(hold up 3 fingers)*.

2. Sing *Baa, baa, black sheep* (line 1).

Lesson 5.1   *(continued)*

3. Repeat as the children sing with you.
4. Continue with each line until you complete the song.
5. "Now we will sing the entire song." (Sing the whole song with the children.) Have the children practice the movements: "When we sing *Baa, baa, black sheep,* we will clap 3 times, like this." Sing and clap each part of the song.
6. Tell the children: "Now let's do all of the movements."

Mulberry Bush

Keep the children in a circle, facing center.

1. Describe and demonstrate the following steps, based on the lyrics:

Here we go 'round the mulberry bush *(walk or skip to the right)*,

The mulberry bush, the mulberry bush,

Here we go 'round the mulberry bush,

So early in the morning.

This is the way we wash our clothes *(stop, drop hands, and turn in place once)*,

Wash our clothes, wash our clothes *(pantomime washing clothes on a washboard)*,

This is the way we wash our clothes,

So early Monday morning.

2. Repeat, having the children use the following actions:

Iron our clothes (Tuesday)

Mend our clothes (Wednesday)

Sweep our floor (Thursday)

Make a cake (Friday)

Build a house (Saturday)

Bake our bread (Sunday)

3. Sing "Mulberry Bush" while having the children practice each action with the song.

Concluding Activities (5 minutes)

Baa, Baa, Black Sheep or Mulberry Bush

Repeat the songs, going through the words and movements several times.

From K.T. Thomas, A.M. Lee, and J.R. Thomas, 2008, *Physical education methods for elementary teachers,* 3rd ed. (Champaign, IL: Human Kinetics). Adapted, by permission, from K.T. Thomas, A.M. Lee, and J.R. Thomas, 2000, *Physical education for children: Daily lesson plans for elementary school,* 2nd ed. (Champaign, IL: Human Kinetics), 204-205.

Lesson 5.2

Rope Activities

Student Objectives   1

- Create letters and shapes with a rope.
- Jump rhythmically back and forth over a rope on the floor.

Equipment and Materials

- 1 small jump rope (6 feet [1.8 m]) per child
- 1 drum
- Music: "Sunshine" from *Modern Tunes for Rhythm and Instruments,* Hap Palmer (AR 523)
- Color cards: 1 red, 1 green, and 1 yellow

Warm-Up Activities (5 minutes)

Traffic Lights

Arrange the children in scatter formation. A leader (you, at first) faces the class while holding movement cards.

1. Describe the warm-up:
   - The leader chooses and calls out a locomotor skill.
   - The leader holds up a red card indicating "freeze," a green card indicating "run," and a yellow card indicating "walk slowly." You perform the movements at the right speeds.
2. Have the children do the warm-up.
3. As a variation, you can select other movements for yellow and green, such as walking in place or walking backward and running sideways or leaping forward.

Repeat the warm-up several times.

Skill-Development Activities (20 minutes)

Jump Rope Activities

Make sure that the children are still in scatter formation, and give each child a jump rope.

1. Challenge the children with the following tasks:
   - Can you make a circle (square, triangle) with your rope?
   - Can you walk (jump, hop) around your triangle?
   - Can you make a letter with your rope?
   - Can you jump (leap, hop) over your letter?
   - Can you think of another way to move over your letter?
   - Can you put your rope in a straight line? With your side to the rope, can you jump from side to side over the rope (facing the rope, jump over the rope and back)?
2. Repeat the challenges several times.

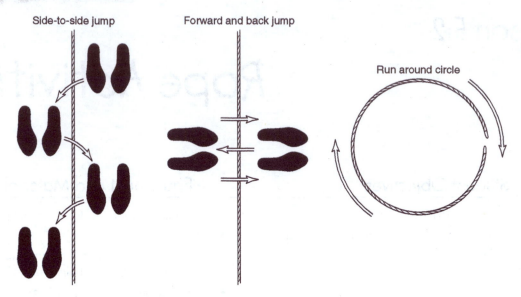

Side-to-side jump   Forward and back jump   Run around circle

Concluding Activities (5 minutes)

Rope Tasks

Have the children stand beside their ropes, which are laid out straight on the ground.

1. Tell the children: "Jump side to side (forward, backward) to a drumbeat (to music) over the rope."
2. Repeat the rope tasks several times.

Lesson 5.3

Rope Jumping

Student Objectives 1

- Jump Hot Pepper and High Water with a long rope.

Equipment and Materials

- 1 long jump rope per group

Warm-Up Activities (5 minutes)

High, Low, Medium

Arrange the children in scatter formation.

1. Describe the activity:
   - I will tell you "high," "low," or "medium."
   - On "high," run high on tiptoe.
   - On "low," run low with your body close to the ground.
   - On "medium," run at an in-between level.
   - I will change commands several times.
2. Have the children do a warm-up.
3. Have the children skip or gallop rather than run.

Skill-Development Activities (20 minutes)

Rope Skills

Divide the children into groups of 3 or 4; each group has a long jump rope.

Have the children practice running in the Front Door and running out the Back Door, using Two-Foot Singles and Doubles (see lesson plan 9.3 for these jumps).

FRONT DOOR

1. Describe and demonstrate Front Door: "In Front Door, turn the rope toward the Jumper. The Jumper runs under the turning rope (runs in the 'front door') and either jumps or runs out."
2. Have the children practice Front Door; rotate Jumpers and Turners.

BACK DOOR

1. Describe and demonstrate Back Door: "In Back Door, turn the rope away from the Jumper. The Jumper begins to run as the rope leaves the ground, entering when the rope is at the top (runs in the "back door"). The Jumper stays and jumps once and then jumps out while the rope is at the top."
2. Practice Back Door; rotate Jumpers and Turners.

Hot Pepper

Keep the same formation.

1. Describe and demonstrate the skill: "Jumping Hot Pepper is jumping with the rope turning very fast."
2. Have the children practice Hot Pepper; one child at a time is in each rope. Rotate Turners so that everyone has a chance.

Lesson 5.3 *(continued)*

High Water

Keep the same formation.

1. Describe and demonstrate the skill: "Jumping High Water is jumping with the rope turning so that it gradually gets higher and higher from the ground. Turners, be careful to move up gradually, instead of quickly, so the jumper will be safer."

2. Have the children practice High Water; one child at a time is in each rope. Rotate Turners so that everyone has a chance.

Mabel, Mabel

Keep the same formation.

1. One by one, say and have the children practice each line of the rhyme:

> Mabel, Mabel, set the table,
>
> Don't forget the salt and pepper.
>
> *(On "pepper," turn the rope faster and faster,*
> *and then the Jumper jumps until he or she misses.)*

2. Practice the entire rhyme.

Fourth of July

Keep the same formation.

1. One by one, say and have the children practice each line of the rhyme:

> I asked my mother for 15 cents,
>
> To see the elephant jump the fence.
>
> He jumped so high he reached the sky,
>
> And never came back 'til the Fourth of July.
>
> *(Use regular jumps for the first two lines. On the third line,*
> *the rope is gradually raised and the Jumper must jump*
> *higher and higher until the end of the rhyme.*
> *Again, Turners, be careful to raise the rope gradually.)*

2. Practice the entire rhyme.

Concluding Activities (5 minutes)

High Water and Hot Pepper

Have the children practice High Water and Hot Pepper again, using the rhymes Mabel, Mabel and Fourth of July.

From K.T. Thomas, A.M. Lee, and J.R. Thomas, 2008, *Physical education methods for elementary teachers*, 3rd ed. (Champaign, IL: Human Kinetics). Adapted, by permission, from K.T. Thomas, A.M. Lee, and J.R. Thomas, 2000, *Physical education for children: Daily lesson plans for elementary school*, 2nd ed. (Champaign, IL: Human Kinetics), 595-596.

Lesson 5.4

Folk Dance

Student Objectives   1

- Combine a step-close and a stamp to perform the Kinderpolka.

Equipment and Materials

- Music: "Kinderpolka (Children's Polka)" (Folkraft 1187)

Warm-Up Activities (5 minutes)

Animal Chase

Mark two goals, 30 feet (9 m) apart. Arrange the children along one goal line.

1. Use the following commands:
   - Animals run backward one time.
   - Animals run sideways two times.
   - Animals jump forward one time.
2. Repeat.

Skill-Development Activities (20 minutes)

Step-Close

Arrange the children in a single circle; partners face each other.

1. Describe and demonstrate the Step-Close: "To do the Step-Close, step to the side and then close with the opposite foot."
2. Have the children practice the Step-Close.

Kinderpolka

Keep the children in a single circle; partners face each other.

1. Demonstrate and describe the movements:
   - Part 1:
     - 2 step-close steps to the center,
     - 3 stamps in place (performed slowly),
     - 2 step-close steps back to original position,
     - 3 stamps in place. (Cue words: "Step, close, step, close, stamp, stamp, stamp.")
   - Part 2: Repeat Part 1.
   - Part 3:
     - Clap your own thighs 1 time,
     - Clap hands together 1 time,
     - And clap hands to partner's hands 3 times.
   - Part 4: Repeat Part 3.

Lesson 5.4   (continued)

- Part 5:
  - Shake your right index finger 3 times at partner.
  - Repeat with left index finger.
  - Turn around 4 steps in place.
  - Stamp 3 times.
2. Have the children practice the movements with cues.
3. Have them listen to the music.
4. Have them clap in rhythm to the music.
5. Say the cues to the music as the children perform.

Concluding Activities (5 minutes)

Kinderpolka

Have the children perform the entire sequence with the music. Repeat.

From K.T. Thomas, A.M. Lee, and J.R. Thomas, 2008, *Physical education methods for elementary teachers*, 3rd ed. (Champaign, IL: Human Kinetics). Adapted, by permission, from K.T. Thomas, A.M. Lee, and J.R. Thomas, 2000, *Physical education for children: Daily lesson plans for elementary school*, 2nd ed. (Champaign, IL: Human Kinetics), 584-585.

Lesson 5.5

Country Dance

Student Objectives   1

- Perform the Grapevine Step to music.

Equipment and Materials

- Music: "Elvira" by the Oak Ridge Boys, *Greatest Hits* (MCA 5496)
- 1 parachute
- Signal

Warm-Up Activities (5 minutes)

Parachute Steps

Arrange the children around the parachute and ask them to hold it with one or both hands.

1. Explain the warm-up:
   - Moving clockwise, slide in a circle.
   - On the signal, change directions.
2. Have the children do the warm-up, repeating the instructions several times. You can also have them try jumping, hopping, and running in place.

Skill-Development Activities (20 minutes)

Elvira

Arrange the children in scatter formation.

1. Have the children listen to "Elvira" and clap to the beat.
2. Have them stand in place and step to the music.

Grapevine Steps

Keep the children in scatter formation.

1. Describe and demonstrate the skill, going to the right:
   - Step to the right with your right foot.
   - Bring your left foot behind and step on it.
   - Step to the right again with your right foot.
   - Bring your left foot in front and lift your left knee across in front of your right knee while balancing on your right foot.
   - Summarize: The Grapevine Step takes 4 counts: step, back, step, cross (or lift).
2. Have the children practice Grapevine Steps, going to the right. Cue the children: "Right, back, right, lift."

Lesson 5.5 *(continued)*

3. Repeat, going left. Cue the children: "Left, back, left, lift."
4. Have the children practice the Grapevine Step, going to the right and left (with a partner, in a line, in a circle).
5. Have the children practice the Grapevine Step to the music.
6. Have the children practice the Grapevine Step with a quarter turn (pivot) on the lift, after completing the right, back, right. Cue the children: "Right, back, right, lift, and pivot."

Concluding Activities (5 minutes)

Grapevine Line

Arrange the children in a single-file line. Have the children perform the Grapevine Step right and left, in a line, to the music, making a quarter turn to the left at the end of each Grapevine Step to the left.

From K.T. Thomas, A.M. Lee, and J.R. Thomas, 2008, *Physical education methods for elementary teachers*, 3rd ed. (Champaign, IL: Human Kinetics). Adapted, by permission, from K.T. Thomas, A.M. Lee, and J.R. Thomas, 2000, *Physical education for children: Daily lesson plans for elementary school*, 2nd ed. (Champaign, IL: Human Kinetics), 983-984.

Lesson 5.6

Rope Jumping

Student Objectives   1

- Perform the Rock Step, Ski Twist, and Straddle Cross Jump with a jump rope.
- Jump rope to music.

Equipment and Materials

- 1 short jump rope per child
- Music: *Aerobic Rope Skipping* (AR 43); *Jump Aerobics* (KIM 2095); *Jump to the Beat* (KIM 8097)

Warm-Up Activities (5 minutes)

Follow the Leader

Divide the children into groups of 4, each group with 4 ropes. Arrange the groups in scatter formation.

1. Explain the warm-up:
   - Each group creates rope obstacles by arranging its 4 ropes into a formation.
   - Choose a leader, who leaps, jumps, or hops through the pattern; the rest of you follow.
   - Give everyone a chance to lead and create a pattern.
2. Have the children do a warm-up.

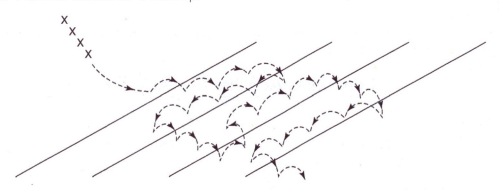

Skill-Development Activities (20 minutes)

Two-Foot Double Jump Forward

Arrange individuals in scatter formation; each child has a jump rope.

1. Describe and demonstrate the skill: "Jump on both feet twice for each turn of the rope."
2. Have the children practice the Two-Foot Double Jump Forward.

Lesson 5.6 (continued)

Two-Foot Double Jump Backward

Keep the children in scatter formation; each child has a jump rope.

1. Describe and demonstrate the skill: "Throwing the rope backward overhead, jump on both feet 2 times for each turn of the rope."
2. Have the children practice the Two-Foot Double Jump Backward.

Rock Step

Keep the children in scatter formation; each child has a jump rope.

1. Describe and demonstrate the skill: "Using a double-jump rhythm, place one foot in front of the other; jump on the front foot, leaning slightly forward and with the same turn of the rope, and rebound on the back foot."
2. Have the children practice the Rock Step with the left leg forward.
3. Have them practice the Rock Step with the right leg forward.

Ski Twist

Keep the children in scatter formation; each child has a jump rope.

1. Describe and demonstrate the skill: "Using a double-jump rhythm, twist your knees and ankles in the same direction."
2. Have the children practice the Ski Twist.

Straddle Cross Jump

Keep the children in scatter formation; each child has a jump rope.

1. Describe and demonstrate the skill: "Using the double-jump rhythm, land first with your feet about shoulder-width apart; and then on the second jump, land with your feet crossed."
2. Have the children practice the Straddle Cross Jump.

Jump to Music

Keep the children in scatter formation; each child has a jump rope. Have the children jump rope to music, using any of the steps learned.

Concluding Activities (5 minutes)

Jump Rope Routine

Keep the children in scatter formation; each child has a jump rope. Direct the children to perform the following routine to music:

- 8 Two-Foot Double Jumps
- 8 Rock Steps
- 8 Ski Twists
- 8 Straddle Cross Jumps

From K.T. Thomas, A.M. Lee, and J.R. Thomas, 2008, *Physical education methods for elementary teachers*, 3rd ed. (Champaign, IL: Human Kinetics). Adapted, by permission, from K.T. Thomas, A.M. Lee, and J.R. Thomas, 2000, *Physical education for children: Daily lesson plans for elementary school*, 2nd ed. (Champaign, IL: Human Kinetics), 973-974.

CHAPTER 6

Physical Activity
for Children

KADEN, AGE 7

Physical inactivity is a major independent health risk factor: Even if you remove all other potential risk factors, physical inactivity still carries health risk. Thus, a physically active lifestyle, which begins during childhood, reduces a person's potential burden on public health. Children respond differently than adults do to training, however; so programs that promote physical fitness for children must accommodate these differences.

Learner Outcomes

After studying this chapter, you should be able to do the following:

- Define and contrast physical activity and physical fitness.
- List and describe the benefits of a physically active lifestyle.
- Use the FITT principle.
- Define the components of physical fitness and describe the training for each of them.

Glossary Terms

physical activity	intensity	flexibility
sedentary	time	systolic pressure
physically active	duration	diastolic pressure
physical fitness	type	anaerobic threshold
body composition	aerobic training	norm-referenced tests
FITT	muscle strength	criterion-referenced tests
frequency	muscle endurance	

During the 1990s, the focus of physical education and exercise shifted from physical fitness to a broader term—physical activity. **Physical activity** covers a continuum from sedentary to physically fit (figure 6.1). **Sedentary** describes a person who is inactive (e.g., a person who sits at work and during leisure time). **Physically active** describes a person who engages in 1 hour per day of whole-body movement (e.g., walking), 30 minutes of which is moderate to vigorous (i.e., it makes them breathe hard and sweat). Lifestyle physical activities include cleaning house, gardening, and using the stairs instead of the eleva-

tor. Physically active people have reduced health risk. **Physical fitness** involves taking a physically active lifestyle to a higher level and is defined by a specific regimen of training and testing.

For several reasons, you, along with parents and coaches, need to know about physical activity, physical fitness, and the physiological responses to exercise, as well as differences between children and adults regarding exercise

- to understand that reducing health risk is a long-term benefit of a physically active lifestyle,

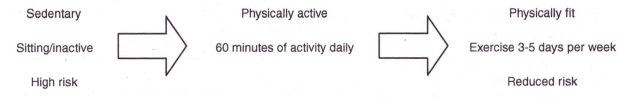

Sedentary	Physically active	Physically fit
Sitting/inactive	60 minutes of activity daily	Exercise 3-5 days per week
High risk		Reduced risk

Figure 6.1 The physical activity continuum demonstrates the relationship between health risk and level of physical activity, and shows characteristics associated with the terms "fitness," "sedentary," and "physically active."

- to understand that the roots of a physically active lifestyle are found in childhood,
- to be able to plan appropriate activities to encourage children to be physically active,
- to be able to provide children with safe environments for physical activity,
- to be able to present knowledge so that children understand the benefits of being physically active, and
- to be able to assess physical activity and fitness appropriately.

In the last 25 years, focus has shifted from physically fit to physically active. There are two reasons for this. First, physical fitness is an outcome of being physically active. Physical activity is a continuum from sedentary to fit. Second, health benefits are the greatest when people move from sedentary to physically active. If you visualize the continuum with sedentary at one end, fit at the other, and physical activity in the middle, the goal is for everyone to be in the space from physically active to fit. Unfortunately, too many people, including children and adolescents, are between sedentary and physically active (Centers for Disease Control and Prevention [CDC] 2000). The goal is for a minimum of 1 hour of physical activity on most days of the week. In a phone survey (CDC 2003), 9- to 13-year-old males and females were asked about participation in organized sport and free-time physical activity. They reported 38.5 and 77.4 percent participation, respectively, during the previous 7 days for sport and free-time physical activity. In the YRBSS (Youth Risk Behavior Surveillance Survey) of high school students, approximately 10 percent reported no moderate or vigorous physical activity during the last 7 days and only 30 percent reported having daily physical education (CDC 2006). Based on these data, many children and adolescents are not meeting the minimum recommended amount of physical activity.

One important goal of physical education is for children to be active outside of class.

The Four Guiding Principles

Now we explore in more detail the four guiding principles outlined on page 35 in regard to physical activity. Keep in mind as you study this chapter that each of the principles is important to understanding how children develop and what this means for physical education.

Principle 1. Children Are Not Miniature Adults

Children are naturally active; however, their activity tends to be in bursts rather than in sustained bouts of exercise. This is because children have less hemoglobin and less muscle mass. Hemoglobin carries oxygen to the muscles. Part of what exercise training does for adults is to train the cardiovascular system to be efficient in delivering oxygen. During exercise, adults are working at closer to their maximum capacity (aerobic capacity) for oxygen delivery than during rest. Children work close to the maximum aerobic capacity all of the time, so they benefit less from cardiovascular training and they fatigue more rapidly during exercise (Bar-Or 1983). Similarly, children improve on flexibility, muscle strength, and muscle endurance with training. Much of the improvement is attributable to improved technique, for example pacing themselves when they are running the mile.

Children often "exercise" in natural settings such as playing games after school and riding bikes. The typical child is significantly more active on a Saturday than on a school day (significant means 5 hours of physical activity on Saturday compared to 1 hour on Wednesday). Increasingly, the tendency for sedentary days is expanding from school days to everyday; this is a trend that must be reversed to address obesity, diabetes, and other chronic health problems.

Physical education classes look like fun and games rather than a day at the fitness center. Enjoyment is one of the important characteristics of quality physical education programs (Wechsler, McKenna, Lee, and Dietz, 2004). However, while they are having fun, children are breathing hard, sweating, moving toward fitness, learning skills, and preparing to be active in a lifelong way. Quality physical education programs recognize that children like varied types of activities, so programs cover a range of activities from dance and gymnastics to sport to fitness. Adults also like variety; some prefer to go to the fitness center, others play golf or tennis, walk the dog, or play basketball.

Principle 2. Boys and Girls Are More Alike Than Different

Several measures of muscle strength and endurance demonstrate this principle: for example, sit-ups, vertical jump, and grip strength (Thomas and French 1985). On these tasks, boys and girls have similar average scores and ranges of scores during childhood. At puberty, scores on most muscle strength and endurance tasks begin to favor males because of the increase in testosterone, a hormone associated with increased muscle mass and sexual maturation in males.

Even before puberty, upper-body strength is often less in girls, as demonstrated in tasks such as push-ups and chin-ups (Thomas and French 1985). Elementary school boys can typically complete between 1 and 10 chin-ups whereas girls complete 0 to 1 chin-ups at the same ages. There is considerable overlap between the performances, and, for both genders, the rather poor performance is likely because of lack of practice. Time and equipment limit the amount of practice that can be devoted to chin-ups in physical education class. A typical class with 25 students has only one chin-up bar. Children who practice climbing on their own are probably those who excel on the tests.

Physical education teachers often use tests of muscle strength and endurance as a teaching tool rather than for evaluation purposes. The tests help children understand the difference between strength and endurance, the relationship between them, the muscle groups worked by various exercises, and the way to develop strength and endurance.

Principle 3. Good Things Are Earned

Fitness is an outcome of physical activity. Children improve on fitness tests from fall to spring in part because the children have grown in the meanwhile; they also improve because of the practice associated with testing and physical education classes. Children often perform more poorly on fitness tests in the fall than they did the spring before, indicating the value of physical education in training fitness. One important component of physical education is to help children understand the satisfaction associated with reaching a fitness goal.

Physical activity in adults is associated with four elements during childhood: enjoying physical activity, competence, and confidence (Whitehead and Corbin 1997) and trying a variety of activities (Robertson-Wilson, Baker, Derbinshyre, and Côté 2003). These elements are important because the most active children tend to remain active as adults; the least active children tend to remain sedentary as adults. Thus, childhood experiences are important for physical activity and adult health.

Enjoyment focuses on fun and is also a result of the other three elements: confidence, competence, and variety. Competence is skill. An important function of childhood is to learn skills. Skill allows participation and thus increases activity. Skill also increases confidence in performance and in the ability to learn new skills. Most of the activities children enjoy are not continued when they become adults. For example, tag is a favorite physical activity for children, but not for adults. Adult confidence in trying something new is likely the result of recollections of mastering activities during childhood. Experimenting with a variety of activities during childhood allows skill and confidence to develop and presents an opportunity to find that special enjoyable activity. This is especially important for girls.

Physical education teachers help children observe skill acquisition. For example, skill tests are often practiced so that children can see their progress. The role of the physical education teacher is to help children achieve learning outcomes, including mastery of motor skills that lead to confidence. The fun and games of elementary physical education teach important skills.

Principle 4. No Body Is Perfect

The obesity epidemic has focused considerable attention on body weight, BMI (a ratio of weight to height), and body fat. Many physical fitness tests include an estimation of the healthiness of body weight or fat (Morrow, Jackson, Disch, and Mood 2005). Care must be taken in the interpretation of categories such as "overweight" and "obese." The goal of these measures is to determine whether or not an individual is at a "healthy weight." The essential issue is whether too much of the body weight is fat; measures that use body weight alone cannot make that determination. A muscular person with an appropriate percentage of body fat may be in the "overweight" category. The emphasis on weight creates two additional potential problems:

- It shifts the focus away from physical activity, a positive behavior, and toward body weight.
- In some people, it may encourage unhealthy eating and a desire to be "too thin."

In terms of health outcomes, it is as important to be physically fit as to be of normal weight (Lee, Blair, and Jackson 1999). So a focus on being physically active, with a goal of physical fitness, is positive, predicts health outcomes, and helps everyone see what is important. Increasing physical activity has the potential to reduce body fat (and excess weight) in those who need to reduce fat and is healthy for everyone.

Because the primary goal is being active, you can organize physical education classes to allow a variety of levels of participation. For example, according to individual contracts and plans of participation, you may have some children walking while others jog or run. Similarly, some children may be doing chin-ups while others are doing push-ups or modified push-ups. Physical educators make these decisions with children, based on individual needs rather than on arbitrary factors such as gender or body weight.

Even though children are naturally active, some children are not getting enough activity or the right kind of activity. A goal of physical education is to ensure that all children—regardless of gender, weight status, or skill—learn the skills, knowledge, and behaviors to be active. Children are less active on school days than on weekend days; schools must accept some responsibility for increasing physical activity in children to ensure health, growth, and fitness. Programs must be based on an understanding of the differences between children and adults in their response to exercise and in their needs and interests. Fitness is not the physical education curriculum; it is an outcome of physical education.

In the following sections, we provide greater detail on many aspects of health benefits of regular physical activity. Depending on your level of interest and need, these sections can add considerably to your knowledge.

Benefits From Being Physically Active

The following are the 10 leading health indicators in *Healthy People 2010* (U.S. Department of Health and Human Services [USDHHS] 2000):

1. Physical activity
2. Overweight and obesity
3. Tobacco use
4. Substance abuse

5. Responsible sexual behavior
6. Mental health
7. Injury and violence
8. Environmental quality
9. Immunization
10. Access to health care

School initiatives to provide healthy environments and reduce disparities based on gender, ethnicity, income, and age include requiring immunizations, providing school nurses and physical education, and banning tobacco and illegal substances. Schools have provided health education and participated in co-curricular programs educating children and adolescents about gangs, substance abuse, tobacco use, sex, and mental health. Schools and teachers embrace improving the health of students as part of their mission (Simons-Morton, Parcel, Baranowski, Forthofer, and O'Hara 1991). You and your school have the opportunity to influence significantly what children do during school, after school, and throughout their lives. With so many other problems to deal with, however, why should physical activity be a priority for schools? The statistics provide the answer to that question.

Adults who are physically active have several advantages over those who are not (USDHHS 2000):

- Lower death rates
- Lower rates of cardiovascular deaths
- Lower incidence of diabetes
- Lower risk for colon cancer
- Lower blood pressure
- Increases in muscle mass, muscle strength, and bone strength

A number of psychological benefits can be gained from regular activity:

- Reduced symptoms of depression
- Improved mood
- Reduced risk of developing depression
- Enhanced psychological well-being

Regular physical activity also has several other benefits for adults:

- Weight control
- Weight loss
- Decrease in body fat

Children and adolescents need regular weight-bearing physical activity to ensure normal skeletal growth (Bailey 2001). Clearly, physical activity is related to lifelong health, and physically active lifestyles begin during childhood. In addition to enhancing physical and mental health, physical activity contributes to development and meets important social needs, which are addressed in chapter 7, Psychosocial Factors in Physical Education.

Concepts Into Practice

Longitudinal research indicates that physical activity and fitness are as important for reducing mortality as obesity. Longitudinal research follows the same individuals across time: Obese physically fit adults had lower death rates than sedentary adults of normal weight (Lee, Blair, and Jackson 1999). This means that being active and working toward fitness is just as important, if not more important, for overweight children in your class. An overweight child can be fit and benefits from being fit.

Adults who are physically active report having learned sport skills as children and developing confidence as a result of those experiences (Welk 1999). Barriers to being active include lack of time, lack of access to facilities, and lack of access to safe environments. People with more education and more income are more active than people with less education and less income (CDC 1997). Women are less active than men, African Americans and Hispanics are less active than whites, and the disabled are less active than the general population. People living in the north central and western states are more active than those living elsewhere in the United States.

Children face barriers similar to those faced by adults—time, access, and safety. Children are more likely to be active, however, when important adults (e.g., parents, teachers, and coaches) encourage them to be active. Children enjoy the social aspect of exercise, so planning family or group activities that include physical activity is a good way to encourage children to be active. Schools can reduce barriers to activity for children and provide social support so that children are more likely to be active.

To summarize, a physically active lifestyle begins during childhood when there is opportunity, including time, place, and social support.

Physical education contributes to health and challenges children to be creative.

Developing skill and confidence during childhood is important to maintaining a physically active lifestyle. Physical activity reduces health risk directly and in a secondary role because activity reduces overweight and obesity.

Physical Fitness

In 1956, European children performed better on fitness tests than did children in the United States. As a result, youth fitness testing was established in the United States by President Eisenhower (Park 1988). At the same time, the Soviet Union was rapidly developing its space program, so the concern about physical fitness doubled as the United States started to train astronauts. Presidents Kennedy and Johnson continued to support the fitness movement, which eventually became the President's Council on Physical Fitness and Sport. Many people at the time took the President's Youth Fitness Test; a more recent version is called the Presidential Test. Early youth fitness tests did not require or even suggest how to train children to do well on the test. Often, the test was given in the fall and spring and then forgotten in between. Depending on the year, only the top 5 to 15 percent of the students could earn an award, so many children who took the test had a failing experience. Fur-

thermore, the test included items that had nothing to do with fitness (e.g., throwing a softball).

Several other fitness tests have emerged to compete with the Presidential Test; among them were Fitnessgram and American Alliance for Health, Physical Education, Recreation and Dance (AAHPERD) Health-Related Fitness Test. The Physical Best Program was developed by AAHPERD during the 1980s. This program had several levels of awards and suggested activities to train for fitness during the year. Recently, Fitnessgram has included a computer program to track physical activity. (Fitnessgram and Activitygram are available from Human Kinetics, Inc. and the Cooper Institute of Aerobics Research.) The changes in fitness testing reflect a change in fitness philosophy during the 1990s: Physically active lifestyles are for everyone and provide the most benefit to health, whereas physical fitness is for some people and provides additional benefits with small additional risks.

The American College of Sports Medicine (ACSM 1995) describes three components of physical fitness: cardiovascular endurance, body composition, and musculoskeletal health (which includes flexibility, muscle strength, and endurance). The most documented benefit from fitness is that it reduces the risk of cardiovascular disease. **Body composition**—specifically, maintaining a healthy body weight and healthy percentage of body fat—also contributes to reduced risk of cardiovascular disease, adult-onset diabetes, and cancer. Flexibility, muscle strength, and endurance reduce lower-back pain and improve posture, functional capacity, and the ability to conduct daily activities.

The cardiorespiratory, flexibility, muscle strength, and endurance components of fitness translate directly into fitness tests and training activities (table 6.1). Body composition does not involve specific activities, but it is positively influenced by training activities for the other components.

Use the acronym **FITT** to remember the terms that describe fitness training:

- **Frequency**—the number of training sessions per week
- **Intensity**—the percentage of maximum heart rate or strength for the training
- **Time**—the amount of training in minutes or repetitions, also called **duration**

Table 6.1 Fitness Components, Tests, Training Activities, Frequency and Duration

Component	Test	Training activities	Frequency and duration
Cardiorespiratory endurance	Mile run, step tests, PACER	Jogging, cycling, swimming, aerobic dance	20 min, 3 days per week at training heart rate
Muscular strength and endurance	Sit-ups, push-ups, pull-ups, chin-ups	Sit-ups or crunches, push-ups, weight training, chin-ups, or pull-ups	3 times per week with 3 sets of 10 repetitions
Flexibility	Sit and reach, back-saver	Stretching of most major muscle groups	3 times per week
Body composition	BMI, skinfolds		

- **Type**—the kind (e.g., swimming vs. running) of activity, which also influences training

To meet the minimum for **aerobic training** (cardiorespiratory fitness), you must exercise (swim, jog, cycle) 3 days per week for 20 minutes at your training heart rate. To calculate the training heart rate, subtract your age from 220 and multiply the result by 0.7. The most familiar training activities for muscle strength and endurance are sit-ups or crunches, push-ups, chin-ups, and pull-ups. Weight training also contributes to muscle strength and endurance. Muscle strength and endurance training also require a frequency of 3 days per week. **Muscle strength** is the maximum amount of force that a muscle can produce at one time. To train strength, the intensity is usually high (close to the maximum) and the time (number of repetitions) is low. **Muscle endurance** activities are low in intensity (50 to 70 percent of maximum) and high in time (3 sets of 10 or more repetitions). Some activities are considered muscle endurance for one person and muscle strength for another. For example, a person who can do 10 chin-ups is training muscle endurance, whereas someone who cannot quite do 1 chin-up is working on muscle strength. **Flexibility**, defined as the range of motion in a joint, is increased by low-intensity stretching with many repetitions, performed 3 or more days per week. One issue complicating physical fitness in elementary schools is that many programs do not allow enough time for physical education (e.g., days per week and time per day) to train fitness in children. Clearly, programs need 3 days per week for approximately 1 hour each day to meet the minimum criteria of fitness.

One of the challenges for you and your school is helping children develop the competence (e.g., skill and knowledge) and initiative to be responsible for their own fitness, beginning in childhood. The challenge results from two factors. First, time is needed to train for fitness. Typically, physical education—whether taught by a classroom teacher or by a specialist—is not offered daily. Although daily physical education might be ideal, it is not common. Even with daily physical education, the time demand of physical fitness training reduces the time available for skill acquisition. Second, the optimal situation is for children to assume responsibility for their own fitness. Adults must decide to train and to continue to train for fitness, and children can begin to learn this habit, with the goal of lifelong fitness becoming a self-responsibility. Some people choose to be active rather than fit. Skill is a predictor of physically active lifestyles, however, so allocating physical education time to skill development is important. How can you decide how much time to allocate? This is partially a personal choice; however, all children need to understand how to train for fitness and need to have a variety of exercises designed for them that meet fitness goals. Furthermore, all children need skill in order to participate in a variety of physical activities that can contribute to a physically active lifestyle. The physical activity continuum in figure 6.1 on page 127 demonstrates the relationship between activity level, health risk, and fitness compared with being physically active.

Being physically active is a goal for everyone, whereas physical fitness is a goal for some. To provide safe and effective programs, you need to understand some of the differences in how children and adults experience exercise. Just as children grow, mature, and have skills that evolve with time and practice, their bodies also change in other ways that cannot be directly observed.

benefit trade-off and potential for injuries. Weight training takes a lot of time, and, for prepubescent children, the gains are small (Faigenbaum, Westcott, Loud, and Long 1999). Therefore, the time might be better spent doing something else, such as practicing skill (COPEC 1998). As children are growing, there is risk of injury; however, low-intensity (low-weight) training regimens can be safe (LePostollec 2002). Specific guidelines for prepubescent weight training are available (Kraemer and Fleck 1992). One critical component of weight training for children is the participation of a teacher or a coach certified to coach young children (Kraemer and Fleck 1992). Generally, weight training is not a good use of physical education time during elementary school.

Most children do well on the sit-up tests, although practice and training are important. Scores often decrease from spring to fall, however, which suggests that practice during physical education improves performance. Girls are more flexible than boys in a comparison of test scores for the sit and reach. Again, practice is the most likely cause of these differences. Flexibility is the easiest

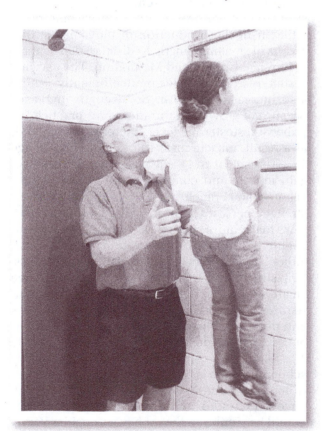

A child performs a muscle strength activity under the watchful eye of her teacher.
Photo courtesy of the authors.

component of fitness to train and the first to deteriorate during periods of inactivity. Most people experience periods when movement is restricted and flexibility is significantly reduced.

Muscle strength, muscle endurance, and flexibility improve with training. Although gender differences are observed in these components of fitness, no biological reason for the differences is evident before puberty. Therefore, you and the children's parents should encourage and expect boys and girls to practice a variety of activities that maintain or enhance skill performance, such as sit-ups, sit and reach, and pull-ups.

Body Composition

Obesity and being overweight are independent health risk factors. Physical inactivity is related to obesity and being overweight. Parents are concerned about children who are overweight. The assumption is that excess weight is fat, so overweight has come to mean too fat. People of all ages need some fat. Too much fat is unhealthy, however. The American College of Sports Medicine recommends maximum body fat of 14 to 19 percent for males and 20 to 24 percent for females ages 20 to 60+ years. Body weight is made up of both fat and lean tissue. The LBM is muscle, bone, organs, and all tissues other than fat. The second assumption about body weight and fat is that bones are a constant density or mass. Bone density differs among races and across age, so this assumption can be a problem. People with "light" bones, or osteoporosis, could be in the normal weight range and still be too fat. Someone with dense bones might be overweight yet have a low amount of body fat. The same could be true of someone who is very muscular. Muscle is dense and heavy as a result. Therefore, very athletic people with more than average muscle mass may weigh more than normal and still not have too much fat.

Body composition is a complex issue. Often, you can make mistakes by trying to take something complex and make it simple. A height and weight chart is simple to use but may not be accurate in determining who is at risk. The Body Mass Index (BMI), a commonly used measurement, is basically a height and weight chart. BMI is body weight in kilograms divided by height in meters squared. LeBron James of the Cleveland Cavaliers is 6 feet 8 inches (1.8 m 20.3 cm) tall and weighs 240 pounds (109 kg); his BMI is 26.4, which labels him with grade 1 obesity. Shaquille O'Neal has a

Biological and Physiological Differences in Children

The discussion in chapter 3, Physical Growth and Maturation, demonstrated that children are not smaller versions of adults. It also means they do not exercise the same way that adults do. How does exercise work? The body makes two major adjustments during aerobic exercise (prolonged, rhythmic exercise such as jogging, running, or cycling). First, muscles do their work during exercise by using fuel (food) and oxygen. The more intense the work is, the more the body uses oxygen and fuel. The oxygen is used very rapidly, so the blood must deliver more oxygen as work continues or increases (more fuel is needed too, but this is not a major issue at most levels and durations of exercise). As a result, the lungs and heart must work harder. Generally, respiration and heart rate increase with the intensity of the exercise. At some point, the circulatory system can no longer keep up in delivering oxygen and removing waste. Fatigue sets in quickly at that point, and work must be stopped or substantially reduced.

The second effect of exercise is the production of heat. The body dissipates some heat by breathing but removes most of it by sweating: The circulatory system increases blood flow to the skin, and the heat is lost by radiation and evaporation of sweat. You need to be conscious of this process, particularly during hot and dry weather, when excessive sweating and evaporation may produce a loss in total body fluid that can result in dehydration. Replace lost fluid by regular water intake during heavy exercise in hot and dry weather. People of all ages are susceptible to dehydration. Always permit children to drink as much water as they want to during and after exercise. Water is as good a fluid replacement as any of the advertised commercial products. The USDA warns that children do not drink enough water and should be encouraged to drink water regardless of whether they are exercising, so encouraging children to drink water meets the demands of exercise and a more general nutritional need.

Children and adults handle heat and oxygen production differently during exercise and physical activity. Children have higher resting heart rates than adults; at rest, children's hearts are working harder than adult's hearts. For example, a 6-year-old boy has a resting heart rate of 86 beats per minute (a girl's at the same age would be 88); by age 13, his resting heart rate would be

You can easily estimate your heart rate by gently pressing your fingers on the carotid artery and counting the beats for 10 seconds and then multiplying by 6.

66 (hers would be 70). The maximum heart rate for a 6-year-old is 215, as compared with 201 for a 13-year-old. The easiest way to estimate heart rate is to press your fingers gently on the carotid artery and count the beats for 10 seconds and then multiply by 6. The carotid artery can be located by placing the fingers next to the Adam's apple (see photo).

Blood pressure increases steadily during childhood and adolescence. **Systolic pressure**, the maximum pressure immediately after a heart beat, increases from 108 to 115 millimeters Hg (Hg is the symbol for the element mercury as read on the gauge) during childhood and adolescence in boys and from 101 to 111 millimeters Hg in girls. **Diastolic pressure**, the minimum pressure just before a heart beat, goes from 72 to 82 millimeters Hg in boys and from 65 to 75 millimeters Hg in girls.

Respiration volume increases directly in relation to the intensity of exercise, but only to about 50 to 60 percent of maximum aerobic power or maximum oxygen uptake ($\dot{V}O_2$max). Maximum aerobic power, maximum oxygen uptake, and $\dot{V}O_2$max are terms used to describe the upper limit of the cardiorespiratory system in its ability to deliver oxygen to the body during exercise. At this point, respiration increases very rapidly. The change from steady to rapid increase in respiration is called the **anaerobic threshold**, the point at which the body can no longer keep up with the oxygen demands or the waste buildup in the muscles. The muscles are working without adequate oxygen and, in this state, fatigue sets in very rapidly. Respiration response is the same for girls and boys. As children exercise, respiration rate can provide information about level of fatigue. For example, a child who can talk easily while jogging is probably breathing steadily; when respiration interferes with talking, the child is moving toward fatigue.

Anaerobic power, the ability to work without oxygen, is also lower in children than adults. This is because children have less of an important enzyme (phosphofructokinase or PFK) in their muscles; this enzyme allows the muscles to work without oxygen. Children produce more PFK after puberty. Anaerobic power is important in activities such as sprinting.

Children also have a lower hemoglobin concentration in the blood than adults. Hemoglobin is the part of blood that carries oxygen to the working muscles (e.g., in the heart and legs), so children transport less oxygen per unit of blood than adults. This means that children can do less work than adults. Hemoglobin content in the blood increases at puberty; however, the increase is not as great in women as it is in men.

Children become more fit as a result of fitness training. The responses to training tend to be lower in children for several reasons:

- Children tend to be more fit at the onset, so training results in less improvement.

- Children have higher resting and maximum heart rates, which limits the intensity of training (0.7 × maximum heart rate = training heart rate).

- Children have less hemoglobin, which limits maximal oxygen uptake.

Exercise training produces three benefits for children and adults. First, hearts become stronger as a result of training as stroke volume (the amount of blood the heart can pump in one beat) increases. Second, more capillaries develop as a result of training, which provides a better supply of blood to the heart and working muscles. Third, better extraction of oxygen from the blood leads to improved enzymatic reactions. In order to benefit from training, children must exercise 3 days per week for at least 20 minutes per day for 10 or more weeks at the training heart rate. Training or target heart rates for various age groups are presented in table 6.2.

Table 6.2 Target Heart Rate (HR) Zones to Estimate the Intensity of Exercise

Age range in years	Target HR zone (beats per minute)
6-12	160-190
12-25	150-185
30-39	140-180
40-49	135-170
50-59	130-170
60-69	125-170

Reprinted from *Basic Stuff Series I: Exercise Physiology* (1981) with permission from the National Association for Sport and Physical Education (NASPE), 1900 Association Drive, Reston, VA 20191-1599, www.naspeinfo.org.

The relationship between the type of cardiorespiratory (aerobic) fitness exercise used for training and the type of testing used is critical. A child who has trained regularly as a swimmer has trained cardiovascular endurance, but if that child is tested using the mile run, the benefits may not show up in the test results. There are two reasons for this: First, the muscles used for swimming (arms) and running (legs) are different, so muscle endurance may be low in the legs and detract from the child's performance. Second, the knowledge of how to pace for the mile run is critical and learned through practice. Failure to pace carefully is one reason many children do poorly on the mile run test. You may remember a classmate running full speed for the first part of the mile run and then stopping or at least slowing considerably for the rest of the mile. The object of pacing in the mile run is to maintain a relatively constant speed with enough energy remaining to run faster at the end. Practice creates immediate improvements in test scores, which are not related to improved fitness.

Aerobic fitness tests fall into two categories: **Norm-referenced tests** are based on the normal (bell-shaped) curve and compare one person to the group. **Criterion-referenced tests** use a standard and generally place people into two groups (pass and fail or master and nonmaster). Early fitness tests were norm referenced and used the levels of the best 5 to 15 percent as criteria for an award.

Recent tests tend to be criterion referenced, with the criterion selected based on predicted health risk. The idea is that a child who is 10 years old and can run the mile in 9 minutes and 48 seconds or less has less health risk than a child who runs the mile in 9 minutes and 49 seconds or more. Unfortunately, the various tests use different standards for passing (Morrow et al. 2005). For example, a 9-year-old boy would have to run the mile at different speeds to pass the various tests: Fitnessgram (12 min), Physical Best (10:30 min), President's National (8:31 min), and Presidential Tests (<10 min), respectively. This is confusing and leads to controversy about the level of fitness of youth in the United States (Blair 1992). Furthermore, there are gender differences at each age for all tests, beginning at 6 years of age. The times for girls are greater (meaning that girls run more slowly and still pass) than those for boys, by 48 seconds or more, at each age for each test (Wilkinson, Williamson, and Rozsdilsky 1996).

Give careful consideration to test selection, use, and interpretation. If you maintain separate, lower standards, the message you send to girls as young as 6 years old is that girls' health is less important than boys' health. Is there a biological reason to expect girls to perform more poorly than boys? The answer to this question is no. Prior to puberty, boys and girls are similar in ability, and their performance should be similar, as should your expectations. The passing rates on the four tests are different: Fitnessgram (84%), Physical Best (51 or 52%), President's National (63 or 65%), and Presidential Tests (21%), respectively (the passing percentage for boys is presented first; if different, the passing percentage for girls is shown second). By selecting the test, you can manipulate the passing rate for all children. If you want to demonstrate that most of your students are fit, use the Fitnessgram. However, if you want to demonstrate a need for fitness, use the Presidential Test. Interpret test results for children, parents, and administration in terms of the test characteristics and the purpose of testing. Often, it is best on any test to compare scores for a particular child rather than to compare scores between children or to test criteria alone. In this way, maintenance or improvement is the focus of the discussion instead of awards and comparisons to highly variable standards.

Take care in the use of fitness training and testing; there is no evidence that being fit or training for fitness actually "carries over" to adult physical activity. Tracking is a term used to describe whether a behavior or characteristic remains constant across time. Unfortunately, no relationship has been demonstrated between physical fitness as a child and adult fitness or activity (Bouchard, Shepard, and Stephens 1994). Furthermore, school programs that train for fitness in children have had little success in maintaining fitness (or activity) levels once the program ends. There is little carryover from during-school programs to out-of-school activity. Clearly, you face many challenges when planning and implementing a fitness program. The existence of challenges does not suggest that fitness is not important or valuable. However, you should keep the role of fitness and fitness testing in physical education in perspective. The goal is maintaining good long-term health and providing a challenge for those children who are interested in taking physical activity to the next level.

Musculoskeletal Function

Girls and boys gain strength during childhood and adolescence. Part of this increase is caused by growth—bigger muscles and longer levers (limbs) generate more force, which translates to greater strength. As children grow, they become more efficient in the production of movements; this results in greater strength, as discussed in chapter 3, Physical Growth and Maturation. The nervous system recruits muscles more efficiently, which also increases strength. So strength increases because of growth, maturation, and practice. At puberty, testosterone levels increase in boys and, as a result, muscle mass increases. At about age 13, girls gain fat and reach maturity, whereas boys gain muscle and continue to grow and mature (Thomas and French 1985). Consequently, muscle strength increases for boys and can be observed in tasks that require strength. Girls and boys are (and should be) similar in strength during childhood, although some tasks have large gender differences. Grip strength, sit-ups, and the vertical jump have small gender differences until puberty. Tasks that require upper-body strength, such as chin-ups and pull-ups, however, show large gender differences: Girls can do 0 to 1 chin-up and boys can do 1 to 10 chin-ups, on average, during elementary school. Practice is the most likely reason for the differences in these tasks; if girls were expected, encouraged, and practiced, their performance would be similar to that of boys. Consider young female gymnasts, who demonstrate upper-body strength; clearly, girls can do chin-ups!

Weight training for children is a controversial topic. The two most important issues are cost—

BMI of 31.6, placing him in the obese category. These BMIs are considerably higher than recommended for health, yet in terms of performance or appearance, neither athlete would be considered at risk. The point is that, in terms of BMI, height and weight can be deceiving, and considerable stigma can result from careless use of norms.

Muscle and bone tissues are healthy and they weigh more than fat. People with large, dense bones and greater than average muscle mass are likely to appear overweight based on BMI or height and weight charts, yet they are probably not too fat. On the other side of the continuum are those who have little muscle and bones that are less dense than expected. Very low BMI is also unhealthy, particularly before 20 years of age. During growth—specifically, before 20 years of age—bones gain density. Dense bones have higher fracture points, which means the bones are more difficult to break. Bone density is a result of three factors: genetics, nutrition, and exercise (Bailey 2000, 2001). Adequate calcium and weight-bearing exercise produce healthy bones. From about 20 years of age onward, bones lose density. Two things can be done about this loss: First, the bones should start out as dense as possible, which means that, during childhood and adolescence, physical activity and calcium are critical. Second, the rate of loss should be as slow as possible; again, the critical factors are physical activity and calcium. For bone health, being underweight—especially of LBM—is a greater risk than being overweight.

In 2006, the American Heart Association released a scientific statement focused on increasing physical activity in children and youth (Pate, Davis, Robinson, Stone, McKenzie, and Young 2006). The paper highlighted the role of schools, specifically physical education in schools, as critical to the health of children. The American Heart Association is concerned about obesity and sedentary lifestyles, as these contribute to heart disease. The same year, the American Academy of Pediatrics released a policy statement calling for the "reinstatement of compulsory, quality, daily PE classes in all schools (grades kindergarten through grade 12) taught by trained qualified educators" (American Academy of Pediatrics 2006, p. 1839).

Body Composition and Gender

Nearly from conception on, girls have more fat than boys because girls have more estrogen. At puberty, when estrogen levels increase, so do fat levels. If girls do not have enough body fat, estrogen drops and menstruation ceases until fat levels increase. Sometimes this secondary amenorrhea happens with athletes who are training. In order to menstruate, girls and women need about 15 percent body fat (Sinning and Little 1987; Morrow et al. 2005). Most girls have more than 15 percent fat. Obesity, or too much fat, begins at 20 percent for boys and 30 percent for girls (Morrow et al. 2005). Approximately 1 in 4 children have too much fat; that is, they are obese based on percentage of body fat above 20 or 30 percent by gender. Girls are typically less active, which contributes to the higher percentage of body fat. The fact that girls are fatter than boys can be blamed partially on biology but is also attributable to environment (Thomas and French 1985). Gaining fat is easier for girls, thanks to estrogen, and encouraged in girls by sociocultural norms that suggest girls should be less active than boys. Physical activity can facilitate weight control and healthy growth. This is an important fact to present to girls and boys.

Understanding What to Do About Body Composition

What does this mean for children who are overweight and overly fat? The cycle of being fat, avoiding activity, and becoming fatter makes the problem worse. Sometimes, teachers and coaches send negative messages to the overweight child. This can be as subtle as focusing on the lean or best performers or as obvious as saying, "If you are fat, you can't also be fit." Being inactive is a greater risk to health than being overweight. So the message should be clear: Activity is important to all people. At the same time, overly fat children are working harder during physical activity because they carry extra fat. Overly fat children may feel self-conscious about their bodies or may have underlying problems that cause or contribute to their obesity.

You can help by making sure that children understand that bodies are different and there is not a perfect or most desirable body shape. Some differences in body shape are attributable to genetics; others are caused by what people eat and by their activity patterns. You can also prepare children for the bodily changes that occur during adolescence. Finally, you can avoid using a simplistic approach to a complex problem. For example, in addition to body weight or fat, you can examine other measures of health risk. Waist-to-hip ratio

(WHR), the circumference of the waist at the narrowest point divided by the circumference of the hips at the widest point, is a predictor of health risk. Large WHR is a predictor of risk; WHRs above 1.0 and 0.9 are identified as points of increased risk for males and females, respectively. Estimating body fat using skinfold calipers is another way to examine risk. Good equipment and practice are necessary to estimate fat accurately. Some experts recommend tracking the sum of skinfolds rather than calculating the percentage of body fat (Lohman 1992). In the absence of good calipers and training, you should probably not estimate body fat. Under the best of circumstances, you should use more than one technique. Consider discussing BMI, WHR, and physical activity together to develop a risk profile. Furthermore, you can encourage all children to seek healthy bodies that are not too fat nor too frail nor too thin.

Summary

Physical activity has important health implications: Those who are physically active have less health risk than those who are inactive. Physical fitness is at the opposite end of the physical activity continuum from sedentary. Physical fitness requires specific training. Boys and girls should be motivated and encouraged to be physically active. Prior to puberty, gender differences in fitness are primarily attributable to differences in the treatment of boys and girls. In American culture, boys are expected and encouraged to be active and fit whereas girls are not.

Children's bodies work harder during exercise than adults' bodies do, so children often fatigue sooner than adults. Furthermore, because of biological differences between children and adults, children's fitness does not improve during training as much as that of adults. As children mature, fitness performance should improve. The long-term goal of physical education and other physical activity programs is for children to develop a physically active lifestyle.

Mastery Learning Activities

1. Calculate your maximum heart rate (220 – your age). Calculate your training, or target heart rate (maximum heart rate × 0.7). Take your nonexercising heart rate (your heart rate while you are sitting down).

2. Locate a physical fitness test. Compare the standards across age and between genders. What are the passing rates on the test? How were the standards selected?

3. Interview a physical education teacher. Ask about the teacher's fitness testing philosophy and the test used.

4. Find one newspaper article from the past week about exercise or activity and health.

5. For each of the following concepts, identify supporting facts.

   a. Lifestyles are sedentary, physically active, or physically fit.

   b. Physical activity directly influences health.

   c. Fitness has specific training criteria (aerobic, muscle strength and endurance, and flexibility).

   d. Physical activity has specific criteria (moderate-to-vigorous activity).

   e. Being too fat is an independent health risk; being overweight does not necessarily mean that the body has too much fat.

   f. Bones and muscles are the heaviest tissues in the body. Bones must become strong during childhood and adolescence.

   g. Muscle strength and muscle endurance are related but different; the training for strength is high intensity, whereas the training for endurance is high repetitions.

   h. The FITT principle guides training for fitness.

   i. Fitness tests vary greatly in the standards and in the passing rates set for males and females.

References

American Academy of Pediatrics. 2006. Active Healthy Living: Prevention of childhood obesity through increased physical activity. *Pediatrics* 117: 1834-1842.

American Alliance for Health, Physical Education, Recreation and Dance (AAHPERD). 1981. *Basic stuff series I: Exercise physiology.* Reston, VA: AAHPERD.

American College of Sports Medicine. 1995. *ACSM's guidelines for exercise testing and prescription.* Philadelphia: Lea & Febiger.

Bailey, D.A. 2000. Is anyone out there listening? *Quest* 52: 344-350.

Bailey, D.A. 2001. Get it right the first time: The importance of leisure activities during the growing years for skeletal health. In *Physical activity in the context of leisure education,* edited by F. Fu and H. Ruskin, 78-86. Hong Kong: Hong Kong Baptist University Press.

Bar-Or, O. 1983. *Pediatric sports medicine for the practitioner.* New York: Springer-Verlag.

Blair, S. 1992. Are American children and youth physically fit? The need for better data. *Research Quarterly for Exercise and Sport* 63: 120-123.

Bouchard, C., R.J. Shepard, and T. Stephens. 1994. The consensus statement. In *Physical activity, fitness and health: International proceedings and consensus statement,* edited by C. Bouchard, R.J. Shepard, and T. Stephens, 9-76. Champaign, IL: Human Kinetics.

Centers for Disease Control and Prevention (CDC). 1997. *Guidelines for school and community programs to promote lifelong physical activity among young people.* [Online.] Available: www.cdc.gov [September 8, 2002].

CDC. 2000. *Promoting better health for young people: A report to the president from the secretary of health and human performance and the secretary of education—fall 2000.* Silver Spring, MD: CDC Healthy Youth.

CDC. 2003. Physical activity levels among children aged 9-13 years: United States 2002. *MMWR Morbidity and Mortality Weekly Report* 52: 785-788.

CDC. 2006. *YRBSS National youth risk behavior survey: 1991-2005.* [Online.] Available: www.cdc.gov/healthyyouth/yrbs/pdf/trends/2005_YRBS_Risk_Behaviors.pdf [November 2006].

Council on Physical Education for Children (COPEC). 1998. *Physical activity for children: A statement of guidelines.* Reston, VA: National Association for Sport and Physical Education (NASPE) Publications.

Faigenbaum, A.D., W.L. Westcott, R.L. Loud, and C. Long. 1999. The effects of different resistance training protocols on muscular strength and endurance development in children. *Pediatrics* 104(1): 5.

Kraemer, W.J., and S.J. Fleck. 1992. *Strength training for young athletes.* Champaign, IL: Human Kinetics.

Lee, C.D., S.N. Blair, and A.S. Jackson. 1999. Cardiorespiratory fitness, body composition, and all-cause mortality and cardiovascular disease mortality in men. *American Journal of Clinical Nutrition* 69: 373-380.

LePostollec, M. 2002. *Weight training for kids. Advances for nurse practitioners: Online edition.* Available: www.advancefornurses.com/pastarticles/mar4_02feature4.html [March 2002].

Lohman, T.G. 1992. *Advances in body composition assessment.* Champaign, IL: Human Kinetics.

Morrow, J.R., A.W. Jackson, J.G. Disch, and D.P. Mood. 2005. *Measurement and evaluation in human performance.* 3rd ed. Champaign, IL: Human Kinetics.

Park, R.J. 1988. Measurement of physical fitness: A historical perspective. *ODPHP Monograph Series:* U.S. Department of Health and Human Services.

Pate, R.R., M.G. Davis, T.N. Robinson, E.J. Stone, T.L. McKenzie, and J.C. Young. 2006. Promoting physical activity in children and youth: A leadership role for schools. *Circulation* 114: 1214-1225.

Robertson-Wilson, J., E. Baker, E. Derbinshyre, and J. Côté. 2003. Childhood sports involvement in active and inactive female adults. *AVANTE* 9: 1-8.

Simons-Morton, B.G., G.S. Parcel, T. Baranowski, R. Forthofer, and N.M. O'Hara. 1991. Promoting physical activity and a healthful diet among children: Results of a school-based intervention study. *American Journal of Public Health* 81: 986-991.

Sinning, W.E., and K.D. Little. 1987. Body composition and menstrual function in athletes. *Sports Medicine* 4: 34-45.

Thomas, J.R., and K.E. French. 1985. Gender differences across age in motor performance: A meta-analysis. *Psychological Bulletin* 98: 260-282.

U.S. Department of Health and Human Services (USDHHS). 2000. *Healthy People 2010: Conference edition.* Washington, DC: Government Printing Office.

Wechsler, H., M.L. McKenna, S.M. Lee, and W.H. Dietz. 2004. The role of schools in preventing childhood obesity. *The State Education Standard* (December): 4-12.

Welk, G.J. 1999. The youth physical activity promotion model: A conceptual bridge between theory and practice. *Quest* 51: 5-23.

Whitehead, J.R., and C.B. Corbin. 1997. Self-esteem in children and youth: The role of sport and physical education. In *The physical self: From motivation to well-being,* edited by K.R. Fox, 175-203. Champaign IL: Human Kinetics.

Wilkinson, S., K.M. Williamson, and R. Rozsdilsky. 1996. Gender and fitness standards. *Women's Sport and Physical Activity Journal* 5: 1-23.

Resources

www.fitness.gov/index.html

www.acsm.org

Lesson Plans

The six lesson plans at the end of this chapter represent several ways to incorporate fitness into elementary physical education. The lessons include circuit training, fitness challenges, and moderate-to-vigorous games. In addition, children enjoy fitness hustles (e.g., aerobic dance) and jump rope. You can do fitness units, in which fitness is the focus for several weeks, or fitness days, in which fitness is practiced intermittently through the year. They can include moderate-to-vigorous activities on a daily basis or assigned fitness homework. You and your school can further encourage physical activity and fitness at recess or after school by sponsoring walking clubs, activ-ity groups, and similar activities. Children enjoy participating in these activities with you and other significant adults (e.g., parents, administrators, and counselors), so running and walking clubs are usually popular. Whether walking, jogging, cycling, or swimming, children can chart the distances; doing this on a map is educational, motivational, and fun for children.

Lesson 6.1

Moderate to Vigorous Games

Student Objectives 2 4 5

- Distinguish between muscular strength and muscular endurance.
- Participate in moderate to vigorous activities.
- Demonstrate cooperation when playing Reveille.

Equipment and Materials

- 4 cones or tape or, if outside, chalk
- Horn or other signal (a horn is best, but a whistle, bell, or other noisemaker will work)
- Enough carpet squares or taped or chalked Xs for half of the children

Warm-Up Activities (5 minutes)

Divide the children into small groups. Have the children do Crunches and Push-Ups.

Crunches

Tell and demonstrate for the children: "Lie on your back on a mat. Cross your legs at the ankle, with your knees slightly bent. Bring your knees toward your tummy or chest until your feet are over your hips or chest. At the same time, place your hands near your ears without gripping your head. Start the crunches by lifting your head and shoulders off the floor, pointing your nose toward your knees. Lower your shoulders to the starting position, but keep your head slightly off the floor. Repeat, twisting at your waist slightly so the opposite elbow and knee touch. Be sure to twist your upper body, not your elbow. One repetition is one to the left, one to the center, and one to the right."

Push-Ups

Gather the children into an information formation.

1. Describe and demonstrate a correct Push-Up:
   - Start with the balls of your feet and hands on the ground; hands are shoulder-width apart, and feet are together or comfortably apart.
   - Stretch out (extend) your legs so that they and your upper body form a nearly straight line.
   - Lower your body toward the ground by bending your elbows; keep your body straight.
   - When your body is nearly to the ground, move back up to the original position.
   - Keep your body stiff as a board.
2. Have the children practice giving you feedback on correct and incorrect push-up form. Emphasize supportive ways to offer feedback.
3. Rearrange the children into partners in scatter formation.
4. Tell the children: "One partner does Push-Ups while the other watches to see that the person is performing the Push-Up correctly."
5. After a few minutes, have the children switch roles. Circulate, helping children give accurate feedback.

Lesson 6.1 *(continued)*

Skill-Development Activities (20 minutes)

Select one or two games to play. Keep group sizes small to increase participation opportunities.

Reveille

Arrange children in 2 groups on parallel lines about 40 feet (12 m) apart, defined by the 4 cones.

1. Describe and demonstrate the game:
   - On the signal, everyone runs for the opposite line.
   - The first group to line up and stand at attention gets 1 point.
   - Take care and cooperate when running past other children so that no one gets bumped or tripped.
2. Have the children play Reveille, repeating several times.

Sneaky Tag

Use the 4 cones to define a square playing area. Place the carpet squares on one side of the square. The starting line is opposite the squares. Arrange children in 2 groups: one group on the starting line, one group on the carpet squares or chalked or taped Xs. (On a hard surface, mark Xs with tape or chalk; on soft ground, carpet squares work well.)

1. Describe and demonstrate the game:
   - The children on the start line are the Sneakers, and the children on the Xs (or carpet squares) are the Taggers.
   - On the signal, the Sneakers move through the Taggers, trying to get to the end line without being tagged. Sneakers must stay inside the boundaries, and Taggers must keep at least one foot on the X.
   - If you are tagged, jog around the end boundary during the next round and then rejoin the Sneakers for later rounds.
   - Sneakers who safely get to the end line use that new line for their starting end for the next round, which begins on the next signal.
2. Have the children play several rounds. Then have Taggers and Sneakers switch roles.

Fitness Relay

Arrange 6 groups of children at one end of the play area.

1. Describe and demonstrate the activity:
   - The first child in each line runs to the other end of the play area (marked with cones), does 5 Sit-Ups, and then runs back to the start.
   - The second child does the same thing, and so forth, until all of the children have had a turn.
   - The first group to finish selects the exercise to be done on the next round (e.g., run and do Push-Ups, Crunches, or Reverse Push-Ups, or the like).
2. Play several rounds to practice a variety of fitness tasks.

Concluding Activities (5 minutes)

Physical Fitness Concept

Gather the children into an information formation.

1. Present the concept to the children: "Muscular endurance is when a muscle or a group of muscles can make the same movement many times without getting too tired. Being able to do several sit-ups, push-ups, and chin-ups demonstrates muscular endurance. Muscular strength is

how much work a muscle can do in one try. Muscles get stronger by exercising (for example, by moving heavy objects)."

2. Begin the discussion: "What activities have we done that call for you to repeat a movement many times?" (Crunches, Sit-Ups, Push-Ups, Reverse Push-Ups.) "What about jogging?" (Yes.) "What about throwing a ball?" (No.) "Jumping rope?" (Yes.) "Now, everyone is going to do a muscular endurance activity. Be sure to stay in your own space."

3. Tell the children: "Everyone switch and do a different endurance activity." (Do this for 30 to 60 seconds.) "Switch again!" (Do this for 30 to 60 seconds.) "OK, sit down and relax. Usually muscular endurance activities are done for at least 10 minutes in activities such as jogging and in 3 sets of 10 repetitions for tasks such as Sit-Ups. This kind of work helps your muscles develop endurance."

Alternative Learning Activities

Gather the children into an information formation for this discussion.

1. Loop a rubber band around the blades of scissors. Open and close the scissors as you describe the action.

2. Begin the discussion by saying, "The rubber band is elastic, which means it stretches. When I open the scissors, the joint—the part where the blades are joined—opens wider and the rubber band stretches. When the scissors are closed, the rubber band contracts (shortens). Your muscles are designed the same way, with muscles on one side of a joint stretching and those on the other side contracting (shortening) to make the bones move."

3. "Put your hand on the big muscle in the front of your upper arm. This is called the biceps. Bend your arm so that your fist moves toward your shoulder. Do you feel the biceps pulling, tightening to move your arm? Now slowly lower your fist until your arm is straight. Do you feel the biceps relaxing? Muscular strength is the greatest amount of weight a muscle can lift in one try."

4. "To train muscles and help them become stronger and able to work longer (increase endurance), we use the overload principle. Can anyone guess what 'overload' means? The overload principle means you make your body do extra work—by moving either more weight at one time or the same or lower weight more times—to increase the muscle's ability to work. At your age, the weight you usually move is your own body weight, so doing a few more repetitions of an exercise each time you exercise helps build your muscular strength and endurance."

From K.T. Thomas, A.M. Lee, and J.R. Thomas, 2008, *Physical education methods for elementary teachers*, 3rd ed. (Champaign, IL: Human Kinetics). Adapted, by permission, from K.T. Thomas, A.M. Lee, and J.R. Thomas, 2000, *Physical education for children: Daily lesson plans for elementary school*, 2nd ed. (Champaign, IL: Human Kinetics), 69-71.

Lesson 6.2

Circuit Training

Student Objectives 2 4

- Demonstrate Fitness Circuit.
- Stay on task.
- Take turns.
- State that physical fitness is an exercise or sport that contributes to health and allows us to do activities throughout the day.
- State that physical activity is any movement that contributes to being healthy.

Equipment and Materials

- 6 cones
- 6 identifying signs (numbers and pictures)
- Tape (to attach signs to cones)
- Music or special signal (e.g., whistle)
- Enough short jump ropes for one-sixth of the class (see station 6 instructions)
- 2 long jump ropes (for crab walk, station 4)

Warm-Up Activities (5 minutes)

Pyramid

Arrange children along one side of the play area in a line, facing the other side.

1. Tell the children: "We are going to move across the activity area very slowly. When we come back, we will speed up a little. We will continue until we are running as fast as we can. This is called 'Pyramid' because we are building from a slow to a fast speed, just as a pyramid is built from low to high. Remember to stay in your own personal space so no one gets hurt."
2. Move across the area at least 6 times, increasing the speed each time.
3. Repeat, moving backward and then sideways.

Skill-Development Activities (20 minutes)

Circuit Training: Fitness Circuit

Set up the 6 stations as described, using the cones to mark their locations. Divide the children into 6 groups, and assign each group to a station.

1. Explain and demonstrate the activities for each station.
2. Rotate the groups through the stations, repeating each station as follows:

Round	Time at each station (seconds)	Time between stations (seconds)
1	15	15
2	20	15
3	25	15
4	30	15

3. As you have children repeat this circuit on other days, increase the time at each station, decrease the time between stations, and increase the number of rounds.

STATION 1: JUMPING JACKS

Tell and demonstrate for the children: "Standing with your feet together and your hands at your sides, bounce up and land with your feet apart while moving your arms and clapping your hands above your head. Then jump back to the starting position. Jumping Jacks help enhance muscular endurance and cardiovascular endurance."

STATION 2: AIRPLANE CIRCLES

Tell and demonstrate for the children: "Standing with feet comfortably apart and arms extended to sides, circle your arms forward; count 1, circle forward (one complete circle for each count). This helps your flexibility and muscular endurance."

STATION 3: SIT-UPS

Gather the children into an information formation.

1. Describe and demonstrate a correct sit-up:
   ○ The Sit-Up is done with a rolling motion.
   ○ Begin by lying on your back, with your legs bent slightly at the knees so that the soles of your feet are flat on the ground.
   ○ Choose one of the two hand–arm positions: you can cross your hands and arms on your chest so that your hands are resting on the opposite shoulders, or you can place your hands on the sides of your head, with a finger placed on each ear; keep your elbows lined up (parallel) with the back of your head (keep them there, without pulling forward past the ears).
   ○ Perform each Sit-Up slowly, rolling your chin to your chest in order to lift your head, your shoulders, and then your lower back off the ground. During the movement, feel the muscles under your belly button working.
   ○ Once your lower back is off the ground, unroll back down to the start position.
2. Have the children practice analyzing your sit-up form. Arrange the children in scatter formation; each child has a carpet square or mat.
3. As you say, "Rolllllll," have each child do a Sit-Up; emphasize slow movement.
4. After one sit-up, tell the children: "Point to the muscles that did the work" (the muscles under the belly button). Repeat several times.
5. Have partners check each other's form.

Tell the children: "This helps make your abdominal muscles stronger."

STATION 4: CRAB WALK

Tell and demonstrate for the children: "Assume a back support position with your knees bent and your body straight; walk on your hands and feet from line A to line B and from line B to line A; continue until the time is up. This helps make your arm muscles stronger."

STATION 5: PUSH-UPS

See lesson plan 6.1 for a description of Push-Ups. Tell the children: "This helps make your arm muscles stronger."

STATION 6: ROPE JUMP

Tell and demonstrate for the children: "Begin with both feet on one side of the rope and then jump up and sideways so that you land on the other side of the rope while moving forward slightly. Repeat, crossing back and forth over the rope. When you reach the end of the rope, turn around and continue until the time is up. This helps make your leg muscles stronger."

Lesson 6.2 *(continued)*

Station 1 — Jumping jacks
Station 2 — Airplane circles
Station 3 — Sit-ups
Station 4 — Crab walk
Station 5 — Push-ups
Station 6 — Rope jump

Line A ← 30 ft → Line B

Concluding Activities (5 minutes)

Physical Fitness Concept

Gather the children into an information formation.

1. Explain the concept to the children: "Physical activity, like walking or doing work in the house or the yard, contributes to health. Physical fitness is a type of physical activity that makes your body work hard; physical activity is moving that helps you be healthier."

2. Begin the discussion by asking the children, "Can you name some jobs that require physical fitness?" Discuss the answers, identifying jobs that require energy (e.g., construction, farming).

3. Ask the children, "What after-work activities can you think of that are not sport, but are physical activity" (e.g., housework, gardening)?

Alternative Learning Activities

1. Using magazines and newspapers, make two collages: one of physical fitness activities (aerobic dance, weight training, jogging) and one of physical activities (e.g., not sport or exercise). Discuss the idea that both physical fitness and physical activities can contribute to health.

2. Make a list of ways people can add physical activity to their lives (for example, taking the stairs instead of the elevator, walking to the store instead of driving, or parking farther from stores).

From K.T. Thomas, A.M. Lee, and J.R. Thomas, 2008, *Physical education methods for elementary teachers*, 3rd ed. (Champaign, IL: Human Kinetics). Adapted, by permission, from K.T. Thomas, A.M. Lee, and J.R. Thomas, 2000, *Physical education for children: Daily lesson plans for elementary school*, 2nd ed. (Champaign, IL: Human Kinetics), 53-55.

Moderate to Vigorous Games

Student Objectives   2   5

- Demonstrate fair play during Crows and Cranes.
- Name a muscular strength and a muscular endurance activity.

Equipment and Materials

- 4 cones or 2 long lines marked on the surface

Safety Tip

- Remind children to watch where they run so they don't hurt anyone else.

Warm-Up Activities (5 minutes)

Fitness Circuit: Stretching Routine

Arrange the children in scatter formation. Perform each stretch for 10 repetitions per minute with 6 seconds for each repetition: Shoulder Pull, Arm Reach-Out, Triceps Stretch, Forward Straddle Stretch, and Frog Stretch.

SHOULDER PULL

Slowly pull your left elbow across the front of your body toward the opposite shoulder. Hold for 10 seconds. Relax and repeat with the opposite elbow.

ARM REACH-OUT

Sit on the floor. Lock your fingers together and, with palms facing out, straighten your arms out in front of you. Stretch and hold for 10 seconds. Relax and repeat.

TRICEPS STRETCH

Lift your arms up over your head and touch your elbows. Hold your right elbow with your left hand and pull gently. Let your right hand drop behind your head as you stretch. Hold for 10 seconds and relax. Repeat, pulling your left elbow with your right hand.

FORWARD STRADDLE STRETCH

Sit on the floor with your legs straight and about 3 feet (0.9 m) apart. Bend forward at the hip. Grasp your right knee, calf, or ankle (as far down your leg as you can go) and pull your body gently toward your leg. Hold for 10 seconds and then relax and repeat on the left side.

FROG STRETCH

Lie down with your knees bent and the soles of your feet together. If you relax, gravity will pull your knees toward the ground and stretch the insides of your thighs. Relax for 10 seconds, and then lift your knees up and toward each other, so that they are no longer relaxed, for 10 seconds (knees do not need to touch at this point). Do not bounce!

Lesson 6.3 *(continued)*

Skill-Development Activities (20 minutes)

Crows and Cranes

Arrange the children in two parallel lines facing each other, with half of the children on each line, 30 to 50 feet (9 to 15 m) apart.

1. Explain the game:
   - The children in one line are Crows; those in the other line are Cranes.
   - As I begin saying "Crrrr . . . ," the two lines walk toward each other.
   - When I complete the word Crow or Crane, the line I call is "It." The children in that line run forward and try to tag the other children, who turn and try to avoid being tagged.
   - You are safe when you cross the line you started from. Tagged children join the other line, and play continues.
2. Have the children play Crows and Cranes.
3. Mix up which line you call to surprise the children.
4. Remind children to watch where they run so they don't hurt anyone.

Variation: Witches and Warlocks

Instead of Crows and Cranes, call the children standing on one line "Witches" and the children on the other line "Warlocks." As you call out one name or the other, draw out the "W" sound, alternating between Witches, Warlocks, and Wizards. When you say Wizards, everyone must freeze. Anyone who moves while frozen runs a lap before the next round of play.

Concluding Activities (5 minutes)

Physical Fitness Concept

Gather the children into an information formation.

1. Present the concept to the children: "Muscular endurance is when a muscle or a group of muscles can make the same movement many times without getting too tired. The number of Sit-Ups, Push-Ups, and Chin-Ups you can do helps demonstrate your muscular endurance. Muscular strength is how much work a muscle can do one time. Muscles get stronger by exercising (for example, by moving heavy objects)."
2. Begin the discussion: "Can you name some activities that call for you to repeat a movement many times?" (Crunches, push-ups, jogging, jumping rope, but not throwing a ball.) "Everyone show me an activity in which you repeat the movement many times." Correct anyone who is not doing an endurance activity. "Now switch to another endurance activity."
3. Tell the children: "Usually, muscular endurance activities are done in sets of 10 to 12 repetitions, so you should build up to doing 10, resting briefly, doing 10 more, resting, and then doing 10 more."
4. Continue the discussion: "Muscular strength varies from person to person and muscle to muscle. Different people have different strength levels, and different muscles on the same person have different strength levels. Muscles get stronger with training. Muscular strength and endurance work together to help us do all of the tasks we need to do. Sometimes we lack the muscular strength to do an activity, but with training we improve and then can do the activity many times. Pull-Ups are sometimes like that. At first, a person cannot do one Pull-Up, but, with training, strength increases and one Pull-Up becomes easy. Then, after more training, we can do many Pull-Ups because we have improved our muscular endurance."

From K.T. Thomas, A.M. Lee, and J.R. Thomas, 2008, *Physical education methods for elementary teachers*, 3rd ed. (Champaign, IL: Human Kinetics). Adapted, by permission, from K.T. Thomas, A.M. Lee, and J.R. Thomas, 2000, *Physical education for children: Daily lesson plans for elementary school*, 2nd ed. (Champaign, IL: Human Kinetics), 441-442.

Lesson 6.4

Fitness Challenge

Student Objectives 2 5

- Use equipment safely.
- Follow directions.
- Demonstrate locomotor skills.
- Define resting heart rate.

Equipment and Materials

- 4 cones or 2 long lines marked on ground
- 1 hoop per child

Warm-Up Activities (5 minutes)

Loose Caboose

Arrange groups of 3 or 4 children in scatter formation. Scatter 3 or 4 extra children about a clearly defined play area.

1. Describe and demonstrate the game:
   - In each group, form a "Train," holding one another at the waist in a line (stay hooked together).
   - The extra children are "Loose Cabooses"; they try to hook onto the backs of the Trains.
   - The Trains move around the play area, trying to avoid being hooked onto by a Loose Caboose.
   - If a Loose Caboose does connect with a Train, the Engine (the first child in that train) becomes a Loose Caboose.
2. Have the children play Loose Caboose.

Skill-Development Activities (20 minutes)

Hoop Challenges

Arrange the children in scatter formation; each child has a hoop.

1. Have the children try the following challenges that develop muscular endurance and aerobic fitness:
   - Spin the hoop on one arm, then on the other arm, and then on one leg. Try to do 10 to 20 spins on each.
   - Spin the hoop on another part of the body (waist, hips, neck).
   - Spin the hoop on your body; try to make it go slowly, then fast, and then slowly.
   - Spin the hoop on the ground like a top.
2. Have the children put their hoops on the ground:
   - Jump in and out of the hoop slowly.
   - Jump in and out of the hoop fast.
   - Move around the hoop, jumping in and out.

   - Hop in and out of the hoop.
   - Run and jump over the hoop.
   - Hop forward (then backward) around the hoop.
3. Have the children pick up their hoops again:
   - Pick up the hoop and stretch with the hoop over your head.
   - Holding the hoop, stretch to one side and then to the other.
   - Roll the hoop from one line to the other.
   - Roll the hoop and run around it as it rolls. Watch out for other hoops and children. Repeat several times.
   - Roll the hoop and try to jump through it as it rolls.
   - Roll the hoop so it returns to you (put backspin on the hoop).

Hoop Relay

Arrange the children in pairs and give each pair a hoop. Have the pairs stand about 30 feet (9 m) away from a line.

1. Describe and demonstrate the activity:
   - The first child in line rolls the hoop to a line 30 feet (9 m) away and back.
   - The second child takes the hoop and rolls it to the line and back; this sequence continues until the time is up. The children can count the number of turns completed.
2. Have the children do Hoop Relay.

Concluding Activities (5 minutes)

Physical Fitness Concept

Gather the children into an information formation.

1. Introduce the concept: "After you have been lying still for 15 to 30 minutes (or when you first wake up in the morning), the number of times your heart beats is called 'resting heart rate.' You can lower your resting heart rate by exercising regularly."

2. Tell the children: "Make a fist with your hand" (demonstrate, pausing for children to close their fists); "your hand is contracted. Now open your hand" (demonstrate, pausing for the children to open their fists) "and relax. Your heart works like your hand. When the heart is relaxed (the open fist), blood enters. Then when the heart beats, or contracts (the closed fist), the blood is pushed out. The blood goes from the heart through arteries to the muscles and organs (stomach, kidneys, intestines, and so on)."

3. Tell the children: "Put your hand on your chest, be very still, and feel your heart beat." Demonstrate and allow children to feel their hearts beating. "Heart rate is the number of times your heart opens and closes in 1 minute. When you sleep, your hearts are still beating, but more slowly. That is why it is called 'resting heart rate.' When you exercise, your heart rate goes up. When you are awake but sitting still, your heart rate is in between the resting and exercising heart rate."

From K.T. Thomas, A.M. Lee, and J.R. Thomas, 2008, *Physical education methods for elementary teachers*, 3rd ed. (Champaign, IL: Human Kinetics). Adapted, by permission, from K.T. Thomas, A.M. Lee, and J.R. Thomas, 2000, *Physical education for children: Daily lesson plans for elementary school*, 2nd ed. (Champaign, IL: Human Kinetics), 450-451.

Lesson 6.5

Wands

Student Objectives 1 2

- Explain the health benefits of physical activity.
- Maintain continuous activity with a wand.
- Perform simple stunts with a wand.

Equipment and Materials

- 1 wand (30 to 36 inches [76 to 91 cm]) per child
- Optional: 2 additional wands per group
- Stopwatch or clock with second hand

Warm-Up Activities (5 minutes)

Running and Dodging Games

Arrange partners in scatter formation. Choose from Follow the Leader, Partner Dodging, or Individual Running and Dodging.

FOLLOW THE LEADER

Have the children do the following activities:

- Run with one child in front and one behind (in typical follow-the-leader style).
- Run beside your partner.
- Run back to back with your partner (one going forward, one backward).
- Take turns leading.

PARTNER DODGING

On a signal, partner 1 runs and dodges, attempting to get away from partner 2. Partner 2 attempts to stay as close to partner 1 as possible. Take turns leading.

INDIVIDUAL RUNNING AND DODGING

Arrange the children in scatter formation. On a signal, have the children do the following challenges:

- Run and turn quickly to the right.
- Run and turn quickly to the left.
- Run and make a small circle and then a large circle.
- Run in a zigzag pattern.

Skill-Development Activities (20 minutes)

Wand Challenges

Keep the children in scatter formation, and give each child a wand to place on the floor. Present the following tasks:

- With your side to the wand, jump back and forth over it.
- With your side to the wand, jump rapidly back and forth over it 20 times.

Lesson 6.5 (continued)

- Face the wand and jump over it. Then turn around completely, and jump over it again. Try adding a turn in the air as you jump.
- Jump over the wand backward.
- Jump over the wand several times, increasing the height of your jump each time.
- Jump over the wand several times, increasing the distance of your jump each time.

Timed Partner Jump

Arrange partners in scatter formation. Have the children try to jump for 1 minute.

1. Explain the activity:
   - One partner holds the wand about knee high.
   - The other partner jumps back and forth over the wand as many times as possible in 30 seconds.
2. Signal the start and end of this period: "Take turns holding and jumping."
3. Have the children do the Timed Partner Jump.

Jump Over the Wand

Arrange the children in scatter formation.

1. Hold the wand in front of you with both hands about shoulder-width apart. The lower you hold the wand, the easier the task will be.
2. Jump up and over the wand.

Wand Follow the Leader

Divide children into groups of 4. Give each group 4 to 6 wands. Direct each group to arrange the wands in various patterns to jump and hop into, out of, and around.

1. Tell the children: "Play Follow the Leader; change leaders every 60 seconds."
2. Here are some pattern suggestions:
   - Place the wands in random order and jump forward, backward, and sideways over them.
   - Place the wands in parallel lines. Jump, leap, or hop through the wands.
   - Place the wands in a square or another geometric shape and jump, leap, or hop through the shape.
   - Place the wands in other patterns. Jump, leap, or hop through the patterns.

Pass-the-Wand Cool-Down

Divide children in groups of 4 or 5 in a relay formation; half of each group is at opposite ends of the play area, facing the other part of the group. Ends should be about 60 feet (18 m) apart.

1. Explain the activity:
   - One child in each group holds the wand for that group. That child walks to the opposite end of the play area carrying the wand and hands the wand to the first child in that part of the line, in relay fashion.
   - The child now holding the wand walks to the part of the group where the first child began and passes the wand to the next child.
   - The activity continues until everyone has had several turns.
   - This is not a race; it is a cool-down.
2. Have the children do the Pass-the-Wand Cool-Down.

Concluding Activities (5 minutes)

Physical Fitness Concept

Gather the children into an advanced information formation.

1. Discuss some of the health benefits of physical activity: "People who exercise tend to feel better about themselves; to be less likely to experience obesity, heart disease, and high blood pressure; and to be better able to cope with stressful situations."
2. Explain that there are some things that exercise cannot do, such as increase your intelligence or change your personality.

An Exercise Quiz

Keep the children in the advanced information formation.

1. Read a list of benefits of exercise to the children.
2. Ask them to give you a "thumbs up" if the statement is true and a "thumbs down" if the statement is false.
3. Regular exercise does the following:
   - Improves physical fitness. (True; training is the only way to increase fitness.)
   - Makes you taller. (False; growth, not exercise, does this.)
   - Turns fat to muscle. (False; exercise can reduce fat and increase muscle, but these are different tissues.)
   - Increases your IQ. (False; but you may be able to think better if exercise helps you feel less stressed.)
   - Helps maintain a lean body. (True; exercise helps reduce fat and increase muscle.)
   - Improves your self-image. (True; exercise helps you be proud of yourselves.)
   - Reduces the risk of heart disease. (True; exercise and diet help keep the heart healthy.)
   - Allows you to read faster. (False; reading practice helps you read better.)
   - Improves your cardiorespiratory endurance. (True; training is based on exercise.)
   - Absolutely assures you of a long life. (False; nothing can do this, but exercise should improve the quality of your life.)

From K.T. Thomas, A.M. Lee, and J.R. Thomas, 2008, *Physical education methods for elementary teachers*, 3rd ed. (Champaign, IL: Human Kinetics). Adapted, by permission, from K.T. Thomas, A.M. Lee, and J.R. Thomas, 2000, *Physical education for children: Daily lesson plans for elementary school*, 2nd ed. (Champaign, IL: Human Kinetics), 834-835.

Lesson 6.6

Moderate to Vigorous Games

Student Objectives 2 4

- Give examples of conditions that are the opposite of health-related physical fitness.
- Perform a stretching routine.
- Execute 3 sets of Crunches, 8 repetitions per set.
- Execute 3 sets each of Regular and Triceps Push-Ups, 3 repetitions per set.
- Participate in a moderate to vigorous game.

Equipment and Materials

- 4 bases
- 1 playground ball (8.5 inches [21.5 cm])
- 1 parachute

Warm-Up Activities (5 minutes)

Stretching Routine

Arrange children in a large circle, facing the center.

1. Describe and demonstrate each of the stretches.
2. Have children do each of the stretches.
   - **Modified Neck Roll.** Sit tall, with one hand on each side of your head covering your ears. Drop your head forward and then roll your head around very slowly in a semicircle, supporting your head with your hands, first to the left and then to the right. Do not move past the shoulders or backward. Repeat several times.
   - **Shoulder Shrugs.** Lift your shoulders to your ears, then return to normal position.
   - **Side Stretch.** Sit with feet apart, toes pointed straight ahead, and knees slightly bent. Place one hand on the hip and extend the other arm up over the head. Slowly bend to the side toward the hand on the hip. Hold for 10 seconds and relax. Repeat in the opposite direction.
   - **Front and Side Lunges.** Facing forward, bend to a squat, with your right leg directly under your torso and your left leg extended to the side. As you bend, place your hands, palms down, on the floor on each side of your right foot for balance. Keep both heels on the floor. Your left leg can be slightly bent at the knee. Your right knee should be directly over your right toes. Look forward while keeping your head up. Your back should be parallel to the floor. Hold this position for 5 to 20 seconds.

     Gradually turn to your right while allowing your heels to leave the floor. Your right knee should touch or be close to touching your chest. Bend the left knee and then gradually straighten both legs to nearly extended (determine this by your comfort level—don't extend if you feel pain; to avoid pulling the ligaments, knees should never be completely straight). Keep your back straight and parallel to the floor and your head up. Turn and "roll" your body over your left knee, repeating the entire sequence.

- **Standing Heel Stretch.** Stand with one foot directly in front of the other, about 1 foot (30 cm) apart. With both feet flat on the ground and your body positioned directly above the back foot, bend your knees. Bend so that your thighs are parallel to the floor but don't allow your heels to leave the floor. Hold for 5 to 20 counts. Reverse feet and repeat.

3. Combine stretches into the following routine:
   - Hold head right, 2, 3, 4; right, 2, 3, 4; and left, 2, 3, 4; left, 2, 3, 4.
   - Lift shoulders up, down, 2, 3, 4; again, 2, 3, 4.
   - Reach up, left, center, right, forward; left, center, right, forward.
   - With your heels flat on the floor, bend your right knee and hold, 2, 3, 4, 5; lift head up.
   - Turn to the right, with your back straight and your head up; allow your heels to come up.
   - Stand, extending your legs; keep your back down!
   - Turn to the front, bend your left knee; lift head up, hold, 2, 3, 4.
   - Turn to the left, with your back straight and your head up; allow your heels to come up.
   - Stand, extending your legs; keep your back down!
   - Do the Standing Heel Stretch (count 5 to 10). Reverse.

Skill-Development Activities (20 minutes)

Crunches and Regular and Triceps Push-Ups

ADVANCED CRUNCHES

Gather the children into an advanced information formation.

1. Describe and demonstrate the exercise:
   - Lie on your back, with your hips bent at a 90-degree angle so that your feet are over your hips or tummy.
   - Cross your ankles and bend your knees slightly.
   - With your fingers gently touching your ears on each side of your head, do the Crunch by lifting your head, neck, and shoulders (to the shoulder blades) off the ground.
   - End the lift when one elbow touches (or nears) the opposite knee or both elbows reach the knees.
   - Do one Crunch each: right elbow to left knee, left elbow to right knee, both elbows to both knees, and then repeat the sequence. Use the count "right, left, both; right, left, both."

   Arrange the children in scatter formation with mats.
2. Have the children repeat this sequence 6 times and then rest.
3. Have the children repeat the entire sequence twice more.

PUSH-UPS

Gather the children into an advanced information formation.

1. Describe and demonstrate regular push-ups:
   - Support your body weight on your hands and feet; your hands are at the side of your body, chest high. Your body should be straight, with feet together.
   - By straightening your arms, lift your body upward; then, in a smooth, continuous motion, lower your body back to the starting position.
   - Repeat.
   - Do 3 Push-Ups, rest briefly; do 3 more and rest; and then do 3 more and stop.

   Arrange the children in scatter formation.

2. Have the children do 3 sets of 3 Regular Push-Ups.

3. Describe and demonstrate Triceps Push-Ups:
   - Support your weight on your hands and heels, with your back facing the floor. Your body should be straight.
   - Gradually lower your body toward the ground and then return to the starting position by bending and straightening your arms. This is a difficult skill, and very little motion is possible at first.
   - Repeat.
   - Try to do 3 Triceps Push-Ups, rest briefly; do 3 more and rest; and then do 3 more and stop.

4. Have the children try to do 3 sets of 3 Triceps Push-Ups.

Line-Up

Divide children in 2 teams: one on the field and the other at bat.

1. Describe and demonstrate the game:
   - The hitter bounces a playground ball and strikes it with his or her hand and then the entire team runs around the bases in a single-file line behind the hitter. Each hitter has only one chance to strike the ball: It is either an out or a run. Foul balls are outs.
   - When the hitter hits the ball fairly, the players on the fielding team all line up behind the player who catches the ball. They pass the ball quickly overhead back to the end of the line and then back to the front of the line; they try to get the ball to the end and back to the beginning of the line before the members of the hitting team all reach home.
   - If the ball moves to the end of the line and back to the catcher before the hitting team is home, it's an out.
   - If the hitting team gets home before the ball gets to the end of the catching line and back to the catcher, it's a run.
   - When the hitting team has 3 outs, the teams switch positions.

2. Have the children play Line-Up (15 minutes).

Cool-Down With Exchange Positions

Arrange children around the outside of a parachute that is spread out on the ground. Assign the children numbers and instruct them to hold the parachute with the left hand and circle counterclockwise.

1. On your signal, the odd-numbered children release the parachute and move forward to take the place of the odd-numbered players in front of them (variations can include moving up 2 places, 3 places, and so on). Repeat with even-numbered players moving.

2. Have children move using a variety of locomotor skills, such as running, galloping, skipping, and walking.

Concluding Activities (5 minutes)

Physical Fitness Concept

Divide children into groups of 5 or 6.

1. Discuss how physical fitness is the opposite of sickness or being unhealthy: "Fitness contributes to being healthy. Fitness influences our daily lives and the length of our lives. Older people who are fit have a better chance of living longer and more active lives. Younger people who are fit say they are happier, have more energy, and are healthier than low-fit people."

2. Ask the children: "Can you give me some examples of opposites?" (Up and down, night and day, cold and hot.) "Opposites are as far apart as possible. Living in New York or living in Los

Angeles is about as far apart as you can be and still be living in the United States. That's like sickness and fitness!"

3. Ask each group to discuss and then describe a fit person and a low-fit person. Say to the children: "Remember, looks don't tell the whole story!"

From K.T. Thomas, A.M. Lee, and J.R. Thomas, 2008, *Physical education methods for elementary teachers*, 3rd ed. (Champaign, IL: Human Kinetics). Adapted, by permission, from K.T. Thomas, A.M. Lee, and J.R. Thomas, 2000, *Physical education for children: Daily lesson plans for elementary school*, 2nd ed. (Champaign, IL: Human Kinetics), 842-843.

CHAPTER 7

Psychosocial Factors in Physical Education

AMY. AGE 9

Children are naturally active and want to learn motor skills; however, participation in these activities and the motivation to do so decline during childhood, with an accelerating decline during adolescence. Competition and rewards can have a negative impact on participation, whereas appropriate motivational techniques can encourage participation.

Learner Outcomes

After studying this chapter, you should be able to do the following:

- Define intrinsic and extrinsic motivation, ego, and task orientation.
- Describe when children are ready for competition.
- Define the four attributions.
- Compare cooperation and teamwork to competition in choices from the physical activity curriculum.

Glossary Terms

motivation	social comparison	anxiety
intrinsic	ego orientation	role taking
extrinsic	task orientation	self-concept
competence	competition	self-efficacy

Many of you may recall how excited you were about physical education class as elementary students. There was probably a different atmosphere in your high school physical education class than in a present-day class. What happened? Is the shift in attitude because high school students are "too cool" to be excited about physical education or because they really dislike physical education? Participation in physical education classes and in physical activity in general clearly declines during adolescence (the middle school and high school years). The decline is greater in girls than in boys. Several factors contribute to this decline: One is the variety of new interests and time demands on adolescents. Many activities compete for their time, both in and out of school. Another explanation is that physical education is repetitive; the curriculum is the same year after

year. Siedentop (1998) suggests that physical education focuses on teaching the same beginning-level sports each year. One cure for the boredom created by that situation is to expect increasingly more from the students each year. Alternatively, many teachers opt to teach new beginning-level activities. Another explanation for the decline in physical activity among adolescents could be that students are turned off to physical activity because their needs are not being met.

You need to understand the psychological and sociological aspects of physical education for children so that

- you can encourage physically active lifestyles,
- the children are motivated, and
- they learn cooperation and teamwork.

This chapter presents information based on physical education, physical activity, and research on youth sport. Many children (more than 20 million at any time of the year) participate in out-of-school sport programs (Ewing and Seefeldt 2002). Those experiences influence how children feel about physical activity and thereby influence physical education. Some of what researchers have learned by studying youth sport applies to physical education. A relatively new area of information is exercise psychology, which provides information about adherence and affect related to physical activity.

One of the challenges of physical education is that performance is public. Unlike the classroom, where many performances are private, a mistake or poor performance in physical education is visible to all. Therefore, even though the psychological factors are the same in the classroom and the gym for young children, the situation is different.

The Four Guiding Principles

Now we explore in more detail the four guiding principles outlined on page 35 in regard to psychosocial factors. Keep in mind as you study this chapter that each of the principles is important to understanding how children develop and what this means for physical education.

Principle 1. Children Are Not Miniature Adults

During elementary school the motivation to learn and master skills is driven by two questions: Am I getting better? Am I normal? Children who answer these questions positively are likely to continue performing and learning (Scanlan 1995). To answer these questions, children must test themselves. One way is to compare a personal performance to that of others; another is to ask questions. Children who are successful in their comparisons (tests) tend to select challenging future tests. Children who are consistently unsuccessful either avoid testing in the future or select tests that are not challenging.

Learning is greatest when the task is challenging but attainable, so it is important to ensure that children are successful in answering the questions. Children must understand the role of practice in success. Children are in control of

effort and therefore practice. You usually select the task and task difficulty in physical education. Because children vary in skill and experience, you individualize the challenge so that it is appropriate for each child. Furthermore, you help children understand what is "normal" and how to track learning (improvement).

Principle 2. Boys and Girls Are More Alike Than Different

Three reasons children voluntarily participate in physical activity are having fun, being with friends, and learning new skills (Weiss 2000). These reasons are the same for boys and girls. However, the emphasis is different. Boys are most motivated to be with their friends; girls are seeking an activity they like, so they focus more on learning new skills (Robertson-Wilson, Baker, Derbinshyre, and Côté 2003; Weiss 2000). The end result is the same. Experiences that meet these needs encourage future participation.

Physical education teachers often group children for practice by saying "everyone find a partner"; after some practice, this is followed up with "now find a new partner." This allows the children to work closely with friends during the learning experience.

Principle 3. Good Things Are Earned

Most children want to be successful and do what is "right"; that is, they have the desire. The problem is that achieving that desire takes "will." In terms of skill, it means practice. Just wanting to be successful or ethical is not enough (Bredemeier 2005). A critical question is how children develop the will to support achievement of their desire to succeed.

Attribution describes the factor by which the child explains a performance. Teachers and coaches can influence attribution (Horn 1987). The goal is to attribute outcomes to effort—practice and hard work. This is critical because the other three attributions (e.g., luck, task difficulty, and ability) are unstable or out of the child's control. The child has no control over luck, it is difficult to change ability, and adults often determine the task difficulty. The child's perception of skill influences attribution such that children who view themselves as more skilled attribute to effort and ability (Weiss and Horn 1990).

Goal setting can bring task difficulty under the child's control and address issues of ability. Task difficulty and a child's ability should be closely matched so that the chances for success are about 50–50. Achievement-goal approaches to motivation identify two classes of goals: task and ego. Ego goals focus on winning, trophies, and recognition; task goals focus on mastery (Roberts 1992). Younger children tend to adopt a mastery or task approach; older children may not. Ego-orientated goals are associated with attrition and should be avoided. Because both you and the coaches can influence children's thinking, the focus should be on task-oriented goals (Weiss and Horn 1990).

Physical education classes are usually organized so that all children are challenged. During the same lesson, you may observe several "levels" of a task; as a result, it is challenging to each child but still attainable. One mini-game might have no defense, another might have defensive players who cannot move their feet (but can use their arms), and another mini-game with a full defense. The game and goals are the same, but the level is modified so that all of the children are challenged and can be successful.

Principle 4. No Body Is Perfect

Competition is neither good nor bad; however, consistently losing can be negative. Children on a consistently losing team predicted a loss on the next game, even after a win (Smith, Smoll, and Curtis 1978). Children who were on winning teams predicted a win on the next game, even after a loss. Because no one is perfect, play, practice, and competition should be organized so that no one is a consistent loser. The negative consequences of competition include anxiety, stress, consistent failure, and decreased intrinsic motivation (Passer and Wilson 2002). Unfortunately, physical activity is important and the performances are public in physical education, so stress and anxiety are present in physical education. Although most of the research has been conducted in sport settings, the results apply to physical education settings.

Physical education classes de-emphasize competition, so the goals are task-oriented and not focused on winning. Often, at the end of a game, children ask, "Who won?" A skilled teacher is likely to answer: "Does it matter? Did you have fun? Did you learn?"

In the following sections, we provide greater detail on many aspects of psychological factors

Setting goals is one way to develop upper body strength as part of fitness.

in physical activity. Depending on your level of interest and need, these sections may add considerably to your knowledge base.

Motivation

The goal of childhood is independence, which is achieved as children develop competence in many domains, including academics and social and physical areas. Infants, children, and adolescents are naturally driven to be independent. But adults, including teachers and parents, can facilitate or undermine this achievement of independence. **Motivation** is the reason behind making choices. Motivation can be **intrinsic** (because the child wants to), **extrinsic** (because something external influences the child), or a combination of intrinsic and extrinsic factors. Infants are motivated to develop skills in order to conquer their environment as part of a quest for independence. Children continue to learn new skills as a natural and normal

162

Table 7.1 Stages of Achievement Motivation

Stage	Age	Description	Outcome if successful	Outcome if unsuccessful
1. Autonomous	Preschool	Exploratory behaviors and learning to cope with the environment, both self-motivated (autonomous)	Master environment, seek future tests of competence	Dependence
2. Social comparison	Primary grades	Learning about one's self by answering "Am I normal?" and "Am I improving?" Peer pressure and a quest for normalcy begin	Information about self, seeks challenging tests of competence	Dependence Bully syndrome Follows peers for most decisions
3. Mature	Upper grades	Uses correct motivation based on the situation—autonomous when peer pressure is negative and social comparison when appropriate	Independence	Dependence

part of development. Achievement motivation is the reason children (or infants) decide to learn a skill. Three stages of achievement motivation have been defined (table 7.1; Scanlan 1995). **Competence** is the skill or capability to do a task. During childhood, however, the focus of learning motor skills shifts from phylogenetic (inherent) to ontogenetic (culturally transmitted). Chapter 4, Motor Performance During Childhood, explains these in detail. Motivation and competence lead to independence.

As skills are mastered, children ask two questions:

1. Am I normal?
2. Am I improving?

Positive answers to these questions move children toward independence. To answer these questions, children compare themselves to others; this is called **social comparison**. Children are intrinsically motivated to master new skills, and they use social comparison to evaluate themselves. You can help children make appropriate comparisons and track improvement. For example, children should compare themselves to other children who are similar in age and experience or to their own previous performance. Children tend to use outcome information for evaluation (e.g., hitting the target or winning the race). However, as discussed in chapter 4, Motor Performance During Childhood, progress is often slower in outcome than in process. Therefore, you can help children recognize improvements

in the mechanics and efficiency of movements or decisions rather than focus on the end product. Using comparison in this way is both informative and normative.

When children answer yes to both questions (i.e., "I am normal" and "I am improving"), intrinsic motivation to try new tasks increases. When children answer no, the outcomes vary, but generally those children do not move to stage 3 of table 7.1. Children who are unsuccessful with tests of competence—who perceive themselves as failing to improve or failing to be normal—often select easy tasks for success, or they avoid any test. You may observe this during practice, as children practice tasks that are too easy or avoid practice altogether. Another outcome is the bully syndrome, in which children select opponents who are younger, smaller, or less skilled. The bully syndrome is an attempt to show competence or skill by selecting a "sure thing" as a task.

Although social comparison is normal, it does not imply that competition is necessary for comparison to occur; the purpose is informative and normative. Furthermore, adults do not need to emphasize comparison to others. You play a critical role in helping children see themselves as normal and improving; thus, you help children maintain or increase their intrinsic motivation (Weiss 1993, 2000). Part of teaching is helping children track improvement. When you describe the relationship between practice and achievement, the normative function is being served. That is, most people have to work hard and practice to master this skill, so the child thinks, *I am normal because I will have to practice to learn this skill; I can't do it now, but, after I practice, I will be able to.*

Related to the notion of intrinsic and extrinsic motivation are task and ego orientations of performers. A person can choose to do a task because it brings status and therefore feeds the ego—this is an **ego orientation**. Alternatively, a person can do a task because improving or mastering the task brings personal satisfaction, which is called **task orientation**. In youth sports, children with ego orientations tend to drop out, whereas children with task orientations persist. You may observe similar patterns in exercise, especially in physical education class. In other words, you should encourage children to participate because improving skill and mastering tasks make them feel good about themselves. The focus should be on how they feel about themselves rather than how others feel about them.

Attribution

For any test of competence, there are four possible explanations for the outcome, regardless of success or failure. These attributions have two dimensions: locus of control (internal or external) and level of stability (stable or unstable), as shown in table 7.2. From previous chapters, you can guess that the preferred attribution is effort, because effort is related to practice. Furthermore, effort is under a child's control and is variable. So the objective is to have a child give maximum effort all of the time.

Table 7.2 Locus of Control

	Internal	External
Stable	Ability	Task difficulty
Unstable	Effort	Luck

Task difficulty is your responsibility. Chapter 4, Motor Performance During Childhood, listed the various methods for altering a task. You should make tasks challenging but doable: children should have a 50–50 chance of success

when they give maximum effort. Tasks that are too easy can be boring and do not help them master new skills. Tasks that are too difficult do not help them learn and may be frustrating. Ability is often viewed as talent. Talent, as discussed in chapter 5, Cognition, Learning, and Practice, is not a powerful predictor of performance in many physical activities. However, talent is often presented as a major factor (Thomas, Gallagher, and Thomas 2000). If talent is the most important factor in performance, practice and instruction become unimportant. The ability to do a task changes slowly with practice, which is why it is viewed as stable. In other words, ability does not change from moment to moment. Most children are more alike in ability than they are different; however, children do have widely varied experience and interests. You should balance ability and task difficulty so that children feel challenged, improve, and find satisfaction in achievement.

Luck is often used as an explanation for outcomes. For example, children on losing teams say luck explains a win. Luck is both external and unstable and therefore a poor choice. The assumption is that children learn attributions, and the most appropriate attribution is effort.

Goals

One way to help children track improvement is to establish goals and to relate performance to those goals. Seeing progress and improvement is motivating. Goals should be specific and challenging. Vague or low-level goals, such as "do your best," produce the poorest performance. Goals can be for a group of children (e.g., a class) or for an individual child. Goals can focus on skill, behavior, or knowledge.

Current best practices in education focus on standards and benchmarks, a formal set of goals discussed in chapter 15, Growing as a Teacher. Referring to benchmarks, standards, and goals helps children understand what is expected so that they can track progress and take responsibility for learning. Whether they are informal goals for a task or a formal system of evaluation, goals are an important part of a quality physical education program. Consider goals during planning and make them evident during practice. They are the foundation for feedback and evaluation.

Concepts Into Practice

Ms. Abernethy knows the value of goal setting; therefore, she sets goals for herself and her students and requires them to set goals for themselves. The goal she sets for herself is to recognize verbally five students in each class each day who are making progress toward the lesson's goal. She does this by making a note at the end of class next to the names of those she has recognized. Her goal for her students is a benchmark for her program. That benchmark is for 75 percent of the students to have 30 minutes of moderate-to-vigorous activity at least 5 days per week reported in their journals. When she reads the journals, she can determine if this goal has been met. She plans on reporting this to the students using a chart. Each week, she adds a bar to the chart showing what percentage of the students met the goal. In Ms. Abernethy's class, each student is required to create personal goals for physical activity. The following two samples represent goals for a less active and a more active student, respectively: "I will go for a 30-minute walk after school on Monday, Wednesday, and Friday of next week." "I will practice running the mile every day next week."

Competition

The earliest **competition** is between the infant and the environment. During the primary grades, this evolves into social comparison. Competition can be institutionalized; that is, it can take the form of tournaments, with rules and formal structure, or it can be inherent, such as when children compare themselves with other children. Competition is neither good nor bad (Passer and Wilson 2002). However, competition—especially highly structured competition—can create negative consequences, including stress and anxiety, consistent failure, awards that undermine intrinsic motivation, and failure to meet basic goals of sport and physical activity.

Stress and anxiety increase as the importance of a performance increases and as the performance becomes public. Physical activity is important in contemporary American culture, and performance in physical education is public because other classmates and teachers observe it (Kimiecik, Horn, and Shurin 1996; Smith, Smoll, and Curtis

1978). Therefore, stress and anxiety are inherent in physical education as well as sport. **Anxiety** is one extreme of arousal—the negative extreme. At the opposite end of the anxiety continuum is a state as relaxed as sleep. In the middle is enough arousal to produce effort without anxiety. Performers experience stress when they perceive an imbalance between ability and task difficulty. Stress is a result of anxiety; sometimes the heart rate is elevated, breathing may be affected, sweating can occur, or the face may flush. Stress may negatively affect performance. and it has emotional consequences beyond the performance. For example, general anxiety may increase. To keep stress and anxiety under control, you can use three strategies:

1. Keep the importance of a performance in perspective; class participation should not be elevated to a major life event.

2. Reduce the public display as much as possible; for example, have several children participate at once or have the potential observers do something other than observe.

3. Reduce competition and focus on skill learning, short-term goals, and cooperation rather than on winning.

In the best-case scenario, half of the participants in competition lose. For example, in team sports, one team (half) wins and the other (half) loses. In individual sports, such as the 100-meter dash in track, many lose and only one wins. Unfortunately, often the same individuals are consistent losers; that is, one team never wins. When teams or individuals have similar records, competition has fewer negative consequences. In fact, the highest situation for motivation is when there is an equal chance to win or lose. Consider playing golf: If your opponent is Tiger Woods, you probably are not motivated to play your best because you know he is so much more skilled at the sport. Conversely, playing your elderly aunt who has never played golf also fails to demand a high level of motivation or to produce your best performance. Consistent losing also affects future performance. Children who are on losing teams predict future losses, even immediately after a win. Children who are on winning teams predict winning, even after a loss. You can see how children could interpret losing as failing to be normal and failing to improve. You can eliminate these problems by making sure that children have a balance of outcomes. For example, rotate children among teams so that, after each game, one-third to one-half of the players move to a different team, or ensure that teams have a balanced skill pool as they are chosen. You might want to omit keeping score or having teams compete during physical education. Another technique used by physical education specialists is to total the scores for both teams in one class and compare that to the total for both teams in a different class. You can compare the total score of the class (both teams) one day to the total score the next day. The key is to keep competition—and the potential negative consequences of competition—under control.

Awards and rewards are part of many competitions and can be contingent on performance—this means the award is earned. Sometimes awards are given to all participants; these are not based on performance. Finally, awards can be unexpected; that is, the award is given, but the recipient did not know prior to the performance about the award. Awards and rewards can shift the motivation from intrinsic (and task oriented) to extrinsic (and ego oriented). Generally, when children want to do something, awards are not necessary. Furthermore, awards can undermine intrinsic motivation, which is undesirable. For young children (children aged 7 and younger), awards

are perceived as fun and tend not to undermine intrinsic motivation. However, for children older than 7, consider the use of rewards and awards carefully. Use the following guidelines:

- Do not give awards to everyone for participating.
- Give contingent awards sparingly or not at all.
- Use rewards (or bribes) to get children to do something they do not want to do.

Competition—especially team sport competition—should teach several valuable skills to participants. Sportsmanship, leadership, and learning skills are what children and adults want sport to teach, but emphasis on competition often decreases the opportunities to learn them. Two major factors that children cite as reasons for participating are being with friends and having fun. When competition overshadows these factors, children are likely to stop enjoying participation. In competitions run by adults, all decisions are made by the adults; as a result, children cannot learn leadership. When competition is high, adults often make decisions that focus on winning rather than on other goals of sport participation. Adults often demonstrate poor sportsmanship, and highly competitive situations

When children participate in organized sports, it is important to emphasize skill learning and enjoyment, not winning.

set the stage for similar behaviors by children. For example, playing the best players most or all of the time means other players do not have a chance to practice skills. Competition often means that the players who need the most practice—the poorest players—get the least practice! In addition, it is not fun to sit on the bench. Children report a preference for playing on a losing team to sitting on the bench of a winning team. Because the three most frequently given reasons for participation are being with friends, having fun, and learning skills (Weiss 2000), you need to organize competitive activities that allow children to do all three. This often means reducing the emphasis on winning and competition. Sport offers opportunities for children to practice making moral decisions. Practicing leadership, cooperation, and decision making are important aspects of sport and physical education.

The decision whether or not to cheat is another "teachable moment." If children are allowed to cheat as long as they don't get caught, the message is that cheating is okay. Children receive mixed messages from after-school experiences, professional sports, and parents. You are important to the children, which means that you can influence what they think and do. On issues related to morality (e.g., cheating, teasing), saying nothing is usually interpreted by children as agreement, so be sure to speak up!

A Teachable Moment

The catcher in a game of scooter pinball was holding the ball but not tagging out the runner coming toward home. The catcher reached toward the runner and then pulled the ball back as the runner hesitated between third base and home. Meanwhile, another runner reached third base, so the first runner had to go to home; however, the catcher had not yet tagged the runner during numerous opportunities. The teacher blew the whistle, asking, "Does anyone know why I stopped the game?" After a few seconds of consideration, a student ventured the following response: "Because the catcher was teasing the runner." The teacher said, "Okay, but why does that matter?" Another student says, "It is mean." The teacher responded, "Okay; anything else?" After a pause, two students responded, "If the catcher dropped the ball, it would let the runner score," and "The catcher is letting the team down." The teacher said to the catcher, "Okay, now you know what to do. We are ready to continue to play. How do you think we should continue?"

Cooperation

American society values cooperation. "Plays well with others" has meaning because of the value of the cooperation implied in the statement. Children learn to be cooperative, so it is important to provide opportunities to practice cooperative behaviors. Expecting young children (under 12 years) to consider others first is asking for behavior that is beyond their developmental capacity. Teaching them to think of others is different. Kohlberg (1971) described three stages of moral reasoning: In Stage 1, children make decisions based on rewards and punishment—for example, "Cheating is wrong because I was punished for cheating." Stage 2 is characterized by making decisions based on the expectations of significant others—in other words, "Cheating is wrong because my parents would be disappointed if I cheated." Finally, Stage 3 finds children making an internalized decision based on right and wrong—"It is not fair to everyone else if I cheat."

Similarly, children do not master role taking, or putting themselves in someone else's place, until about 12 years of age (Passer and Wilson 2002). Cooperation without guidance is very difficult for children until they understand how someone else feels and how someone else can contribute. Part of development is learning to see the value of others and the contribution they can make and becoming sensitive to their feelings. Without guidance, cooperative activities often become variations on competition. Children work together not for the joy of sharing, but because it is the only way to win.

Cooperation implies that everyone is working together. Two ideas related to cooperation are leadership and cohesion, which help foster cooperation. First, most groups have a leader. Everyone in the group does not always have to do what the leader says. A leader must gain consensus from and provide guidance to the group. Second, to be cohesive, groups need to learn to work as one; the group members must work together. This happens best if each member makes a contribution to the mission of the group. Several things can facilitate cooperation: First, young children should practice cooperation with small groups, perhaps only two children. The pairs should have specific problems to solve and should contribute equally to the solution. For all ages, it is helpful to select a leader with specific duties (e.g., poll the group for opinions about possible solutions). Each member of the group should have a job that contributes to the mission. With practice, more responsibility should be shifted to the children themselves for organizing the group activities. Group leadership can be changed frequently so that all of the children are leaders at some time. Competition should not always be the motivating factor for cooperation. Each day, every activity can be a venue for learning about cooperation. Cooperation is easier among those who respect one another. Children are likely to follow your lead; thus, you must encourage all of the children, respect their contributions to the learning environment, and provide them with opportunities to practice cooperation.

One way to encourage cooperation is to end class with the children in a circle. Each child must say something nice or something that she or he likes about the person on the right. Children are cued to look for the good in everyone. A variation is to have children say what they liked best in class.

Self-Concept and Self-Efficacy

Self-concept is the way people view themselves. It is an overall feeling based on specific subcomponents, such as how they feel about physical activity and sport or social settings. The quality of children's experiences influences how children view themselves, which is translated to self-concept. Self-concept is relatively stable; that is, after about 8 years of age, children have a view of themselves across a variety of settings that is translated into an overall feeling. If children receive positive reinforcement from you, their parents, and their peers about performances in physical activity and sport (and other areas), their self-concept is positive. The critical element is a child's competence—or skill (Weiss 2000). Your goal is simple: Increase the child's skill because this positively influences self-concept. Three suggestions are as follows:

1. Explain success in movement and how errors and mistakes should be used to adjust movements for future success.

2. Discuss how other children should be treated when they make mistakes so that errors are viewed as a normal part of learning and are not threatening.

3. Be positive!

Self-efficacy is the confidence people have in accomplishing a specific task. For example, are you 25, 50, 75, or 100 percent confident that you can lift a 100-pound (45.3 kg) box? What about a 50-pound (21.6 kg) box? Self-efficacy is situational, whereas self-confidence is more general and stable. Self-efficacy contributes to self-

Physical education activities provide an important place for children to practice cooperation.

concept (Weiss 2000). Confidence is related to both. Confidence is critical to continued patterns of physical activity. Adults who are active report having high self-confidence and competence regarding physical activity. Their self-concept about sport and physical activity is positive, and they have high self-efficacy when asked about participating in and adhering to physical activity and exercise programs. This suggests the importance of developing confidence, high self-efficacy, and movement competence (skill) during childhood.

Exercise Adherence and Affect

Being physically active is a one- or two-stage process. If you are active, the goal is to maintain an active lifestyle. If you are not active, however, the first step is to initiate an activity program; the second step is to maintain the program. Children are naturally active, so it is a matter of maintaining that activity. Patterns suggest that activity drops between 9 and 13 years of age, especially for girls (Welk 1999). The two-stage model applies to many adolescents. Logic suggests that it would be easier to maintain activity by preventing the decline than to initiate and maintain activity in a sedentary population. So one goal for elementary physical education is to encourage lifelong physical activity.

Physical activity, even as little activity as going for a walk, produces positive changes. In other words, activity can produce feelings of happiness (Ekkekakis, Hall, VanLanduyt, and Petruzzello 2000). Physical activity reduces depression and its symptoms. Chemicals released during exercise, which promote a sense of well-being, cause some of these changes. Furthermore, the psychological benefits of feeling in control, a sense of accomplishment, and social support are likely contributors to the improvement in affect.

A sedentary person may become depressed and avoid more activity, therefore becoming more depressed and creating a cycle. Often, sedentary people gain weight and fat. Obesity has an additive effect: being inactive and overweight leads to more depression, which leads to less activity, and so forth. Physical activity has immediate and long-term benefits for mental health.

The positive feelings associated with an active lifestyle reinforce the activity. Feeling good and being happy are translated into exercise adherence. Unfortunately, in adults, approximately half of those initiating an activity program drop out within 6 months of starting the program (Dishman 1994). Dropping out can bring feelings of inadequacy and then depression. Clearly, keeping children active is easier than getting adults to initiate and maintain activity programs.

Summary

Children are naturally motivated to be active and to learn skills. They participate because they want to be with friends, have fun, and learn skills. Focusing on the enjoyment of accomplishment and effort encourages lifelong participation and increases motivation. You and the children both need to use goals to monitor progress, focusing on task mastery while minimizing competition. Physical activity brings psychological as well as physiological benefits—another reason to encourage active lifestyles. Sport and physical education offer the opportunity to develop important social skills, such as cooperation and leadership. These skills are facilitated through cooperative activities.

Mastery Learning Activities

1. Select a sport. Identify the major skills in the sport. Using those skills and equipment, develop a cooperative activity for children in grade 5.

2. Make a list of 20 statements that reinforce effort.

3. Write a story that portrays to children the concept of doing something because it makes you feel good about what you are doing rather than because someone else wants you to do it.

4. Find one of the articles in the reference list, read it, and write a one-page summary.

References

Bredemeier, B.L. 2005. *Excellence made good: Exploring moral and civic character*. McCloy Lecture presented at the Annual Meeting of the American Alliance of

Health, Physical Education, Recreation and Dance, Chicago, IL, April 14.

Dishman, R.K. 1994. *Advances in exercise adherence.* Champaign, IL: Human Kinetics.

Ekkekakis, P., E.E. Hall, L.M. VanLanduyt, and S.J. Petruzzello. 2000. Walking in (affective) circles: Can short walks enhance affect? *Journal of Behavioral Medicine* 23(3): 245-275.

Ewing, M.E., and V. Seefeldt. 2002. Patterns of participation in American agency-sponsored youth sport. In *Children and youth in sport: A biopsychosocial perspective,* edited by F.L. Smoll and R.E. Smith, 39-60. Dubuque, IA: Kendall/Hunt.

Horn, T.S. 1987. The influence of teacher-coach behavior on the psychological development of children. In *Advances in pediatric sport science: Vol. 2. Behavioral issues,* edited by D. Gould and M.R. Weiss, 121-142. Champaign, IL: Human Kinetics.

Kimiecik, J.C., T.S. Horn, and C.S. Shurin. 1996. Relationships among children's beliefs, perceptions of their parent's beliefs and their moderate-to-vigorous physical activity. *Research Quarterly for Exercise and Sport* 67: 324-336.

Kohlberg, L. 1971. Stages of moral development as a basis for moral education. In *Moral education: Interdisciplinary approaches,* edited by C.M. Beck, B.S. Crittenden, and E.V. Sullivan, 23-92. Toronto: University of Toronto Press.

Passer, M.W., and B.J. Wilson. 2002. At what age are children ready to compete? In *Children and youth in sport: A biopsychosocial perspective,* edited by F.L. Smoll and R.E. Smith, 83-103. Dubuque, IA: Kendall/Hunt.

Roberts, G.C. 1992. Motivation in sport and exercise: Conceptual constraints and convergence. In *Motivation in sport and exercise,* edited by G.C. Roberts, 3-29. Champaign, IL: Human Kinetics.

Robertson-Wilson, J., E. Baker, E. Derbinshyre, and J. Côté. 2003. Childhood sports involvement in active and inactive female adults. *AVANTE* 9: 1-8.

Scanlan, T.K. 1995. Social evaluation and the competitive process: A developmental perspective. In *Children and youth in sports: A biopsychosocial perspective,* edited by F.L. Smoll and R.E. Smith, 298-308. Dubuque, IA: Brown & Benchmark.

Siedentop, D. 1998. *In search of effective teaching: What we have learned from studying teachers and students.* McCloy Lecture presented at the Annual Meeting of the American Alliance for Health, Physical Education, Recreation and Dance, Portland, OR, April 7.

Smith, R.E., F.L. Smoll, and B. Curtis. 1978. Coaching behaviors in Little League baseball. In *Psychological perspectives in youth sport,* edited by F.L. Smoll and R.E. Smith, 173-201. Washington, DC: Hemisphere.

Thomas, K.T., J.D. Gallagher, and J.R. Thomas. 2000. Motor development and skill acquisition during childhood and adolescence. In *Handbook of sport psychology,* 2nd ed., edited by R.N. Singer, H.A. Hausenblas, and C. Janelle, 20-52. New York: John Wiley.

Weiss, M.R. 1993. Children's participation in physical activity: Are we having fun yet? *Pediatric Exercise Science* 5: 205-209.

Weiss, M.R. 2000. Motivating kids in physical activity. *President's Council on Physical Fitness and Sports Research Digest* 3(11): 1-8. Washington, DC: President's Council on Physical Fitness.

Weiss, M.R., and T.L. Horn. 1990. The relation between children's accuracy estimates of their physical competence and achievement-related characteristics. *Research Quarterly for Exercise and Sport* 61: 250-258.

Welk, G. 1999. The Physical Activity Promotion Model: A conceptual model to advance the promotion of physical activity in the population. *Quest* 51: 5-23.

Lesson Plans

The lesson plans at the end of this chapter focus on cooperation and minimizing competition. The first lesson requires that young children work together in a continuous relay with no winner. The second lesson focuses on developing passing and catching skills and teamwork but has an element of competition. Generally, the children do not keep score, so the emphasis on competition is very low. The game can be adapted to a variety of age groups by increasing the number of balls, calling the "fouls" more closely, or being more relaxed. Sharon's Shoot Around provides the most practice for the least skilled children. In order for a team to be successful, the team must work together for success. Raging River requires children to cooperate and to use equipment in a unique way to solve a problem.

Most games and activities can be modified to reduce competition. Children should never be eliminated from games; they should be rewarded for teamwork, cooperation, and skill. Other cooperative activities include rhythmic activities, in which partners or groups work together in partner gymnastics stunts (lessons 7.3, 7.6, and 12.1).

Lesson 7.1

Laundry Basket Express

Student Objectives 3 5

- Work together.
- Continue the activity with little adult intervention.
- Remain active for the entire time.

Equipment and Materials

- 1 laundry basket or box per pair of children
- Many balls or beanbags
- 4 cones
- 1 towel or similar size cloth for every 2 to 4 children

Warm-Up Activities (5 minutes)

Len's Ball Mix-Up

Arrange the children on a line in the middle of the gym. Scatter balls and beanbags around the gym on the floor. Identify 2 marked areas on the floor (mark with cones or use the basketball key) for the "zone." Tell the children: "Oh, dear, I made a mistake and it is a mess! When I say go, pick up all of the balls and beanbags and place them in the zone. Pick up only one at a time. Once you place that one in the zone, get another one. Here is the zone." (Show them one of the areas you are using as the zones; use the other area later.) "Now, please, quickly and carefully put all of the balls into the zone!" Give the signal to start. When all or nearly all of the balls are in the zone, stop the activity and reassemble the children on the line. Now overact and say, "Did I say I wanted you to put those in that area? Oh my, I really wanted them at the other end." (Now point to the other zone.) "Can you do that? Ready?" Give your signal to start. This sequence can be repeated, with many mentions of "mistakes" and "oh, dear."

Skill-Development Activities (20 minutes)

Laundry Basket Express

Arrange the children in pairs; each pair has a laundry basket. Place the 4 cones in each corner of a large rectangular area.

The object of the activity is to move the balls or beanbags using the basket from one cone to the next, place the balls in a pile, and then return to the original place with the basket to gather the "new" balls, which were delivered by other children. More than one pair of children can be stationed at a cone; just stagger their starts. The children should move the balls continuously and as quickly as possible.

Concluding Activities (5 minutes)

Arrange children in groups of 2 or 4. Give each group a towel (or cloth rectangle) and a beanbag. Each child should grasp a corner of the towel. The object is for the groups to try to move the beanbag by tossing it into the air with the towel. Give the following challenges:

- Toss and catch.
- Toss it high.
- Toss it away from you.
- Think of other ways to move the beanbag.

From K.T. Thomas, A.M. Lee, and J.R. Thomas, 2008, *Physical education methods for elementary teachers*, 3rd ed. (Champaign, IL: Human Kinetics).

Lesson 7.2

Len's Scooter Ball

Student Objectives 1 5

- Work cooperatively with all teammates.
- Pass (throw) and catch accurately.
- Follow the rules.

Equipment and Materials

- 1 scooter for each child (all but 4 to 6 children)
- 1 to 3 foam balls (8.5 inches [21.5 cm])
- 8 cones
- 4 mats (4 by 6 to 8 feet [1.2 by 1.8 to 2.4 m])

Skill-Development Activities (25 to 30 minutes)

Len's Scooter Ball

Arrange 1 cone in each corner of a rectangle (the corners of a basketball court work well). Place 4 more cones along the longest two sides to divide the area into 3 approximately equal sections. Place one mat on the floor and one against the wall (or standing like a screen) at the middle of both short ends of the court.

Divide the class into 2 teams, divide each team into 3 groups. One group from each team plays in each of the 3 sections of the court marked by the cones. Each team defends one of the two "goals," which are the mats. In order to score points, the children must throw the ball so that it hits the standing or leaning mat. Two or three players on a team are goalies. Goalies stand on the mat that is on the floor and try to stop the ball from hitting the other mat. All players except goalies are on scooters. The game is played in 6 or more units of time. At the end of a unit (generally 3 minutes), the players in each section rotate to the adjacent section. New goalies are selected, and the former goalies use their scooters (at the opposite end of the court) so that goalies rotate with their group. Have all of the children play goalie each time that the game is played. To begin the game, bounce the ball in the middle section. The rules are as follows:

- Players must pass (throw the ball) to teammates.
- Players pass the ball from adjacent areas; they may not throw the ball over an area to the opposite end of the court.
- Players may not move scooters while they are holding a ball.
- Only the players in the area closest to the goal can score.
- If a player with the ball falls off the scooter, the ball goes to the other team.
- A player can only hold the ball for 3 seconds before passing it.

These rules are followed more strictly with older or more experienced children. Put additional balls in play as the children demonstrate skill and cooperation.

From K.T. Thomas, A.M. Lee, and J.R. Thomas, 2008, *Physical education methods for elementary teachers*, 3rd ed. (Champaign, IL: Human Kinetics).

Lesson 7.3

Partner Stunts

Student Objectives 1 2 5

- Work cooperatively with a partner.
- Understand the terms "base," "top," and "balance."
- Demonstrate two partner stunts and attempt other partner stunts.

Equipment and Materials

- 1 or more mats (4 by 8 feet [1.2 by 2.4 m]) per group
- Background music (optional)

Safety Tips

- Use spotting on difficult stunts.
- Children should be as equal in size as possible when they are working in pairs.

Warm-Up Activities (5 minutes)

Warm-Up Routine for Grades 2 and 3

Arrange the children in a line along one side of the mat.

1. Teach all parts of the warm-up as a routine.
2. Have the children perform the following sequence of steps:
   - Do a Head Circle right and then left.
   - Do Shoulder Circles forward (3 times) and backward (3 times).
   - Stretch torso (side, back, side, front); repeat 3 times.
   - Stretch hamstrings (squat to straighten); repeat 5 times.
   - Rotate ankles (3 times inward, 3 times outward).
   - Arch the back (5 times).
   - Do Crunches (20 times).
   - Do Push-Ups (10 times).
   Move the children into a circle formation.
   - Do Skips (24 clockwise, 24 counterclockwise).
   - Do Vertical Jumps (10 times).
   - Run continuously for 1 minute around the circle.

Skill-Development Activities (20 minutes)

Wring the Dishrag

Match pairs of children according to size.

1. Describe and have two children demonstrate the stunt:
    - Stand facing each other, with hands joined.
    - Lift arms (one partner's left, the other's right), turn toward and under the lifted arms, and continue turning until you are facing each other again.
2. Have the children practice Wring the Dishrag.

Partner Get-Up

Have partners sit facing each other.

1. Describe and have two children demonstrate the stunt:
    - Join hands and touch toes.
    - Pull on each other's hands while pushing feet against the other's until standing.
    - Keep feet about shoulder-width apart.
2. Have the children practice Partner Get-Up.

Partner Hopping

Have partners stand facing each other, about as far apart as one leg length.

1. Describe and have two children demonstrate the stunt: "Hold each other's right (or left) leg and then hop in the same direction using only two of the four legs you and your partner have."
2. Have the children practice Partner Hopping.

Human Top

Have partners stand facing each other, with hands joined and toes touching.

1. Describe and have two children demonstrate the stunt:
    - Lean backward until your arms and legs are straight and your two bodies form a V.
    - Then turn clockwise, keeping your toes together and your arms straight.
2. Have the children practice Human Top.

Back-to-Back Get-Up

Have partners sit back to back.

1. Describe and have two children demonstrate the stunt:
    - Lock your elbows and bend your legs so that your heels are close to your seat.
    - Push with your legs to stand while your backs are still touching.
2. Have the children practice Back-to-Back Get-Up.

Lesson 7.3 (continued)

Quad Leg Lift

Arrange partners on the mats.

1. Describe and have two children demonstrate the stunt:
   - Lie on your backs, with your heads touching, and extend your feet in opposite directions. Put your hands out to the side.
   - Bend your knees so that your feet are on the floor.
   - Each of you lifts up one leg at the same time until your toes touch in the air. Then lift your other leg until all four legs touch.
   - Keep your legs up for a count of 5, and then go back to the starting position.
2. Have the children practice the Quad Leg Lift.

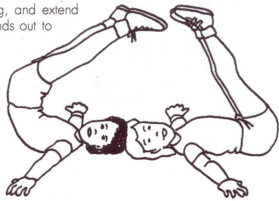

Wheelbarrow

Continue with pairs of children on the mats.

1. Describe and have two children demonstrate the stunt:
   - One partner lies on his or her tummy; the arms are bent, supporting the body near the chest. The other partner stands near the feet of the partner on the floor and squats down (bending knees and keeping back straight).
   - The standing partner lifts the feet of his or her partner off the ground. The standing partner lifts with the legs while keeping the back straight.
   - Then both partners walk forward; one uses hands to walk, and the other uses feet.
2. Have the children practice the Wheelbarrow.

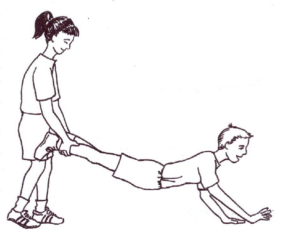

Two-Person Pyramid

Continue with pairs of children on the mats.

1. Describe and have two children demonstrate the stunt:
   - One partner, called the "base," begins on all fours (with feet and hands shoulder-width apart).
   - The other partner, called the "top," places both feet on the base's hips below the base's waist and stands. Both partners face the same direction.
   - Partners take turns being the base and the top.
2. Have the children practice the Two-Person Pyramid.

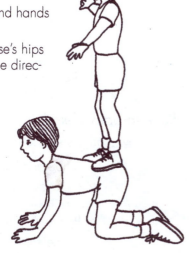

Individual Front Fall

Arrange 4 to 6 children in 2 to 3 pairs on a mat.

1. Describe and have a child demonstrate the stunt:

   ○ Stand with your arms at your sides and feet together.

   ○ Lean forward and fall to the mat. At the last possible second, move your arms forward to catch your body weight and break the fall.

   ○ As your hands touch the mat, bend your arms at the elbows gradually to absorb the force as your body continues to fall to the mat.

   ○ Finish in a facedown position on the mat.

2. Have the children practice the Individual Front Fall. Encourage all of the children to try it.

Concluding Activities (5 minutes)

Wave

Have the children stand on one side of the mat, facing the width of the mat.

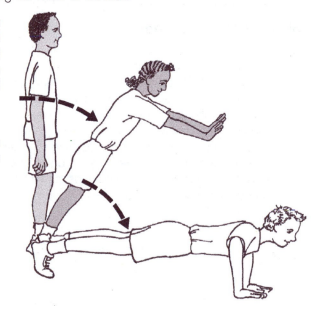

1. Describe and have one group demonstrate the stunt: "Line up shoulder to shoulder and do the front fall, one after the other. The first child begins the fall, and, before he or she hits the mat, the next child begins the fall, and so forth."

2. Have the children practice the Wave.

3. Repeat with all of the children and mats in one long line, beginning at one end of the mats and ending at the opposite end.

From K.T. Thomas, A.M. Lee, and J.R. Thomas, 2008, *Physical education methods for elementary teachers*, 3rd ed. (Champaign, IL: Human Kinetics). Adapted, by permission, from K.T. Thomas, A.M. Lee, and J.R. Thomas, 2000, *Physical education for children: Daily lesson plans for elementary school*, 2nd ed. (Champaign, IL: Human Kinetics), 654-660.

Lesson 7.4

Sharon's Shoot Around

Student Objectives 1 5

- Work together cooperatively.
- Keep score for the team.
- Help others.
- Practice basketball shooting.

Equipment and Materials

- 1 basketball goal
- 4 bases
- 1 basketball or playground ball

Skill-Development Activities (30 minutes)

Sharon's Shoot Around

Set 4 bases on one end of a basketball court.

Divide the children into 2 teams. Scatter one team around the basketball goal and give that team the basketball. Line up the other team near one of the 4 bases (one of which you designate as home). The running team begins running the bases—2 children at a time—on the go signal. Each time the two children make a circuit around the 4 bases, they score 1 point and another pair begins to run. The shooting team shoots baskets, beginning on the go signal. Once a child makes a basket, he or she may not shoot again but assists in retrieving balls for the remaining shooters. Children are awarded 1 point for each basket made (e.g., 1 point for each team member). Once all of the players on a team have made a basket, the round ends, and the teams switch positions. The game continues, ending with an equal number of rounds.

Lesson 7.5

Raging River

Student Objectives 5

- Work cooperatively to solve a movement problem.
- Use equipment creatively to solve a problem.

Equipment and Materials

- 1 balance beam or line on the floor per group
- 1 mat per beam
- 1 hoop per group

The following equipment is what is needed for each "river" that you set up. Try to keep group size around 6 children in order to increase participation opportunities.

- 1 mat
- 1 cone
- 1 rope
- 2 carpet squares
- 1 ball
- 1 scooter
- Polyspots or polydomes to mark the "river"

Warm-Up Activities (5 minutes)

Select one of the following cooperative games.

Balance Challenge

Have small groups of children stand in a line on a line or balance beam, which is over a mat.

1. Describe the game:
   - The object is to reverse the order of the children in the group without any children stepping off the beam (or line). For example, the last child on the right end of the line reverses places with the last child on the left of the line, and so forth.
   - Balance while climbing over and around each other.
2. Have the children try the Balance Challenge.

Hoop Circle

Have each small group of children stand in a circle, with hands joined; use one hoop per group.

1. Describe the game:
   - Place the hoop over your heads (hands are joined through the hoop, or the like).
   - The object is to move the hoop around the entire circle without releasing hands.
2. Have the children play Hoop Circle.

Lesson 7.5 *(continued)*

Circle Untangle

Have small groups of children stand in a close circle, with hands extended inward.

1. Describe the game:
   - Join hands and follow three rules: you can't join hands with the child on either side, you can't join both hands with the same child, and you can't let go of hands at any time.
   - The object is to make one large circle with hands joined. Give the children a hint: "Some of you may end up facing in, while others end up facing out."
2. Have the children play Circle Untangle.

Skill-Development Activities (20 minutes)

Assign each small group of children a set of equipment, including 1 mat, 1 scooter, 1 cone, 2 carpet squares, 1 rope, and 1 ball. For each group, define a "river" (2 lines) about 30 feet (9 m) apart.

Raging River

1. Describe the game:
   - The object is to cross the "river" (the area between the 2 lines) without touching the "water" (the floor). Each group must get all of the group members and all of the equipment to the other side of the river without touching any body part to the floor. If a person touches the floor, the group must start that round over.
   - Each time your group successfully crosses, you must return, using one fewer piece of equipment. Remove equipment in the following order: ball first, rope second, cone third, carpet squares fourth, scooter fifth. Your final trip is with the mat only.
2. Have the children play Raging River. Be aware that some groups may make all seven trips, while other groups may not be able to complete one trip in the time allotted.
3. Encourage children to work cooperatively and explore as many solutions to the problem as possible. Provide feedback as the game goes on.

Concluding Activities (5 minutes)

1. Discuss the various strategies that groups used to be successful in Raging River. You may want to have groups demonstrate their strategies.
2. As an expansion idea, use a variety of equipment to alter the game (e.g., cardboard boxes, walking cans, balance beams).

From K.T. Thomas, A.M. Lee, and J.R. Thomas, 2008, *Physical education methods for elementary teachers*, 3rd ed. (Champaign, IL: Human Kinetics). Adapted, by permission, from K.T. Thomas, A.M. Lee, and J.R. Thomas, 2000, *Physical education for children: Daily lesson plans for elementary school*, 2nd ed. (Champaign, IL: Human Kinetics), 948-949.

Lesson 7.6

Partner Stunts

Student Objectives 2 5

- Attempt 3 new partner stunts.
- Name at least 8 partner stunts.

Equipment and Materials

- 1 or more mats (4 by 8 feet [1.2 by 2.4 m]) per group

Warm-Up Activities (5 to 7 minutes)

Warm-Up Routine for Grades 4 and 5

Use the Warm-Up Routine for Grades 4 and 5 from lesson 3.4, page 56.

Skill-Development Activities (18 to 20 minutes)

Triple Roll

Create groups of 3 children, and assign each group to a mat.

1. Describe and have three children demonstrate the stunt:
   o All of you get down on all fours about 3 feet (.9 m) apart, facing the same side of the mat.
   o The middle child begins to roll to the right. The child on the right hops over the middle child and rolls toward the child on the left, who jumps to the middle over the rolling child.
   o Continue.
2. Have the children practice the Triple Roll.

Lesson 7.6 *(continued)*

Jump-Through

Continue with groups of 3 children at the mats.

1. Describe and demonstrate the stunt:
   - Hold hands to form a circle.
   - One of you jumps over the joined arms of the other two children, who help lift the jumper's weight.
   - Take turns jumping.
2. Have the children practice the Jump-Through.

Shoulder Balance

Arrange pairs of partners on the mats.

1. Describe and have two children demonstrate the stunt:
   - One child (the base) lies flat on his or her back, with knees bent.
   - The other partner (the top) stands between the knees of the base, leans forward, and rests his or her shoulders on the extended arms of the base.
   - The top holds the base's knees and kicks his or her legs up to a handstand position.
2. Have the children practice the Shoulder Balance, with one pair spotting another pair.

Spotting for the Shoulder Balance

Have four children demonstrate the spotting technique:

- Spotters stand on each side of the base near the waist of the base.
- They guide and balance the top by holding the top's thighs and shoulders, being careful not to interfere with the base's grasp on the top.

Concluding Activities (5 minutes)

Discussion

Arrange the children in a semicircle. Discuss what the children have learned today:

- What new partner stunts did we learn today? (Shoulder Balance, Jump-Through, Triple Roll.)
- Which is the best stunt you and your partner can do? Which is the hardest? Show me your best!

From K.T. Thomas, A.M. Lee, and J.R. Thomas, 2008, *Physical education methods for elementary teachers*, 3rd ed. (Champaign, IL: Human Kinetics). Adapted, by permission, from K.T. Thomas, A.M. Lee, and J.R. Thomas, 2000, *Physical education for children: Daily lesson plans for elementary school*, 2nd ed. (Champaign, IL: Human Kinetics), 1048-1050.

PART III

Preparing to Teach Physical Education

The previous section helped you understand *whom* you will teach and how they learn. Now you will prepare to teach. One of the first questions that expert teachers ask before teaching in a new setting is, "Can I see the room?" They want to know what the classroom looks like, what resources are available there, how long the class period lasts, and how other practical information might affect their teaching. Experts then leverage those resources in personal ways to create a learning process that is clearly their own. Therefore, this section begins, in chapter 8, Planning Your Curriculum, with both long- and short-term (e.g., annual, unit, and lesson plans) planning to help you decide what to teach.

The next question is "How should I teach?" Chapter 9, Organizing for Teaching, covers factors such as group size and how information is delivered. Expert teachers are good at preventing problems that might interfere with learning; thus, they are expert classroom managers.

Chapter 10, Managing Students, covers management, including class rules, formations, transitions, equipment handling, and getting students' attention.

You may already feel the weight of responsibility that goes with being a teacher. Chapter 11, Teachers' Rights, Responsibilities, and Best Practices, explores the responsibilities, rights,

and best practices associated with becoming a professional teacher.

The final chapter in this section, chapter 12, Equipment and Facilities, covers the "where" and "what" of physical education: playgrounds, gymnasiums, equipment, and so on.

CHAPTER 8

Planning Your Curriculum

KYLEAKIN, AGE 9

The goal of physical education is for students to become physically educated. Planning allows teachers to reach that goal and others with developmentally appropriate programs. Planning includes curricular philosophy, long- and short-term objectives, activities, and evaluation.

Learner Outcomes

After studying this chapter, you should be able to do the following:

- Explain the relationship among teacher values, learner objectives, instruction, and evaluation.
- Define and demonstrate curriculum alignment.
- Explain basic concepts of health, physical activity, and fitness.
- Create developmentally appropriate outcomes for students.
- Define concepts related to health promotion and disease prevention.
- Define warm-up, progression, and closure activity.

Glossary Terms

vertical alignment	static balance	force
horizontal alignment	dynamic balance	flow
progression	personal space	objectives
sequence	general space	warm-up
scope	speed	closure

Developmentally appropriate physical education is based on three principles:

1. Motor skill development is sequential and age related.
2. Motor skill development is similar for all children.
3. The rate of motor development varies among and within children.

Curriculum Planning

In American schools, you usually have complete freedom to develop your own physical education curriculum, including choosing a curriculum emphasis, setting objectives and goals, selecting and sequencing content, and deciding how to assess learning and the program. Your curricular choices are a reflection of your values and beliefs about what children should learn and how they should spend their time in physical education classes. Regardless of the approach used to select content, recent concerns about childhood obesity and sedentary lifestyle patterns in today's children have led most of you to focus on a program emphasizing health and promotion of physical activity. Today, a quality physical education program is designed to provide children with an opportunity to engage in a range of developmentally appropriate movement activities and to teach them fundamental skills that make participation in lifelong physical activity enjoyable. You play a critical role by giving students the knowledge to make good activity choices and help them develop the skills they need to be confident in physical activities.

Because another purpose of physical education in school is the development and maintenance of physical fitness, children also need to acquire the knowledge, skills, and confidence needed to accept responsibility for their own personal fitness. A quality physical education program should also provide opportunities for them to develop sport skills and to understand rules and strategies of various sport activities. Although there are many choices to make in designing a curriculum, with careful planning, the important outcomes of physical education can be achieved—that is, your students can be physically educated. One way to achieve this is by providing developmentally appropriate lessons and instruction (see Is Your Program Developmentally Appropriate? on page 210). You are likely to have strong beliefs about the value of educational experiences from physical skills, structured and unstructured games, and a variety of dance activities. The result is a curriculum that reflects these preferences and is a blend of aspects from meaningful options that match your values and objectives. Activities can include fundamental movement skills, traditional individual and team sports, and specialty options such as adventure activities, outdoor pursuits, and martial arts.

To begin the planning process, study the National Standards (or your state standards) and identify the skills and knowledge that children need to meet these standards. The standards offer a framework that defines what they need to know and be able to do as a result of a physical education program. You should evaluate the content chosen in terms of the overall contributions to a physically educated person. As discussed in chapter 2, Meeting the Mission of the Elementary School, you are more likely to use a blend of several curriculum theories because you select what is best for your students, what you are comfortable with, and which aspects of a curriculum theory are most important. Every teaching situation is unique, and it is impossible for a single curriculum to fit every school and every teacher. Thus, you must adapt or create programs for your own situations. As you develop your physical education curriculum, your primary goal should be

to design developmentally appropriate experiences that will help all of your students become physically educated. It is important to ensure that the curriculum content is sequenced so that children progress toward the standards at each developmental level.

One goal of curriculum development for physical education teachers is to make physical education an integral part of the mission of the school. For classroom teachers who teach physical education, meeting the entire mission of the school—including physical education—is a goal of the curriculum. Integration of physical education into the mission of the school is important, and you can accomplish it by recognizing the important and unique contributions that physical education makes to child development.

You need to understand curriculum design so that

- your programs are based on developmentally appropriate principles,
- your students understand and adopt physically active lifestyles, and
- your programs accomplish their goals and objectives.

Fitness Education as Part of the Curriculum

As you learned in chapter 6, Physical Activity for Children, physical activity is a continuum, with sedentary lifestyles at one end and a physically active lifestyle resulting in physical fitness at the other end. Thus, the physical education curriculum should facilitate many opportunities for exercise, with the primary goal of developing and maintaining a health-enhancing level of fitness. Children spend a good part of their physical education time in physical activity and learn many ways to develop fitness outside of class. Programs should be designed for children to gain health-related fitness benefits with the long-term goal of developing a commitment to lifelong participation in physical activity. The fitness phase of the curriculum integrates physical fitness testing as a learning experience and is usually organized around the four components of health-related fitness: cardiorespiratory endurance, muscular strength and endurance, flexibility, and body composition. You should also incorporate instruction in the principles for improving and maintaining physical fitness: frequency, intensity, duration, and specificity.

Iowa's National standards?

One goal of variety is to ensure that every student loves at least one activity.

A Developmental Framework for Curriculum Planning

A curriculum based on developmental constructs derives its structure from research on how motor skills develop in children, as explained in chapters 3 through 7. You can design a learning hierarchy around task complexity that develops prerequisite skills for each task and requires mastery. The stages of control in the execution of motor skills follow a predictable sequence; however, the rate at which motor skills are acquired varies within and across children. The program must provide opportunities for children to progress individually. Developmental physical education provides activities to enhance the rate and quality of individual development. The curriculum in the lower grades focuses on fundamental skills such as locomotion, nonlocomotion, receiving and projecting objects, and stability. You can combine and refine these skills through a variety of lead-up games, gymnastics, and rhythmic activities. Eventually, you can present more specialized skills required for traditional sports and activities. As you follow a developmental philosophy, select and organize movement activities according to needs, interests, and skill capabilities of children at different ages. The developmental status of children is your basis for planning, with special attention given to the proficiency barrier described in chapter 4, Motor Performance During Childhood. Children who have not mastered fundamental motor patterns cannot modify these patterns to form specialized skills; they must still focus on technique in individual movements and consequently cannot integrate them to form specific sport skills. Sport skill development begins at about third grade as fundamental patterns are combined, with both skill and accuracy stressed. At about fifth grade, emphasis shifts to developing skill in complex sport, rhythmic, and gymnastics activities. By the sixth grade, you can refine many specific skills for participation in competitive and creative activities. This model is consistent with the hierarchy of the psychomotor domain presented in chapter 1, Health and Developmental Benefits of Physical Education. A sample of how the activities might differ across the grades is shown in table 8.1.

Selecting Desired Outcomes

Once you choose your curriculum emphasis, you can set your goals and objectives. The National Standards for Physical Education (National Association for Sport and Physical Education [NASPE] 2004) introduced in chapter 1 are the standards for elementary school children. Children who are physically educated have mastered the skills needed to perform a variety of physical activities, they are physically fit, and they participate in physical activity on a regular basis. Specifically, a physically educated person does the following:

1. Demonstrates competency in motor skills and movement patterns needed to perform a variety of physical activities.

Table 8.1 Percentage of Time Spent in Various Activities by Grade Level

Grade level	pre-K–K	1-2	3-4	5-6
Basic locomotor and manipulative skills	30	20	5	
Games of low organization	10	20	5	
Rhythmic activities	20	20	20	
Stunts and tumbling	20	20	20	10
Fitness	20	20	20	20
Team sports			10	10
Individual sports			5	10
Recreational games			5	10
Dance			5	10
Novelty activities			5	10
Adventure and outdoor pursuits				10
Aquatics				10

2. Demonstrates understanding of movement concepts, principles, strategies, and tactics as they apply to the learning and performance of physical activities.

3. Participates regularly in physical activity.

4. Achieves and maintains a health-enhancing level of physical fitness.

5. Exhibits responsible personal and social behavior that respects self and others in physical activity settings.

6. Values physical activity for health, enjoyment, challenge, self-expression, and social interaction.

These are the desired outcomes for the developmental curriculum that we propose.

The National Health Education Standards (Joint Committee on Health Education Standards 1995) can be integrated with the Physical Education Standards to define what children should know about health-enhancing practices. Many of the health standards are linked to the broad notion of a healthy lifestyle and the reduction of health risks. A developmental curriculum recommends an integration of health and physical activity content, and some of the health concepts and behaviors are closely related to physical activity. The health standards identify the health skill and knowledge essential to the development of health literacy. Health-literate students do the following:

1. Comprehend concepts related to health promotion and disease prevention.

2. Analyze the influence of family, peers, culture, media, technology, and other factors on health behaviors.

3. Demonstrate the ability to access valid information and products and services to enhance health.

4. Demonstrate the ability to use interpersonal communication skills to enhance health.

5. Demonstrate the ability to use decision-making skills to enhance health.

6. Demonstrate the ability to use goal-setting skills to enhance health.

7. Demonstrate the ability to practice health-enhancing behaviors and avoid or reduce risks.

8. Demonstrate the ability to advocate for personal, family, and community health.

Adapted from L.M. Summerfield, 1995, *National Standards for School Health Education*. ERIC Digest. Washington, DC: ERIC Clearinghouse on Teaching and Teacher Education. (EDRS No. ED387483).

Understanding Curriculum Alignment

Curricular alignment is expressed in two directions—vertical and horizontal. **Vertical alignment** describes the relationship of the benchmarks and content across grades. Good vertical alignment begins with standards describing what children can do and what they will know at the end of the program—in this case, grade 12. Benchmarks are specific skills and knowledge that represent progress toward the standards. We recommend benchmarks for every 1 or 2 grades, for example, at the end of kindergarten, second, fourth, and sixth grades (see figure 8.1). Others use slightly different age or grade divisions. Tables 8.2 through 8.7 show the benchmarks presented in PECAT (Physical Education Curriculum Assessment Tool). These benchmarks describe what children should do

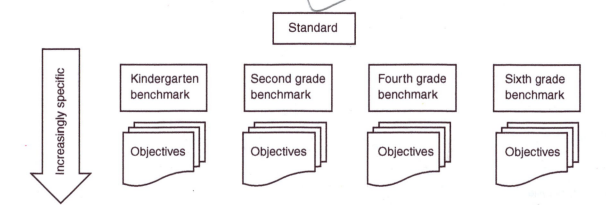

Figure 8.1 The NASPE standards provide a goal that physical educators want students to reach but that is accomplished via smaller steps: Daily lesson objectives contribute to accomplishing unit objectives, which, in turn, are directed toward mastering annual or biannual benchmarks that ultimately lead to achieving the NASPE standards.

and know at the end of grades 2, 5, 8, and 12. By looking at the benchmarks for one standard across the grades, you should see evidence of progress toward the standard. What is expected becomes increasingly more difficult or complex and more similar to the standard as children get older. This concept is consistent with developmentally appropriate physical education. PECAT provides 4 to 6 benchmarks for each standard at each of the four levels (grades K-2, 3-5, 5-8, and 9-12).

You can develop benchmarks based on the critical components of the standard. For example, standard 5 includes responsible behavior and respect. Critical skills or knowledge might include following the class rules; working independently, with others, and leading; understanding social responsibility; and using social skills. Table 8.8 on page 196 presents those four concepts at four grade levels as benchmarks. The first row represents class rules (see chapter 11, Teachers' Rights, Responsibilities, and Best Practices, for more information on class rules); the second row,

working independently, with others, and leading; the third row, understanding social responsibility; and the fourth row, using social skills.

Vertical alignment is usually a shared responsibility. In most school districts, more than one teacher provides physical education, so vertical alignment is the result of a plan that is developed and executed by more than one person. What is critical to the success of this part of the curriculum plan is that each of you accepts responsibility for your portion of the plan. You should understand vertical alignment and be familiar with the plan for your district. Vertical alignment of standards and benchmarks may be done at the state, district, or building level, so, in many cases, you do not create this part of the plan. In all cases, you are critical because you must accept responsibility for your portion of the learning outcomes of your students. Horizontal alignment is vested in individual teachers. In this case, you are responsible for ensuring progress toward those standards on a continual basis. This may be viewed as annual

Table 8.2 Sample PECAT Benchmarks for National Standards

National Standard 1: Demonstrates competency in motor skills and movement patterns needed to perform a variety of physical activities.

End of grade 2 benchmark	End of grade 5 benchmark	End of grade 8 benchmark
Achieve mature forms in the basic locomotor skills and vary how these skills are performed in relationship to changing conditions and expectations.	Develop maturity and versatility in the use of fundamental skills for more enjoyable movement experiences.	Use skills successfully in modified games or activities of increasing complexity and in combination with other basic skills.
Show progress toward achieving mature form in the more complex manipulative skills (e.g., foot dribble) and achieve mature form in the less complex manipulative skills (e.g., underhand throw).	Achieve mature forms in the basic nonlocomotor and manipulative skills.	Perform the basic skills of the more specialized sports, dance, and gymnastics activities with mature form.
Demonstrate control in traveling (walking, running, skipping), weight-bearing, and balancing activities on a variety of body parts.	Demonstrate locomotor, nonlocomotor, and manipulative skills for performance outcomes (e.g., hitting targets).	Demonstrate use of tactics within sport activities.
Demonstrate smooth transitions between sequential locomotor skills.	Use fundamental, nonlocomotor, locomotor, and manipulative skills in dynamic and complex environments (e.g., formal dance to music) and in combination with each other.	
	Use specialized skills basic to a movement form (e.g., basketball chest pass, softball fielding with a glove).	Participate with skill in a variety of modified sport, dance, gymnastics, and outdoor activities.

National Standard 1 from *Moving into the Future: National Standards for Physical Education*, 2nd Edition (2004) reprinted with permission from the National Association for Sport and Physical Education (NASPE), 1900 Association Drive, Reston, VA 20191-1599.

Table 8.3   Sample PECAT Benchmarks for National Standards

National Standard 2: Demonstrates understanding of movement concepts, principles, strategies, and tactics as they apply to the learning and performance of physical activities.

End of grade 2 benchmark	End of grade 5 benchmark	End of grade 8 benchmark
Mature in basic movement abilities.	Participate in complex motor skills, transfer concepts learned in other skills or games for performance of the new skill or game (e.g., bending the knees lowers the center of gravity and increases stability).	Exhibit an increasingly complex discipline-specific knowledge.
Apply concepts such as body parts, actions and planes, and personal or general space.	Comprehend more complex concepts and principles and apply them in structured settings.	Identify principles of practice and conditioning that enhance movement performance.
Identify and use concepts of the body, space, effort, and relationships that vary the quality of movement.	Use knowledge of critical elements of form or simple biomechanical or motor development principles to provide feedback to others.	Have higher levels of understanding and application of movement concepts or principles and game strategies, critical elements of activity-specific movement skills, and characteristics representing highly skilled performance.
Identify elements of correct form for fundamental skills and use them in performance.		Know when, why, and how to use strategies and tactics within game play.
Use feedback to improve motor performance.	Use performance feedback to increase cognitive understanding of a skill and to improve performance.	Use information from a variety of internal and external sources to guide and improve performance.

National Standard 2 from *Moving into the Future: National Standards for Physical Education*, 2nd Edition (2004) reprinted with permission from the National Association for Sport and Physical Education (NASPE), 1900 Association Drive, Reston, VA 20191-1599.

progress measured by benchmarks, within a unit of instruction, or within an individual lesson. Alignment of standards, benchmarks, objectives, curriculum content, and assessment demonstrates accountability. Alignment is logical, so there are educational objectives for each standard that are more short term—annual, unit, or lesson. Those objectives are directly related to the curriculum plan and the educational experiences during class. Finally, assessment is done to measure the learning. Accountability means that you and your program can demonstrate their contribution to student achievement of the outcomes (standards). Table 8.9 on page 197 presents the objectives for each kindergarten benchmark for standard 5. These would be followed by lesson objectives, activities, and assessments to demonstrate horizontal alignment.

In a well-aligned program, the connection among standards, objectives, activities, and assessment is obvious. So, an observer could watch a lesson and know what standard(s) was being addressed. Similarly, the assessment plan would lead to a clear image of what had been taught. Chapter 15, Growing as a Teacher, provides greater detail on evaluation and assessment. However, you need to consider alignment during the planning process. As you plan the curriculum, think about what activities align with each objective and how you might assess progress toward the standards and your objectives.

A Focus on Integration

A developmental curriculum can best achieve the NASPE standards for elementary students by using an integrated approach to planning and teaching. This approach combines skill development with an emphasis on the value of physical activity as a health benefit. For example, the children work on movement skills in such a way as to stay highly physically active. Then, in teachable moments, you briefly point out health-related fitness concepts. All of your classes are not fitness classes, but you do want to teach concepts and basic knowledge related to the components of health-related fitness. All children should be

Table 8.4 Sample PECAT Benchmarks for National Standards

National Standard 3: Participates regularly in physical activity.

End of grade 2 benchmark	End of grade 5 benchmark	End of grade 8 benchmark
Participate in physical activities largely for the enjoyment gained from them.	Develop an awareness of participation in physical activity as a conscious personal decision, choosing activities for both the enjoyment and the health benefits produced.	Be able to set physical activity goals independently and participate in individualized programs based on personal goals and interests, as well as the results of fitness assessments.
Engage primarily in nonstructured physical activities on an intermittent basis outside physical education class and have fun while doing so.	Voluntarily participate in moderate-to-vigorous physical activity for longer periods outside of physical education class.	Participate regularly in moderate-to-vigorous physical activities in both school and out-of-school settings.
Participate in a wide variety of gross motor activities that involve locomotion, nonlocomotion, and manipulation of objects.	Be able to identify and make use of opportunities at school and within the community for regular participation in physical activity.	Have an increasing awareness of the opportunities for participation in a broad range of physical activities and interests.
Select and participate in moderate-to-vigorous activities during leisure time.	Begin to recognize and use critical elements and movement concepts to sustain participation in enjoyable activities.	Select and use physical activities appropriate for the activity goals set.
Recognize that participation in moderate-to-vigorous physical activity has temporary and lasting effects on the body and choose to engage in activities that contribute to improved health.	Be capable of using information from a variety of internal and external sources to regulate participation in an activity.	Have a level of knowledge and understanding of physical movement principles and tactics that allows them to apply these concepts to their participation in more situations.

National Standard 3 from *Moving into the Future: National Standards for Physical Education*, 2nd Edition (2004) reprinted with permission from the National Association for Sport and Physical Education (NASPE), 1900 Association Drive, Reston, VA 20191-1599.

taught the FITT principles that are described in chapter 6, Physical Activity for Children, and should learn the basic anatomy of the cardiovascular system. Young children can feel their hearts beating fast and understand that physical activity causes this to happen. In the older age groups, they can monitor the physiological indicators that accompany vigorous physical activity and adjust their level of activity accordingly.

One way to integrate fitness concepts and guidelines is to ask children to think about what health-related fitness component is needed for various sport skills and lead-up activities. For example, playing the game of soccer requires cardiorespiratory endurance and football passing requires arm strength. In volleyball, you need to develop muscular strength and endurance in the legs for jumping. Provide a variety of fitness activities that correspond to the specific skill you are teaching. It is essential that you help children develop the competence and initiative to be responsible for their own fitness; this begins when children enter school.

If your goal is to promote healthy, active lifestyles, children need to comprehend concepts related to overall health and to demonstrate the ability to use decision-making skills to enhance overall health. The National Health Standards further specify that students need to demonstrate the ability to practice health-enhancing behaviors and avoid or reduce risks. One critical area that is related to a healthy, active lifestyle is learning information about nutrition and following a healthy diet that reduces the risk of disease. MyPyramid is an educational tool that integrates information about healthy eating and physical activity. Its design is simple, and it serves as a reminder of the importance of daily physical activity and makes suggestions for how much food a person should choose from each of the five food groups: grains, vegetables, fruits, milk, and meat and beans. The United States Department of Agriculture developed the plan; it is personalized, and the kinds and amounts of food to eat are individualized. The plan can be found at www.MyPyramid.gov.

Table 8.5 Sample PECAT Benchmarks for National Standards

National Standard 4: Achieves and maintains a health-enhancing level of physical fitness.

End of grade 2 benchmark	End of grade 5 benchmark	End of grade 8 benchmark
Engage in a variety of activities that serve to promote health-related physical fitness.	Regularly participate in physical activity for the purpose of improving physical fitness.	Monitor their own heart rate, breathing, and recovery rate during and after strenuous physical activity.
Enjoy physical activities for the pleasure experienced from moving, and not necessarily associated with the development of physical fitness.	Participate in moderate-to-vigorous physical activity for longer periods without tiring.	Participate in moderate-to-vigorous physical activities on a regular basis without undue fatigue.
Participate in physical activity intermittently for short periods and accumulate a relatively high volume of total activity while having fun doing so.	Begin to engage in physical activities specifically related to each component of physical fitness and be capable of monitoring the physiological indicators that accompany moderate-to-vigorous physical activity and adjusting personal activity accordingly.	Participate in moderate-to-vigorous activities that address each component of health-related fitness, including cardiorespiratory endurance, muscular strength and endurance, flexibility, and body composition.
Possess basic knowledge of the components of health-related fitness (cardiorespiratory endurance, muscular strength and endurance, flexibility, and body composition).		Know the components of health-related fitness and how these relate to their overall fitness status.
	With teacher assistance, interpret the results and understand the significance of information provided by formal measures of physical fitness.	Assess their personal fitness status for each component and use the development of individualized physical fitness goals with little help from the teacher.
		Show progress toward knowing the concepts and theories of physical fitness (e.g., threshold, overload, specificity) and how to use these principles to improve their level of physical fitness.

National Standard 4 from *Moving into the Future: National Standards for Physical Education*, 2nd Edition (2004) reprinted with permission from the National Association for Sport and Physical Education (NASPE), 1900 Association Drive, Reston, VA 20191-1599.

The curriculum is also designed to teach cooperation, social skills, and personal responsibility by blending these important outcomes into the overall plan. Educators have long stressed the importance of students' being able to make the social adjustments necessary for success in individual and group-play environments. They need to understand concepts of cooperation, rules, fair play, and honesty in motor skill settings. By the end of grade 2, children should discover the joy of playing with friends and how social interaction can make activities more fun. Then, by grade 8, they are expected to have well-developed cooperation skills and be able to accomplish group or team goals in both cooperative and competitive situations.

Experiences in physical education should allow children to learn, solve problems, and make significant decisions about their own learning. Physical activity is integrated with other subject areas across the curriculum with the goal of helping children develop confidence and grow into responsible, self-directed, physically educated adults. You can provide short bouts of activity time throughout the day, either between lessons or between classes. The Take 10 curriculum integrates academic goals in language arts, math, social studies, and science with movement and physical activities. The Take 10 materials can be found at their Web site: www.Take10.net. Children get out of their seats to spend 10 minutes in some physical activity that is related to a subject lesson; the activities require no equipment and can be easily performed in a classroom.

Table 8.6 Sample PECAT Benchmarks for National Standards

National Standard 5: Exhibits responsible personal and social behavior that respects self and others in physical activity settings.

End of grade 2 benchmark	End of grade 5 benchmark	End of grade 8 benchmark
Discover the joy of playing with friends and how social interaction can make activities more fun.	Be active participants in class and learn to work independently and with small groups enjoying the diversity of others.	Have well-developed cooperation skills and accomplish group or team goals in both cooperative and competitive situations.
Know safe practices, physical education class rules, and procedures and be able to apply them with little or no reinforcement.	Identify the purposes for and follow activity-specific safe practices, rules, procedures, and etiquette.	Move from identifying and following rules, procedures, safe practices, ethical behavior, and positive forms of social interaction to reflecting on their role in physical activity settings.
Know how to use acceptable behaviors for physical activity settings and be able to build a foundation for successful interpersonal communication during group activity.	Continue to develop cooperation and communication skills to enable completion of a common goal while working with a partner or in small groups.	Understand the role of diversity in physical activity and continue to include and support each other, respecting limitations and strengths of group members.
Have improved motor skills that provide a basis and appreciation for working with others in cooperative movement, sharing, and working together to solve a problem or tackle a challenge.	Work independently and productively for short as well as progressively longer periods during and outside of physical education classes.	Understand the concept of physical activity as a component of modern culture and social life.
	Continue to develop cultural or ethnic self-awareness, appreciate their heritage, and appreciate the differences in others.	Seek greater independence from adults and effectively work independently and in groups to complete assigned tasks.
		Make appropriate decisions to resolve conflicts arising from the influence of peers and practice appropriate problem-solving techniques to resolve conflicts when necessary in competitive activities.

National Standard 5 from *Moving Into the Future: National Standards for Physical Education*, 2nd Edition (2004) reprinted with permission from the National Association for Sport and Physical Education (NASPE), 1900 Association Drive, Reston, VA 20191-1599.

Practical Considerations for Curriculum Planning

The physical education content you select depends on factors such as the following:

- Your school and physical education objectives and goals
- School and community environment and cultural influences
- Size of your class
- Student abilities
- Equipment and facilities
- Scheduling of classes
- Your own likes, dislikes, strengths, and weaknesses

No two teaching situations are the same. You must tailor the specific content you choose to your situation in order to maximize learning for all of the children, based on those factors. Thus, in addition to forming your grade-level physical education objectives, answer the following questions before selecting specific units and activities:

- Can you manage the unit or activity, given the number of students you have?

Table 8.7 Sample PECAT Benchmarks for National Standards

National Standard 6: Values physical activity for health, enjoyment, challenge, self-expression, or social interaction.

End of grade 2 benchmark	End of grade 5 benchmark	End of grade 8 benchmark
Be physically active because of the enjoyment accomplished by participating.	Identify activities they consider to be fun.	Seek experiences involving physical activity for group membership and positive social interaction.
Like the challenge of experiencing new movements and learning new skills.	Choose an appropriate level of challenge in an activity so as to experience success and engage in activity with students of similar skill levels.	Recognize that challenge is found both in high levels of competition and in learning new or different activities.
	Be challenged by learning a new skill or activity and enjoy broadening their repertoire of movement skills.	Understand that physical activities can help them take steps toward independence.
Feel joy in movement as they gain competence.	Attribute success and improvement to effort and practice.	Experience a greater awareness of feelings toward the avenues of self-expression provided through dance, gymnastics, and other artistic sports.
Begin to function as a member of a group and to work cooperatively for brief periods.	Relate enjoyment directly to competence in a particular activity.	Participate in physical activities that provide a positive outlet for competition with peers and a means of gaining respect and recognition so that they can increase self-confidence and self-esteem.

National Standard 6 from *Moving into the Future: National Standards for Physical Education,* 2nd Edition (2004) reprinted with permission from the National Association for Sport and Physical Education (NASPE), 1900 Association Drive, Reston, VA 20191-1599.

Table 8.8 Sample Benchmarks for National Standard 5 at Four Elementary Grade Levels

National Standard 5: Exhibits responsible personal and social behavior that respects self and others in physical activity settings.

Kindergarten benchmark	Grade 2 benchmark	Grade 4 benchmark	Grade 6 benchmark
Moves under control all or most of the time, for example, by not bumping into other students or equipment, and by maintaining an upright posture.	Quietly listens to instructions and watches demonstrations while standing still all or most of the time.	Follows class rules without reminders all or most of the time.	Demonstrates initiative in personal responsibility at least once, for example, by appropriately handling something that is out of place, volunteering to help, or other similar behavior.
Maintains personal space all or most of the time, for example, by not touching other students.	Works effectively with a partner all or most of the time.	Contributes meaningfully to group success on tasks all or most of the time.	Demonstrates leadership or mediating in a group at least once, for example, when the group is struggling finding a compromise or solution agreeable to the group.
Identifies one personal attribute or example of a personal attribute.	Identifies one example of personal behavior that is responsible.	Sets a personal responsibility goal.	Sets and meets a personal responsibility goal.
Regularly says "please" and "thank you" in the appropriate context.	Compliments another student on verbal request at least once.	Encourages another student at least once.	Regularly encourages other students.

National Standard 5 from *Moving into the Future: National Standards for Physical Education,* 2nd Edition (2004) reprinted with permission from the National Association for Sport and Physical Education (NASPE), 1900 Association Drive, Reston, VA 20191-1599.

Table 8.9 Alignment of Benchmarks and Objectives for National Standard 5: Kindergarten

National Standard 5: Exhibits responsible personal and social behavior that respects self and others in physical activity settings.

Critical component	Benchmark	Objective
Following class rules	Moves under control all or most of the time, for example, by not bumping into other students or equipment, and by maintaining an upright posture.	TLW walk or jog, staying within the boundaries while maintaining an upright posture at least once in three trials. TLW walk and jog, beginning in scatter formation and moving through group space, maintaining upright posture and not touching other students in 2 out of 3 one-minute trials.
Working independently, with a group or leading	Maintains personal space all or most of the time, for example, by not touching other students.	TLW find and maintain personal space for the warm-up with polyspots (or other markers) 3 out of 5 times. TLW find and maintain personal space for the warm-up without polyspots or other markers at least once.
Understanding personal responsibility	Identifies one personal attribute or example of a personal attribute. For example, a respectful person listens while another is talking and follows the rules.	TLW state one personal attribute from the following list: listens quietly, stops on the signal, takes turns, "is nice," or uses equipment appropriately. TLW state one reason why personal attributes are important; those reasons are safety, learning, respect.
Using social skills	Regularly says "please" and "thank you" in the appropriate context.	TLW name one time during class when it is appropriate to say "please" (e.g., when you need help). TLW identify an appropriate time to say "thank you."

TLW = The learner will

National Standard 5 from *Moving into the Future: National Standards for Physical Education*, 2nd Edition (2004) reprinted with permission from the National Association for Sport and Physical Education (NASPE), 1900 Association Drive, Reston, VA 20191-1599.

- Does the unit or activity meet the needs of all of your students?

- Is the unit appropriate for your students' developmental level (readiness)?

- Does your choice of unit or activity respect the cultural needs and interests of your students?

- Does the unit or activity have the potential to stretch your students' cultural awareness?

- Do you have access to a gym, all-purpose room, outdoor space, or community facility appropriate for conducting the unit or activity?

- Do you have, or can you borrow or make, the equipment you need to conduct the unit or activity so that all students are actively involved in learning all of the time?

- How much time are you able to set aside for each lesson? Is it enough to accomplish each lesson's objective? Is block time a possibility?

- How many class periods per week are you able to mandate for physical education? Is the total time enough to accomplish your objective?

- Given your facilities, training, equipment, and individual students, can you conduct the unit or activity safely?

- Is the content meaningful, challenging, and motivating to all of your students? Is the overall value of the activity equal to the cost?

- Based on the overall physical education schedule, is this activity compatible with other units and lessons being taught?

A perfect world would contain unlimited equipment, facilities, and instructional time to accomplish the goals of physical education. Unfortunately, in the real world, you must consider certain issues as you plan. Several formats are used for scheduling physical education that bring these practical issues to life:

- The school offers 25- to 30-minute back-to-back classes with a physical educator.

A Teachable Moment

Ms. King's class has been playing Nose Tag on the playground for 5 minutes; their movement is slowing, and many children are moving to the fringe of the area. Earlier in the game, all of the children were playing vigorously and staying in the center of the play area where the action was greatest. One of the children runs to her and says, "I am really hot; can I have a drink?" Ms. King stops the activity and explains, "When you exercise, your body produces heat. Today, the temperature is also warm, making it more difficult for your body to get rid of the heat from exercise. One way you cool yourself is by sweating. The air passes over the sweat, the sweat evaporates, and your skin cools down. It is important to drink water when you sweat. If you do not drink enough water, you can become dehydrated and your body gets too hot. This is bad for your health. We will continue to play, but one child at a time may get water by using the water pass. Remember to wait for the pass and then get your drink and return promptly so others can have a turn." Ms. King has addressed the immediate health needs of her students—remaining hydrated—and she has used this opportunity to teach about heat, activity, and dehydration.

- Physical education is taught by classroom teachers during the last 30 minutes of the day.
- Physical education is taught by classroom teachers in rotation with art and music at each grade level.
- The school offers 25 to 30 minutes of physical education, 2 days per week, by a physical educator, and 3 days per week with the classroom teacher at the end of those 3 days.

When one person is teaching physical education, and classes are back to back, there is no time for extensive equipment set-up; so regardless of the grade level, activities requiring similar set-ups must be taught throughout the day. Accommodations for age and skill differences must be made, but as much of the same equipment as possible must be used in all classes. If several teachers are teaching physical education, the use of facilities and equipment can be coordinated among them. When more than one teacher is teaching the same students, the curriculum must also be coordinated among the teachers. When both classroom and physical education teachers are teaching the same students, the physical education teacher may be willing to create a master curriculum so

Novel activities like this one can enhance student motivation, but make sure you have enough equipment to keep everyone involved.

that classroom teachers know what to teach. In schools where many teachers are teaching their classes at the same time, considerable planning and coordination of facilities and equipment are necessary. Clearly, the best circumstance for children is to have physical education as often as possible—ideally, 5 days per week for at least 30 minutes per class. This may not happen, however, and when it does, curriculum may be influenced by practical issues related to facilities and equipment. Even when there is time between classes, issues of equipment and facilities are part of curriculum planning. For example, weather can influence outside activity choices; alternating gymnastics and volleyball is impractical because the equipment differs radically.

Developing Appropriate Content for Physical Education

Curriculum planning should consider several factors:

- Progression
- Sequence
- Scope

In a model developmental curriculum, you need to ensure that your students progress from inefficient and ineffective skill performance to an efficient and effective level. The curriculum we propose includes not only content suggestions but also student assessment analyses that are divided into subsections corresponding to the grade levels used in the national standards for physical education. **Progression** means improvement, or mastery, of increasingly difficult tasks. Generally, progression refers to steady increases in the qualitative (efficiency) and quantitative (effectiveness) aspects of the skills, and the task demands are increased. One way to observe progression is to see a task presented in a more challenging way each day of a unit. You can accomplish this goal by planning appropriate practice, regulating the difficulty of activities, and assessing children's progress along the way to ensure that they are learning what you want them to learn. It is important to determine exactly how much time and in what order you teach the physical education content so that you reach your objectives and the outcomes stated in the standards. **Sequence** involves the order in which you teach the progression of curriculum from year to year, reflecting the timing and depth of the program. Then you must define

your program's **scope**, the content of the program in terms of its breadth or range throughout the academic year. Children do not develop efficient patterns in one year. Rather, the fundamental skills are emphasized over several years, as you guide students toward skilled performance. Children are assessed to determine their status and progress and to give you information about when students are ready for greater challenge. The National Standards are the ultimate goal—"being physically educated" (NASPE 2004); however, NASPE provides sample benchmarks for each of the standards across the grade levels as biannual objectives (figure 8.1 on page 190). This chapter shows you how to align lesson and unit objectives with benchmarks for each of the standards. Then you should be able to design your own complete series of checkpoints or benchmarks.

Fundamental motor skills (locomotor and manipulative skills) and movement concepts (body awareness, body parts, nonlocomotor skills, shapes, awareness of space, effort, and relationships) serve as organizing centers for instruction in the lower grades and provide a foundation for more complex skills and fitness activities. You can use the Movement Alphabet (Buschner 1994) to develop a sequence of developmentally appropriate movement skill and concept lessons (table 8.10). Chapter 4, Motor Performance During Childhood, describes the fundamental skills, and the following sections provide suggestions for incorporating the movement concepts into lesson development. We have outlined procedures for using concepts to elicit a variety of responses from children. Finally, we have provided sample benchmarks to illustrate how you can check to make sure that your students are progressing.

Locomotor Patterns

Children must practice and master the basic locomotor patterns (e.g., walking, running, and jumping) that require coordination of the body's large muscles before they can master sport skills. Locomotor skills are considered prerequisites for many sport, dance, and gymnastics skills. Lessons involving locomotor skills should progress from movement in free space to movement requiring close control and complex interactions with objects. Because efficient performance of locomotor skills is a prerequisite to later skill development in sport activities, you should be able to design appropriate tasks and make important corrections; the rubrics in chapter 4 provide

Table 8.10 Movement Alphabet

MOTOR SKILLS = VERBS		Body awareness	Spatial awareness	MOVEMENT CONCEPTS = ADVERBS	
Locomotor patterns	Manipulative patterns	Body awareness	Spatial awareness	Effort	Relationship
Walking	Throwing	Body parts	General	Speed	Objects
				slow fast	
Jogging	Catching	Shapes	Personal	Force	Partner
		curved twisted		light strong	
Running	Kicking	Base	Directions	Flow	Others
		narrow wide		left right	
Jumping and landing	Punting	Form	forward backward	bound	
		symmetrical asymmetrical			
Galloping	Dribbling (feet)	Nonlocomotor	up down	free	
Hopping	Dribbling (hand)	Balance	clockwise counterclockwise		
		static dynamic			
Skipping	Striking		Levels		
			high medium low		
Sliding	Volleying		Pathways		
			straight curved zigzag		
Leaping			Extensions		
Faking			short long		
Fleeing Chasing Dodging			To body		
			near far		

Reprinted, by permission, from C. Buschner, 1994, *Teaching children movement concepts and skill: Becoming a master teacher* (Champaign, IL: Human Kinetics), 10.

guidance for evaluating and correcting locomotor skills. You can develop similar rubrics for combinations of locomotor skills, such as walking, jogging, running, hopping, jumping, skipping, galloping, leaping, and sliding.

Manipulative Patterns

Manipulation includes giving force to objects (e.g., throwing, kicking, striking, and volleying), gaining control of objects (catching), and maintaining control of objects (dribbling). Development of efficient locomotor skills is likely to precede the mastery of manipulative skills, although they are introduced simultaneously in the program (table 8.11). Skills needed to interact accurately with stationary objects (e.g., to hit a ball off a tee) are less complex than those needed to move objects in space (e.g., to hit a thrown ball). Thus, compe-

Table 8.11 Ages of Children When 60 Percent of Them Master Motor Skills

Running	4-4.5 yr
Throwing	4-7.5 yr
Skipping	6-6.3 yr
Catching	6.5-7 yr
Kicking	6.5-8 yr
Hopping	7.5 yr
Striking	6.5-8.5 yr
Jumping	10 yr

Adapted from V. Seefeldt and J. Haubenstricker, 1982, Patterns, phases, or stages: An analytical model for the study of developmental movement. In *The development of movement control and co-ordination*, edited by J.A.S. Kelso and J.E. Clark (New York, NY: John Wiley & Sons), 314.

tency in manipulating stationary objects should precede competency in manipulating moving objects. Chapter 4 presents additional suggestions on how to design and alter tasks to increase or decrease difficulty.

Body Awareness

Before children can perform locomotor skills in an efficient way, they must be able to maintain their bodies in a stable position and understand what the body does while moving (e.g., how posture and balance interact and how they are influenced by environment). Body awareness refers to knowing the body's actions. During the early elementary years, children need to learn names, locations, and functions of the body and body parts. You can present tasks to challenge children to explore movement with different body parts. The gymnastics lesson for kindergarten and grade 1 shown at the end of this chapter demonstrates the use of body parts, directions, and movements. Through body awareness activities, children also learn to control body shapes (curved, twisted, narrow, wide, symmetrical, asymmetrical) and nonlocomotor activities (swing, sway, twist, turn, bend, curl, stretch, sink, push, pull, and shake). **Static balance is** the ability to maintain a stationary position for a specified period—the center of gravity remains inside the base of support. Activities that require static balance are balancing on one foot and balancing on three different body parts. **Dynamic balance is the ability** to maintain a balanced position while moving

through space. Activities that require dynamic balance include walking on stilts and walking on a balance beam.

Body Parts

Knowing the location of body parts and surfaces is an important cognitive concept. Being able to apply these terms during movement is a basic skill necessary for understanding instruction and feedback. The movements associated with demonstrating understanding provide practice of important nonlocomotor skills. The following movement challenges combine body awareness with body parts:

- Touch the right elbow to the left knee; touch the head with both hands.
- Twist the arms; twist the right arm and the left leg; twist the whole body.
- Run and make large circles with the arms; walk and twist the trunk.
- Travel around the room; on the drum beat, balance on the right foot and the left hand.
- Balance on four body parts, three body parts, and two body parts.
- Make a complete turn while balancing on one foot.
- Balance on different body parts (knees, seat).

Nonlocomotor Skills

Nonlocomotor skills are movements done while the body remains in one location. This is contrasted with locomotor skills, in which the body moves from location to location. Nonlocomotor skills include balancing tasks and other movements such as bending, stretching, curling, and swaying. The following challenges are examples of nonlocomotor skills:

- Balance on one foot and swing the opposite leg.
- Bend one, two, or three body parts.
- Bend up and down and side to side.
- Bend the neck (arms, legs, fingers) in different ways.
- Lie on the floor and bend different body parts.
- Stretch the body in different directions (up, down, to the side).
- Stretch different body parts.

- Balance on different body parts (knees, seat) and stretch.
- Shake the arms (legs, trunk, neck).
- Shake the top (bottom) part of the body.
- Shake one or both arms or legs.
- Swing the trunk from side to side.
- Swing one arm and one leg.
- Push with one or both arms (legs).
- Push from a kneeling (sitting) position.
- Pull with one hand, both hands, and one hand and then the other hand alternately.
- Pull from over the head or from the side.
- Make yourself round.
- Twist your arms, legs, trunk.
- Make a narrow shape.
- Curl your arm, back, body.
- Wiggle your arm, leg, hand, body.
- Swing your arms; swing one leg.
- Sway your body.

Nonlocomotor skills include bending, stretching, and balancing.

Spatial Awareness

Spatial awareness refers to sensing where the body moves. **Personal space** is the area around the body; it extends as far as the reach from side to side and front to back. Personal space moves with the body as it travels around a room. Children need to understand that individual space is the area around the body; the play area is **general space**, which is shared by the whole class. Through exploratory movement tasks in general space, children can learn to manage their bodies to avoid collisions. Moving under control is an important skill and safety concept that is closely related to understanding personal and general space. The concept of space also includes awareness of directions and levels.

Directions Movement can be performed in place, left, right, forward, backward, sideways, up, down, clockwise, and counterclockwise. The concept of directions includes awareness of up, down, left, right, in front of, in back of, above, below, in, out, over, under, and around. Direction can also be referred to as the pathway or pattern of a movement. The body can move in straight, curvy, diagonal, and zigzag pathways. Children can adapt and refine fundamental movement patterns through exploring movement in different directions. The following are examples of movement tasks designed to explore directions:

- Walk (run, jump, hop, slide) and change direction on a drum beat.
- Move four slides to the right and four slides to the left.
- Jump, making a quarter, a half, and a whole turn to the left or right.
- Gallop forward 4 times, jump backward 4 times, and hop sideways 4 times.
- Kick one leg forward and move backward.
- Kick to the side and move sideways.
- Move through a hoop while it is rolling.
- Travel around the room in a zigzag (or curvy) pathway.

Levels Movement can occur at high, medium, and low levels (referring to the height of the movement). Children can jump high and make wide shapes with their bodies or catch a ball high over the head. You can combine low, medium, and high movements into a sequence to provide an array of experiences. The following movement tasks are designed to explore different levels:

- Stretch (curl, roll, rock, twist) at a low level (lying on the floor), medium level (sitting or kneeling), and high level (standing and in the air).
- Combine 1 roll, 4 running steps, and 4 leaps.
- Toss a beanbag over the head and catch at a high, medium, or low level.
- Make a bridge with the body using four body parts to balance.
- Walk at a low level while keeping hands at a high level.
- Jump high, "melt" to a sitting position, stretch, and balance on three body parts.

Effort

Awareness of qualities, or the effort aspect, of movement refers to sensing how the body moves. The qualities of movement are speed, force, space, and flow. Skill in movement is the ability to select the right combination of these qualities. Children must have the opportunity to experiment with varying degrees of each so they can learn to select the appropriate blend. **Speed** of the movement can range from slow to fast. **Force** is the amount of energy expended for a movement; it can range from light to heavy. **Flow** is the amount of control present in a movement; it ranges from free to bound. A bound movement is under the complete control of the performer and can be stopped at any moment. Free flow is a continuous movement that cannot be stopped after the action is initiated, such as a flip in gymnastics.

These are some examples of movement tasks of varying qualities:

- Run (jump, hop, skip, gallop, slide) quickly and quietly.
- Run fast, and on the signal run slowly.
- Walk or run with long, heavy steps.
- Move like a robot, a wooden soldier, or a rag doll.
- Show a hard, forceful movement (striking or hitting motion) with the arms, legs.
- Bend and stretch body parts using slow, strong movements.

Relationships

The relationship concept is movement that interacts with others or with an object. Children can perform movement alone, with a partner, or in a group:

- Move toward, away from, around, or behind a partner.
- Copy the movements of a partner.

You can refine and vary basic locomotor, nonlocomotor, and manipulative patterns by using different objects. You can adjust play objects in size and weight to children's developmental levels to make successful practice possible:

- Put the beanbag in front of (behind, beside, above, below, under) you.
- Walk around the hoop, stand beside the hoop, and stand in front of the hoop.
- Strike a balloon above your head and then hit it below your knees.
- Jump forward, backward, and sideways over a rope.

Developmental Progression and Benchmarks

The learning outcome is "to be physically educated," as documented by the six NASPE content standards. Standards 1 and 2 focus on motor skills, so the developmental curriculum is first based on appropriate sequence and progression to meet standards 1 and 2. The progression from grade to grade is demonstrated as fundamental skills are combined and refined to create more complex movement patterns. When practiced in the early elementary grades (kindergarten, first, second, and third), the basic locomotor, nonlocomotor, and manipulative skills become automatic and can then be combined into a variety of higher order, more comprehensive skills needed for game, gymnastics, and rhythmic activities. Children should acquire these specific skills in the middle grades (fourth and fifth) and then refine them in the upper grades (sixth, seventh, and eighth). Gradually, they can apply the skills to lead-up games, modified games, and specific sports; stunts; tumbling and apparatus activities; and creative, folk, social, and square dance. You need to check along the way to ensure that the children are making progress toward becoming physically educated. For each of the fundamental motor skills and movement concepts, you can establish benchmarks to indicate whether the children are on track in the process. We provide examples of PECAT benchmarks for assessing fundamental skills and concepts for three different levels (at the end of grades 2, 5, and 8) in tables 8.2 through 8.7. You should develop your own benchmarks for assessing student progress toward specific goals, but you can use the PECAT benchmarks as a guide.

Program of Physical Activity and Fitness

We have focused our discussion on the development of fundamental movement and movement concepts. It is also important, however, to plan a curriculum that encourages vigorous physical activity for health benefits. In defining a physically educated student, the National Content Standards (NASPE 2004) emphasize the importance of regular participation in physical activity and the development of health-related fitness as important goals. In defining skills and knowledge related to health literacy, the National Health Education Standards stress the importance of students' comprehending concepts related to health promotion and practicing health-enhancing behaviors. Health-related fitness has four components that are defined in detail in chapter 6, Physical Activity for Children:

- Cardiorespiratory fitness
- Muscular strength and endurance
- Flexibility
- Body composition

Using an integrated approach to curriculum planning, you can teach health-related physical fitness and physical activity in such a way as to encourage children to seek a healthful, active lifestyle long after they leave your classroom. Fitness is temporary: Becoming fit in class does not have lasting benefits if the children choose to be sedentary as adults. The fitness content standard focuses on learning about fitness, using individualized programs, and being active, as shown in the description (table 8.12).

Children should understand the difference between the following terms: health-related physical fitness, physical activity, skill-related fitness, and exercise (see chapter 6). You should introduce the benefits of physical activity, and children should leave elementary school understanding the basic concepts and principles of fitness education (figure 8.2).

Table 8.12   General Descriptions of Content Standards in Physical Education: Physical Fitness and Activity

Standard 3: Exhibits a physically active lifestyle	The intent of this standard is to establish patterns of regular participation in meaningful physical activity. This standard should connect what is done in the physical education class with the lives of students outside physical education. Although participation within the physical education class is important, what the student does outside of the physical education class is critical for developing an active, healthy lifestyle. Students are more likely to participate if they have had opportunities to develop interests that are personally meaningful to them. Young children should learn to enjoy physical activity. They should participate in developmentally appropriate activities that help them develop movement competence, and they should be encouraged to participate in vigorous and unstructured play.
Standard 4: Achieves and maintains a health-enhancing level of physical fitness	The intent of this standard is for the student to achieve a health-enhancing level of physical fitness. Students should be encouraged to develop higher levels of basic fitness and physical competence as needed for many work situations and for leisure participation. Health-related fitness components include cardiorespiratory endurance, muscular strength and endurance, flexibility, and body composition. Expectations for students' fitness levels should be established on a personal basis, taking into account variation in entry levels rather than setting a single standard for all children at a given grade level. For elementary school children, the emphasis is on an awareness of fitness components and having fun while participating in health-enhancing activities that promote physical fitness. Middle school students gradually acquire a greater understanding of the fitness components, how each is developed and maintained, and the importance of each in overall fitness.

- Reduces the risk of heart disease, diabetes, and high blood pressure
- Promotes emotional wellness
- Enhances neural development
- Helps an individual perform nonphysical activities better
- Saves society money through improved health
- Enhances skeletal health, muscular strength, and cardiorespiratory fitness
- Improves posture

Figure 8.2 Benefits of physical activity.

From the U.S. Department of Health and Human Services (USDHHS), 2000, *Healthy people 2010: Conference edition* (Washington, DC: Government Printing Office).

Principles for Maintaining and Improving Physical Fitness

- Overload
- Frequency
- Intensity
- Time
- Type

Guidelines for Teaching Health-Related Fitness Concepts

6 Seconds x 10

You can teach the concepts of cardiorespiratory fitness during physical education at any grade level. Introduce one fitness concept each day at the beginning of each class. For example, you can introduce young children in grades K-2 to concepts such as resting heart rate, aerobic fitness, and basic knowledge related to the cardiorespiratory system. You can teach them to recognize changes in heart rate during exercise. You can show a picture of the heart and explain how blood moves through the heart, arteries, and veins. As children age, they can monitor their own levels of activity using pedometers or heart monitors and can identify aerobic fitness activities. They can measure their own level of aerobic fitness and understand and interpret the results. Three fitness lessons and one health lesson that can be used to teach cardiorespiratory fitness are provided at the end of this chapter. The circuit training lesson for K-1 children (Lesson 8.3) introduces the concepts of regular exercise

and moderate-to-vigorous participation. You can revise the circuit plan for variety and adjust it for different age groups. You can use jumping rope, stepping through hoops or running through cones, crawling through tunnels, and stepping on and off a bench in a circuit. You can adjust the time at each station for increases in intensity and vary the amount of rest between stations. Older children can create their own stations. The health lesson (Lesson 8.4) introduces physical activity as a part of a healthy lifestyle and explains what sedentary versus active means and what it means to be physically fit. For grades 2 and 3, the lesson on moderate-to-vigorous games (Lesson 8.6) introduces concepts of cardiorespiratory and aerobic fitness. The concluding activity presents information related to a trained heart and introduces the children to pulse counting. For grades 4 and 5, there is a lesson on rope jumping (Lesson 8.8). Look at these examples and then create some activities of your own. — recovption

You can teach the concepts of muscular strength and endurance and relate them to the principles of overload, progression, and specificity. Training for strength is a program using weights or activities such as curl-ups, push-ups, or other exercises using the child's body weight. You can also use partner resistance activities and weight training for developing muscular strength and endurance. The overload principle refers to the need to increase the workload to make improvements in strength and endurance. Progression implies that the increase in workload be gradual. The principle of specificity refers to the need for training to be specific to a muscle group for an effect to occur. The principle of regularity means that the training activities must be performed on a regular basis. The rope jumping lesson (Lesson 8.8) at the end of this chapter introduces the overload principle and explains what overload means in terms of strength and endurance.

You can introduce flexibility in the early grades as the ability to bend, stretch, or twist. As children progress through the grades, you can explain their ability to move a joint through a complete range of motion. You should define the different types of stretching and discuss the benefits of regular stretching. A static stretch is a slow stretch that is held for 10 to 30 seconds and is usually the recommended approach. Children should not bounce or stretch to the point of pain. The specificity principle is important to remember when training for flexibility because the benefits are gained only in the muscles and joints used in the stretching exercise. You can teach the specificity principle as it relates to flexibility by presenting pictures of the different bones and muscles that are being used in a stretch. Look at the stretching routine for the warm-up activity in the lesson on moderate-to-vigorous games (Lesson 8.6) at the end of this chapter. One of the objectives for this lesson is for the children to demonstrate the correct technique for each stretch.

Body composition is an important topic to include in physical education because of its relationship to overall health-related fitness, but it is also a sensitive topic because it is related to obesity and being overweight. Beginning in kindergarten, children need to understand that physical activity can affect body composition and help maintain a healthy weight. As recommended in chapter 6, Physical Activity for Children, your primary goal in introducing body composition concepts is to encourage all of the children to seek healthy bodies that are neither too fat nor too thin. It is important for children to understand that bodies are different and that there is not one perfect weight or amount of body fat. If you have access to skinfold calipers, practice so that your estimates are accurate, and then you might choose to estimate body fat in your students. Even then, you should combine several techniques if your goal is to develop a risk profile. Review the descriptions of BMI and WHR in chapter 6 for help with your decisions about estimating body fat and determining risk. Review the lesson on cooperative teams and discussion groups for grade 6 (Lesson 8.11) at the end of this chapter. Notice that, in cooperative learning groups, the children are asked to explain about individual differences in body shapes and weight. Discussion groups should be able to explain that different body shapes are partly the result of genetics but also of patterns of diet and activity.

Motivating Children in Fitness

To encourage lifelong regular physical activity, physical education activities must leave each child feeling competent and confident. Offering praise, encouragement, and meaningful and varied activities helps motivate children to seek physical activity on their own. Criticizing, embarrassing, and shaming them just turns them off. The Council on Physical Education for Children (COPEC 1992) has developed examples of appropriate and inappropriate practices that can help you distinguish between what you should do and what you should avoid doing. Table 8.13 presents our own examples, which focus on fitness.

Individualize your fitness lessons so that the children build confidence. The following are some ideas to inspire them:

- Instead of assigning a predetermined number of exercises, give children a range to complete, such as a choice of doing between 10 and 25.
- List several exercises for one component and allow children to choose the ones they want to do (you can set up stations).
- Instead of having all of the children run a mile, let each child keep track of how far he or she runs in 12 minutes.
- Another way to motivate children is to focus on the personal effort and improvement of all of them rather than on the prowess of a few elite children. Encourage children to cheer one another on in small

Table 8.13 Examples of COPEC Appropriate and Inappropriate Practices

Appropriate practice	Inappropriate practice
Fitness activities are used to demonstrate the concepts of fitness and the benefits of a physically active lifestyle. The activities allow the children to experience the difference between cardiorespiratory fitness and flexibility.	Fitness test scores are used to identify and highlight the most fit and least fit children to the entire class. This is done in an effort to motivate the least fit students to improve and to reward the most fit children.

groups instead of having them compete to see who can do the most or run the fastest.

- Finally, praise and reward individual effort and improvement as well as group cooperation, inspiring confidence and competence in each child.

The fitness program should focus on the definition of physical fitness, the components of fitness, the benefits of exercise, and the requirements for being physically fit and maintaining fitness levels (see chapter 6).

For example, a benchmark at the end of second grade for National Standard 4—Achieves and maintains a health-enhancing level of physical fitness—could be that the children possess knowledge related to cardiorespiratory endurance, muscular strength and endurance, flexibility, and body composition. By the end of grade 5, the children should begin to engage in physical activities specifically related to each component of physical fitness and be capable of monitoring the physiological indicators that accompany moderate-to-vigorous physical activity. Finally, by the end of grade 8, they should be able to assess their personal fitness status for each component and use the development of individualized physical fitness goals with little help from you. See tables 8.2 through 8.7 for other PECAT benchmarks.

The Obese Child

Children who are overweight are most likely self-conscious about their bodies, making them reluctant to attempt to participate in physical activity. This attitude, of course, perpetuates the obesity and compounds the complications that can arise from obesity. We recommend the following guidelines for helping obese or overweight children:

- Create a fun physical education program to encourage all of the children to participate and to send the message that physical activity is worth engaging in.

- Always build in ways to individualize physical education lessons so that all of the children, including the obese child, can succeed.

- Approach family members privately and diplomatically and point them in the direction of professional help, such as a family physician.

- Privately recognize and reinforce small improvements in lifestyle choices, such as eating fruit instead of potato chips with lunch or walking to school instead of riding in a car.

- Encourage all of the children to focus on how individual choices can lead to a healthy lifestyle instead of focusing on weight or body composition as the sole or most important indicator of health and fitness.

- Allow the obese child to choose his or her own intensity level. Even mild exercise is beneficial.

This approach increases the likelihood that the child will continue to participate in physical activity outside of school Increasing physical activity can have a positive impact on obesity. Activity expends energy; if nothing else changes (e.g., diet, growth), increasing activity has the potential to burn calories and therefore reduce body fat. Physical activity also reduces depression, which is often associated with obesity and being overweight.

All children benefit from participating in physical activity.

Planning for the Year

You have a choice of many approaches in developing a schedule for the year. We recommend that you do this using a weekly calendar that lists the 36 weeks of the school year and a category or topic selected for each week. You should develop an annual plan that is appropriate for your school situation. An example of a yearly program for pre-K through grade 6 is shown in table 8.14. The plan distributes activities across the year for pre-K through grade 4. For grades 5 and 6, the activities are more often blocked into units, which are taught during adjacent weeks. Notice that the first week or two in each yearly plan is dedicated to the creation of a learning atmosphere. During this time, you can introduce the children to the rules and consequences associated with appropriate class behavior, and they can learn efficient protocols for making transitions, creating formations, obeying boundaries, and handling equipment. More information about these protocols or management techniques is presented in chapter 11, Teachers' Rights, Responsibilities, and Best Practices. The other categories taught during the year are games and sports, rhythmic activities, gymnastics, and

fitness-related activities. The weekly units are then defined by activities that correspond to the outcome goals. The plans for pre-K through grade 4 repeat content representing locomotor, nonlocomotor, manipulative, and body management skills because the primary focus of the program at this level is on development of fundamental skills. Children learn best when the topics are revisited throughout the year rather than grouped together as a long series of lessons. Locomotor skills, for example, are first introduced in week 4 or 9 and then reviewed several times during the year. In the sample plan for grades 5 and 6, the activities selected are the more traditional sport, gymnastics, and rhythmic activities, and they are presented in longer, theme-related units. In grades 3 and 4, we recommend introducing sport skills. Then children practice the sport skills in grades 5 and 6, using lead-up games and modified games. In all grades, competition is not emphasized, allowing a focus on skill development.

You should check the annual plan to be certain that it is developmentally appropriate. During a year, the activities in your plan should demonstrate the four characteristics listed in the sidebar on page 210. Progression (increased

Table 8.14 Weekly Format for Pre-K Through Grade 6

Week	Category	Activity pre-K–K	Activity 1-2	Activity 3-4	Activity 5-6
1	Creating a learning atmosphere	Organizational protocols	Organizational protocols	Organizational protocols	Organizational protocols
2	Fitness	Hustles	Hustles	Hustles	Hustles
3	Fitness	Assessment	Assessment	Assessment	Assessment
4	Gymnastics	Locomotor skills	Pretumbling and review	Tumbling	Tumbling
5	Gymnastics	Pretumbling	Stunts and tumbling	Tumbling	Tumbling
6	Games and sports	Body parts, throwing, and catching	Throwing and catching	Tossing, throwing, and catching	Juggling
7	Games and sports	Throwing, catching, and moving objects	Tossing and kicking	Frisbee	Frisbee
8	Gymnastics	Tumbling	Stunts and tumbling	Tumbling	Large equipment
9	Games and sports	Running, dodging	Locomotor skills	Vigorous games	Tennis
10	Games and sports	Moving objects with feet	Kicking and striking	Soccer	Soccer
11	Fitness	Circuit training	Circuit training	Circuit training	Circuit training

	Category	Activity pre-K–K	Activity 1-2	Activity 3-4	Activity 5-6
12	Gymnastics	Tumbling	Stunts and tumbling	Tumbling	Small equipment
13	Gymnastics	Partner activities	Partner activities	Partner and group stunts	Partner stunts
14	Games and sports	Kicking	Striking and dribbling	Soccer	Football
15	Rhythmic activities	Body shapes, non-locomotor, and locomotor	Locomotor skills	Locomotor and nonlocomotor	Dance steps
16	Rhythmic activities	Singing games	Nonlocomotor skills	Folk dances	Folk dances
17	Rhythmic activities	Lyrics and action words	Singing games and folk dance	Country dances	Rope jumping
18	Games and sports	Striking with hand	Frisbee	Basketball	Basketball
19	Games and sports	Manipulative skills stations	Parachute	Volleyball	Basketball
20	Gymnastics	Small equipment	Small equipment	Small equipment	Partner stunts
21	Games and sports	Striking with extension	Manipulative skills	Basketball	Volleyball
22	Gymnastics	Large equipment	Large equipment	Large equipment	Large equipment
23	Games and sports	Locomotor skills, jumping	Locomotor combinations	Basketball	Cooperative games
24	Rhythmic activities	Rhythm sticks	Rhythm sticks	Rhythm sticks	Tinikling
25	Rhythmic activities	Long ropes	Rope jumping	Rope jumping	Tinikling
26	Rhythmic activities	Short ropes and marching	Folk dances and singing games	Tinikling	Advanced tinikling
27	Games and sports	Manipulative skills stations	Manipulative checklist	Juggling	Track and field
28	Games and sports	Locomotor skills and combinations	Locomotor checklist	Track and field	Track and field
29	Games and sports	Locomotor games	Locomotor games	Track and field	Softball
30	Games and sports	Manipulative games	Manipulative games	Softball	Softball
31	Games and sports	Cooperative games	Cooperative games	Cooperative games	Bowling
32	Fitness	Moderate-to-vigorous games	Vigorous games	Vigorous games	Circuit training
33	Rhythmic activities	Parachute play	Scarves	Juggling	Juggling
34	Fitness	Challenges	Challenges	Rope jumping	Rope jumping
35	Fitness	Assessment	Assessment	Assessment	Assessment
36	Field days				

difficulty), breadth (variety), depth (improved skill development via ample time and goals), and sequence (order) should be present from year to year. Including all four characteristics is difficult for a physical education specialist, and nearly impossible for a classroom teacher, because you only teach for one year! Many states provide curricula that give the scope and sequence of activities so that individual grade-level teachers can determine where these activities fit into the physical education curriculum as a whole. Your knowledge of child development is another source of information for decision making, as are the lessons, activities, and material in this book. Optimally, classroom teachers who are responsible for physical education have either the time to plan together, a specialist to plan the vertical curriculum for them, or a state or district curriculum to guide this process. Physical education specialists may have similar resources. In either case, this chapter demonstrates the vertical nature of the curriculum, which is a concern for all of you.

Is Your Program Developmentally Appropriate?

Use these four criteria to judge whether physical education programs are developmentally appropriate (COPEC 1992):

1. Orderly sequence of motor skill learning
2. Provisions for individual differences
3. Appropriate goal structures
4. Ample learning time

Another way to approach the annual plan in elementary school is to devote one day of the week to a specific type of activity. Three examples are presented in table 8.15. The activity categories are the same as in the first method—games and sports, fitness, gymnastics, and rhythmic activities. The "day-of-the-week" method guarantees that children revisit activities throughout the year, and it is consistent with the format of after-school activities, in which children have dance one day and soccer another. The order of activities should provide progression and follow a sequence, as presented in table 8.15. Another way to approach the annual plan in elementary school is to devote one day of the week to a specific type of activity or to use a "free choice" technique. You can use the free choice technique in any curricular organization.

Free choice days are earned by the entire class for skill mastery, good behavior, or both. You can offer choices as a reward or recognition of performance by allowing the class to select one activity for the free choice or by providing several activities from which individual children select a choice.

There is no one right way to go about selecting the activities for a year, as long as your choices are consistent with your outcome goals. We have provided an example, but adjust it in any way that works for you and your class and that is consistent with developmentally appropriate physical education.

Guidelines for Writing Objectives

The NASPE standards (2004) specify the knowledge, skills, and ways of thinking that students are expected to master in elementary physical education. Understanding these long-term goals is important, but a more immediate concern for you is the ability to work backward to set daily lesson **objectives.** Learner outcomes for daily lessons are usually stated in three domains: cognitive, affective, and psychomotor. Regardless of the domain, you should use the following guidelines to write good objectives:

1. Write the objectives in a way that makes it clear that the expectation is for the learner. It is not acceptable to write in terms such as "the teacher will" or "the lesson will." State objectives in terms of observable student behavior. The objective must specify the kind of behavior that you are looking for. For example, appropriate verbs for the psychomotor domain include dribble, jump, trap, and throw. A meaningful objective describes the end desired behavior so well that no mistake in judgment can be made as to whether the student performed in the desired manner.

2. Define the expected behavior in terms of the important conditions under which it is to occur. Catching a ball thrown overhand from a distance of 50 feet (15 m) is more difficult than catching a ball thrown underhand from 10 feet (3 m). Describing the conditions is essential because this component determines the level of difficulty. The type and size of the equipment, the size of the area, and whether the movement is initiated by the learner or by another person are all examples of conditions that must be defined.

Table 8.15 Daily Approach to Curriculum: Day-of-the-Week Plan

Monday	Tuesday	Wednesday	Thursday	Friday
Games and sports	Gymnastics	Fitness	Rhythmic activities	Games and sports
Games and sports	Gymnastics	Games and sports	Rhythmic activities	Free choice
Games and sports	Gymnastics	Fitness	Rhythmic activities	Free choice

ACTIVITY PROGRESSION AND SEQUENCE

	Pre-K–K	1-2	3-4	5-6
Games and sports	Locomotor Manipulative Low-organization games Combination skills	Locomotor Manipulative Lead-up games Combination skills Novelty skills	Locomotor and manipulative skills, combinations Beginning sport skills	Soccer Football Basketball Volleyball Softball Frisbee Tennis Track and field
Gymnastics	Locomotor Pretumbling Tumbling Partner stunts Small equipment Large equipment	Tumbling Partner stunts Small equipment Large equipment	Tumbling Partner stunts Small equipment	Tumbling routines Partner and group stunts Apparatus routines
Rhythmic activities	Locomotor Nonlocomotor Singing and word tasks Folk dances	Loco com Folk Rhythm Ropes		Folk dances Country dances Rhythm sticks Ropes
Fitness	Fitness assessment Hustles Challenges Circuits Games	Fitness a Hustles Challenge Circuits Games	assessment Hustles Circuits Ropes Wands	Fitness assessment Hustles Circuits Ropes Resistance

3. Describe the criteria of acceptable performance. The level of performance for success can be subjective (e.g., using correct technique) or objective (e.g., hitting the target 8 out of 10 times). Both subjective and objective criteria for mastery are important, and you should include them both in a student objective. The following is a sample objective that includes both criteria:

Without losing control, the student will dribble the ball 10 yards (9.1 m) and back using the dominant hand and exhibiting the following technique:

a. Head up and eyes forward

b. Knees slightly bent

c. Elbows close to body

d. Force applied with fingers of cupped hands

You may shorten the objective by not stating the specific points of technique. In the following example, subjective criteria for the child's technique are implied but not spelled out precisely: "The student will dribble the ball 10 yards and back using the dominant hand with good form."

Writing Objectives in Three Domains

The psychomotor domain is the category of objectives that deals with motor skills. In chapter 4, Motor Performance During Childhood, we discussed the factors to consider when you are establishing a simple-to-complex sequence of movement tasks. If you establish the instructional sequence during preplanning and include the criteria for specific objectives, writing objectives for motor skill instruction (psychomotor domain) should be a simple task. To dribble the ball down the basketball court and pass off to a teammate without traveling, the child must be proficient in dribbling and must have both declarative and procedural knowledge of traveling. The affective domain is the category of objectives dealing with the ability to get along with others and exhibiting responsible social behavior. The simple-to-complex notion is also valid for the affective domain. If you expect children to work effectively as a team toward a common goal, you should stress learning to work cooperatively with a partner at an early age.

The cognitive domain is the category of objectives that deals with learning and understanding concepts and that emphasizes problem solving. The learning outcomes in this domain are also hierarchical, which means that children must develop lower-level cognitive skills before you can expect higher-order outcomes. Following is a sample objective for one of the benchmarks associated with Content Standard 5. Using this example, develop objectives for other benchmarks.

Standard 5. Exhibits responsible personal and social behavior that respects self and others in physical activity settings.

Kindergarten Level

- Benchmark: Moves under control all or most of the time: for example, by not bumping into other children or equipment, and by maintaining an upright posture.
- Objective: The learner will walk or jog, staying within the boundaries while maintaining an upright posture at least once in three trials.

For example, the learner will do the following correctly formulated behavioral objectives for Standards 5 and 6:

- Demonstrate cooperation by working with a partner.
- Give two or more examples of sharing and cooperation in physical education (grade 2).
- Name dances or activities from at least two countries other than the United States (grade 4).

- Describe how team members of different skill levels can contribute to the team effort (grade 6).
- Use movement to express correctly the feelings of happy, sad, and angry.
- Name one new activity that he or she enjoyed as a result of trying it for the first time with the class (grade 2).
- List one accomplishment in physical education for himself or herself and one for a classmate (grade 4).
- Identify two emotions felt and provide sport (or physical activity) examples of those emotions (grade 6).

Writing a Daily Lesson Plan

When you are getting ready to write daily plans, realize that there is no specific or correct way to write them. Although the format for a lesson plan may differ according to the book you are reading, all of the lessons should have the same general components for effective learning. The lesson plan outlines expected learning outcomes (objectives) and describes the procedure to use daily to reach the outcomes. It outlines which learning activities to introduce, how to present and organize these experiences (instruction and demonstration), what cues you need to emphasize (feedback), and how you can determine success (evaluation). The format we recommend includes a warm-up at the beginning of each lesson. The **warm-up** activities usually focus on moderate-to-vigorous movement designed to get the body ready for the activities to follow. Our plans also list all of the equipment and materials that you need for each lesson, important safety tips, and a concluding activity.

Depending on level of experience, your lesson plans for a particular activity can look quite different from those of other teachers. Veteran teachers do not have to write as much on paper as the novice teachers. You can compare writing and teaching from lesson plans to cooking. When you first attempt to make a dish, you consult a cookbook, purchase and prepare the ingredients, and carefully follow the order of activities laid out in the recipe. As you make the same dish over and over, you consult the recipe less often and begin to add your own ideas to the mix. Planning and teaching are much like this. You become more comfortable as you teach the lessons year after year; then you can add your own touch to the lessons, making the experience more exciting and enjoyable. The lessons presented in previous chapters demonstrate one format for developing lesson plans. Find a format that works best for you. Table 8.16 presents another format that new teachers can use for planning. You should develop a format acceptable to your supervisors and one that suits your individual preferences. Both of these formats have similar components. Having written lesson plans is essential for several reasons:

- To guide instruction
- To reduce liability via careful planning
- To improve planning for future lessons
- To serve as a reminder of past activities

It is important for you to know the content of the lesson well. By being familiar with many activities and understanding developmental progressions, you can then adapt the learning activities according to the needs of each child. You can note these activities in the daily plan as alternative activities to use "just in case." They

help meet the objectives in the lesson plan, but perhaps with another approach.

You should include several essential components in every lesson plan: objectives, equipment, warm-up activities, skill-development activities, and closure.

Objectives Objectives should describe precise learner outcomes for the day. When writing objectives, keep in mind the amount of time available to practice the skill. Too often, teachers write objectives that are impossible to achieve in a 30-minute period. Write objectives according to what the child should know and be able to do by the time the class has ended. Use the sample benchmarks for specific grade levels provided by the NASPE standards as a guide when you are writing objectives.

Equipment List all of the items needed for the lesson, such as mats for gymnastics, music for dance lessons, sport equipment for skill development, and cones for boundaries. You should

Table 8.16 Sample Lesson Plan

Objective	Activity	Formation (draw)	Equipment	Cues	Evaluation
Demonstrate slow and fast movements	Move about the area walking or running, slow or fast as instructed	Scatter	None	"Move under control" "Walk or run, slow, fast"	Observe children changing as instructed.
Name 3 locomotor skills	Practice run, hop, gallop, and slide	x—o x—o x—o x—o x—o	Polyspots	"Fast" "One foot" "One foot leads" "One side"	Ask children to name a skill as teacher demonstrates.
Demonstrate 3 locomotor skills	Practice run, hop, gallop, and slide	x—o x—o x—o x—o x—o	Polyspots	"Fast" "One foot" "One foot leads" "One side"	Observe children doing the skills.
Identify feelings resulting from movement	Demonstrate favorite locomotor skill individually.	x—o	None	Children's names	Ask why this is a favorite.
Understand straight and curved movement patterns	Move using any locomotor pattern in the appropriate pattern based on cue; switch with drum signal	Scatter	Drum Pencils and paper	"Straight" "Curve" "Move under control"	Children draw lines indicating straight and curved on paper.

The objective is specified first and then an activity is designed to accomplish the objective. The formation (the position and location of students for the learning activity) and the equipment for each activity are specified; teacher cues and an evaluation for each activity follow.

use all of the equipment you have available so that each child gets maximum participation and practice.

Warm-Up Include a 3- to 5-minute vigorous activity in each lesson. This provides the children with immediate activity to get their hearts pumping before they settle down into the learning activities. The warm-up may or may not relate to the lesson for the day.

Skill-Development Activities The skill-development phase of the lesson plan describes how you progress through the lesson. This should include a description of the learning tasks and a diagram of formations, groupings, and the arrangement of each learning activity. This part of the lesson plan addresses how you communicate the content to the children as well as the progression you use to teach each skill.

To meet the needs of all developmental levels in the class, you should be prepared to offer a wide variety of skill practice activities. Include cue words or major points in technique that need to be emphasized in this part of the plan. If you want to stress concepts or strategies, include a note as a reminder to yourself. Keep in mind that all activities planned for the day should directly relate to the objectives of the lesson.

Closure The **closure** summarizes the day's learning and allows you to do a quick check for understanding. An effective lesson closure should firm up learning by reviewing the purpose and objectives of the lesson and reflect on or review what was learned. It allows children a chance to cool down after activities and gives you a chance to check for understanding by asking questions or administering some form of assessment. Finally, it should give you the opportunity to "bait" the children and get them excited and looking forward to the next lesson.

Summary

The curriculum is a plan for the physical education program. The first step in creating a curriculum is to develop goals and objectives that are based on your values. The seven National Content Standards for physical education provide a framework to begin planning the curriculum. Activities and instruction should be developmentally appropriate. Although the overall learning outcome (goal) of physical education is the same for all of the children, the learning activities and expectations are different. Younger children should experience a wide variety of movements that begin with fundamental skills as well as combinations of fundamental skills. With age and skill development, you can introduce the children to sport-specific skills, fitness, and other specific skills for use during leisure time. Vertical and horizontal alignment of the curriculum ensure that benchmarks for each grade level become increasingly more difficult and more similar to the standards as children get older. The overall goal is to enable children to be physically active adults who are competent, confident, and knowledgeable.

Mastery Learning Activities

1. Locate a unit plan. Does it meet the four criteria for a developmentally appropriate program?

2. Find a Web site that has physical education lesson plans. Critique one lesson plan. Does it include all of the important components?

3. What do you value and how does that influence what you teach in physical education? Which curricular model best meets your values? How can you ensure that your program meets the content standards for physical education?

4. Considering the weather, typical school facilities, and your personal interests, develop a yearly plan for grades K, 3, and 5.

5. Write five lesson plans that demonstrate progression and that are developmentally appropriate. Each lesson should cover at least three content standards.

References

Buschner, C. 1994. *Teaching children movement concepts and skill: Becoming a master teacher.* Champaign, IL: Human Kinetics.

Council on Physical Education for Children (COPEC). 1992. *Developmentally appropriate physical education practices for children.* Reston, VA: National Association for Sport and Physical Education (NASPE) Publications.

Joint Committee on Health Education Standards. 1995, 2006. *The National Health Education Standards: Achieving health literacy.* Atlanta: American Cancer Society.

National Association for Sport and Physical Education (NASPE). 2004. *Moving into the future: National standards for physical education.* 2nd ed. Boston: WCB/McGraw-Hill.

Resources

International Life Sciences Institute (ILSI). 1997. *Improving children's health through physical activity: A new opportunity, a survey of parents and children about physical activity patterns.* Washington, DC: ILSI.

Seefeldt, V., and J. Haubenstricker. 1982. Patterns, phases, or stages: An analytical model for the study of developmental movement. In *The development of movement control and co-ordination,* edited by J.A.S. Kelso and J.E. Clark, 309-318. New York: Wiley.

Lesson Plans

The following sample lesson plans demonstrate how you can design learning experiences to accomplish the desired outcomes for a developmental curriculum. Lessons 8.1 and 8.2 are intended to develop movement competency in locomotor skills, with a special emphasis on movement concepts and principles. These K-1 lessons are focused on walking, running, and jumping within the context of personal and general space. At this level, the children are asked to adapt the fundamental patterns by moving forward, backward, and sideways. Lessons 8.3 and 8.4 extend the work on locomotor skills and concepts by introducing a fitness circuit and concepts related to fitness and health.

At grades 2 and 3, children refine and vary locomotor skills by moving in different directions and performing with a partner (lesson 8.5). Lesson 8.6 introduces moderate to vigorous games as a fitness activity.

Lesson 8.7 is designed to allow students in grades 4 and 5 to combine locomotor movements in a creative sequence. The intent of this lesson is to encourage patterns of behavior that promote personal and group success in an activity setting by providing opportunities for children to participate in partner and cooperative group activities. Lesson 8.8 for grades 4 and 5 reviews fitness principles and emphasizes the importance of regular participation in physical activity and the development of health-related fitness.

The intent of the lessons for grade 6 is to encourage patterns of behavior that promote personal and group success in an activity setting by providing opportunities for children to participate in cooperative activities and express their feelings (lessons 8.9, 8.10, and 8.11). Lesson 8.9 introduces cooperative discussion groups, and the last two lessons use this technique. Children are asked to share their feelings about physical education and to participate in cooperative discussion groups on a variety of health-related topics.

Lesson 8.1

Body Parts, Positions in Space, Directions

Student Objectives 1 5

- Identify body parts and spatial directions.
- Explain the signals per direction.
- Follow instructions.
- Cooperate when playing Identify the Body Part.

Equipment and Materials

- Whistle
- 1 hoop (30 to 36 inches [76 to 91 cm]) per child or pair of children
- Music: "Hokey Pokey" (with and without words) from *Hokey Pokey*, Melody House (MHD 33)

Warm-Up Activities (5 minutes)

I See

Arrange the children in scatter formation.

1. Begin by saying, "I see." The children respond with "What do you see?"
2. Give a movement command, such as "I see everybody running in place." The children run in place.
3. After a short time, begin again with "I see." The children freeze and respond with "What do you see?" and so on.
4. Include other activities such as clowns marching, children running fast, children jumping, children chopping wood, horses galloping, and children skipping.

Skill-Development Activities (20 minutes)

Movement Challenges

Arrange the children in scatter formation or in a semicircle; all of the children should be visible to you.

1. Tell the children: "Touch your foot (head, chest, knees, toes, elbows, legs, thighs, calf, back, shoulder, arm, hip, wrist, ankle, finger, front, bottom, neck, tummy, forearm, face) with both hands."
2. Repeat step 1 with this command: "Wiggle (or move) your foot." Continue with the remaining body parts. Give each child or pair of children a hoop. Keep the children standing near their hoops in scatter formation or in a semicircle.
3. Have the children perform the following challenges:
   - Put your elbow (leg, knee, head, foot) inside your hoop.
   - Get inside the hoop (in front of the hoop, beside the hoop, part in and part out of the hoop, under the hoop).
   - Walk around the hoop.

- ◦ Move the hoop around you.
- ◦ Next, arrange partners in scatter formation.
4. Tell the children: "Touch your partner's foot." Continue with the body parts previously listed. Continue with modified formations: "Stand beside (back to back with, elbow to elbow with) your partner."

Identify the Body Part

Keep partners in scatter formation. Designate one partner as the Caller and the other as the Mover.

1. Describe the activity: "The Mover moves a body part, and the Caller says the name of the part out loud. We will repeat this several times, then switch Caller and Mover."
2. Have the children play Identify the Body Part.

Movement Challenges

Arrange children in scatter formation. Challenge the children with the following tasks:

- Raise your right (left) hand.
- Move your left (right) foot.
- Walk to your right (backward to the left).

Concluding Activities (5 minutes)

Hokey Pokey

Arrange the children in a circle, facing center.

1. Play a record or tape of the music. The first few times, use a voice singing the words and then let the children sing to an instrumental version. As they follow the directions, have the children rock—or move back and forth as if in a rocking chair—with the music.
2. On the chorus ("You do the Hokey Pokey and you turn yourself around; that's what it's all about!"), direct the children to turn in individual circles while pointing their fingers to the sky and shaking hands. Then ("You do the Hokey Pokey, H-o-o-key P-o-o-key") have the children get on their knees and bow with their arms extended and hands wiggling.

From K.T. Thomas, A.M. Lee, and J.R. Thomas, 2008, *Physical education methods for elementary teachers*, 3rd ed. (Champaign, IL: Human Kinetics). Adapted, by permission, from K.T. Thomas, A.M. Lee, and J.R. Thomas, 2000, *Physical education for children: Daily lesson plans for elementary school*, 2nd ed. (Champaign, IL: Human Kinetics), 250-251.

Lesson 8.2

Locomotor Patterns and Combinations

Student Objectives 1 2 5

- Demonstrate various locomotor patterns and at least one combination of two patterns.
- Distinguish between personal and general space.
- Cooperate while playing Partner Follow the Leader.

Equipment and Materials

None

Safety Tip

- Remind the children of personal and general space.

Warm-Up Activities (5 minutes)

Point and Run

Arrange the children in scatter formation; stand at the front of the area facing the children.

1. Have the children run through general space. Have the children continue to run in one direction until you signal them to change direction.
2. Whistle to gain their attention and then use a hand signal to indicate a change in direction: Signal with the thumb (toward yourself so that the thumb points in the direction the children are to move front) or finger (left, right, or away from you so that the finger points in the direction the children are to move back).
3. Remind the children not to bump into each other.

Skill-Development Activities (20 minutes)

Movement Challenges

Keep the children in scatter formation.

1. Tell the children: "Walk from your space to another space."
2. Describe the route taken (for example, from your classroom to the physical education area). Call it a "pathway," "pattern," or "route."
3. Describe an alternative route from your classroom to the physical education area. Call it a "pathway," "pattern," or "route."

4. Tell the children: "Walk back to your space another way, using a different route or pathway. Are there more ways to travel between spaces, other than a different route or path? We might use various levels (high, low) or walk backward."

5. "Walk backward on your toes (on heels, bent over, sideways)."

Sliding

Keep the children in scatter formation.

1. Describe and demonstrate the skill: "Sliding is a kind of walking in a sideways direction with a slight hop in the middle, in which the following foot never passes the leading foot."

2. Have the children practice sliding. Add this guideline: "Slide with your arms out."

3. Have them practice sliding at various speeds in both directions.

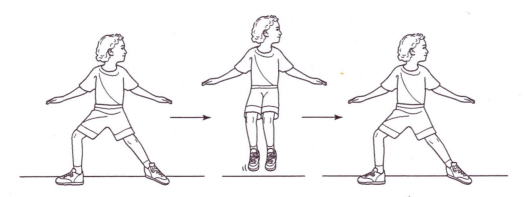

Galloping

Arrange the children in scatter formation.

1. Ask the children: "What is the name for the kind of running a horse does?" (Galloping.) "Galloping is like sliding. Can you tell me how? Can you show me galloping?"

2. Have the children practice leading with each foot.

3. Ask the children: "Who can gallop with one foot leading and then switch to the other foot leading?"

4. Discuss and demonstrate "right," "left," "front," and "back."

5. Challenge the children with the following tasks:
   ○ Slide right.
   ○ Gallop forward.
   ○ Run backward.
   ○ Slide to the right.
   ○ Gallop with your left foot leading.

Movement Challenges

Arrange partners in scatter formation.

1. Tell the children: "One partner stands still; the other partner walks around the partner. Stop!"

2. Have the pairs switch the partner who stands still and the moving partner.

3. Repeat; then continue: "Move until you are in front of your partner."

Lesson 8.2 *(continued)*

Concluding Activities (5 minutes)

Partner Follow the Leader

Keep partners in scatter formation.

1. Have partners alternate being leader at 1-minute intervals.
2. Direct the leader to use one of today's locomotor patterns to move about the area with the partner following using the same pattern: "Leaders, you can walk, slide, or gallop. Change which foot you lead with. Partners, follow the leader!"

From K.T. Thomas, A.M. Lee, and J.R. Thomas, 2008, *Physical education methods for elementary teachers*, 3rd ed. (Champaign, IL: Human Kinetics). Adapted, by permission, from K.T. Thomas, A.M. Lee, and J.R. Thomas, 2000, *Physical education for children: Daily lesson plans for elementary school*, 2nd ed. (Champaign, IL: Human Kinetics), 256-258.

Lesson 8.3

Circuit Training

Student Objectives 2 4 5

- Demonstrate Fitness Circuit.
- Stay on task.
- Take turns.
- State that regular exercise means exercising 3 times every week.
- State that physical fitness means having enough energy to move all day and be healthy.

Equipment and Materials

- 6 cones
- 6 identifying signs (Use numbers and pictures reminding children of what to do at the stations; photos of previous or older children performing the exercises are helpful.)
- Tape (to attach signs to cones)
- Music or special signal (e.g., whistle)

Warm-Up Activities (5 minutes)

Use Pyramid in lesson 6.2 on page 144.

Skill-Development Activities (20 minutes)

Fitness Circuit

Place 6 cones with either numbers or pictures for identification in a circle with 30 feet (9 m) between each cone. Divide the children into 6 small groups, and place one group at each cone.

1. Spend 5 or 6 minutes explaining how to use the circuit and how to do each exercise. (When this is a repeat lesson, quickly review the circuit by describing and demonstrating the activities for only 1 or 2 minutes.)

2. At first, have the children spend about 1 minute at each station, with 30 seconds to travel between stations.

3. Over time, as the children gain experience, strength, and endurance, have them spend 2 minutes at each station and 15 seconds in between. In addition, altering the time frames makes the activity fun; for example, sometimes go slowly between cones (1 minute) and make short stops (5 seconds) at cones.

4. Tell the children:

   ○ At each cone, do a different exercise until the signal. When the music stops (or the whistle blows), run to the next cone and do the exercise for that cone.

   ○ Run clockwise, in this direction (point).

   ○ When you hear the music, what should you be doing? (Exercising.)

   ○ When the music stops, what should you be doing? (Running to the next cone.)

   ○ If you get to the cone and the music has not started, run in place until the music signals for you to start the exercise.

5. Have the children practice running between and stopping at the cones on the signal. Alter the amount of time between the cones by saying: "Change, move s-l-o-w-l-y, at normal speed, or fast." You may want to accompany the verbal instruction with an arm signal. For example,

Lesson 8.3 (continued)

move your arm in a circle so that the children can judge the amount of time to move between stations by the speed of your arm (e.g., slow arm circle for long times between).

6. Begin the activity and then continue as time permits.

STATION 1: BIG SWING

Tell and demonstrate for the children: "Stand with your feet shoulder-width apart and knees slightly bent. Bend at the waist and knees and swing both arms between your legs, reaching backward as far as possible. Change directions of the arm swing; move both arms in front of your body and then up and over your head and back as far as possible. Do this as continuously as possible in a rhythmic motion. This exercise helps your body bend or become more flexible."

STATION 2: BIG STEPPERS

Tell and demonstrate for the children: "Standing and staying in one place, take big marching steps" (exaggerate, bringing knees toward chest).

STATION 3: BIG CURLS

Tell and demonstrate for the children: "Standing with feet shoulder-width apart and arms hanging relaxed to the side, look at your belly button by curving your backbone slightly. Tighten your abdominal muscles and hold for 5 counts; then stand straight, relax 5 counts, and repeat."

STATION 4: BIG JUMPS

Tell and demonstrate for the children: "Pretend you are standing at the back of an imaginary box. Jump over the box going forward; then jump to the side, backward, and to the other side, in a pattern as if you were jumping over the edges of the box." (Note: A picture of a box may be a good reminder of what the children should do at this station.)

STATION 5: BIG APPLES

Tell and demonstrate for the children: "Stand with feet shoulder-width apart and hands on waist. Reach with one hand as far to one side as possible, and pretend you are picking an apple off a high branch on a tree beside you. Now move the apple above your head and put it in the pretend basket on the opposite side of your body. Remember to stretch throughout the movement. Repeat with the other hand to the other side." (Note: A picture of an apple may be a good reminder of what the children should do at this station.)

STATION 6: BIG CIRCLES

Tell and demonstrate for the children: "Jog in your own circle forward, backward, sideways facing in, and sideways facing out. Repeat. Remember to stay in your own space!" (Note: You may need to have groups practice this all at once—spread out through the play area—before sending the children through the circuit.)

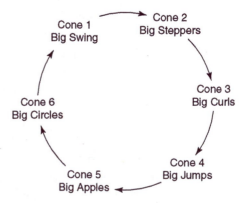

Concluding Activities (5 minutes)

Physical Fitness Concept

Gather the children into an information formation.

1. Explain the concept to the children: "Regular exercise helps you develop physical fitness. Physical fitness means that you are healthy and have enough energy to move all day without becoming too tired. Regular exercise means that you do moderate to vigorous exercise at least 3 times a week for at least 10 minutes at a time, 3 times each exercise day."

2. Discuss these concepts: "'Moderate to vigorous' means that the movements make you breathe hard and possibly sweat. Can you name some things you do that are moderate to vigorous exercise?" Allow children to respond, helping them distinguish between moderate to vigorous and sedentary activities.

3. Continue the discussion:
   ○ Do members of your family exercise regularly? How? (Long walks, tennis, jogging.)
   ○ Being healthy and having enough energy to move all day long without becoming too tired probably means you are physically fit.
   ○ Can you name someone from the movies or television who is physically fit? (Michael Jordan, Sylvester Stallone, Mia Hamm.)
   ○ Why do you think these people are physically fit? (They exercise regularly, they look healthy, and they appear to have a lot of energy, so it is a combination of exercise and energy.)

4. Finish the discussion: "Can you walk like a person with a lot of energy?" Encourage children to move about the area with a lot of energy, and point out children who are especially energetic. Ask the children: "Can you move like a person with little or no energy?" Children should move slowly, with poor posture, sad faces, and so on.

Alternative Learning Activities

1. Ask the children to bring in (or select from magazines and newspapers you provide) pictures of "fit" and "not fit" people. Those who are fit should be demonstrating high energy. Make a collage of the two types of pictures and draw a large circle with a slash through it on those of "not fit."

2. Ask children to draw pictures of people doing moderate to vigorous activities.

3. Invite a parent or person from the community to talk about his or her exercise program. (Police and firefighters are good sources.)

From K.T. Thomas, A.M. Lee, and J.R. Thomas, 2008, *Physical education methods for elementary teachers*, 3rd ed. (Champaign, IL: Human Kinetics). Adapted, by permission, from K.T. Thomas, A.M. Lee, and J.R. Thomas, 2000, *Physical education for children: Daily lesson plans for elementary school*, 2nd ed. (Champaign, IL: Human Kinetics), 50-52.

Lesson 8.4

Physical Activity and Fitness

Student Objectives 2

- Name a benefit of physical activity.
- Name two or more components of health-related physical fitness.

Equipment and Materials

- Magazines, scissors, glue, paper, markers or crayons for collages

---

Health Concept (30 minutes)

Gather the children into an information formation for the entire discussion.

Physical Activity

1. Introduce the concept: "Physical activity is part of a healthy life; physical fitness means being able to do a specific amount of physical activity." Introduce the following definitions:
   - A sedentary person is one who sits and rests most of the time.
   - A physically active person is one who walks or moves around. For example, a "physically active person" may have three 10-minute bouts of activity each day. A physically fit person is one who trains his or her body so that it can do certain physical tasks, including everyday living tasks. Physical fitness has five parts: cardiovascular (aerobic) fitness, muscular strength and endurance, flexibility, and a healthy amount of body fat.
2. Ask the children: "Can you name some jobs that are sedentary?" (Typist, bus driver, cashier.) "Can you name some jobs that are physically active?" (Construction worker, train conductor, janitor.) "Who can you name that is physically fit?" (Michael Jordan, Tiger Woods.) "How do you know?" (They are able to perform well in their sports because they have trained their bodies.)

Identify Sedentary Versus Active Activities

1. Tell the children: "For each activity listed, say 'active' or 'sedentary.'"
   - Using the elevator
   - Riding the bus
   - Cleaning the house
   - Watching television
   - Taking the stairs
   - Walking to school
   - Playing basketball
   - Taking a nap
   - Mowing the grass

2. Ask the children: "Can you name some ways you could be more physically active?" (Take several responses, making sure the children understand that chores and other nonsport and nonplay activities, such as yard work and house cleaning, can be good for health.)

Physical Fitness and Health

1. Introduce this idea: "A physically fit person should be able to do the following things:"
   - Jog (or any other combination of aerobic activity) for 3 continuous 10-minute segments 3 days each week, do 10 sit-ups and 10 push-ups
   - Touch his or her toes (with knees slightly bent for safety); have some body fat, but not too much

2. Tell the children: "Being physically active regularly leads to being physically fit, reducing health risks. People who are sedentary are often sick and sometimes die when they are young. What could a person with a sedentary job do to be healthier?" (Exercise after work to be more physically active.)

3. Have the children draw or cut pictures out of magazines to make a collage of sedentary and active people.

From K.T. Thomas, A.M. Lee, and J.R. Thomas, 2008, *Physical education methods for elementary teachers*, 3rd ed. (Champaign, IL: Human Kinetics). Adapted, by permission, from K.T. Thomas, A.M. Lee, and J.R. Thomas, 2000, *Physical education for children: Daily lesson plans for elementary school*, 2nd ed. (Champaign, IL: Human Kinetics), 335-336.

Lesson 8.5

Galloping, Sliding, and Skipping

Student Objectives 1 2 5

- Distinguish between galloping, sliding, and skipping.
- Gallop, slide, and skip in different directions.
- Gallop, slide, and skip with a partner.

Equipment and Materials

- 1 drum
- 1 parachute

Warm-Up Activities (5 minutes)

Magic Movements

Arrange the children in a circle.

1. Explain the activity:
    - Run in a circle.
    - On "freeze!" stop and create a movement to express a feeling, such as happy, sad, frightened, ugly, or gentle.
2. Name some feelings and have the children express them, and then ask the children for additional suggestions.

Skill-Development Activities (20 minutes)

Locomotor Tasks

Arrange the children in scatter formation.

GALLOPING

1. Describe and demonstrate galloping: "To 'gallop' you step and leap (one leg leads, the other joins)."
2. Use a drum for your start and stop signal. Challenge the children with the following tasks:
    - Gallop freely in general space.
    - Gallop so that your body goes high with each step. Push off hard with your back leg, and swing your arms.
    - Take very large steps as you gallop.
    - Gallop backward. This is very hard. Use your arms.
    - Think of a movement to do with the arms (head, shoulders) as you gallop.
    - Gallop with a partner.

SLIDING

Make sure the children are still in scatter formation.

1. Describe and demonstrate sliding: "To 'slide' means you step and then close (move your foot up to the other foot) going sideways."
2. Challenge the children with the following tasks:
   - Slide to the right (left).
   - Look in the direction in which you're sliding.
   - Look in the opposite direction.
   - Try other pathways.
   - Slide while holding both hands with a partner.

SKIPPING

Make sure the children are still in scatter formation.

1. Describe and demonstrate skipping: "To 'skip' you step-hop."
2. Challenge the children with the following tasks:
   - Skip freely in general space.
   - Skip and think of different positions for your arms (in front, to the side, folded in front of chest, behind back).
   - Skip high (low, fast, slowly).
   - Skip with a partner (two other children).

Concluding Activities (5 minutes)

Parachute Activities

Space the children around the parachute; each child holds the edge with one or both hands. Moving clockwise or counterclockwise, have the children gallop, slide, and skip, stopping on the start or stop signal.

Lesson 8.6

Moderate to Vigorous Games

Student Objectives 4 5

- Cooperate with two other children when playing Three-on-Three.
- Demonstrate correct technique in stretching.
- Define cardiorespiratory, or aerobic, fitness.

Equipment and Materials

- 4 cones
- 10 playground balls

Warm-Up Activities (5 minutes)

Fitness Circuit: Stretching Routine

Arrange and mark 6 stations in the center of a large rectangle defined by 4 cones. Divide the children into 6 groups, and assign each group to a station.

1. Describe and demonstrate the stretching exercise at each station. The first time the children do the circuit, use 5 to 6 minutes to explain the stations and rotation, and allow 2 minutes at each station. In subsequent lessons, allow 3 minutes at each station after a brief review of the 6 stretches and safe-stretching guidelines.
2. Remind the children of the importance of stretching slowly to the point of tension, not pain. No bouncing!
3. After the first station, signal the children to leave their station, run to the outside boundary, and return to the next station in order. Continue until each group has visited each station.

STATION 1: SHOULDER PULL

Slowly pull your left elbow across the front of your body toward the opposite shoulder. Hold for 10 seconds. Relax and repeat with the opposite elbow.

STATION 2: ARM REACH-OUT

Sit on the floor. Lock your fingers together and, with palms facing out, straighten your arms out in front of you. Stretch and hold for 10 seconds. Relax and repeat.

STATION 3: TRICEPS STRETCH

Lift your arms up over your head and touch your elbows. Hold your right elbow with your left hand and gently pull. Let your right hand drop behind your head as you stretch. Hold for 10 seconds and relax. Repeat, pulling your left elbow with your right hand.

STATION 4: FORWARD STRADDLE STRETCH

Sit on the floor with your legs straight and spread about 3 feet (0.9 m) apart. Bend forward at the hip. Grasp your right knee, calf, or ankle (as far down your leg as you can go) and pull your body gently toward your leg. Hold for 10 seconds; then relax and repeat on the left side.

STATION 5: SHOULDER-LIFT STRETCH

Lie on the floor with your knees bent and your fingertips touching your ears. Slowly lift your head forward while stretching your upper back and neck. You should feel a gentle pull along your spine (backbone) to the shoulder blades. Hold for 5 seconds; then slowly relax to the starting position. Relax for 10 seconds and repeat.

STATION 6: FROG STRETCH

Lie down with your knees bent and the soles of your feet together. If you relax, gravity will pull your knees toward the ground and stretch the insides of your thighs. Relax for 10 seconds, and then lift your knees up and toward each other, so that they are no longer relaxed, for 10 seconds (knees do not need to touch at this point). Do not bounce!

Skill-Development Activities (20 minutes)

Three-on-Three

Define a large rectangle with the cones. Divide the children into groups of 3, and give a ball each to half of the groups. Have this half of the class line up along one short side of the rectangle. Have the remaining groups stand in the rectangle about one-third of the way from the short side where the other groups are lined up. Pair each group on the line with a group inside the rectangle.

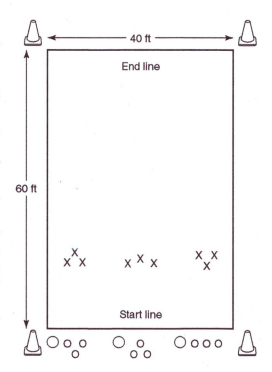

1. Describe and demonstrate the game:
   - The object of the game for the team with the ball is to move the ball from the starting line across the far end line.
   - You may take 5 steps carrying the ball; then you must stop and pass, bounce, or roll the ball toward the end line.
   - You must carry the ball or pass it to another group member such that the ball goes over the end line. Remember to use no more than 5 steps when carrying the ball.
   - The object of the game for the other team is to take the ball away.
   - When and if you take the ball away, by catching it or by a tie (taking hold of the ball when a child from the other team is holding the ball), go immediately to the start line; from there, try to get the ball over the end line.
   - Whenever the ball goes over the end line, your team trades roles with the other team.
2. Have the children play Three-on-Three.

Concluding Activities (5 minutes)

Physical Fitness Concept

Gather the children into an information formation.

1. Present the concept to the children: Cardiovascular fitness, or heart fitness, is also called "aerobic fitness." A person who can jog, ride a bike, or swim for 20 minutes is demonstrating aerobic fitness. Cardiovascular, or aerobic, fitness has three major benefits:
   - A trained heart has a lower resting heart rate because the heart pumps more blood each beat, and so fewer beats are needed to pump the same amount of blood.

- A trained heart has more pathways for blood to travel in and around the heart.
- Training lowers blood pressure (how hard the blood pushes against the artery walls).

2. Tell the children: "All of these benefits reduce the risk of illness related to the heart."

3. "When I say, 'Start,' count the number of beats that your heart makes. You can count your heartbeats by putting your fingers on each side of your Adam's apple and pushing gently. Swallowing helps you locate the Adam's apple. Start."

4. Stop the count at 10 seconds.

5. Tell the children: "Now, jump up and down quickly 20 times." Have the children count their heart rate again. The heart rate should be higher.

From K.T. Thomas, A.M. Lee, and J.R. Thomas, 2008, *Physical education methods for elementary teachers*, 3rd ed. (Champaign, IL: Human Kinetics). Adapted, by permission, from K.T. Thomas, A.M. Lee, and J.R. Thomas, 2000, *Physical education for children: Daily lesson plans for elementary school*, 2nd ed. (Champaign, IL: Human Kinetics), 439-440.

Lesson 8.7

Creative Movement

Student Objectives 1 5

- Combine several locomotor skills while you are moving.
- Duplicate a partner's movement sequence.
- Work cooperatively with a group to achieve a goal.

Equipment and Materials

- 2 rhythm sticks
- 1 drum
- 1 tambourine
- Polyspots or polydomes to mark lines

Warm-Up Activities (5 minutes)

Use Movement to Sounds from lesson 4.4, page 89. Variation: Have children gallop.

Skill-Development Activities (20 minutes)

Movement Combinations

Make sure the children are still in scatter formation.

1. Have the children perform the following movement combinations:
   - Leap forward (4 counts), leap backward (4 counts), leap while turning (4 counts), jump in place (4 counts), and collapse.
   - Hop right (4 counts), hop left (4 counts), run forward (4 counts), stretch (2 counts), and curl (2 counts).
   - Swing right leg forward and back (8 counts), swing left leg forward and back (8 counts).
   - Hop in place (4 counts), hop forward (4 counts), hop backward (4 counts), hop in place (4 counts).
   - Walk forward (8 counts), jump in place (8 counts), walk backward (8 counts), jump in place (8 counts).
   - Slide right (8 counts), slide left (8 counts).
   - Run (3 counts), leap (1 count). Repeat several times.
   - Run (2 counts), leap (2 counts). Repeat several times.
2. Repeat challenges as time allows.

Partner Copy Activity

Arrange partners in scatter formation.

1. Select two or more locomotor or nonlocomotor skills you wish to target and a variety of counts (e.g., 4, 8, 12, 16, 24).
2. Explain the activity:
   - The goal of the activity is for the leader to use the skills in a sequence with the specified number of counts. For example, the task might be to use walk, hop, and jump for 16 counts. The sequence could be walk (8 counts), hop (4 counts), and jump (4 counts).

- One of you creates the movement sequence and the partner watches.
- The partner then repeats the sequence.
- Then you trade roles and repeat the activity using other skills and counts.

3. Present the following tasks for partners:
   - Walk, run, stretch, and twist for 12 counts.
   - Gallop forward, gallop backward, jump forward, and jump backward for 24 counts.
   - Walk forward, walk backward, and hop in a circle for 12 counts.
   - Skip and slide for 16 counts.

4. After several practice trials, have the children select their own movements and number of counts.

Advanced Movement Sequences

Divide the children into groups of 4 to 6 and place each group behind a line. If your space is large enough, create smaller groups so that more children can move at once.

1. Describe and demonstrate the following sequence: "Take 3 jumps forward; 5 walking steps backward; 8 galloping steps with the right foot leading; 8 galloping steps with the left foot leading."

2. Have children take turns helping each other learn and practice the sequence in their groups. Practice the sequence with the children moving across the floor until it becomes easy.

3. Repeat with the following sequences:
   - Take 3 hops forward on right foot; 3 hops forward on left foot; 6 leaps forward; 4 jumps forward; 8 walking steps backward.
   - Take 4 walking steps forward; 4 walking steps backward; 2 hops right; 2 hops left; 4 jumps forward.
   - Take 2 galloping steps with right foot leading; 2 galloping steps with left foot leading; 4 walking steps forward; 8 jumps side to side.

Concluding Activities (5 minutes)

Movement Sequences

Ask each group of children to create a movement sequence to perform while they are moving across the floor.

From K.T. Thomas, A.M. Lee, and J.R. Thomas, 2008, *Physical education methods for elementary teachers*, 3rd ed. (Champaign, IL: Human Kinetics). Adapted, by permission, from K.T. Thomas, A.M. Lee, and J.R. Thomas, 2000, *Physical education for children: Daily lesson plans for elementary school*, 2nd ed. (Champaign, IL: Human Kinetics), 957-958.

Lesson 8.8

Rope Jumping

Student Objectives 2 4 5

- Explain how to use the overload principle to develop strength.
- Maintain continuous activity with a long rope.
- Jump a short rope cooperatively with a small group for 10 minutes.

Equipment and Materials

- 4 jump ropes per group (12 to 16 feet [3.7 to 4.8 m] long)
- 1 short jump rope per group of 3 children

Warm-Up Activities (5 minutes)

Jumping Through Long Ropes

Divide the children into groups of 6 or 8, and assign each group to a rope pattern made with 4 parallel long jump ropes.

1. Explain the activity:
   - Starting at one end, jump over the ropes into the spaces between the ropes; first go forward and then sideways.
   - Repeat several times, hopping on the right foot, hopping on the left foot, and leaping.
   - Play Follow the Leader; each child gets a turn to lead the group.
2. Have the children do the activity.

Skill-Development Activities (20 minutes)

Review Front Door and Back Door with the children (see lesson plan 5.3, page 117).

Swinging

Divide the children into groups of 4 or 5, each group with a long jump rope, in a scatter formation. Establish a rotation system for each group, with 2 children turning and 2 or 3 jumping.

1. Describe and demonstrate swinging: "In swinging, the Turners swing the rope slightly from side to side. Jumpers stand next to the rope and jump over it as it swings."
2. Have the children practice swinging; rotate so that Turners get a chance to practice jumping.

Swing and Turn

1. Describe and demonstrate Swing and Turn: "In Swing and Turn, the Turner swings the rope over the head of the Jumper. The Jumper jumps over the rope."
2. Have the children practice Swing and Turn; rotate Jumpers and Turners. Continue practice until most children can jump at least 3 jumps without missing.

Lesson 8.8 *(continued)*

Continuous Jumping to Chants

Divide the children into pairs in scatter formation; each pair has a rope.

1. Say each chant; then have children practice it. Explain that jumping rope continuously is good aerobic exercise.
2. Have each pair select one of the chants and jump continuously up to 50 or until a miss occurs.

10-Minute Jump

Divide the children into groups of 3, and give each group a short jump rope. Have the groups get into scatter formation.

1. Explain the game:
   - The object of the game is for one team member to be jumping at all times.
   - One child should start jumping. When he or she begins to tire, the second child should begin jumping.
   - When the second child begins to tire, the third child should begin jumping. Continue taking turns and resting for 10 minutes.
2. Have the children play 10-Minute Jump.

Cool-Down

Walk one lap forward, one backward.

Concluding Activities (5 minutes)

Physical Fitness Concept

Gather the children into an advanced information formation.

1. Review the definition of muscular strength: "Do you remember what 'muscular strength' is?" (The greatest amount of weight that your muscles can lift in one try.)
2. Review the meaning of overload: "Do you remember what the 'overload principle' is in terms of muscular strength and endurance?" (Exercising with more weight than usual.)
3. Discuss exercises for strength training: "Overload training is a way to help your muscles get stronger. You want to make your muscles work harder. If you can lift a 5-pound (2.3 kg) weight easily with one hand, but a 10-pound (4.5 kg) weight is very hard to lift, then use a 10-pound (4.5 kg) weight to exercise for strength. You won't be able to perform many repetitions because you have overloaded your muscles."
4. Ask the children the following questions:
   - If you can lift a 10-pound (4.5 kg) weight easily, can you develop strength by using a 5-pound (2.3 kg) weight and performing many repetitions? (No.)
   - If a person can lift a 30-pound (13.5 kg) weight but can only do one or two repetitions, can he or she develop strength using the 30-pound (13.5 kg) weight? (Yes.) What does overload training mean in terms of muscular strength and endurance? (Increasing weight to develop strength or increasing number of repetitions to develop endurance.)

From K.T. Thomas, A.M. Lee, and J.R. Thomas, 2008, *Physical education methods for elementary teachers*, 3rd ed. (Champaign, IL: Human Kinetics). Adapted, by permission, from K.T. Thomas, A.M. Lee, and J.R. Thomas, 2000, *Physical education for children: Daily lesson plans for elementary school*, 2nd ed. (Champaign, IL: Human Kinetics), 822-823.

Lesson 8.9

Signals, Boundaries, Groupings, and Rules

Student Objectives 2 5

- Change direction on a visual signal.
- Move diagonally, lengthwise, and crosswise across an area.
- Move in an area within an area.
- Give situational examples of rules.
- Cooperate in a discussion group.

Equipment and Materials

- Physical Education Rules poster
- 4 cones

Warm-Up Activities (5 minutes)

Moving to Visual Signs

Arrange 4 cones to form a rectangle. In response to the following visual signals, the children move in the indicated directions and stop. Movement should be continuous unless you give the stop signal.

- Thumb pointed over your shoulder. (Children move forward.)
- Finger pointed right. (Children move left.)
- Finger pointed left. (Children move right.)
- Finger pointed straight ahead. (Children move backward.)
- Hand held up with palm facing front. (Children stop.)
- Finger pointed to either back corner. (Children move diagonally.)
- Hand held up with palm facing front. (Children stop.)

Skill-Development Activities (20 minutes)

Form Two Teams

Children form a line on a boundary line and count off by twos.

1. The number ones move across the area to the other boundary line.
2. The ones are Team 1 and the twos are Team 2.

Touch Down

Team 1 lines up on a boundary line; each player holds both hands out in front, with the hands placed together to form a pocket. Team 2 lines up on the opposite boundary line. You hold a small object that is used as the bait.

1. Holding the small object, walk to each player; pretend to drop the object in that player's hands.

Lesson 8.9 *(continued)*

2. Give the object to a player on the team, but don't let the opposing team know who that player is.
3. On a signal, the teams run to the opposite boundary lines; each player on Team 2 attempts to tag a player on Team 1.
4. If the player with the object gets to the opposite boundary line without being tagged, Team 1 scores a point.
5. Repeat the game with Team 2 as the carrying team.

Moving Within a Rectangle

Arrange the children in 4 groups. Divide the rectangle into quarters (point out imaginary lines), and place one group in each of the quarters.

1. Ask the children to move within their own areas.
2. The children stop on a signal and, on the next signal, they move together to another area.
3. Repeat; include the rule that they cannot go to the same area twice.

Concluding Activities (5 minutes)

Rules

Show the Physical Education Rules poster. Ask the children to recall and verbally list the rules. Watch for situations in the remainder of the organization lessons that are examples of good behavior regarding rules; stop the class activity and point out these examples.

Cooperative Discussion Groups

Arrange the children in groups of 4 to 6 to form heterogeneous discussion groups. Have equal representation of children of different races, ethnic origins, social classes, and gender.

1. Establish guidelines for cooperative discussion groups. Tell the children that everyone must participate in the discussion, only one child can talk at a time, the others must listen, and everyone must show respect for others.
2. Present a topic for the groups to discuss. Here are some examples:
   - Describe a child who takes responsibility for his or her own behavior.
   - What should we do with children in our class who fail to take responsibility for their own behavior?
   - How should we deal with children who do not follow the class rules?
   - How should we deal with children who do not try?
   - How should we deal with children who do not take care of the equipment?

From K.T. Thomas, A.M. Lee, and J.R. Thomas, 2008, *Physical education methods for elementary teachers*, 3rd ed. (Champaign, IL: Human Kinetics). Adapted, by permission, from A.M. Lee, K.T. Thomas, and J.R. Thomas, 2000, *Physical education for children: Daily lesson plans for middle school*, 2nd ed. (Champaign, IL: Human Kinetics), 6-7.

Lesson 8.10

Forming Groups and Journal Writing

Student Objectives   5   6

- Use task cards in a station formation.
- Share feelings about physical education in writing.

Equipment and Materials

- Task cards
- A notebook and pencil for each child

Warm-Up Activities (5 minutes)

Forming Groups

Review forming groups with adaptations. Make cards before class and distribute them to the children as they enter the gym. Each card should be either red, blue, yellow, or green; cards should have various team names printed on them (e.g., Cubs, Cardinals, Rangers, or Orioles). Cards should be numbered from 1 to 28 or up to the total number of children in the class. With 28 children in the class, there should be 7 red, 7 blue, 7 yellow, and 7 green cards. Each team name should be printed at least once on each color.

1. Present the following tasks:
   - Find a partner who has the same color card. Children should ignore the team name and the number.
   - Now find a partner who has the same number on the card. Children should ignore the team name and the color.
2. Form two groups. Cardinals and Cubs make up the first group; Rangers and Orioles make up the second group. Children should ignore the color and the number.
3. Continue with other combinations.
4. Form two groups. Group 1 = numbers 1 through 14 and Group 2 = numbers 15 through 28.
5. Form four groups. Group 1 = Cardinals, Group 2 = Cubs, Group 3 = Rangers, and Group 4 = Orioles.

Skill-Development Activities (20 minutes)

Task Cards

Fitness tasks are printed on cards large enough for the children to read (8.5 by 11 inches [21.5 by 28 cm] or larger).

1. Place one of the cards at each of the 4 stations.
2. Children are assigned to a station, and, on a signal, they move to the next station. Allow 2 or 3 minutes at each station.
   - Task Card #1: Run in place 50 steps or more without stopping.

Lesson 8.10 *(continued)*

- o Task Card #2: Moving in circles or figure-eights, gallop or skip for 50 steps without stopping.
- o Task Card #3: Hop 25 times on the right foot and 25 times on the left foot.
- o Task Card #4: Jump in place at least 50 times.

Partner Relay

Arrange the children in pairs and assign each pair to 1 of 5 relay teams. Mark a starting line and a return line.

1. At the return line, place a stack of cards for each relay team.
2. Specify on the cards (one for each pair) how the pair returns to the starting line. Here are some examples:
    - o Run with one child going forward and one going backward.
    - o Hold hands, face each other, and slide.
    - o Gallop with opposite feet forward.

Concluding Activities (5 minutes)

Feelings About Physical Education

Arrange the children in scatter formation. Each child needs a notebook and a pencil.

1. Ask the children to think about their own feelings when they were in physical education last year.
2. Stimulate the children's thinking by asking them to complete the following open-ended statements:
    - o I feel good in physical education when I . . .
    - o My favorite activity is . . .
    - o If I were the teacher, I would change . . .
    - o Some things I do not like about physical education are . . .
3. This should be a serious activity; children's responses should be private and not discussed in class.
4. Read the journals to get ideas about how the children think and feel about their experiences in physical education.

From K.T. Thomas, A.M. Lee, and J.R. Thomas, 2008, *Physical education methods for elementary teachers*, 3rd ed. (Champaign, IL: Human Kinetics). Adapted, by permission, from A.M. Lee, K.T. Thomas, and J.R. Thomas, 2000, *Physical education for children: Daily lesson plans for middle school*, 2nd ed. (Champaign, IL: Human Kinetics), 10-11.

Lesson 8.11

Cooperative Teams and Discussion Groups

Student Objectives 2 5	Equipment and Materials
• Work successfully in a learning group. • Cooperate in a discussion group.	• 6 playground balls

Warm-Up Activities (5 minutes)

Forming Groups

Review forming groups with adaptations. See lesson plan 8.10, page 237.

Skill-Development Activities (20 minutes)

Cooperative Learning Groups

Arrange the children in groups of 4 to 6 to form heterogeneous learning teams.

1. Review the guidelines for cooperative group work (see lesson plan 8.9, page 236).
2. Discuss the importance of cooperative effort in group work.
   - Each child is responsible for his or her own work and the work of the team. The group is not successful unless all of the children accomplish the goal.
   - Children must help each other.
   - Each child must try hard.
3. Present a problem for the groups to solve. Here are some examples:
   - Create a ball game that uses throwing and catching.
   - Create a ball game that uses kicking.
   - Discover ways to explain the meaning of balance.
   - Discover ways to explain the meaning of strength.
   - Discover ways to explain differences in body shapes and weight.
   - Discover ways to explain how "normal" includes a range of sizes and shapes.

Concluding Activities (5 minutes)

Cooperative Discussion Groups

1. Continue work with cooperative grouping by asking children to discuss a variety of topics.
2. Present open-ended questions for the groups to discuss and try to solve. All of the groups discuss the same question. Here are some examples:

Lesson 8.11 *(continued)*

- ○ What should we do about children in our class who do not like physical education?
- ○ Why is physical education important?
- ○ What are the most important things that we can learn in physical education class this year?
- ○ What does playing fair mean?
- ○ Why is it important to accept individual differences in sizes and shapes?

3. A representative from each group shares the solution with the entire class.

CHAPTER 9

Organizing for Teaching

RACHEL, AGE 7

Many instructional strategies are available to you. One way these strategies can be described is in terms of learner involvement in decision making. Effective teachers employ a variety of teaching strategies.

Learner Outcomes

After studying this chapter, you should be able to do the following:

- Define indirect and direct styles of teaching.

- Distinguish among station teaching, guided discovery, exploration, contracts, cooperative learning, and task sheets.

- Modify a game for contextual practice.

Glossary Terms

direct instruction approach	task sheets	guided discovery
indirect instruction approach	learning contracts	exploration
station teaching	cooperative learning	contextual practice

After selecting content, you must decide how to organize the children for instruction and how to communicate the content to them. These decisions ultimately define your responsibilities and those of the learner in a particular teaching context. They also determine the extent to which tasks are appropriate for individual learners. Chapter 8, Planning Your Curriculum, discussed factors that you should consider in determining learner outcomes and planning for a developmentally appropriate program of physical activities. This information should ensure that the content you select is generally age appropriate. Another of your responsibilities is to implement a quality lesson for individuals within each class. You can accomplish some lesson objectives most effectively by presenting a specific series of activities or tasks to a group of children and asking them to respond according to directions. For these lessons, all of the children perform the same task at the same time. You might organize some class periods to allow children to practice different tasks, however. There is always more than one way to organize and deliver a lesson. You can choose from a number of teaching approaches and organizational patterns, depending on the objectives of the lesson, the characteristics of the students, the resources available, and your own abilities and interests. Good teachers use more than one approach and might do so even within one lesson.

This approach—using a method appropriate to the content and objective—is no different than what classroom teachers do every day in math, science, reading, and other academic subject areas. The approach may be different than what physical education specialists are used to. In fact, you can probably think of several stereotypes of a physical education teacher. These may not be accurate or fair, but they do demonstrate why physical education specialists should model a variety of approaches and patterns. In chapter 10, Managing Students, we present management routines. Do not confuse having routines—which are good—with having only one teaching approach and one organizational strategy. Limited approaches and strategies are not the best practice.

You need to understand how to organize for teaching so that

- you can individualize lessons to optimize learning,

- you have numerous instructional approaches available, and

- you can select instructional approaches based on the content, the learner, and your characteristics.

Teaching Approaches

Teaching approaches, teaching styles, and instructional strategies all refer to how you go about delivering the content of the lesson. Various styles or approaches are usually defined in terms of the amount of teacher control versus learner involvement in the lesson. You might select a **direct instruction approach**, in which the emphasis is on class control, with little opportunity for children to choose between alternatives and make decisions about their own learning. Using this style, you would give explicit instructions and provide a clear description of what learners are to do. The instructions would specify how children should respond and direct all aspects of the class. Think of teaching styles on a continuum, with a direct approach at one end and an indirect approach at the other (figure 9.1). An **indirect instruction approach** is characterized by opportunities for student involvement with teachers establishing a learning environment that helps students discover solutions on their own. Indirect teaching involves children in decision making at a maximum level. You can select an approach that falls anywhere along the continuum from direct to indirect, depending on the goal of the lesson and the intended outcome. Examples that fall between direct and indirect are station teaching, individualized instruction, and cooperative learning. Indirect approaches are consistent with the constructivist approach and active learning discussed in chapter 2, Meeting the Mission of the Elementary School. Another way to organize teaching is to consider the context. Some of you may prefer to remove skills from the context for practice, and some skills fit this approach well.

For example, you might decide to teach the Grapevine Step in a progression that begins with a drill, then with practice in a circle using the parachute, and finally in a dance. Another teacher, who is teaching in the context, might begin with the actual dance. Another example is learning basketball shots in drills versus during game play. The amount of learner involvement and the degree of context specificity are two variables that you need to consider during planning.

Approaches Without Learner Involvement: Direct Teaching

You can teach many lessons most appropriately with the direct style. If the lesson objective is for all of the children to perform a particular movement in a particular way and learning can be enhanced by listening to a verbal description and observing a model, direct teaching is appropriate. You can effectively teach skills such as the Forward Roll, the Standing Long Jump, or Three-Beanbag Juggling by the direct style. The organizational arrangement for direct approaches is usually teaching the whole class, but you can use other formations, such as partners or small groups. The goal is for you to direct all aspects of the class, but you can offer movement tasks of varying difficulty for children at different developmental levels. You should arrange the children so that all of them can see and hear you, because you deliver all of the content and determine the pace of the class. You explain the movement or movement sequence, including well-selected cues; demonstrate all or part of the skill; signal the children to repeat the movement one or more times; observe their performance and provide feedback; and, eventually, evaluate the final achievement. In a direct approach, the teacher controls all aspects of the class.

The direct style is a good choice when your lesson involves introduction of a new skill or when safety is an issue. This format allows you to have complete control and is useful with classes

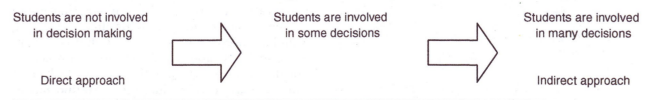

Figure 9.1   Continuum of teaching styles.

From J.R. Thomas, K.T. Thomas, and A.M. Lee, 1988, *Physical education for children: Concepts into practice* (Champaign, IL: Human Kinetics), 107. Adapted by permission of J.R. Thomas, K.T. Thomas, and A.M. Lee.

that are difficult to manage. Often, after students spend some time in controlled practice, they should be able to manage their own behavior well enough that you can give them more opportunities for decision making and individualized practice. Several guidelines are important for successful use of direct teaching:

- Always have a signal (e.g., a drumbeat or a verbal command) to get the attention of the class.

- Provide for maximum practice (e.g., use small groups for drills). Never have children standing in long lines.

- Most important, remember your responsibilities in motor skill learning, as discussed in chapter 4, Motor Performance During Childhood. Identify the skill level of the child on a task and provide for developmentally appropriate practice so that every child finds success.

The direct style can also be applied in lessons in which children play a new game of low organization, learn an aerobic dance or jump rope routine, or practice a folk or square dance. In these situations, guide the class through the steps or sequence using a structured approach.

Concepts Into Practice

Kimi is student teaching. The first lesson she teaches to her fourth-grade class is the Grapevine Step. She recognizes how important it is for the children to master this step, because she will use it in line dances during the next two lessons. As she discusses her teaching options with her cooperating teacher, she decides to use a direct approach to introduce and practice the Grapevine Step. Then, at the end of the lesson, if the children have mastered dancing the step to music, she concludes with a challenge for them to create ways to use the step in small groups. If they have not mastered the step, she can use the concluding time for additional practice. Everything goes smoothly using the direct style, and Kimi sees that all of the children can do the Grapevine Step. She presents the challenge to her class. Most of the groups begin trying ways to use the step, but two groups are standing still, arguing, and becoming frustrated. Kimi visits those groups. The first group has no idea what to do, so she says, "See if you can do the Grapevine Step and put a turn at the end, so that you change directions each time." The second group has many ideas but cannot agree on what to do first. Kimi says, "Try Erin's idea first, then Joe's, then Carrie's. See which one you like best." Kimi's cooperating teacher praised her for identifying the problem and trying two styles of teaching. Kimi realized that the indirect approach may work better for some groups than for others.

Peer demonstrations provide benefits to both motivation and knowledge of skills.

Teaching Approaches With Some Learner Involvement

Some teaching approaches fall between the two extremes of the direct and indirect approaches: station teaching, individualized instruction, and cooperative learning. You can practice many movement tasks and sport skills effectively using a station approach to teaching. With this format, you usually decide which activities to practice, but the children can practice various tasks and can progress at individual rates. **Station teaching** is an effective way to practice after the initial introduction of a skill or movement. You can use it in both primary and upper grades. When you use learning stations, set up several practice areas in the gymnasium or on the playground. This arrangement is similar to learning centers in a classroom and circuit training in physical fitness. You can design lessons for practicing different skills or different levels of a particular skill. Divide the children into groups; assign each group to a station. Signal when the groups are to rotate. After children have some experience working independently at completion of all of the tasks or activities, they can progress individually to the next group. (You can communicate the tasks to the children with task sheets or posters.) This frees you to work with children who are having trouble or to evaluate individual children.

One example of a station learning arrangement is shown in figure 9.2. The tasks shown in the figure are appropriate for children in grade 2. Each station should have enough equipment for five children to participate at the same time. To make sure that the children understand what to do at each station, explain and demonstrate. The task sheets, posters, and other reminders at each station are also helpful. You can use the same activities effectively for practice of sport skills in the upper grades. Ability grouping for sport-skill practice allows a range of skill levels within an age group. Usually, you plan each station with progressive tasks, but you can also design some stations specifically for those children who would benefit from modified (lower-level) or extended (higher-level) tasks. In most sport-skill lessons, children tend to accomplish more if grouped with children of similar skill (Thomas 1994). This is especially important if safety is a concern. Figure 9.3 shows a layout for soccer stations and provides sample tasks. See also "Lesson #3 Gymnastics Lesson" on the DVD-ROM for a video clip showing station teaching.

Individualized Teaching With Task Sheets and Contracts

You can use **task sheets** to communicate the activities to be accomplished to individual children. They can work alone or with partners, but there is always opportunity for individual progression. You can design the sheets for varying lengths of time, and children can work on the same or on different skills. Task sheets may provide some tips for performance, but you should give initial instruction and demonstration for new skills. More often, you might use task sheets to refine skills. When a child works with a partner, this approach allows for valuable evaluation and feedback. Figures 9.4 and 9.5 show two types of task sheets.

Learning contracts provide an excellent way to begin shifting decision-making responsibility from you to the learner. A teacher–student contract is a written agreement of what the student is to accomplish in a specified period. There are several types of contracts; each requires a different amount of student responsibility. Contract teaching should allow varying amounts of time for completing tasks and should provide opportunity for independent work. The choice contract provides a list of activities, and each activity usually has a point value. Students can choose from the tasks and then work at individual rates, but they should be encouraged to select tasks that match beginning competency levels. Figure 9.6 shows an example of a student choice contract.

An open-ended contract gives the student the most responsibility: The student lists the skills to be mastered and the time needed to accomplish them. Figure 9.7 is an example of a contract designed for basketball by a student in grade 5. You can also use open-ended contracts for physical fitness activities outside class.

Cooperative Learning

Cooperative learning is a teaching approach designed to encourage students to take responsibility for their own learning and to work cooperatively with a group to accomplish a goal. Using this format, you can assign children to heterogeneous groups, with equal representation of races, ethnic origins, social classes, and gender. Present the children with a problem or a question and give them time to solve the problem or answer the question. The problem might be to create a ball game that uses throwing and catching or to discover ways to explain the meaning of balance. It is important to establish guidelines for cooperative work. Everyone in the group must participate in the assigned work; however, only one child may talk at a time, and the others must listen quietly. Everyone must show respect for others. It is important that the children assume responsibility for their own work as well as for the work of the entire group. The group is not successful unless all of the children accomplish the goal, so they are encouraged to help each other. Before assigning a cooperative activity, you should set the stage by discussing the following concepts with the class:

- Why groups fail to solve the problem (the problem is too difficult; group members fight with one another)

| 1 Throwing and catching | 2 Kicking | 3 Dribbling |
| 6 Rope jumping | 5 Striking | 4 Jumping and landing |

Station 1—Throwing and catching

- Toss the beanbag over your head and catch it with your right hand (5 times).
- Repeat, using your left hand.
- Stand on the red line and hit the red target on the wall 5 out of 10 times.
- Repeat, using the blue line and the blue target.

Station 2—Kicking

- Kick the ball with your right foot from the red line so that it goes between the cones and hits the wall (5 times).
- Repeat, using your left foot.
- Kick the ball with your right foot from the blue line so that it goes between the cones and hits the wall (5 times).

Station 3—Dribbling

- Dribble the ball in place 10 times using your right hand.
- Repeat, using your left hand.
- Dribble the ball in place 5 times with your left hand and 5 times with your right hand.
- Dribble 10 times, alternating right and left hands.

Station 4—Jumping and landing

- Using two feet, jump through the hoops on the floor.
- Repeat, going backward and sideways.
- Run and jump for distance.

Station 5—Striking

- Strike the balloon up and over your head 5 times using your right hand.
- Repeat, using your left hand.
- Stand on the red line and strike the large ball so that it hits the red target on the wall (5 times).
- Repeat, using the blue line and the blue target.

Station 6—Rope jumping

- With your rope on the floor, jump back and forth over it 10 times.
- Jump rope forward 10 times without missing.
- Repeat, jumping backward.

Figure 9.2 Skill stations.

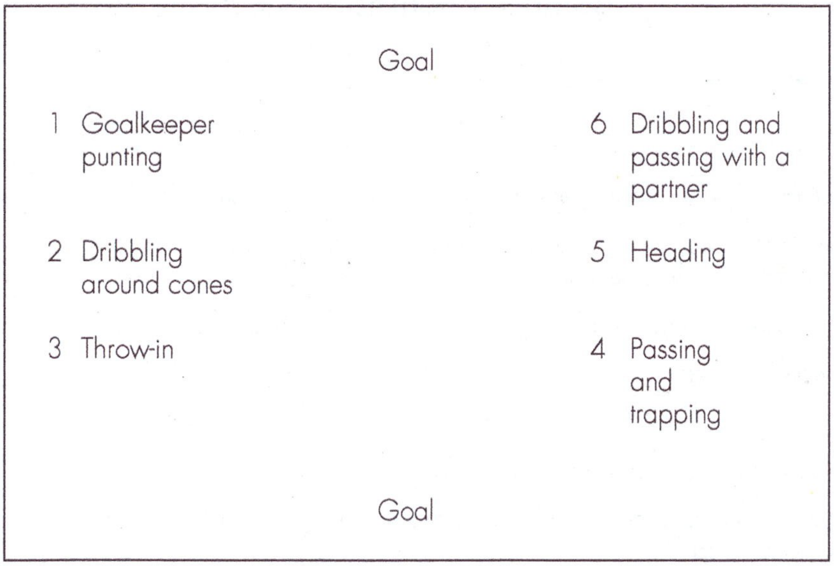

```
                            Goal

    1  Goalkeeper                   6  Dribbling and
       punting                         passing with a
                                       partner

    2  Dribbling                    5  Heading
       around cones

    3  Throw-in                     4  Passing
                                       and
                                       trapping

                            Goal
```

Station 1—Goalkeeper punting

- Punt the ball 10 times to a partner who is 30 yards (27.4 m) away.
- Punt to the right 10 times and to the left 10 times.

Station 2—Dribbling around cones

- Dribble the 30-yard (27.4 m) course several times, weaving in and out of the cones.

Station 3—Throw-in (two-hand overhead)

- Throw for accuracy at the targets placed at 10, 15, and 20 yards (9.1, 11.6, and 18.2 m) (5 times at each distance).

Station 4—Passing and trapping

- Using the inside of the foot, kick a stationary ball to a partner 10 feet (3 m) away 10 times. Partner traps using the sole of the foot.
- Repeat, using nondominant foot.

Station 5—Heading

- Head a ball thrown by a partner 10 times.
- While moving to your right, head a ball thrown by a partner 10 times.
- Repeat while moving to your left.

Station 6—Dribbling and passing with a partner

- Running with a partner at moderate pace 10 yards (9.1 m) apart, dribble and pass with the partner while running a distance of 20 yards (18.2 m).
- Repeat several times with rest.

Figure 9.3 Soccer stations.

From J.R. Thomas, K.T. Thomas, and A.M. Lee, 1988, *Physical education for children: Concepts into practice* (Champaign, IL: Human Kinetics), 111. Reprinted by permission of J.R. Thomas, K.T. Thomas, and A.M. Lee.

Balance Beam Task Sheet

Name _____

	Completed?	
	Yes	**No**
1. I can walk the beam slowly without falling.	☐	☐
2. I can walk the beam slowly with my hands on my hips without falling.	☐	☐
3. I can walk forward, balance on one foot at the center, and continue walking to the end without falling.	☐	☐
4. I can walk the beam with a beanbag balanced on my head without falling.	☐	☐
5. I can walk the beam sideways with my right foot leading without falling.	☐	☐
6. I can walk the beam sideways with my left foot leading without falling.	☐	☐
7. I can walk the beam backward without falling.	☐	☐
8. I can walk forward, pick up a beanbag at the center, and continue to the end without falling.	☐	☐
9. I can walk to the center, make a half turn, and continue to the end of the beam without falling.	☐	☐
10. I can walk to the center, perform a swan balance on my left foot, and continue to the end of the beam without falling.	☐	☐

Figure 9.4 Sample individual task sheet.

From J.R. Thomas, K.T. Thomas, and A.M. Lee, 1988, *Physical education for children: Concepts into practice* (Champaign, IL: Human Kinetics), 113. Reprinted by permission of J.R. Thomas, K.T. Thomas, and A.M. Lee.

- How group members have their feelings hurt (others are not listening; they are unable to help)

- What makes groups successful (taking turns, sharing responsibility, respecting others)

After the activity, discuss with the class what worked and what did not. Focus on groups with positive interactions and results.

You can use cooperative discussion groups to get children to think about the importance of individual effort and social responsibility. For example, you could use the following topics at the beginning of the school year to emphasize the importance of working hard and following the rules set for the class:

- Describe a child who doesn't try in physical education.
- What should we do if some children don't try?

- What would our class be like if nobody tried?
- How should we deal with children who always want to argue with others and with me?
- How should we deal with children who shove or hit others?

Other topics for discussion might be the following:

- Why is physical education important?
- What does "playing fair" mean?
- Why is it important to follow the rules when you are playing a game?

During a fitness lesson, you can ask cooperative groups to discuss and make decisions about ways to increase activity levels or burn calories. After you explain target heart rate to them, you can ask older children (grades 4 and 5) to calculate a training heart rate range for a particular

Soccer Task Sheet

Name _____   Partner _____

Skill

Dribble and pass with a partner.

Checkpoint

- Keep the ball in front of your partner when passing.
- Control the dribble and the pass.
- Pass using your right foot and your left foot.
- Pass using the inside and the outside of your foot.

Task 1

Run at a moderate pace, approximately 10 yards apart; dribble and pass with your partner for 50 yards. (Repeat three times with rest in between.)

Evaluation

Place an X in the space that you think best represents *your* performance in dribbling and passing.

Rating	Trial 1	Trial 2	Trial 3
Poor			
Fair			
Good			

Task 2

With your partner, dribble and pass for 50 yards. After passing the ball, move behind your partner. Your partner then moves to where you were and passes to you. Partner moves behind you, and you take his/her place. (Repeat three times with rest in between.)

Evaluation

Place an X in the space that you think best represents *your* performance in dribbling and passing.

Rating	Trial 1	Trial 2	Trial 3
Poor			
Fair			
Good			

Figure 9.5 Sample task sheet for soccer.

From J.R. Thomas, K.T. Thomas, and A.M. Lee, 1988, *Physical education for children: Concepts into practice* (Champaign, IL: Human Kinetics), 113. Reprinted by permission of J.R. Thomas, K.T. Thomas, and A.M. Lee.

Jump Rope Contract

Your objective is to earn 20 points this week. From the list of options, select the tasks that you want to accomplish. To compete an option, you must perform the activity without error.

I, _____, will earn 20 points from the list below.

Points	Options	Times
2	1. Two-foot doubles: jump on both feet twice for each turn of the rope.	20
2	2. One-foot doubles: jump on one foot twice for each turn of the rope.	20
2	3. Two-foot singles: jump on both feet once for each turn of the rope.	10
2	4. One-foot singles: jump on one foot once for each turn of the rope.	10
2	5. Alternate: jump on each foot for each turn of the rope.	10
2	6. One-foot continuous: jump on the same foot for each turn of the rope.	10
2	7. Leg swings: jump using a one-foot single while the free leg swings across.	10
2	8. Ski twists: jump two-foot singles with knees and ankles together and twisting.	10
2	9. Two foot, one foot: jump on two feet and then on one foot for each turn of the rope.	10
5	10. Straddle jumps using two-foot double rhythm: First jump is out; rebound is in.	10
5	11. Straddle cross using two-foot double rhythm: First jump is out; rebound is in with feet crossed.	10
5	12. Rock, placing one foot in front of the other. Jump on front foot, leaning slightly with feet crossed.	10
5	13. Arm cross, jumping continuously, crossing and uncrossing arms after each jump.	10
5	14. Make up a routine using at least four different jumps.	10

Figure 9.6 Sample student choice contract for the jump rope activity.

From J.R. Thomas, K.T. Thomas, and A.M. Lee, 1988, *Physical education for children: Concepts into practice* (Champaign, IL: Human Kinetics), 112. Reprinted by permission of J.R. Thomas, K.T. Thomas, and A.M. Lee.

child. The following topics or problems are examples:

- Name some ways that people who want to lose weight can increase the amount of physical activity they get. (Walk to school instead of riding, plan an exercise program, or use the stairs rather than the elevator.)

- Name some ways to increase your activity level after school each day. (Take a bike ride, mow the lawn, walk to the park, go roller-skating, play sports, or rake leaves.)

- Calculate a target heart rate range. Give each cooperative group a card or sheet of paper with the following formulas:

Training heart rate = 220 − age × 0.75
(lower end)

Training heart rate = 220 − age × 0.90
(upper end)

Basketball Contract

Activity _____ Date _____

	I will	Goal	Time
1.	Practice one-hand set shots from the foul line.	At least 5 shots from each area	15 minutes
2.	Practice dribbling around cones using alternate hands.	Complete the course 5 times without losing control of the ball.	10 minutes

Signed _____

Evaluation

Did you reach your goal today?

What do you need help with?

Figure 9.7 Sample open-ended contract (basketball).

From J.R. Thomas, K.T. Thomas, and A.M. Lee, 1988, *Physical education for children: Concepts into practice* (Champaign, IL: Human Kinetics), 112. Reprinted by permission of J.R. Thomas, K.T. Thomas, and A.M. Lee.

As children work together toward a common goal, they learn about role taking and cooperation.

For a 12-year-old, the range would be

$$220 - 12 = 208 \times 0.75 = 156 \text{ (lower end) and}$$
$$220 - 12 = 208 \times 0.90 = 187 \text{ (upper end).}$$

The cooperative task is to calculate the training heart rate range for each child in the group. Remind the children that everyone in the cooperative group must understand the formula and how to use it before the group is successful.

Teaching Approaches Involving Learners in Many Decisions: Indirect Styles

Indirect teaching styles involve discovering, exploring, selecting from alternatives, and seeking solutions to problems or tasks that you design and present. You can usually preplan a sequence of challenge tasks or movement questions with more than one answer. Indirect teaching calls for varied responses, whereas the direct style calls for a particular response from each child. As the children are solving a given problem in a series, you can move around the playground and give individual assistance, which may include some direct teaching. You can arrange the children in any formation, and they can work alone, with a partner, or in groups. You present the problem, provide time for the children to experiment and explore, and encourage them to think critically about a solution.

At the primary level, an indirect approach can be quite effective in teaching lessons designed to vary movement patterns using the elements of movement (space, qualities, and relationships). Older children can explore relationships, direction, and variations using basic sport skills. Examples of movement problems for younger children and possible responses and extensions are presented in table 9.1. You might design movement problems for older children for a specific sport. Table 9.1 presents problems for soccer.

Guided discovery is an indirect approach used when you want the children to discover a solution through a series of questions. This approach is a convergent, problem-solving process in which you want a predetermined answer or response. With a series of well-designed questions, you lead the children to the desired movement response. Another indirect approach that you can use is **exploration**, an open-ended, divergent, problem-solving process. In this style, there are no predetermined or correct answers; the goal is for children to explore and create solutions on their own. Figure 9.8 shows sample activities for the direct approach, guided discovery, and exploration.

Physical education teachers have recently been encouraged to promote a learning environment that encourages students to think critically (Werner 1995). The more indirect styles of teaching are needed to accomplish this goal (Anderson, Reder, and Simon 1998). Critical thinking involves choosing from alternatives, applying knowledge in new situations, and analyzing and evaluating information. Children who think critically process information at a higher level. Figure 9.9 shows some examples of ways to encourage critical thinking in physical education.

Table 9.1 Examples of an Indirect Approach

Teacher	Responses	Extension
Show me three ways to travel around your hoop.	Walking backward Jumping sideways Crab walk	Try again. This time show me how your three movements can be made at a low level.
Discover different ways to toss your ball to your partner.	Underhand using two hands Underhand using one hand Overhand using two hands	Can you send the ball to your partner with other body parts?
Can you find three ways to send the soccer ball a short distance to a partner with your foot?	Kick with inside of foot Kick with outside of foot Kick with heel	Continue practicing. Decide which part of the foot provides a more accurate kick.
How can you stop a soccer ball coming toward you in the air?	With the head With the body With the leg	Can you find other ways?

Sample Activities

Direct Approach

Follow the Leader, mirroring, finger plays, and Simon Says (played without the elimination process, of course) are examples of developmentally appropriate activities taught with a direct style of instruction. Also in this category are songs accompanied by unison clapping or movement, and rituals such as the Mexican Hat Dance and the Hokey Pokey. If these activities are to be performed in a traditional manner, with all of the children doing the same things at the same time, the only expedient way to teach them is with a direct approach using demonstration and imitation.

Guided Discovery

The ultimate goal of the following questions and challenges is a Forward Roll. However, because guided discovery allows children to respond to challenges at their own developmental level and rate, accept their responses even if they don't manage to perform the desired Forward Roll. Ultimately, you can lead all of the children to the "correct" answer through convergent problem solving. Specific challenges and questions vary according to the responses elicited, but the following is an example of the process:

- Show me an upside-down position with your weight on your hands and feet.
- Show me an upside-down position with your weight on your hands and feet and your tummy facing the floor.
- Can you put your bottom in the air?
- Can you look behind yourself from that position?
- Can you look at the ceiling? Try to look at even more of the ceiling.
- Show me you can roll yourself over from that position. Can you do it more than once?

Exploration

Any challenge that results in a number of responses falls under the heading of exploration, or divergent problem solving. For example, a challenge to the children to make a crooked shape can result in as many shapes as there are children. A challenge to balance on two body parts can result in one child balancing on the feet, another on the knees, and still another, who may be enrolled in a gymnastics program, doing a handstand. Encourage children to continue producing divergent responses, but your encouragement should take the form of neutral feedback (e.g., "I see your two-part balance uses one hand and one foot").

Figure 9.8 Sample activities for teaching with different methods.

Reprinted, by permission, from R. Pica, 1995, "Exploration, guided discovery, and the direct approach," *Teaching Elementary Physical Education* 6(5): 5.

Contextual Practice

The most contextually valid practice is practice during an actual activity. In this circumstance, the learner uses skills and knowledge together. Some of you may prefer to introduce a new activity by starting at the end—in other words, beginning with the actual activity. One reason is to help children understand how individual skills, strategies, and rules are used. This can motivate them to practice those skills. One approach is to try out the game first: children readily see that skill is necessary for both success and increased enjoyment. At this point, you may switch to a drill that uses the skill necessary in the game. After some practice, the children may play the game again. Repeat the process until they learn the skills and the game. This approach is based on what we know about how to organize practice to maximize learning. Unfortunately, the acquisition time may be longer, but as you learned in chapter 5, Cognition, Learning, and Practice, retention is better.

Direct Style

1. Hop forward 5 times. Then jump sideways 3 times.
2. Run straight across the room. Hop on one foot back.
3. Bounce the ball with your fingerpads.
4. Rise suddenly, directly, and with a lot of power (explode up), and then slowly, directly, and gently sink as you make your body come to rest on the floor.
5. Balance on one foot in a scale position. Then do a Forward Roll.
6. Hit the ball with a flat racket as you hit your tennis forehand.
7. When dribbling the ball against the opponent, protect the ball by keeping your body between it and the opponent.

Indirect Styles

1. **Select:** Travel around the gymnasium using the steplike weight transfer actions. Each time you hear the drum, change the way you travel. Now each time you hear the drum, change the direction of your travel. Finally, change both your method of travel and direction when you hear the drum.
2. **Classify:** Today you are going to work on ways to use your feet to travel as you move in general space. You may use only your feet to travel. Ready, go . . . stop. Who can tell me one way? Yes. Walk, run (one foot to the other, alternating). Hop (one foot to the same). Can you try other ways? Yes, I see two to two (jump).
3. **Compare:** Try bouncing the ball with stiff fingers and slap at it with your palm (make lots of noise). Now try pushing the ball down with your fingerpads. Keep your fingers spread and try not to make any noise as you push the ball down to the floor. Which way seems to give you the most control?
4. **Explain, compare, contrast:** Try various rising and sinking actions. Vary the way you use time, force, and effort. Make the way you rise different from the way you sink. Perform your sequence for a partner by taking turns. Then compare and contrast your solutions. How were they the same? Different?
5. **Sequence:** Use a roll of your choice to link two balances smoothly.
6. **Apply:** I'm noticing that, as you hit your forehand strokes, a lot of balls kind of pop up and go high into the air. Others often hit their ball down into the net. What can you do to change this and hit the balls over but close to the net? How would this change your grip? Swing?
7. **Analyze:** Dribble a ball against an opponent in this space (15 by 40 feet [4.5 by 12m]). Start at one end and try to get to the other end without your opponent stealing the ball from you. How can you best protect the ball while dribbling down the court?

Figure 9.9 *Examples of ways to encourage critical thinking.*
Reprinted, by permission, from P. Werner, 1995, "Moving out of the comfort zone to address critical thinking," *Teaching Elementary Physical Education* 6(5): 7.

Another way to use **contextual practice** is with modified games. In this case, you can reduce the scale so that you reduce the playing area, the team size, and the range of skills while the major elements, such as scoring, defense, and offense, remain the same. Think about a tee-ball or baseball game with only three players. There is still batting, throwing, catching, and running that lead to scoring or stopping scoring. With only three players in the game, each player has more opportunity to practice important skills.

At this point, you may be wondering how context relates to learner involvement. Of course, you could use direct instruction, although in the games with reduced scale the children are involved in many decisions within the context of the games. Those of you who are more comfortable with direct instruction may choose to reduce the choices for children as much as possible while still using the modified game for practice. Clearly, if you use whole game, you can maintain control and use the direct instruction approach. Using the tee-ball example, if you use an indirect approach, you might allow each group of children to decide how much defense to establish for their group. So one group might decide that, once the ball is fielded, it has to be thrown to another player; another group might allow running with the ball; yet another group might allow tagging a runner; and other groups might decide that only the base could be tagged.

Often, you can use stations to practice individual skills; however, you can also use them to practice modified games. For a basketball unit, one station might focus on free-throw shooting and rebounding, another on in-bounds passes to a lay-up, another on a zone defense and three-point shots. As the children learn skills within the context of the game, you can shift the approach increasingly toward guided discovery or exploration as children are challenged to solve game-related problems. You might ask the children to demonstrate a play or situation in which one skill or strategy is more appropriate than another.

The use of contextual practice has the advantage of providing you with many teachable moments, and the disadvantage of requiring your knowledge to take advantage of those moments. Although the examples are primarily from sport, the contextual approach works for other activities, such as dance and fitness. (See "Lesson #2 Games and Sport Lesson" on the DVD-ROM for a video clip showing a contextual practice approach to teaching a soccer lesson.)You might play a piece of music and ask the children to move to the beat. Your goal would be for the children to determine what steps might work with the music; you might ask them, for example, "Will a two-step, a waltz, hopping, or galloping work best?" With guidance, you can urge the children to try the target steps with the music.

a health-enhancing level of physical fitness in classes that use either a direct or an indirect approach. They can demonstrate responsible personal and social behavior, develop respect for differences among participants, and develop an awareness of the intrinsic values of participation with a combination of the two approaches. If critical thinking is a goal, you can incorporate more indirect approaches.

Mastery Learning Activities

1. Write three paragraphs: the first, a summary of what you value; the second, a contrast of direct and indirect styles of teaching; and the third, matching a teaching style to your values. The reader should understand what you value, what the direct and indirect styles involve, and why one style is better for you based on your values.

2. Select a concept based on one of the National Content Standards (NASPE). Develop a cooperative learning or critical thinking activity that would help children understand the concept.

3. For children in kindergarten, grade 3, and grade 5, contrast the advantages and disadvantages of the direct and indirect methods for each age level.

4. Select a skill and a grade level. Develop either a contract or an individual skill sheet for that skill.

5. Develop a station teaching lesson for a specific grade. Make a time line for the lesson that indicates how much time to spend introducing the stations, how long a group stays at each station, and how long it takes to rotate. Be sure that the total time is less than or equal to a class period so that all of the children can rotate through all of the stations during one lesson. Describe how you can stay on time.

Summary

You can use a number of teaching approaches in physical education. Each approach has a set of assets and liabilities. Children can become competent in many movement forms, learn to apply concepts and principles to learning, and achieve

References

Anderson, J.R., L.M. Reder, and H.A. Simon. 1998. Radical constructivism and cognitive psychology. In *Brookings papers on education policy: 1998,* edited by D. Ravitch, 227-255. Washington, DC: Brookings Institution.

Thomas, K.T. 1994. The development of expertise: From Leeds to legend. *Quest* 46: 199-210.

Werner, P. 1995. Moving out of the comfort zone to address critical thinking. *Teaching Elementary Physical Education* 6: 7.

Resources

Metzler, M.W. 2000. *Instructional models for physical education.* Needham Heights, MA: Allyn & Bacon.

Mosston, M., and S. Ashworth. 1994. *Teaching physical education.* 4th ed. New York: Macmillan College Publishing.

Pica, R. 1995. Exploration, guided discovery and the direct approach. *Teaching Elementary Physical Education* 6: 5.

Siedentop, D., J. Herkowitz, and J. Rink. 1984. *Elementary physical education methods.* Englewood Cliffs, NJ: Prentice Hall.

Lesson Plans

The lesson plans at the end of this chapter show examples of the various approaches to teaching. The first lesson uses a direct teaching approach for introducing vigorous games. A fitness concept is introduced as a concluding activity. The second lesson uses a station formation, but the teaching approach is direct. The next two lessons use a direct approach to teach jumping rope and stunts. The following lessons illustrate a station approach and an individualized contract. The lesson on games and sports uses stations to teach soccer skills, and the lesson on fitness combines stations and a fitness contract. The final lesson demonstrates a contextual approach to floor hockey. If you prefer, you can easily apply the lesson to soccer and play it outdoors.

Lesson 9.1

Moderate to Vigorous Games

Student Objectives 4 5

- Demonstrate correct stretching technique in a warm-up routine.
- Follow the rules in moderate to vigorous games.
- Describe how much exercise is needed for physical fitness.
- Demonstrate cooperation by playing one of the games.

Equipment and Materials

- 4 cones, polyspots, or polydomes
- 1 hoop or carpet square per group
- 1 playground ball
- 1 foam or small playground ball per group

Warm-Up Activities (5 minutes)

Arrange the children in scatter formation.

Stretching Routine

SHOULDER SHRUG

Lift your shoulders to touch your ears; return to relaxed position.

SIDE STRETCH

Sit with your feet apart and knees slightly bent. Place one hand on your hip and extend the other arm up over your head. Slowly bend to the side toward the hand on your hip. Hold for 10 seconds and relax. Repeat in the opposite direction.

SIDE LUNGE

Stand with your feet and shoulders facing forward. Take a large step to the right with the right foot. The right knee bends; make sure that knee does not extend over the toes. Hold for 10 seconds and relax. Repeat in the opposite direction.

ANKLE ROTATION

Standing on one leg, make as large a circle as possible with the foot of the opposite leg. Your knee and hip should not move—only your ankle.

Stretching Routine 2

Keep the children in scatter formation.

1. Describe and demonstrate the four stretches.
2. Direct children to do the stretches in the following order:
   - 8 Shoulder Shrugs
   - 8 Side Stretches (4 each side)

Lesson 9.1 (continued)

- ○ 8 Side Lunges (4 each side)
- ○ 8 Ankle Rotations (4 each ankle)
3. Repeat entire sequence.

Skill-Development Activities (20 minutes)

Select one or two games to play. Keep group sizes small to increase participation opportunities.

Leader Ball

Divide the children into groups of 4 or 5. Each group has a leader and a ball.

1. Describe and demonstrate the game:
   - ○ Take turns being the leader.
   - ○ Stand behind the starting line. Children should stand shoulder to shoulder, facing the leader, who should stand about 10 feet (3 m) away.
   - ○ Jog in place during the activity.
   - ○ The leader throws the ball to the first child at one end of the line, who throws the ball back to the leader.
   - ○ The leader throws the ball to the second child, who also throws it back to the leader. This continues until each child has caught and thrown the ball.
   - ○ When the leader catches the ball tossed by the last child, the entire group runs to the end line (point to a line parallel to the starting line), and the child who was originally first in line becomes the new leader.
   - ○ Play continues until every child has had a turn being the leader.
2. Designate a spot to put the ball while the children are running, such as a hoop or carpet square.
3. Have the children play Leader Ball.

Pair Tag

Arrange children, each holding hands with a partner, in equal numbers on 2 facing lines, 50 to 60 feet (15 to 18 m) apart. One pair (also holding hands) is in the center between the lines: These two are the "It" pair.

1. Describe and demonstrate the game:
   - ○ With hands joined, the It pair tries to tag other pairs, who run from It to the opposite side of the play area on the go signal.
   - ○ As pairs are tagged, they also become It and join the other taggers in the middle.
   - ○ When all pairs have been tagged, the last pair stands alone in the center for a new game. Any pair that drops hands must also join the taggers in the middle. Work with your partner so that, when you're running, one of you doesn't drag the other around.
2. Have the children play Pair Tag.

Delivery Relay

Divide the children into groups of 4; have 2 groups stand across from each other on each side of 2 lines, 60 feet (18 m) apart.

1. Describe and demonstrate the game:
   - ○ One child in each group gets a ball (or other small object).
   - ○ On the signal, that child carries (delivers) the ball to a teammate at the other line. That child returns the ball to a child at the first line, and so on, until each child has carried the ball over the distance.

○ Jog in place while waiting for your turn.

2. Have the children play Delivery Relay, repeating as time allows.

Concluding Activities (5 minutes)

Physical Fitness Concept

Gather the children into an information formation.

1. Present the concept to the children: "A physically fit person exercises regularly—jogging, cycling, or swimming, doing Sit-Ups and Push-Ups, or stretching. These exercises can help our muscles stay healthy and keep our bodies from storing too much fat. To be physically fit, we must exercise at least 3 times each week. It is best to spread the exercise throughout the week, rather than 3 days in a row. But, if you can, exercising more than 3 days a week is great! Fun, active games also improve our health-related physical fitness."

2. Ask the children: "How could we do this?" Discuss possible scenarios; for example, doing fitness activities on Monday, Wednesday, and Friday or on Tuesday, Thursday, and Saturday.

3. Discuss activities that the children could do at home in addition to the program at school.

Alternative Learning Activities

1. Make a fitness contract and help the children fill it out.

2. Make a fitness calendar. For the current month, have each child mark days when he or she has done 30 minutes of total activity (at least 10 minutes at a time). Children may write the actual activities themselves or parents can help.

From K.T. Thomas, A.M. Lee, and J.R. Thomas, 2008, *Physical education methods for elementary teachers*, 3rd ed. (Champaign, IL: Human Kinetics). Adapted, by permission, from K.T. Thomas, A.M. Lee, and J.R. Thomas, 2000, *Physical education for children: Daily lesson plans for elementary school*, 2nd ed. (Champaign, IL: Human Kinetics), 64-66.

Lesson 9.2

Jumping and Hopping With Hoops

Student Objectives 1 5

- Demonstrate jumping and hopping with good control.
- Work cooperatively with a group on hopping and jumping tasks.

Equipment and Materials

- 1 hoop (30 to 36 inches [76 to 91 cm]) per child

Warm-Up Activities (5 minutes)

Tortoise and Hare

Arrange the children in scatter formation.

1. Describe the activity:
   - Run very slowly when I say, "Tortoise," and very fast when I say, "Hare."
   - Start with running in place, and move on to running in general space.
2. Have the children play Tortoise and Hare.

Skill-Development Activities (17 minutes)

Tasks for Hoops

Keep the children in scatter formation; give each child a hoop.

1. Challenge the children with the following hoop tasks:
   - Balance on your right (left) foot in the center of your hoop.
   - While balancing on one foot, stretch your body tall (bend over and touch the ground, stretch your arms wide, swing your free leg).
   - Jump around your hoop, forward (backward).
   - Jump in and out of your hoop.
   - Jump forward into your hoop. Jump backward out of your hoop.
   - With one foot inside the hoop and one foot outside the hoop, jump around the hoop. Repeat, going backward.
   - Hop inside your hoop 5 times on your right (left) foot.
   - Hop forward around the outside of your hoop.
   - Hop in and out of your hoop.
   - Jump around the outside of your hoop; jump into the hoop and balance on one foot.
   - Rearrange children in groups of 3 or 4; each group has 1 hoop.

2. Challenge the groups with the following tasks:
   - Jump around the hoop with your right side toward the hoop (clockwise).
   - Take 5 giant steps away from the hoop; then hop back toward the hoop.
   - Everyone stand in the hoop. (Combine groups to see how many children can fit into 1 hoop!)

Concluding Activities (8 minutes)

Jumping and Hopping Through Hoop Patterns at Stations

Set up the 4 stations as shown in the figures. Divide the children into 4 groups, and place each group at one of the 4 stations.

1. Briefly describe and demonstrate each station.
2. Have the children perform the tasks.
3. Rotate the children to a new station every 2 minutes.

STATION 1

Jump forward and backward through the hoops. Hop forward and backward through the hoops.

Station 1

STATION 2

Straddle jump (one foot in each hoop) forward and backward through the hoops. Hop through the hoops, creating a pattern.

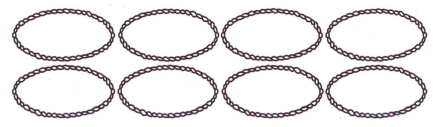

Station 2

STATION 3

Hop forward and backward through the hoops. Jump through the hoops.

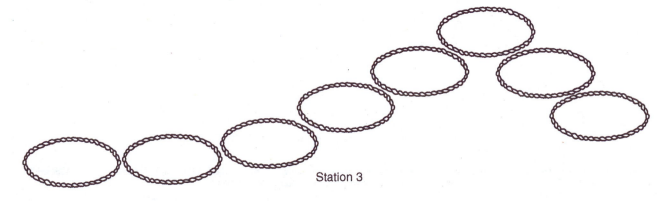

Station 3

Lesson 9.2 *(continued)*

STATION 4

Jump sideways through the hoops. Hop sideways through the hoops.

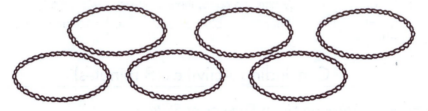

Station 4

.From K.T. Thomas, A.M. Lee, and J.R. Thomas, 2008, *Physical education methods for elementary teachers*, 3rd ed. (Champaign, IL: Human Kinetics). Adapted, by permission, from K.T. Thomas, A.M. Lee, and J.R. Thomas, 2000, *Physical education for children: Daily lesson plans for elementary school*, 2nd ed. (Champaign, IL: Human Kinetics), 155-157.

Lesson 9.3

Rope Jumping

Student Objectives 1	Equipment and Materials
• Perform Two-Foot Singles and Doubles (forward and backward) with a short jump rope.	• 1 short jump rope per child • Signal

Warm-Up Activities (5 minutes)

Use High, Low, Medium from lesson 5.3, page 117. Variation: Specify another locomotor skill or allow the children to select a skill.

Skill-Development Activities (20 minutes)

Two-Foot Singles

Arrange the children in scatter formation; each child has a jump rope.

1. Describe and demonstrate the activity: "To do Two-Foot Singles, jump on both feet once for each turn of the rope."
2. Have the children practice Two-Foot Singles, starting slowly and then going faster.

Two-Foot Doubles

Keep the children in scatter formation; each child has a jump rope.

1. Describe and demonstrate the activity: "To do Two-Foot Doubles, jump on both feet twice for each turn of the rope. The rope turns more slowly for Two-Foot Doubles."
2. Have the children practice Two-Foot Doubles.

Basic Jump Backward

Keep the children in scatter formation; each child has a jump rope.

1. Describe and demonstrate the activity: "For this jump, throw the rope backward and jump with both feet together as the rope hits the floor. This is a variation of the Two-Foot Single."
2. Have the children practice the Basic Jump Backward.

Helicopter

Keep the children in scatter formation; each child has a jump rope.

1. Describe and demonstrate the activity: "With both ends of the rope in one hand, swing the rope in a circle overhead. Make sure that you keep a tight grip on the rope and watch out for your classmates."
2. Have the children practice the Helicopter.

Lesson 9.3 (continued)

Single-Side Taps

Keep the children in scatter formation; each child has a jump rope.

1. Describe and demonstrate the activity: "With both ends of the rope in one hand, swing the rope in a circle to the side of your body."
2. Have the children practice Single-Side Taps.

Double-Side Taps

Keep the children in scatter formation; each child has a jump rope.

1. Describe and demonstrate the activity: "Holding both ends of the rope in one hand, swing the rope in a circle once on one side of your body and once on the opposite side of your body."
2. Provide a drumbeat, and have the children practice Double-Side Taps, to a drumbeat, with each hand.
3. Have the children practice jumping in place to a drumbeat while doing Double-Side Taps.

Extension Activities

Have the children create routines using Helicopters, Single- and Double-Side Taps, and Two-Foot Single and Double Jumps.

Concluding Activities (5 minutes)

Don't Miss

Divide the class into 4 groups; each child has a jump rope. Each group should have jumpers of all achievement levels.

1. Describe the activity:
   - Choose a type of jump and, on the signal, jump as many times as possible without a miss. Jumps can be Two-Foot Singles or Doubles or Basic Backward Jumps.
   - I will time you for 1-minute periods; count the number of misses during each session.
   - The group with the lowest number of misses wins. You are on your honor to count accurately.
2. Have the children do the activity. Repeat several times.

From K.T. Thomas, A.M. Lee, and J.R. Thomas, 2008, *Physical education methods for elementary teachers*, 3rd ed. (Champaign, IL: Human Kinetics). Adapted, by permission, from K.T. Thomas, A.M. Lee, and J.R. Thomas, 2000, *Physical education for children: Daily lesson plans for elementary school*, 2nd ed. (Champaign, IL: Human Kinetics), 589-590.

Lesson 9.4

Tricky Stunts

Student Objectives 1 6

- Perform individual stunts.
- Have fun!

Equipment and Materials

- 1 or more mats (4 by 8 feet [1.2 by 2.4 m]) per group

Safety Tips

- Children who have identified or who complain of lower-back problems should not do the Double-Jointed Walk.
- The Double-Jointed Walk should only be done for short distances.

Warm-Up Activities (5 minutes)

Follow the Leader

Arrange the children in a line.

1. Ask the first leader to perform locomotor skills, such as skipping, running, and jumping, as the group follows.
2. Ask a second leader to perform additional locomotor skills that the first leader did not think of.
3. If there are no additional locomotor skills, ask the new leader to do the Warm-Up Routine for Grades 2 and 3 from lesson 7.3, page 174.
4. When that exercise is finished, ask the next child in line to lead another warm-up exercise, and so on, until the children have done all of the warm-up exercises.

Skill-Development Activities (21 minutes)

The stunts and skills today are special; each is unique. Encourage the children to learn and have fun with these activities!

Around the World

Create small groups, and assign each group to a mat.

1. Describe and have a child demonstrate the stunt:
   - Begin by sitting with your legs tucked tightly against your chest, knees apart, and ankles together. Put your upper arms between your legs, and wrap your lower arms around your lower legs. Keep your wrists flexed so that your hands meet in front of your ankles.
   - Tuck your chin tightly against your chest, and roll your body to one side.
   - Continue the circular motion by lifting and rolling your torso.
2. Have the children practice Around the World.

Lesson 9.4 *(continued)*

Walking in Place

Continue in small groups; each group has a mat.

1. Describe and demonstrate the stunt:
   - The object is to appear to walk while actually staying in one place.
   - Move your arms back in an exaggerated way while stepping forward and dragging the supporting leg backward.
   - Get the support leg back a step before putting the swing leg down to avoid moving across the floor.
2. Have the children practice Walking in Place.

Heel Click

Continue in small groups; each group has a mat.

1. Describe and demonstrate the stunt: "Jump as high as possible into the air, tap your heels together one or more times, and land on both feet."
2. Have the children practice the Heel Click.

Double-Jointed Walk

Children with lower-back problems or those who complain of discomfort when attempting this stunt should not do the Double-Jointed Walk.

1. Describe and demonstrate the stunt:
   - Begin by squatting with your knees apart, feet together, and arms threaded through your legs. Try to clasp your hands in front of your ankles.
   - Keep your shoulders close to your knees; both upper arms are between your legs.
   - Wrap your forearms around your lower legs; bend your wrists so that you can join your hands in front of your ankles.
   - While holding your head high and looking forward, walk using a side-rocking motion.
2. Have the children practice the Double-Jointed Walk.

Knee Touch

Continue in small groups; each group has a mat.

1. Describe and demonstrate the stunt:
   - Standing on one leg, hold the foot of the opposite leg behind your seat.
   - Dip down until the knee of your bent leg touches the floor.
2. Have the children practice the Knee Touch.

Scoot-Through

Continue in small groups; each group has a mat.

1. Describe and demonstrate the stunt:
   - Begin in the push-up position; your arms support your body weight and your legs extend to the rear, with your body in a straight line.
   - Without moving your hands or arms, slide your legs forward; keep your legs as straight as possible until they pass between your arms. Continue sliding your legs through until your body is extended in front of your arms.
2. Have the children practice the Scoot-Through.

Concluding Activities (4 minutes)

Simon Says

Divide the children into small groups and scatter the groups around the play area; each group is at a different mat. If there is room on the mats, all of the children can perform at once; otherwise, have the children perform in order. Pick one child in each group to start as Simon.

1. Describe the game:
   - Simon tries to trick the group into doing something that Simon does not "say" to do. Use the individual stunts learned in this lesson.
   - Simon gives commands, some of which begin "Simon says" (and then Simon names individual stunts from this lesson). The group should perform those tasks.
   - When Simon gives a command without saying "Simon says" (e.g., if Simon were to say, "Do the Heel Click"), the group should not perform the task.
   - Take turns, in order, for being Simon.
   - A turn ends as soon as Simon tricks someone.
   - When another child becomes Simon, the old Simon moves to the end of the order.
   - A child doing a task that Simon did not say moves to the end of the order—for performing and for being Simon—but keeps playing.
2. Have the children play Simon Says.

Lesson 9.5

Soccer

Student Objectives 1

- Make progress toward refining the instep kick.
- Kick a ball in various directions.

Equipment and Materials

List is for one station circuit. (For more than one station circuit, you need more equipment. See relevant text.)

- 1 soccer ball per pair
- Station 1: 2 goals or targets
- Station 2: 1 cone
- Station 3: 1 large cardboard box
- 1 jump rope per child
- Polyspots, polydomes, or tape to mark lines
- Signal

Warm-Up Activities (5 minutes)

Rope Jumping

Arrange the children in scatter formation; each child has a jump rope.

1. Describe and demonstrate the activity: "Turn the rope at a slow tempo and do Two-Foot Doubles (two jumps on both feet simultaneously for each rope turn)."
2. Have them do this for 2 minutes, rest 30 seconds, and then jump rope for 2 more minutes, followed by another 30-second rest.

Skill-Development Activities (20 minutes)

Instep Kicking

Assign a group of 3 or 4 children to each station; each child has a ball. (Duplicate stations as needed to keep group size small.)

1. Describe and demonstrate instep kicking at each station.
2. Have the children practice Instep Kicking at the stations.
3. Signal groups to rotate to a new station every 5 minutes.

STATION 1: PASSING FOR GOAL

Mark a kicking line 25 feet (7.6 m) from a goal line on which you have set up 2 targets or goals.

Kick to the right and to the left so that the ball travels between the goal markers; practice until you can hit the target 3 times in a row before moving to a longer distance. (Distance can vary according to skill.)

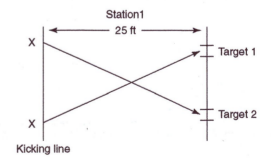

STATION 2: KICKING TO HIT AN OBJECT

Mark a field about 30 by 30 feet (9 by 9 m) and place a cone in the center of the field.

Kick from any boundary of the square and attempt to hit the cone in the center. Gradually increase the distance you kick from.

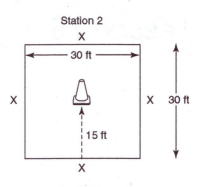

Station 2

STATION 3: KICKING THE BALL OFF THE GROUND

Mark a field 20 by 20 feet (6 by 6 m) and place a large cardboard box in the center of the field.

Kick a ball so that it travels off the ground and lands in the box. Gradually increase the distance you kick from.

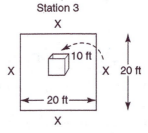

Station 3

STATION 4: KICKING FOR DISTANCE

Mark two kicking lines 30 yards (27.4 m) apart.

Take turns with a partner kicking a ball as far as possible.

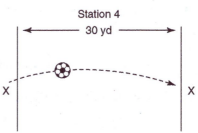

Station 4

Concluding Activities (5 minutes)

Kickover

Create fields that are 10 by 20 feet (3 by 6 m), with a 5-foot (1.5 m) goal marked by cones at one end. Mark kicking lines at 5, 10, 15, and 20 feet (1.5, 3, 4.5, 6 m) (see figure below). Place 2 teams of 3 or 4 children on each playing field; each team has a ball.

1. Describe the game:
   - Give each player a chance to kick the ball (using the instep kick) toward the goal.
   - Your team scores 1 point if the ball goes over the end line and 2 points for a successful hit into the goal area.
   - Begin at the 5-foot (1.5 m) line. After each player gets a kick from the 5-foot (1.5 m) line, both teams move to the 10-foot (3 m) line, and so on.
   - The team with the most points at the end of the playing time wins.
2. Have the children play Kickover.

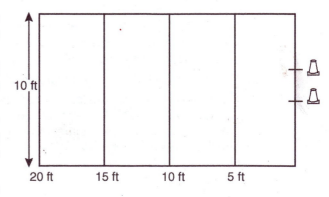

From K.T. Thomas, A.M. Lee, and J.R. Thomas, 2008, *Physical education methods for elementary teachers*, 3rd ed. (Champaign, IL: Human Kinetics). Adapted, by permission, from K.T. Thomas, A.M. Lee, and J.R. Thomas, 2000, *Physical education for children: Daily lesson plans for elementary school*, 2nd ed. (Champaign, IL: Human Kinetics), 884-886.

Lesson 9.6

Developing a Fitness Contract

Student Objectives 2 4

- Make a fitness contract based on fitness evaluation.
- State one reason fitness is important.
- Participate independently in fitness activities.

Equipment and Materials

- Fitness Contract form
- Equipment needed for fitness stations
- Large task cards (at least 8.5 by 11 inches [21.5 by 27.9 cm]); if you are using stations, include 1 task card per station

Skill-Development Activities (30 minutes)

Learning About Fitness Plans

Set up enough stations to create a circuit with task cards for groups of 4 to 6 children. First gather the children into an advanced information formation.

1. Discuss the importance of exercising on a regular basis; help the children develop realistic goals for exercise.
2. Show the children a sample set of fitness test scores. Ask the following questions:
   - In what areas does this person need to improve to enjoy a basic level of health-related fitness? (If the flexibility score is low, this is a target area.)
   - What might be a realistic, specific goal in each of those areas? (Goals range from participation for low-fit individuals to a specific time or score.)
   - What activities might this person do to reach each goal? (Walking and other aerobic activities, as well as stretching, are good.)
   - How often should this person do those activities to have a good chance of reaching his or her goals? (3 times per week or more)
3. Help the children develop a similar personal fitness plan.
4. Divide the children into groups of 4 to 6. Have the groups rotate through a circuit, practicing fitness activities, while you meet with each child at one station to discuss his or her personal plan and to sign a written agreement to try to improve personal fitness level outside of class. Use the fitness contract shown on the next page or develop one that meets your needs.
5. Explain that you will give the fitness tests again later during the year so that they can see improvement.

Contract for Cardiorespiratory Endurance Program

I, _____, do hereby agree to exercise for 20 minutes 3 times a week for 10 weeks. My exercise heart rate will be _____.

Week	Days	Type of exercise	Duration
1			
2			
3			
4			
5			
6			
7			
8			
9			
10			

Approved by _____

Date _____

From K.T. Thomas, A.M. Lee, and J.R. Thomas, 2008, *Physical education methods for elementary teachers*, 3rd ed. (Champaign, IL: Human Kinetics). Adapted, by permission, from K.T. Thomas, A.M. Lee, and J.R. Thomas, 2000, *Physical education for children: Daily lesson plans for elementary school*, 2nd ed. (Champaign, IL: Human Kinetics), 797-798.

Lesson 9.7

Floor Hockey: Striking, Passing, and Traveling

Student Objectives 1 5

- Demonstrate striking the puck for a shot, traveling, and passing to a partner.
- Work cooperatively with a small group.

Equipment and Materials

- 1 hockey stick (or pillow polo) per child
- 1 plastic puck (a beanbag or cheeseburger puck may be substituted) for every 4 children
- 1 net or 2 cones for every 4 children
- 2 polyspots for every 4 children

Warm-Up Activities (5 minutes)

Hockey Shuttle

Arrange the children in groups of 4; 2 children from each group are opposite the other 2 children at the other end of the gym.

1. Describe the activity: The first child with the puck runs to the other end of the gym toward the teammates carrying the puck. Once you reach the line at the other end, place the puck on the line and move behind your teammates. The next child in line picks up the puck and runs back to the other end of the gym, placing the puck on the line. Repeat so that each child makes the trip several times.

2. Have one group demonstrate the procedure. Ask if there are questions and answer them.

3. Have the children play the game until the time is up or they are too tired to continue.

Skill-Development Activities (18 minutes)

Striking for a Shot

Arrange the children in groups of 4; you may use the same groups as in the warm-up. Place a goal (or 2 cones about 5 feet [1.5 m] apart) on the line at the ends of the gym. Place 1 polyspot, centered, 10 feet (3 m) in front of the goal; place the other polyspot, centered, about 15 feet (4.5 m) from the goal. Two players are defenders and stand with at least one foot on a polyspot. The other two players are the offense. All players have a hockey stick. To begin play, one offensive player starts about 20 feet (6 m) away from the goal near the center. That player travels toward the goal while moving the puck with the hockey stick. Both the stick and the puck should be on the floor. The other offensive player can stand anywhere except in the goal and is the only player who can score a goal. The player with the puck passes it to the other offensive teammate, who tries to shoot a goal.

The defense begins the game "cold," which means that the players are standing with both feet on the polyspot. The defense players can move their sticks on the ground toward the puck. After one shot at goal, the players rotate so that the shooter moves to the first defensive position (nearest the goal); that player moves to the other defensive position. The 15-foot [4.5 m] defender moves to the offense, and the remaining offensive player becomes the new shooter. Play this game one or more times.

As players demonstrate skill on offense, allow the defense to become more active. The next level of defense is "warm," which means that players keep one foot on the polyspot and the stick on the floor. A "hot" defense is when players start on the polyspot but are allowed to move when the puck is passed to the second offensive player or when the first offensive player passes a line 15 feet (4.5 m) from the goal. Continue play, allowing groups to use different levels of defense as appropriate.

Playing Goal

Maintain the groups of four with the same equipment. In this game three players are offense and one player is goalie. The goalie defends the goal by deflecting shots with the hockey stick. Place one polyspot to the left of the goal, 10 feet (3 m) away, and the other polyspot to the right, 10 feet (3 m) away. Offensive player 1 travels with the puck—from about 20 feet (6 m) away from the goal—toward the other offensive players and passes the puck to one of them. That player passes to the other offensive player. Once all three offensive players have touched the puck with their sticks, any one may shoot for a goal. If the shot is successful, the offensive players rotate among the three offensive positions and play again. If the shot fails, all three players must touch the puck again before anyone can attempt a shot. Once a player has made a goal, he or she may not shoot again until all of the players have made a goal.

Once all three players have made a goal, the goalie moves to offense, and one of the offensive players becomes goalie. This sequence continues until everyone has played goalie.

Concluding Activities (2 minutes)

The goalie collects the hockey sticks and places them according to your directions. The offensive player with the puck or closest to the goal cleans up the goal, putting it away or moving it out of the way. The other two offensive players pick up polyspots and the puck according to your directions. Once clean-up is completed, the children line up to leave the gym. Once everyone is in line, ask the children to rate themselves on the following skills from 1 to 5 (5 is outstanding) by holding up the number of fingers:

- Listening to instructions (I was a good listener today.)
- Following instructions (I followed instructions today.)
- Learning skills (I learned a new skill today.)
- Demonstrating sportsmanship (I was a good sport today.)

From K.T. Thomas, A.M. Lee, and J.R. Thomas, 2008, *Physical education methods for elementary teachers*, 3rd ed. (Champaign, IL: Human Kinetics).

CHAPTER 10

Managing Students

BRYNN, AGE 9

Management is a precursor to instruction. It allows you to prevent problems, keep students safe, and maximize time for instruction and practice.

Learner Outcomes

After studying this chapter, you should be able to do the following:

- Describe the relationship and differences between management and instruction.

- Define and demonstrate at least five management techniques.

- Explain how to adjust management techniques for use with various grade levels of students.

Glossary Terms

management	concluding activity	class rules
class signals	transition	desist
initial activity	formation	time-out

Darryl Siedentop (1998) has said that all expert teachers are good managers; however, all good managers are not expert teachers. Management is a precursor to instruction. Some teachers manage students effectively but do not provide instruction (especially challenging tasks, feedback, and practice). The students are under control and seem busy and happy, but this does not mean they are learning. Other teachers use management techniques to facilitate teaching and learning. Teaching includes planning, instruction, directions, demonstrations, practice, goal setting, cues, feedback, and evaluation. **Management** is a set of techniques that you can use to control students and create a safe environment, including routines and rules. Management—especially class control—is the goal for some teachers; but for expert teachers, management is a tool to achieve educational objectives. You need to know about and be able to use management techniques for several reasons:

- To enhance student safety
- To ensure time and opportunity for learning

- To prevent problems during physical education

The most basic skill of teaching is managing students, including keeping them safe and under control; taking care of administrative tasks (e.g., attendance); and holding the students' attention. Perhaps because these tasks are obvious and inherent in the description of being a teacher, or perhaps because expert teachers make management look easy, novice teachers assume the management of students is easy. Planning for management is critical for successful teaching and learning; it is what makes management look effortless! Physical education, because of the facilities and activities involved, requires careful planning and execution of management. You need to be a good manager during physical education class for several reasons. First, the physical location of children is more challenging in the gym or on the playground than in a classroom. In the classroom, each child has a desk or chair; that spot is a clear and personal location, unlike location in the gym. Second, noise and movement complicate the physical education environment; even if the children are quiet, the equipment often is noisy (e.g., bouncing balls). Third, children are often excited during physical education class, where both performance and emotions are on public display. In a classroom, student work is often private—no one can see it—whereas performance is conducted in front of others in physical education class—often important others. As discussed in chapter 1, Health and Developmental Benefits of Physical Education, movement skills are important; this places additional stress on children to do well in front of others. The additive effect of these factors can make physical education a volatile subject that demands good management. Good management can also help students achieve National Content Standard 5: "Demonstrates responsible personal and social behavior in physical activity setting."

Management Components

Management has six components: class signal, initial and concluding activities, transitions and formations, handling equipment, class rules, and intrusive events. As you introduce children to your management system, we recommend positive reinforcement of good behaviors: "I really like the way you lined up today," "Thank you for stop-ping and listening so quickly," or "Chris did a great job putting away our equipment today, let's say 'thanks.'"

Class Signal

Getting the children's attention in the gym is a challenge; doing so outdoors is even more challenging. The purpose of most **class signals** is for children to stop, look, listen, and be quiet as quickly as possible. Signals include noise makers (e.g., tambourine, bell) and hand signals. You may recall physical education teachers using a whistle. In elementary school, a whistle is generally not the best signal. Sometimes it is easy to become dependent on the whistle and use it rather than planning carefully. But you can use whistles for starting and stopping activities, refereeing games, and expressing dissatisfaction. A raised hand is a popular signal; children like to be among the first to notice. A variation is the "give-me-five" signal, in which your raised hand is mirrored by the children. The five fingers mean feet still, hands at sides, eyes looking, ears listening, and brain thinking. Another signal that requires children to respond is the mirror clapping signal. In this case, you clap a pattern and the children respond with that pattern. Signals that require children to respond with an

Sitting with children allows eye contact and control during class discussion.

answer (e.g., with raised arm or clapping) are fun and inclusive but usually take more time.

You might use the same signal every day and all year. Or you might use a variety of signals. As long as children know the signal and what to do when you give the signal, either technique works well.

Initial and Concluding Activities

Classroom teachers usually escort students to the gym for physical education, turning them over to the physical education teacher. The first thing children do at or in the gym is the **initial activity**. Some teachers use squads first; others use a line. But, at some point, the class has a routine that signals the beginning of physical education. When classroom teachers teach physical education, the same type of initial activity signals the beginning of physical education. Opening the door to the gym and having children run chaotically around the gym is not an initial activity. They need to know what to do first, where to go, and what to expect. If attendance is part of the routine, you can handle it during the initial activity. The following are some ideas for initial activities:

- On a 20-foot (6 m) square on the floor, marked with four tape lines of different

colors, group the children by color at the beginning of the year. For grades 2 through 5, write instructions for challenges on a dry erase board (e.g., balance on your right foot for 10 counts, 10 jumping jacks); for grades K and 1, the challenges remain the same for several weeks (e.g., touch toes 10 times; stretch to the sky 10 times).

- Tape three rows and 25 columns of symbols to the wall. Row 1 is shapes (square, triangle, or circle; red, blue, green, or yellow); row 2 is numbers (1 through 25); and row 3 is balls (tennis, basketball, football, or soccer). Assign children a spot (one of the columns) to stand in front of after entering the gym. Take attendance by recording the numbers without children. This system helps manage class later, too, as you make groups by selecting the row that forms the size and number appropriate to the activity. If you want four groups, you say, "Footballs to station 1, tennis to station 2, basketball to station 3, and soccer to station 4" or "Squares and triangles are in the field; circles and rectangles at bat" (figure 10.1).

- Children enter the gym and run (or hop, skip, or gallop) until the music stops. The pattern

Figure 10.1 One of the ways you can help manage children is to use wall markers of shapes and numbers for rapid grouping.

(cones, lines, circle) is predetermined and remains the same for every class.

Each of these activities establishes a routine so that the children know exactly what to do once they enter the gym. Class ends in a similar way, with a routine. Students transition from physical education teacher to their classroom teacher (or gym to classroom) in the same way each class. The following are ideas for a **concluding activity**:

- A set of footprints marks a spot for the line leader to stand (away from the door); other children line up behind the line leader. You give them "high five" as they leave the gym.

- The children stand on a line, and you ask them to rate themselves on skill, behavior, and cooperation for the day. Once you and the children agree on the ratings, they walk quietly out of the gym.

- Children sit on markers. The class must add a physical education vocabulary item to the word list on the wall. The word must have been used in class and must be new (not already on the wall). You write the word and tape it to the wall.

These activities are not the same as instructional warm-ups or closure activities. These are part of the class routine, established to make children comfortable and to keep control. The initial and concluding activities do not have to be long; 10 to 60 seconds is enough time to set clear beginning and ending points to the physical education class.

Transitions and Formations

Two types of **transition** occur in physical education class: the physical transition and the cognitive or activity transition. The physical transition moves students from one location, or **formation**, to another. The cognitive or activity transition changes "gears"; students may stay in one place but be expected to do something different after the transition. Both transitions require planning. Generally, the cognitive transition starts with closure on the previous idea or activity and then provides an anticipatory set or introduction to what comes next. This is easier if the two activities are related or can be related. If the activities have nothing to do with each other, you can help students make the transition by saying, "Now we are changing gears; we are going to do something completely different."

Formations for groups of children include shapes, groups, and spacing. The easiest are those made with a landmark—a line on the floor, a cone, carpet square, or polyspot. You can purchase polyspots in a variety of shapes and colors from companies that sell physical activity equipment. Children often use landmarks, such as the line or circle formation, to create shape formations. Formations include boundaries; that is, where does the line end? Establishing boundaries is important; they should not be made by default. Often, boundaries are the walls. Wall boundaries may be inadequate for running activities, however; running to the wall may cause injury. Cones, lines, and other markers can be used to establish boundaries. Outdoors, the edge of the hard surface often makes a good boundary. You should clearly mark and state boundary locations for any space and sometimes for each activity.

Groups come in all sizes, from 2 partners to 10 or more. (See "Lesson #5 Games and Sport Lesson" on the DVD-ROM for a video clip showing a manipulative skills lesson using small groups.) Spacing can be either close or far and personal or general. Close spacing occurs when children are near enough to each other to touch; far spacing occurs when they are far enough apart so that touching is not possible. Personal space is the area around each child's body, defined by extending arms in all directions. General space is all the space that is not personal space. Scatter formation is when children are randomly placed in far spacing.

To spend as little time as possible when moving children into formations, note the following hints:

- Have a system in place to put children in groups of various sizes (e.g., squads, marks on the wall, alphabetical groups).

- Use physical landmarks to form lines, circles, and other shapes.

- Change formations as seldom as possible.

- If possible, order the activities so that those using the same formation are presented together.

Poor cognitive or activity transitions are apparent when children answer questions with comments that are off the topic, an answer appropriate for the previous topic but not the current topic, or a motor response that is no longer appropriate. Use these three techniques to keep children with you during these transitions:

1. Presenting an overview at the beginning of class that outlines the content for the day (this alerts children of upcoming transitions)

2. Reminding children during the transition of the change (e.g., "Now we are changing gears")

3. Using different terminology or a different voice (e.g., tone or loudness) after the transition

Handling Equipment

Equipment creates two problems for management. First, equipment can change the excitement, noise, or self-control of children to an inappropriate level. Second, handling equipment can take too much time away from instruction and practice. Distribution of playground balls creates an irresistible situation, even for college students, but then the students are bouncing the balls as you try to give directions. One strategy is to keep the equipment out of sight and out of reach until it is needed. Another is to separate equipment and students but have the equipment ready and distributed around the gym. A constant tension exists between the time available to distribute equipment and class control. The type of equipment, class routine, and student characteristics (e.g., age, experience, self-control) influence the decisions you make about how to handle equipment.

Handle equipment efficiently by locating it where it will be used and ready for use, although this can still be tempting to students. For older students and classes with well-established routines,

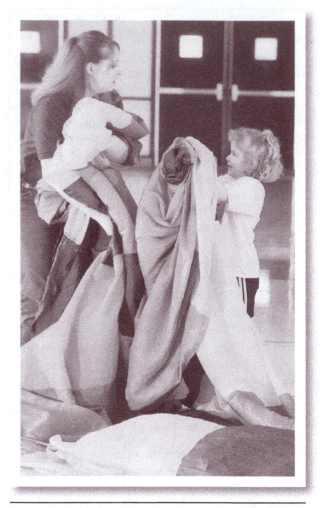

Expert teachers help students learn how to handle equipment properly.

Concepts Into Practice

Mark was struggling with one of his classes. Too much time was spent during each class reminding the class of the rules. He decided a new strategy was in order, so he made a small chart with a pyramid of stars. The five stars at the top represented following all five class rules, four stars meant following four of the rules, and so forth. At the end of class, he assigned stars to students based on their behavior and how well they followed the rules. This was reported to the teacher on an index card that had the appropriate number of stars. The card also had a place to recognize a class "superstar" for the day so Mark could recognize one student he "caught doing the right thing." Using the strategy improved class behavior and allowed Mark to focus on skills.

this method is preferred. Alternatively, one student can get equipment for several students. This works especially well when a group of children will be using the equipment but can also work when each child in a group needs equipment. Finally, the most conservative and time-consuming method is for you to distribute equipment to each child or for the children to get their equipment one at a time.

Practice with distributing and returning equipment improves the process if you provide instruction and feedback. Clear instructions and expectations, with cues and reminders, are also helpful. Learning how to deal with equipment is an important part of physical education class. Children can learn self-control, listening, sharing, and helping when you make these learning objectives.

Class Rules

Class rules have two purposes: to keep children safe and to allow learning. Center class rules on those two purposes. National Content Standard 6 is that the student should demonstrate understanding and respect for differences among people in physical activity settings. One way that you can help children achieve this goal is through comprehensive rules that are clearly explained. Children cannot follow the rules unless they know them. State the rules in the positive rather than in the negative. Make the rules broad enough to handle a variety of situations. For example, use "Hands to self" rather than "Don't hit, don't kick, don't touch, and don't take." Older children can help make the rules for the class; however, you may have to guide them to cover all of the necessary areas. Therefore, before allowing children to make up their "own" rules, outline the rules yourself. If the children do not mention one of your rules, you may be able to guide them to suggest it by giving an example of a situation calling for the rule. For example, if children do not propose a rule related to equipment, you might stimulate thought by saying, "What happens at home if one of your toys is broken?" Usually, this means they have less to play with and thus suggests that they should be careful with equipment. Often management is a direct approach to instruction, but this is a clear opportunity for indirect instruction by guiding or questioning children. Most children prefer to know and follow the rules. For many children (and adults), it is embarrassing to do something wrong. So explain the rules, give examples, and help children understand why rules are important (e.g., to keep them safe and allow them to learn). Posting the rules is helpful (table 10.1).

When children are disruptive or break a rule, several options are available:

- Ignore the child and behavior.
- Give a general reminder.
- Desist.
- Issue a warning.
- Punish the child.

Hint

To improve behavior, catch children doing something right and reinforce the good behavior.

You should handle misbehavior by adhering consistently to the discipline plans of your school or school district. Generally, these policies focus on punishment systems; for example, issue a warning, declare a time-out, send the child to the office, and call the parent. However, your management and class rules can be preventive and reduce the need for punishment. First, determine why the child is breaking the rule. If it is to gain your attention, ignoring the behavior may be your best solution. Catching children doing something right and recognizing or reinforcing the good behavior are the best ways to encourage good behavior. The child may not remember the rule or know that the rule applies in this behavior situation. In that circumstance, a general reminder to the class about the rule may work best. A **desist** is another way to handle problems; use it when a child is talking while you are talking or a child is touching another child. Move close to the offending child without interrupting instruction. In a desist, you gain proximity, do not point out the infraction, and continue

Table 10.1 Sample Class Rules

Grade 1	Grade 5
1. Be nice.	Avoid hostile gestures, fighting, and game disruptions.
2. Hands off.	Keep hands, feet, and objects to yourself.
3. Be careful.	Use equipment only as it is intended.
4. Listen and do.	Follow instructions the first time they are given.
5. Do your best.	Stop, look, and listen on the signal.

[handwritten note: the problem w/ recognizing good behavior—]

with class as though nothing happened. There are several useful variations on the desist:

- Looking at the offending child and attempting to make eye contact until the target behavior stops.
- Giving a pat on the back—touch the child (e.g., on the shoulder) as a reminder that you are paying attention.
- Changing the subject—ask the child a question or for assistance with a task.

Deciding how to change behavior is based on several factors. The first guideline is to interrupt instruction as little as possible, which is the advantage of a desist. Second, change the behavior with as few consequences as possible. Consequences range from embarrassment to punishment. The desist and its variations meet these requirements; that is, you do not interrupt instruction and the consequences are very low, although children often change behavior immediately.

If children or classes are a continual source of disruption, an action plan may be your best solution. Behavior letters (figure 10.2), awards (figure 10.3), monitoring-reporting forms (figure 10.4), and behavior contracts (figure 10.5) all work toward changing behavior in the long term. You should recognize and reinforce good behavior out loud and in writing. Typically, bad behavior is difficult to ignore, so it is recognized and

reported; but recognizing good behavior is also important. Reporting disruptive behavior can be a reminder to report good behavior; each time you note a bad behavior, note at least one good behavior as well.

The time-out is often recommended to change behavior. **Time-out** involves isolating a child physically and in terms of instruction. In physical education class, a time-out allows a child time to calm down, which is often what is needed. However, some children may prefer to sit on the sidelines, so time-out is not a punishment. For any consequence to be effective, the consequence must actually force the child to change the behavior. Therefore, consequences—even for the same behavior—must be individualized for each child. For the child who really wants to play, time-out works; however, for the child who does not care about playing, time-out is not effective. This principle applies to all consequences (e.g., send to office, call parents). Physical activity is never an appropriate punishment because you want the children to learn from it and enjoy it.

Intrusive Events

Intrusive events interfere with teaching. Two examples are when children get a drink of water or go to the bathroom. In chapter 6, Physical Activity for Children, you learned that water is important. If children leave the instructional area to get water,

---

Dear (parent name):

    You will be pleased to know that your child, (child's name), has been exhibiting the following good behavior in physical education class:

- Following instructions
- Using equipment appropriately
- Participating in all activities
- Being courteous to other children

    You and your child are to be commended. Thank you for your cooperation.

Sincerely,
(teacher's name)

Figure 10.2 Sample letter to notify parents of good behavior.

Teacher's Award for Good Behavior

presented to _____

for
following behavior rules

_____   _____
Principal   Teacher

Figure 10.3 Award for good behavior.

[handwritten: Use these @ Conference Time (positive & negative } beh)]

Name of child _____   Date _____

Behavior Report

Fails to follow instructions. ☐
Is verbally hostile. ☐
Physically abuses another child. ☐
Disrupts a game or activity. ☐
Misuses equipment. ☐
Fails to stop on the signal ☐

_____
Teacher's signature

Figure 10.4 Observation form for monitoring and reporting behavior.

safety is a primary concern; secondary to that is maintaining class continuity. Assuming it is safe, how will you allow children to get a drink without having each child ask individually? Another consideration is having more than one child gone at a time; this can increase risk and can disrupt play or instruction. You might use a pass system. This works well until the pass is lost. A recommended method is to put a two-sided, colored sign in a pocket on the wall: The red side says "stop" and the green side says "go." When children go for a drink or to the bathroom, they switch the sign to "stop"; on returning, they switch it back to "go." You can glance at the sign, as can all of the other children, and know that a child is gone.

Other intrusive events include messages, delivered over the public address system or directly to you, and emergencies. The school plan covers

[handwritten: Teacher Talking the drinks will have to wait]

Behavior Contract

I, (student's name), will do the following:

1. Practice the skills at each station.
2. Not push or hit other children during physical education class this week.

_____
Student's signature

I, (teacher's name), will do the following:

1. Allow (student's name) to select the game for the day.
2. Appoint (student's name) equipment manager for the day, next week.

_____
Teacher's signature

Figure 10.5 Behavior contract.

some emergencies (e.g., fire drills, tornado drills); others are part of the class plan for first aid and emergency. Write the procedure for an injury and post it on the wall of the gym. Critical information includes what information is needed for using the 911 emergency phone (school name, address, and phone number), who should be notified in the school (e.g., the nurse or principal), where the first aid supplies are located, and what the children should do during the emergency. Once you develop a plan, share the plan with the principal and the school nurse and then revise the plan after talking to them. Once everyone agrees with the plan, share and discuss it with the children. Ice packs, a first aid kit, accident reports (figure 10.6), and a phone are essential emergency supplies (see chapter 12, Equipment and Facilities, for a more complete list).

Legal Liability

Chapter 11, Teachers' Rights, Responsibilities, and Best Practices, provides greater detail on legal liability. The purpose of this section is to demonstrate the relationship between management and liability. You are responsible for the care and safety of your students. Because you care about them and therefore want them to be safe, you need to understand your legal responsibility. Your legal responsibility is based on negligence. Negligence is defined as an act that does not meet the standards established by law for protection of children against unreasonable danger or risk of injury. In legal terms, this is often called the "standard of care" and refers to "best practices" in educational terms. To establish negligence, it must be proven in court that you failed to take necessary action to ensure the safety of a student and that this failure to act resulted in an injury. Negligence may also be established if you commit an act that a reasonable person would have realized involved risk of injury, and an injury resulted. Thus, you can fail to act, can act inappropriately, or can act in a way that falls below a certain standard required by law and is then considered negligent. In fulfilling the responsibility to maintain a safe environment for children, you should provide adequate supervision, plan activities appropriate for the participants, maintain a safe play area, provide adequate instruction, and establish procedures for emergency care. Four factors influence negligence: adequate supervision, safe environments, adequate instruction, and appropriate emergency procedures.

Incident Report Form

Name of student _____ Grade _____ Age _____

Date of incident _____ Time of incident _____

Did the incident occur during

   ❑ Class? If checked, what class? _____

   ❑ Recess?

   ❑ Other? If checked, please explain. _____

   _____

Nature of incident

   ❑ Injury (accidental)

   ❑ Injury (not accidental)

   ❑ Verbal abuse

   ❑ Other (explain) _____

   _____

Describe the incident:

Location _____

People involved _____

What happened _____

_____

Immediate action taken _____

Was there an injury? Yes ❑ No ❑ If yes, describe the degree (nondisabling, temporarily disabling).

_____

Was a teacher present at the time? Yes ❑ No ❑ Name _____

Other witnesses: Name _____

Class _____

Was a parent notified? Yes ❑ No ❑ _____

What could be done to prevent similar incidents? _____

_____

Signature _____

Figure 10.6 Accident and incident report.

285

Never leave children unsupervised on a playground or in the gymnasium—even if you are in the area. Supervisors need to be aware of what is going on, make children aware of safety factors, and be accessible to any child needing help. Children must learn to move under control and to think about their actions. Select a location for observing children that provides the best view of most of them. Two other factors influence the location you select for observing: the risk associated with the activity or equipment and student characteristics. If the activities or equipment used in a lesson are generally low risk, but one activity is of greater risk, consider locating near the activity with the highest risk. Sometimes, however, risk is associated with particular children—those most likely to misuse equipment or move out of control. You must decide where the risk is greatest and locate yourself there.

One technique to facilitate supervision is orientation with "your back to the wall." This means no children can get behind you and out of view. You can walk the perimeter, trying to view as much as possible of the class. When it is impossible to see the entire area, scan the area constantly. Typically, an experienced teacher's vision is captured by an out-of-boundary activity—something that looks different than expected. For example, you are expecting to see all of the children moving across the gym floor in about the same way; however, three boys in the back row are several steps behind the group—a sure sign that they are not on task. If no harm has been done and the boys are back on track, continue to scan. On the other hand, you need to intervene if the boys continue misbehaving by pushing and shoving each other. Good scanning captures these events; you decide how to handle them and then continue scanning. Even when you must respond to an event that captures your vision, resume scanning as soon as possible. When you are forced to stop scanning, you may need to stop all activity until you can begin scanning again. You may stop all activity and ask, "Why did I ask everyone to stop?" Or say, "There is no reason for anyone to touch another child during this activity." You might reorganize the children so that the three boys are no longer together, or decide to stand closer to them but still in a position to see the whole class. At times, you may need to leave the perimeter, moving through or into the instructional area. You should know that this can increase risk, especially if children are then behind you. Scan in the classroom, too, where it may be more difficult to identify inappropriate behaviors—for example, children off task—than in the gym. Scanning is an important skill any time children are present (e.g., playground, bus duty, cafeteria, classroom, gym).

Examine small equipment for damage and inspect large equipment regularly. An excellent source of information about equipment and facilities is the U.S. Consumer Product Safety Commission Web site (www.cpsc.gov). Guidelines on the site for safe equipment and recall information are updated regularly. When ensuring a safe environment, check surfaces, making sure that indoor surfaces are clean and dry and outdoor hard surfaces are dry and free of debris. Soft outdoor surfaces should be appropriately maintained (e.g., grass mowed and reasonably dry, sand deep and raked, bark or shavings deep). Even under the best circumstances, accidents can happen. The point is to avoid injuries that *can* be avoided. Find out who at the school is responsible for checking equipment and maintaining facilities. Although it would be ideal to have these duties assigned to maintenance staff, you cannot assume this. A checklist of the times and dates that equipment and facilities are checked is helpful. In any case, do not let the children use equipment or facilities that are unsafe; do everything reasonable to prevent anyone from being injured.

Adequate instruction has two components: instruction for skill and instruction for safety. This applies to both free play (e.g., recess) and class time. Good management practices cover this instruction for class time. Be proactive, making sure that recess and other free play periods are safe by instructing children about safety and skill.

Use good judgment when making decisions based on natural hazards, such as weather conditions (e.g., heat and humidity), insects, and animals. It is better to be too conservative than to increase risk for children. Generally, when you aim to do the "right thing" and have reasons for your decisions, your liability is low. Using good management reduces liability.

Summary

Management is important because it reduces risk, increases safety, and allows more time for learning. Routines, a basic component of management, make children comfortable. Good management reduces your liability. Management also allows children to develop the skills necessary to be physically educated as they learn to demonstrate responsible personal and social behaviors and to show respect for differences among people by following class rules.

Mastery Learning Activities

1. Examine lesson 10.1 for grades K and 1 and lesson 10.5 for lessons for 4 and 5. What are the differences between the grades? List the management techniques used in the lessons.

2. Write an emergency plan to be posted on the gym wall.

3. Fill in the table below.

4. Describe the four factors determining legal liability (negligence).

References

Siedentop, D. 1998. *In search of effective teaching: What we have learned from studying teachers and students.* McCloy Lecture presented at the Annual Meeting of the American Alliance for Health, Physical Education, Recreation and Dance, Portland, OR, April 7.

U.S. Consumer Product Safety Commission. *Handbook for public playground safety,* Publication 325. Washington, D.C: United States Government Printing Office.

Resources

National Playground Safety Commission. www.cpsc. gov.

Siedentop, D., J. Herkowitz, and J. Rink. 1984. *Elementary physical education methods.* Englewood Cliffs, NJ: Prentice Hall.

Lesson Plans

The six lesson plans at the end of this chapter demonstrate how to teach children about rules, formations, handling equipment, and other management techniques. The lessons are fun and teach important skills. The techniques and practice change as children mature. You should cover the basics of class organization at the beginning of the school year and again as necessary throughout the school year. The investment of time in planning is worthwhile because, in the long run, it prevents problems and increases instructional time.

	Definition	Example 1	Example 2	Example 3
Signal				
Rules				
Formations				
Boundaries				
Intrusive event				
Initial activity				
Concluding activity				
Emergency procedure				

Lesson 10.1

Signals, Rules, and Boundaries

Student Objectives 5

- Identify safety and learning as benefits of having and following rules.
- Identify the class signals.
- Demonstrate starting and stopping on signal.
- Move into information formation on a signal.
- Move within and around boundaries.

Equipment and Materials

- Chalkboard or flip chart (or poster board, large paper) for writing
- 1 carpet square per child
- 5 to 10 beanbags

Warm-Up Activities (5 minutes)

Islands in the Ocean

Arrange carpet squares with 6 feet (1.8 m) or more between each square. Each child should be sitting on a carpet square.

1. Explain that each carpet square is an island, so each child has his or her own island. The islands are small, and the children must try to stay "dry" by staying on the carpet square.
2. Call out the following movements and positions, reminding children to stay on the squares: "Stand up, walk, lie down, sit on your knees, sit down and touch your feet, stand up and touch your feet, jump, turn around, and sit down." Repeat movements and speed up or slow down changes in movements, depending on how successful the children are at each movement.
3. Compliment children who stay on the squares.

Skill-Development Activities (20 minutes)

Physical Education Rules

Arrange the children in a close group; they sit on the floor on the carpet squares.

1. Explain the formation: "This is called an information formation. When I say, 'information formation,' move to this close group and sit on the floor. We will practice this again later."
2. Ask the children: "What might happen if we did not have rules or laws? For example, how do traffic rules help us?" (If there were no stop signs or cars did not stop at the signs, there would probably be many accidents. Many people could be hurt. Having and following rules keeps us safer.)
3. "What rules should we have in physical education class so everyone can be safer?" Lead a discussion of rules 1 through 3. Write the rules on the chalkboard or paper:
   o Rule 1: "Keep your hands off: This means we do not put our hands, feet, or other body parts on anyone else so that everyone will be safe."
   o Rule 2: "Be careful: Do not damage equipment. Do not move wildly; this way, everyone is safe and the equipment stays in good condition for physical education class."

- Rule 3: "Listen and look for the stop signals: When you hear or see the signal, stop, listen, and look at me." Demonstrate the stop signal. Tell the children: "Show me the stop signal. Good remembering! Following the stop signal helps everyone hear instructions and stay safe."

4. "These rules give everyone the same opportunity, or chance, to learn. What other situations should we have rules for?" (When one child does not hear the instructions because another child is talking, when one child keeps a piece of equipment [e.g., a ball] too long so other children do not have the chance to practice, and so on.) Lead the discussion to rules 4 through 6.

- Rule 4: "Be nice. Do not fight; do not bother others; be helpful. Being nice keeps everyone safe while learning and having fun!"

- Rule 5: "Listen and do: When I am talking, please don't talk; when another child has permission to talk, please don't talk; it is OK to talk quietly at other times; do what you are instructed to do." You may prefer to have a signal for quiet that differs from the stop signal, such as a raised hand or finger over the mouth. If so, explain and demonstrate it now.

- Rule 6: "Do your best: Always try everything and work hard. This rule makes sure everyone learns and feels good about physical education class."

5. Continue the discussion about the importance of following rules until you think the children have a good understanding of acceptable behavior in the physical education setting. Most of the rules the children come up with are variations or examples of the 6 rules already listed. Help the children to categorize these as such. Write any further rules on the chalkboard or paper.

6. Note: After class, make a poster of your final version of class rules for future reference.

Moving Within and Around Boundaries

Using the 4 cones, mark a large rectangle in the playing area.

1. Relate this activity to rule 5: Listen and do. Tell the children: "Having boundaries helps us to be safe and learn; if you are too far away, you might not be able to hear what to do or you might be in danger."

2. Walk the entire class around the sides of the rectangle formed by the 4 cones.

3. Show them the boundary lines between the cones. Describe the boundary lines: "These are like invisible walls; the area 'inside' is like a room. On the other side of the wall is the 'outside.'" Scatter the children inside the "room."

4. Signal the children: "Move carefully but freely (randomly) inside." Signal stop. Compliment those who stop quickly and quietly.

5. "Move along the boundaries on the outside of the line." Signal stop. Offer compliments.

6. "Move along the boundaries on the inside of the line." Signal stop. Offer compliments.

7. "Move along the boundaries on the outside." Signal stop. Offer compliments.

8. Repeat steps 4 through 7 as time permits.

Concluding Activities (5 minutes)

Physical Education Rules

Signal the children to create the information formation.

1. Compliment those who remembered the formation and gathered quickly and quietly.

2. Repeat the rules that were written earlier and ask: "Can you give a reason for each rule?"

3. "Do you have any questions?" Allow the children to raise any concerns.

4. If this is your last class of the day, ask one child to gather the cones and two or three others to gather the carpet squares and bring them to you.

From K.T. Thomas, A.M. Lee, and J.R. Thomas, 2008, *Physical education methods for elementary teachers*, 3rd ed. (Champaign, IL: Human Kinetics). Adapted, by permission, from K.T. Thomas, A.M. Lee, and J.R. Thomas, 2000, *Physical education for children: Daily lesson plans for elementary school*, 2nd ed. (Champaign, IL: Human Kinetics), 6-8.

Lesson 10.2

Rules, Consensus, and Formations

Student Objectives 5	Equipment and Materials
• Recognize the rules.	• Physical Education Rules poster
• Give examples of the rules.	• 1 carpet square per child plus a few extra
• Reach consensus on the class rules.	• 4 cones or other markers
• Move from a line to a circle formation.	• Polyspots, polydomes, string, or tape circle
• Participate in a game.	• 5 to 10 beanbags

Warm-Up Activities (5 minutes)

Wild One

Use 4 cones to define a rectangular play area. Scatter carpet squares and beanbags randomly in the play area; leave spaces between them. Have each child begin by standing on a carpet square. There should be extra squares.

1. Review and emphasize rule 2, Be careful, before introducing the game.
2. Designate one child as the Wild One ("It") and direct him or her to move randomly about the play area, making faces, waving arms, and generally acting wild while the other children walk from carpet square to carpet square. Tell the children: "Only one child may be on a square at a time. Keep moving all the time from square to square."
3. After a while, signal stop and select a new Wild One. Stop the game if more than one child ends up on a square; remind the children to move to another square.
4. After the children have learned to move continuously from square to square, tell them to run between squares.
5. Repeat the game with new Wild Ones, stopping as necessary to remind the children that there is only one Wild One or that only one child may be on each square.

Skill-Development Activities (20 minutes)

Rules Consensus

Gather the children into an information formation.

1. Show the children the rules. Ask the children:
   ◦ Who remembers a rule? Continue until the children have repeated each one.
   ◦ Why are rules important? (Stay safe; save time.)
2. Give an example of when each rule might apply:
   ◦ Rule 1: Hands off. If a child is a Wild One, other children may not be able to listen, do, and learn.

- Rule 2: Be careful. If our equipment is broken, no one can learn; a child who is hurt cannot learn.
- Rule 3: Listen and look for the stop signals. Remember yesterday when we practiced moving in and out of our area? If everyone had not stopped when I signaled, some people might not have heard the directions.
- Rule 4: Be nice. Children fighting can keep many of the other children from learning.
- Rule 5: Listen and do. As a new activity begins, we must listen for instructions and then do them in order to learn as much as possible.
- Rule 6: Do your best. Each of us must try everything, even if we think we are not very good at the activity.

3. Ask if children understand each rule. Discuss if necessary:
   - Are these good rules?
   - Can you agree with them? (If yes, continue; if no, discuss and resolve any problems or misunderstandings so that all of the children can agree with the rules.)
   - Can you follow the rules? We are all counting on you.
4. Ask one child to gather the beanbags and two children to gather the carpet squares for you.

Circle and Line

Arrange the children in a line between 2 cones. Mark a large circle with cones, polyspots, or polydomes 20 to 30 feet (6 to 9 m) from the line.

1. Describe the line formation. Tell the children:
   - Look at your present location and remember it.
   - Look for some special landmark, such as a line, a clover, or a bare spot.
2. Describe and point out the circle.
3. Signal the children: "Move, in any way you want, to the circle and stand still on the line." Adjust the children's positions in the circle as necessary. Signal the children: "Move back to your positions on the line."
4. Repeat several times until the children master the skill.

Moving Within and Around Boundaries

Using 4 cones, mark a large rectangle in the playing area around the circle. Create the rectangle in a different position from the previous lesson.

1. Remind the children what they have learned about boundaries.
2. Ask the children: "Who can show me the boundaries marked by the cones?" Allow one child to demonstrate by running between the four cones marking the boundaries of the rectangle.

Concluding Activities (5 minutes)

Circle Boundaries Game

Arrange half of the children in a circle that is inside the rectangle formed by the 4 cones. Scatter the remaining group outside the circle but inside the rectangle.

1. Explain that the scattered children can move three places on your command: (1) inside the rectangle but outside the circle, (2) inside the circle, and (3) around the boundaries.
2. Explain the activity: "When I say, 'rectangle,' 'boundaries,' or 'circle,' walk or run until I signal for you to stop or change locations." Repeat several times; then reverse the roles of the two groups.

Lesson 10.2 *(continued)*

For additional steps, place a line somewhere in the rectangle.

3. Expand the activity: "Now let's add another word. When I say, 'Line!' form a line as quickly as possible."

4. Have the circle group walk along the circle. Each time you signal for the other group to change locations, have these children change the direction in which they are walking.

5. If this is your last class of the day, ask one to four children to gather the cones.

From K.T. Thomas, A.M. Lee, and J.R. Thomas, 2008, *Physical education methods for elementary teachers*, 3rd ed. (Champaign, IL: Human Kinetics). Adapted, by permission, from K.T. Thomas, A.M. Lee, and J.R. Thomas, 2000, *Physical education for children: Daily lesson plans for elementary school*, 2nd ed. (Champaign, IL: Human Kinetics), 9-11.

Lesson 10.3

Equipment and Spacing

Student Objectives 5

- Demonstrate getting and returning equipment.
- Demonstrate near and far spacing.

Equipment and Materials

- 4 cones
- Enough beanbags for one-fourth of the class
- Enough hoops for one-fourth of the class
- Enough balls for one-fourth of the class
- Enough jump ropes for one-fourth of the class
- 6 carpet squares

Warm-Up Activities (5 minutes)

Review of Formations

Arrange the children in scatter formation inside a large rectangle defined by the 4 cones.
Ask the children to complete the following tasks:

- Move into a circle formation around me.
- Jog clockwise.
- Freeze!
- Jog counterclockwise.
- Freeze!
- Move to a line formation between me and that cone (point).
- Jump up and down in personal space.
- Freeze!
- Move to a scatter formation.
- Run in general space inside the boundaries.
- Freeze!
- Jog clockwise around the outside of the boundaries.
- Freeze!
- Move to the line I'm pointing to (on one side of the rectangle).
- Hop across the rectangle to the opposite line.
- Make a circle around me.

Lesson 10.3   *(continued)*

Skill-Development Activities (20 minutes)

Station Rotation

Place 1 carpet square on each of the long sides of the rectangle and 1 carpet square in each corner. Divide the children into 6 groups.

1. Assign each group to a carpet square.
2. Number each carpet square, saying the numbers for each group aloud as you point to the square: "Say each number aloud with me."
3. "On the signal, the children in each group should move from their carpet square to the next higher number; number 6 should go to number 1." Continue until all of the groups are back to the starting positions.
4. "Repeat in reverse (1 goes to 6, 6 to 5, 5 to 4, and so on)."

Giving Out Equipment

Divide the children into 4 groups; assign 1 group to each corner of the play area.

1. Assign each group a type of equipment (e.g., beanbags to group 1, hoops to group 2, balls to group 3, and ropes to group 4).
2. Name a group. Have each child in the group get one piece of equipment from you, return to the group's station, and sit down with the equipment.
3. Repeat with the other groups.

Concluding Activity (5 minutes)

Nose Tag

Arrange the children in scatter formation. Designate two players as "Its."

1. Describe and demonstrate the game:
   - Two children begin as Its and try to tag the other children, who run and try to avoid being tagged by the Its.
   - You are safe from being tagged if you are standing on one leg with the other leg looped over one arm while the hand on that arm holds your nose.
   - If you let go of your nose, lose your balance, or begin to run, you are no longer safe and can be tagged by an It.
   - Once tagged, you become an It and switch places with the original It.
2. Have the children play Nose Tag.

From K.T. Thomas, A.M. Lee, and J.R. Thomas, 2008, *Physical education methods for elementary teachers*, 3rd ed. (Champaign, IL: Human Kinetics). Adapted, by permission, from K.T. Thomas, A.M. Lee, and J.R. Thomas, 2000, *Physical education for children: Daily lesson plans for elementary school*, 2nd ed. (Champaign, IL: Human Kinetics), 379-380.

Lesson 10.4

Stations and Rotations, Rules and Consequences

Student Objectives 5

- Work cooperatively to decide the consequences for infractions of rules.
- Move to station formation and rotate.

Equipment and Materials

- 4 cones
- Enough hoops for one-fourth of the class
- Enough balls for one-fourth of the class
- Enough carpet squares for one-fourth of the class
- Enough jump ropes for one-fourth of the class

Warm-Up Activities (5 minutes)

Near–Far Concepts

Arrange partners in scatter formation. Ask the children to respond quickly to the following statements:

- Stand close to your partner.
- Move as far away as possible from your partner.
- Make a double circle, one partner standing beside the other, so that one partner is on the inside and the other is on the outside circle.
- Move sideways so that the inside circle is smaller, the outside circle is larger, and you and your partner are in far position.
- One partner moves outside the boundaries while one partner stays inside the boundary in near position.
- One partner moves outside the boundaries while one partner stays inside the boundary in far position.
- One partner makes a line on this side (point); the rest of you make a line over there (point).
- Make the lines as short as possible so that you are in near position.
- Make the lines longer so that you are in far position.

Skill-Development Activities (20 minutes)

Consequences

Gather the children into an information formation.

1. Read the rules.
    - Rule 1: Follow directions.

- Rule 2: Hands off other children.
- Rule 3: Be careful of equipment and others.
- Rule 4: Stop, look, and listen on the signal.
- Rule 5: Do not fight or stop practice or play.

2. Ask the children: "Are there any questions about the rules?" (Pause.) "We talked about why it is important to follow the rules. Following rules makes it easier for everyone to learn, saves equipment, and keeps us safe. What happens if someone breaks a rule?" (It interferes with learning, it may be dangerous, equipment may be broken, and there should be consequences for the rule breaker.)

3. Ask the children: "What consequences would be fair?" Discuss. Suggested consequences include the following:

- First offense: 3-minute time-out.
- Second offense: 6-minute time-out.
- Third offense: Call parents.
- Fourth offense: Send to principal.

4. Note: Use behavior contracts, good behavior rewards, and good or poor behavior letters to parents. After class, make a poster of the consequences.

Stations

Use the cones to define a rectangle. Divide the children into 4 groups, and assign 1 group to each corner of the play area. Assign 1 type of equipment to each group.

1. Name a group and have one member of that group get the equipment for the entire group.
2. Allow the children to do creative movements with the equipment for 1 to 3 minutes.
3. Have each group rotate to the next station and repeat.
4. Continue until all four groups have been at all four stations.
5. Have one child from each station return the station's equipment.

Concluding Activities (5 minutes)

Movement Patterns

Arrange the children in scatter formation in the middle of the play area. Tell the children to move in the following patterns and to change patterns on the signal:

- Hop forward (backward, left, right). Repeat.
- Jog in a circle (clockwise); turn and jog in a circle the opposite direction (counterclockwise).
- Skip forward; then jump backward.
- Walk forward, change direction, change direction, change direction (any direction).
- Move in a zigzag pattern.
- Move in a straight line.
- Move in a curved line.

From K.T. Thomas, A.M. Lee, and J.R. Thomas, 2008, *Physical education methods for elementary teachers*, 3rd ed. (Champaign, IL: Human Kinetics). Adapted, by permission, from K.T. Thomas, A.M. Lee, and J.R. Thomas, 2000, *Physical education for children: Daily lesson plans for elementary school*, 2nd ed. (Champaign, IL: Human Kinetics), 381-383.

Lesson 10.5

Signals, Boundaries, Groupings, and Rules

Student Objectives   5

- Move diagonally across an area.
- Move in an area within an area.

Equipment and Materials

- Physical Education Rules poster
- 8 cones or markers
- Large sign cards (8.5 by 11 inches [21.5 by 27.9 cm] or larger)
- 8 foam balls
- Polyspots, polydomes, or tape for marking lines

Warm-Up Activities (5 minutes)

Single File

Arrange the children in squad formation. Designate a leader of each squad. Practice working in single file:

- On the signal, the last child in each line runs to the front of that line and becomes the new leader.
- All leaders jog or walk around (across, inside) the area as you hear me call out the pattern.

Skill-Development Activities (20 minutes)

Advanced Information Formation

Arrange the children in concentric semicircles, with the first row seated, the next row kneeling, and the last row standing. Tell the children: "This as an 'advanced information formation.'"

Rules

1. Ask the children to recall and state the rules.
   - Rule 1: Follow directions.
   - Rule 2: Hands off.
   - Rule 3: Be careful.
   - Rule 4: Stop, look, and listen on the signal.
   - Rule 5: Do not fight.
2. Watch for situations during the remainder of the lesson that are examples of good behavior; stop the class activities and point out these examples.

Lesson 10.5   *(continued)*

Changing Direction to a Verbal Signal

Arrange the children in scatter formation within a large rectangle marked with 4 cones.

Have the children move to commands; give a signal for each change of direction: "Run (walk, hop, jump) left (right, back, forward, sideways)."

Task Cards

Print movement tasks on cards large enough for the children to read (8.5 by 11 inches [21.5 by 27.9 cm] or larger).

1. Show the cards to the entire group or place the cards at the activity stations. Direct the children to read the tasks and respond with the appropriate movements.
2. Use the following examples of task card instructions or choose other tasks that fit with your skill-development plans:
   - Slide right, slide left, and hop in a circle.
   - Jump forward, jump backward, spin, and sit down.
   - Run 10 steps backward, and leap back to starting place.
   - Gallop in a circle, hop three times, and jump high.

Station Formation

Place 1 of the cards at each of 4 stations. Direct the children:

- Move to the stations, forming squads with no more than 8 children (or one-fourth of the class) per squad.
- Rotate (1 goes to 2, 2 to 3, and so on).

Partner Relay

Arrange the children in pairs, and assign each pair to a 4-person relay team. Mark a starting line and a return line. At the return line, place a stack of cards for each relay team; each pair of children has a card. The cards specify how the pair returns to the starting line. Use the following examples of task card instructions or choose other tasks that fit with your skill-development plans:

- Hold one hand with your partner and hop on opposite feet.
- Run backward.
- Skip with one child in front of the other.
- Join both hands and slide.

1. Explain the activity:
   - On the signal, travel with your partner; use any type of movement to the return line. Then select a card from the stack of cards and read the task.
   - Travel back to the starting line; use the movement specified on the card. This is not a race.
   - Continue until each pair in your group has had a turn.
   - Shuffle the cards and repeat the game until the time is up.
2. Run the Partner Relay.

Moving Diagonally

Have the children get back into 4 groups, and place 1 group in each corner of a large rectangle defined by 4 cones.

1. Have group 1 switch with group 3.
2. Have group 2 switch with group 4.

3. Repeat steps 1 and 2.

4. Have the children move to scatter formation.

5. Present the following tasks:
   - Can you move diagonally? Stop when you hit a boundary.
   - Move to a corner if you are not in a corner.
   - Move diagonally.

Concluding Activities (5 minutes)

Moving Within an Area

Use a second set of 4 cones to mark out a square in the center of the large rectangle. Divide the children into 5 squads. Send squads 1 and 2 to one end of the large area. Send squads 3 and 4 to the other end of the large area. Send squad 5 into the small square.

1. Explain the activity:
   - Squads 1, 2, 3, and 4 throw the foam balls over the small square and play catch between those squads. Squad 5 players try to catch the balls.
   - If a member of squad 5 catches a ball, that child switches places with the thrower.

2. Run the activity. If squad 5 is having trouble catching the balls, enlarge the center square.

From K.T. Thomas, A.M. Lee, and J.R. Thomas, 2008, *Physical education methods for elementary teachers*, 3rd ed. (Champaign, IL: Human Kinetics). Adapted, by permission, from K.T. Thomas, A.M. Lee, and J.R. Thomas, 2000, *Physical education for children: Daily lesson plans for elementary school*, 2nd ed. (Champaign, IL: Human Kinetics), 757-759.

Lesson 10.6

Signals, Boundaries, Groupings, and Rules

Student Objectives 5

- Move among line, circle, scatter, pair, and station formations.
- Form squads.
- Start, listen, and stop on an auditory signal.
- Move in, across, around, and outside boundaries.
- State rules for class behavior.
- Work cooperatively with a group to accomplish a goal.

Equipment and Materials

- Physical Education Rules poster
- 4 cones or markers
- 1 carpet square per squad
- 1 basketball or a playground ball (8.5 inches [21.5 cm]) per group

Warm-Up Activities (5 minutes)

Boundaries

Divide the children into 4 groups. Arrange one group on each boundary line of a large rectangle defined by the 4 cones. Name or number the boundaries (1 to 4, or North, South, East, and West).

1. Call out the following exchanges; children on the boundaries named exchange places with each other:
   - 1 and 3 (North and South)
   - 2 and 4 (East and West)
   - 1 and 4 (North and West)
   - 3 and 2 (South and East)
   - 1 and 2 (North and East)
   - 3 and 4 (South and West)
   - 3 and 1 (South and North)
   - 4 and 2 (West and East)
2. Tell the children: "Everyone return to starting position!"

Skill-Development Activities (20 minutes)

Physical Education Rules

Arrange the children in the advanced information formation.

1. Use this section by reading the following rules or working with the children for a consensus on the rules.

- Rule 1: Follow directions (on the first time that they are given).
- Rule 2: Hands off (keep hands, feet, and objects to yourself).
- Rule 3: Be careful of equipment and others.
- Rule 4: Stop, look, and listen on the signal.
- Rule 5: Do not fight or interfere with the practice or play of others (avoid hostile gestures, fighting, and game disruption).

2. "Are there any questions about the rules?" Discuss.

Cooperative Groups

Arrange the children in groups of 4 to 6 heterogeneous learning teams every time you create cooperative groups. Place the children carefully by combining those who lack social skills with others who are more socially mature. Separate the children who tend to be disruptive by placing them in different groups. Also strive to create equal representation of children of different races, ethnic origins, social classes, and gender in each group. Finally, keep group sizes as small as possible to increase participation opportunities. Have each squad line up at a carpet square, arranged at one end of the play area.

1. Assign a role for each member of the group. Roles can include organizer or leader, timekeeper, encourager, praiser, equipment handler, facilitator, and summarizer. Explain the roles you wish the children to use:
   - The "organizer" is the child who gets the group started on the group project and serves as the group leader.
   - The "timekeeper" keeps time and makes sure that the task is completed in the allotted time.
   - The "encourager" encourages each child to work productively and reminds each child that his or her role is important.
   - The "praiser" encourages positive interaction by making supportive remarks to each child.
   - The "equipment handler" is responsible for getting and returning the equipment that the group needs.
   - The "facilitator" asks you for help when needed.
   - The "summarizer" keeps mental notes of the process and provides a summary at the end of the session.

2. Establish guidelines for cooperative work:
   - Everyone must contribute to the work.
   - Only one child can talk at a time, and the others listen.
   - Everyone must show respect for the others.
   - Each child has a unique role to fill.

Problem Solving

Continue with small groups.

1. Present a problem, such as one of the following, for the groups to solve:
   - Create a ball game that requires a circle and uses the skills of throwing, catching, and running.
   - Design a play to be used in halfcourt basketball.
   - Design an exercise plan for 1 week.

2. Share how you score the work of each group on a 5-point scale, ending with this reminder: "Your group can earn 5 points only if you collaborate and work according to the guidelines and if all children fulfill their assigned roles."

Squad Formation

Teach the children to divide themselves into their small groups (assigned in the previous section) with a designated meeting place and a set formation (short parallel lines at each carpet square arranged at one end of the play area).

Lesson 10.6 *(continued)*

1. Tell the children: "On the signal, move behind the squares and form lines with the groups I've already assigned."
2. Adjust children, if necessary, so that the lines are straight and nearly equal in length. Tell the children: "Remember your squad and your position in your squad."

Concluding Activities (5 minutes)

Formations

Start this activity with the children still in their squads. Define the play area with the 4 cones. Ask the children to create the following formations:

- Make a line facing me.
- Move to scatter formation.
- Make a circle around me.
- Find a partner and stand back to back.
- Move to scatter formation.
- Move to squad formation.
- Squad 1 go to station 1. (Point to a corner; stations 1 to 4 are the corners of a rectangle.)
- Squad 2 go to station 2, (and so on; use the long sides or center of the rectangle if you have more than 4 squads).
- Rotate (squad 1 goes to station 2, squad 2 to station 3, and so on).
- Players at each station make a circle.
- Make one big circle with the entire class.
- Move back to squad formation.
- Move to scatter formation.
- Select a partner and get back in scatter formation.
- Move back to squad formation.

Single File

Continue in squad formation. Designate a leader of each squad. Practice working in single file:

- On the signal, the last child in each line runs to the front of that line and becomes the new leader.
- All leaders jog or walk around (across, inside) the area as you hear me call out the pattern.

From K.T. Thomas, A.M. Lee, and J.R. Thomas, 2008, *Physical education methods for elementary teachers*, 3rd ed. (Champaign, IL: Human Kinetics). Adapted, by permission, from K.T. Thomas, A.M. Lee, and J.R. Thomas, 2000, *Physical education for children: Daily lesson plans for elementary school*, 2nd ed. (Champaign, IL: Human Kinetics), 753-756.

CHAPTER 11

Teachers' Rights, Responsibilities, and Best Practices

HILDEGARD, AGE 9

At least three levels of rules, regulations, and responsibilities apply to teachers: criminal laws, professional standards, and best practices. As professional educators, you are held to a higher standard than the general public. In fact, you are expected to establish challenging standards for yourselves. Meeting or exceeding these expectations provides a safe and nurturing environment for students.

Learner Outcomes

After studying this chapter, you should be able to do the following:

- Define liability, negligence, standard of care, and best practice.
- Explain the three levels of teacher responsibility.
- Discuss your responsibilities as these relate to safety.
- Describe why best practices (and beyond) are important.
- List expectations for professional teachers.
- Relate at least one principle to one or more statute.
- Describe the characteristics of a professional educator.

Glossary Terms

breach of contract	tort	supervision
professional ethics	negligence	active supervision
statutes	liability	chain of command
individualized education program (IEP)	standard of care	best practice
Buckley Amendment	instruction	

Unfortunately, the media presents almost daily accounts of teachers and schools in the context of criticism or legal action. The accounts may tell of poor student achievement or illegal behavior by a professional educator. Actions that would not be newsworthy for the typical citizen may create a media frenzy in the case of a teacher because they are held to a higher standard as professionals and as caretakers of children. As teachers, you appreciate the recognition that goes with your reputation for shaping the future by teaching tomorrow's leaders, but with that recognition comes considerable responsibility. You are expected to be exemplary models for children! Because most schools are supported by tax monies from the state government, the legislatures of each state have the opportunity to set criteria for your behavior and licensing. Usually, these are expressed in codes of professional conduct as part of state rules and regulations. Professional organizations also outline performance and ethical codes for you and identify best practices. In addition, federal statutes (laws) require both you and your school to meet a variety of requirements. Finally, you must also abide by the civil and criminal codes that apply to every person.

You need to understand your rights and responsibilities and the laws, statutes, and regulations that apply to you for two reasons:

1. to provide the optimal educational environment for your students so that you can be a professional educator and

2. to protect yourselves and your school from litigation.

This chapter provides an overview of legal concepts, prevention, safety, and liability issues and introduces your rights, responsibilities of professional conduct, and best practices. Prevention and knowledge are critical tools for you to avoid problems with the law. Professional legal problems can result from three areas of law: contracts, statutes, and tort. In addition, as citizens, you may have personal legal problems when your behavior falls under the realm of the criminal code.

Professional teachers willingly accept the responsibility of being good role models for their students.

Criminal Code

You are bound and guided by several sets of laws, regulations, and expectations. Civil and criminal laws apply to you just as they apply to everyone else. Laws, whether you agree with them or not, allow democratic society in the United States to operate in a reasonably safe, secure, and smooth manner. These laws are similar to your class rules, which are designed so that the class runs in a smooth and orderly manner. As citizens in a free country, you can lobby to change the laws, but you are expected to abide by those laws until they are changed. Your values and moral development influence your beliefs, and society protects your right to hold different values and beliefs. Your society also protects the majority, however, by expecting citizens to follow laws.

Laws and regulations about automobile operation, taxes, substance use, and public conduct, among many others, apply to everyone. You may not agree with the speed limit, but you have the right to lobby for changes in speed limits and are subject to punishment if you are guilty of breaking it. You may be thinking, *How does this matter if I am a teacher?* Under most circumstances, speeding is not relevant to your professional life. However, it could be relevant if you were speeding with students in your car or while operating a school district vehicle.

Any criminal or civil law might affect your professional life, especially as a prospective or new teacher. For example, many states (e.g., Iowa) require you to report any convictions (other than a parking ticket) on the application for a license. Some states (e.g., Missouri) require you to report arrests or charges even when there has been no conviction. There is no clear answer as to how this information is used in determining who is licensed. Schools require similar self-reporting on job applications. It is not clear how this information influences who is employed. Many teachers and prospective teachers must undergo a criminal background check for licensing and employment. Although these specific laws do not focus on you or on school-related activities, they can influence your opportunity to be hired. The use of criminal background information undoubtedly has evolved during your career because these procedures are new and changing rapidly.

Areas of the law that are most likely to influence your opportunity to teach are those that deal with minors, such as providing alcohol to a minor or having an illegal personal relationship with a minor. One of the reasons behind self-report and criminal background checks is to keep child predators out of the schools. Breaking a law with a minor or breaking a law designed to protect a minor does not have to happen on school property. Whether you are on or off the school premises, these behaviors are likely to have serious legal and professional consequences. Convictions less likely to create a problem are status crimes—acts that are illegal when you are of one age but not illegal at an older age, such as breaking curfews.

The culture and government in the United States are based on the notion that society is better served by people who act responsibly and who adhere to rules created for the greater good. Public education is expected to teach and follow that notion. Thus, as citizens and as a part of a public entity, you are bound in two ways to the laws. Codes of ethics for teachers may require other teachers to intervene when students or colleagues are not abiding by the law. Therefore, you are bound to the criminal laws in three ways: as citizens regulating your own behavior, as professionals meeting professional standards, and as enforcers who may be obligated to report illegal acts committed by students or colleagues.

Contracts

Generally, you should not have legal problems related to contracts. A contract is a promise, and breaking the promise, or **breach of contract**, is cause for legal action. You do have connections to contracts in three areas: your personnel contracts, school activities related to a district contract, and contracts that you initiate for your school.

Most school districts use contracts to describe your duties and the responsibility of the district to compensate you (e.g., salary and benefits). You and your school district are expected to live up to the contract from the moment of verbal acceptance of a job through the completion of the job. Once you sign a contract with a school, you are obligated to work for that district for the duration of the contract, even if a better job is offered to you after you sign the contract. You can be sued for failing to meet the obligations of the contract, but schools may agree to release you from a contract at your request. This is a matter of **professional ethics** as well as a legal issue. Professional ethics suggest that, once you verbally agree to accept a job offer, you should follow through. Think about

loyalty, why loyalty is important, and how breaking a contract reflects on your loyalty.

Schools and districts often have contracts with businesses or individuals, such as a food service contract with a company to provide the school meals or a contract with a sporting goods store to provide equipment. Sometimes these contracts have special provisions, such as "exclusive rights," meaning that no competing business or individual is allowed to do business with the school during the time of the contract. You are expected to respect these contracts. Often, you may not be aware of these contracts and breach the contract out of ignorance. It is best to check with the principal or business manager before purchasing anything, because you might not be reimbursed for purchases outside of the contract or you could involve the school in a lawsuit.

Finally, you are not usually allowed to commit the school or district to a contract. An official of the agency must sign contracts, or else the contract is invalid or the signer is responsible for the contract obligations. This may seem like a small matter, but consider a field trip that may have a contract for transportation, food, and admission for a group of children. If you sign the contract, you are likely to be responsible for the costs. Part of the reason for district policy about who can make a contract is to protect individual teachers from financial debt; another is to avoid conflict of interest. You might go to a business to purchase equipment because your cousin owns the business even though another business may have better prices. The fact that the chosen business benefited someone you knew is a conflict of interest. Beware of purchasing if gifts are associated with the purchase. If you order materials—even through regular school channels—and are given a free gift as a result of the order, the gift belongs to the school, not to you.

Two of the three statutes (Title IX and IDEA) flow from the principles presented in part II of this book. Reviewing the section on variability in chapter 5, Cognition, Learning, and Practice, provides the evidence base or science for the statutes.

Statutes

Statutes are established by the government and guide operations of many entities. Three examples are the Americans with Disabilities Act, Title IX, and the Buckley Amendment. These affect all of you—classroom teachers and physical education specialists. We discuss each briefly as related to physical education class.

Inclusion of Students With Special Needs

For more than 30 years, schools have been charged with finding, identifying, and educating people with disabilities. Physical educators have been proud that physical education was classified as a direct service from the inception of laws defining special education (e.g., P.L. 94-142). This means that all students with identified disabilities have physical education instruction in the most inclusive and appropriate setting. An important strength of physical education has been inclusion. Inclusion is defined as meaningful participation in the least restrictive environment. The spirit of inclusion is to provide an educational setting that is "regular" or as similar to regular as possible without increasing liability or reducing learning for any students. The term *regular* refers to the regular classroom or physical education class for the age or grade of the student. Claudine Sherrill (1998) points out that adapted physical education and inclusion are "good practices" in elementary physical education. A quality program with expert instruction individualizes and adapts activities so that all students benefit. The developmental approach suggests that inclusion is part of sound teaching. Furthermore, everyone learns from inclusion; it is an integral part of diversity and a multicultural perspective that is inherent in education in the United States.

The **individualized education program (IEP)** describes the placement for physical education—regular physical education, special (or adapted) physical education, or a combination. Therefore, whether you are a classroom teacher or a physical education specialist providing physical education to the student with a disability, you must understand the IEP and ideally should attend the IEP meeting. The law requires that students with disabilities have, at a minimum, the same amount of physical education as provided for other students in the district. If the district (or state) requires daily physical education, the student with special needs must have daily physical education. Providing physical education in the least restrictive environment less often than daily is a violation of these statutes. Schools are required to comply with these regulations. The law does not make exceptions for students with health impairments or with disabilities. No one has the right to make an arbitrary decision to exclude a student with special needs from physical education for a class, a week, or a year, including parents, classroom teachers, educational aides, and physical education specialists. The spirit of the law suggests that everyone work together to provide a successful educational experience for everyone!

Quality physical education programs include students with disabilities in meaningful learning experiences.

Physical education is a valuable and viable part of every child's education, as recognized in the original legislation and continuing with the most recent version of the Americans with Disabilities Act. In a "regular" physical education class that includes students with disabilities, you face three challenges. The first is meeting the potentially wider range of abilities. The second is ensuring the safety of all of the children in the class. The third is meeting the demands set forth in the statutes. The learning environment is enriched with diversity, so the first challenge is one that enhances learning and should be your focus. Unfortunately, the remaining two often are the focus of your efforts. Chapters 3 through 7 presented principles to guide your thinking about the differences among children. Of course, the most relevant is "Children are more alike than different." Help with adapting activities was covered in chapter 4, Motor Performance During Childhood. If you meet the first challenge, it is unlikely that you will have trouble with the other two. However, some suggestions might help.

When the IEP specifies inclusive placement in regular physical education, the assumption is that any limitations to participation in regular physical education or supports necessary for participation are specified in the IEP. Supports include special equipment, an education assistant, and other modifications to allow the student to be successful. Unfortunately, the limitations may not always have been specified in the IEP. For example, the physical education department may not have been represented at the IEP meeting. Alternatively, the child with special needs may not need any supports and may perform well in physical education but could cause a threat to other children in the class. So, first, do not assume anything. Second, gather as much information about this situation as possible from the IEP, the parents, the people who were at the IEP meeting, and from the student. Third, keep an open line of communication with parents and the student. As with all physical education students, you should apprise the students and parents of your plan for activities, expectations, and approach. You may want to meet with the student and parents to discuss the plan of activities. Clarify what you know based on the IEP and what you need to know from parents and others. At this point, you should have all of the information necessary to satisfy the IEP and to offer a safe learning environment to your student with special needs. If, at any time, you have concerns for the safety of this student or others, use a backup plan: Change the class activity and

seek help as soon as possible. For example, suppose you are supervising a throwing and catching activity with tennis balls and a wheelchair-bound student is hitting other students or being hit with the balls. You are concerned because the hits are to the head. Stop the activity quickly and move as seamlessly as possible into a safe rhythmic activity. Good teachers have a selection of backup activities to use at any time. An example for young children might be the action song "Head, Shoulders, Knees, and Toes"; for older children, "Hi, My Name Is Joe" would be an example.

"Hi, My Name Is Joe"

Chant or sing the following lyrics; the actions are in parentheses.

Hi, my name is Joe
(wave left hand and arm)
and I have a wife and kids and a dog and work at a button factory *(still waving)*.
One day
My boss said to me, "Hey, Joe"
(now wave both hands),
"can you push this button with your right hand?"
I said sure *(now pretend to push a button with the right hand while waving)*.
(Continue pressing the button with your right hand.)
Hi, my name is Joe *(wave left hand and arm, push button with right hand)*
and I have a wife and kids and a dog and I work at a button factory
(still waving and pushing button).
One day
My boss said to me, "Hey, Joe"
(wave between pushing with right hand),
"can you turn this dial with your right foot?"
I said sure *(now twist right foot, push button with right hand)*.

Repeat, adding a new body part on each verse, as follows:

- Left foot tapping pedal
- Left hand turning knob
- Head pressing lever

The laws provide a framework for including students with special needs; however, responsible teachers implement the law with best practices—in other words, back to the "spirit" of the law. Research and planning help caring teachers provide optimal experiences for all of the children in their class. Use the following background information to help you think about how inclusion might work, depending on the disability and school circumstances. Children with learning disorders, behavioral disorders, and mental disabilities are often placed in physical education class with developmentally normal children of the same age. As the first step, understand the disability and the individual child's manifestation of the disability. Read about the disability and talk to knowledgeable people about the individual situation; the classroom or resource teacher, school psychologist, and parents are good sources of information. With information about the disability and the individual, you can plan ahead to manage the disability and maximize learning. Transitions and waiting are often difficult for students with behavioral disorders, so a reminder to "be patient" or to "wait for the signal" may help. Contracts for behavior and learning are helpful for students with learning disabilities and behavior problems (figure 11.1). Consider each lesson and determine at what point a student may have trouble. Plan to provide information designed to prevent problems before they occur.

Setting behavior goals and recording daily performance are helpful tools when you are working with children with behavioral disorders. First, identify the target behaviors as well as those to eliminate and those to reinforce. Perhaps the child has difficulty when other children do not follow your directions and when others do not do what he or she wants them to do. The child becomes upset and tries physically to force others to do what he or she wants. The behaviors to eliminate are using physical force and losing control. Reinforce alternatives such as using words instead of physical force and encourage students to focus on self rather than others during class. Occasionally, the child may use a loud and frustrated voice, as an alternative to physical force, to let you know what is happening. This disrupts instruction and

---

Date _____

I, (student's name), will follow instructions the first time given. I will keep my hands to myself. I will treat the equipment with respect.

(Signature)_____

I, Ms. Helpful, will allow (student's name) to select the class choice activity when he or she has successfully met this contract for five physical education classes.

*Ms. Helpful*_____

Daily record on an index card (3 by 5 inches [5 by 12.7 cm])

✓ = Always

= Needs work   Monday   Tuesday   Wednesday   Thursday   Friday

Instructions

Hands to self

Equipment

Figure 11.1 Behavior contract and daily record card.

Concepts Into Practice

The fall festival is about to begin and the fourth graders are very excited. The excitement is almost too much for Sam, a special needs student. Sam is in a self-contained Behavior Disorder class, but he has been placed in a regular class for physical education. Sam and Ms. Anderson, the fourth-grade classroom teacher teaching this physical education class, are very proud that Sam has earned this opportunity. Ms. Anderson has planned to play Scooter Ball (see the lessons in chapter 7, Psychosocial Factors in Physical Education). After the warm-up activity, it takes a little time to set up the equipment. Ms. Anderson anticipates that the class will become more excited, and this may be too much for Sam. She asks Sam and one other child to be her helpers. Ms. Anderson asks the class to sit quietly while she and the helpers set up the equipment. This plan has made Sam feel special and has kept Sam busy, under control, and close at hand for direct supervision. In addition, Sam feels like part of the group because Ms. Anderson selected two children to help, Sam and a child without a disability.

alienates the other children. These disruptions comprise a third target behavior to address; you need to work to reduce their frequency and to redirect the focus from "tattling" to employing a calm verbal description of what is interfering with the child's learning. The second step is to develop a plan; older children should participate in developing it. The plan might include the following five parts:

1. Positive reinforcement when the child uses words instead of physical force.

2. A reminder to the child to focus on himself or herself and on learning rather than on the behavior of others.

3. The opportunity to remove himself or herself from a situation that may be frustrating. Generally, this is limited to two to three times per class and reduced as other positive behaviors become more frequent.

4. A limit of one to three times that the child may talk to you. The comments must be in a quiet calm voice (you may remind the child of this), and the number should be

reduced as other positive behaviors become more frequent.

5. A rating at the end of each class that identifies the child's performance on each target behavior.

Your planning is also a major factor in dealing with children with mental or learning disabilities. Identifying the supports necessary for success in a lesson or activity before the lesson and providing those supports are critical to success. Often, misbehaviors are a result of frustration; you can reduce or eliminate them with planning. Supports for children with mental or learning disabilities are similar to the supports necessary in the classroom. Classroom teachers can typically use the same techniques in the gymnasium as in the classroom. Physical education specialists should discuss these supports with the classroom teacher to gain insight into the child concerned. Both classroom teachers and physical education specialists should be part of the IEP committee and have access to the IEP as necessary.

"So much has been given to me that I have no time to ponder over that which has been denied."

—Helen Keller

Children with sensory (e.g., hearing or visual) impairments need assistance coping with the environment. Adapting the learning environment is one strategy to help children with sensory impairments; several examples of this approach follow:

- Locate the child in a position to see, hear, or read lips.

- Use assistive devices, such as sound or visual signals for targets to move, throw, or kick toward.

- Provide a peer guide to help the child as necessary with environmental conditions.

Perhaps the most valuable source of information is the child with the sensory disability. Ask the child how you can help, talk about what will happen during class and what you will do to help, and ask permission to talk about the disability with the other children; these are important strategies that can facilitate inclusion and learning.

Concepts Into Practice

Mr. Moore is the physical education teacher. Ryan is a student in his first-grade class. Ryan has cerebral palsy and, because he is nonambulatory, most of the time Ryan is in either a wheelchair or uses a walker. Mr. Moore is starting a tumbling unit. "Today you are going to use the mats and do tumbling. There are three special things I want to tell you before we begin. These three things are important, so listen and remember. First, a special rule is that only one person can be on the mat at a time. Ryan is going to be out of his chair today and working on the mat. Second, I want to remind you to move under control. This means that you are careful and do each skill correctly when it is your turn. Third, you are going to cheer for each other, so everyone does his or her best. Can someone tell me one of the three special things?" Mr. Moore has provided special rules to promote safety and learning for the whole class. He is including Ryan fully in the lesson, and he is encouraging the children to appreciate each other's performances.

Physically challenged children need physical education and benefit from physical activity. Children who spend their day in a wheelchair, walker, or other assistive device need time to do weight-bearing activity to stimulate bone growth and increase circulation to the lower limbs. Many activities (such as log rolls, the seal walk, using a scooter, and parachute activities) are appropriate, safe, and beneficial and do not need adaptation for nonambulatory children. Other activities need some modification. Children with physical disabilities should be included, which means doing the same activity as the class, with the class. Inclusion does not mean doing different activities or the same activities in a different location. One of the benefits of inclusion in physical education is the social interaction that results from practicing and performing together. For able-bodied children, participating in an inclusive class helps to achieve National Content Standard 6: Demonstrates understanding and respect for differences among people in physical activity settings.

Teaching children with physical disabilities requires extra research, planning, and communication. First, you must learn as much as possible about the condition, the assistive devices (walkers, wheelchairs, braces, helmets), and the child as possible. Once again, classroom teachers, parents, and physical therapists are good sources of information. Physical education specialists may have to develop these relationships to gather appropriate information. Classroom teachers have the relationships and information and thus can view their instruction of physical education as an extension of what happens in the classroom. Furthermore, physical education is another aspect of inclusion for the child with special needs. Second, you must plan, focusing on including all of the children and mastering objectives. Many children have both walkers and wheelchairs at school. If the lesson focus is moving in patterns, the walker is a better choice. For a catching lesson, the wheelchair may work best, and, for tumbling, the child is not going to use any device and may need a helmet. You can see why planning ahead and communication are critical!

Sometimes children with disabilities are accompanied to physical education class by the classroom teacher or an educational assistant or aide. One challenge is to take advantage of the assistant without isolating the child. Generally, to increase inclusion, spend some time planning the activity and training the aide. For example, the aide can supervise his or her student while working with other students but should not replace interaction with other students; for example, if the activity is playing catch, the aide should assist but not actually play. The parallel play of a disabled child and his or her aide is no more inclusive than having the disabled child in a one-on-one class. Sometimes new teachers or physical education specialists are reluctant to tell the aide what to do, so the aide stands idle or makes decisions better made by the teacher. Although most states require training to be an aide, the training is not the same as that for a certified teacher. The job of the aide is to provide the support necessary for the student to be included as is appropriate. Physical education should not be break time for the aide, nor should a child with a disability be excluded from physical education because the aide is not available, willing, or able to assist. Working with the aide, so that he or she understands the importance of physical education and how to assist, is critical to this process. Use the following guidelines as you work with the aide to maximize the benefits of physical education:

- The child should be a part of the class formation for activities (in the circle, part of the line, a team member).
- The child should participate with other children (not with the aide), such as when playing catch with another child.

- The activity is adapted to meet the needs of the child; the child is not eliminated because of the activity.

- You provide cues or instructions before or during the lesson so that the aide can do an effective job.

- Occasionally, you can "trade places" with the aide so that he or she can supervise the class and you can work one-on-one with the child with special needs.

Gender Inclusion

Because of Title IX, schools are obligated to provide equal opportunities for boys and girls. Title IX has the greatest impact on competitive sport opportunities. In part II of this book, we presented information suggesting that boys and girls are more alike than different. As a result of Title IX, you can put that knowledge into action! We do not recommend separating boys and girls during elementary physical education for any reason. Group children for instruction and practice by skill level, but not by gender. When the opportunity is not equal because of gender, a lawsuit can ensue based on Title IX. Doing what is right, however, is more important than the possibility of a lawsuit. Allowing all of the children the opportunity to reach their potential is optimal.

A Student's Right to Privacy

The **Buckley Amendment**, also called the Family Right to Educational Privacy Act, may be violated more than any other statute. This law stipulates that educational information must be confidential. Only students and their parents are to be aware of most information about student progress. The following are examples of violations:

- Posting of student grades by name or social security number

- Casual discussions of student performance, even among teachers

- Discussing student performance over the phone without being able to verify the caller's relationship to the student

- Providing parents of students over 18 years of age with educational record information

Does this mean that you cannot discuss a student? No, but you should do so in a professional context. If the identity of the student is not important (i.e., if you are asking a more experienced teacher for help and the teacher does not know the student or the student's identity is not critical to the problem), you should not identify the student. On the other hand, you may seek advice from the student's previous teacher as long as this is done in a professional manner. Casual discussions about students in the teachers' lounge are not appropriate. Nor are conversations about a student with another student. You need written permission from the parents and additional permission from students over 7 years of age in order to report any information about academic performance to someone other than your school administration, the parents, or the student. The permission should include what can be discussed or provided, to whom, and for what period of time. If you have questions about requests, ask your principal for advice. It is always okay and usually safer to respond to a request by saying, "I do not have that information in front of me; can I get your name and number and call you back?" This allows you to make sure it is permissible to provide information. Noncustodial parents, insurance companies, and coaches often seek information without permission.

Look for a problem where you least expect it. Mentioning the highest grade or best score on a test or measurement may embarrass the best student. This is a violation of that student's rights. So, although your intention is to share the joy of the great performance, you need to do so privately. In physical education, many performances are public. It is easier to maintain a student's privacy in a classroom situation. Examples are the movement away from reading aloud or the care taken to maintain privacy when handing back graded work. There is no reasonable way to keep each performance private in physical education class. However, you can be sensitive to the students, especially when you are doing assessments and grading.

Torts

Circumstances arise when you may have legal problems but have not broken a criminal law. When a student is hurt, someone gets blamed. The result can be a lawsuit where the plaintiff (the student or the parents) alleges a breach in the standard of care (or duties of care). Usually, both you and the school are the defendants (the ones being sued). These lawsuits are examples of a **tort**, a civil legal action. Sometimes criminal actions accompany these civil actions. You are often the first to ask the question "Could I have prevented this?" An accident is an unintentional and unavoidable event. Accidents happen everywhere, including in school. Because physical education is a high-risk activity, accidents are a concern. You must consider four sources of risk for children: the activity, the equipment or facility, your behavior, and the other children's behavior. Careful planning reduces the risk in physical education class and other physical activity experiences because you consider all four sources of risk. Chapter 12, Equipment and Facilities, tells how to increase safety on the playground and in the gymnasium. The focus is on how you can reduce risk while facilitating learning. Chapter 10, Managing Students, helps with controlling students, reducing risk and increasing learning. Answering the question "Is this developmentally appropriate?" also assists you in reducing risks. Finally, other teaching behaviors, such as supervision and your response to an injury, prove important. As a teacher, you want to be able to answer, "Yes, I did everything possible to prevent this injury, and I responded appropriately after the injury."

Negligence occurs when you are responsible for an injury; that is, you did not act in a reasonable and prudent way to prevent the injury based on the situation. **Liability** cases attempt to prove that the responsible person did not meet the standard of care and that damage resulted from the injury. The law recognizes the **standard of care** as the test for liability cases. Standard of care is defined as what a reasonable and prudent person would do under the circumstances. Negligence, the most frequent level of all tort lawsuits, is a result of a specific relationship, in this case between you and your student. As a teacher, you are expected to provide both instruction and supervision while avoiding acts or omissions that could hurt your students. The standard of care depends on the relationship and what should be expected. Three other levels of torts exist: intent to cause harm, knowledge of potential harm, and recklessness that causes harm. Anyone, including you, can be charged with or found guilty of any of the four levels of torts. However, intent, knowledge, and recklessness do not require a special relationship. For example, a person who punches a stranger can be sued for intent. The key to educational negligence is this: Because you are trained and in a position of trust, the standard of care is greater for you than for many other people.

In physical education, the idea of assumed risk is a moderating variable. Every physical activity (and everything else) has some risk; for example, even when wearing appropriate shoes and clothing, a normal, healthy child can fall down and be injured running across a clean, perfectly maintained gymnasium floor. That type of risk is assumed in any physical activity. Add another well-behaved child to the scenario; they bump and fall, and an injury results. This is also a likely part of assumed risk. However, if there is water on the floor, the risk has changed, and the questions become, "Did you know about or do anything about the water?" "Was it reasonable for you to know about the water?" If yes, "Was it reasonable for you to do something different?" You can help parents and children understand the risk inherent in physical education class by informing them about the types of activities planned. As a part of this, you can inform parents of rules, especially the reason for the rules. Send home a letter that explains the rules and the activities. Have the parents sign the letter and return it to you. End your letter with an offer to answer any questions they may have. This opens the lines of communication. This letter does not eliminate all chance of a lawsuit, but it is good practice.

Reading about lawsuits and injuries can be a bit overwhelming. Instead, consider this: You are generally reasonable and prudent. Thus, you are in a position to make good decisions about the risk for your students. When you suspect that something is not safe, follow up and make a good decision. You can prevent injuries and the resulting legal complications. If you think equipment is faulty (e.g., the bolts on the playground climber are loose) or a facility looks unsafe (e.g., the gym floor is damp, wet, or slippery), do not use it; rather, report it to the appropriate authority, and follow up to be certain that repairs are made. Use an appropriate level of concern about liability and injuries to guide your careful planning. Part of your desire to be a teacher stems from your concern for children; that concern, combined with knowledge about safety, reduces your chances of negligent behavior. The next section examines your duties of care in more detail.

Standard of Care (Duty of Care)

Although all aspects of teaching are important, the first obligation is safety. Fortunately, doing a good job in the other aspects of teaching generally enhances safety. Recall the four sources of risk for your students. These educational concerns are aligned with the five duties of care representing the legal perspective: proper instruction, proper supervision, proper classification, a safe environment, and response to an injury (Pettifor 1999).

Instruction

Instruction begins with a plan. A written lesson plan demonstrates that you have considered what to teach and how to teach it. Specifically, your plan should fulfill several objectives:

- It should be developmentally appropriate.
- It should allow for differences among children.
- It should consider both progression (improvement) and previous experience.
- It should identify the objective of the lesson, safety issues, and equipment needed.
- It should include, in writing, management and safety because both are important parts of a lesson plan.

- It should include demonstrations and questions to determine understanding; it should use corrective feedback; and it should specify this on the lesson plan in writing.
- It should be consistent with district, state, or national guidelines.

Chapter 9, Organizing for Teaching, and chapter 13, Instructing Students, provide greater detail for planning and instruction. Three concepts can guide you: Do not assume anything, plan for the worst, and be more careful rather than less careful (figure 11.2). Assumptions are not a legal or moral defense. Do not assume that your students have had previous experience or that all children listen and are careful. Having all children active as much of the time as possible is ideal for learning and health, but it may be problematic for safety. As a new teacher or the teacher of a new class, exert more control at first. As you learn which children need more guidance or which activities have lower risk, you can gradually allow more freedom and reduce your control. In the classroom, having children sit is a great way to keep control. As classroom teachers increase in confidence (and

Checklist for Instruction

- ❑ Parents and children were informed of the class rules and rationale for the rules (in writing).
- ❑ The rules are posted at the venue, and additional activity-specific rules are reviewed before each class.
- ❑ Parents and children were informed of the curriculum plan (over the semester or year).
- ❑ Parents were offered the opportunity to ask questions and to communicate about the curriculum and rules.
- ❑ A written lesson plan is available (see chapter 9, Organizing for Teaching, for more detail).
- ❑ The activity is developmentally appropriate.
- ❑ The children have been adequately prepared for the activity.
- ❑ The lesson accommodates a variety of skill levels and groups the children appropriately.
- ❑ Alternative activities are available as needed.
- ❑ An emergency and accident procedure is posted at each activity venue.
- ❑ A first aid kit is readily available.
- ❑ The equipment and venue are checked regularly for hazards (see chapter 12, Equipment and Facilities, for more detail).
- ❑ Incident reports are kept on file.
- ❑ The principal (and other teachers, as appropriate) is notified about the incident.
- ❑ After an accident, follow-up with the children and parents is completed.

Figure 11.2 The checklist will help you determine whether you have considered many issues related to quality physical education.

control), they gradually allow more freedom of movement around the room. The same principle works here! Let your students know that you ask them to go one at a time, to sit or stand still, or to follow other safety rules because you care about them. Your message to them is "Many activities that are fun are also risky, so you must be responsible and earn the opportunity to participate in fun and challenging activities." Do not teach an activity unless you feel competent and confident about it. If you are unsure, ask another teacher for help or substitute a different activity.

During instruction, a fine line exists between a child who is rebellious and one who is afraid. As described in chapter 10, Managing Students, fear of failure often breeds behavior problems in physical education class. Another type of fear is related to failure and also to injury: Occasionally, children refuse to participate in risky activities because they are afraid. Generally, when a child says, "I'm afraid," it is true. Children often encounter negative outcomes for admitting fear. These are learned at an early age, so they are often reluctant to admit fear. Do not force a child who is afraid to do an activity. Encourage, break the task down, offer help, but never say, "Oh, come on, it is easy"; this only makes the child feel worse about the fear! Look for signs of fear, such as holding on tightly to a source of security. Children who are afraid grab onto something—including you—and do not let go! It is difficult to force a fearful child to do a task. It is wrong, especially if the child is hurt in the attempt, and it is not a productive educational procedure. Instead, be patient, help the child gain confidence, and reduce the pressure on the child. Also, be sensitive to how the child is portrayed to the other children. Being afraid is difficult, but being afraid in front of your peers is much worse. Once again, you may reduce the stigma and gain a child's confidence by recognizing the fear as valid, identifying the difficulty of the task, and even admitting personal fears of a similar nature.

Supervision

Supervision is the most basic of your responsibilities. You are responsible for supervising children in the classroom, before school, at recess, and at many other times. Although being present is the prerequisite for **supervision**, being present does not guarantee adequate supervision. When you physically (direct removal) or mentally (indirect removal) leave the area, the children are at greater

risk. Most of you think very carefully before leaving the children alone. Most of the time nothing happens—no one is injured and no one discovers that the students were alone. If a child is injured, however, you may be held responsible because you failed to provide proper supervision. At other times, you may be in the area with the children physically, but you may not be fully aware of what is happening. Of course, this may be the goal of a child—to do something inappropriate without your being aware of it! Examples of indirect removal include talking to a class visitor during class, handling a disruptive or injured child, and fixing a piece of equipment. It is best to be with the children at all times, but sometimes you must leave a class unattended. What happens if a child gets hurt when you are not present? Pettifor (1999) suggests, "Courts will consider these factors in determining liability":

- Reasons for the absence
- Length of the absence
- The age and maturity level of those children who were left unsupervised
- Location of the injured child who was left unsupervised
- The activity in which the children were engaged immediately prior to your absence
- Your ability (compared with a reasonable person) to foresee the potential dangers (p. 289)

Provide active rather than passive supervision for the children in your care (Thompson, Hudson, and Olsen 2007). What does this mean? **Active supervision** has three characteristics:

1. Proximity—noting the distance that you are from the activity
2. Scanning—looking at the entire area regularly
3. Positioning—placing yourself so that you can see everyone and everything

Active supervision applies to any supervision. The courts recognize three types of instructional supervision in physical education (Dougherty 1993). General supervision means that you are physically present. Specific supervision means that you are assisting a child or group of children. Transitional supervision occurs when there is a change in activity or change in venue. You (or a qualified substitute) should be present at all times during physical education class. Supervision is

Grouping students for activities is appropriate when matches are based on skill or physical size.

constant, and you should provide assistance, such as spotting, when necessary. Spotting is physical guidance provided to a learner by another person for the purpose of increasing safety. Thus, the children are under continuous supervision by a qualified adult. For example, when going from the playing field to the classroom, the children should not be sent ahead while you are putting away equipment.

Classifying Students

You frequently need to group children for activity. For most activities, you should group them per logical criteria. For example, in partner activities, size may be important, so children of similar size may be paired, or one large and one small child may work together on partner balances where the larger child serves as the base. Skill level is another way to pair children. Except when peer tutoring and using equalized teams, you can usually pair children by skill level. A very strong and well-skilled thrower paired with a weaker and less-skilled catcher is

a formula for disaster in a catching activity. For many activities, random groups or pairs work well because one child is unlikely to hurt another child. Rhythmic activities are good examples of relatively low-risk activities and thus are good for randomizing the groupings. Generally, do not group by gender (e.g., all boys in one group or boy and girl pairs). Also, avoid allowing children to make up their own groups. Certain combinations, pairings, or groups can create trouble regardless of the activity. It is your job to form pairs, groups, or teams in a way that is safe, productive, and efficient. Be cautious, however: You may be the biggest "kid" in the class, so consider whether it is safe for you to participate. Your size may endanger a child; you must serve as a role model, and you must be able to supervise. It is unlikely that your participation is justified in view of those three points.

Safe Environment

Equipment, facilities, or venues must not contribute to an injury. Poor maintenance and developmentally inappropriate uses of equipment and facilities frequently lead to injuries. Schools should inform children (and parents) about playground and facility rules. Equipment and facilities need to be checked routinely—that is, on a regular, documented schedule. Upkeep and repairs should be conducted in a timely and efficient manner, and someone should be responsible for these activities. Maintenance also includes routine cleaning of the areas. Sand on a gym floor, rocks on asphalt, water on surfaces, and dirt and debris in fans and ventilating systems can all contribute to risk. Do not assume that someone else has taken care of these responsibilities, however. View yourself as the last line of defense in ensuring the safety of your students. If you find equipment or a facility unsafe, do not use it! Report the problem—preferably in writing—and follow up to be sure that repairs have been made.

Select small equipment, such as balls and bats, based on the size and skill of the children. Similarly, large equipment, including outdoor play structures, should be age appropriate. Playgrounds should have areas designated for age groups (or grades). Chapter 13, Instructing Students, offers more information and sources for playground regulations. Thus, if you take older children to an area designated for younger children, or vice versa, you may be placing them at risk because the new area does not meet their developmental needs.

Venues and facilities are subject to another category of potential safety hazards. Weather and other transient factors such as overcrowding increase risk for children. The weather itself can be a risk (too cold or hot) or can create a risk (water on the field). Scheduling physical education during lunch or recess, when the area is crowded, and scheduling more than one class in an area both increase risk. Even in a large gymnasium, having a volleyball game at one end and a dance or gymnastics lesson at the other is not a safe practice. Stray balls can trip students who are concentrating on another activity. Chapter 12, Equipment and Facilities, includes examples of environmental factors to consider as you determine the appropriateness of a venue or facility.

If you know of a hazard, you are obligated to report it to your supervisor. Suppose you see a hole in the outdoor court and decide not to use the area for your class. When the next physical education class enters the area, a child is hurt by stepping into the hole. In this case, you are partially at fault because you did nothing to prevent the injury! So, report the hazard to the principal, mark the hazard (e.g., post a "keep out" sign or mark the area with yellow hazard tape), and inform anyone else who may use the area about the hazard.

When an activity requires safety equipment (e.g., protective eye wear for floor hockey), make sure that you and all of the children have and use the safety gear. Be a good role model! Allowing children to bring equipment from home can be a good solution to equipment shortages. However, two problems can arise when they are using equipment from home: The equipment can be lost or stolen, or it can fail to be properly maintained. Before deciding to allow children to bring equipment from home, check with the principal.

Responding to Injuries

Unfortunately, there is no way to avoid all injuries. Therefore, you need to have a plan for dealing with them. Your plan should include the following:

- Getting help
- Having a first aid kit on hand
- Receiving first aid training

With cell phones and intercoms, you should be able to get help easily, but when a crisis arises, everything that can go wrong will go wrong. First, have a written plan posted at each venue (e.g., the playground and the gym). Include in the plan whom to contact first and how. Make sure there is a backup plan. For example, if you call the office, but the line is busy or no one answers, what can you do? Include the phone number of the school nurse. In your instructions, include the address and phone number of the school so that when you are calling for emergency medical help you can quickly indicate where you are located. This plan should be developed by a team (e.g., the principal, school nurse, and one or more teachers) and clearly understood by everyone. Each school differs in procedures about who should be called first and how the emergency should be handled. The point is to have a plan, in writing, and have available at all times the materials that are necessary to carry out the plan. The school gymnasium is likely to have a phone; many have an intercom. You can use a student messenger in grades with older students. Clearly, in an emergency, your first two obligations are to get help and to stabilize the injured child. Thus, you need to have current first aid training, and you must have a first aid kit readily available.

Contents of a First Aid Kit

- Copy of the emergency plan
- Emergency contact numbers for fire, police, and ambulance
- Disposable gloves
- Blanket
- Antibacterial hand cleaner
- Adhesive bandages, tape and gauze pads, elastic wraps
- Antiseptic and burn ointment
- Insect sting kit
- Eye wash kit
- Scissors and tweezers
- Cotton pads and cotton-tipped applicators
- Cold pack
- Splints and triangular bandages

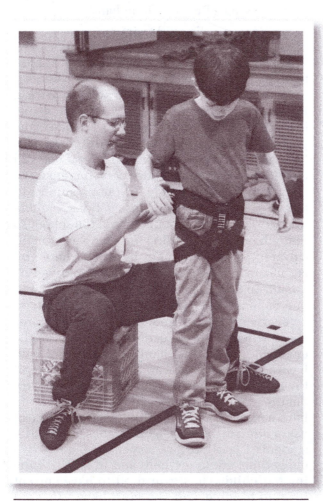

Teachers must ensure that safety equipment is used properly so that the equipment will work as intended.

A third issue concerns the rest of your class while you are occupied with the emergency. Again, a plan is helpful. The children are safest sitting quietly a reasonable distance from the injured child, but do not allow them to gather around the injured child. A reasonable plan is to discuss with them before an injury occurs what should happen in case of an injury. Children are often curious and afraid, and they want to be helpful. Let them know how they can help. A sample of what you might present follows.

Responding to an Emergency

- Tell me immediately if you or someone else is hurt.
- All of the children who are not injured should continue working until I say "Stop."
- When I say "Stop," move to a safe place and sit quietly until a grown-up tells you what to do.
- Be a helper by waiting patiently.
- If I ask you to do something, listen carefully and do it immediately.

Professional Responsibility

Educators are held to higher standards than other people. You are expected to meet certain responsibilities in order to maintain you job and teaching license; in doing so, you also avoid being sued or arrested. You may no longer be allowed to teach after you have failed to meet professional standards. Many states offer two or more levels of a teaching license. The first license allows you to teach for a set period; to qualify for your next license, you may have to meet specific additional requirements. For example, you may have to be observed while teaching or take additional courses. The following list provides some examples of professional responsibilities:

- Keeping up to date (keep learning!)
- Doing your job as an instructor and supervisor
- Doing mandatory reporting
- Demonstrating ethical behavior
- Seeking help when necessary

You are familiar with the need to continue to learn and to do your job as an instructor and supervisor, and you have probably heard of mandatory reporting. Mandatory reporting includes those of you who are obligated to report suspected abuse (e.g., physical, sexual, emotional) to the appropriate authority (usually the principal). You should also intervene or report instances in which you have reason to believe that a student is breaking the law. This frequently happens with substance abuse—the student talks about using an illegal substance. The fact that you overhear this or that a student takes you into his or her confidence does not relieve you of your duty to do something. Schools have varying policies; find out how you are obligated to handle the situation. Many times, students confide in you as a plea for help. Allowing students to continue endangering their lives is not helping. Let them know you care and that you are obligated to help. Hopefully, you feel comfortable telling them that you can provide support during this time and are able to follow through. The first step in helping is reporting.

From an ethical standpoint, you need to follow the **chain of command**. If you have a problem or concern, your first obligation is to address this with the appropriate person. You may observe a colleague doing something that seems inappropriate, such as giving a student a ride home from school, appearing to be under the influence of alcohol or drugs at school, or using equipment that is unsafe. Ethical behavior demands that you discuss this first with the colleague. There may be a logical explanation that satisfies your concern. The explanation may even teach you something!

Sometimes the colleague is clearly doing something that seems wrong, has no explanation, and seems determined to continue. If students are not in immediate jeopardy, express your concern and provide a reasonable period for change. However, if students are at risk, seek help immediately at a higher level. Discuss the situation discreetly with your supervisor or a trusted senior colleague; under most circumstances, follow his or her advice. You always have the right to continue moving up the administrative ladder with your concerns, but be certain of the facts and know that you have informed all of the people in the chain. The first question that most school superintendents ask is, "Have you discussed this with your principal?" If you have not, the superintendent may not speak with you. You have two obligations under ethical behavior in this regard: Follow the chain of command and do not gossip or complain casually about colleagues or school policy.

Professional responsibility recognizes that everyone needs help—even professionals. Standards encourage you to seek help from colleagues and supervisors as necessary. This is not viewed as a sign of weakness, but of strength and determination to do what is right.

Best Practices and Beyond

Most of this chapter has been devoted to the minimum expected of you. You probably entered education to be the best, not to do the minimum. Therefore, a brief discussion of best practices is appropriate. A **best practice** is a way to do something that maximizes the opportunities to be gained from the experience. Several best practices have been presented in previous sections of this chapter. For example, although it is acceptable to cancel a physical education class because of unsafe conditions (and this is certainly better than continuing under unsafe conditions), there is a better way. Have a backup plan. Identify and learn several activities that do not require equipment or a specific venue. Use one of those activities instead of canceling class.

We suggested earlier in the chapter that you inform parents and children of rules and activities via a letter. This is clearly better than not informing them at all. However, including parents and children in the planning of rules is even better. This helps them buy into the rules and encourages greater understanding between you and them. Afterward, parents and children see rules as a means to safety and maximal learning. For example, rather than viewing a special shoe requirement as an inconvenience and unnecessary expense, parents may see it as a way to protect their children from injury. This is a best practice, not just meeting the minimum!

Summary

One of the many responsibilities that you face is keeping your students safe. Most of you enter teaching because of a caring attitude and concern for children that translates into a desire to make and keep them safe. In addition to these values influencing your behavior, the laws that regulate society also apply to you. Professional organizations and state regulations reiterate this responsibility for you. Your desire for continuous improvement leads many of you to seek the best practice in each situation, including student safety. In addition to safety, you accept many other responsibilities, such as arranging field trips, purchasing equipment for the school, and managing school events. These activities often require you to have some understanding of laws, statutes, contracts, and torts.

Mastery Learning Activities

1. Search the newspaper for an article on a lawsuit against a school or teacher. In 100 words or fewer, describe the case. Was it negligence, intent, knowledge? Were criminal charges filed? What are the professional issues involved?

2. Find the code regulating teacher behavior for your state or a state where you hope to teach. (Look on the Internet or ask the State Department of Education for a reference.) What is covered in the code?

3. Observe a teacher during physical education class. Where did the teacher stand and why? In your description, consider proximity, scanning, and position of the teacher, as well as the activity and the age and skill of the children.

4. Search the literature and find an article on best practice (in the classroom or gymnasium). How did reading this change your view?

5. Using the Department of Education Web site, select two states and identify the similarities and differences in each in applying for a teaching license. Do both states require self-reporting? Do they perform criminal background checks?

References

Dougherty, N., ed. 1993. *Principles of safety in physical education and sport.* Reston, VA: American Alliance for Health, Physical Education, Recreation and Dance (AAHPERD).

Pettifor, B. 1999. *Physical education methods for classroom teachers.* Champaign, IL: Human Kinetics.

Sherrill, C. 1998. *Adapted physical activity, recreation and sport: Crossdisciplinary and lifespan.* 5th ed. Boston: WBC McGraw-Hill.

Thompson, D.M., Hudson, S.D., and Olsen, H.M. 2007. *S.A.F.E. play areas: Creation, maintenance, and renovation.* Champaign, IL: Human Kinetics.

Resources

Hart, J., and R. Ritson. 1993. *Liability and safety in physical education and sport.* Reston, VA: American Alliance for Health, Physical Education, Recreation and Dance (AAHPERD).

www.uni.edu/playground/

Lesson Plans

The first lesson plan is partner stunts for grades K and 1. The lesson works well with little or no adaptation for children with sensory impairments. The partner can provide cues and physical guidance for each activity. The second lesson is dribbling and bouncing in patterns for grades 2 and 3. For a child with a physical disability in a walker or wheelchair, you can adapt the lesson to use taped circles on the floor rather than hoops. The wheelchair or walker moves over the tape, but not the hoops. A smaller ball may help the child keep the ball under control and closer to the walker or wheelchair. Another child can assist with retrieving a ball that bounces away from the chair or walker. You can place the cones farther apart for children dribbling from walkers or wheelchairs. If necessary, make the group smaller (3 versus 5 children in a group) for the group with the disabled child. The third lesson is a softball lesson for grades 4 and 5. The lesson begins with a review of catching. The game is flexible, to allow success for all skill levels. The most skilled players move farthest away to catch the ball, or you can challenge them by having them run up from a distance of 10 to 20 feet (3 to 6 m) from the left, the right, or behind the catching line before catching the ball. You can individualize virtually any lesson plan for children with special needs or exceptional skill.

Lesson 11.1

Partner Stunts

Student Objectives   1   5

- Demonstrate two partner stunts.
- Cooperate with a partner.

Equipment and Materials

- 1 mat (4 by 8 feet [1.2 by 2.4 m]) per group
- Background music (optional)

Safety Tip

- For Back-to-Back Get-Up, limit practice to the mats.

Warm-Up Activities (5 to 10 minutes)

Warm-Up Routine for Grades K and 1

Arrange the children in a large circle facing the center.

1. Teach all parts of the warm-up as a routine.
2. Have the children perform the following sequence of steps:
   - Slide right (16 counts).
   - Slide left (16 counts).
   - Run clockwise (32 counts).
   - Run counterclockwise (32 counts).
   - Stretch upward (8 counts).
   - Stretch forward (8 counts).
   - Stretch right (8 counts).
   - Stretch left (8 counts).
   - Stretch downward (8 counts).
   - Do 2 Waist Circles (4 counts).
   - Do 2 Straddle Stretches (4 counts).
   - Do 2 Back Arches (8 counts).
   - Do Sit-Ups and Push-Ups.

Skill-Development Activities (20 minutes)

Partner Walk

Designate one partner as the leader in each pair.

1. Describe and demonstrate the stunt:
   - The leader stands with feet shoulder-width apart, facing his or her partner. The follower (the other partner) stands close to the leader with toes on top of the leader's feet. The partners place their arms on each other's shoulders.

Lesson 11.1 (continued)

- o The leader begins to walk (forward, sideways, or backward). The object is to keep your feet joined at all times.

2. Have the children practice the Partner Walk. Verbal cues are helpful.

3. Variation: Have everyone change partners on signal (music stopping, a whistle, or a hand signal). Continue and then change again.

Leapfrog

Keep the pairs of children in scatter formation.

1. Describe and demonstrate the stunt:
   - o One partner squats, with hands placed firmly on the floor, arms between the legs, and head tucked against the chest.
   - o The other partner places both hands on the shoulders of his or her partner from behind and jumps (with legs spread apart) over the squatting child.
   - o The jumping partner immediately gets into a squatting position, and the squatting partner becomes the leaping partner. Keep trading off.

2. Have the children practice Leapfrog.

3. Once the children have mastered Leapfrog with their partners, join two pairs of partners so that the leaping partner jumps three children successively and then squats and the last child in line becomes the leaper, and so on.

4. Variations: Have the children do Leapfrog with the entire class in a long line! The first leaping child leaps over the entire line; the second child in line begins when the first leapfrog has leapt over five or more children. The game continues until everyone has had a turn leaping the line.

Wring the Dishrag

Keep pairs of children in scatter formation.

1. Describe and demonstrate the stunt:
   - o Begin facing each other, with hands joined. Lift both arms on one side (one partner's right arm, the other's left arm).
   - o Rotate (turn) your bodies, turning in the direction of the lifted arms but keeping your hands joined.
   - o Keep turning so that your backs are to each other and then return to the starting position.

2. Have the children practice Wring the Dishrag.

3. Variations: This stunt looks quite nice when the class (or half of the class) stands in 2 lines with partners facing each other. The first pair in line begins to Wring The Dishrag; when they have lifted their lead arms, the next pair begins, and so on. You can also arrange children in a circle (one partner facing in, the other facing out) so that, when the last pair finishes, the first pair begins again.

Back-to-Back Get-Up

Arrange small groups of children in pairs at the mats.

1. Describe and have two children demonstrate the stunt:
   - o Stand on the mat with your partner, with your backs together and arms hooked at the elbows. Place your feet at about shoulder-width apart.
   - o Sit down together slowly. Press your backs against each other in order to prevent bumping your heads or backs.

- You should end up sitting with your legs tucked up to your body and your feet flat on the floor, arms still locked at the elbow, and backs pressed together.
- Now push with your feet and slowly straighten your legs to stand up again.

2. Have the children practice Back-to-Back Get-Up.

Concluding Activities (5 to 10 minutes)

Simon Says

Arrange pairs of children in scatter formation.

1. Describe the game:
   - Each pair, working together, does what Simon says and tries not to do the task if Simon doesn't say to.
   - For example, suppose Simon says, "Simon says partner walk forward four steps, Simon says wring the dishrag, Simon says hop three steps backward with your partner, do leapfrog with your partner." Partners would not do leapfrog, because "do leapfrog" did not start with "Simon says."
   - If you make a mistake, carefully move to the front of the play area and continue playing.
   - Help your partner be a good listener!

2. Have the children play Simon Says.

From K.T. Thomas, A.M. Lee, and J.R. Thomas, 2008, *Physical education methods for elementary teachers*, 3rd ed. (Champaign, IL: Human Kinetics). Adapted, by permission, from K.T. Thomas, A.M. Lee, and J.R. Thomas, 2000, *Physical education for children: Daily lesson plans for elementary school*, 2nd ed. (Champaign, IL: Human Kinetics), 290-292.

Lesson 11.2

Dribbling and Bouncing in Patterns

Student Objectives   1

- Dribble in a pattern.
- Demonstrate catching, dribbling, and throwing in a series.

Equipment and Materials

- 1 playground ball
- 1 hoop (30 to 36 inches [76 to 91 cm]) per child
- 15 cones or filled 2-liter plastic bottles

Warm-Up Activities (5 minutes)

Use Delivery Relay from lesson 4.2, page 85.

Skill-Development Activities (20 minutes)

Dribbling in Hoops

Arrange the children in scatter formation; each child has a hoop and a ball. Have them place their hoops on the ground.

1. Tell the children: "Keep your ball close to your body; look where you are going, not at the ball."
2. Challenge the children with these tasks:
   - Bounce your ball in your hoop while standing outside your hoop. Repeat several times.
   - Dribble your ball inside your hoop and walk around the outside of your hoop.
   - Change directions! Repeat several times.

Movement Tasks

Arrange small groups of 3 to 5 children with their hoops and balls. Have each group lay their hoops on the ground in a row.

1. Have the children dribble the balls as they walk around and through the hoops.
2. Repeat.
3. Set up 3 lines of 5 cones, with about 5 feet (1.5 m) between cones (or use hoops spaced 5 feet [1.5 m] apart). Divide the children into 3 groups, and assign each group to a line of cones.
4. Have the children dribble a zigzag pattern around the cones.
5. Repeat.
6. Rearrange the hoops in a row (to dribble inside), followed by the cones spread in a row (to zigzag around). Make 3 sets of each.
7. Have the children dribble inside the hoops and then dribble a zigzag pattern around the cones.
8. Repeat several times.

Concluding Activities (5 minutes)

Dribble-and-Throw Relay

Arrange the children into short relay lines along one end of the play area; each group has a cone about 15 feet (4.5 m) away.

1. Have the first child in each line dribble around the cone and then throw the ball back to the next child in line; continue this action for all of the children.
2. After throwing the ball, each child returns to the end of the team's line.
3. Play continuously in the available time. If you wish, determine which team has gone "through the line" the most times.

From K.T. Thomas, A.M. Lee, and J.R. Thomas, 2008, *Physical education methods for elementary teachers*, 3rd ed. (Champaign, IL: Human Kinetics). Adapted, by permission, from K.T. Thomas, A.M. Lee, and J.R. Thomas, 2000, *Physical education for children: Daily lesson plans for elementary school*, 2nd ed. (Champaign, IL: Human Kinetics), 479-481.

Lesson 11.3

Softball

Student Objectives 1 5

- Catch below the waist a ball thrown by a partner from a distance of at least 15 feet (4.5 m).
- Cooperate with a group to accomplish a task.

Equipment and Materials

- 1 softball per pair
- Polyspots or polydomes to mark lines
- Signal

Warm-Up Activities (5 minutes)

Circle Conditioning

Have the children stand in circle formation. With one child as the leader, have the children perform the following calisthenics. Encourage each child to try to increase the number each day.

BENT-KNEE SIT-UPS

Lying on the floor with arms folded across your chest and your hands on your shoulders, bend your knees 90 degrees and raise your body until your arms touch your knees. Perform as many Bent-Knee Sit-Ups as possible in 60 seconds.

PUSH-UPS

On hands and toes (regular push-ups) or hands and knees (modified push-ups), bend your arms and lower your trunk to touch your chin to the ground. Then raise your body back up to the starting position, performing as many Push-Ups as possible in 60 seconds.

STRADDLE SIT STRETCH

Sitting with legs in a straddle position, bend at your waist, extending your arms to your right foot, touch your head to your right knee, and hold for 10 to 30 seconds. Reach up as you move to repeat to the left, performing the Straddle Sit Stretch at least 3 times to each side.

LATERAL JUMP

With feet together, jump side to side over a line as many times as possible in 30 seconds, rest 15 seconds, and repeat.

Skill-Development Activities (20 minutes)

Catching Balls Below the Waist

Arrange pairs of children in scatter formation about 15 feet (4.5 m) apart; each pair has a softball.

1. Describe and demonstrate the skill:
   - Get into a ready position and move in front of the incoming ball. Your little (pinky) fingers should be coming together and your palms facing upward.
   - As the ball makes contact with your hand (or glove), cover it with your other hand.
   - Stand with your weight forward on the foot opposite your throwing arm when you are making the catch so that you can throw quickly.

2. Have the children practice throwing and catching above and below the waist with the following variations:

   o Throw so that your partner can catch above (below) the waist. Keep your little fingers together for a ball below the waist.

   o Throw so that your partner must move forward (backward, to the left, to the right) to catch.

3. Gradually increase the distance between partners.

Concluding Activities (5 minutes)

Throw and Catch Game

Arrange teams of 4 or 5 along 2 lines, 20 feet (6 m) apart. On each team, player 1 stands on one line facing the rest of the team, and the remaining players line up behind the other line, across from player 1 (see figure below). Give each team a softball. Allow the catcher to vary the distance between the thrower and catcher for each throw so that children at different skill levels can be successful.

1. Describe and demonstrate the game:

   o The goal of the game is for each team to work together to make sure that all children are successful.

   o On the signal, player 1 selects a distance and throws the ball to player 2. Player 2 throws it back and goes to the end of the line.

   o Player 1 throws to each player until all are back in their original positions. Then player 1 goes to the end of the line, and player 2 becomes the new thrower.

   o Rotate through all of your players.

   o Score 1 point for each successful catch.

   o The team with the most successful catches wins.

2. Have the children play the Throw and Catch Game; remind them to help everyone succeed.

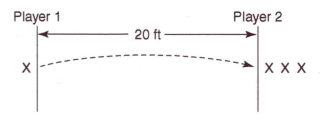

From K.T. Thomas, A.M. Lee, and J.R. Thomas, 2008, *Physical education methods for elementary teachers*, 3rd ed. (Champaign, IL: Human Kinetics). Adapted, by permission, from K.T. Thomas, A.M. Lee, and J.R. Thomas, 2000, *Physical education for children: Daily lesson plans for elementary school*, 2nd ed. (Champaign, IL: Human Kinetics), 914-915.

CHAPTER 12

Equipment and Facilities

ANTHONY. AGE 7

Equipment and facilities enhance student learning but present safety challenges both for you and for your school.

Learner Outcomes

After studying this chapter, you should be able to do the following:

- Evaluate the appropriateness of equipment for skill development.
- State and apply safety guidelines for equipment and facilities.
- Plan instructional or free time to maximize physical activity when you are using equipment and facilities.
- Distinguish between structured and unstructured physical activity.
- State the benefits of unstructured physical activity.

Glossary Terms

proximity	scanning	structured physical activity
visual angle	decision making	unstructured activity time

Equipment and facilities present unique challenges for you and your school. Trade-offs exist between practical issues and potential for learning. Practical issues include cost, maintenance, space, and storage; these must be balanced with the ideal for engaging students in meaningful play and instruction to facilitate learning. Furthermore, many of you—even physical education specialists—may not have the expertise or the time to plan and monitor effectively the physical education equipment and facilities. Finally, the same equipment and facilities are usually multipurpose; that is, they are used for instruction (physical education), free time (recess), recreation (before and after school), and, often, at lunchtime or assemblies. Various people may supervise the use of facilities, with varying degrees of ownership or investment. For example, the physical education teacher may take great care in managing the gym and equipment compared with someone who is renting the gym after school. Consider what a common practice this is and how a classroom teacher might feel if the school rented his or her classroom to someone else for use after school!

Knowing about equipment and facilities enables you to do several things:

- Enhance student learning
- Make the environment as safe as possible
- Balance practical concerns and learning issues

Small Equipment

Small equipment falls into three general categories: manipulatable objects (e.g., balls), single-use equipment (e.g., batting tee), and support materials (e.g., cones, music). You need to balance practical issues, such as cost and storage, with instructional issues (e.g., developmentally appropriate level, variety, specificity, practice) when you consider small equipment. For example, in a class of 25 children, you would ideally have one piece of equipment for each child. However, when you purchase 25 footballs, volleyballs, basketballs, soccer balls, bats, baseball gloves, goals, and bases, clearly, both storage and cost are practical issues. You may prefer to purchase 25 playground balls and only a few of each other type. Consider what is necessary for instruction at all grade levels and across activities. For example, organizational equipment is used in all physical education classes, so it makes sense to purchase one set of cones, polyspots, and carpet squares for the school. Every teacher does not need a set of cones or playground balls in his or her classroom. Generally, the decision is to invest in multiuse rather than single-use equipment. For example, purchase and store playground balls rather than soccer balls, if you must choose; or purchase many playground balls and a few specialty balls. Physical education specialists face equipment issues as well; storage and expense are at the top of the list. In addition, many specialists travel from school to school, so transporting equipment is an additional problem.

Support materials include management items and other equipment that facilitates learning. Schools should have enough markers (polyspots) so that at least one is available for each child in a class. Cones are another necessity. Sometimes homemade equivalents are helpful, such as colored masking tape to mark spots on the floor and two-liter plastic bottles (filled with sand or water and sealed) for cones. You can use a CD or tape player to play music for fitness, dance, and gymnastics (National Association for Sport and Physical Education [NASPE] 2001a). When purchasing a player, select one that is as adaptable as possible. For example, choose one that works with a remote microphone so that your voice can be amplified when necessary.

For the lower grades, playground balls (rubber 8.5 and 13 in. [21.5 cm and 33 cm]), foam balls (8.5 in. [21.5 cm] with plastic coating), hoops, and beanbags are essential. Sport-specific balls are helpful in the upper grades (volleyball trainers, footballs, softballs, soccer balls, and junior basketballs). Other helpful equipment includes carpet squares and hoops (30 to 36 in. [76 cm and 91 cm] size). Have one for each child, if possible; but class can still be effective with one for each two or three children. Selecting equipment for a variety of students can help meet individual needs. For example, rather than order a dozen identical bats, order three or four each of two or three types of bats, selecting from traditional metal bats to large plastic bats. Younger and less skilled children are more successful with the larger plastic bats, whereas well-skilled and older children

Beanbags can be used in a variety of ways and in many games.

are challenged by the "regular" bats. The variety meets the needs of children within and between classes. If you are the physical education specialist, you need to have equipment on hand that is appropriate for all grades. Classroom teachers may want to pair up by grades as a practical approach to equipment. In both cases, the information here is a guide to what you need for the school, your class, or your grade.

You may use specialty equipment less often, but it is helpful; this includes items that enhance manipulative skills, balance, and teamwork. Examples include scooters, foxtails, batting tees, nets, walking cans, wands, rhythm sticks, beanie launchers, jump ropes, bowling balls and pins, quoits, Frisbees, fluff balls (yarn), Hacky Sacks, beach balls, balloons, rackets, bats, bases, goals, targets, and floor hockey sticks. Music for dance,

fitness, and gymnastics is also considered specialty equipment. Sample equipment lists are presented in tables 12.1 to 12.3. The National Association for Sport and Physical Education (NASPE 2001a), an association of the American Alliance for Health, Physical Education, Recreation and Dance (AAHPERD), provides a list of equipment (table 12.4) as part of their guidelines for elementary physical education materials.

How do you decide what you need? First, think about what you teach and what you have on hand. Next, prioritize the list so that what you need most often is at the top of the list. Finally, consider budget and storage issues. Buy what you use most frequently, what is within your budget, and what you have room to store. Each year, add to the equipment on hand, remembering to replace items because of wear and tear.

Table 12.1   Necessary Equipment

	K-1	2-3	4-5	6-8
30-40 polyspots	▓	▓	▓	▓
30 wands	▓	▓	▓	▓
8-12 cones	▓	▓	▓	▓
6 gymnastics mats (6 by 12 feet [1.8 by 3.7 m])	▓	▓	▓	▓
1 balance beam (4 inches by 10 feet [10 cm by 3 m])	▓	▓	▓	▓
30 playground balls (8.5 inches [21.5 cm])	▓	▓		
4 batting tees	▓	▓	▓	▓
30 beanbags	▓	▓		
30 foam balls (8.5 inches [21.5 cm])	▓	▓		
30 hoops (30 to 36 inches [75 to 90 cm])	▓	▓	▓	▓
1 parachute	▓	▓	▓	▓
12 long jump ropes (16 feet [4.9 m])		▓	▓	▓
30 jump ropes (5 to 7 feet [1.5 to 2.1 m])	▓	▓	▓	
30 Frisbees		▓	▓	▓
2 volleyball nets			▓	▓
12 junior or foam footballs			▓	▓
12 trainer volleyballs			▓	▓
12 softballs			▓	▓
12 junior basketballs			▓	▓
4 junior bats			▓	▓
1 set of softball bases			▓	▓
8 batons			▓	▓

Shading identifies appropriate grades

Table 12.2   Suggested Equipment

	K-1	2-3	4-5	6-8
4 shapes (to climb through)	▓			
3 pairs of walking cans	▓			
3 jumping cubes (2 feet square [61 cm])	▓			
30 ribbon streamers	▓	▓	▓	▓
2 sets of pillow polo (24 sticks total)	▓	▓		
30 carpet squares	▓	▓	▓	▓
60 rhythm sticks	▓	▓	▓	
30 scooters	▓	▓	▓	▓
1 drum or tambourine	▓	▓	▓	▓
1 climbing rope			▓	▓
1 vaulting mat			▓	▓
2 sets of floor hockey sticks (24 total)			▓	▓
2-6 soccer goals			▓	▓
6 bowling balls			▓	▓
6 sets of bowling pins			▓	▓
30 tennis rackets (half short handle)			▓	▓
90 tennis balls			▓	▓
4 sets of bamboo poles (for tinikling)			▓	▓

Shading identifies appropriate grades.

Table 12.3 Optional Single-Use Equipment

	K-1	2-3	4-5	6-8
Juggling scarves	▓	▓		
Scoops and balls	▓	▓		
Buddy walkers (2 person)	▓	▓		
Foxtails	▓	▓	▓	
Kosh-kosh balls		▓	▓	
Juggling beanbags		▓	▓	▓
Ominkin ball or Earth ball		▓	▓	▓
Hacky Sacks		▓	▓	
Pogo sticks			▓	▓
Stilts			▓	▓
Buddy walkers (4 person)			▓	▓

Shading identifies appropriate grades.

Homemade Equipment

Once again, a trade-off exists, this time between the cost effectiveness and the safety of homemade equipment. Homemade equipment is usually less expensive, but it may present problems in maintaining safety. Equipment manufacturers are responsible for making their products safe, and manufacturers stand behind their products as long as you use the product as intended. You are the only person standing behind homemade equipment, however! Certain items, such as fluff or yarn balls, are relatively safe; thus, if these are less expensive to make than to purchase, homemade is a good substitute. Some items present safety issues, however, such as coat hangers covered with nylon used instead of paddles. The coat hanger is a hazard; do not substitute it for purchased paddles or rackets.

Table 12.4 NASPE (2001a) Elementary Physical Education Equipment

General equipment	Quantity
Chalk or white board	1
Bags to carry balls	6
Ball inflator	1
Ball repair kit	1
Bulletin board	1 or 2
Clipboards	Enough for one-half of class
First aid kit	1
Measuring tape (100 feet, 50 feet [30 m, 15 m])	1
CD or tape player	1
Crates or baskets for storage	5
Field marker (for chalking lines)	1
AV cart with electrical outlet for CD or tape player	1

EDUCATIONAL GAMES

Skill themes: bouncing, striking, kicking, catching, throwing

Equipment items	Equipment size	Quantity for class size of 20-25
Playground balls	5, 6, and 8.5 inches (12.7, 15, and 21.5 cm)	17, 17, and 30
Balls for striking with body	8 and 9 inches (20 and 22.5 cm)	15-18 of each
Beach balls	24 inches (60 cm), 45 inches (112.5 cm)	18, 25
Foam balls	7 or 8 inches (17.5 or 20 cm)	25
Fleece or yarn balls	3 inches (7.5 cm) (washable)	25
Balloons	11 inches (27.5 cm)	36-72
Squish balls	3 inches (7.5 cm)	17 or 18
Foam balls (bounceable)	4.75 inches (11.9 cm)	30
Beanbags	4 inches (10 cm), 5 inches (12.7 cm)	30

(continued)

Table 12.4 *(continued)*

Skill themes: bouncing, striking, kicking, catching, throwing

Equipment items	Equipment size	Quantity for class size of 20-25
Flying disks	11 inches (27.5 cm)	30
Deck rings	7-inch diameter (17.5 cm)	17 or 18
Rag balls	9 inches (22.5 cm)	17 or 18
Plastic bottle bats	11.5-inch (28.8 cm) handles	17 or 18
Soft bat	24, 27, and 29 inches (60, 67.5, and 72.5 cm)	5 of each
Lollipop paddles (styrofoam heads)	8- and 10-inch (20 and 25 cm) diameter with 12-inch (30 cm) handles	17 or 18 of each
Scoops		30
Youth tennis rackets	21 and 24 inches (52.5 and 60 cm)	30, 30
Foam blade hockey sticks with styrofoam pucks	40- and 45-inch (100 and 112.5 cm) sticks	30 of each
Portable gym standards (150 lb) (67.5 kg)		Minimum 8 (or 4 pairs)
Net for standards		4
Cones or jug markers	12, 18, and 24 inches (30, 45, and 60 cm)	26, 14, 14
Pinnies, sashes, or vests (three or more colors)		30
Scooter boards with handles		30
Spotmarkers		20
Basketballs (junior size)		30
Adjustable basketball goals	7-10 inches (17.5-25.4 cm)	4-6
Soccer balls	Sizes 4 and 5	18 and 30
Parachute		1

EDUCATIONAL DANCE

Skill themes: locomotor and nonlocomotor skills

Equipment items	Equipment size	Quantity for class size of 20-25
Plastic hoops	30- and 36-inch (75 and 90 cm) diameter	20, 20
Styrofoam hoop holders (2 per hoop)		30
Rhythmic equipment—		
• Ankle wrist bells		8
• Rain stick		8
• Rap stick		8
• Drum with mallet		1
• Lummi sticks	12 inches (30 cm) long and 0.75-inch (1.9 cm) diameter	30
Stretchy material bands	36 inches (90 cm) long and 6 inches (15 cm) wide	30
Nylon scarves	54 by 54 inches (135 by 135 cm)	30
Tinikling sticks or boards and jump bands		15 pairs
CD or tape player		1
Cordless microphone		1
Sound system		1

EDUCATIONAL GYMNASTICS

Skill themes: rolling, jumping and landing, balance, transfer of weight, hanging and swinging

Foam vaulting trapezoid	(3-4 sections)	1
Styrofoam shapes (circles, triangles, ovals, wedge)		8
Mats	4 by 6 feet (1.2 by 1.8 m) or 5 by 10 feet (1.5 by 3 m), 2 inches (5 cm) thick	7 or 8 mats (3 or 4 students per mat)
Landing mats	4 inches (10 cm) thick	Minimum of 1
Incline mats	36 inches (90 cm) wide by 72 inches (180 cm) long	1
Balance beams and benches	12 feet (3.7 m) long, 12 inches (30 cm) wide	1 or more
Jumping boxes (foam shapes of varying heights)	12-24 inches (30-60 cm)	4-6
Trestles	5, 6, and 7 feet (1.5, 1.8, and 2.1 m)	2 of each
Sliding boards to connect to trestles	12 inches (130 cm) long, 10-12 inches (25-30 cm) wide	2
Connecting ladder		1
Hanging ropes		1 or 2
Jump ropes (plastic segments for beginners; speed rope for experienced jumpers)	7, 8, 9, and 16 feet (2.1, 2.4, 2.7, and 4.9 m) in length	13, 13, 13, 13
Stretch jump ropes ("magic ropes")		8-12
Wands		12 or 13

PHYSICAL FITNESS ASSESSMENT

Sit-and-reach box for measuring flexibility		2-4
Stopwatches		4-6
Skinfold calipers		6
Modified chin-up bar and standards		1
Fitness assessment package		1

Adapted from *Guidelines for Facilities, Equipment and Instructional Materials in Elementary School Education*, with permission from the National Association for Sport and Physical Education (NASPE), 1900 Association Drive, Reston, VA 20191-1599.

Other typically safe, inexpensive, homemade items include wands from broom handles and rhythm sticks from dowels. You can create a foxtail by putting a tennis ball inside a tube sock. Generally, you can make soft equipment at home, but you should purchase items that inflate or have hard surfaces.

Items that are readily available but not specific to physical education are also helpful. For example, cardboard boxes, laundry baskets, and milk crates make excellent storage containers and targets. The school cafeteria staff may be able to supply you with boxes; if you have a ready supply, dispose of them after use (e.g., one for a target) rather than storing them for reuse.

Another source of low-cost (and sometimes free) help is the local bowling lanes. Bowling lane personnel can add additional holes to purchased gymnasium balls so that the balls fit more children. They may be able to donate bowling pins as well. Because the children use their facilities, these businesses are usually willing to help. Other businesses often donate items you need—for example, carpet squares from the flooring store, dowels from the lumber yard (to make wands and rhythm sticks), and storage containers (garbage cans on wheels, milk crates, laundry baskets) from the local discount or home supply store. You can make many of the equipment storage racks using materials purchased or donated locally. Determine your storage needs and share pictures of what matches your needs with parents and others.

Large Equipment

Large equipment falls into three categories: outdoor equipment, such as playground structures; indoor moveable equipment, such as mats and balance beams; and indoor fixed equipment, such as climbing ropes, rock walls, and chinning bars. There is some overlap between large equipment and facilities; that is, playground structures are considered both a facility and large equipment. Playground equipment is discussed in the next section.

The same practical challenges (cost, storage, and number) that apply to small equipment also apply to large equipment. Large, fixed equipment also presents safety hazards; these items are often an "attractive nuisance." Once large, fixed equipment is installed, you and your school are responsible for its supervision and maintenance. Many schools use the gym for other purposes or allow outside groups into it after school. A student at lunch or a visitor may find it impossible to resist climbing up and hanging from the chinning bar, which is very attractive and thus a nuisance, but one for which you are responsible in terms of safety. If a student or visitor is injured using the chinning bar, you are likely to be sued! To make such equipment less attractive, select large, fixed equipment that can be stowed out of the way. For example, if possible, choose chinning bars that can be raised or removed from the wall, nets and ropes that can be raised to the ceiling when not in use, or rock walls for which the rocks can be removed when not in use. Take care when you

place large equipment. Do not place fixed equipment in walkways, especially near exits. Have a plan for securing equipment when it is not in use. At the least, post a sign that indicates potential danger (figure 12.1). Additional information about fixed hazards is presented in the next section.

Facilities

Three or four different facilities are found in most schools: indoor physical education facilities and outdoor grass surfaces, playground structures, and hard surfaces. Inside are the gymnasium or multipurpose room, designed for physical education, and other spaces such as hallways and classrooms that can be used when other facilities are not available for physical education. Gymnasiums or multipurpose spaces should provide 110 square feet (10 m^2) of space per child in an area of approximately 70 by 100 feet (21 by 30 m) (NASPE 2001a). The ceiling should be at least 20 feet (6 m) high; the room must have adequate lighting, sound absorption, and smooth and hard walls at least 10 to 15 feet (3 to 4.5 m) above the floor. Windows may be higher; mats are used for padding below that height. Depending on the age and original design of indoor facilities, safety hazards may exist, even in facilities designed spe-

DANGER
No Climbing

Figure 12.1   Warning sign.

cifically for physical education. One of the most common safety issues indoors is the size of the space. For example, a gym may be large enough for a basketball court, but the out-of-bounds lines are very close to the wall. Children running to catch a ball may not be able to stop, so the walls are a hazard. Walls with protruding doorknobs or hanging equipment present even greater hazards. In small facilities, establish boundaries inside the court lines. Consider the size of the facility, the size of the children, the number of children, and the type of activity before you decide what is safe. Games of chase (e.g., tag) may be appropriate in the gym for younger children (grades K through 3) who are slower and smaller, but unsafe for older children (grades 4 through 6) who are larger and faster. A distance of 7 to 9 feet (2.1 to 2.7 m) between the activity and a hazard (e.g., the wall or stored equipment) is recommended. Furthermore, drinking water and restrooms should be nearby.

Concepts Into Practice

Mr. Astor, a fourth-grade teacher, realizes that the gym is too small for his large class of older students. The new gym will be ready next semester. He wants to teach physical education every day, but rainy days are a challenge. After a lot of thought, he decides to split his class in two and teach 30 minutes of physical education to each group on rainy days. One group will work on physical activity journals and have free reading time while the other group is being active. Then the groups will reverse roles. This works well because the bleachers are available for the writing group to use, and Mr. Astor can position himself across the gym from the bleachers so that he can see all of the students.

Other indoor hazards include the surface, permanent objects, and moveable objects. Debris or water makes nearly any surface dangerous. This means that the floor should be dry-mopped frequently and wet-mopped regularly (i.e., with water or a cleaning solvent). Dry mopping should remove sand, dirt, and other debris. Wet mopping is appropriate for regular cleaning and for sanitizing the surface. Once the floor has been wet-mopped, it should dry thoroughly before being used. One way to reduce sand and other debris on the floor is for children to have athletic shoes used only for physical education. Although this creates expense for parents, it can reduce risk. Constantly

wearing one pair of shoes reduces their tread, which can cause slipping, even on a clean floor. In addition, shoes worn outdoors track in dirt, sand, and debris. So, indoor-only shoes specifically for physical education are helpful. Alternatively, the floor could be cleaned after every class.

Virtually anything that protrudes into the gym or other indoor area creates a hazard. Doorknobs are common in older facilities, and so are drinking fountains. Sometimes physical education equipment is positioned so that it protrudes into the activity area. Chin-up bars, bleachers, fire alarms, and storage cabinets are examples of possibly protruding items. Sometimes you can solve the problem by moving the chin-up bar to a position that is taller than any child. At other times, there is no way to move the equipment. In that case, padding is helpful. You can purchase or make mats that protect children from doorknobs, posts, the edges of stages, and other equipment that protrudes into the space. NASPE (2001a) provides guidelines for facilities, including specific recommendations for avoiding dangerous problems with facilities (figure 12.2).

Even in the newest of facilities, storage is at a premium. The solution is often to store some items along the edge of the gym, but a rack of folding chairs pushed against the gym wall the morning after a meeting may seem harmless until a child is injured falling into the chairs. Placing a stack of mats in a corner seems as though it is a good solution because the mats are padded. However, the mats are an attractive nuisance. Unsupervised children may climb on the pile and risk falling and injuring themselves. Thus, moveable items may be a hazard. If possible, remove the items; if not, create a safety zone around them so that children are less likely to injury themselves. NASPE suggests 400 to 600 square feet (37 to 56 m²) of storage with 12- to 15-foot (3.6 to 4.5 m) ceilings to avoid problems associated with storage.

Outdoor hard surfaces (asphalt, concrete, or synthetic) should be separated from general playground areas so that instruction is not interrupted by recess and other events. The area should be 50 by 80 feet (15 by 24 m) or greater and provide 110 square feet (10 m²) of space per child. Outdoor field space should be well drained, with appropriate turf that is cared for regularly. Check the permanent equipment on fields (such as backstops) regularly for wear or disrepair and service as needed. Generally, the playground of a typical elementary school should measure 8 to 10 acres (3.2 to 4 hectares).

1. Boards of Education, through their school budget process, fund

    (a) the purchase and maintenance of appropriate and sufficient physical education supplies and equipment, and

    (b) equitable physical education facilities and maintenance of these facilities for each school.

2. Physical education teachers, physical education program administrators, and school administrators should jointly

    (a) develop standards for appropriate supplies and equipment and procedures for purchasing, and

    (b) provide input to plans for new physical education facilities.

3. School and community facilities and programs are designed and implemented to support and complement one another in serving children's needs.

4. There is a dedicated facility for the physical education instructional program.

5. Adequate space, ranging from 110 square ft to 150 square ft per child, for learning movement activities in which children can move freely and safely. The student-to-teacher ratio should be 25:1 per class. Intact classes should not interfere with one another.

6. Adequate space, ranging from 400 to 600 square ft with a height of 12' to 15', is available for safe and proper storage of physical education equipment.

7. Physical activity space is designed to facilitate instruction free of distractions and pass-through traffic patterns.

8. Restrooms and drinking fountains should be located close to the instructional facilities; if drinking fountains are in the instructional area, they should be recessed.

9. Office space, ranging from 120 to 240 square ft in size, for the physical education teacher is provided to allow students convenient access to their teacher for consultation and assistance.

10. A learning environment with adequate acoustics ("sound baffles") permits children to participate safely in all phases of instruction.

11. Indoor facilities, with proper flooring and lighting, are clean and sanitized on a daily basis. Floor surface should be either hardwood with cushion or a roll-out synthetic product. The minimum amount of light should be 30 foot-candles.

12. All-weather outdoor surfaces are properly marked with circles, lines, and courts to permit participation in a wide variety of activities and are appropriate for students with varied ability levels.

13. Outdoor areas are available for teaching and

    (a) are free from safety hazards (such as glass, debris, water),

    (b) located away from occupied classrooms,

    (c) have clearly defined physical boundaries,

    (d) are far away from parking lots or streets (no closer than 100 yd) or are separated by barriers that prevent vehicles from entering the area,

    (e) are close enough to school building to permit access to equipment, and

    (f) provide shelter in case of inclement weather.

14. Natural play areas are available to facilitate and encourage creative and exploratory play.

Figure 12.2 NASPE guidelines for facilities.

Adapted from *Guidelines for Facilities, Equipment, and Instructional Materials in Elementary School Education,* with permission from the National Association for Sport and Physical Education (NASPE), 1900 Association Drive, Reston, VA 20191-1599.

Multipurpose playground equipment challenges children to try new skills and encourages playful creativity.

acceptable locations, three additional areas of concern arise.

The first area of concern is proper installation, the second is maintenance, and the third is the surface. Follow the manufacturer's instructions for installation of playground equipment carefully and monitor for compliance after the equipment is installed. Updated information is available from the National Playground Safety Commission (NPSC; www.cpsc.gov, then search for playground safety) on the current standards for various ages of children and maintenance of equipment. These standards change, and safety warnings and recalls occur; therefore, check with the NPSC regularly to be certain that your playground is in compliance. Regular maintenance is critical for safety. Equipment may be damaged during use, or bolts and other parts may wear or become loose. Monthly inspections generally catch these problems. The surface of the equipment is the most difficult feature to maintain. Each material has advantages and disadvantages, and all require regular maintenance. Sand is a good surface, but it requires regular raking and replacement. Pea gravel works well in wet weather but is dangerous when children throw it. For all materials, the depth determines absorption during impact from falling or jumping. Guidelines for the proper depth of each material are provided by the NPSC.

You can use the playground, specifically the playground equipment, as a learning center during instruction. Children find challenges in using the equipment to solve problems, develop upper-body strength, and practice jumping and landing. Traditional single-use playground equipment (e.g., swings, slides, and merry-go-rounds) is being replaced by multiuse structures. Many playgrounds have both types of equipment; the safety issues are generally the same. Select the equipment based on the age of the children and its general use. Is the purpose to develop skill, to promote social interaction or fitness, or to foster creativity? What age range will use the equipment? Equipment catalogs provide you with helpful information for making decisions about what to purchase. Provide a separate area for pre-K and kindergarten. The size and skill of this age group demand different, specifically, smaller equipment than for older children. Furthermore, younger children may be injured by older children because younger children get in the way or cannot get out of the way of older children during vigorous play. Once you have selected age-appropriate equipment and identified the

Safety

Safety is a result of proper installation, maintenance, supervision, and training. Planning is essential for safety. Selection of the facilities and equipment for the age, skill, and ability of the children is the first step. Second is planning for maintenance so that equipment and facilities are checked regularly. For example, the gym floor may need to be cleaned between classes if shoes are dirty or wet. The NPSC safety checklist, presented in figure 12.3, outlines 10 steps to a safer playground. This checklist is a starting point for safety; you, your school, and the children's parents should strive to go beyond the minimum!

Supervision begins with training of the personnel who supervise the use of equipment and facilities. Supervision must be adequate in quality and quantity; this means having enough trained supervisors to manage the size of the area and the number of children. Training applies to the children and often to their parents. Children should learn the rules for the equipment and facilities and

Concepts Into Practice

Ms. Blount has taken her class to the playing field for a lesson on soccer. The field is very wet, even though it is late afternoon. She decides that it is unsafe and moves her class to the hard-surface play area that is nearby and dry. She knows the soccer lesson will not work—or be safe—on the hard surface. Fortunately, she has a back-up plan. She uses the extra playground balls she brought and teaches Four Square.

why each rule is important. It helps for parents to be informed about the rules because they can reinforce the school playground rules after school and on weekends. In addition, parents should be informed about playground safety before it becomes an issue. Children must learn to move under control when using the equipment and facilities. Safety prevents accidents, but it does not eliminate risk. Children, their parents, and the supervisors need to understand the risk involved and work as a team to promote safety.

Supervision has four aspects: proximity, visual angle, scanning, and decision making.

1. **Proximity** means the distance between the supervisor and the object of supervision.

The need for proximity is based on the risk or hazard presented by the equipment or activity and on the individual children. For example, a large piece of playground equipment might require that you stand nearby, or a group of risk-taking children might demand your presence.

2. **Visual angle** is the range or percentage of the area that you can see from a particular location. Generally, standing at one corner and farther away from the area provides you with the greatest angle.

3. **Scanning** means sweeping the area with your eyes to observe. Scanning is preferred over fixed vision, in which you look at one object or event. Scanning the entire area every 6 seconds is recommended (Thompson, Hudson, and Olsen 2007).

4. **Decision making** occurs when you observe something that seems out of range, such as a child who is higher than normal, a large cluster of children, or a ball where it should not be. Generally, you fixate on the out-of-range area to determine whether the situation demands intervention. If the decision is no, continue scanning; if the answer is yes, increase proximity (e.g., move toward the situation). The aspects interact, so, in order to gain proximity, reduce visual angle. To identify a problem

1. Make sure surfaces around playground equipment have at least 12 inches (30 cm) of wood chips, mulch, sand, or pea gravel, or mats are made of safety-tested rubber or rubberlike materials.

2. Check that protective surfacing extends at least 6 feet (1.8 m) in all directions from play equipment. For swings, be sure that surface extends, in back and front, twice the height of the suspending bar.

3. Make sure that play structures more than 30 inches (75 cm) high are spaced at least 9 feet (2.7 m) apart.

4. Check for dangerous hardware, such as open S hooks or protruding bolt ends.

5. Make sure spaces that could trap children, such as openings in guardrails or between ladder rungs, measure less than 3.5 or more than 9 inches (less than 8.8 or more than 22.5 cm).

6. Check for sharp points or edges in equipment.

7. Look for tripping hazards, such as exposed concrete footings, tree stumps, and rocks.

8. Make sure that elevated surfaces, such as platforms and ramps, have guardrails to prevent falls.

9. Check playgrounds regularly to see that equipment and surfacing are in good condition.

10. Carefully supervise children on playgrounds to make sure that they are safe.

Figure 12.3 CPSC (NPSC) checklist for public playground safety.

Children are eager to explore and accept challenges inherent in large, multipurpose playground equipment.

and make a decision, you may have to stop scanning.

With training and practice, supervision improves. Consider the position you select from which to begin supervision. Move as the situation demands. When you must stop scanning, return to scanning as soon as possible. As children talk to you, continue monitoring playground behavior. Generally, do not stand near other supervisors. This can be distracting to all of you and is not the best way to provide optimal supervision.

Recess

Physical education class and recess cross paths in two dimensions: facilities and goals. Although each serves a unique role in a child's education and each is important, practical and educational issues arise because of the crossed paths. Both recess and physical education class contribute to the amount of physical activity that children receive during the school day. Children need at least 1 hour of physical activity each day, including 30 minutes of moderate-to-vigorous activity

during that hour. When physical education is a sequential instructional program that focuses on skill acquisition, it is **structured physical activity**. Recess is **unstructured activity time**, in which children practice using skills learned in physical education class as well as social skills and have the opportunity to release stress (Pellegrini and Smith 1993; Pellegrini and Davis 1993). Consider that three 10-minute recesses and one 30-minute physical education class daily provide the minimum of 1 hour of activity that children need each day. Evidence suggests that children who do not have recess may be more distracted, less able to concentrate, and more restless than those who have recess. Children may learn social skills in solving problems and conducting conflict resolution during recess (Thomas, Lee, McGee, and Silverman 1987). The NASPE and the National Association of Elementary School Principals support recess as an essential part of a child's learning (NASPE 2001b). The Council on Physical Education for Children (COPEC) provides eight recommendations for recess that specifically establish that recess and physical education are both important and independent components of a quality educational program (figure 12.4).

- Physical education provides a sequential instructional program with opportunities for children to learn about and participate in regular physical activity, to develop motor skills, and to use skills and knowledge to improve performance.

- Schools should develop schedules that provide for supervised, daily recess in grades pre-K through grades 5 or 6. The use of facilities for recess activities should not interfere with instructional classes (separate locations for each activity). If possible, recess should not be scheduled back to back with physical education classes.

- Recess should not be viewed as a reward but as a necessary educational support component for all of the children. Children should not be denied recess as a means of punishment or to make up work.

- Periods of moderate physical activity should be encouraged and facilitated while recognizing that recess should provide opportunities for children to make choices. NASPE recommends that children ages 6 to 11 participate in at least 1 hour and up to several hours of physical activity each day. This activity may occur in periods of moderate-to-vigorous activity lasting 10 to 15 minutes or more. Recess may provide some of this activity time.

- Schools should provide the facilities, equipment, and supervision necessary to ensure that the recess experience is productive, safe, and enjoyable. Developmentally appropriate equipment, as outlined in the NASPE *Guidelines for Facilities, Equipment, and Instructional Materials*, should be made available. Adults should regularly check equipment and facilities for safety.

- Physical education teachers and classroom teachers should teach children positive skills for self-responsibility during recess.

- Adults should direct or intervene when a child's physical or emotional safety is an issue. Bullying or aggressive behavior must not be allowed, and all safety rules should be enforced.

Figure 12.4 COPEC recommendations for recess (NASPE 2001b).

Summary

Consider the size of the children, class, and facility when you are deciding the appropriateness of an activity for that facility. When selecting equipment, consider the size, ability, and age of the children and how the equipment fits the intended learning outcome. Prevent injuries by regular maintenance of equipment and facilities and appropriate supervision. Using a variety of equipment and facilities can enhance learning. Structured and unstructured opportunities to learn and create when children are using gross motor skill is an important part of their development. Being safe means reducing risk as much as possible.

Mastery Learning Activities

1. Using a catalog or Internet site, find a list of physical education equipment and determine the cost of such equipment for class.

2. Travel to an elementary school playground. Conduct a safety inspection using the 10 points from the Consumer Product Safety Commission (CPSC) Public Playground Safety Checklist.

3. Identify the physical education facilities in the elementary school you attended (or one you have observed as a college student).

4. Using the CPSC Web site (www.cpsc.gov), determine the following for slides:

   a. Rung sizes, stair treads, and ramp slopes

   b. Heights of guardrails

   c. Angle and guardrail sizes

References

National Association for Sport and Physical Education (NASPE). 2001a. *Guidelines for facilities, equipment, and instructional materials in elementary education*. Council on Physical Education for Children. A position paper from the National Association for

Sport and Physical Education. Reston, VA: NASPE Publications.

NASPE. 2001b. *Recess in elementary schools.* Council on Physical Education for Children. A position paper from the National Association for Sport and Physical Education. Reston, VA: NASPE Publications.

Pellegrini, A.D., and P.D. Davis. 1993. Relations between children's playground and classroom behaviour. *British Journal of Educational Psychology* 63: 88-95.

Pellegrini, A.D., and P.K. Smith. 1993. School recess: Implications for education and development. *Review of Educational Research* 63: 51-67.

Thomas, J., A. Lee, L. McGee, and S. Silverman. 1987. Effects of individual and group contingencies on disruptive playground behavior. *Journal of Research and Development in Education* 20: 66-76.

Thompson, D.M., Hudson, S.D., and Olsen, H.M. 2007. *S.A.F.E. play areas: Creation, maintenance, and renovation.* Champaign, IL: Human Kinetics.

U.S. Consumer Product Safety Commission. 2002. *Handbook for public playground safety.* Publication 325. Washington, DC: Government Printing Office.

Herkowitz, J. 1984. Developmentally engineered equipment and playgrounds. In *Motor development during childhood and adolescence,* edited by J.R. Thomas, 139-173. Edina, MN: Burgess.

Mack, M.G., S.D. Hudson, and D. Thompson. 1999. Playground safety: Using research to guide community policy. *Journal of Health Education* 30: 352-357.

Sallis, J.F., T.L. McKenzie, B. Kolody, M. Lewis, S. Marshall, and P. Rosengard. 1999. Effects of health-related physical education on academic achievement: Project SPARK. *Research Quarterly for Exercise and Sport* 70: 127.

Thompson, D., S.D. Hudson, and M.G. Mack. 1998. Keep school playgrounds safe. *The Education Digest* 64: 60-64.

Resources

Bruya, L.D. 1988. *Play spaces for children: A new beginning.* Reston, VA: American Alliance for Health, Physical Education, Recreation and Dance (AAHPERD).

Bruya, L.D., and S.J. Langendorfer. 1988. *Where our children play: Elementary school playground equipment.* Reston, VA: American Alliance for Health, Physical Education, Recreation and Dance (AAHPERD).

Lesson Plans

The first two lessons demonstrate the use of large equipment in gymnastics and games as children use balance beams and other climbing or jumping apparatus. Lesson 12.6 adapts several facilities (indoor and outdoor) for use in fitness testing and training.

The other four lessons demonstrate the use of small equipment in lessons. For younger children, the lesson uses stations to practice manipulative skills. The parachute is used to foster cooperation and following directions. Beanbags are used for juggling in grades 4 and 5; scarves can be used first and then balls once juggling is mastered.

Lesson 12.1

Large Equipment

Student Objectives   5

- Perform independent work.
- Demonstrate following rules.

Equipment and Materials

- Station 1: 1 low balance beam (e.g., 2 by 4 inches [5 by 10 cm]; 4 by 4 inches [10 by 10 cm]; 4 by 6 inches [10 by 15 cm]) and bean-bags or 1 rope per child (optional: 2 wands per child)
- Station 2: 1 jumping cube (24 inches [60 cm]) per child
- Station 3: 1 climbing rope (10 to 20 feet [3 to 6 m] in length and 2 inches [5 cm] in diameter) attached to the wall
- Station 4: 1 tunnel, or 2 or 3 other shapes, several beanbags
- Station 5: 1 vaulting cube (wider at the bottom than at the top, 24 to 30 inches [60 to 76 cm] high, or large paper boxes stuffed with paper) and 1 beanbag per child
- Station 6: 1 wooden climbing ladder, a wall, mats, and several beanbags
- Mats (4 by 8 feet [1.2 by 2.4 m]) as needed for safety
- Carpet squares (for use if there are too many children per spot at the stations)

Safety Tip

- Emphasize following the rules. Sit all of the children on carpet squares before you begin the rotations and whenever it becomes necessary to calm them down.

Warm-Up Activities (5 minutes)

Use Warm-Up Routine for Grades K and 1 from lesson 11.1, page 321.

Skill-Development Activities (24 minutes)

Stations

Set up the 6 stations as described in the text and shown in the figures on pages 345 to 346. Arrange small groups at the stations.

1. Use 6 to 7 minutes to describe and demonstrate the 6 stations.
2. Review the stop and rotate signal.

3. Have the children practice at each station for 3 minutes and then rotate. (When revisiting this lesson, you can use more time at each station because explanations will take less time.)
4. Move from station to station—spotting, observing, and managing.

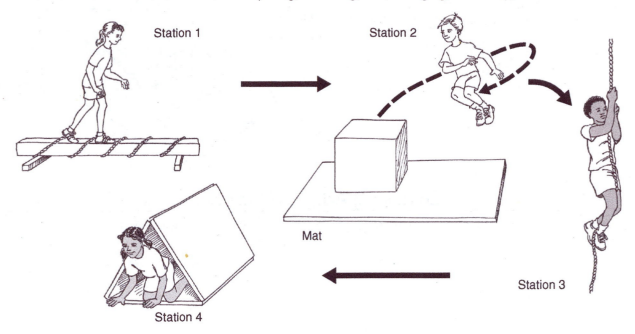

STATION 1: BALANCE BEAMS

Step over the objects on the balance beam (beanbags spaced on a beam or a rope wound around the beam). Wands (broomsticks) make good aids for children who are having trouble on the beam. Allow children to use them as canes (one in each hand) to facilitate balance.

STATION 2: JUMPING CUBES

Perform the following activities while jumping from the cubes:

- Clap hands in flight.
- Spin all the way around (360 degrees) in the air.
- Jump higher. (Someone can hold an arm up as a target or barrier.)

STATION 3: CLIMBING ROPE

Practice climbing the rope:

- Go feetfirst with hands below the feet.
- Go no-legs (hold them in the air).

STATION 4: SHAPES OR TUNNEL

Perform these tasks while navigating the shapes:

- Carry an object (a beanbag).
- Go with your eyes closed.

STATION 5: VAULTING CUBES

Practice the following vaulting skills:

- Use only one arm.
- Use no arms.
- Carry an object (a beanbag).

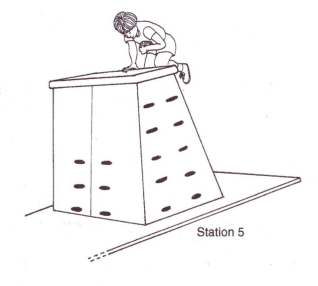

Lesson 12.1 *(continued)*

STATION 6: LADDER

Practice ladder-climbing skills:

- Carry an object (a beanbag).
- Climb at a steeper angle (by raising the ladder).

Station 6

Concluding Activities (1 minute)

Have the children help set the stations in order for the next class or put the equipment away.

Lesson 12.2

Large Equipment

Student Objectives 1 5

- Demonstrate skills on a large apparatus.
- Follow other children.
- Cooperate with a large group.

Equipment and Materials

The following list is given per obstacle course that you set up. Keep group sizes small to increase participation opportunities.

- 1 jumping cube (24 inches [60 cm])
- 3 balance beams (2 by 4 inches [5 by 10 cm]; 4 by 4 inches [10 by 10 cm]; 4 by 6 inches [10 by 15 cm]; 8 to 14 feet [2.4 to 4.2 m] long)
- 2 vaulting cubes (wider at the top than at the bottom, 24 to 30 inches [60 to 76 cm] high, or large paper boxes stuffed with paper)
- 1 tunnel, or 2 or 3 other shapes
- 1 wooden climbing ladder
- 1 climbing rope (10 to 20 feet [3 to 6 m] in length and 2 inches [5 cm] in diameter) attached to the wall
- 1 triangle mat
- Mats (4 by 8 feet [1.2 by 2.4 m]) as needed for safety
- Carpet squares (for use if children must wait turns)

Warm-Up Activities (5 minutes)

Use Warm-Up Routine for Grades K and 1 from lesson 11.1, page 321.

Skill-Development Activities (24 minutes)

Obstacle Course

Set up the courses as shown. Divide the children into the same number of groups as obstacle courses. Keep groups small to increase participation opportunities.

1. Describe and demonstrate the obstacle course.
2. Have the children go through the obstacle course using the skills shown in the figure.
3. Send one child at a time (or space the children so that no child catches another).
4. Repeat for all of the children as many times as possible.

Start

Concluding Activities (1 minute)

Have the children help set the stations in order for the next class or put the equipment away.

Lesson 12.3

Manipulative Skill Stations

Student Objectives 1

- Work independently.
- Record own progress.
- Improve performance in the six tasks as a result of practice.

Equipment and Materials

Plan to set up 2 complete sets of stations.

- Station 1: tennis balls, targets, rope, 2 standards (or other supports to suspend the rope from 5 to 15 feet [1.5 to 4.5 m] high)
- Station 2: bowling pins or weighted plastic bottles, playground balls
- Station 3: 4 barrels, 5 hoops, rope, beanbags, tennis balls, foam balls, 2 standards (or other supports to suspend the rope 5 feet [1.5 m] high)
- Station 4: playground balls, launchers, bean-bags
- Station 5: playground balls, rope and 2 standards, wall or fence
- Station 6: balloons, foam balls, playground ball, wall or fence
- 4 student progress sheets per child (see end of this lesson for sample)
- Tape, polyspots, polydomes, cones, or chalk to mark lines as needed
- Signal

Safety Tip

- Remind children of the signals used to stop activity, change stations, and so on.

Warm-Up Activities (5 minutes)

Slap Tag

Arrange the children into 2 equal groups on 2 parallel lines, about 50 feet (15 m) apart. Designate one group as the Runners and the other as the Chasers. Have the Chasers stand with their backs to the play area and their hands stretched out behind.

1. Describe the game:
   o The Runners sneak across and slap the hands of the Chasers.

- As soon as the hands are slapped, both the Runners and the Chasers turn and run for the Runners' baseline at the other side of the play area.
- The Chasers try to tag the Runners before they reach base.
- Every Runner who is tagged moves to the other side and joins the Chasers.
- Each round, Runners and Chasers switch roles.

2. Have the children play Slap Tag.

Skill-Development Activities (25 minutes)

Ball Stations

Set up 2 complete sets of stations. Arrange the children into 12 groups of 2 or 3. You may want to group the children in the classroom (e.g., red, blue, gold, silver, orange, and green stars); this will help you send groups to their starting stations quickly (red stars to station 1, blue stars to station 2, and so on).

1. Spend 6 to 7 minutes explaining stations. Then send the children to the stations on the first day.
2. Rotate each group to a new station after 6 minutes on the first day (8 or 9 minutes on subsequent days). Rotate the children through 3 stations each day.

STATION 1

Mark lines 10, 15, 20, 30, 40, 50, and 60 feet (3, 4.5, 6, 9, 12, and 18 m) from the wall. Suspend a rope 5 feet (1.5 m) above the ground and 30 feet (9 m) back from the wall.
   Throw tennis balls at the wall. Throw tennis balls over the rope from the various distances.

STATION 2

Set up a bowling pin and mark lines 5, 10, and 15 feet (1.5, 3, and 4.5 m) from the pin.
   Play one-pin bowling (from increasingly difficult distances of 5, 10, and 15 feet [1.5, 3, and 4.5 m]) using a playground ball.

STATION 3

Place ice cream barrels (marked a, b, c, and d) 2 feet (60 cm) apart, with the nearest one 5 feet (1.5 m) away. Place hoops (marked a, b, c, d, and e) 5 feet (1.5 m) apart, with the nearest hoop 5 feet (1.5 m) away. Mark lines 5 and 10 feet (1.5 and 3 m) away from the hoops and barrels. Suspend a rope 5 feet (1.5 m) high and mark a line 10 feet (3 m) away.
   Toss balls into the barrels. Toss foam balls into 5 hoops. Toss over and under a rope 5 feet (1.5 m) high from 10 feet (3 m) away.

STATION 4

Mark lines 5, 10, and 15 feet (1.5, 3, and 4.5 m) from a wall.
   Bounce the ball to the wall, let it rebound, and catch it from 5, 10, and 15 feet (1.5, 3, and 4.5 m). Launch the beanbag and catch it with both hands (same hand as launching foot, opposite hand as launching foot). Toss the beanbag into the air and catch it.

STATION 5

Mark lines 10, 20, 30, and 40 feet (3, 6, 9, and 12 m) from a wall. Suspend a rope 3 feet (0.9 m) above the ground in front of the wall.
   Kick the ball to the wall from each line. Kick the ball above the rope from the 10-foot (3 m) line. Kick the ball under the rope from the 10-foot (3 m) line.

STATION 6

Mark lines 5, 10, and 15 feet (1.5, 3, and 4.5 m) away from a wall.
   Hit the balloon up as many times as possible. Hit the foam ball from your palm. Hit the playground ball on a bounce from the ground to the wall from the lines.

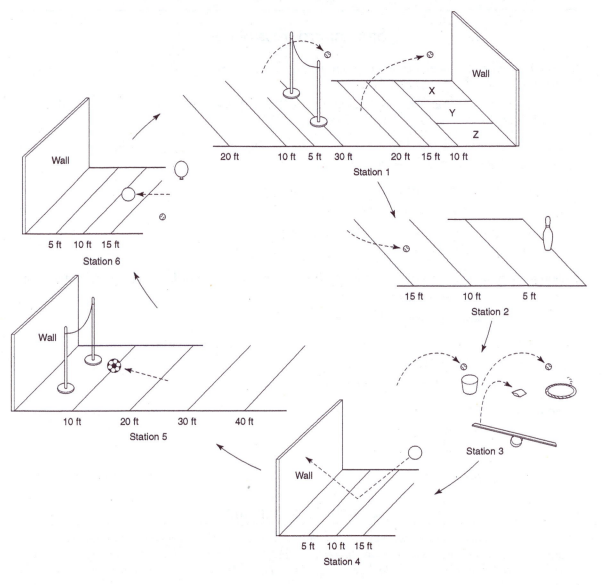

Station 1

Station 2

Station 3

Station 4

Station 5

Station 6

20 ft   10 ft   5 ft   30 ft   20 ft   15 ft   10 ft

Wall

X
Y
Z

15 ft   10 ft   5 ft

5 ft   10 ft   15 ft

10 ft   20 ft   30 ft   40 ft

5 ft   10 ft   15 ft

Wall

Student Progress Sheet

Have one sheet per child to use each day. Have a red pencil at each station the first two days, and a blue pencil the second two days. Have or help each child circle his or her best score for the day at each station. Using the colored pencils allows you, the children, and their parents to see progress.

Student Progress Sheet

Station 1: I can hit the wall with the ball standing on the line marked 10, 15, 20, 30, 40, 50, and 60 feet (3, 4.5, 6, 9, 12, and 18 m).

I can throw the ball over the rope to zone X, Y, Z, from the line marked 10, 15, 20, 30, 40, 50, and 60 feet (3, 4.5, 6, 9, 12, and 18 m).

Station 2: In 10 rolls, I hit the pin _____ times from 5 feet (1.5 m); _____ times from 10 feet (3 m); and _____ times from 15 feet (4.5 m).

Station 3: I can throw the foam ball into hoops a, b, c, d, and e.

I can throw the tennis ball into barrels a, b, c, and d.

I can throw the ball over the rope: Yes _____ No _____

I can throw the ball under the rope: Yes _____ No _____

Station 4: I can bounce the ball to the wall and catch it from 5, 10, and 15 feet (1.5, 3, and 4.5 m).

I can launch and catch the beanbag: Yes _____ No _____

I can toss the beanbag over my head and catch it: Yes _____ No _____

Station 5: I can kick the ball 10, 20, 30, and 40 feet (3, 6, 9, and 12 m).

I can kick the ball high (over the rope): Yes _____ No _____

I can kick the ball low (under the rope): Yes _____ No _____

Station 6: I can hit the balloon _____ times.

I can hit the foam ball _____ times.

I can hit the playground ball 5, 10, and 15 feet (1.5, 3, and 4.5 m).

Concluding Activities

There is no concluding activity because the children should spend all of their time at the stations. As you rotate children to the last station, however, tell them that you will give a 3-minute warning when class is ending and that they should circle their last best score and replace the equipment so that it is ready for the next class.

From K.T. Thomas, A.M. Lee, and J.R. Thomas, 2008, *Physical education methods for elementary teachers*, 3rd ed. (Champaign, IL: Human Kinetics). Adapted, by permission, from K.T. Thomas, A.M. Lee, and J.R. Thomas, 2000, *Physical education for children: Daily lesson plans for elementary school*, 2nd ed. (Champaign, IL: Human Kinetics), 137-140.

Lesson 12.4

Locomotor Skills Obstacle Course

Student Objectives 1

- Travel through an obstacle course using various locomotor skills without touching the obstacles.

Equipment and Materials

- Polyspots or polydomes for marking lines

For each obstacle course:

- 4 cones
- 10 hoops
- 8 milk crates
- 2 low balance beams

Arrange obstacle courses as shown below, 1 course per group.

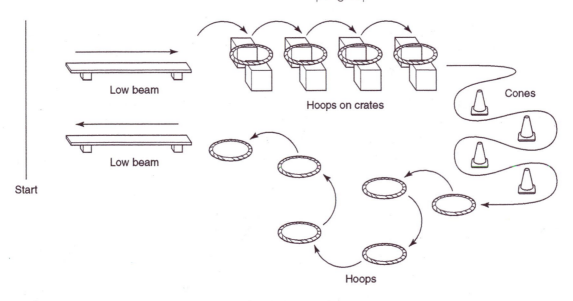

Low beam

Hoops on crates

Cones

Low beam

Start

Hoops

Warm-Up Activities (5 minutes)

Reveille

Arrange the children in two groups along parallel lines.

1. Describe the game:
   - On the signal (a horn is best, but a whistle, bell, or other noisemaker will do), everyone runs for the opposite line.
   - The first group to line up, standing at attention, gets 1 point.

Lesson 12.4 *(continued)*

- Take care when running past other children so that no one is bumped or tripped.
- Play several rounds.

2. Have the children play Reveille.

Skill-Development Activities (20 minutes)

Obstacle Course

Divide the children into groups of 4 to 6, and arrange each group at the beginning of an obstacle course.

1. Describe the activity: "Hop (on right foot) down the balance beam, jump through the elevated hoops, weave around the cones, hop (on left foot) through the hoops on the ground, and walk backward down the second balance beam."

2. Have them repeat, using different arrangements of the equipment and other locomotor skills (e.g., gallop, slide, skip).

3. Have each group make a pattern for their course, learn it, and teach it to the other groups.

Concluding Activities (5 minutes)

Crows and Cranes

Arrange two groups facing each other on lines 20 feet (6 m) apart. Two additional lines are needed 30 feet (9 m) outside the first pair of lines (adjust starting lines closer together or farther apart as needed). Designate one group as "Crows" and the other as "Cranes."

1. Describe and demonstrate the game:
   - I will call out Crows or Cranes (extend the first consonants of the word so that the children do not know which name will be called, C-r-r-r-rows or C-r-r-r-ranes).
   - The team whose name is called turns and runs to its goal line as the other team chases, attempting to tag the runners.
   - All tagged players become members of the other team, and play continues. Play ends when all of the runners cross the line or are tagged.

2. Have the children play Crows and Cranes.

3. Variation: Have both groups walk toward each other; as they get close together, the group called runs back to the goal line.

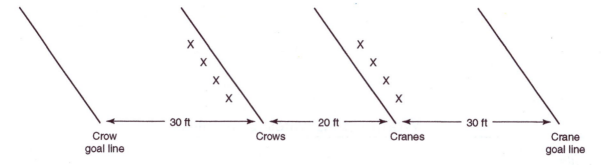

From K.T. Thomas, A.M. Lee, and J.R. Thomas, 2008, *Physical education methods for elementary teachers*, 3rd ed. (Champaign, IL: Human Kinetics). Adapted, by permission, from K.T. Thomas, A.M. Lee, and J.R. Thomas, 2000, *Physical education for children: Daily lesson plans for elementary school*, 2nd ed. (Champaign, IL: Human Kinetics), 532-533.

Lesson 12.5

Parachute Games

Student Objectives   1

- Perform parachute activities, demonstrating cooperation.
- Follow verbal instruction to learn new activities.

Equipment and Materials

- 1 parachute
- Several fluff balls
- Several large playground balls (13 inches [33 cm])
- Several smaller balls (2 or more colors) (6 inches [15 cm])
- Stopwatch or clock with second hand
- Polyspots or polydomes to mark lines

Warm-Up Activities (5 minutes)

Use Sneaky Tag from lesson 2.2, page 29.

Skill-Development Activities (20 minutes)

Parachute Activities

Arrange the children around the outside of the parachute, which is spread out on the ground.

EXCHANGE POSITIONS

Assign the children numbers, one through the total number of children.

Tell the children to hold the parachute with the left hand and circle counterclockwise. Remind them which numbers are odd and which are even. Tell the children: "On the signal, the odd-numbered children release the parachute and move forward to take the place of the next odd-numbered player in front of them" (variations can include moving forward two places, three places, and so on). Repeat with the even-numbered players moving. Have the children use a variety of locomotor skills (walk, run, skip, gallop, slide) to move.

RUN UNDER

Assign the children numbers from 1 to 4.

Tell the children: "Begin in a squat position, holding the parachute with both hands. When you hear the signal, lift up the parachute to form an umbrella. I will call a number from 1 to 4. All of you let go of the parachute, and the players with the number called must move across the circle under the parachute to the opposite side (and into the former position of another player with the same number) before the parachute floats down." You can specify the type of movement you want the children to use (e.g., different locomotor skills, animal walks, moving backward).

POPPING POPCORN

Place several fluff balls on the parachute.

Tell the children: "Shake the parachute up and down, attempting to 'pop' the balls into the air, but not off the parachute."

BALL ROLL

Have the children grasp the parachute, which you have laid on the ground. Place a large playground ball on the parachute.

Explain and have the children do the activity: "I will tell one child to stand and raise his or her part of the parachute. Then the next child counterclockwise (point) in the circle raises the parachute, and so on. The object is to keep the ball rolling around the edge of the parachute." After the ball passes, the children may lower the parachute to keep the ball going. After children gain some proficiency, include changing the direction of the ball or add additional balls.

Parachute Games

Keep the children around the outside of the parachute, which is spread out on the ground.

POPCORN GAME

Place several fluff balls on the parachute. Assign the children numbers, one through the total number of children.

Describe and have the children play the game: "The odd numbers form one team and the even numbers another. The odd-numbered team releases the parachute and each member takes two or three steps backward. The even-numbered players have 30 seconds to pop all of the balls off the parachute. Players then exchange places, and the odd-numbered team has a turn. The team with fewer balls on the parachute after the 30-second period wins."

CENTER BALL

Have two teams stand on opposite sides of the parachute (you can use the teams already created, but they don't need to remember their numbers), holding it about waist high. Place two different colored balls (6 inches [15 cm]) on the parachute.

Describe and have the children play the game: "Each team tries to shake the opponent's ball into the center pocket and at the same time keep their own ball from going into the pocket. Your team scores a point every time it puts the opponent's ball in the pocket."

BALL SHAKE

Two teams stand on opposite sides of the parachute (keep teams from Center Ball or make two new teams). Place several different balls (e.g., one foam, one playground, etc.) on the parachute.

Describe and have the children play the game: "On a signal to begin, each team tries to shake the balls off the other team's side of the parachute. You may not use your hands to keep the balls on the parachute. Your team earns 1 point each time that a ball leaves the parachute on your opponent's side and touches the ground."

Concluding Activities (5 minutes)

Parachute Games

Let the children choose one of the parachute games to repeat.

From K.T. Thomas, A.M. Lee, and J.R. Thomas, 2008, *Physical education methods for elementary teachers*, 3rd ed. (Champaign, IL: Human Kinetics). Adapted, by permission, from K.T. Thomas, A.M. Lee, and J.R. Thomas, 2000, *Physical education for children: Daily lesson plans for elementary school*, 2nd ed. (Champaign, IL: Human Kinetics), 536-538.

Lesson 12.6

Practicing the 1-Mile Run and Sit-Ups

Student Objectives   1

- Demonstrate pacing in the 1-mile run.
- Perform correct sit-up form.

Equipment and Materials

- Cones for marking the 1-mile running course
- Stopwatch
- Mats (optional)
- Setting up a distance run test: 1 mile is 5,280 feet, or 1,760 yards (about 1,610 m); use any configuration that equals that distance.

20 yd on each side; run 22 laps

110 yd between lines; run back and forth 8 times

Skill-Development Activities (30 minutes)

1-Mile Run and Sit-Ups

Divide the children into 2 groups.

1. Discuss the need for pacing in the 1-mile run.
2. Describe and demonstrate a correct Sit-Up:
   - The Sit-Up is done with a rolling motion.
   - Begin by lying on your back with your legs bent slightly at the knees so that the soles of your feet are flat on the ground.
   - Choose one of the two hand–arm positions: You can cross your hands and arms on your chest so that your hands are resting on the opposite shoulders, or you can place your hands on the sides of your head with a finger placed on each ear, keeping your elbows lined up (parallel) with the back of your head (keep them there, not pulling forward past the ears).

Lesson 12.6 *(continued)*

- o Perform each Sit-Up slowly, rolling your chin to your chest to lift your head, your shoulders, and then your lower back off the ground. During the movement, you should feel the muscles under your belly button working.
- o Once your lower back is off the ground, unroll to the start position.

3. Have the children practice analyzing your sit-up form.

4. Have one group practice the pacing of the 1-mile run. Encourage each child to find the fastest pace that he or she can maintain while running the total distance.

5. Have the other group select partners. One partner in each pair does Sit-Ups for 60 seconds while the other partner holds feet; then have them switch roles.

6. After 15 minutes in each activity, allow a 2-minute rest; then have groups switch activities.

7. If the weather is hot, make sure that the children have the opportunity to get water when they want it.

From K.T. Thomas, A.M. Lee, and J.R. Thomas, 2008, *Physical education methods for elementary teachers*, 3rd ed. (Champaign, IL: Human Kinetics). Adapted, by permission, from K.T. Thomas, A.M. Lee, and J.R. Thomas, 2000, *Physical education for children: Daily lesson plans for elementary school*, 2nd ed. (Champaign, IL: Human Kinetics), 793-794.

Lesson 12.7

Juggling

Student Objectives   1

- Attempt to juggle two, then three, beanbags.

Equipment and Materials

- 3 beanbags per child

Warm-Up Activities (6 to 8 minutes)

Use Walk or Jog from lesson 4.3, page 87.

Skill-Development Activities (17 minutes)

Juggling

Arrange the children in scatter formation; each child has 3 beanbags. Describe, demonstrate, and have the children practice only one or two steps of juggling at a time (see next section for descriptions of each step).

1. Describe and demonstrate steps 1 and 2.
2. Have the children practice steps 1 and 2 until they achieve some skill.
3. Encourage them to establish a good rhythm.
4. Describe and demonstrate steps 3 and 4.
5. Have the children practice steps 3 and 4 until they achieve some skill.
6. Describe and demonstrate step 5.
7. Have the children practice step 5 until they achieve some skill.
8. Describe and demonstrate step 6.
9. Have the children practice step 6 until they achieve some skill.

Steps in Juggling

Describe, demonstrate, and have the children practice only one or two steps of juggling at a time (see outline in previous section):

Step 1—"Using your right hand, throw one beanbag up and catch it. The beanbag should go slightly above your head."

Step 2—"Using your left hand, throw one beanbag up and catch it."

Step 3—"With one beanbag in each hand, toss the right-hand beanbag and then the left-hand beanbag, catching each with the same hand that tossed it. This should be toss right, toss left, catch right, catch left. Now, after tossing the beanbag in your right hand, toss the one in your left hand under it, catching each beanbag with the same hand that tossed it."

Step 4—"Repeat step 3, but catch each beanbag with the opposite hand."

Step 5—"Hold two beanbags in your right hand. Toss one in the air and then the other. Catch the first and toss it again. Catch the second and toss it again; continue." Cue the children: "Toss the beanbag underneath (toward the left side) each time. Repeat with your left hand."

Lesson 12.7 *(continued)*

Step 6—"Hold two beanbags in your right hand and one in your left. Toss one beanbag from your right hand, toss the beanbag from your left hand, and then toss the third beanbag. Repeat." Cue the children: "Toss each beanbag underneath (toward the inside of the body) the one in the air."

Concluding Activities (5 minutes)

Children who cannot do step 6 will not be able to do this activity; for those children, go back and help them practice the needed skills during this time.

Continuous Juggling

Arrange the children in scatter formation; each child has 3 beanbags.

1. Explain the following modification: "In step 6" (previous section) "after tossing and catching the third beanbag, stop and begin again. In continuous juggling, keep tossing until you miss or stop."

2. Have the advanced children practice continuous juggling while you help the other children master step 6 (see previous section, Steps in Juggling).

PART IV

Teaching Physical Education

Finally, you are ready to teach! Now what? This section focuses on what you do when children are present—what you do to facilitate learning during class. Close your eyes and picture a physical education class. What do you see? Maybe you can picture yourself giving instructions, demonstrating, or providing feedback to students. Or maybe you see yourself spending time watching students; observation is an important part of teaching. Chapter 13, Instructing Students, covers those activities. Because you also assess student performance as an integral part of the learning process, chapter 14, Evaluating Students, covers evaluation activities. Finally, in chapter 15, Growing as a Teacher, you can explore ways to enhance your teaching skills through the use of reflection, portfolios, continuing education, and professional engagement.

CHAPTER 13

Instructing Students

RACHEL, AGE 9

Instruction includes teaching behaviors such as positioning, scanning, observing, interacting, cuing, demonstrating, reinforcing, and giving feedback. These are enhanced by personality variables: voice, body language, eye contact, and facial expression. Teaching and learning are dynamic processes that require constant monitoring so that optimal learning takes place. You can learn to optimize these behaviors and thereby have an impact on student learning.

Learner Outcomes

After studying this chapter, you should be able to do the following:

- Define and demonstrate appropriate teaching behaviors (directions, cues, demonstrations, reinforcement).
- Discuss and enhance instruction with personality variables.
- Define and use observation for skill and behavior.
- Identify a plan for improving observation.
- State how and when teaching expertise develops.

Glossary Terms

volume	facial expression	directions
tone	location	demonstrations
pace	scanning	teachable moment
body language		

Just as the phrase "natural athlete" is used to describe expert athletes, "she or he is a natural" has been applied to teachers. However, expert teachers recognize that hard work and practice contribute to teaching expertise. Expert teachers make it look easy! Teachers *learn* to be expert instructors; they are not born to teach. We believe that no one wants to be a poor teacher. Unfortunately, most of you can identify at least one teacher who was not effective. With knowledge and practice, anyone can be a good teacher. The goals of methods courses, practical experience, and student teaching are to help you develop the skills necessary to teach and to continue improving as a teacher. This chapter describes important behaviors for teachers during instruction and much of what has been learned about expert teachers. Table 13.1 provides a guide for effective instruction, including information from this chapter, plus elements of planning from the previous chapters. Refer to the table as you read this chapter.

You need to understand and apply information about instruction so that

- student learning is optimal,
- you are ready to assume the responsibility of teaching, and
- continuous improvement of teaching is a realistic goal.

Table 13.1 Rubric to Guide Instruction

	Novice	Emerging	Mastery
Initial activity (not warm-up)	Routine is not evident	Students organize eventually	Immediate initial activity with little or no instruction
Transition	Planning is not evident	Some time spent moving into formations or groups	Smooth, brief transitions for groups or formations; planning is evident
Equipment	Planning is not evident	Planning is evident, could improve	Quick and efficient, planning is evident
Special events	Restroom or water requests, behavior problems, and other events interrupt instruction	Planning is evident, but some interruptions occur; behavior problems are handled with desist or other techniques	Planning is evident and minimizes interruptions; behavior problems are generally prevented
Concluding activity (not cool-down)	Routine is not evident	Students organized to leave after instructions	Clear routine is evident and requires few or no cues
Voice	Inappropriate—too soft, loud, assertive	Occasionally too loud or not loud enough, generally good	Appropriate—clear, loud enough
Body language	Negative or low energy	Generally reflective of the message and energetic	Consistently energetic, reflective of the message
Eye contact	None	Some	Consistent
Facial expression	Negative, neutral	Neutral or smiling	Smiling most of the time—occasionally reflective of situation
Student interaction	Unclear whether you like the students or activities	Generally clear that you like the students and activities	Clear that you like the students and activities
Enthusiasm	Low energy, seems tired or apathetic	Demonstrates sufficient energy	High energy, seems disappointed when time is over, appears to be able to go on indefinitely
Positioning	Poor choice, cannot see or be seen by all students	Back to the wall most of the time	Selects optimal location for each phase of lesson
Focus	Consistently distracted	Occasionally distracted	Focused on students and learning
Scanning	Not evident	Scans every 6 seconds and identifies some problems	Constantly scanning (every 6 seconds), identifies most problems
Instructions	Not clear	Generally clear	Clear and concise
Demonstration (teacher or peer)	Fails to demonstrate or provides incorrect demonstrations or more than three demonstrations	Correctly demonstrates, no more than three times	Correctly demonstrates (no more than three times) with appropriate cues
Reinforcement	Fails to provide verbal or physical reinforcement	Uses same phrase or physical reinforcement repeatedly	Consistently applied using varied phrases and physical reinforcements

(continued)

Table 13.1 (continued)

	Novice	Emerging	Mastery
Feedback	No performance-contingent feedback	At least two performance-contingent statements	At least two performance-contingent statements, uses both corrective and reinforcing, uses the sandwich technique (encourage, correct, encourage)
Evaluation	Not evident	Attempt to evaluate skill or lesson	Clearly relating objectives, practice, feedback, and assessment
Objectives	Not clear	Somewhat clear	Evident and related to the instruction, practice, and feedback or evaluation
Practice organization	Inappropriate or ineffective	Acceptable (multiple trials)	Optimal (random, student-paced)
Warm-up activity	Not evident or inappropriate	Appropriate	Facilitated mastery of the objectives or supported skill development
Skill-development activity	Not evident or inappropriate	Children active	Learning (skill or knowledge acquired) evident or fitness objective met
Closure or culminating activity	Not evident or inappropriate	Somewhat related to lesson	Takes skill development to a higher level (e.g., use in game or evaluate, increase understanding)

Practice

Practice and feedback are two of the most important learning variables. Generally, practice is considered a planning variable. When you plan practice well, learning activities go smoothly and instructional variables are your focus. Unfortunately, this may not always be the case. Even the best plans, by the most expert teachers, sometimes fail. Therefore, you need to monitor practice organization to determine whether the practice is helping children learn. The key variables in practice are type of practice (e.g., constant, blocked, variable, and random), amount of practice (e.g., number of trials), and content of practice (e.g., whole skill, part or progressive part, contextual).

Motor skill learning takes time—and lots of practice. Regardless of the quality of practice, children may not improve during a lesson. Therefore, you may have difficulty determining whether the problem is with the amount of practice, the organization of practice, or some other factor. One way to evaluate the effectiveness of practice is to examine the range of performance on a task. If some children are improving and others are not, your practice organization and content are probably fine. However, when no one is successful or improving, you need to reorganize either the practice or the content. Likewise, when everyone has mastered the task, it is time to move on in the content. You may need to provide additional practice for those who are struggling, or you may need to alter the task for individuals or groups so that practice challenges those children who are mastering the skill and allows success for those who are struggling. Another way to evaluate practice is to determine whether the quality of the skill is improving or the children's understanding is increasing. These variables are more sensitive to change than outcome variables. If understanding of the skill has increased or if performance of the skill has become more efficient, practice is working.

Several events should cause you to reorganize practice quickly:

- The children are having trouble following instructions; for example, they do not know what to do, they do the wrong thing, or they do nothing.

- None of the children are making progress in qualitative aspects of the skill.
- The children cannot explain what they are trying to accomplish with the practice.
- After considerable time, skill is not improving.

Children learn new skills through effective practice. You provide effective practice and instruction. The next section focuses on instruction.

Personality Variables

Discussion of personality generally includes such characteristics as outgoing, shy, and reserved. Your personality may influence how you teach and certainly affects how easy it is for you to learn to be an effective teacher. A shy person may have to overcome anxiety about being in front of a group. A quiet person may have to develop enthusiasm. A loud and assertive person may need to quiet, calm, and control natural tendencies in order to be effective with young children. A person who is enthusiastic, friendly, humorous, caring, and expressive may have a head start as a teacher compared with a person who is shy, quiet, solemn, and low key. However, to be an effective teacher, you need to develop specific skills related to instruction.

Voice is important because the size of a gym and the environment on the playground tend to dissipate **volume**, so children have trouble hearing. There is a balance between being loud enough and yelling. Yelling often influences the tone of your voice, making you seem angry when you are just trying to be heard. Often, those with deeper voices are heard more easily, so if your voice is not deep, practice using a deeper voice. If volume is still a problem, use a microphone (the wireless kind works well in the gym) or whisper so that children get in the habit of listening carefully. The **tone** of your voice is especially important in elementary school. Children are sensitive to anger, frustration, sarcasm, and apathy in voices. Be sure that your voice expresses what you want to convey. Talking too fast makes it difficult for children to understand, so **pace** what you have to say. Pause occasionally to allow them to reflect. Silence from you is not always a bad thing. We suggest listening to an audiotape to identify aspects of your voice that may need to be changed.

Body language lets students know that you are a focused, energetic teacher.

Body language is more important than words to most listeners. If you stand with your arms crossed, the observer may think you are angry or unapproachable. Other body language might reflect fatigue (slouching), impatience (hands on hips), or disinterest (turning away). Generally, you do not want to seem unapproachable or disinterested, and you should not ever appear that way to students! Using your hands to emphasize a point or to maintain student interest is one form of positive body language. Walking around—without pacing—demonstrates enthusiasm and shows concern for all of the students. A videotape can help you evaluate your body language.

Using eye contact does two things: First, it sends a positive message to students—you like them and feel comfortable with them. Second, it helps keep students focused on you. For younger children, you may have to kneel or squat down to have eye contact; being at eye level with children is helpful. Practice making eye contact with every child during class.

Facial expression, especially smiling, is one of the most powerful tools you have. Young children (7 years and younger) interpret a neutral facial expression and an angry expression the same way (i.e., The teacher is angry with me or doesn't like me) (Passer and Wilson 2002). Smiling sends positive messages to children: "I like what I am doing, I like you, I am happy." You can use other facial expressions to convey information or to emphasize a point. For example, showing surprise, concern, or excitement may be useful. Many expert teachers entertain their students—at least part of the time; somewhere inside those teachers is an actor or comedian. Every teacher does not have to entertain; however, it is a useful tool for those who are comfortable using it.

You have many interactions with your students; this is probably why you decided to become a teacher. The interactions are positive for you and the child. Therefore, interact with all of the children and learn to do so in a variety of ways, as time allows. If you began each class with individual greetings, the class would be over before the greetings ended. Similarly, you have general as well as specific ways to interact with the children, sometimes recognizing the child for no particular reason, sometimes making contact as a reaction to a specific event. Both recognitions are important—especially to the child. So, how do you interact? Smiles, comments, a touch, and a look (not "the look") are all interactions (table 13.2).

You can most often express enthusiasm as energy. However, your enthusiasm is also apparent in careful planning, feedback, and every phase of instruction. In physical education, energy is one of your implied characteristics. If you were tired, lazy, or ill, you would have trouble portraying enthusiasm for physical activity and the health benefits related to physical activity. Enthusiasm for what you do helps others see why it is important and why they should participate. Passionate teachers have enthusiasm that shows in every phase of their teaching. Their energy is transmitted to their colleagues and students, and their mission is to create the same passion in everyone.

You are not required to have a sense of humor, but it is useful. Humor directed at yourself is especially helpful. Making fun of children or others is not an acceptable educational practice, however. You can use humor as an effective teaching tool. Children generally like physical education and sport because they are fun, and humor can make learning fun. Humor brings novelty to class; for example, throwing a rubber chicken into the parachute as children shake the edges of the parachute to make "popcorn fluff balls" with foam balls is fun and funny.

Teaching requires that you juggle several things at once—lesson content, management and safety of students, and instruction. The balance between being aware of what is happening generally and concentrating on student learning is a challenge. You need to focus on students and student learning and not be distracted by unimportant events. At the same time, you need to pay attention to important events—within the class and outside

Table 13.2   Teacher–Student Interactions

List the students' names in the left column. Each time your observer notices you looking, speaking, touching, or smiling at a student, a mark is placed in the appropriate box. The goals are to have at least one interaction with each student in a class and to balance the interactions among students.

Name	Looked at	Spoke to	Touched	Smiled at

Using Humor

Ms. Heath is going to play Len's Ball Mix-Up (described in chapter 7, Psychosocial Factors in Physical Education). She saw Len teach this game to kindergarteners when she was a student. He held their attention by walking in front of them carrying a box with the balls and beanbags. The box had a hole; when he tipped the box backward, the balls fell out through the hole. This left a trail of balls behind him. When he turned, he looked surprised to see the balls! The children laughed and were very excited to pick up the balls as part of the game. Ms. Heath decides to use humor to make the activity more fun, even though she is usually quiet and serious.

it. For example, a signal for a fire drill is important and demands your response, whereas a stray bell going off should not interfere with learning. One of the most difficult times occurs early in your student teaching, when observers are more likely to be present. Your focus needs to be on the students and what they are learning, so making eye contact with or monitoring the cooperating teacher or other visitors is an example of "loss of focus." On the other hand, you should notice when someone enters the gym or playground. You should immediately make a quick visual check to decide if the event is important. Most of the time, your focus should immediately return to instruction. For example, suppose that you see your principal enter the gym. You glance at the principal and notice that he or she has just stopped by to see what you are doing. Class continues as though the principal is not there. Alternatively, the principal signals that he or she needs to speak with you. Immediately, give the children something to do and move toward the principal as you continue to observe your students.

Teaching Behaviors

Instructions, cues, feedback, and demonstrations are among the teaching behaviors that are most important to physical education. You can learn to do each of these and, with practice, improve the effectiveness of each. The first step is understanding each behavior so that you know what you eventually want to accomplish.

Teaching is a series of teacher–student and student–teacher interactions, but student–teacher interactions are not as frequent as you might expect (Rink 1996). Consider only interactions that are related to learning. Eliminate management interactions and all group interactions (e.g., giving instructions to the class). Student–teacher interactions—those times related to skill learning when you speak to, look at, or touch a student—are often infrequent. The overall message of one-on-one, skill-related interactions is "I like you; I like this activity." It is helpful if you truly like the children and the activity, but what really matters is that they believe that you do. You should try to have many interactions that portray these positive ideas.

In the gym and probably in the classroom, you spend more time with group interactions than with one-on-one interactions. In the classroom, you have the opportunity for one-on-one interaction through written work. In the gym, feedback, reinforcement, and encouragement must come directly and often take the form of a one-on-one interaction. At the same time, you must instruct and supervise the whole class. Optimally, you provide instruction to the class as a whole and have one-on-one interactions with individual children as frequently as possible.

Location

Where should you stand when you teach? In part, this is related to the formation in which you have placed the children. For example, when they are arranged in a circle, you are usually well positioned by becoming part of the circle: If you are standing in the middle of the circle, at least half of the children are behind you. Three guidelines determine **location**, where you should position yourself for an activity. First, position yourself so that you can see as many of the children as possible, preferably all of them. Stand with your back to the wall (or to the boundary) to keep all of the children in front of you. Second, position yourself nearest to the activity with the highest risk; third, stay close to the highest-risk children. When you temporarily move out of position to stand near a child who is misbehaving, this is called a "desist" (see chapter 11, Teachers' Rights, Responsibilities, and Best Practices). A desist is temporary, and, typically, you can immediately move back to the best location. Classroom teachers use this technique frequently by moving from the front of the room to stand near a child or group of children; once the children return to the task, the teacher moves away. Sometimes optimal location (deciding which is the greater risk) is a difficult decision and may require a change in the lesson. For example, you need to spot an activity. You place that activity near the boundary so that you can see most of the class as you spot. However, you have one child who often moves out of control. Once that child leaves the activity you are spotting, ask yourself, "Am I close enough to monitor and maintain a safe environment?" You may need to ask that child to stay with you or to sit out for a while, or you may need to alter the activity itself so that it is safe for the children to do without spotting. For example, you could switch from handstands, which generally need spotting, to the Donkey Kick, which does not need spotting. Moving among the children is often a positive action. Consider the cost-to-benefit trade-off: The benefits are increased opportunities for interaction, better vision of individual performance, and possibly more effective evaluation for feedback. The cost is that you cannot see all

of the children. As you do low-risk activities with children who move and work under control, you have more freedom to move among the children. The optimal position allows you to see all of the children and yet to be near the highest-risk activity and the highest-risk children (figure 13.1).

Scanning

Scanning is visually searching the learning area. Specifically, you are looking at the children and at what they are doing, pausing only when something demands your attention. Make a visual sweep of the entire area every few seconds (6 seconds is a good goal). When something captures your attention, decide quickly whether you need to do something. Safety issues are a major concern in your scanning: you are looking for "out-of-bounds" actions such as children moving too fast or out of control, using equipment improperly, or touching or interacting with other children when they should not be. As your scanning improves, you

Figure 13.1 Optimal position to guide students and activities.

can capture other behaviors related to instruction rather than safety, including children who are off task, trying but doing the wrong skill, or making errors in skill execution. Expert teachers can scan to monitor behavior while maintaining focus on learning. You can spot or provide feedback to one child while monitoring the rest of the class. To use scanning effectively takes practice. One way to gain this practice is during observation of other teachers. Scanning and observation are similar and usually done at the same time. The subtle difference is that observation focuses on skill and learning whereas scanning focuses on safety and monitoring management. You have to do both. Observation is covered next in this chapter.

Concepts Into Practice

Ryan is observing Mr. Lyon teach. Mr. Lyon changed positions. During the first few observations, Ryan did not know why Mr. Lyon moved across the gym. By the fifth observation, Ryan was scanning and could see that Mr. Lyon was using a desist. That is, he moved across the gym because two students were not participating.

Observation for Skill and Confidence

Spend a significant amount of class time watching children. Consider the rubrics in chapter 4, Motor Performance During Childhood, for locomotor skills and manipulative skills. You can use those and similar rubrics to guide instruction and practice, conduct formative evaluation, provide corrective and reinforcing feedback, and evaluate at the end of a unit. Observation is a learned skill, so practice improves two dimensions of observation. First, it improves *what* you see. Watching for specific movements or behaviors starts with knowing what to look for. What you are looking for depends on the situation. For example, the goal of a game may be passing the ball to many team members; thus, you are looking for many passes. Another activity may focus on accuracy or distance of passes, so you are watching for those characteristics. Sometimes you observe for behavior because a child, class, or activity demands that listening, following instructions, and cooperating are the most critical educational objectives.

When the lesson objective is problem solving or cooperation, you should be observing for groups who are not functional. You might see one child standing apart from the others or two subgroups working rather than one. Rubrics developed for each activity help you focus on the target skills. You can glance at the rubric and be reminded of what you are hoping or expecting to observe.

You can also observe student confidence. Children who are eager for a turn or who avoid turns show their range of confidence! Observe for confidence, behavior, and skill. Unfortunately, some teachers tend to focus on behavior rather than on skill or confidence. Children who lack confidence may avoid physical activity. Identify children who lack confidence and work with them to increase confidence. First, identify the child's actual skill level and compare that to the perceived skill level. Children may lack confidence because they think they are "below average." Second, help the child recognize that skill improves with practice and that it is normal to need practice. Third, assist the child in understanding that each person is different and that a variety of skill levels is normal. Finally, recognize improvement and help the child focus on improving. All of this begins with observing for confidence.

The second dimension of observation that improves with practice is remembering. With practice, you can recall information about performances in considerable detail. Often, you do not have time to take notes about performance during class, so you sometimes need to remember information about children's skills until the next time you see them. Remembering can be incidental (things you recall without trying) or central (things you remember because you try). Remembering children's performance is important; make it central to your observation! Watch and remember what children are doing. Typically, this is easier for the best and worst performers and most difficult for the average students: Focus in order to remember several of the average students' performances. You are likely to remember the best and worst incidentally!

Strategies for Improvement

Practice, goal setting, and obtaining feedback can help you improve your observational skills. Experience with teaching allows you to focus on observation: Management becomes automatic and you master the lesson content so that it no longer demands your full attention. In addition, more experienced teachers know what to look for, which makes observation more effective. Student teachers frequently report seeing much more during an observation of another teacher's lesson after, rather than before, student teaching.

To develop observational skills, first select an objective for the observation. Begin with a specific target—for instance, the same foot leading in galloping. Second, observe several children doing the activity and then close your eyes and recall the performance of three of the children. Third, watch those three again and see if your were correct in your recollection. As you master observing and remembering the performance of three children, challenge yourself with remembering that of five or seven students. Gradually shift to remembering only those who did not succeed on the task; in other words, begin to see those who are "outliers." You may want to group students in your mind: those succeeding, those needing specific work, and those needing practice on every aspect of the skill. With practice, you can observe and remember which children did not master the skill objective or demonstrated unacceptable behavior and whether there were trouble spots in the lesson itself (e.g., safety or management issues). The key to expert observation is knowing what you are looking for before the observation.

Videotaped teaching allows you to observe the lesson and see what actually happened. This can provide feedback and guide improvement. A peer or mentor can also provide feedback that can help improve your observational skills. This occurs frequently during field experience and student teaching when your supervisor asks, "What did you notice about the two girls in the front row during the warm-up?" or points to a child who needs special help during practice. They are guiding you to observe what they observe. Practice, with challenging goals and feedback, results in better observation. For example, your cooperating teacher during student teaching may say, "Next time you teach, I want you to say something to the students—so I know you see them—every time one steps outside the boundaries." Seeing more allows you to provide more information to the children so that they learn more.

Directions and Demonstrations

Directions, or instructions to the students, are one way to communicate what you want them to do. Instructions should be limited to three or fewer

actions (Gallagher, French, Thomas, and Thomas 2002; Rink 1996), for example, "First person in each line, move across the gym, pick up a ball, and return to your place." Another example is "Step, then hop; do this on each foot." According to the age and skill of the students, your instructions can be more detailed and can sometimes be increased in number. Associate instructions with cues that serve as reminders of larger ideas. The cue for the previous example is "step hop" and, as skill increases, "skip." Instructions often include examples or stories; these metaphors help children get the whole idea. After giving an example, review the steps or instructions again: "Remember three important things: (1) Move under control. (2) Change levels. (3) On the signal, change directions." Follow with the cues "control," "levels," and " directions."

Demonstrations, or the use of models, have been the focus of motor learning research. As a result, several important guidelines suggest which student to use as the model, how often to use a model, and when to use the model (Thomas 1994):

- Correct demonstrations are important.

- Demonstrations help children understand what to do the first time they try something new; models presented before practice help the most.

- Limit demonstrations to three; then allow practice.

- Once a skill has been stabilized, use additional demonstrations to help older children.

- Help the children know what to look for (e.g., watch their feet).

- Use peer models, which are effective for learning and motivation when the demonstration is correct.

- Avoid expert models, which may not be helpful because children can be intimidated by advanced skill.

Reinforcement and Feedback

Reinforcement, or encouragement, is important to students in three ways. First, it lets them know you are watching. Second, it lets them know that you care about their learning and effort. Third, encouragement suggests that you believe the children are capable of learning the task. The best situation for reinforcement is to use the sandwich technique, which combines reinforcement with feedback. Feedback is information that specifically identi-

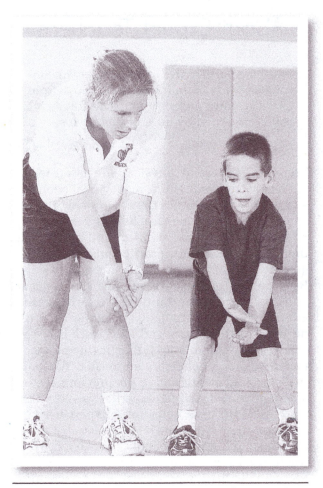

Demonstrations require you to model proper form in performing skills.

fies errors in skill execution or correct aspects of skill. The sandwich technique provides positive reinforcement with corrective feedback, followed by reinforcement, for example: "Good try; now take a bigger step. I know you can do it!"

Feedback is one of the two most important learning variables (practice is the other) and is one of the most difficult for teachers to master. Children associate feedback with skill development, which is important to them. Therefore, even though correcting errors may be difficult for you—probably because it feels negative—this is an important part of teaching. Generally, you will find it easier to correct misbehaviors than errors in skill (Gallagher et al. 2002; Rink 1996; Thomas 1994). The implication is that skill errors are not under the child's control, whereas behavior is. Consider this another way. Children who receive corrective feedback gain control over their skill; without feedback, children clearly do not have control. Feedback is empowering. Use the sandwich technique to make feedback a positive experience.

Because feedback and practice help children learn and are therefore important issues for you, explore them carefully. Observe a teacher and record his or her practice, feedback, and reinforcement behaviors, or ask someone to watch your teaching and to use the recording sheet in table 13.3. The object is to provide each child with many practice trials and to provide feedback as often as possible to each child.

Table 13.3 Feedback and Practice

An observer should record the practice and feedback that you provide during a lesson. Record the number of trials, corrective feedback, and reinforcing feedback for each student in the appropriate box.

Name	Number of trials	Corrections	Reinforcements

Effective and Expert Teachers

Expert teachers are opportunistic, which means they take advantage of an unplanned situation and use it as a **teachable moment**. Leadership, sportsmanship, and behavior are often best learned during teachable moments. You can also convey sport strategies through unplanned events. Clearly, you must plan for teaching content but should also use unplanned opportunities to enhance learning. Experienced teachers use these opportunities more frequently than do beginning teachers. Reflection is one way to develop these skills: At the end of the class or of the day, you may realize that you missed a teachable moment. That is okay, as long as you use this to prime yourself for the next time a similar teachable moment occurs. More information about using reflection to improve your teaching is presented in chapter 15, Growing as a Teacher.

Concepts Into Practice

In his first kindergarten class of the morning, Ben introduced the concept of energy balance (i.e., calories in versus calories out) by relating snacks to activities. He asked the children what snacks they ate after school and what physical activities they enjoyed at home. The children did not name a snack until he specified, "What do you eat when you get home from school?" Then children mentioned cookies, juice, and chips. Several children offered activities such as gymnastics, soccer, and bike riding; then one boy said Monopoly. Ben then told the class that each time they moved—played sports or exercised—they used energy from the foods they ate, so eating was important for being able to play. After class, Ben realized he had missed a teachable moment, so he revised his lesson for the second class and was ready in case another opportunity presented itself. In the second class, Ben said, "After school, I am hungry and I usually eat a few of those baby carrots as a snack. Do any of you eat snacks after school?" Many children responded; several said, "Carrots." Then Ben asked about sports and activities. When a girl answered, "Playing Barbie," Ben was ready. He said, "I am sure playing with dolls is fun, but it is not very active. I bet you also ride a bike or play tag—those are more active!" He gave the girl a chance to respond and praised her for understanding the concept. Ben reflected, corrected, and used the teachable moment.

About Expert Teachers

"Each has an effortless, fluid, largely unconscious quality to their work that results from a certain automaticity and comfort level seldom reached by most of their peers."

—*Dodds (1994)*

The effectiveness of physical education teachers has been examined in many ways (Housner and Griffey 1985; Ennis 1994). However, the key characteristic of expert teachers is automaticity. Expert teachers use, monitor, and revise routines for management, practice, and instruction quickly and effectively, often while multitasking. Because the routines are efficient and demand so little cognitive attention, these behaviors are described as automatic. Teaching expertise develops with practice and hard work over several years (Graham 2001). Practice (experience) helps make the behaviors automatic. Although the behaviors mentioned in the previous section are important, teaching expertise is more than a series of discrete behaviors. Expert teachers automate those behaviors into routines that can be adapted quickly and accurately as needed. Thus, teaching begins as a set of skills, similar to those presented in the previous section (e.g., scanning, feedback). In addition, these teaching skills are combined with knowledge of the content (e.g., knowledge about physical activities). As a result, you can progress from declarative knowledge to procedural knowledge; that is, you know what to do first and, after practice, develop if-then-do routines. Ten characteristics of experts are listed in figure 13.2.

Expert teachers typically begin class with a review. For example, in an algebra class, the teacher might review the assigned and completed homework before going on to the next topic. The purpose is to determine whether the students understand and are ready for more difficult information. If students are not ready based on the review, the teacher provides additional instruction or practice before moving on. At other times, when students indicate readiness, the teacher uses a review to set the stage for the new information. Expert teachers often end class with a "teaser" by using homework or today's content to introduce what will happen in the next class and to pique student interest.

Expert teachers are proactive and take more time to make decisions than novices. For example, at the beginning of the year, expert teachers may

Characteristics of Experts

1. Novices tend to hold literal views of objects and events, whereas experts make inferences about these objects and events. Experts are better able to make predictions than novices.
2. Experts categorize problems to be solved at a higher level, whereas novices categorize problems by the surface characteristics of the problem.
3. Experts have extraordinarily fast and accurate pattern recognitions.
4. Experts may be slower than novices in the initial stages of problem solving.
5. Experts are sensitive to the task demands and social structure of the job situation.
6. Experts have been shown to be opportunistic planners.
7. Experts show self-regulatory or metacognitive capabilities that are not present in less experienced learners.
8. Experts develop their expertise over long periods.
9. Experts have knowledge that shows up in relation to the goal structure of the problem.
10. Experts possess a higher level of sport-specific motor skills as sport participants, compared to novices.

Figure 13.2 Ten characteristics of expert teachers.

devote several class periods to student routines, whereas novice teachers tend to start immediately with content. Novices often have control problems, which interfere with student learning. The time that expert teachers spend establishing routines allows for more learning in the long term. Expert teachers take more time to make decisions but less time to implement the action plan based on the decision compared with novices. Experts may reflect on a problem longer; this is most likely related to two other characteristics of experts. First, unlike novices, experts rarely make judgments based on surface characteristics—the way something looks. The novice may see several children standing in a group and assume that the group is off task, but the expert may see that the groups are actually working strategically or trying to solve a problem. Second, experts tend to categorize problems at a higher level and make accurate predictions. In order to do so, they probably need more time.

Novice teachers have less experience on which to make decisions and less knowledge; therefore, they can make more rapid—but often poor—decisions. Expert teachers deliberately spend time trying to improve their teaching (instruction, planning, and evaluation). Expert teachers take advantage of the teachable moment and plan for maximal learning. Expert teachers want to see the instructional setting and plan around those constraints (along with others, such as equipment and time). Experts recognize the impact of those factors on instruction (figure 13.3).

Berliner (1994) presents a five-stage model for teacher expertise:

- Novices are student teachers and new teachers (stage 1); context-free rules are essential for them.
- Advanced beginner teachers (stage 2) are those in year two or three of teaching; they

```
Novice . . . . . . . . . . . . . . . . . . . . . . . . .deliberate
Advanced beginner . . . . . . . . . . . . . .insightful
Competent performer . . . . . . . . . . . . . .rational
Proficient performer . . . . . . . . . . . . . .intuitive
Expert . . . . . . . . . . . . . . . . . . . . . . . . .arational (beyond rational rules)
```

Figure 13.3 Berliner's five-stage model.

combine experience with verbal knowledge.

- Competent teachers (stage 3) emerge by year four; they make good decisions and know what is important.

- Some teachers become proficient performers (stage 4) by year five; they use intuition, procedures, and pattern recognition.

- Expert teachers (stage 5) are characterized by fluid performance; decisions are automatically rapid and accurate.

As student teachers and new teachers (stage 1), novices are taught definitions and context-free rules. Context-free rules are generalized in order to fit almost any situation; in other words, one size fits all. Experience is more important to novices than verbal information. The list of seven considerations for demonstrations and the guidelines on where to stand during class that were presented earlier in this chapter are examples of context-free rules. This is essential for novice teachers, although not sufficient for expertise. Advanced beginner teachers are in stage 2, which occurs in years two and three. At this stage, teachers combine experience with verbal knowledge and continue to gather experience. New teachers sometimes fail to find solutions for problem situations, but, after two or three exposures to these situations, the advanced beginner has a solution and is learning when to follow and break those context-free rules. In stages 1 and 2, teachers do not accept full responsibility for their actions, and they are not fully directing instruction. Stage 3, the competent teacher, is achieved by most fourth-year teachers. Competent teachers make good choices about what to do and how to achieve goals, and they can distinguish between what is important and what is not important. This stage is characterized by emotional responses to success and failure and full acceptance of responsibility. A few teachers become proficient performers (stage 4) at about year five. Intuition, procedures, and pattern recognition are new characteristics of this stage; decision making is still deliberate. The expert level (stage 5) is primarily distinguished from the proficient level by the fluid performance of the expert. The expert is not deliberate, but automatic. The expert seems to operate on intuition because decisions are rapid and accurate. Experts tend to monitor or reflect on problems, but not on successes. For example, expert physical education teachers break the rules by moving into the center of the gym; they evaluate more frequently and are

Expert teachers are opportunistic, taking advantage of teachable moments to enhance learning.

better prepared to complete complex teaching scenarios such as cooperative learning and peer tutoring. Thus, the expert teacher may bypass the most rational approach—in other words, he or she does not always follow the rules that have been established as a "safety net" for less experienced teachers.

Four categories of pedagogical knowledge have been identified by Grossman (1990):

1. The teacher understands how to accommodate instruction to the developmental level of the student (e.g., cognitive, emotional, social, and physical development).

2. The teacher understands what the student knows about the skill—correct and incorrect information—and the context in which the skill is used.

3. The teacher can select and apply curricular knowledge of a skill so that students practice the skill.

4. The teacher has multiple strategies for teaching content such as sports, dance, fitness, fundamental movements, and knowledge.

These four categories of knowledge apply to all teachers and work well with the standards of the Interstate New Teacher Assessment and Support Consortium (INTASC) presented in chapter 1, Health and Developmental Benefits of Physical Education. You need to be able to apply knowledge of your field and of child development. Furthermore, you must have and apply specific pedagogical knowledge of management, instruction, curriculum, and evaluation. "Apply" means to use during instruction when students are present. So, although the chapters in this book may be discrete areas of information, each is designed to work with the other chapters to provide the knowledge that you need to be a proficient or expert teacher. It is possible to learn to become an expert teacher, but moving through the stages of teaching takes time and effort. Therefore, set challenging but realistic goals for your teaching. The following are examples of instructional goals for a class:

- To provide concise instructions so that most students (except one or two at most) follow the instructions the first time

- To provide one to three correct demonstrations per skill

- To provide a cue for each skill

- To provide specific feedback about the skill to at least two students using the sandwich technique

- To provide at least 10 practice trials for each student (for most skill activities)

- To name, touch, or make eye contact with every student in the class (other than when taking attendance)

- To stand where all students can see and be seen

- To scan the class during practice every 6 seconds

- To evaluate student learning for each skill (the percentage of the students who were able to do the skill effectively)

Summary

Teaching depends on planning and comprises personality and instruction. Instructional variables include directions (instructions), cues, demonstrations (modeling), feedback, evaluation, teacher position, and observation. Personality variables include voice, body language, eye contact, and facial expression. Each of these important variables contributes in varying degrees to your success. For example, one teacher may be an expert in planning lessons for maximal learning but is rather boring. Another teacher may be entertaining and able to adjust instruction during the lesson, which is necessary because his or her planning is relatively weak. Optimally, a teacher is strong in all areas, but, practically speaking, you must take advantage of your strengths and minimize your weaknesses. Furthermore, at all levels from novice to expert, you must plan, work, and reflect to continue improving. To be effective, you must integrate what you know about children, the content, and teaching. Effectiveness increases with practice when you reflect and select goals for improvement.

Mastery Learning Activities

1. Create a paired adjective list with characteristics of teachers. On the left are descriptors of ineffective teachers, on the right, descriptors of effective teachers. Here is an example:

   Unprepared   Prepared

2. Make a list of as many ways as possible that you can interact with students to demonstrate that you like them.

3. List as many different ways as possible to say each of the following:

   good effort

   good work

   good citizenship

   good behavior

4. Write a series of specific objectives for yourself, directed at developing teaching skills. The objectives should show progression (become increasingly demanding) and be focused on one of the teaching behaviors.

5. Describe your personality. Which characteristics are strengths or weaknesses as a teacher? What can you do to make the most of your strengths?

6. Observe a physical education class. From memory, recall skill details for five students. Alternatively, after teaching a physical education lesson, identify one student each with high, average, and low skill.

7. Observe a physical education teacher. How many of the characteristics of expert teachers did you see?

References

Berliner, D.C. 1994. Expertise, the wonder of exemplary performance. In *Creating powerful thinking in teachers and students,* edited by J.N. Mangieri and C.C. Block, 161-186. Fort Worth, TX: Holt, Rinehart and Winston.

Dodds, P. 1994. Cognitive and behavioral components of expertise in teaching physical education. *Quest* 46: 153-163.

Ennis, C.D. 1994. Knowledge and beliefs underlying curricular expertise. *Quest* 46: 164-175.

Gallagher, J.D., K.E. French, K.T. Thomas, and J.R. Thomas. 2002. Expertise in sport: Relations between skill and knowledge. In *Children and youth in sport,* 2nd ed., edited by F.L. Smoll and R.E. Smith, 475-500. Dubuque, IA: Kendall/Hunt.

Graham, G. 2001. *Teaching children physical education: Becoming a master teacher.* 2nd ed. Champaign, IL: Human Kinetics.

Grossman, P.L. 1990. *The making of a teacher: Teacher knowledge and teacher education.* New York: Teachers College Press.

Housner, L.D., and D.C. Griffey. 1985. Teacher cognition: Differences in planning and interactive decision making between experienced and inexperienced teachers. *Research Quarterly for Exercise and Sport* 56: 44-53.

Passer, M.W., and B.J. Wilson. 2002. At what age are children ready to compete? In *Children and youth in sport: A biopsychosocial perspective,* edited by F.L. Smoll and R.E. Smith, 83-103. Dubuque, IA: Kendall/Hunt.

Rink, J. 1996. Effective instruction in physical education. In *Student learning in physical education: Applying research to enhance instruction,* edited by S.J. Silverman and C.D. Ennis, 171-198. Champaign, IL: Human Kinetics.

Thomas, K.T. 1994. The development of expertise: From Leeds to Legend. *Quest* 46: 199-210.

Resources

Berliner, D. 1986. In search of the expert pedagogue. *The Educational Researcher* 15: 5-13.

Lesson Plans

The following lesson plans represent the use of instructions, demonstration, and cues. In the gymnastics lesson for grades K and 1, notice how instructions and demonstration are used to give the children the idea of each skill. This is followed by practice, which uses cues or instructions. The skills are generally practiced using the whole method. For safety, a few children do each skill while you provide guidance and keep control. At the end of the lesson, the children are challenged to practice the skill that was most difficult—in other words, the skill that needs the most practice. For the gymnastics lesson for grades 2 and 3, the instruction is similar in format, but notice that the skill expectations are higher. At the end of the lesson, children are asked to practice a variety of skills rather than focus on the most difficult. Two lessons for grades 4 and 5 are presented. Notice how new skills are presented similarly to those for the previous grades. At the end of the lesson, students are asked questions about the important parts of the skill and are asked to assist peers with skill analysis and combining skills. Responsibility and freedom are encouraged in older, more experienced students.

The rhythmic lesson for grades K and 1 allows you to observe children. Observe for following instructions, for skill (e.g., keeping the beat), for creativity (e.g., walking and creating movements to the beat), or for remembering (sequence of four movements to a beat). For grades 2 and 3, the lesson affords similar opportunities to observe children. In grades 4 and 5, the lesson focuses on learning and using a simple dance step, the Schottische. If you are well organized and give good instruction (directions, cues, and demonstrations), students succeed. If students have trouble with this lesson, reflect on your teaching. At the end of the lesson, observe students for understanding and creativity.

Lesson 13.1

Pretumbling and Animal Walks

Student Objectives 1 2 5

- Take turns practicing.
- Follow the safety rule of waiting for a turn.
- Perform one additional Animal Walk and one new balance activity.
- State the cues for the Forward Roll.

Equipment and Materials

- 1 mat (4 by 8 feet [1.2 by 2.4 m]) per group
- 1 jump rope per mat
- Background music (optional)

Safety Tip

- During practice time, stop the music as a signal for children to sit and get organized.

Warm-Up Activities (7 minutes)

Use I See from lesson 8.1, page 216.

Skill-Development Activities (18 minutes)

Bear Walk

Arrange small groups of children, each at a mat. Remind the children that there should be only one child practicing at a time on each mat.

1. Describe and demonstrate the stunt: "With your hands on the floor and arms and legs straight, move one hand and then the foot on that side, then the other hand, then the foot on that side, rolling your body and 'lumbering' while walking."

2. Have the children practice the Bear Walk.

Puppy Run

Keep the same setup.

1. Describe and demonstrate the skill:
   - Bend your knees, crouching down on all fours.
   - Let your hands support some of your body weight; look forward, and run.
   - Now sit and lie on the floor like a dog.

2. Have the children practice the Puppy Run.

Lesson 13.1 *(continued)*

Animal Walk Game

Have groups of 4 to 6 children line up.

1. Describe and demonstrate the game:
   - The first child in each line begins to walk like an animal. The rest of the children in the group follow.
   - The leader changes to another animal walk, and each child in that line follows.
   - I will surprise you and (at random times) call out the name of the animal walk a group is doing. When a group's animal walk is called out, the first child in that line goes to the end of the line, and the second child becomes the leader.

2. Have the children play the Animal Walk Game.

3. Variations: "Does a cat move the same way as a dog?" Cue the ideas of stretching, moving quietly, and dragging the feet a bit pigeon-toed. Have the children move like cats. Then have half of the children be cats and the other half be dogs. "How do cats and dogs play together? How does an injured dog move? Sometimes they run on three legs or limp on one of the four." Have the children move like an injured dog.

Rocker, One-Leg Balance, Log Roll

ROCKER

Arrange small groups of children, each at a mat. The children take turns practicing, so line them up to emphasize that only one child goes at a time.

1. Describe and demonstrate the skill:
   - Begin in a tight tuck while sitting with hands and arms tightly holding knees, chin on chest, and forehead against knees; roll backward onto your back.
   - While your body weight is on your shoulders, change the direction of the roll and rock back toward your feet until your bottom and feet are the only parts touching the ground. Continue rocking from your bottom and feet to your shoulders, and then reverse.

2. Have the children practice the Rocker. Cue the children: "As you rock, try to get your shoulders off the mat and then your legs and hips off the mat."

ONE-LEG BALANCE

Continue with the same setup.

1. Describe and demonstrate the skill:
   - Standing with your hands on your hips or waist, lift your left foot and place it against your right knee.
   - Stand in this position for as long as possible.
   - Then repeat, touching your right foot to your left knee.

2. Have the children practice the One-Leg Balance. Give the children this tip: "Look at a place on the wall to maintain your balance."

LOG ROLL

Continue with the same setup; remind the children to take turns practicing one at a time.

1. Describe and demonstrate the stunt:
   - Lying on one side, with your arms and legs together and stretched out (extended), roll onto your tummy and quickly over onto your other side; continuing rolling over until you reach the other end of the mat.
   - Start the rolling motion by turning your head and shoulders and then your trunk and legs. Your hands and feet should not push to turn your body.

2. Have the children practice the Log Roll with their heads all in the same direction.

3. Have the children repeat the Log Roll, but rolling in the opposite direction. Cue the children: "Keep your arms and legs straight."

Forehead Touch

Continue with the same setup.

1. Describe and demonstrate the stunt: "Kneeling with hands joined behind your back, slowly lower your head and chest until your forehead touches the mat. Keep your hands behind your back. Keep your knees and feet together throughout the whole movement."
2. Have the children practice the Forehead Touch.
3. If children are having trouble with this stunt, especially overbalancing to avoid hitting their heads, allow them to practice a few times with one hand behind their backs and the other in front of them on the mat. But allow them to support their weight with one finger only!
4. Remind the children: "Be sure that your knees and feet are together throughout. Be sure to keep your hands behind you. Go slowly!"

Tightrope

Keep the same setup, but place 1 jump rope at each mat.

1. Describe and demonstrate the skill, relating it to the circus tightrope walking, which some children may be familiar with: "Walk on the jump rope as though it were above the ground, trying not to step off." Ask the children: "What helps us balance?" Demonstrate balancing by using arms, looking at a spot, and watching the rope about 18 inches (45 cm) in front of your feet.
2. Have the children practice walking the Tightrope. Remind children to use their arms to balance.
3. Variation: Expand the activity by making the rope curved, wiggly, and into other shapes.

Forward Roll

Keep the same setup.

1. Describe and have a child demonstrate the skill:
   - Begin in a squat with your hands on the mat shoulder-width apart and your chin on your chest; look at your tummy.
   - Bend your arms to bring your shoulders closer to the mat, overbalance, roll onto your shoulders, and continue to roll with your legs tucked.
   - Keep your heels close to your bottom and your knees close to your chest until your feet touch the ground and you are squatting again. (Discuss variations presented later for the take-off, roll, and landing phases. See lesson plan 13.6, page 392.)
2. Have the children practice the Forward Roll. Cue each child in line: "Bend, hands on mat. Look at tummy. Straighten legs and roll onto your back. Stand up." Or tell them: "Hands on mat, chin on chest, bend arms, and straighten legs. Roll."
3. Remind the children: "Land on your back."
4. Don't worry if the children do not get all of the way around to their feet. Stress the landing on their shoulders and keeping their heads out of the way.

Concluding Activities (5 minutes)

Regroup the children on mats according to what they need to practice (e.g., put those practicing the Tightrope on one mat, the Log Roll on another, and the Rocker on another).

Use this time to observe skills and offer individual instruction.

From K.T. Thomas, A.M. Lee, and J.R. Thomas, 2008, *Physical education methods for elementary teachers*, 3rd ed. (Champaign, IL: Human Kinetics). Adapted, by permission, from K.T. Thomas, A.M. Lee, and J.R. Thomas, 2000, *Physical education for children: Daily lesson plans for elementary school*, 2nd ed. (Champaign, IL: Human Kinetics), 273-275.

Lesson 13.2

Keeping Time to a Beat

Student Objectives 1

- Move body parts to a beat.
- Step in place to a beat.
- Tap rhythm sticks to a beat.

Equipment and Materials

- 1 drum
- Music: "Sunshine" from *Modern Tunes for Rhythm and Instruments*, Hap Palmer (AR 523)
- 2 rhythm sticks per child

Warm-Up Activities (5 minutes)

Fitness Circle

Arrange the children in a large circle.

1. Have the children move continuously in a large circle, counterclockwise, changing movements on a drum beat or other signal. Cue the children: for example, "Walk with big steps, walk with tiny steps, run, walk on all fours, jump, hop, run lifting knees high, skip, leap."
2. Use a drumbeat to set the pace once the children have the idea of keeping a beat.
3. Speed up the movement by speeding up the drumbeat.
4. Stop the drum, stopping the movement to change movement patterns.

Skill-Development Activities (20 minutes)

Keeping Time to a Beat

Have the children sit down, still in a large circle.

1. Play a rhythmic pattern on the drum as follows, providing a continuous sound, so that the underlying beat is evident, and varying the tempo (speed):
   - Clap your hands to keep the beat.
   - Tap your hands on your thighs (your shoulders, the floor) to keep the beat.
   - Tap your feet on the floor.
   - Move your head (shoulders, elbows, fingers) to the beat.
   - Make punching movements overhead (in front of your body, to the side of your body) with your arms to the beat.
2. Keep the rhythmic pattern going on the drum.
3. Keep encouraging the children to keep the beat.
4. Repeat all methods of keeping the beat to the song "Sunshine."

Extension Activities (5 to 10 minutes)

Keep the children in a large circle.

1. Tell the children: "Walk in a circle to the beat, creating body movements to the beat of the music."
2. Ask the children to create other ways to keep time to the beat.

Concluding Activities (5 minutes)

Movement to a Beat

Arrange the children in a large circle.

1. Play "Sunshine" and have the children perform the following sequence:
   - 8 steps in place.
   - 8 claps.
   - 4 punch movements overhead.
   - 4 punch movements forward.
2. Repeat 4 punches overhead and 4 punches forward.
3. Repeat the entire sequence.

From K.T. Thomas, A.M. Lee, and J.R. Thomas, 2008, *Physical education methods for elementary teachers*, 3rd ed. (Champaign, IL: Human Kinetics). Adapted, by permission, from K.T. Thomas, A.M. Lee, and J.R. Thomas, 2000, *Physical education for children: Daily lesson plans for elementary school*, 2nd ed. (Champaign, IL: Human Kinetics), 200-201.

Lesson 13.3

Locomotor and Tumbling Skills

Student Objectives   1

- Complete a Forehead Touch, a Forward Roll, or a Donkey Kick.
- Maintain a balance position after executing a locomotor pattern.
- State the reason for the head position when doing the Forward Roll.

Equipment and Materials

- 1 or more mats (4 by 8 feet [1.2 by 2.4 m]) per group
- Background music (optional)

Safety Tips

Review the class rules and the following safety rules:

- Rule 1: Take turns. Only one child should be on a mat at a time. Take a turn and then allow the next child to have a turn.
- Rule 2: Do all of the tumbling on a mat.
- Rule 3: Stay at your mat until I tell you to move.
- Rule 4: Keep your hands to yourself.
- Rule 5: Perform only those activities that are assigned to the mat.
- Rule 6: Be a good spotter.

Warm-Up Activities (5 to 7 minutes)

Listen and Move

1. Give the following instructions as quickly as the children can complete the tasks:
   - Run 20 steps to the right.
   - Make 10 big arm circles.
   - Run 20 steps to the left.
   - Touch your toes (bend knees slightly) and then reach for the sky. (Repeat 5 times.)
   - Slide 10 steps to the right.
   - Skip 10 skips forward.
   - Jump as high as you can 10 times.
   - Hop backward 20 hops on your right foot and then on your left foot.
   - Twist your torso right and then left. (Repeat 5 times.)
2. Repeat the entire sequence at least once.

Warm-Up Routine

STRETCHES

Arrange the children in a long line on one side of the mat.

- **Head Stretches.** Slowly move your head while providing support with your hands (chin to chest and up, ear to shoulder and up, ear to opposite shoulder and up, chin on chest). Repeat. Place your hands with palms above ears, fingers over top of skull.
- **Shoulder Circles.** Roll your shoulders in circles forward and then backward (hands on hips).
- **Torso Stretch.** With arms extended overhead, stretch to the side, rear, opposite side, and front.
- **Hamstring Stretch.** Bend to a squat position with hands on the floor in front of your body and then slowly straighten your legs upward until your knees are only slightly bent.
- **Ankle Rotations.** Sitting on the floor, with legs extended in a "V" position in front, move your ankles so that your feet and toes make circles.
- **Back Arch.** Rolling over onto your tummy, with your legs stretched out (extended) and together behind and your arms extended in front, look up to the ceiling, and lift your legs and feet as high as possible. Keep your tummy on the floor and your legs straight and together.
- **Crunches.** Do as many Crunches as possible, up to 20. Bend your knees, place your fingers near your ears, with your hips at 90 degrees (making a corner of a square) and your feet over your hips or abdomen.
- **Push-Ups.** Do as many Push-Ups as possible, up to 10. Keep your body straight, with your arms bending at the elbows to raise and lower your body.
- **Locomotor.** Arrange the children in a large circle.
- **Skip Clockwise.** Skip 24 steps clockwise (point) and then go the other way and do 24 skips counterclockwise (point).
- **Vertical Jumps.** Jump straight up, 5 to 10 inches (13 to 25 cm) high (show height clearly).
- **Jog or Run.** Try to jog or run in the circle for 1 minute without stopping.

Warm-Up Routine for Grades 2 and 3

Arrange the children in a line along one side of the mat.

1. Teach all parts of the warm-up as a routine.
2. Have the children perform the following sequence of steps:
   - Do Head Stretches right and left.
   - Do Shoulder Circles forward (3 times) and backward (3 times).
   - Do a Torso Stretch (side, back, side, front); repeat 3 times.
   - Do a Hamstring Stretch (squat to straighten); repeat 5 times.
   - Do Ankle Rotations inward (3 times) and outward (3 times).
   - Do 5 Back Arches.
   - Do 20 Crunches.
   - Do 10 Push-Ups.
   - (Move the children into a circle formation.)
   - Skip 24 skips clockwise and 24 counterclockwise.
   - Do 10 Vertical Jumps.
   - Run around the circle continuously for 1 minute.

Skill-Development Activities (18 to 20 minutes)

Review the safety rules before introducing the new skills.

Lesson 13.3 *(continued)*

Forehead Touch

Arrange small groups of children at the mats. If there is no danger of children bumping into each other or falling off the mats, allow two or three children on a mat at once—for this stunt only.

1. Describe and demonstrate the stunt:
   - Kneel with your feet and knees tightly together and your hands clasped behind your back.
   - Slowly lower your head until your forehead touches the mat.
   - To finish, rise back to the kneeling position without using your hands for balance or support.
2. Have the children practice the Forehead Touch.

Forward Roll

Arrange the children in small groups; each child is in a line at the side of the mat.

1. Describe and demonstrate the stunt:
   - Begin by squatting on the mat, with your hands placed just in front of and outside your feet and your arms placed outside your legs.
   - In one motion, straighten your legs (look at your tummy with your chin on your chest if possible) and shift about half of your body weight onto your hands and arms.
   - Bend your arms to support more weight until you are using only your feet for balance.
   - Then move your hips above your shoulders and forward.
   - At some point, your hips overbalance, and your body rolls forward.
   - Land on your shoulder blades.
2. Have the children practice the Forward Roll. Tell the children: "Keep your chin tucked close to your chest. The momentum carries your body around in a circle, but your legs must stay tucked tightly. Keep your whole body curled into a ball to help you roll!"
3. Ask the children: "What is the correct head position for the Forward Roll?" (Chin tucked.)
4. Ask them: "Why is this position important?" (To protect the head and neck, especially to keep the head from suffering impact during the roll.)

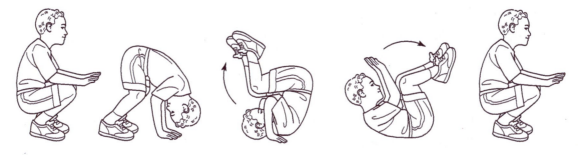

Donkey Kick

Continue with small groups, with only one child at a mat.

1. Describe and demonstrate the stunt:
   - The object of this task is to get both feet off the mat at the same time and to support all of your body weight with your hands.
   - Begin by standing in the middle of the mat, facing the length of the mat. Place both hands on the mat about shoulder-width apart.
   - Keep your arms straight, but bend your legs slightly. Let your hands carry some of your body weight.

- As you kick your feet up and back, take all of your weight on your hands. Keep your eyes focused on the mat directly between your hands.
- Be careful not to kick very hard because this may cause overbalancing and you may flip over onto your back. The purpose is to get both feet off the ground and support your weight with your arms, not to get into a vertical position (45 degrees is safer).

2. Have the children practice the Donkey Kick.

Concluding Activities (5 minutes)

Pretumbling Skills

Review with the children the skills practiced earlier (basic Leap, Log Roll, Rocker, One-Legged Balance, and Needle Scale).

1. Ask the first child in line at each mat to select and perform one of those stunts.
2. Then the next child has to perform another stunt, and so on, until each child has had a turn.
3. If there is time, rotate to another first child in line and repeat. You may want to incorporate the tumbling from today's lesson as well.

From K.T. Thomas, A.M. Lee, and J.R. Thomas, 2008, *Physical education methods for elementary teachers*, 3rd ed. (Champaign, IL: Human Kinetics). Adapted, by permission, from K.T. Thomas, A.M. Lee, and J.R. Thomas, 2000, *Physical education for children: Daily lesson plans for elementary school*, 2nd ed. (Champaign, IL: Human Kinetics), 624-626.

Lesson 13.4

Tumbling

Student Objectives   1

- Demonstrate balancing in various positions and on various body parts.
- Practice and refine the basic rolls.
- Observe and evaluate the technique of a partner.
- Create a movement sequence.

Equipment and Materials

- 1 or more mats (4 by 8 feet [1.2 by 2.4 m]) per group

Warm-Up Activities (5 to 7 minutes)

Use Movement to Sounds from lesson 4.4, page 89.

Skill-Development Activities (18 to 20 minutes)

Organize small groups of children, and assign each group to a mat for each activity.

1. Describe and demonstrate the Two-Knee Balance, V-Sit, and 360-Degree Turn.
2. Have the children practice each stunt.

Two-Knee Balance

Kneeling with feet extended behind and hips straight, lift your feet off the mat and balance on your knees only.

V-Sit

Sit and lift your legs straight and together as high as possible, with your torso forming the other side of the V.

360-Degree Turn

Begin, standing still and straight. Bend your knees and rotate your arms and torso away from the direction you are planning to turn. Jump up and turn your head, torso, and arms as hard as possible in the direction of the turn. Land on both feet.

Skill Practice

Create partners within the small groups, and continue with each group at a mat.

1. Have the children practice the Forward Roll, Straddle Forward Roll, Backward Roll, Straddle Backward Roll, Heel Slap, Run and Take-Off, Needle Scale, and Regular and Straddle Splits. Say to the children: "Observe your partner to see if he or she is using the correct technique."
2. Ask the children: "Are there pointers you can give your partner about technique? For example, you might say, 'Your head was tucked on the roll, but you crossed your ankles.'"

Concluding Activities (5 minutes)

Movement Challenges That Combine Skills

1. Challenge the children with the following movement combinations:
   - A Forward Roll, immediately followed with a Backward Roll
   - Backward roll from straddle to straddle and then a Straddle Forward Roll
   - A regular scale into a Needle Scale
2. Have the children create their own combinations.

From K.T. Thomas, A.M. Lee, and J.R. Thomas, 2008, *Physical education methods for elementary teachers*, 3rd ed. (Champaign, IL: Human Kinetics). Adapted, by permission, from K.T. Thomas, A.M. Lee, and J.R. Thomas, 2000, *Physical education for children: Daily lesson plans for elementary school*, 2nd ed. (Champaign, IL: Human Kinetics), 1024-1026.

Lesson 13.5

Body Shapes and Levels

Student Objectives 1 6

- Create movements at various levels.
- Create a short dance using body shapes and levels.

Equipment and Materials

- 1 drum

Warm-Up Activities (5 minutes)

Use Magic Movements from lesson 8.5, page 226.

Skill-Development Activities (20 minutes)

Levels and Collapse

Gather the children into an information formation.

1. Describe and demonstrate levels: "Movement can occur at various heights: high, medium, and low (e.g., on tiptoe, normal standing, and squatting)."
2. Describe and demonstrate collapse: "Drop to the floor, letting gravity pull you down in a way that looks as if you have no bones."

Movement Challenges

Arrange the children in scatter formation.

1. Tell the children: "Stretch high and, on the signal (drum beat), collapse to the floor."
2. Repeat rapidly.
3. Repeat slowly.
4. Tell the children: "Pretend you are a puppet and the puppet master is pulling your strings to lift you tall and high. All of a sudden, the strings begin to break. Collapse your wrists, your arms, your head, your shoulders, and your legs."
5. Challenge the children with the following tasks:
   - Make another stretched shape and, on the signal, collapse into a low shape.
   - Pretend that you are a block of ice melting.
   - Combine four walking steps, a high shape, and a low shape. Cue the children: "Walk, walk, walk, walk, high shape, low shape." Repeat, having the children jump (hop, leap, skip).
   - Make a medium shape.
   - Each time you hear a drum beat, show me another shape. Try wide, narrow, big, and small shapes. Beat the drum while the children practice making shapes.

○ Combine four walking steps and then a high shape (a medium shape, a low shape). Repeat, having the children jump (hop, turn, leap).

Concluding Activities (5 minutes)

Have each child create a rhythmic activity, using walking, jumping, or hopping and a high, medium, or low shape.

Lesson 13.6

Tumbling

Student Objectives   1

- Change directions while skipping.
- Combine running and leaping and running and jumping.

Equipment and Materials

- 1 or more mats (4 by 8 feet [1.2 by 2.4 m]) per group
- 1 yardstick or ruler
- Paper and pencil

Warm-Up Activities (5 to 7 minutes)

Use Warm-Up Routine for Grades 4 and 5 from lesson 3.4, page 56.

Skill-Development Activities (18 to 20 minutes)

Skipping Backward

Keep the children in scatter formation.

1. Describe and demonstrate the skill: "Step back, hop, step back, hop."
2. Have the children practice Skipping Backward.

Skipping Sideways

Make sure that the children are still in scatter formation.

1. Describe and demonstrate the skill: "Step across the forward leg, hop, step, hop; step across the forward leg, hop."
2. Have the children practice Skipping Sideways.
3. Have them practice skipping in each direction.

Change Directions

Make sure that the children are still in scatter formation. Introduce changing directions while they are skipping.

1. Tell the children: "Without breaking rhythm, turn toward the open side of your body (the direction you can turn without moving your feet)."
2. Have the children practice skipping and changing directions.

Run and Jump

Make sure the children are still in scatter formation.

1. Describe and demonstrate the skill:
   - You can jump for height or distance. Begin running, take off from one foot (a running step), and land on both feet.
   - If the purpose is height, the angle of your takeoff should be steeper, and your arms should move straight up and remain overhead on the follow-through.

○ If the purpose is distance, the angle of your takeoff should be lower, and your arms should reach forward toward your intended landing area.

2. Have the children practice Run and Jump.

Leap

Make sure the children are still in scatter formation.

1. Describe and demonstrate the skill:

○ A leap is an exaggerated running step with a very long nonsupporting phase.

○ Take off from one foot and land on the other foot; lift your body high into the air and spread your legs into a splitlike position. The arms can be held at shoulder height or to the side, or they can be used to lift the body by working in opposition.

2. Have the children practice leaping.

Run and Leap

Organize small groups of children, and assign each to a mat.

1. Describe and demonstrate the skill: "Take several small steps, then a long exaggerated one (leap), and continue with several steps, another leap, and so on."

2. Have the children practice Run and Leap.

Jump From Knees

Continue with the same setup.

1. Describe and demonstrate the stunt: "Kneeling on the mat, with your arms extended in front of your chest, swing your arms down and backward and then quickly upward as your legs straighten and push against the mat to lift your body to a standing position."

2. Have the children practice Jump From Knees.

Donkey Kick

Organize small groups of children, and assign each to a mat.

1. Describe and demonstrate the stunt:

○ The object of this task is to get both feet off the mat at the same time and to support all of your body weight with your hands.

○ Begin by standing in the middle of the mat, facing the length of the mat. Place both hands on the mat about shoulder-width apart.

○ Keep your arms straight, but bend your legs slightly. Let your hands carry some of your body weight.

○ As you kick your feet up and back, take all of your weight on your hands. Keep your eyes focused on the mat directly between your hands.

○ Be careful not to kick very hard because this may cause overbalancing and you may flip over onto your back. The purpose is to get both feet off the ground and support your weight with your arms, not to get into a vertical position (45 degrees is safer).

2. Have the children practice the Donkey Kick.

Lesson 13.6 *(continued)*

Skill Practice

Assign each child a partner within the groups at the mats.

Have the children practice the Forward Roll, Straddle Forward Roll, Backward Roll, Straddle Backward Roll, Heel Slap, and Regular and Straddle Split. Say to the children: "Observe your partner to see if he or she is using the correct technique."

FORWARD ROLL

Organize small groups of children, and assign each to a mat.

1. Describe and demonstrate the stunt:
   - Bend over and place your hands on the mat shoulder-width apart and, while looking at your tummy and bending your arms, shift more and more body weight onto your hands as your legs provide less and less support.
   - As your center of gravity moves forward, your body overbalances and rolls forward as you hit the mat on your shoulder blades. Continue to roll in a curved position.
   - Bend your legs at the knees and accept weight on your legs as your shoulders leave the mat.
   - Return to standing with your arms extended overhead.
2. Have the children practice the Forward Roll.

STRADDLE FORWARD ROLL

Arrange partners on the mats.

1. Describe and demonstrate the stunt:
   - This is actually two consecutive rolls. Start by doing a Forward Roll and then add the straddle part. Begin in closed standing position, with feet together and arms extended overhead; bend, placing your hands on the mat shoulder-width apart.
   - Look at your tummy, bend your arms, and accept more and more of your body weight onto your hands as your legs decrease support.
   - As your center of gravity moves forward, your body overbalances and rolls forward as you hit the mat on your shoulder blades. Continue to roll in a curved position.
   - This stunt differs from a regular Forward Roll. Keep your legs straight and spread apart in the straddle position so that you land on your legs for the first roll with your feet spread, body bent slightly forward, and arms extended forward.
   - Begin the second roll immediately from the straddle position, with your head tucked under and your body moving forward to a landing on the shoulder blades.
   - Recover to standing, with your feet closed, as in the regular Forward Roll.
   - Work with your partner—one partner stands in front of the Roller after the roll phase to help him or her recover. Roller, reach out to your partner and try to shake hands as you come up. This gets your arms and weight forward by moving your center of gravity forward.
2. Have the children practice the Straddle Forward Roll.

BACKWARD ROLL

Continue with the same setup except that partners are not necessary.

1. Describe and demonstrate the stunt:
   - Begin in a standing position, with arms extended overhead (palms up) and your back toward the length of the mat and your chin moving to your chest. Lower your body to a tuck position by bending the knees. Overbalance your body backward to begin the roll, and remain in tuck position as your shoulders and hands contact the mat.
   - Push with your hands to lift your body (hips, legs, and torso) over your head. Your head and neck should not support your weight and you should touch the mat as little as possible.

○ As your feet touch the mat, straighten your arms until your feet are supporting your weight. Rise to standing with your arms extended overhead.

2. Have the children practice the Backward Roll.

STRADDLE BACKWARD ROLL

Continue with the same setup.

1. Describe and demonstrate the stunt:
   ○ Begin standing in a straddle balance position, with your back toward the length of the mat.
   ○ Move your hands between your legs as your torso moves forward to lower your body, with your hips moving back and down, until your seat touches the mat.
   ○ Move your hands to your shoulders as in the regular Backward Roll. Immediately roll your body backward while your legs remain in the straddle position.
   ○ Recover to the straddle balance position.
2. Have the children practice the Straddle Backward Roll.
3. Have the children extend the skill by beginning in closed standing position and rolling to a straddle balance and then rolling again from the straddle balance to a closed standing position (two rolls).

HEEL SLAP

Continue with the same setup.

1. Describe and demonstrate the stunt:
   ○ The object is to touch your heels with your hands just under your seat and then land on both feet.
   ○ Jump up from both feet, lifting both feet toward your seat while reaching back with your arms.
2. Have the children practice the Heel Slap.

STRADDLE SPLIT

Begin in the straddle balance position and end with your legs extended as far apart as possible. If you are very flexible, recover into a Regular Split. Otherwise, lean forward, taking your weight on your arms and chest, and then swing both legs together to the rear to lie on your front.

REGULAR SPLIT

Begin with your feet together in a "T" position, where one foot faces front and the other foot is perpendicular to and behind the front foot, with the feet meeting the heel of the front foot to the arch of the rear foot. Slowly slide one foot forward and the other backward until your legs are fully extended.

Note: A child may also do Regular Splits with only one leg moving, while the other leg remains stationary. To recover, the child leans forward with the torso over the front leg and swings the back leg around to the side until it is touching the front leg.

Concluding Activities (5 minutes)

Movement Challenges That Combine Skills

Have the children create their own combinations.

Split Measurement

Measure the distance from the floor to the bottom of the leg at the hip for each child in either split position. Record the information. Use this later to show improvement. Reassure the children that, as they work on this skill, they will get better at it.

From K.T. Thomas, A.M. Lee, and J.R. Thomas, 2008, *Physical education methods for elementary teachers*, 3rd ed. (Champaign, IL: Human Kinetics). Adapted, by permission, from K.T. Thomas, A.M. Lee, and J.R. Thomas, 2000, *Physical education for children: Daily lesson plans for elementary school*, 2nd ed. (Champaign, IL: Human Kinetics), 1022-1023.

Lesson 13.7

Dance Steps

Student Objectives 1	Equipment and Materials
• Perform a sequence of Schottische steps and Step-Hops to music.	• Music: "Military Schottische" from *Basic Dance Tempos*, Honor Your Partner (LP 501A) (or other Schottische music)

Warm-Up Activities (5 minutes)

Schottische

Arrange the children in scatter formation.

1. Have the children listen to the Schottische music.
2. Using the Schottische step, have the children travel to the music.
3. Have them repeat, using forward and backward Schottische steps.

Skill-Development Activities (20 minutes)

Schottische and Step-Hop Sequence

Arrange the children in a double circle, facing counterclockwise.

1. Have the children practice combining 2 Schottische steps and 4 Step-Hops. Cue the children: "Walk, walk, walk, hop; walk, walk, walk, hop; step-hop, step-hop, step-hop, step-hop."
2. Have them practice in place, repeating several times.
3. Variations:
   ○ Perform 2 Schottische steps moving forward (begin on the right foot) and then 4 Step-Hops in place.
   ○ Replace the 4 Step-Hops with Rock Steps: forward left, back right, forward left, back right.
   ○ Perform the Schottische steps diagonally to the right and the left.
   ○ Perform Step-Hops while moving forward (or turning in a circle).

Concluding Activities (5 minutes)

Schottische Step-Hop Routines

Assign each child a partner. Ask each pair to create a routine using 2 Schottische steps and 4 Step-Hops.

From K.T. Thomas, A.M. Lee, and J.R. Thomas, 2008, *Physical education methods for elementary teachers*, 3rd ed. (Champaign, IL: Human Kinetics). Adapted, by permission, from K.T. Thomas, A.M. Lee, and J.R. Thomas, 2000, *Physical education for children: Daily lesson plans for elementary school*, 2nd ed. (Champaign, IL: Human Kinetics), 989-990.

CHAPTER 14

Evaluating Students

MUNA, AGE 9

Evaluation, or making a judgment, is an important part of the teaching and learning process; it guides planning and instruction and is the basis for feedback and grading in physical education.

Learner Outcomes

After studying this chapter, you should be able to do the following:

- Define evaluation and describe the relationship among evaluation, instruction, objectives, and planning.

- Use evaluation appropriately for feedback, screening, assigning grades, adjusting objectives, and continual improvement of student learning.

- Identify a variety of assessment tools, including checklists, rating scales, rubrics, and tests.

- Compare and contrast norm- and criterion-referenced measurement.

- Define and give examples of validity, reliability, and objectivity.

Glossary Terms

evaluation	norm-referenced tests	rubrics
validity	criterion-referenced tests	checklists
reliability	authentic assessment	rating scale
objectivity	grading	

The terms "grading" and "evaluation" are often used synonymously. However, grading is one of many applications of evaluation. Consider evaluation in the context of Bloom's taxonomy (see chapter 5, Cognition, Learning, and Practice). **Evaluation** is the highest level of cognition and is defined as making a judgment. Evaluation in the informal sense is used for feedback; in the formal sense, it is used to judge performance. This chapter is near the end of the book not because evaluation is an afterthought, but because evaluation must be firmly based on knowledge, comprehension, application, analysis, and synthesis. Evaluation is an integral part of the teaching and learning process.

Assessment is an integral component of accountability. Both you and your school assess student progress toward standards by measuring performance on benchmarks. As described in chapter 9, Organizing for Teaching, horizontal alignment is the foundation for this process. Thus, it is critical for you to understand the benchmarks, horizontal alignment, and evaluation. The ultimate decisions about student progress toward standards is evaluated (e.g., judged) by others in the educational system (e.g., your principal, the superintendent, state or other agency), but you are the first and, arguably, the most important part of the evaluation system. The accurate and systematic evaluation of your students is an important step in ensuring that they will become physically educated.

NASPE has provided broad guidelines for evaluation, which are presented in figure 14.1. You develop objectives, plan, instruct (practice and feedback), and evaluate. Although NASPE advo-

---

We Believe That . . .

Based on our experiences and knowledge, we believe that the planning, implementation, and assessment of elementary physical education should be a continuous process. Assessment serves two functions: It evaluates the process of students in achieving program and individual goals, and it guides lesson planning and instruction. Thus assessment is essential in order to

- guide diagnostic and prescription processes during teaching and learning;
- guide and motivate children toward established goals;
- evaluate the learner's response to the learning experience; and
- inform parents, learners, the school, and the community of the program's values and outcomes.

Many evaluative techniques should be used to better understand children in the program, including knowledge testing, anecdotal records, motor skills assessments, decision making in games and practice, health-related fitness testing, and teacher observations of performance, attitudes, and feelings. *The single most important aspect of assessment is to review children's progress rather than rank children or compare them to norms.*

Finally, the physical education program is accountable to the children, school, and community for quality teaching and learning. Periodic assessment of the program is essential to the development of student potential; this assessment should include guiding philosophy, student achievement, facilities and equipment, allocation and use of resources, and administrative and community support.

Figure 14.1   Statement of the authors' beliefs about evaluation developed from experience as well as use of NASPE documents (Holt/Hale 1999a, b; Mitchell and Oslin 1999).

---

cates the use of evaluation in program planning, assessment, and teacher improvement, the focus of this chapter is on evaluating students. However, we use student evaluation to guide curriculum and instruction decisions and to evaluate our teaching. You can see this relationship in figure 1.3 (page 12), which is the foundation for the teaching and learning described in this book.

You can use evaluation for feedback and grading (figure 14.2). In addition, you may be asked to monitor health and other behaviors, such as height and weight, or to do scoliosis screening by checking for curvature of the spine. You should evaluate the motor skills of young children or developmentally delayed children. Generally, you use screening tests for referral to healthcare professionals (e.g., school nurse) rather than your own interventions. However, these are first steps in the screening process. This chapter covers performance evaluation of students and grading in physical education. The principles of evaluation apply to setting objectives, screening, reflecting, and giving feedback, as well as grading and evaluating performance.

You need to understand the principles of evaluation and grading so that you can use

- appropriate measurements and assessments per instructional objectives,

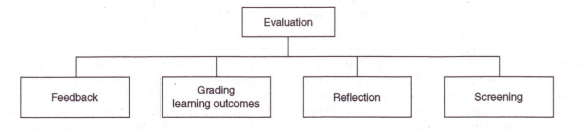

Figure 14.2   Purposes of evaluation in elementary physical education.

- evaluation measurements that are valid, reliable, and objective,
- evaluation to improve student understanding and performance,
- evaluation for continuous improvement of student learning, and
- grading practices that are fair and represent important physical education objectives.

The overall goal of elementary physical education is for children to be physically educated, or exposed to a physically active lifestyle based on participation in a variety of games or sports, dance, gymnastics, and fitness activities. Participation requires two areas of competency: knowledge and skill. Physically active lifestyles and physical fitness flow naturally from development and practice of those competencies. You can conceptualize evaluation of knowledge as declarative (evaluation of facts and rules) or procedural (use of the knowledge). Objectives of physical education that involve leadership or sportsmanship would also be part of the evaluation plan. Whatever domain you are evaluating (psychomotor, cognitive, or affective), the following principles of evaluation apply:

1. The evaluation focuses on an important educational objective.
2. Tests and measurements must be developmentally appropriate.
3. Validity, reliability, and objectivity are important considerations in evaluation.
4. Evaluation is used for continuous improvement.

Validity in Evaluation

A valid test measures what it is supposed to measure and is both reliable and objective. **Validity** is the single most important concept in measurement and evaluation. You must first determine whether the evaluation is valid—that is, does it represent the objective? **Reliability** means that the result represents a typical performance—you get the same answer each time. **Objectivity** means that the test or measurement is without bias. In other words, the test does not unfairly discriminate against a student. Thus, a student from a different cultural background has an equal opportunity to perform well. You may be afraid to make judgments because of the issue of objectivity. This means that objectivity has

become more important in your practice than validity. Because evaluation is a judgment, you must use your knowledge and experience to make fair judgments. Avoiding making judgments is as poor a practice as being biased! Multiple-choice and true-false tests are called objective tests. It is easy to see you might give multiple-choice and true-false tests frequently. The question is whether they are valid measures of the objective. The trade-off between validity and objectivity is discussed in greater detail later in this chapter. Physical education presents the same evaluation challenges. It is safer—more objective—to evaluate using a knowledge test, factors such as attendance or proper attire, and analysis of quantitative skills (e.g., how fast a child runs or the number of times that a child can hit the target). However, these measures may not be valid compared with those based on objectives such as "play basketball, demonstrate teamwork, adopt a physically active lifestyle."

A frequent problem in testing arises when students are sick or have personal problems at the time of the test. On one hand, you need to have a test score that is representative of the student's typical performance. On the other hand, you must be unbiased in dealing with students. You might place more emphasis on "fair to all"; consequently, everyone takes the test at the same time, regardless of individual circumstances. You can view validity, reliability, and objectivity as a hierarchy, with validity as the most important and the others subordinate and embedded. An evaluation should be valid, reliable, *and* objective. You might make a "judgment" and allow the individual student to take the test at a different time. The unbiased teacher would do this for any student with a circumstance that would produce potentially unrepresentative scores. Ideally, an evaluation is perfectly valid, reliable, and objective. Unfortunately, in the real world, compromise is often necessary.

Validity is most important partly because it includes reliability and objectivity. However, validity is independent of reliability and objectivity (Morrow, Jackson, Disch, and Mood 2005). Likewise, reliability issues are more important than objectivity issues. So, in the example of a cultural problem interfering with obtaining a representative score, you can view reliability as having priority over objectivity.

You can apply this same concept to the type of test or measurement that you select for the evaluation. If a multiple-choice test is a valid measure of the objective, using a multiple-choice test is good. However, if the objective is about playing a game or using knowledge in a game, a multiple-choice test may not be a sound educational choice. Once again, you can see a trade-off between validity and reliability or objectivity. The more valid, or real world, the test is, the less reliable and objective the test may be. This problem applies to all tests, measurements, and evaluations. Sometimes objectives seem to contradict each other when measured; this complicates the issue further. For example, children need to demonstrate motor skills during game play, and working as a group is important. A child may demonstrate being a good team member by passing the ball to a teammate; however, this means the child does not practice or demonstrate the skill of shooting a goal. Thus, the less valid way of measuring shooting skill is better. The same challenge applies in the classroom, for example, if you wanted to encourage the development of vocabulary but realized that penalizing spelling errors often reduces student experimentation with new words. The conflict is between two equally important and opposing objectives.

Children are evaluated for a variety of reasons in physical education, including mastery of learning outcomes.

These examples demonstrate why validity is a consideration. You can reduce student and parent concern over these issues by

- explaining the purpose of the test to the children,
- describing how the test results are used,
- allowing children appropriate practice or experience with the test material before the test, and
- following acceptable and consistent testing procedures.

Knowing: Traditional Assessment

Two general categories of traditional assessment, norm-referenced and criterion-referenced testing, apply to evaluation of knowledge, motor skills, and fitness. **Norm-referenced tests** show an expected range of performance; in fact, the assumption is that the scores fit the bell-shaped curve. This means that most students have similar scores in the middle of the distribution and fewer students are spread among the higher and lower scores. The vertical axis is the number of people and the horizontal axis is the scores (figure 14.3). **Criterion-referenced tests** are based on mastery learning and place students into two categories: master (successful) and nonmaster (unsuccessful). The criterion can be established in three ways: based on norms from a norm-referenced test, based on an arbitrary standard, or based on the contrast between two groups. An example of an arbitrary standard is the height required to go on certain rides at the amusement park. Contrast between groups involves comparing two known groups on the test (e.g., beginners and experts), using the cut-off as the point where the curves for the two groups cross (figure 14.4). In the example, the score (average) where the curves overlap is used to separate the two groups. You could use this to group children for play so that those with more equal skill play with and against each other. You can use similar groupings to determine which children are ready for more advanced skills and which ones should continue practicing basic skills. Many prepared tests presented in books or journals are created using either norm-referenced or criterion-referenced methods. This is one characteristic that you should consider when you are selecting published tests. Most often, you can construct your own tests; sometimes you can use one of these techniques to provide feedback to the children. In case of norm-referenced tests, you can report the percentile for a child (e.g., 50th percentile equals the middle) or a child's rank on the test (e.g., in the top 10). In the case of criterion-referenced tests, you can report a successful or unsuccessful performance, tell a child, "You met the goal," or place a child in a group based on the test score.

Neither type of test (norm- or criterion-referenced) is necessarily better or worse than the other. The critical issue is that you select the appropriate type of test based on the objective and then interpret the test results appropriately. The four frequently measured aspects of physical education are knowledge, skill, fitness, and game play. So, one way to decide how to evaluate is to consider the aspect being evaluated.

Declarative knowledge is necessary, but not sufficient, for success in games and sport. Children must know the rules, definitions, and basics of the movements before they can participate. If you teach rules, definitions, and movement parameters, you should evaluate the students' declarative knowledge. You can use traditional tests, such as multiple-choice tests, to provide information about student knowledge; comprehension; and even application of the rules, definitions, and basics of the movements.

Sport and motor skills tests often examine skills out of context and focus on product rather than process. For example, you could examine free-throw shooting skill as a skill test or use free-throw shooting performance from actual games. Because performance in a game is probably the objective, the latter would probably be more valid. However, sometimes using actual play is not practical. In

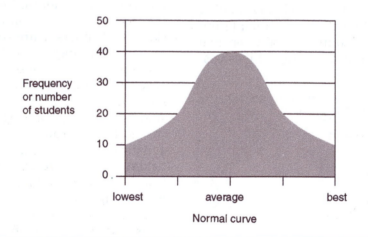

Figure 14.3   Normal curve.

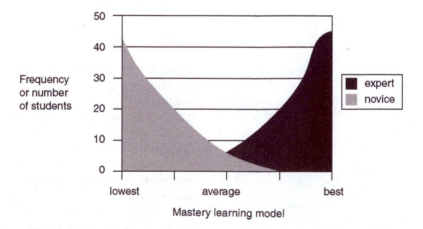

Figure 14.4   Using overlapping curves to determine masters and nonmasters.

a game, players have different opportunities and are influenced by the play of others. It would be possible to play a game, or even several games, and never shoot a free throw. You can use skill tests to determine readiness to play a game. Game play, although valid, might not be the best way to determine readiness to begin game play or to evaluate skill. Children with experience playing have an unfair advantage, and they do not have equal opportunities for performance in a game. Techniques for measuring sport skills and knowledge in context, as well as process evaluations, are covered in the next section.

Sometimes you can test higher-level thinking skills (analysis, synthesis, and evaluation) and procedural knowledge using traditional tests, such as essays. However, two limitations are evident with the traditional approach: First, children's language, reading, and writing skills influence the outcome. This is a particular problem for young children. Second, time is critical in many

Teachers must devote time to observing students to evaluate learning.

physical activity settings, and traditional tests take time. A related problem is the difference between knowing what to do and actually being able to do it. A sports fan may know what to do in a game, but the fan may not be able to execute the skill. This is typical in novices; they know what to do before they can actually perform the skill in the context of the game.

Careful construction and use of tests to measure knowledge are important because they produce the most accurate information and because the evaluation is stronger and more defensible. Validity, reliability, and objectivity are part of careful test construction. Expert teachers use tests carefully in several ways:

- They include evaluation in the planning process so that they are considering how objectives will be evaluated as they are written and lessons are developed.

- They spend time searching for tests, modifying those tests if necessary, and, as a last resort, constructing their own tests.

- They know the answers to written tests before administering the tests.

- They evaluate tests twice—before and after administering the tests. To do this, have a colleague look at the test before you give it, asking, "Is it developmentally appropriate? Is this a valid test of the objective?" After the test, look at the results. Did the best students do well? Did several students have the same problem? Is there a reasonable explanation for the problem?

- They make tests challenging but fair. Expert teachers do not make tests difficult. You do not have to make tests difficult to obtain a range of scores, because some students do not prepare for the test and are unsuccessful. Artificially difficult tests are not valid.

- They help students understand that testing and evaluation represent their work and performance. Evaluation guides students to improvement.

Some things you may want to test do not fit the norm-referenced model, including activities in which only a few scores are possible, such as the number of free throws made in 10 attempts. Furthermore, criterion- and norm-referenced measurements focus on outcomes, which may be a limitation. For beginners, progress is slow and, as you learned in chapter 4, Motor Performance During Childhood, often observed in the way a skill looks (process) long before the outcome changes. This means that many outcome-based tests do not capture valid performance and change. Consider again the free-throw example: A child might throw zero free throws and then, after practice, still throw zero free throws. Nevertheless, you might be able to observe improvements in form; perhaps, after practice, the ball hits the basket's rim, indicating that the shot was actually closer, but not in the basket itself! There are times when traditional testing, either norm- or criterion-referenced, is appropriate. Alternatives are presented later in this chapter. Traditional testing can provide the following information:

- Tracking improvement to motivate the students
- Comparing to normative data for screening (health, fitness) or fun
- Determining readiness
- Grouping students
- Assessing your program

Applying Authentic Assessment

You can use **authentic assessment**, as an alternative to traditional testing, to evaluate performance. Traditional tests, such as multiple choice, number of free throws made, and timed mile run, are sometimes criticized for poor validity; the tests did not represent the target skills or knowledge. Authentic assessment and performance evaluation shift the focus to learning outcomes rather than test scores. The U.S. Congress (1992) defined performance assessment as "testing methods that require students to create an answer or product that demonstrates knowledge or skills." The shift in assessment philosophy is parallel to a shift in instructional style from teacher-centered (lecture) to student-centered (engagement). There are three characteristics of authentic assessments:

1. They represent higher-order cognitive skills.
2. They simulate real-world tasks.

3. They shift responsibility to the student for documenting learning.

Examples of authentic assessments are observations, portfolios, checklists and rating scales, performances, and projects. Authentic assessment is consistent with both a constructivist approach and active learning and also with mastery learning and criterion-referenced measurement. One difference is that authentic assessments often use more than two categories of performance (successful and unsuccessful). Norm-referenced testing is at the opposite end of the assessment continuum from authentic assessment.

The emergence of authentic assessment and the learner-centered approach is part of the framework of standards and benchmarks favored by many school districts (Lambert 1999; Mitchell and Oslin 1999; Morrow et al. 2005). Samples of benchmarks for grades K, 2, and 4 and assessments for those representing the National Content Standards are presented in table 14.1. Validity is generally less problematic when you are using authentic assessments. However, children may have difficulty understanding what a written assignment has to do with physical education. One reason validity is not such an issue with authentic assessment is that children are given the assessment criteria at the beginning of instruction. Often, they do not know how they will be evaluated in norm-referenced testing situations until the time for evaluation. When using a norm- or criterion-referenced test, inform children about the test early in learning, explain how it will be used, and allow them to practice the test. Reliability and objectivity are still challenges in authentic assessment. To improve reliability and objectivity, you can

- develop clear and specific criteria for the assessment,
- ensure that the person doing the assessment understands the criteria, and
- practice the assessment.

You can develop rubrics for virtually any skill, knowledge, or behavior. One advantage of rubrics is that both the student and the evaluator have the same information before the assessment. We have presented rubrics in previous chapters (e.g., the locomotor and manipulative rubrics in chapter 4, Motor Performance During Childhood, and the

Table 14.1 Sample Benchmarks and Assessments Based on National Content Standards

Content standard	Grade	Benchmark	Assessment
Demonstrates competency in many movement forms and proficiency in a few movement forms	K	Runs, walks, hops (one foot), and gallops forward using mature form Moves at fast and slow speed Moves at high, medium, and low levels	Teacher observation using rubric Teacher observation Teacher observation
	2	Runs, walks, hops (each foot), gallops (each foot), slides, and skips forward using mature form Combines locomotor patterns Throws, catches, kicks, or strikes using mature form Catches and strikes a tossed object	Teacher observation using rubric Teacher observation Teacher observation using rubric Checklist
	4	Throws, catches, kicks, and strikes using mature form Combines balancing and other nonlocomotor skills with locomotor skills, using smooth transitions Demonstrates a sequence of two or more gymnastics skills Performs movements to music with the beat and in proper sequence	Teacher observation using rubric Teacher observation Checklist Checklist
Applies movement concepts and principles to the learning and development of motor skills	K	Correctly names walk, run, gallop, hop, and jump	Teacher observation
	2	States the characteristics of a mature walk, run, gallop, hop, and jump	Written or oral report
	4	Detects and corrects errors in locomotor skills and manipulative skills	Written test
Exhibits a physically active lifestyle	K	Participates in vigorous activity during class	Teacher observation
	2	Participates in a variety of physical activities	Journal
	4	Describes the benefits of a physically active lifestyle	Written test
Achieves and maintains a health-enhancing level of physical fitness	K	Demonstrates moderate-to-vigorous activity for at least 10 minutes without stopping	Teacher observation
	2	Understands why heart rate goes up during vigorous exercise	Class discussion
	4	Completes activity necessary for a test of cardiovascular fitness	Mile-run test
Demonstrates responsible personal and social behavior in physical activity settings	K	States class rules	Teacher observation
	2	Uses equipment safely and as intended	Teacher observation
	4	Accepts personal responsibility for following the rules	Teacher observation

(continued)

Table 14.1 *(continued)*

Content standard	Grade	Benchmark	Assessment
Demonstrates responsible personal and social behavior in physical activity settings	K	Willingly plays with others	Teacher observation
	2	Cooperates and takes turns during activities	Teacher observation
	4	Participates willingly in activities that represent a variety of cultural views	Student project
Understands that physical activity provides opportunities for enjoyment, challenge, self-expression, and social interaction	K	Works with a partner to solve a movement challenge	Teacher observation
	2	On verbal request, moves in a way that expresses joy, sadness, or fatigue	Observation
	4	Writes about three physical activity experiences that have brought enjoyment, challenge, self-expression, or social interaction	Journal entries

Moving Into the Future: National Standards for Physical Education, 2nd Edition (2004) adapted with permission from the National Association for Sport and Physical Education (NASPE), 1900 Association Drive, Reston, VA 20191-1599.

teaching rubric in this chapter). Table 14.2 is a rubric for leadership, sportsmanship, and teamwork. Student checklists are a recommended step in the learning process before you apply the final rubric (Baker, Costa, and Shalit 1997). The checklist begins with "Did you do the following?" The tasks leading to success are listed, with a place to check "not yet," "partially," or "complete." The tasks could include skills practice (e.g., completed three types of forward roll, did 10-second handstand, balanced on three body parts 4 times each for 15 seconds each), homework (e.g., selected two pieces of instrumental music), or written work (e.g., wrote a sequence of tumbling that included one roll, one balance, and two other movements). For more advanced students, the checklist might also include a fitness program to train for the activity, a performance goal, and a self-assessment of the process (e.g., Did I work hard? Did I review and revise my work? Did I consider alternative solutions? Did I seek advice?).

Burke (2006) emphasizes the importance of encouraging students to go beyond the minimum described in the standards in rubrics. Of course, this means that you must develop rubrics and activities that allow students to see how to extend beyond the standard. In a four-part rubric, the third level is "meets the standard" and the fourth level is "exceeds the standard."

Feedback to Children and Parents

One goal of evaluation is continuous improvement. Therefore, children and their parents need to be informed of the children's status. Feedback should occur during regular grading cycles and as information becomes available. Providing information only during regular grading periods limits continuous improvement because the information needed for the improvement is not available during the practice period. At the beginning of the school year, parents and children should be informed about the goals and objectives of the physical education program, the activities included in the program, and administrative policies (e.g., attendance, participation, dress code). Formal feedback is provided through the formal grading cycles. Informal feedback, such as portfolio checks, rubric results, and journals, should be provided as appropriate. For example, pretest information from a rubric could help parents provide practice at home and would identify for children the aspects of a skill. Providing informal feedback to parents from evaluations allows parents to be partners in education. Furthermore, the additional information can help parents understand the meaning of grades in physical education.

Table 14.2 Rubric For Leadership, Sportsmanship, and Teamwork

Use this rubric to assess student performance on these three skills. Discuss the information with the children (and possibly the parents) so that they can learn how and where to improve.

	Take some time to think before acting	Thumbs up	Double thumbs up
Leadership	Interferes with the learning of others, bullies or bosses others, has tantrums or pouts	Leads when asked, coaches when asked	Coaches classmates, knows when to lead and when to listen
Sportsmanship	Does not follow or understand rules, does not share or play well with others, does not try	Follows rules most of the time, shares with others, demonstrates efforts	Voluntarily follows rules all of the time, gives maximum effort all of the time
Teamwork	Refuses to work with others, fights or argues with others, makes negative comments to others, has difficulty understanding feelings of others	Willingly works in pairs or groups most of the time, does not say negative things to others, when prompted understands feelings of others	Supports all classmates with positive comments, works with any classmate all of the time, takes turns fairly, understands feelings of others

Concepts Into Practice

Ms. Corey used a rubric to evaluate students on three skills: jumping a self-turned rope, bouncing a playground ball, and skipping. She sent the rubric home with each child; a parent was asked to sign the rubric and send it back to school with the child. Ms. Corey left a place for parents to comment. A mother made the following comment: "I had no idea that Jason could not jump rope. We bought one on Friday and have practiced all weekend! The next time you give this test, he will be ready. P.S. It was fun to practice jumping rope together."

Continuous improvement also applies to you. Good teachers adjust instruction and practice after evaluating student learning. Informal evaluations for feedback, pretests, and other on-going measurements can provide you with information that should influence your behaviors, planning, and practice. Continuous improvement is impossible for you without evaluation of your students.

Using Tests

Standardized tests, such as the Fitnessgram or President's Challenge, are often used for fitness. Other standardized tests are published in books and journals. Before using any test, read the explanation of the test. This usually includes information about validity, reliability, and objectivity; the purpose of the test; and the intended audience. Many tests come with manuals that explain how to administer the test, scoring methods, and other information. Following the test instructions is important because the results are influenced by how the test is administered. The advantage to standardized tests is that the work of creating the test is done for you. However, you must still learn how to administer and interpret the test.

Fitness tests are often used to monitor physical activity in children. If children do well on the test, the assumption is that the child is physically active. Sometimes, you can use the results to check for improvement if you train children for fitness during class or as assigned homework. You can also use fitness scores in grading. However, this is only acceptable when you train children for fitness as part of the physical education program; even then, some components of fitness are difficult to influence. You can also use evaluation of fitness as an educational tool to describe the components of fitness and typical activities that train those components. Using the information from a fitness test as a tool for understanding is appropriate.

Generally, you can use motor performance tests for screening to assess developmental level in young children or to determine placement for adapted physical education. Although there is a place for these tests, it is not in elementary physical education.

Sport skills tests can support teaching and learning of sports. You can use them in several ways:

- for motivation,
- for information about student competence to inform planning and instruction,
- as practice drills, or
- as part of a grading system, but not as the only or primary form of evaluation.

Select sport skills tests carefully based on the age and skill of the students, and match them with your educational objectives. The primary goal of all tests is to enhance student learning. Contrast the best and inappropriate practices in figure 14.5 as you think about the previous examples of fitness and sport skills tests.

Grading

Schools, districts, and states have a variety of policies on grading in physical education. Sometimes a grading system is mandated; for example, all subjects are graded "satisfactory," "needs improvement," or "unsatisfactory" or they are graded with letter grades (passing grades usually include A, B, C, and D). At other times, you are responsible for developing a grading system. The most important factor in any **grading** system is to convey important information about performance. A grade of "C" or "needs improvement" does not outline for the child or parents what to do. Physical education report cards are helpful because more information can be presented to both the child and the parents. Whatever grading system you use, several guidelines apply to assigning grades:

1. For children in elementary school, base the grades on as many components as possible. No single event (e.g., a test, game, or day) should contribute more than 10 percent of the final grade; you should base the grade on at least 10 elements.

2. Grades should represent distinct performances: Student performances earning a specific grade are similar to each other and different from those of students earning other grades.

3. Grades should represent important physical education objectives. Therefore, grading on attendance, shoes, and other administrative criteria is not a "best practice." Base grades on motor performance and knowledge.

Best practice	Inappropriate practice
The grade is focused on important student learning outcomes (e.g., skill and knowledge).	The grade is focused on dress, attendance, effort, and class rules.
The grade is based on many (at least 10) different performances.	The grade is based on a single score (e.g., a fitness test or skill test).
Assessment is used to make curriculum decisions, identify children with special needs, and interpret the program to stakeholders.	Assessment is used only for grading.
Fitness tests are used as part of an ongoing fitness program in which tests and scores are used privately to enhance student learning.	Fitness testing is conducted one or two times each year because it is required or for the purpose of awards.
Assessment is authentic and considers the context.	Skills, knowledge, and behavior are assessed in trivial or artificial situations.

Figure 14.5 Best practices and inappropriate practices in physical education measurement.

4. Grades should provide children and parents with information that facilitates improvement.

We recommend a physical education report card. If a single grade is required, you can design the report card so that it demonstrates how you determined the final grade. Although comments are not required on any report card, parents and children usually appreciate your individualized comments.

You could base a physical education report card on the national standards and benchmarks for each grade (table 14.3). Using the guidelines,

Table 14.3 Sample Physical Education Report Card and Grade Based on National Content Standard

Content standard	Benchmark	Yes	or No
Demonstrates competency in motor skills and movement patterns needed to perform a variety of physical activities	Mature form (see rubric) Locomotor skills:		
	• Walk	☐	☐
	• Run	☐	☐
	• Hop	☐	☐
	• Gallop	☐	☐
	• Slide	☐	☐
	• Skip	☐	☐
	• Jump	☐	☐
	Manipulative skills:		
	• Throw	☐	☐
	• Catch	☐	☐
	• Kick	☐	☐
	• Strike	☐	☐
Demonstrates understanding of movement concepts, principles, strategies, and tactics as they apply to the learning and performance of physical activities	Names three locomotor skills	☐	☐
	Demonstrates fast and slow	☐	☐
Participates regularly in physical activity	Participates actively during class	☐	☐
	Reports being active out of class	☐	☐
Achieves and maintains a health-enhancing level of physical fitness	Participates for 15 to 20 minutes without stopping	☐	☐
	Can hang by the arms for 30 seconds	☐	☐
	Can do 10 crunches	☐	☐
Exhibits responsible personal and social behavior that respects self and others in physical activity settings	Moves under control	☐	☐
	Does not interfere with others	☐	☐
	Helps others	☐	☐
	Treats equipment well	☐	☐
Values physical activity for health, enjoyment, challenge, self-expression, and/or social interaction	Demonstrates enjoyment, sadness, and fatigue by moving	☐	☐
	Cooperates with a partner	☐	☐
	Demonstrates effort	☐	☐
Final grade	Needs improvement	☐	☐
	Meets standards	☐	☐

Moving Into the Future: National Standards for Physical Education, 2nd Edition (2004) adapted with permission from the National Association for Sport and Physical Education (NASPE), 1900 Association Drive, Reston, VA 20191-1599.

you would evaluate several benchmarks in each of the six standards. The report could end there or you could turn it into a grade based on the individual components from each standard. This would inform parents and be consistent with the standards approach to assessment. You must decide at the beginning of a year the value for each component of the grade. For example, you might use each of the six standards equally for a grade, or you might place greater value on standards 1 (movement skill) and 3 (physically active lifestyle). You might combine scores from standards 2, 4, 5, and 6 at 10 percent each and standards 1 and 3 at 30 percent for a final grade. In either case, you must convert the individual benchmarks and standards to a component grade and then a final grade. Two ways to do this are subarea grading and assigning numeric values.

In subarea grading, you count letter grades (e.g., "A," or "satisfactory") and assign the most frequently occurring as the grade. So, a student who had A, A, A, A, B, A, for the six standards would receive a final grade of A. When subarea grade is not obvious, you can convert the letter grades to numbers: A = 4, B = 3, C = 2, D = 1, and F = 0. Sum the scores and divide by the number of scores. Then convert the average number to a letter grade. Thus, the grades of A, B, B, C, B, A equal 4, 3, 3, 2, 3, 4, for a total of 19; this divided by 6 is 3.17, for a final grade of B. If you weight the subareas (in this case, standards) differently so that standard 1 is 30 percent, standards 2 through 5 are 10 percent each, and standard 6 is 30 percent, using the previous example, the scores would be AAA, B, B, C, B, AAA, (4 + 4 + 4 + 3 + 3 + 2 + 3 + 4 + 4 + 4 = 35/10 = 3.5, or 6 of 10 grades of A) for a final grade of A.

Converting to mathematical scores works similarly. Assign to each standard a point value. If the standards are equally valued, the points are 100/6, or 16 points each. Assign points to various performances: perfect performance, 16; average performance, 13; and so forth. Sum the points to create total points of 100, which you can then convert to a letter grade using a grading scale (e.g., 90 to 100 = A; 80 to 89 = B). You can also assign standards to point values: You can assign 30 points each to standards 1 and 3, and then assign 10 points each to the remaining standards.

You and your school should give careful consideration to what the grade means in terms of the distribution of students. Clearly, every child cannot be above average. In fact, according to the normal curve, only half can be above average and two-thirds are about (or around) average. If a "C" represents average, then 4 to 6 of 10 students are average ("satisfactory" or "C"), 1 to 3 are above average, and 1 to 3 are below average. Unfortunately, many parents and children feel that a grade of average is unacceptable. This notion is related to the issue of grade inflation, in which grades are higher than predicted by the normal curve. Anchor points are the performance that a grade represents (e.g., "C" as average or "C" as satisfactory). "Average" implies that 40 to 66 percent of the children perform in this range. "Satisfactory" may mean the minimum acceptable score, with more students electing to be above this point. So satisfactory and average can represent two very different messages, although both are represented by "C." In schools or classrooms where criterion-referenced measurement and mastery learning are the philosophical orientation, grades are most likely to be successful or unsuccessful. Schools, school districts, and teachers should consider carefully how grades are conceptualized—that is, criterion- or norm-referenced—and determine the anchor points for grades. The same issue is relevant in the classroom when the two differences are the content and the information conveyed by the grade. In the classroom, parents and students are likely to see many grades representing performance before a report card. In physical education, the only representation of performance may be the grade on the report card. Neither classroom teachers who teach physical education nor physical education specialists are likely to send home daily, weekly, or monthly reports about a progress in physical education. Classroom teachers send home written work, representing performance in spelling, math, reading, and other subjects, on a regular basis.

These methods apply to any system for evaluating benchmarks and standards. To be valid, the weighting of an objective, standard, or benchmark should represent three concepts:

1. Time spent
2. Emphasis
3. Importance

So, you can consider weighting of objectives or standards based on time spent; this should also be representative of what you thought was most important and what you emphasized. Sometimes, you may spend less time, but a concept is very important and you have emphasized it; then you should weight it heavily compared to the time spent. Ultimately, grades should be valid, reliable, and objective. Regardless of the method that you use to calculate grades, you need to consider three important issues:

1. Grades inform parents and students about performance (skill and knowledge).

2. Grades represent important educational objectives.

3. Students with the same grade are similar, and students with different grades are meaningfully different.

Informing parents and students at the beginning of the year of the grading method and the expected grade distribution is a good practice. After you have assigned grades, reporting the actual grade distribution is also a good practice. Under no circumstance should you post or report individual students' grades; students and their families have the right to expect that grades and other performance information be confidential (chapter 11, Teachers' Rights, Responsibilities, and Best Practices, provides more information on this issue). You should respect students by restricting discussions of grades and performances to professional conversations. Casual talk in the teachers' lounge is not a professional context.

Sample Instruments for Evaluation

You can use rubrics, rating scales, and checklists to evaluate skills for children in elementary school. **Rubrics** must define at least two levels of performance. The descriptions show the evolution of the skill from a lower to a higher level. Several rubrics have been presented in previous chapters. **Checklists** usually employ two categories—observed and not observed—whereas rating scales use multiple categories. The **rating scale** for creative rhythmic activities uses three categories (seldom, sometimes, and nearly always) and allows you to observe on three occasions. The checklist for basketball skills (grades 4 and 5) provides a yes–no response scale for the observation. These instruments focus on the way a skill

is performed (process) rather than the outcome (product). Rubrics provide information about the steps along the way that are not provided in rating scales or checklists. All provide valuable information to the children and their parents about learning and performance.

Table 14.4 shows how you can turn a rubric into a checklist or rating scale. For comparison, table 14.5 shows a rating scale, and table 14.6 shows a checklist. When the performances of students in a class are similar, a rating scale or checklist works well; however, these may not cover all of the levels of performance and may not provide necessary information for improvement. Rubrics show what came before and what comes after, whereas checklists extract information and often focus only on the most advanced skill level.

Portfolios and Journals

Portfolios have become an important part of authentic assessment in education because portfolios can document what you are doing and provide evidence of student learning.

You must make several decisions before using portfolios:

- What will be placed in a student portfolio?

- Who will enter the material?

- Why is this information included?

- How will the information be used?

Traditionally, teachers have recorded student work by class or groups of students (e.g., squads, grades). Portfolios shift the focus to organizing by individual students. Each student has a folder, and both you and the children place materials in the folder. You can use the portfolio to monitor their work and evaluate their progress. Students assume responsibility for many of the items placed in the portfolio, thus reducing your workload. For example, students may complete a journal that they place in the portfolio each week; or they may have homework that they complete and file in the portfolio. Parents may see the entire portfolio during a parent–teacher conference, or you can send portions of the portfolio home for parents to review. Student portfolios may follow students from grade to grade, where the progression of learning is most obvious.

Table 14.4 Rubric for Hopping

Circle the best descriptor in each column or row.

	Most effective	Still improving	Improving	Needs improvement
Leg swing	• Swing leg leads projection	• Swing leg pumps but is in front of the body	• Swing leg is inactive in front	• Swing leg is high in front or to the side
Body position	• Weight transferred smoothly from foot to ball for take-off	• Projected take-off for several steps	• Body leans forward	• Momentary flight from pulling motion for 1 to 2 steps
Arm action	• Arm opposition	• Arms assist from front of body position • Arms in semi-opposition	• Arms reactive and winging	• Arms stationary

Checklist for Hopping

Check yes or no for each skill:

Swing leg pumps but is in front of body	Yes ☐	No ☐
Projected take-off for several steps	Yes ☐	No ☐
Arms assist from front of body position or arms in semi-opposition	Yes ☐	No ☐

Rating Scale for Hopping

Check appropriate box:

	Always	Sometimes	Never
Swing leg pumps but is in front of body			
Projected take-off for several steps			
Arms assist from front of body position or arms in semi-opposition			

Consider Including These Items in Student Portfolios

- Fitness assessment data
- Self-assessment of skills
- Student journals
- Skills rubrics
- Student drawings of PE activities
- Quizzes and other written work
- Charts recording growth

You can include two types of information or "artifacts" in student portfolios: those that you have required and those that are optional. Consider carefully what to require and how it will be used as well as what optional material to include and how that will be used. For example, you may organize artifacts around the six NASPE content standards (see chapter 1, Health and Developmental Benefits of Physical Education), around other themes (e.g., skill, knowledge, fitness and activity, cooperation), or around the grading criteria. Regardless of the organizing themes and content, a summary sheet or checklist of the required items and a log for

Table 14.5 Grades 2-3: Rating Scales for Rhythmic Activities

Name _____ Class _____

Skill	First			Second			Third		
	3	2	1	3	2	1	3	2	1
Is able to vary the *rhythm* of locomotor skills: • Walk • Run									
Is able to vary the *speed* of locomotor skills: • Walk • Run									
Is able to demonstrate • heavy movements • light movements									
Is able to create a movement to a stimulus • (word, feeling, rhyme)									
Can create a simple dance using locomotor skills and shapes									
Is able to produce the actions for singing games: • Bingo • Paw Paw Patch									

Date _____   Date _____   Date _____

3 = nearly always, 2 = sometimes, 1 = seldom

Reprinted, by permission, from K.T. Thomas, A.M. Lee, and J.R. Thomas, 2000, *Physical education for children: Daily lesson plans for elementary school*, 2nd ed. (Champaign, IL: Human Kinetics), 1146.

Journal writing is one of many authentic assessments.

Table 14.6 Checklist for Basketball Skills

Name _____ Class _____

Observation date _____

	Yes	No
CHEST PASS		
Ball is held with fingers.		
Elbows are bent and close to body.		
Feet are in stride position at release.		
Wrists are snapped at release.		
Arms follow through toward receiver.		
DRIBBLING		
Ball is controlled with fingers.		
Knees are slightly bent.		
Body is flexed over ball.		
Head is up with eyes looking forward.		
ONE-HAND PUSH SHOT		
Ball is held with shooting hand behind and under ball.		
Ball is supported by nonshooting hand.		
Knees are flexed in preparation.		
Legs and arms are straightened as ball is released.		
Shooting hand follows through toward target.		

Reprinted, by permission, from K.T. Thomas, A.M. Lee, and J.R. Thomas, 2000, *Physical education for children: Daily lesson plans for elementary school,* 2nd ed. (Champaign, IL: Human Kinetics), 1154.

the users (e.g., students, teachers, and parents) are helpful.

At this point, most of you may be wondering, *How am I going to organize information for all of my students?* (For a physical education specialist, the total could be 400 students!) You can handle portfolios several ways: The most common is to use file folders—one for each child. Place one class or grade in a crate or other similar container to store and transport the portfolios. This container is available to students during specific times (e.g., during class or before school). Generally, you should keep the portfolios because children may lose or damage artifacts or entire portfolios.

Portfolios can also be electronic: you, the students, and the parents can access portfolios via a Web page or CD or in a computer laboratory. You can set up a physical education Web site, make folders for each child (older students can create their own folders), and make the information secure so that only a specific parent or child can read or enter information. Your school can have an electronic record of performance by using the Healthier US Challenge (www.healthierus.gov) and it is free!

Student journals are also popular. For classroom teachers, journaling about physical education or physical activity may seem a natural way to assess physical education and provide writing practice. This may seem less obvious for the physical education specialist. Clearly, journaling is an integrated activity. More important, though, is the information gained from reading journals. Student understanding is evident in journals; you can assess it for grading purposes or to inform teaching and learning.

Summary

Evaluation is the final link in the teaching and learning circle. Evaluation informs teaching and is a major factor in learning. You must plan evaluation during the curriculum and lesson planning process. As you select objectives, you need to consider how to evaluate the objectives. Validity, reliability, and objectivity provide meaning and substance to the evaluation process; therefore, these sometimes influence the objectives of instruction. Objectives should focus on important educational outcomes. Evaluation is then based on educational outcomes, as are grades. Evaluation has many purposes, including screening, grouping, and grading. Grading must follow the principles of evaluation and must provide information to children and parents about learning as well as specific information to facilitate improvement. Use many types of assessment, such as norm-referenced, criterion-referenced, and authentic assessments, as well as a variety of measurements, including cognitive tests, rubrics, portfolios, and journals.

Mastery Learning Activities

1. Find a physical education test for children in elementary school. If the test does not have a stated objective, write one. Critique the test based on validity, reliability, and objectivity.

2. Select one National Content Standard and write a benchmark for each grade (K-5), using the same skill or a variation of the skill. The benchmarks should clearly demonstrate progression from grade to grade.

3. Select one skill and develop a norm-referenced, criterion-referenced, and authentic assessment for that skill.

4. Write a one-page description for parents of a physical education grading system for grades 2 and 3.

References

Burke, K. 2006. *From standards to rubrics in six steps.* Thousand Oaks, CA: Corwin Press.

Baker, B., A. Costa, and S. Shalit. 1997. The norms of collaboration: Attaining communication competence. In *The process-centered school: Sustaining a renaissance community,* edited by A. Costa and R. Liebmann, 119-142. Thousand Oaks, CA: Corwin Press.

Holt/Hale, S.A. 1999a. *Assessing motor skills in elementary physical education.* Reston, VA: NASPE Publications.

Holt/Hale, S.A. 1999b. *Assessing and improving fitness in elementary physical education.* Reston, VA: NASPE Publications.

Lambert, L.T. 1999. *Standards-based assessment of student learning: A comprehensive approach.* Reston, VA: NASPE Publications.

Mitchell, S.A., and J.L. Oslin. 1999. *Assessment in games teaching.* Reston, VA: NASPE Publications.

Morrow, J.R., A.W. Jackson, J.G. Disch, and D.P. Mood. 2005. *Measurement and evaluation in human performance.* 3rd ed. Champaign, IL: Human Kinetics.

U.S. Congress, Office of Technology Assessment. 1992. *Testing in American schools: Asking the right questions.* OTA-SET-519 February. Washington, DC: Government Printing Office.

Resources

Schiemer, S. 2000. *Assessment strategies for elementary physical education.* Champaign, IL: Human Kinetics.

Thomas, J.R., and K.T. Thomas. 1983. Strange kids and strange numbers: Assessing children's motor development. *Journal of Physical Education, Recreation and Dance* 54: 19-20.

Lesson Plans

Three lessons plans using various types of assessment are presented. A checklist is used to assess gymnastics at the end of a unit. Student names go at the top of the column. The lesson suggests that you place children in the order in which they are listed on the checklist to do the tasks; this saves time because you do not have to search the list for a name. A health lesson on fitness and activity for grades 2 and 3 uses a crossword puzzle to check for understanding. Finally, a lesson conducting the 1-mile run test is presented for grades 4 and 5.

Lesson 14.1

Tumbling Checklist

Student Objectives 2

- Evaluate one's own performances of the various skills.

Equipment and Materials

- 1 mat (4 by 8 feet [1.2 by 2.4 m]) per group
- Background music (optional)
- 1 copy of the Checklist for Tumbling per group

Warm-Up Activities (5 minutes)

Use Warm-Up Routine for Grades K and 1 from lesson 11.1, page 321.

Skill-Development Activities (20 minutes)

Skills Checklist

Arrange the children at the mats in small groups corresponding to the order on your checklist. See Checklist for Tumbling on the following pages.

Repeat one at a time the following skills: Log Roll, Rocker, Two-Knee Balance, Forward Roll, Backward Roll, One-Leg Balance, Forehead Touch, Donkey Kick, Tripod, and Elbow–Knee Balance.

Extension Activities

Set up the mats as described for the checklist. Invite another teacher, your principal, or other honored guest to observe the children.

1. Have the children run through the tumbling activities. You could also review the animal walks and locomotor skills.
2. Have each group of children select one stunt per group member and decide the order in which their group will present the stunts.
3. Allow each group to demonstrate for the rest of the class.

Concluding Activities (5 minutes)

Keep the children with their groups at their mats. Tell the children: "Show your group the one skill you did the very best today!"

Checklist for Tumbling

(Kindergarten children's competencies are noted with #.)
(First-grade children should do all skills competently.)

Name													
FORWARD ROLL#													
Begins squatting on mat, hands placed on mat in front of and outside feet.													
Has arms outside of legs.													
In one motion, straightens legs while looking at tummy.													
Begins to support body weight with arms; keeps hips above shoulders and moving forward.													
Lands on shoulder blades.													
Keeps legs tucked.													
Lands on feet (first).													
Does not use hands to push under hips.													
BACKWARD ROLL#													
Begins in squat position with back to length of mat.													
Places hands on shoulders, palms up.													
Presses chin close to chest.													
Begins motion with rocking movement.													
Touches mat with bottom, back, shoulders–hands, head–hands, in sequence.													
Pushes by extending arms when hands touch.													
Recovers (lands) on feet (first).													
LOG ROLL#													
Begins lying crosswise on mat with arms and legs extended.													
Initiates rolling motion by turning head and shoulders.													
Keeps body straight and doesn't use hands or feet to make motion.													
Makes three complete turns, or moves length of mat.													
ROCKER#													
Begins lying on back with hands grasping knees.													
Initiates motion by thrusting head forward and "pumping" body.													
Achieves 90-degree range of motion without releasing grasp of hands and knees.													
Does three consecutive repetitions.													

TWO-KNEE BALANCE#

Begins kneeling (with hips extended so that buttocks do not touch legs), with arms extended to each side.

Lifts feet from mat so that only knees are supporting body weight.

Keeps both feet off floor while maintaining balance. Balances for 5 seconds.

ONE-LEG BALANCE

Begins standing with hands on hips.

Keeps one leg raised until foot clears floor, stopping near knee of support leg.

Maintains balance for 10 seconds.

FOREHEAD TOUCH

Begins in kneeling-squat position (knees, legs, and feet on floor; buttocks on calf of leg), with hands joined behind back.

Bends slowly forward until forehead touches mat.

Raises to kneeling position without using hands for balance.

DONKEY KICK

Begins standing.

Bends at waist, hands placed shoulder-width apart on mat.

Kicks feet and legs out and up behind while supporting body weight with arms.

Moves feet up and down together.

TRIPOD

Begins in squat with hands and arms on mat outside knees and legs.

Bends forward until forehead touches mat.

Bends arms and touches knees to elbows.

Supports body weight with arms.

Maintains balance for 5 seconds.

ELBOW–KNEE BALANCE

Begins in squat with hands on mat outside legs.

Touches elbows to knees.

Holds up head.

Shifts weight from feet to hands.

Maintains balance for 5 seconds.

Physical Activity and Fitness

Student Objectives 2

- Distinguish between physical fitness and physical activity.
- Name one benefit of physical activity.

Equipment and Materials

- 1 copy of crossword per child
- 1 pencil per child

Health Concept (30 minutes)

Gather the children into an information formation for the entire discussion.

Physical Fitness and Physical Activity

1. Introduce the concept: "Physical fitness and physical activity are part of good health and help us grow. Physical fitness is being able to meet some standards for muscle strength and endurance, flexibility, and cardiorespiratory (aerobic) endurance. Having a healthy amount of body fat is also part of fitness."

2. Tell the children: "Physical activity means a person does things that require the large muscles to work, and such a person does not spend all day sitting down. If we take a walk, use the stairs, clean house, or work in the garden, we are being physically active. Being physically fit or active reduces the risk of certain diseases (e.g., diabetes, heart disease), encourages bones to grow stronger, helps make bigger muscles, and keeps our bodies from storing too much fat."

3. Do the crossword on the next page individually. The puzzle words running down are associated with health-related fitness; the words running across are related to physical activity.

Lesson 14.2 *(continued)*

CROSSWORD

Across

1. Don't ride in a car if you can _____.
2. A place where you can grow flowers and make good health
3. To play baseball, you need a ball and a _____.
4. Traveling on two wheels

Down

1. Lifting a heavy object shows your muscular _____.
2. Doing something over and over again shows your _____.
3. This kind of activity helps build your heart fitness.
4. Stretching and bending demonstrates your _____.
5. Your body needs some of this, but not too much and not too little.

From K.T. Thomas, A.M. Lee, and J.R. Thomas, 2008, *Physical education methods for elementary teachers*, 3rd ed. (Champaign, IL: Human Kinetics). Adapted, by permission, from K.T. Thomas, A.M. Lee, and J.R. Thomas, 2000, *Physical education for children: Daily lesson plans for elementary school*, 2nd ed. (Champaign, IL: Human Kinetics), 713.

Lesson 14.3

Testing Aerobic Fitness

Student Objectives   1   5

- Perform the 1-mile run.
- Work cooperatively with a partner.

Equipment and Materials

- Stopwatch
- Cones to mark testing area
- Recording forms
- Music

Warm-Up Activities (5 minutes)

Individual Stretching Exercises

Arrange the children in scatter formation.

1. Briefly discuss the importance of good flexibility and how stretching can improve flexibility.
2. Describe and demonstrate the individual stretching exercises. Emphasize safety guidelines:
   o Move slowly into each stretch, stopping when you feel a slight tug. Stretching should not hurt!
   o No bouncing!
3. Have the children complete the individual stretching exercises.

SITTING TOE TOUCH

Sitting with legs straight and feet together, reach your fingers toward your toes, bringing your face toward your knees, and hold for 5 seconds. Relax. Repeat several times.

TRUNK TWISTER

Sitting with feet shoulder-width apart and hands clasped in front of your chest, keep your arms horizontal (demonstrate). Rotate slowly to the right and left, holding each position for 5 seconds. Repeat several times.

FORWARD LUNGE

Standing with feet together and hands on your hips, lunge forward with your right leg, keeping your left leg straight. Your right knee should form a right angle (corner of a square). Hold the lunge position for 5 seconds and return to starting position. Then lunge with your left leg forward. Repeat several times, alternating right and left legs.

Skill-Development Activities (25 minutes)

1-Mile Run Test

Create partners in two groups, one partner from each pair in each group.

Lesson 14.3 *(continued)*

1. Tell the children:
   - One child from each pair runs the mile first. The other counts the number of laps.
   - I call out each child's time as he or she crosses the finish line; each child's partner records the time.
   - Then we switch and let the other group run.
2. Give the children a short break and the opportunity to get water after running.

From K.T. Thomas, A.M. Lee, and J.R. Thomas, 2008, *Physical education methods for elementary teachers*, 3rd ed. (Champaign, IL: Human Kinetics). Adapted, by permission, from K.T. Thomas, A.M. Lee, and J.R. Thomas, 2000, *Physical education for children: Daily lesson plans for elementary school*, 2nd ed. (Champaign, IL: Human Kinetics), 795.

CHAPTER 15

Growing as a Teacher

DELANEY, AGE 7

Just as an education is more than a collection of courses, becoming a teacher is more than completing a program of study. Teaching is a daily and long-term learning opportunity. Reflection and self-evaluation contribute to teacher growth and are possibly the most powerful forces in creating positive change. Other sources of information include external reviews of your work, continued learning, professional activities, and extending the mission of your school and your work to a wider audience.

Learner Outcomes

After studying this chapter, you should be able to do the following:

- Explain reflection and the benefits of being a reflective teacher.
- Describe portfolios and how to use working, professional, and employment portfolios.
- Understand why lifelong learning is important.
- Describe collaboration and list several of its benefits.
- Identify several ways that you can extend learning beyond the walls of your school.
- Present one or more ways to develop as a professional.

Glossary Terms

reflection	vita	employment portfolio
working portfolio	professional portfolio	service
teaching philosophy statement		

As you observe experienced teachers—particularly expert teachers—you may think, *Teaching looks easy.* However, although rewarding, student teaching is also the most difficult semester of the college careers of many prospective teachers. Good teachers make it *look* easy—in part because of all the unobserved hard work that they do. Another factor is experience. Practice does make for better teaching—but not easier teaching. During student teaching, you are probably going to wonder how your cooperating teacher can do so much over so many years! Unfortunately, the dropout rate for new teachers is high. Teaching is hard work and often offers a low salary. New teachers feel inadequate and isolated; they feel disappointed in their performance and sometimes in the profession. The dropout rate has become a crisis in education for three reasons: First, the costs associated with preparing and inducting new teachers is high—so a teacher dropping out is expensive to the system. Second, most teachers improve during the first five years, so dropping out early means the efficiency of the system is reduced; optimally, teachers would have at least five years of experience. So it may be difficult to get your first job and easier to get your second job! Third, children perform better with more experienced teachers. Student test scores improve each year for the first five to seven years of a teacher's experience (Berliner 1994). (See the DVD-ROM for teacher interviews on commitment to teaching.)

The information in this chapter is important for you for several reasons:

- You want to improve your teaching.
- You must be able to document your teaching performance.
- You may need assistance in obtaining a job.
- You need to transition from student in teacher education to professional teacher.
- You do not want to drop out of teaching.
- You often seek new challenges.

Thus, this chapter covers reflection as a technique to improve teaching; portfolios as learning, professional, and employment tools; collaboration; service; and professionalism.

Reflection

"In the domains in which they are acquiring their abilities, developing experts learn more from experience than do the rest of us. It is highly motivated learning in which they are engaged, whether it is the acquisition of baseball knowledge, chess moves, or computer programming. Their learning probably is also reflected upon more than is the learning in which others engage."

—*David Berliner (1986)*

Reflection is a necessary tool in the process of becoming an expert teacher. Expertise can begin after 10,000 hours of practice, but practice does not guarantee expertise. The practice must be deliberate, with feedback and corrections (Ericsson, Krampe, and Tesch-Römer 1993). **Reflection** on the teaching learning process—thinking, feedback, and correction—is critical when improvement is the goal.

Thus, you should evaluate your own teaching and may evaluate the teaching of others. For example, students observe experienced teachers, student teachers observe cooperating teachers, and you observe your peers. Teaching and learning are complex; examine them together because they influence each other. You plan, manage, instruct, demonstrate, provide feedback, and evaluate, generally in that order. Each of those categories includes many behaviors that provide information about your success (Lee 1991).

Many teacher education programs require students to keep a journal during field experience because this forces you to reflect on your teaching. Supervisors can read the journal and provide feedback—to improve the reflection or to solve teaching problems. The critical ingredient is not the writing, but the thinking. However, writing tends to clarify thinking; the phenomenon has been called "communicating to learn." Most communication education focused on learning to communicate; the reverse process is now the accepted educational procedure—communicating to learn. Whether written, oral, or cerebral, reflection about teaching is critical to improvement.

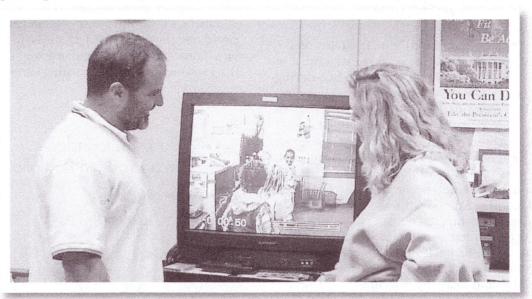

Peer evaluation and self-evaluation are excellent techniques for improving teaching skills.
Photo courtesy of the authors.

Table 15.1 Lesson Evaluation Form

Name of teacher: _____ Date: _____

Name of observer: _____

Objective	Activity	Formation (draw this)	Cues	Number of trials or time	Feedback and evaluation

You can use videotaping to watch your teaching and then reflect and plan for change. You can also ask a colleague to observe and provide feedback (table 15.1). You can use student performance and learning to inform your teaching. In fact, you should use each of these sources of feedback. Some reflection is spontaneous: You realize that something is not working, and you ask yourself, *How can I change this so it will work?* Other reflection is more deliberate and covers longer periods. Both types of reflection are important. (See the DVD-ROM for teacher interviews on goals for the beginning of the year and goals for the rest of the year for new teachers.)

Portfolios

Portfolios have been used in many fields as the primary documentation of work; for example, in art or advertising, students use portfolios during training and while searching for employment. Recently, portfolios have become an important part of authentic assessment in education because they can document what you are doing (Melograno 1999). Portfolios communicate this information in several ways. First, you think about and refine what you believe and what you do to enhance student learning. As you write about your teaching and student learning, the written communication becomes a learning experience, communicating to learn. Second, portfolios demonstrate your communication skills as well as your planning, philosophy, and teaching activities.

Portfolios help you grow, address licensing and certification issues (e.g., INTASC standards), and assist schools and universities during reviews.

They may also enhance your employment opportunities. Three types of portfolio are discussed here: a working portfolio in which to store information about your teaching, a professional or presentation portfolio that highlights your best or most recent work, and an employment portfolio that extends the presentation portfolio to include information required in the job market.

Working Portfolios

You can view a **working portfolio** as a storage system for activities, ideas, and other support materials. A working portfolio is more than a filing system, but it certainly includes a filing system. As a preservice teacher, begin saving and systematically filing samples of your work. No unit plan, bulletin board, or philosophy statement should be considered the final product, at least not until you retire from teaching! You can organize systems for filing around themes (or learning centers) and by age group.

Items to Include in a Working Portfolio

- Teaching statement
- Short-term and long-term goals
- Resume or vita (updated regularly)
- Unit plans
- Lesson plans
- Sample bulletin boards
- Evaluation instruments

- Teaching evaluations
- Journals
- Reflections
- Photos
- Videos

Begin with broad themes (e.g., locomotor skills and manipulative skills) or team sports. As you collect more information, add more specific categories, such as softball, soccer, and basketball. Organize by the class in which the work was completed, especially early in your college career. As you collect materials, document the source. For example, one lesson might be downloaded from a Web site, another might be a class handout, and a third might be a lesson plan given to you by a colleague. Recording this information is important for two reasons. First, you may need to give credit to the source at a later time and, as your portfolio grows, you may not be able to remember every source. Second, you may want to go back and get additional information from that source later. You can use materials from your working portfolio in your professional portfolio or as resources for you as you plan and teach. Working portfolios document, for you and others, the progress you are making as a teacher.

Working portfolios contain many types of materials, including computer storage of important work (always keep a paper copy as well); videotapes of teaching and other performances; papers; critiques; written class work; evaluations by employers, supervisors, and teachers; samples of creations; and virtually anything else. Generally, you need filing boxes to handle the volume of materials in a working portfolio. Hints: Use dividers and labels and color code materials. A working portfolio is a source of information that you may need to access quickly. Keep information in electronic files. For example, update your resume or vita on a regular basis, review your teaching philosophy statement before each school year, and add awards and performance evaluations at the end of each school year.

Base your **teaching philosophy statement** on your values and be specific about how those values affect your curriculum decisions and instructional strategies. Describe a typical class, overview your curriculum and evaluation procedures, and present your point of view on diversity issues such as gender and disabilities (Seldin

1997). A philosophy statement is usually five to seven pages, double spaced, but you can present it in a one-page abstract form. The key to a good philosophy statement is to avoid generalities such as "I want to cure all of the problems in the world by being a teacher" or "I will be the best teacher ever" and to focus on specific activities, behaviors, and beliefs: For example, "By shifting responsibility to students for _____, _____, and _____, I will help them learn to be independent thinkers and better team members" is a specific action tied to a personal value. The teaching philosophy statement should reveal a great deal about you as a person and as a teacher.

The resume or **vita** is a record of what you have accomplished. Ideas vary about the amount of personal information included in a vita. You may feel comfortable including your age, gender, family status, and other descriptive information; however, you do not have to reveal this in your resume or during an interview. Still, your vita should include certain information. Figure 15.1 provides a suggested format. Two critical aspects of a resume or vita are that all information must be accurate (i.e., truthful) and the document should be neat and error free (i.e., no typographical or spelling errors).

Presentation or Professional Portfolios

The purpose of a presentation or **professional portfolio** is to highlight your best work. The portfolio is often used in evaluation of your performance for career ladder programs, merit pay, master teacher programs, and recognition award programs. In creating the professional or presentation portfolio, select materials from the working portfolio. For most professional uses, include the philosophy statement or at least part of it. Photos and other visual material are helpful. Include portions of units or lessons to reduce reading and increase visual impact. Dividers and color coding help guide the reader through the portfolio. You can use presentation portfolios during parent conferences to share with them information about you and your program. An electronic version, rich in visual elements, may be even more practical: CDs, Web pages, and videos capture the imagination of the audience and present your best work. Another alternative, depending on the use, is a large presentation board that uses photos and other visual materials to demonstrate your best work.

Bjorn T. Teach
Physical Education Specialist

Work address:

B. Pettifor Elementary School
1507 Market Street
Champaign, IL 61825
Phone: 555-555-1212
e-mail: borntoteach@champaign.edu.k-12

Home address:

123 School Street
Urbana, IL 61822
555-555-2121

Education

Institution	Degree	Year
Iowa State University	BS in health and human performance	2006
Podunk Center High School	High school diploma with honors	2000

Licenses, endorsements, certifications, and authorizations

Agency	Title	Date
Iowa Department of Education	Initial beginning teacher	2006
Iowa Department of Education	Coaching authorization	2006
Illinois Department of Education	Professional teacher	2006
American Red Cross	First responder	2004-2007

Teaching experience

School name and address	Position	Dates
B. Pettifor Elementary School 1507 Market Street Champaign, IL 61825	Physical Education Specialist	2006-
K. Thomas Elementary School 3345 Jewell Drive Ames, IA 50010	Student teacher	2005

Other work experience

Employer	Job duties	Dates
ISU Clone Kids	Gymnastics instructor	Summer 2003, 04, 05
Ames Public Schools	Substitute educational assistant	2004-2005
Kids Care	Child care provider	2003-2004

Awards and other recognitions

ISU College of Education Dean's List (6 times)	2003-2005
College of Education Outstanding Student Teacher	2005
Harry Schmidt Outstanding Male Senior Award	2005
Phi Kappa Phi National Honorary	2004

Figure 15.1   Sample of a resume or vita.

Employment Portfolios

The **employment portfolio** displays your best work. However, you should target employment portfolios at a specific employer. Doing your homework about the prospective school or school district is critical. Include in your employment portfolio, as well as in your letter of application, a section that matches your goals and skills to the characteristics of the school (e.g., mission statement, school improvement plan, demographics, and organization). This section demonstrates that you have a genuine desire to work in the setting, you understand the needs, and you match those needs perfectly. Select work samples that target the unique aspects of the school (or district); the artifacts may vary depending on the job for which you are applying. Each district and school is different; at various schools within a district, each person who interviews you or looks at your credentials may place greater value on one aspect of your materials over another. Every part of your application package or employment portfolio should be the best that you can produce and should represent you as well as possible. What will people say when they look at your materials? Samples of positive comments are presented in the Concepts Into Practice box on this page.

Components to Include in an Employment Portfolio

- Letter of application (a copy of the one you mailed with your application), which describes why you want to teach, why this school is perfect for you, and what highlights of your credentials relate to this job
- A copy of the district application
- Your resume or vita
- A list of references and your relationship to them (highlight how and what they know about your teaching); obtain prior permission to use them as references
- A statement of your short- and long-term goals
- Your teaching philosophy statement
- Sample unit and lesson plans, including evaluation instruments and bulletin board photos or sketches
- Evaluations of your teaching by supervisors and peers; other related evaluations
- Other materials (videos, awards, samples of written work, copy of teaching license)

Concepts Into Practice

Chris is applying for a job in the Newcastle School District. His employment portfolio has been reviewed by several people in the district. When they meet to discuss each candidate, they say the following about Chris:

Director of human resources: "The application is complete and has no errors. I like his letter of application because it demonstrates his ability to communicate."

Curriculum director: "His unit plans are clear and creative, and he includes many support materials, such as the bulletin boards and handouts. He included evaluation materials for each lesson and unit."

Principal: "Two things were important to me— First, I can see from his philosophy statement that he cares about the kids and works hard to help them learn. Second, his letters of recommendation from his supervising and cooperating teachers say he is a team player—I need that in my school."

Teacher: "He doesn't have any years of experience, but he has a number of service learning and related work experiences on his vita. He is probably ahead of a new teacher, and he has worked hard to learn about teaching before his first job."

Parent: "As a parent and school board member, I am impressed with his computer and technology skills. His CD has video clips of his teaching! I think he can help us in that area, too."

Assistant principal: "Everything looks great. I am impressed with the letter from his methods professor. I could almost see him teaching, just from reading her letter and evaluation."

Lifelong Learning

Educators value learning. Educators want their students to value learning and to continue to learn during vacations and after graduation, You model this behavior, as demonstrated by reading, traveling, and searching the Internet for new information. You provide those tools to your students and have them yourselves. Your learning as teachers continues in the informal sense of reflection, in the formal sense of evaluation by supervisors, and in other ways as well.

Professional learning may occur in workshops and advanced university courses and by securing additional endorsements or certificates. School districts and professional associations provide opportunities for you to learn—some voluntary and others mandatory. Some of these experiences are intended to help you meet the mission of the school; others are more content specific. In addition, you have the opportunity to select meaningful experiences from a variety of professional organizations. Attending a conference is one way to meet other professionals, to learn from them, to share with them, and to learn from experts. Schools often provide the opportunity for you to take professional leave days to attend conferences. We encourage you to try this!

Personal lifelong learning is also important. Your life is more than just teaching, and your teaching is enhanced by a variety of interests. Reserve some time for yourself; try something new each year. You may better understand your students' likes and dislikes if you try new activities, because you may like some better than others. Classroom teachers are accustomed to reading the popular books their students are reading. Physical education specialists benefit from this activity as well for two reasons: First, it opens new areas of communication with their colleagues and students. Second, it opens opportunities for integration of physical education and classroom subjects.

Select a popular book that elementary students are reading, such as one of the books in the *Harry Potter* series. Create a game or physical activity based on the book.

Collaboration

Working with others is inherent in your job description. You need to work with administrators, parents, other teachers, and, of course, your students. In addition to those job-related collaborations, we encourage you to seek community support for your teaching. This may not be something for your first year of teaching, but, as you have time and feel comfortable, look for those in the community who may be able to help you. For example, if you are doing a unit on India or Australia, you may find a person or group who plays cricket—a popular game in those countries. If you are near a university, you can contact the international student group for that community. This collaboration could lead to a demonstration or instruction in a new activity, learning about language and customs—a perfect integration and collaboration. Other sources of collaboration are the local health clinic or medical society, the public health department, the recreation department,

Collaboration is essential for vertical alignment and provides valuable support for new teachers.

and local businesses and service groups. Service clubs (e.g., Rotary, Lions, fraternities) are capable and often willing to support your school projects. Some schools have intergenerational projects in which elderly community members work with you and the students in a variety of forms, from reading to young people to intergenerational meals. To arrange such a project, collaborate, go into the community to build a relationship, and follow through to bring the community into the classroom. Collaboration with the state department of education or the nearest university faculty is also a possibility. Sharing ideas and sharing workload are two benefits of collaboration.

Outreach

Earlier in the book, we discussed the expectations for teachers and how they are higher than for other people, including the idea that you do **service** beyond your teaching job. Sometimes you can complete service by working with a food drive or advising a yearbook committee. At other times, service uses your skill, interests, and expertise in other ways. Perhaps you serve on the advisory committee for the parks and recreation department or YMCA, or you are a member of a service group (e.g., Lions, Rotary). You may write grants to bring preschool programs or nutrition education to your school. Each of these is a service beyond your job.

Professionalism

In chapter 11, Teachers' Rights, Responsibilities, and Best Practices, we presented information on professional ethics and behavior. You also demonstrate professionalism by belonging to and participating in professional educators' associations, mentoring, continuing formal education, and extending professional horizons.

Organizations are available at the national, state, and often local or regional levels for a variety of specializations. Two groups you should know about are the National Education Association (NEA) and the American Alliance for Health, Physical Education, Recreation and Dance (AAHPERD). NEA (www.nea.org) is a politically powerful organization open to all of you. AAHPERD (www.aahperd.org), the primary organization for teachers of health, physical education, and dance, provides membership benefits such as

publications, low-cost insurance, and advocacy. You can learn more by going to the respective Web sites. These are two of the oldest and largest teacher organizations; you can investigate other organizations yourself. The point is that you can demonstrate your professional loyalty by joining and participating, reading the association literature, attending meetings, and perhaps becoming an officer or presenter. Mentoring is another professional act. You work hard and you are busy. You provide advice and opportunities to preservice or new teachers as part of your professional service. This allows you to leave a professional legacy and is often a rewarding and invigorating experience. Being a good mentor requires time, effort, and knowledge. Thus, mentoring is recognized as a valuable part of your work.

Master teacher and national board certification programs are designed so that you can extend yourselves. These programs recognize excellent teaching and are usually highly selective. Generally, you must have several years of experience before entering the program; completion of the program takes two or more years. Why would you want to do this? Challenge, recognition, and learning are all factors in your decision to enter one of these programs. Moving into administration has been the traditional way for excellent teachers to achieve increased status and salary. But this is counterproductive to education: The best teachers are forced to leave teaching to gain recognition. These programs are an answer to that dilemma: you are recognized and rewarded for *teaching*.

Graduate education is another venue for growing as a teacher. Many options are available, from online and commercial degrees to traditional full-time graduate programs. AAHPERD produces a list of graduate programs, which can help you make a decision. If you are interested in a graduate program to increase pay (usually called steps), the type of program does not make much difference. If you want to learn more about teaching or about the fields in which you are teaching, the program does matter. You can pursue three categories of graduate degrees: master of science (MS), master of education (MEd), and master of arts (MA). The MS and MA degrees usually require a thesis; they prepare you for a variety of professional experiences. For example, you may continue in a doctoral program, teach at a community college, or remain in your present teaching position. The MEd is tailored to teachers and is considered the terminal degree. Usually, it does not involve a thesis, but it often involves a final project or internship or both. Graduate education is expensive in terms of tuition and time invested, so careful consideration is a must. Check into the school, consult with the faculty, and ask your principal and other mentors what they think before you decide what to do and where to go. Many graduate schools require you to take a test before admission, the Graduate Record Exam (GRE). A good time to take this test is while you are an undergraduate student, in your junior or senior year. Consider doing this even if you do not want to enter graduate school right away.

Summary

The teaching profession presents several challenges to new teachers:

- Continuing to learn
- Meeting the expectations of parents, students, and administrators
- Transitioning from student to teacher
- Dealing with the frustrations of a challenging new career
- Developing partnerships and collaborations
- Maintaining your personal identity

Supports are available to help you deal with these challenges. Your primary challenge is to improve as a teacher. (See the DVD-ROM for teacher interviews on what new teachers have learned.) Professional associations and continuing education are sources of additional information that can help you increase your effectiveness. The most important and effective method is reflection and self-evaluation. Portfolios and journals are helpful tools for reflection and self-evaluation. You can participate in service activities within your school and outside the school in the community. These activities are important to your professional development. Your personal life is also important because it influences your teaching directly and indirectly.

You need to collaborate and, with experience, go beyond required collaborations. You can seek collaborations in the community or through outside professional connections. Each collaboration has the potential to be a learning experience for you and your students. Formal learning, in the form of workshops and graduate education, also contributes to growing as a teacher.

Mastery Learning Activities

1. Create a vita or resume for yourself.
2. Begin a working portfolio. Develop an organizational system to store materials.
3. Develop five activities based on the NASPE standards to include in a student portfolio.
4. Find the national board certification standards for physical education teachers and make a list of what should be in the portfolio.
5. Identify the strengths and weaknesses of various types of presentation portfolios (e.g., electronic, video, paper, and presentation board).
6. Design or make a Web page, CD, or video portfolio.
7. Compare the graduate programs at two universities on the following characteristics:
   a. The goal of the program
   b. The ranking of the program (or the university graduate program if the program is not ranked)
   c. The course work and other expectations (do they require you to attend full-time?)
   d. The time and cost of a master's degree
8. Investigate a professional organization. Find out the cost and benefit of membership. When does the group meet and where? What is the mission of the organization?

References

Berliner, D.C. 1986. In search of the expert pedagogue. *The Educational Researcher* 15: 5-13.

Berliner, D.C. 1994. Expertise, the wonder of exemplary performance. In *Creating powerful thinking in teachers and students*, edited by J.N. Mangieri and C.C. Block, 161-186. Fort Worth, TX: Holt, Rinehart and Winston.

Ericsson, K.A., R.T. Krampe, and C. Tesch-Römer. 1993. The role of deliberate practice in the acquisition of expert performance. *Psychological Review* 100(3): 363-406.

Lee, A. 1991. Research on teaching in physical education: Questions and comments. *Research Quarterly for Exercise and Sport* 62: 374-379.

Melograno, V.J. 1999. Preservice professional portfolio system. In *Assessment series physical education teacher preparation,* edited by D. Tannehill. Reston, VA: NASPE Publications.

Seldin, P. 1997. *The teaching portfolio: A practical guide to improved performance and promotional/tenure decisions.* 2nd ed. Boston: Anker Publishing.

Resources

Dodds, P. 1994. Cognitive and behavioral components of expertise in teaching physical education. *Quest* 46: 153-163.

Ennis, C.D. 1994. Knowledge and beliefs underlying curricular expertise. *Quest* 46: 164-175.

Graham, G. 2001. *Teaching children physical education: Becoming a master teacher.* 2nd ed. Champaign, IL: Human Kinetics.

Grossman, P.L. 1990. *The making of a teacher: Teacher knowledge and teacher education.* New York: Teachers College Press.

Hebert, E., A.M. Lee, and L. Williamson. 1998. Teachers' and teacher education students' sense of efficacy: Quantitative and qualitative comparisons. *Journal of Research and Development in Education* 31: 214-225.

Housner, L.D., and D.C. Griffey. 1985. Teacher cognition: Differences in planning and interactive decision making between experienced and inexperienced teachers. *Research Quarterly for Exercise and Sport* 56: 44-53.

GLOSSARY

academic learning time—Time on tasks associated with improved outcomes for some sectors of the population.

active supervision—Has three characteristics: proximity, scanning, and positioning.

aerobic training—Designed to improve cardiovascular fitness. You must exercise (swim, jog, cycle) 3 days per week, for 20 minutes at your training heart rate ([220 − your age] × 0.70).

allocated time—The time spent in school for instruction and practice.

anaerobic threshold—The point at which the body can no longer keep up with the oxygen demands or the waste build-up in the muscles.

anxiety—The negative extreme of arousal.

attention—Cognitive capacity or space in short-term memory, vigilance, or focus.

authentic assessment—A form of evaluation as close to the real-world setting as possible and that places responsibility on the student and demands higher-level thinking or critical thinking.

best practice—A way to do something that maximizes the opportunities to gain from the experience.

blocked practice—Practice order for several skills: practices all of one, then moves on to another skill, practicing all of that skill.

body composition—Dividing body mass into components of lean and fat tissue.

body language—Nonverbal messages sent by your positions and movements.

breach of contract—Breaking a promise (usually a written contract).

Buckley Amendment—Educational information must be confidential; only students and their parents are to be aware of most information about student progress.

capacity—The size of memory.

chain of command—A specific order in which to do something (e.g., report an accident).

checklists—Assessment instruments that have a list of criteria evaluated as performed or not performed.

class rules—Have two purposes: to keep students safe and to allow learning.

class signals—Most are indicators for students to stop, look, listen, and be quiet as quickly as possible.

closure—Summarizes the day's learning and allows you to do a quick check for understanding.

cognition—Thinking.

competence—The skill or capability to do a task.

competition—Playing against an opponent (e.g., two tennis players compete, two baseball teams compete).

concluding activity—Event used to end each class (not the same as a closure activity).

constant practice—Repeating one skill over and over.

contextual practice—Practice in the actual activity or a modified situation as similar to the activity as possible.

control processes—Specific cognitive actions that facilitate memory.

cooperative learning—A teaching approach designed to encourage students to take responsibility for their own learning and to work cooperatively with a group to accomplish a goal.

coordinated school health program—The eight-component (health education, physical education, health services, nutrition services, staff health promotion, counseling and psychological services, healthy school environment, and parent and community involvement) program recommended by the Centers for Disease Control and Prevention (CDC).

criterion-referenced tests—Test is based on mastery learning and places students into two categories: master (successful) and nonmaster (unsuccessful).

decision making—When something unusual is observed, then the teacher must take appropriate action.

declarative knowledge—Factual information stored in memory.

demonstrations—Using a model (teacher or child) to show how to do a skill.

desist—Use of teacher proximity to control misbehavior.

development—A combination of growth, maturation, and experience.

developmentally appropriate—Programs that meet the needs of children based on their age, maturation, and interests.

diastolic pressure—The minimum pressure just before a heart beat.

direct instruction approach—Emphasis is on class control with little opportunity for students to choose between alternatives and make decisions about their own learning.

directions—Communications to students (e.g., where to go, what to do).

duration—Same as *time*; the amount of training in minutes or repetitions.

dynamic balance—The ability to maintain a balanced position while moving through space.

educational outcomes—Desired student learning in content areas.

effect sizes—Calculated by dividing the difference between two means (e.g., boys' running speed minus girls' running speed) by the standard deviation of the means; if the answer is zero or close to zero, the effect size suggests the two groups are not different; an effect size of 0.5 is moderate and 0.8 is large.

ego orientation—Undertaking a task because doing so brings status.

employment portfolio—A sample of a professional's best work used to demonstrate competence during the employment search.

evaluation—The highest level of cognition (in Bloom's taxonomy) and is defined as making a judgment.

experience—External or environmental; includes factors such as nutrition, education, and home life.

expertise—The knowledge possessed by a high-level performer; in sport often an athlete "ranked" by some standard (top 10 golfers in the world).

exploration—An open-ended, divergent, problem-solving process.

extrinsic—Doing something because of an inducement (parents' desire, trophy).

extrinsic feedback—Information about performance that cannot be obtained by the performer.

facial expression—Nonverbal messages sent by the face (e.g., happy, sad).

FITT—Acronym for training involving frequency, intensity, time, and type.

flexibility—Range of motion for a joint.

flow—The amount of control present in a movement; ranges from free to bound. A bound movement is under complete control of the performer and can be stopped at any moment.

force—The amount of energy expended for a movement; can range from light to heavy.

formation—Includes shapes, groups, and spacing typically used to organize students.

frequency—The number of training sessions per week.

fundamental movement patterns—General movement patterns such as throwing, catching, running, and jumping.

fundamental skills—General patterns of skills that emerge and are refined during early childhood.

general space—Space in which the group is participating.

grading—Assigning values to performance (grading a paper).

growth—Change in body size that results from more and bigger body cells and more intercellular material.

guided discovery—An indirect approach used when the teacher wants the students to discover a solution through a series of questions.

horizontal alignment—The relationship of standards, benchmarks, objectives, content, and assessment within a grade.

indirect instruction approach—Provides opportunities for student involvement, with teachers establishing a learning environment to help students discover solutions on their own.

individualized education program (IEP)—Instructional plan for a child with one or more disabilities.

information processing—A model to examine problem solving and memory, a part of cognition; it includes perception, working memory, and long-term memory.

initial activity—Event used to begin each class (not the same as a warm-up activity).

instruction—Includes directions, demonstration, feedback, cues, and evaluation as behaviors teachers complete to influence student learning.

INTASC standards—Ten learning outcomes to teacher education programs that apply to all teachers, including those teaching physical education.

intensity—The percent of maximum heart rate or strength for the training.

intrinsic—Doing something because the child wants to.

intrinsic feedback—Information about a performance gained from sensory information.

learning—Four definitive characteristics: Learning results from practice; learning is permanent; learning is dependent on feedback; and learning is demonstrated by retention and transfer.

learning contracts—A written agreement of what the student is to accomplish in a specified time period.

liability—Cases that attempt to prove that the responsible person did not meet the standard of care and that there was damage resulting from the injury.

location—Where you stand during teaching.

locomotor skills—Movements that take us from one place to another, including running, jumping, and hopping.

management—A set of techniques used to control students and create a safe environment; these include routines and rules.

manipulative skills—Movements used to interact with an object, such as object projection (kicking, striking, throwing) and object interception (catching).

maturation—Rate of progress toward a mature state, which is controlled genetically by the child's chronometer (biological time clock).

memory—Comprising two parts: working (short-term) memory, which is limited in capacity; and long-term memory, which is unlimited and where knowledge is stored.

mission—Elementary schools help children become contributing members of our society; the schools serve children, their parents, and the wider community or society.

motivation—The reason behind making choices; can be *intrinsic* or *extrinsic*.

motor milestones—Rudimentary movements (e.g., sitting, rolling over) that can be observed during the first year of life (infancy).

muscle endurance—Repeated muscle contractions at less than maximum effort.

muscle strength—The maximum amount of force a muscle can produce at one time.

negligence—When you are responsible for an injury (i.e., you did not act in a reasonable and prudent way based on the situation to prevent the injury).

nonlocomotor skills—Skills that do not move one from place to place (e.g., balancing, stretching, bending).

norm-referenced tests—Test expectation is for a range of performance (in fact, the assumption is that scores will fit the bell-shaped curve).

objectives—Should be stated in terms of observable student behavior.

objectivity—Is the measurement without bias (i.e., fair to all children)?

ontogenetic skills—Learned skills that vary by cultural and peer group (e.g., roller-skating, skiing).

opposition—In motor skills, refers to the arms working in tandem with the legs (i.e., when the right arm goes forward, the left leg goes forward).

overexclusive attention—To focus attention on one aspect of the stimulus array and ignore all others.

overinclusive attention—The inability to select the critical element to solve a task.

pace—Rate of talking.

personal space—Space surrounding each child.

phylogenetic skills—Movements observed in all individuals in a group (e.g., walking).

physical activity—Sport, exercise, physical education, and play that make an important contribution to child development.

physical education—A planned sequential K through 12 curriculum that provides cognitive content and learning experiences in a variety of activity areas such as basic movement skills; physical fitness; rhythms and dance; games; team, dual, and individual sports; tumbling and gymnastics; and aquatics.

physical fitness—Three components to physical fitness: cardiovascular endurance, body composition, and musculoskeletal health (flexibility, muscle strength, and endurance).

physically active—Describes a person who engages in a minimum of 60 minutes per day of movement, 30 minutes of which is moderate to vigorous.

physique—Description of the way a body looks, an example being somatotyping.

practice—Repetition and a critical ingredient in learning.

procedural knowledge—Information gained by learning about how to do something.

professional ethics—Often a code of conduct established by some group. Here, the teachers' code of conduct.

professional portfolio—Used to highlight your best work.

proficiency barrier—An explanation for children's not mastering the fundamental skills; usually a result of too little practice or ineffective instruction.

progression—Moving from inefficient and ineffective skill performance to an efficient and effective level; improvement or mastery of increasingly difficult tasks.

proximity—The distance between the supervisor and the object of supervision.

puberty—When the genital organs mature, the secondary sex characteristics (facial and body hair and a deeper voice) develop, and we become sexually mature (able to reproduce).

random practice—Practice order for several skills: same skill cannot be practiced two times in a row.

rating scale—An assessment instrument that uses numbers to denote levels of performance.

readiness—Capability of a child to do a task (e.g., reading readiness means the child has all the skills prerequisite to reading).

reflection—Studying the teaching and learning process—thinking, feedback, and correction—is critical when improvement is the goal.

reinforcement and general encouragement—General positive statements, such as "good job," "nice try," and "keep it up."

relative age effect—In sports with an age "cutoff," the oldest athletes are identified as the best.

reliability—Is the measurement consistent? Does it represent a typical performance?

role taking—Putting yourself in someone else's place.

rubrics—A form of authentic assessment with at least two levels of verbal description of the levels of performance.

scanning—Sweeping the area with the eyes to observe.

scope—The content of the program in terms of its breadth or range throughout the academic year.

sedentary—A person who is inactive (e.g., a person who sits at work and during leisure time).

selective attention—Appropriate information is used and all other information is ignored.

self-concept—The way a person views himself.

self-efficacy—The confidence an individual has in accomplishing a specific task.

sequence—The order for teaching the progression of curriculum from year to year, reflecting the timing and depth of the program.

service—Working with groups inside (e.g., school yearbook staff) and outside (community food drive) the school.

skill—Competence to perform a task, specifically a physical movement task such as catching a ball.

social comparison—When children evaluate themselves against others.

speed—Rate of movement; can range from slow to fast.

speed–accuracy trade-off—Effects of movement speed on movement accuracy and vice versa.

standard of care—What a reasonable and prudent person would do under the circumstances.

static balance—The ability to maintain a stationary position for a specified period of time.

station teaching—Equipment, tasks, and types of practice are located at various places; but students can practice different tasks and can progress at individual rates.

stature—Height.

statutes—Established by the government and guide operations of many entities (e.g., Title IX).

strategic knowledge—An understanding of control processes and how to use them.

structured physical activity—Physical education as a sequential instructional program that focuses on skill acquisition.

supervision—State of a responsible adult being present, mentally and physically, to assure reasonable safety for students.

systolic pressure—The maximum pressure immediately after a heart beat.

task orientation—Undertaking a task for personal satisfaction.

task sheets—Used to communicate to individual students the activities to be accomplished.

teachable moment—Unplanned opportunity for learning.

teaching philosophy statement—Should be based on your values and be specific in how those values will affect your curriculum decisions and instructional strategies.

time—The amount of training in minutes or repetitions; also called *duration*.

time-out—Isolating a student, physically and in terms of instruction.

tone—Emotion of your voice (e.g., angry, happy).

tort—Civil legal action, often when parents of a student sue the school (and possibly the teacher).

transition—Physical transition moves students from one location, or formation, to another; cognitive or activity transition changes "gears"; students may stay in one place but be expected to do something very different.

type—The kind of activity.

unstructured activity time—Recess; when children have a chance to be physically active and relieve stress.

validity—Does the test measure what it is supposed to measure? Does it represent the objective?

variability—Differences within or between people (e.g., a single child may perform the same task in different ways; likewise, two children may perform very differently).

variable practice—When one dimension of the task changes (e.g., distance to the target).

vertical alignment—The relationship of the benchmarks and content across grades.

vigilance—Length of time that one can allocate attention to a particular task.

visual angle—The range or percentage of the area one can see from a particular location.

vita—A record of what you have accomplished.

volume—Loudness of your voice.

warm-up—A 3- to 5-minute vigorous activity at the beginning of the lesson.

working portfolio—Viewed as a storage system for activities, ideas, and other support materials.

INDEX

Note: Page numbers followed by an italicized *f* or *t* refer to the figure or table on that page, respectively.

ABOUT THE AUTHORS

Katherine T. Thomas, PhD, is an associate professor at the University of North Texas, where she teaches a variety of teacher education and motor development courses. Dr. Thomas also has taught at Iowa State University, Arizona State University, Southeastern Louisiana University, and Southern University at Baton Rouge. Her research and numerous publications focus on skill acquisition in sport and exercise and the relation of physical activity to health. She has external grant funding in excess of $1,000,000 to study physical activity and is the physical activity consultant for the USDA's Team Nutrition. However, Dr. Thomas says that the most relevant experiences to the writing of this book were her early positions as a graduate assistant and as an instructor in elementary schools and a college teaching laboratory. Those experiences enabled her to find out firsthand what does and does not work in a physical education class.

Dr. Thomas is a member of the American Alliance for Health, Physical Education, Recreation and Dance (AAHPERD) and the North American Society for the Psychology of Sport and Physical Activity (NASPSPA). She received her doctorate in physical education from Louisiana State University in 1981.

Amelia M. Lee, PhD, is a professor and chair of the department of kinesiology at Louisiana State University. In addition to her 30 years as a teacher educator, Dr. Lee has 10 years of experience as a physical educator at elementary schools in Louisiana and Texas. She has published many articles on children's learning and motivation in physical education and has served as a physical education consultant to more than 20 school districts. Dr. Lee is a member of the American Educational Research Association (AERA), and she has received the Scholar Lecture Award from the AERA's Special Interest Group on Learning and Instruction in Physical Education. She is a member of AAHPERD, received an Honor Award from AAHPERD's Curriculum and Instruction Academy, was selected to present the Research Consortium McCloy Lecture, and was named the 2003-04 Alliance Scholar. Dr. Lee earned her doctorate in physical education from Texas Woman's University in 1972.

Jerry R. Thomas, EdD, has taught elementary physical education methods and children's motor development for more than 30 years. He is dean of the College of Education and a professor in the department of kinesiology, health promotion, and recreation at the University of North Texas. Dr. Thomas also has been a professor at Iowa State, Florida State, Louisiana State, and Arizona State Universities. He has written more than 125 published papers, including many on children's motor skills. Dr. Thomas is former president of the American Academy of Kinesiology and Physical Education and NASPSPA. In addition, his scholarly work in physical activity has earned him the titles of C.H. McCloy Lecturer for children's control, learning, and performance of motor skills; Alliance Scholar for AAHPERD; and Southern District AHPERD Scholar.

HOW TO USE THE DVD-ROM

DVD icons have been placed throughout the book to identify discussions that are supported by a video clip. The clips demonstrate how three expert and two young elementary physical education teachers conduct lessons. The clips include a mastery lesson, a contextual practice lesson, a station teaching lesson, a locomotor skill lesson, and a manipulative skill lesson. The DVD also contains interview clips with the teachers and all the lesson plans from the book in PDF format.

You can view the video content either on a television set with a DVD player or on a computer with a DVD-ROM drive. The reproducible lesson plan documents can be accessed only through the DVD-ROM on your computer (see further instructions at the end of this section).

The DVD includes a main menu where you can select clips for each of the five lessons or click Teacher Interviews to display a submenu of clips. After you have viewed a lesson, the DVD will automatically return to the main menu. After you have viewed a teacher interview, the DVD will return to the submenu.

To use the DVD, place it in your DVD player or DVD-ROM drive. A title screen will welcome you to the program. Then the main menu, with buttons for each of the five lessons and a button for the teacher interviews, will appear. When you click on one of the buttons for a lesson, the video will play. When you click on the Teacher Interviews button at the bottom of the screen, the submenu will appear. Click on a button for each interview clip and the video will play.

To access all lesson plan documents from Windows®,

1. Insert the DVD into your DVD-ROM drive.
2. Open "My Computer" and right-click on the DVD-ROM drive.
3. Select "Open."
4. Double-click on the "Lesson Plans" folder.
5. Select the PDF file you want to view.

To access all lesson plan documents on a Macintosh® computer,

1. Insert the DVD into your DVD-ROM drive.
2. Double-click on the DVD icon on your desktop.
3. Double-click on the "Lesson Plans" folder.
4. Select the PDF file you want to view.

Note: If your DVD viewing program is set to automatically launch, the video content will automatically run. You will need to close out of the DVD viewing program before accessing the PDF files.

You will need Adobe® Reader® to view the PDF files. If you do not already have Adobe Reader installed on your computer, go to www.adobe.com to download the free software.